Great Lakes Suite

Great Lakes Suite

A Trip Around Lake Erie

A Trip Around Lake Huron

A Trip Around Lake Ontario

David W. McFadden

Talonbooks
1997

Copyright ©1997 David W. McFadden

Published with the assistance of the Canada Council.

Talonbooks
#104—3100 Production Way
Burnaby, British Columbia
Canada V5A 4R4

Typeset in Garamond Condensed and printed and bound in Canada by Hignell Printing Ltd.

First Printing: September 1997

Talonbooks are distributed in Canada by General Distribution Services,
30 Lesmill Road, Don Mills, Ontario, Canada, M3B 2T6; Tel: (416) 445-3333; Fax: (416) 445-5967.

Talonbooks are distributed in the U. S. A. by General Distribution Services Inc., 85 Rock River Drive,
Suite 202, Buffalo, New York, U.S.A., 14207-2170; Tel.: 1-800-805-1083; Fax: 1-800-481-6207.

Revised and updated from the previous publications of: *A Trip Around Lake Erie* (Coach House
Press, 1980); *A Trip Around Lake Huron* (Coach House Press, 1980); and *A Trip Around Lake
Ontario* (Coach House Press, 1988).

Canadian Cataloguing in Publication Data

McFadden, David, 1940-
  Great Lakes suite

  ISBN 0-88922-382-3

  1. McFadden, David, 1940-   —Journeys—Great Lakes Region.
2. Great Lakes Region—Description and travel. I. Title.
PS8525.F32G75 1997   C818'.5403   C97-910723-7
PR9199.3.M3145G75 1997

Great Lakes Suite

A Trip Around Lake Erie

GREAT LAKES SUITE

VOLUME ONE

A TRIP AROUND LAKE ERIE

A Trip Around Lake Erie is dedicated to Ray Woodworth—painter, sculptor, writer, union organiser and conservationist—accidentally shot to death in Nova Scotia January 3, 1979.

"Although there is plenty of space on a gravestone to contain, bound in moss, the abridged version of a man's life, detail is always welcome."

—Vladimir Nabokov, *Laughter in the Dark*

Contents

A Trip Around Lake Erie

1. There's Something Magical About Your Place of Birth

Hamilton, Ontario, appears on the road map as a little blob of yellow at the western tip of Lake Ontario. It's a dirty, dreary, burnt-out industrial city, a place covered by a perpetual black cloud, and it's not considered a great place to live. Yet I love its junkyards, its other-worldly skyline, the mysterious combination of Victorian and art-deco architecture glimpsed through the swirling clouds of soot.

My motto has always been Do Nothing Unless It's Absolutely Necessary. I've always had a phobia for passivity and although I think it's made my life more interesting I'll never really know for sure. That's the cutting edge of life: knowing that you'll never know what would have happened if you'd followed the left ventricle of your heart rather than the right and so on. I've often thought about leaving this city but my desire to leave has never been strong enough to overcome the inertia. Actually it's something mystical. There's something magical about your place of birth. But everybody knows that.

There should be a Greek word for overpowering love of birthplace but I can't think of what it might be. Since earliest childhood I've felt that the further one gets from Hamilton, Ontario, the less interesting things become, the less magic there is in the air. I can't remember ever being bored in Hamilton but I'm almost always bored outside it. Is it just me or have others had that experience with their place of birth? As if I am bound by delicate threads, frozen by the utter mysteriousness of my immediate surroundings.

For the past nine years I've been living on the Niagara Escarpment that bisects this city, the same escarpment over which the Niagara River falls forty miles to the east. We live in the shadow of the hospital where I was born, where my wife was born, and where our two children were born.

There is much about the city I hate. The Chamber of Commerce and daily newspaper are Hamilton's Bobbsey Twins. The business community, as in all Canadian cities, is blatantly anti-Canadian and pro-American. But the contempt they display toward their own urban area, the sort of contempt that sees progress in tearing down nineteenth-century mansions to make way for parking lots, is something that no longer exists in most cities of the United States.

Perhaps I'm talking over my head. Such large problems are beyond me. My interests are in the smaller things in life, such as wondering about the magic of your place of birth and how it will magnetise you and immobilise you if you allow it to.

2. Emily

The great city of Toronto is only an hour's drive but one cannot pretend that one lives there. What one gives to a neighbouring city is something that has been taken away from one's own city, and everyone becomes poorer.

The Canadian painter John Boyle and his wife Janet moved to Hamilton last year during the last few months of Janet's pregnancy so they could be close to the McMaster University Medical Centre. During his time in Hamilton John spent hours walking around the city and loved its strange beauty. With their new baby, Emily, they've returned to their home near Owen Sound. The poet Christopher Dewdney lived here for six months last year but he's returned to his home town, London, Ontario. Loneliness is an important part of my life.

3. The View from the Mountain

The Renaissance-style series of fountains at Gage Park is still beautiful though fallen to ruin. My series of paintings, Thirty-six Views of the Gage Park Fountains, was shown at the Hamilton Artists' Coop recently and I actually sold one, to my mom.

From the Niagara Escarpment, when the view is not obstructed by apartment towers or smog from the steel companies, you can see Hamilton Harbour, the Beach Strip, the Skyway Bridge and the entire west end of Lake Ontario as if it were a huge map. And one can drive all the way up the escarpment, passing through millions of years of rock sediment, and see this view spring to life. I keep thinking of starting my own little tourist bureau, printing up bumper stickers to read WE CLIMBED HAMILTON MOUNTAIN. One often sees bumper stickers reading WE CLIMBED PIKE'S PEAK and certainly Pike's Peak is much higher than Hamilton Mountain. But it probably isn't as steep.

4. The Old Extra-Terrestrial Convention

If someone from another planet were examining the surface of Earth to determine a landing point I'm sure they'd be drawn to the Great Lakes. They're so weird-looking, you just know it must be a key area of the Earth's surface. If there is intelligent life on Earth it would have to be around the Great Lakes.

The little wings of Lake Michigan like a chicken trying to fly, the stubby banana of Lake Ontario, the shark-like fierceness of Lake Superior, the ballet-like grace of Lake Huron and Georgian Bay, the strategically placed points and peninsulas of sad-eyed Lake Erie—all this must tell the thoughtful observer that the Great Lakes were not formed by blind nature. There must be something more to it! Such a vista is so overwhelming it serves to emphasise the insignificance of the individual human being.

And if these extra-terrestrials did decide on the Great Lakes as a landing area I feel they would have to be drawn to the western tip of Lake Ontario: the Hamilton area. It seems such a likely spot on the map, so central to the lakes themselves.

And if there really are extra-terrestrials observing the surface of this planet their name for the Great Lakes would have to be the same as ours: Great Lakes.

5. A Faint Blue Ridge

When I was a kid my parents used to take me to Lake Erie. We had a cottage there. I would sit on the beach on a clear day looking at a faint blue ridge on the other side of the lake, until, in my imagination, the faint blue ridge would get closer and closer until I'd be able to see trees, buildings, towns, factories, little trucks, trains, cars speeding along the little roads, and sometimes even people who had no idea they were being observed from a great distance.

"What's that faint blue ridge over there?" I asked my dad.

"I don't know, son," he said, thoughtfully. He was always honest when kids asked him questions, unlike many other dads I could mention who find themselves incapable of uttering the words, "I don't know." He promised to ask around for me.

He went and asked Ken Featherstone, the old farmer who rented the land out for the city people to build their cottages.

"Mr. Featherstone says it's the Blue Ridge Mountains of Pennsylvania," he told me a few days later.

"What is?"

"That faint blue ridge over there that you asked me about?"

"Oh yeah," I said. "You know, Dad, I've been thinking that when I'm old enough I'm going to buy a brand new camper van and drive right around this lake."

6. A Life-Size Map of the Great Lakes

So I decided to write this book. I'd forgotten about my vow to drive all the way around Lake Erie, but now, thirty years later, it became somehow urgent to take my family on this trip. I tried to shake the idea but I couldn't. I simply had to write a series of five books based on trips around each of the Great Lakes. I vowed to paint a life-size map of each of the Great Lakes with the flaming brush of my crocus-coloured Volkswagen van.

I explained the whole thing to a mercenary friend who writes scripts for movies and television and makes a lot of money. He told me that in order to make the book more saleable I should have someone chasing us. But, like most of the writers I really admire, I don't want to be any richer or any more famous than anyone else. There is simply an urge to have the voice linger on after an imagined death, an urge to make permanent descriptions of what is dying all around us. And I want to be able to take this book with me when I make my next trip around Lake Erie, perhaps twenty years from now. By that time I'll still be writing but "I" will not be in my writing. "I" will be beyond all that. So this is a farewell of sorts. As is everything.

7. What Lake Should We Go Around First?

When Joan said she'd like to go on a short motor-camping trip, I suggested the idea of taking a series of trips around the Great Lakes. She thought it was a good idea. She'd been complaining because she and the kids hadn't been appearing much in my recent writing. She was furious when she read an article which said: "Joan and the kids have been taking a back seat to McFadden's new concerns." She threw the magazine across the room and said: "That does it! I knew it all along but it really hurts to see it in print."

So the timing was right.

Joan had to go to summer school to take an advanced course in special education starting Wednesday, July 6. So we'd have to be home Tuesday night.

"What lake should we go around first?" I said.

"I don't know," said Joan. "We don't have much time. Which lake is the smallest?"

FRIDAY, JULY 1

8. The Bluegrass Festival at Courtcliffe Park

It was about three o'clock on the afternoon of July 1, Canada's 110th birthday. If you'd been hitchhiking up the Clappison Cut west of Hamilton, Ontario, about that time you would have seen a canary-coloured Volkswagen van chugging up the hill. The present writer was the driver. Sitting next to him was his wife Joan. His daughters Alison, 13, and Jennifer, 9, were in the back seat along with their dog, Bruce, 3. Earlier we'd dropped the cat off at the boarding kennel.

We needed some propane for the camp stove so we headed up to Courtcliffe Park just off Highway 6 on the way to Guelph. It was the only propane place open on Canada Day.

We still didn't know which lake we were going to go around although we had narrowed the choice down to two. It would be either Lake Erie or Lake Huron. When we got to Courtcliffe Park we paid $5.15 to the girl in the store. She gave us a slip of paper and we took it out back. On top of the store was a huge, forty-foot-tall papier-mâché sculpture of a woman in a bathing suit. We took a picture of this image from classical antiquity. As I focussed the camera and set up the shot the girl came out of the store to watch. She was laughing, although it was hard to imagine that no one had ever stopped to take a picture of this giant Aphrodite before.

When we drove around the back we found a large green propane tank set on a cement platform which in turn was surrounded by a barbed-wire fence six feet tall. On the fence was a yellow sign with blue lettering:

NO SMOKING

WITHIN 20 FEET

PROPANE

FOR SALE

I told Joan and the kids to take a walk. There was always the possibility of an explosion. A guy about seventeen with torn jeans and a bushy Afro haircut was operating the pump. "Guess what," he said with a friendly grin. "This is the first tank I ever filled."

He inserted the hose but he couldn't get the propane turned on. He thought it was already filled but he wasn't sure. "No, I'm sure it's empty," I said. "Why don't you go and get your boss and see what he says?"

While he was away I sat on the grass and watched Joan and the kids and Bruce as small as beetles on the other side of a vast green field. The guy returned a few minutes later—alone.

"Now I know what I was doing wrong," he said. He gave the hose a yank and a twist this time as he inserted it and in a few moments the tank was filled.

The guy's name was Court Belinsky. I guess the park was named partially after him. Anyway he was the grandson of S. Radcliffe Belinsky who runs a massage parlour on the top floor of the Holiday Inn in Hamilton. Radcliffe was a dignified old gentleman who liked wearing expensive three-piece suits. His masseuses were some of the most beautiful young ladies imaginable.

I used to see him going into the hotel in the morning. He always walked several paces ahead of his wife. Back a few years when there was a bit of a civic controversy over the tearing down of an old stone armament depot from the War of 1812, Belinsky used to write letters to the editor urging it be torn down. It was in the way of progress, in this case a highway-widening project.

He said he'd actually been born in the depot—owing to some rather unusual but vague events concerning his mother's family—but he certainly wasn't sentimental about the place at all.

In a brilliant compromise the city decided neither to tear it down nor leave it standing. They had it moved at a cost of a million dollars (Canadian).

It was such a nice day, and it looked as if the park employees were getting ready for a busy weekend.

"Anything good going on this weekend?" I asked Court.

"No," he said. "Just camping."

"Don't you usually have a bluegrass festival on the Canada Day weekend?"

"Well, we did last year. But it didn't work out very well. Too many drunks, too many fights."

"The low-lifes spoiling it for everybody, eh?"

"Yeah. Even the musicians said they'd never come back again."

9. Boycott American Culture

One summer a few years earlier, during a preliminary exploration of the shore of Lake Erie, we were driving west of the town of Fort Erie, Ontario, along the north shore. It was solid private-cottage country, with almost no public access to the beaches. Very depressing. All the cottages flew American flags. Joan was really getting browned off.

We drove down a public road to the lake but when we came to the end the beach was all fenced off. So we had to turn around. There was only one way I could turn and that was by pulling a little way, just a few feet, up somebody's driveway.

A woman came running out of her cottage and stood on the verandah screaming at us. There was an American flag flying from her roof.

"Don't you people know this is private property?" she screamed.

Joan was so steamed she yelled back: "If you don't like it, lady, why don't you go back where you came from?"

This is strange, because Joan isn't really that nasty a person, nor is she ordinarily anti-American in the slightest. She is very fond of some of my American relatives, and some of them are dedicated U.S. patriots.

Nevertheless, Joan later became enthused about the Canadian Liberation Movement which was in the news at that time. So we invited Barry Lord to our place to talk about it. Barry was one of the organisers. He was keeping a pretty high profile in those days. I remembered him from when he went to Delta Secondary School in the east end of Hamilton. I was a couple of years behind him. He used to wear saddle shoes with plaid shoe laces. One year he had the lead role in the annual production, *Harvey*. My father went with me to see the show. He was terribly impressed with Barry. "That boy is really going to make something of himself," he said. "You wait and see." Being a semi-continentalist and a Pearsonian Liberal, a person who distrusts political extremism of all kinds, father now winces whenever I remind him that he said that, which isn't often.

So Barry sat in an armchair all evening telling us about the Canadian Liberation Movement. Joan was getting impatient. She wanted to know when the Movement was going to start throwing Molotov cocktails through the windows of American cottages on the north shore of Lake Erie.

"The time might come for that but the time isn't ripe yet," Barry said.

I'd been playing around with the idea of a YANKEE GO HOME bumper sticker campaign and a total boycott of American culture—a boycott of American movies, American TV, American magazines, American junk food outlets and all that stuff. I was convinced it would work, although I found the idea a little frightening at the same time. It takes a special kind of scoundrel to get involved in political movements in relatively comfortable times.

Barry said the Movement would consider the ideas I'd brought up. But it never came to anything. He spent a lot of time talking to us that evening but we never signed up. To me, it was a little frightening, not on a personal level as much as on a national level. To Joan it all seemed just too dull.

Later I heard that the poet Milton Acorn had left the Movement and nobody knew the where-abouts of Barry Lord. Milton was telling people the Canadian Liberation Movement had been infiltrated by the Central Intelligence Agency which should have been no surprise.

"Why don't you denounce them?" somebody was supposed to have asked Acorn. He reportedly replied that he didn't want to demoralise the handful of non-CIA members that were still involved.

We were talking about this as we drove up Highway 6 toward the Macdonald-Cartier Freeway, more familiarly known as Highway 401. As we took the ramp onto the west-bound lane of the 401 we made up our mind. We decided to take the counterclockwise route around Lake Erie. From that point on we seemed to enter Magic Time, when every movement of the hand, every breath, every word sends little waves into the future. My notebook and pen sat on the dashboard in front of me. We felt a little nervous about the whole thing. We were far from the point where one realises there is no future, there is no past.

10. Art Can Make Boring Things Interesting

Aren't expressways boring? They're the worst part of any trip. They're so safe they're dangerous. They're about as much fun as eating at McDonald's. And they've only been in existence since the sixties.

After driving west on the 401 for about thirty miles I began to get a little sleepy. We passed an accident. One car looked scarcely damaged. The other was on its top. Garbage and items of blood-stained clothing were strewn all around. The people had been taken away. It looked bad.

So when we stopped for gas I bought a Coca-Cola and took a few sips. I felt more alert immediately. Caffeine has a strong effect on me because I drink so little of it. My heart started beating faster with each sip. It was just like a snort of cocaine. I was bug-eyed for the rest of the day. We drove on the 401 past London where I'd taken Jennifer a few days earlier to drop off the manuscript of my new book, *Animal Spirits*, at Greg Curnoe's studio. Greg was going to design the book and illustrate it. As we arrived the whole Curnoe family was leaving for the movies. They were going to see *Star Wars*. So Jenny and I went along with them. There were seven of us. We took up one entire row.

"Did you have any trouble following the plot?" I asked Jenny later. It seemed a little too sophisticated for a nine-year-old.

"No," she said. "I understood it perfectly."

So now as we got closer to London Jenny said from the back seat: "Daddy?"

"Yes?"

"Pretty soon we'll be passing a big green sign saying LONDON NEXT FOUR EXITS, right?"

"Right!"

And pretty soon we did.

Driving the 401 has become less boring lately. Seeing Jack Chambers' famous painting of the 401 had an effect on my way of seeing that expressway. Art can make boring things interesting. When I drive the 401 now one of the things I try to do is find the exact spot where that painting was painted. Last week I was driving along and as I approached London I flicked on the radio and heard that Chambers had died the night before. I later found out his painting of the 401 was a composite rather than one specific view. That was why I had problems finding the spot.

My friend Russell Seaworthy had a Volkswagen van. When he drives along the 401 he sometimes amuses himself by imagining what the van looks like from a point half a mile ahead and a thousand feet in the air. In the same way my father, pumping away on his exercise bicycle every morning, pretends he's in the Tour de France.

It's still boring for the kids though. After passing London we took the St. Thomas exit and stopped for a brief rest at Talbotville. We'd go along the lakeshore route the rest of the way, and stay off the expressway as much as possible.

11. A Phone Call to an Unnamed Friend

Just before pulling into a gas station in Talbotville we passed a motel with a sign out front reading SPEND A NIGHT NOT A FORTUNE. "That's not bad," said Joan. "Just twelve dollars for a single." She still wasn't crazy about camping. Some day I might regret buying this van and bullying her into taking these trips. But it seemed like the right thing to do at the time.

While Joan and the kids were in the washroom the entire Glenn Miller Orchestra went by in a bus. GLENN MILLER ORCHESTRA DIRECTED BY JIMMY HENDERSON was painted on the side. Then another bus came by, a church bus. It had on the side BAPTIST BIBLE TEMPLE WHERE GOD DWELLETH HIS WORD DWELLETH TOO and on the back A GOING BUS FOR A COMING LORD. The sun was shining over Lake Erie. I felt happy I was alive in the twentieth century. We were entering a Belle Epoque that would last till our days were done.

I ran across Highway 4 to a telephone booth, and called a friend in a distant city to discuss some personal matters that are of no interest in the present context. As we talked a beautiful woman got out of a Buick Century with Ohio licence plates and went into the telephone booth next to mine. She started phoning around looking for motel accommodation. She sounded worried, because all the motels were booked for the night.

12. A Cleveland Radio Station

Joan offered to drive for a few hours along Highway 3 and I was happy to let her. She wouldn't want to drive once we crossed the border into the United States of America. Besides, I had taught her to drive and I was proud of her skill. She'd been taking lessons from her uncle, who was a professional driving instructor, and it didn't work out. Then her father gave her a few lessons and that didn't work out. But she took to my style of instruction with enthusiasm and learned quickly.

It was a beautiful afternoon, a blue sky, no haze, occasional puffy white and grey clouds like in an A.Y. Jackson painting. Highway 3 is the highway that connects Buffalo and Detroit and tends to be a short cut through Canada for a lot of American traffic between those two cities. It's certainly a lot faster than going south of Lake Erie.

Frank Daville, a former colleague of mine, was an older man, in his sixties, had had a tracheotomy after a bout with throat cancer, and spoke in agonising stage whispers, the little cloth filter covering the hole in his neck flapping in the breeze. He said that in his earlier years, in the fifties presumably or maybe even earlier, he ran a gas station on Highway 3 somewhere around here, and he had nasty things to say about the Americans.

"Every bloody one of them," he said, "had a bottle of whiskey in the glove compartment and a loaded revolver under the front seat."

We rolled along the two-lane, tree-lined road, gradually getting closer and closer to the Lake Erie shore, passing tobacco farms and corn fields and families picking berries and tomatoes. It was so much more pleasant than driving along the angry, mechanical, poisonous Highway 401, and probably safer even though occasional cars whizzed past you the opposite way with only inches to spare.

We passed a water hole with three cows standing thigh deep drinking and a fourth cow walking away as if she'd had enough.

Bruce was lying on the floor. We'd called the Rainbow Bridge in Niagara Falls before leaving home and asked if it would be all right to take a dog across the border. The guy said we'd need a certificate saying he'd had his rabies shot. We got out his medical certificate and the rabies section wasn't marked off although we knew he'd had his shots so we checked it off ourselves and forged the vet's initials.

As we passed the Chatham Boy Scout Camp I flicked on the radio. We got an FM station from Cleveland just as clearly as if we were on the other side of the lake. It was WDNT FM 108. They played a lot of John Denver songs and stuff like that. I'd heard of John Denver but had never actually been conscious of hearing his songs before. I thought the songs were kind of schmaltzy and full of self-pity. I left the station on though because I didn't want to impose my (lack of) taste on Joan and the kids. They seemed to be enjoying the music although they weren't saying anything. Maybe they disliked it too but didn't want to force their taste on me. After all, I was the one who turned the radio on in the first place. And let's not forget it was my radio: Joan had bought it for me for Christmas. It came with an eight-track tape player and we had a little box of eight-track tapes in the back.

13. The Life and Times of Archibald Lampman

> *A magic is laid*
> *upon land,*
> *upon lake....*

Just past the village of Palmyra we caught sight of grey, shallow Lake Erie, the smallest and shallowest of the Great Lakes, the one that is sick and dying, and, according to scientific reports, the one that will be the first to disappear, turn to marsh with a thin stream trickling through the middle. But today, viewed from the highway across a mile of low, flat tobacco fields, Lake Erie looked healthy, huge, deep, blue, truly great, and maybe even happy, its choppy waves like white lips trying to kiss the sun, to steal a line from Malcolm Lowry, the early Malcolm Lowry that is....

"There's Archibald Lampman," cried Joan.

I looked. Sure enough, there was the cairn commemorating Canada's first postal-employee poet. We'd been there last summer and I'd forgotten about it. He was actually buried in Ottawa, the scene of his final series of humiliations, where in 1883 he had taken a job as a clerk in the post office, a job obtained for him by a friend whose father was Canada's postmaster general. Then he began writing a series of scandalous Baudelairian sonnets to a little Lolita and finally married her. They moved in with his father and mother and three teenaged sisters and quarreled bitterly. He soon started addressing his sonnets to other little girls and died at thirty-eight—of a broken heart, it's said! It's apparently very difficult to get information about Lampman because, after his death, members of the Lampman clan clammed up and refused to cooperate with potential biographers. If we'd known about this when we had to memorise Lampman's poems in school we would have been more enthusiastic.

But here, a mile west of the village of Morpeth, was the peaceful Anglican manse in which Lampman grew up and the church in which his father preached. Dozens of Lampmans are buried in the nineteenth-century cemetery behind the church. Both the church and the cemetery have been maintained much as they must have been in Lampman's childhood. It certainly is a mysterious place, guaranteed to make you feel strangely weepy.

Because Lampman was so much a reflection of this land and this lake he's mine whether I want him or not. It's quite healthy to be schizophrenic in your appreciation of poets who are close to you in time and space. The poet Dorothy Livesay is far too young to have known Lampman—he'd been dead a few years before she was born. But I once asked her what the poets of my generation would have thought of people like Bliss Carman, Charles G.D. Roberts and Raymond Knister, all of whom she had known as a young woman: the Canadian avant-garde of the twenties.

"I think you would have found them boring," she said.

What more is there to say? We had them to feed on.

14. In the Sunny Southland

In Morpeth itself there is a cluster of old brown-brick buildings that must have been around in Lampman's day, must have seen him coming to town on foot or on horseback or horse-drawn wagon or whatever. Hanging out in front of one of the buildings—now used as a variety store— is a spiffy new sign reading ENJOY THE STAR WEEKLY. That the sign looks so new is remarkable because the *Star Weekly* folded ten years ago. Perhaps I could add here that as a child I delivered the *Star Weekly*. I had twenty-three customers, paid ten cents for each paper, sold them for twelve cents, and made a profit of forty-six cents a week.

There are fewer clouds in the sky now. The sun is hot on the forehead. It looks as if we're going to miss the hailstorms forecast for the western parts of Lakes Erie and Huron tonight. As Joan drives I open the biscuits and cream cheese. In the back the kids are screaming at each other. "Come on, Joan, let's turn around and go home," I say. Suddenly the kids are best friends again.

We pass through Blenheim where the Cadillac Hotel looks like an interesting old place, and where nine years earlier I'd paid a visit with the painter Greg Curnoe and the photographer Ian MacEachern. I still have a collection of wonderful photos Ian took on that trip.

We pass the Cherry Growers' Co-operative Cold Storage Plant which reminds me we're now entering the sunny southland of Canada, the "Canadian Tropics."

15. How I Came to Give up Using the Ampersand

We passed the Cedar Springs/Erie Beach area and the road began skirting the naked sandy thighs of the shore. You could watch the road with one eye and the little waves rippling against the shore with the other. There were cars parked at the side of the road and people swimming and sunbathing.

We were still listening to the Cleveland radio station when we passed a fruit farm with a sign reading ROBERT CLEVELAND & SONS. An ampersand! My mind reeled back to Winnipeg where I'd been playing the role of the Visiting Poet a few months earlier. A neurotic high-school teacher was reprimanding me for using ampersands in my writing.

"Why can't you use 'and' like everyone else?" she kept saying.

"I like the various shapes of the ampersand in the various type styles," I said. But she wasn't listening.

"I just can't understand why your writing is so full of ampersands."

"It's a tribute to William Blake who always used them."

"I don't understand why you won't explain to me why your writing is so full of ampersands," she said, as if for the first time. I was beginning to realise there was something seriously the matter here—and compassion began to set in.

"Look lady," I said. "If it'll make you feel any better I hereby vow and you're my witness that I'll never use an ampersand again as long as I live."

I looked at her. She had that funny look in her eye. I realised she hadn't heard me.

"Irving Layton never uses ampersands," she said.

She had a tremendously pained expression on her face as if she were having trouble breathing. Each time I spoke you could tell she couldn't hear me because she was too busy thinking about how much she hated me and how unfair it was that I got my poems published but she didn't.

Sure enough, someone later told me she was asthmatic, suffered from migraines, wrote sonnets about leprechauns and enchanted forests, and had a broken-down drunk for a husband.

I wasn't about to knock on the door and ask Robert Cleveland or his sons but I bet no one ever gave them heck for using an ampersand on that sign. Further, I bet they were direct descendants of Moses Cleveland, the seventeenth-century Englishman who came to the U.S.A. and founded the city of Cleveland just across the lake.

Moses Cleveland was a contemporary of the English poet John Cleveland and was the great-grandfather of Grover Cleveland, a U.S. president and mayor of Buffalo in the nineteenth century.

I don't think I ever met anyone named Cleveland. It's certainly not an extinct name though. There's only one Cleveland in the Hamilton phone book, an S.R. Cleveland, but there are twenty-eight Clevelands in the Toronto phone book, not counting Cleveland Controls, Cleveland Tramrails, Cleveland Trencher Division, Cleveland Twist Drill Canada Ltd., and Cleveland House.

Cecil Cleveland lives at 20 Tinder Crescent in Toronto and his phone number is 755-7855.

Bill Cleveland is Dean of Arts at Simon Fraser University.

I would mention Reggie Cleveland, the major-league pitcher who once had the pleasure of beating the Cleveland Indians, but I don't know anything about baseball.

16. Beyond the Blue Horizon

No matter how fast Joan drove, Lake Erie was still there on our left and would be for days. The lake was blue and choppy. At certain places the water was Mediterranean blue all the way from the horizon to the shore. At other spots it developed layers of colour like an exotic drink: a yellow band close to the shore, a green band further out and a blue band stretching out to the horizon, corresponding to the various depths and water temperatures, I suppose.

We passed some small peach orchards. There are only three places I know of in Canada where peaches can be grown: the Okanagan Valley, the Niagara Peninsula, and here. Soft fruit country. Like Georgia.

I didn't know what the kids were doing but they were quiet. I was looking past Joan at the water. Joan might have thought I was looking at her, admiring her profile and her magnificent nose. She was looking straight ahead at the unwinding road.

"I'm okay, aren't I?" she said. She must have been having a moment of existential doubt, a rare thing with Joan as she is basically highly secure. Like the Royal Canadian Mint.

"Okay about what?"

"About everything?"

"Yeah, I guess so. Sure you are."

"We've come through a lot together, haven't we?"

"Yeah. We sure have. I was just thinking that."

There must have been something in the air. I'd heard an interview with Gore Vidal on the radio a day or two before. He was saying that whenever he hears the word "love" he checks his wallet. There is only lust, he said, and there can be no lust between two people who have been living together for any length of time. Just then I began feeling a wave of love toward this woman with whom I'd been living for so many years, fifteen or so. But then again, Gore, maybe I didn't feel it. Maybe I just thought I did. You better check your wallet.

On the western horizon I noticed something. At first I thought it was the faint distant skyline of a large city—maybe Detroit. But no it couldn't be Detroit yet. I refocussed my eyes and the faint line became not the tops of buildings but the tops of trees.

"There's Point Pelee," I averred.

"Where?" said Joan.

"Over there! Look!"

The kids were a-stir. "Are we going to Point Pelee?" said Jenny.

"Yes we are," said Joan. "And we're going to take the ferry to Pelee Island and then across to the United States of America."

"A ferry? Tonight?" said Jenny, trying to disguise her excitement.

"I don't know," said Joan. "We're not going on the ferry tonight, are we Dave?"

"No. Tomorrow morning."

17. The Ketchup Drips All Over the Chips

As we approached Wheatley, Joan wanted a decision on whether we'd camp at Wheatley Provincial Park for the night or head down into Point Pelee and try to locate Russell Seaworthy. It occurred to me that maybe Russell wouldn't want us camping in his front yard but after some hesitation I said, "Let's go to Point Pelee."

"He might be on a field trip," warned Joan.

But as we passed Wheatley Provincial Park Joan said, "Oh, look! All the campsites are filled. No vacancies. I bet we're going to have trouble getting campsites all the way around Lake Erie." After all, this was a special long weekend: Friday, Saturday and Sunday for Canadians and Saturday, Sunday and Monday for Americans.

Point Pelee juts down into Lake Erie in much the same way that Prince Edward County juts down into Lake Ontario. The two towns at the north end of Point Pelee are Leamington and Wheatley. The two corresponding towns at the north end of Prince Edward County are Belleville and Trenton. Prince Edward County is a much larger peninsula than Point Pelee, and likewise Belleville and Trenton are much larger towns than Leamington and Wheatley. Highway 3 runs through Leamington and Wheatley while Highway 2 runs through Belleville and Trenton. And Highway 2 continues all the way across Southwestern Ontario before meeting Highway 3 just outside Windsor. Windsor is the centre of a clock—with one hand, Highway 2, pointing at Montreal and passing through Belleville and Trenton, and the other hand, Highway 3, pointing at Buffalo and passing through Leamington and Wheatley.

Al Purdy is the poet of Prince Edward County. Russell Seaworthy is the poet of Point Pelee.

Past Wheatley we noticed that the corn looked a lot further along than it had forty miles back, but it also looked as if there'd been an awful storm. There was too much water lying in the fields and branches had been knocked off trees and were lying around. When we approached Leamington we saw a huge tall old birch which had been completely uprooted in front of a stately old home. The tree had probably been there since the home was built. And now it was finished. Never to be replaced.

Joan was following the green signs indicating the route to Point Pelee. We turned left at the main intersection of Leamington and started heading south. We passed the familiar old Heinz plant which straddles the road. A sign in front said NO TOURS.

"Hey kids, that's where they make ketchup," said Joan.

"Heinz ketchup," I said, for no special reason.

"Hey," said Jenny, "I've been here before."

I started singing Stompin' Tom Connors' song about Leamington:

> *They romp and run around Leamington*
> *And boy when they get hungry*
> *The ketchup drips all over the chips*
> *Way down in tomato country.*

18. Dropping in on D.H. Lawrence

At the entrance to Point Pelee National Park there was a small gatehouse where a self-important woman checks people entering and leaving. She looked up at me as if I were a criminal. She flipped through a couple of sheets of paper on a clipboard and said she knew of no Russell Seaworthy renting a cottage within the park. I could hear the kids cracking peanuts in the back of the van. "It's not allowed, you know," she said. At first I thought she meant eating peanuts. Then I realised she meant staying in the park overnight.

"Perhaps you've seen his van?" I said. "It's a bright blue Volkswagen with a Michelin man mounted on top."

"No," she said sternly. She wanted me to know she didn't want to hear any more about it. She was above that kind of public-relations work. She took my two-dollar entry fee. It was almost dark. She obviously thought there was something suspicious about someone entering the park so late in the day and was a little annoyed that there was nothing she could do about it except to say what she did say. "There's no overnight camping," she said.

"Yes, I know," I said, politely. I was trying to be as polite as Russell Seaworthy would be under these circumstances. "We'll just look for our friend and if we can't find him we'll leave."

We drove about two miles into the park before seeing Russell's van. We pulled up beside it. Russell came out on the verandah of a nice freshly painted cottage. The cottage looked as if it had been built around 1936. Russell was bathed in the golden light of early evening. He was dressed in a blue shirt and a pair of white drawstring pants. He was barefoot and very tanned. He looked wonderful.

"The entire McFadden family!" he said. "You're the last people I expected to see here."

Diane came out behind him. She said she had been ill with a lung infection for the past two weeks. In fact she came to join Russell at Point Pelee simply to try to shake the stubborn infection. Perhaps the hot sun and clear skies might do the trick. Her daughter Junie stood beside her stark naked as usual. The first time I saw Junie she was fully dressed and for some reason I said to her, "Why don't you take off all your clothes and jump up on my lap and we'll hug and kiss and stuff like that." Expecting her to say, "No sir, not on your life." But, as Diane watched with a bemused smile, Junie whipped off her clothes and jumped up on my lap, which was kind of embarrassing. Latency periods seem to be going the way of the passenger pigeon.

Russell said he'd been cycling, hiking, bird watching, swimming, sunbathing, and reading Wyndham Lewis novels since arriving at Point Pelee. He'd been doing a lot of painting in water colours, acrylics and pencil crayons. And he'd been doing a lot of late-night writing on a small portable typewriter at the kitchen table. Altogether he'd written seventy pages on his science fiction novel and about twelve pages of a long poem. I kept glancing at an old bus that had been wheeled into a space next to the cottage maybe thirty years before and simply left there. It looked as if it had been a church bus at one time. The wheels had been removed. It was sitting at the side of the cottage and first had been used as extra living quarters. Later it had been used strictly for storage. Now it was just mouldering away, the evening sun slanting through its dirty, paint-smeared windows. It looked as if it might have been the British Columbia painter Emily Carr's caravan from the 1930s.

I was swamped by déjà vu after déjà vu. It was as if I'd decided against visiting Russell at Point Pelee on this trip. And now I was an old man, looking back over my life and bitterly regretting not having paid Russell that visit. I was imagining what it would have been like. Isn't that strange? It struck me as being totally strange, a very eerie feeling as befits someone on a trip around Lake Erie. I had to reach out and touch Russell to make sure he was really there, and it was really only 1977.

And then the strangeness transformed itself. It was as if we had gone back in time and were visiting D.H. Lawrence. The sun seemed to have reversed itself. You could see *Kangaroo* on the typewriter.

19. Bruce Pukes on the Floor of Russell Seaworthy's Cottage

"Now we've got someone to challenge at Scrabble," said Diane who looked a little grey.

"Are you on medication?" said Joan.

"Oh, I've got bottles and bottles of pills."

We were standing inside the cottage. It was a comfortable place. There were partitions dividing it into a living room, with a bedroom at the rear, and a kitchen with a washroom at the front and another bedroom at the rear.

The furnishings were all circa 1940: lamps, armchairs, bed-sofas, kitchen tables and chairs in painted wood.

"We'll have to rent it next year," said Joan. As I said before she's really not crazy about camping. Neither am I. I don't know why we do it.

"Sure," said Diane.

Just then Bruce puked on the floor. He stood there looking kind of stupid, an orange pool of guck on the floor at his feet, just inside the front door.

What an intrusion on such a peaceful scene! I grabbed a rag and cleaned up the mess. Joan patted the dog lovingly, saying, "Ah, Brucie, poor doggy, poor Brucie-Wucie." I thought he'd been eating peanuts in the shell although there weren't any shells in the vomit and peanuts aren't orange.

"Maybe he's caught what Diane's got," said Joan, in her own inimitable brand of humour.

"So soon?" said Diane.

20. The Collingwood Poetry Festival

"There's something strange in the air," I confided to Russell, "as if we're time travelling, visiting some writer from the past like Charles G.D. Roberts or Raymond Knister or maybe even Archibald Lampman." I didn't want to say D.H. Lawrence, because Lawrence wasn't Canadian and it might have sounded a little over-blown. Besides I don't think Russell had ever been interested in Lawrence.

"God," said Russell, "I hope it's someone better than Charles G.D. Roberts or Raymond Knister."

For a moment there I'd forgotten how highly Russell regarded himself as a writer. He's such a humble person up front it's easy to disregard the highly structured ego at the back of his brain. His dedication is incredible, all the more so when you think of how his three published books have been so widely ignored by all but a few enthusiasts.

A month or two earlier he had been bird watching in the Collingwood area. He was listening to the radio in the van and found out that there was a poetry festival going on in Collingwood, with big-name poets—if that's not a contradiction in terms—from all over Canada in attendance. You know, the ones who get interviewed by Robert Fulford on television and on Sunday morning arts programs and CBC radio. The ones who are easily understood because they keep reworking the same poem and deal with one very limited, highly monotonous and easily recognisable theme.

"It sounded just dreadful," said Russell. "The interviewer was chasing Joe Rosenblatt around because he'd just won the Governor General's Award. She asked what he did when young poets show him their work. He said, "Oh, if they have any talent at all I'll spend a few minutes with them. Otherwise it's boring."

"Do you wish you'd been there?"

"Oh I was glad I wasn't there. That's for sure. But it sort of irked me, I must admit, that I hadn't been invited."

"Perfectly normal."

21. The Seacliffe Hotel

Russell and I left the women and girls at the cottage and drove off in his van. We were going to the Seacliffe Hotel to check the ferry schedule for the following day.

Back at the gatehouse we asked the same self-important woman if she had a ferry schedule. The asphalt road looked for a moment as if it were on fire. I looked again. It was just the reflection of the setting sun through a curtain of poplars.

I half-expected the woman to say, "Oh, a bright blue Volkswagen van with a Michelin man on top. Someone is looking for you." But no, she just looked at us characteristically as if we were criminals. Maybe she always looked like that and it was really no indication of her mental state. Maybe she was born looking like that, or born to look like that. Needless to say she had no schedule and didn't offer any ideas where we could get one.

We went through the park exit and onto the highway. I took the opportunity to extend a sincere apology to Russell for having missed his poetry reading in Toronto a while back. I hadn't found out about it until it was too late. However, aside from me, the small band of Seaworthy aficionados was in attendance. Greg Curnoe, who had been the first to tell me about Russell, had been there and said it was good. "Russell's a real comic, you know," he said. "He knows exactly how to play an audience. He was reading these poems about sharp objects falling from the sky and people picking them up and cutting themselves. What a funny guy!"

Russell accepted my apology gracefully. Then he began telling me about seeing a legless hitchhiker on the side of the highway as he drove down to Point Pelee. I think this was his way of paying me back for missing his reading, punishing me when I perhaps seemed to be most asking for it.

"He was lying on the ground pointing his crutch at the passing cars," he said.

"Did you stop for him?"

"No. But if you'd been in the van I would have. You could have written his life story."

So it had come to this, had it? Less than two years ago Russell had come to me expressing intense admiration for my writing and now he was making fun of me. I suppose I'd asked for it. There always seemed to be a certain sense of cruelty in Russell. You could see it occasionally in his writing also.

Then as we drove along I told Russell I was planning to write a short documentary novel called *A Trip Around Lake Erie*. He seemed to like the idea. So I told him I wanted to write a similar book for each of the Great Lakes, a five-book series. There was a slight hesitation, my animal instincts telling me he was briefly wondering if I were trespassing on his territory. But no, that's ridiculous, he seemed to be thinking, I can't stake claims to the entire Great Lakes.

"Sounds like a great idea," he said.

As we entered the hotel we stepped over the date of construction, 1938, inlaid in a kind of mosaic pattern in the floor just inside the front door. I'd just been wondering when it was built. It was a three-storey brick structure with an interesting pattern of first-floor lounges and dining rooms. It looked like Hartley House in Walkerton but smaller. We walked through a hallway and into a lounge with a four-foot-high television screen showing a baseball game in progress, with the brand-new Toronto Blue Jays franchise rallying for three runs in the eighth but still losing 11-8 to the Texas Rangers. At the other end of the lounge an outmoded three-piece rock group was performing along with an overly amplified female singer. There were about a dozen people in assorted small groups ignoring both the television and, with much more difficulty, the band. Some of the windows were open and the special melancholic atmosphere of Lake Erie was filtering in, a grey mystery that seemed to be funnelling out of an earlier part of the century, a melange of silent desperation arising from people now dead who once inhabited the area and were pleading to be remembered by the living.

We walked past a large horseshoe-shaped bar behind which a fat woman in her forties was reading the *TV Guide*, and entered another lounge with pool tables and pinball machines and less comfortable tables and chairs.

Another fat woman about twenty-four years old and boasting a withered arm was energetically playing one of the pinball machines. There were quite a few fat people around. There were several fat and surly men in their twenties looking as if they would become violent if they caught you looking at them.

"Hey, whaddaya think you're lookin' at, eh?"

I looked away.

"It's kind of rednecky around here," said Russell. He'd spent a few evenings here during the ten days or so he was at the cottage before Diane and Junie arrived.

There was a public telephone behind the pinball machine and I made a few phone calls trying to get ahold of someone in charge of the ferry docks at Leamington, Kingsville, Pelee Island, or even Sandusky, Ohio. But there were no answers to any of the numbers.

22. Russell Dines Out with Some Biologists

"There are some biologists drinking in the other room," said Russell. "They'd probably know the schedules."

We went into the other room. Russell introduced me to two women and three men relaxing after a hard day answering tourists' questions at the Point Pelee Nature Interpretive Centre. We were sandwiched between the huge television screen where someone had just hit a pop fly and the bandstand where the singer's double-play breasts seemed about to pop out. My eardrums were screaming.

Russell asked about the schedules but I couldn't hear their answers. They were looking at me and moving their lips and I just smiled back.

I figured out this much: the biologists were going to drive to Windsor as soon as they finished their beer. There was going to be a great fireworks display in honour of Canada Day. They wanted us to come along with them, at least the two women did.

It turned out a ferry was to leave at nine in the morning but no one knew whether it left from Leamington or Kingsville. They knew it stopped at Pelee Island but they didn't know how long it stayed there before going on to Sandusky—maybe a week, nobody knew.

We went back into the other room where the pinball machines and pool tables were located. We ordered beer.

One of the women biologists came over to our table. "Are you sure you can't come to Windsor with us?" she said. She was lovely, with tiny blue eyes, a wide mouth and extremely thin lips.

"Afraid we can't tonight," said Russell.

When she left Russell said the biologists had been very nice to him throughout his stay, patiently answering all his complex questions about the natural history of the area, and they even took him out to dinner at the Seacliffe Hotel one memorable night.

"I didn't say a word throughout the whole meal," said Russell with a gentle laugh. "I felt totally out of place."

"I guess they weren't talking about the natural history of Point Pelee?"

"Oh no. They were just talking about university and various people they knew. I don't know what they must think of me."

That was very ill-mannered of them, I thought. But I didn't say anything. "They probably just think you're quiet," I said. "And probably very romantic." I remembered that Russell didn't eat meat.

"What did you have?"

"Fresh Lake Erie perch fillets."

23. On Being Fascinated with What Is Going on Around You

"I'd love to be able to go back in time and see this hotel as it was in the late thirties and forties."

"Yeah," said Russell. "That would be great."

In the van Russell began speaking of his writing. I knew he'd eventually get around to it. He went on and on talking about the transforming effect his writing was having on his personality, and the difficulty he was having getting his characters to obey his orders.

"The novel is being written in the third person so there's no earthly reason why the main character can't simply ride away from the action," he said. I think he was hoping I'd give him some magic word that would solve the riddle.

"But you don't want to force him out of there," I said.

"That's right. Come to think of it, I suppose maybe he'll ride out of the action when he feels the right time has come."

I thought that was a good attitude to take. I mentioned Charles Dickens' *Pickwick Papers*, which was written in the third person (more or less) and the main character Samuel Pickwick, although quite able to run away from the action, was nevertheless always in the action, for all eight hundred pages. And it turned out to be a pretty good book, to say the least.

Russell seemed pleased. He said he'd have to read that book.

24. Full Moon Over Point Pelee

As we drove through the early night the trees parted and there it was: a full moon rising over Point Pelee. The waves on the west shore were smashing into the breakwater rocks and exploding into the air, each drop reflecting a miniature moon, millions of miniature moons.

Russell agreed that each of the lakes has a totally different character. He said Lake Erie was melancholy, gloomy, misty. I said I expected Lake Erie to have the same atmosphere all the way around and I was anxious to find out. We agreed that Lake Erie is our favourite lake. I told him I didn't want to live my entire life without having travelled completely around each of the lakes. It just had to be done.

At the same time I realised the notion was ridiculous. What a silly ambition! It would be more sensible to try to become a millionaire philanthropist or something like that. The world often seems an unfit place for people of modest ambition. You have to be a bit of a killer before anyone will respect you. So who needs respect? I used to know, and very well respected, a fellow who often said that if he ever got rich he would drive all the way along Barton Street till he found out where it ended. This fellow later built an airplane in his backyard, and, in his maiden flight, crashed and killed himself.

But the Great Lakes are an important part of my life. I'm conscious of being surrounded by them. The writing was a way of justifying the trips, a way of making them seem suitably important. But it was also a way of giving evidence of these feelings at this point in the planet's history. That this is one of the ways consciousness felt about these lakes in the twentieth century, if that doesn't sound too terribly pretentious.

25. The Moose Population of Quebec

Again the woman at the gatehouse looked as if we should be arrested and held without bail. Two men in a van entering a national park this late at night? They must be degenerates of the worst imaginable sort. Although Russell's van was quite distinctive in appearance, she didn't want to let on she recognised him and knew he had rented a cabin in the park. No overnight camping was allowed and since the park had been established no new cabins had been allowed to be built. The government had bought up all the old cabins they could. And although government policy fell short of outright expropriation, they had a million ways of letting cottagers know they weren't wanted.

This was one of the ways. This woman had somehow absorbed the unspoken attitude existing between the lines of official policy. Another form of human corruption, the same process no matter what the system. A human being will not hesitate to make another human being feel uncomfortable if there is any advantage at all to be gained. I'll never forget the car-wash attendant in Brunswick, Georgia, who glared hatefully at me for an astounding five seconds because I hadn't put on my brakes at exactly the moment he dropped his hand. I could imagine squadrons of goons like him breaking into tiny Vietnamese villages and hacking away at the screaming men, women and children. But we're supposed to forget all that now.

At least she wasn't armed. The Point Pelee woman, that is. A while back I was driving down to Montreal from the north of Quebec and had to pass through La Verendrye National Park. The guard had a huge revolver in a holster strapped to his belt. He handed me a leaflet, in French, warning drivers to beware of moose on the road.

It said, in part: "Not only can a collision with a moose result in damage to the car and perhaps serious injury to the motorist and passengers, it is also not very beneficial to the moose population of Quebec."

But the eyes of the woman at the Point Pelee gatehouse were incredibly evil. She said nothing but looked as if she knew what unspeakable crimes we were in the habit of committing.

"You'd think she'd recognise me by now," said Russell, mildly.

26. Playing Games

Back at the cottage we ate sandwiches and peanuts and played Scrabble. It wasn't a very exciting game. The words didn't come right for any of us. I kept having the feeling we were intruding, although Diane and Russell were most hospitable. Yet with Diane's illness, she obviously would have been more comfortable without the McFadden family around. Russell would probably be writing right now if we hadn't arrived not only unannounced but uninvited.

Russell kept getting Point Pelee words such as BIRCH and DUNE. Joan went out first, but Diane won as far as points were concerned. Diane scored 117, Joan 96, and Russell and I tied with 105 each. Funny, the last time we'd bowled together we tied too. At this point in the story I wanted to record every detail of the game and go into it with a detailed commentary, even though the game wouldn't be as worth recording, say, as the Go games in Kawabata's *The Master of Go*. I have the complete record of the game right here next to my typewriter. But I won't bother.

Just before sitting down at the typewriter today I was talking to Russell on the phone and reminded him of our Point Pelee Scrabble game. "Oh yeah, that was a good game," he said brightly, after I read him the list of the words he'd used. "That was a great visit," he said. "I'm going to be up there in June and July and you're welcome to come whenever you want."

27. Seeing Canada Vanish Under the Waves

After the game, Diane began stretching and yawning. Soon Russell and I were the only ones up. Russell got out his typewriter and set it up at the kitchen table where we'd been playing Scrabble. In spite of the visitors and Diane's illness Russell seemed to be at some kind of spiritual peak. You could see him quietly smouldering, and occasionally bursting into flame. The stay at Point Pelee was obviously doing him a lot of good. You could see little Point Pelees in his eyes.

"It's really beautiful on nights when there is no moon," he said. "I take a flashlight and get on my bicycle and ride down to the point. The whole peninsula is totally black. It's a spooky experience."

I'd been to the point once, and that had been a year ago. Yet even then, in full daylight, there was something decidedly mysterious about it. You know exactly where you are geographically, right at the southernmost tip of Canada, and it is a very clear experience somehow. You just know you're standing at some kind of significant point although that doesn't make any kind of pragmatic sense. You can see the point continue on under the water, and you can see the waves from the west meet the waves from the east at the place where the land would be if the water level were lower. The biologists stationed in the park say the point over the years keeps swinging back and forth through the water. It's like a dog's tail, they say. It never stops wagging. But the motion is too slow to see.

It was a hot summer afternoon when I last visited Point Pelee and tourists were taking turns walking out to the point then wading further out to the narrow sandbar and having their pictures taken at Canada's southernmost point. Being there was one of those rare Canadian experiences, like watching a lacrosse game between Six Nations and Owen Sound at the Brantford Arena, or finding copies of Fred Cogswell's Fiddlehead books in a bookstore in Yellowknife or Whitehorse. The painter Greg Curnoe once mailed a postcard from Pelee Island to Alert, from the southernmost Canadian post office to the northernmost. Or was it the other way around?

Anyway, it's fun to have your picture taken smiling, pants rolled up, wading off the point of Point Pelee, even though the camera may catch a small island sitting there mindlessly on the horizon. That's Pelee Island, also part of Canada, and even further south. But that doesn't really count. It's the southernmost part of *mainland* Canada that is the magical point.

And the Americans don't bother walking to the point. They just lie on the beach in their bathing suits, drinking American beer from cans, cooking American hot dogs and grumbling about Communism and Ralph Nader. I heard one of them say: "We're smarter than the Russians. We got a man on the moon."

28. Dog-Eating Dragons

"I've got about two hours worth of work to do," said Russell as he started typing. Someday you may read his novel and remember having read this story in which part of that novel was written. The working title is *Planet of Heavenly Peace*. So watch for it. Strange that both "heaven" and "heavy" would have similar Old English roots.

It was a warm summer's night and I decided to take Bruce for a walk. We walked south on the road banked by poplar trees sixty feet tall. The full moon was low in the southern sky, and the road appeared to be heading right into it. Everything was warm silver and voluptuous black. There were no street lights, no traffic lights, no lights from all-night restaurants, not the slightest whisper of even remote traffic in the distance. Just the odd cottage with a slight candle glimmering through the trees like a low-lying star.

Slight wind currents made the tall trees crack occasionally like knuckles.

I was certain I wouldn't want to bicycle all the way to the point with a flashlight on a moonless night. Russell was right. It would be spooky.

We walked about two miles, with Bruce giving low barks whenever a tree would crack its knuckles. I invented a good definition of the word bark: "The outer sheath of trees and dogs."

Point Pelee is on a major North American flyway but there didn't seem to be any nocturnal birds around, at least no noisy ones. Bruce kept close. He seemed aware of being in extraordinary circumstances and he was a little cautious. He probably thought we were approaching the gates of hell. I really couldn't tell if he was staying close to me because he wanted to protect me or because he wanted me to protect him.

For me, it was just like a return to the nineteenth century. An average narrow country road in night-time Ontario. Something out of *Wacousta*. I didn't know who I was. There was something about the atmosphere of the place that made the notion of chucking civilisation even more attractive—just coming out of the woods on dark nights to smash the windows of McDonald's hamburger joints or slash the tires of municipal politicians. Oh, what a wonderful life! Probably *Wacousta* accelerated the deforestation of Southern Ontario by several decades.

As for Bruce, I guess he was expecting to be attacked by man-eating dragons at any moment—or rather dog-eating dragons. As an experiment I made a slight hissing sound. Bruce froze, his ears fully erect.

SATURDAY, JULY 2

29. The First Mention of Dead Fish

In the morning Bruce and I were awake before anyone else so we ran over the dunes and down to the west beach. Out there on the horizon, as it had for ten thousand years, sat Pelee Island, a fringe of dark blue-grey between the light blue-grey sky and the green-grey lake. It's about fifteen miles and takes ninety minutes to get there by ferry from Seacliffe or Kingsville. I sat in the sand and watched a couple of fishing-boats inching along the horizon.

I kicked off my sandals and ran along the beach, careful to avoid stepping on the dead fish. Bruce ran in front of me, occasionally looking back over his shoulder. His tongue was hanging out as if he had swallowed a bright red tie.

The sand became too soft. My feet went down four or five inches with each step. It became too difficult to run. I began slowing down. Then I couldn't run anymore. I fell to my knees. Bruce stopped and cocked his head as if to say, "What's wrong?"

There was quite a breeze and the breeze was churning the waves. Thick whitecaps appeared on the horizon, moved in like low-flying gulls, then disappeared. There was a feeling of being in the sub-tropical rain forest—vines curling up the trunks of small trees and Spanish moss hanging from tall branches like the dry unkempt beards of old hermits.

I performed my regular morning calisthenics with the sandy wind on my back and in my hair. It felt wonderful. Then I remembered that last night, when Russell and I were at the hotel, Joan had taken the dog down to the beach. All the time the dog was down there he kept rolling on top of the dead and rotting fish that dotted the shoreline. He became so smelly that Joan had to bathe him.

So I looked and sure enough he was doing it again. How stupid of me! Joan would kill me. He was rolling over and over back and forth on every dead fish he encountered.

And then he would stand there and piss on each one. And then roll over on it a few more times for luck.

I quickly brought him back up to the cottage and hoped Joan wouldn't notice the smell. It was kind of sad. I'd have liked to have joined Bruce in pissing on the fish and rolling over and over on them.

30. A Skeleton in the Trust Company

The sun came up over the giant poplar trees surrounding the sad little cottage and we ate a hearty breakfast and took dozens of photos of each other with Russell's camera. We said goodbye, see you in time, in Hamilton, in Toronto, somewhere, and drove off.

In Leamington I parked the car and went into a trust company to buy some U.S. money. The town was flooded with the most intense sunlight but it was cool and shady inside. It was Saturday and there were only two women working, no customers. Here I made the kind of faux-pas anyone could have made.

"Skeleton staff today?" I said to the women, innocently trying to make a cheerful joke. As I said it I sucked my cheeks in and opened my eyes wide to try to look like a skeleton.

Neither woman laughed. Then I noticed that one of them did indeed look like a skeleton—sunken eyes, drawn face, extremely thin arms and legs. She looked a hare's breath from death. They doubtlessly thought that I was making some extremely thoughtless and cruel joke, and there was no way I could apologise without making the whole thing worse.

Can you imagine me trying to apologise? What would I say: "Oh, I'm sorry. I had no idea that you looked like a.... Well, I just said that as a joke before really looking at you.... Er, I wasn't referring to your physical appearance at all." It just wouldn't work.

Thin people are often more sensitive about their appearance than the biggest fattest tubs of lard. One woman I know always bursts into tears whenever anyone draws attention to her thinness. Yet the thinnest person of my acquaintance, a Jewish poet who is obsessed with concentration camps, takes great pride in his emaciated body. He puts saccharine in his coffee and refuses to eat bread and pastries, or much of anything. That's understandable though. I think most of us would be a lot happier and less neurotic if we cut our food consumption by 90 per cent.

The thin woman waited on me. It cost me $106.65 in Canadian funds to buy $100 U.S. She gave me five funny-looking twenties with pictures of some guy in a nineteenth-century beard.

Just to remind you: This was the summer of 1977, just a few months before it became obvious to everyone that Canada was heading inevitably for total union with the United States, the country so terrific it doesn't even need a real name.

I looked at the thin woman again just before I pocketed the money. She had a long scar running along the inner half of her left arm. It looked as if the entire ulna had been removed.

31. The Crests of the Provinces of Canada

We decided against taking the ferry across to Ohio. The schedules were just too awkward. The kids were disappointed but we told them there was a ferry marked on the map at Amherstburg at the western end of Lake Erie. We'd zip across there.

So we drove along beautiful sunny Highways 18 and 18A past black families from Detroit fishing in roadside pools where egrets and herons brooded, past fruit farms and small fields of tomatoes, fields swarming with poor-looking families of pickers, past huge cottages owned by Americans and flying the U.S. flag, past monasteries and convents with the ever-blue Lake Erie to the left sitting there like a handful of holy water held up to the parched lips of God.

We stopped at a little place called Colchester situated on a sort of nipple on the long breast-like curve of shore bulging out into the lake from Point Pelee to Windsor. We walked down to the water and waded a bit. There was a small house trailer set there on the lake, almost on the beach itself. The wheels had been removed and it looked as if it were there to stay, or at least until the next strong wind off the lake.

A wooden patio had been built on one side of the trailer. The wood was painted in red and white stripes. There was an ornate railing running around the patio on three sides. Attached to the railing were several hand-painted crests, one for each of the Canadian provinces. There was a large Canadian flag attached to the top of the trailer. And there was a foot-high picket fence marking what appeared to be the boundaries of the owner's property.

I was looking at the crests, from a respectful distance, when the owner pulled up on a bicycle. He was in his mid-thirties.

"Did you paint those crests?" I said.

"Yes, I sure did." You could tell he thought he'd done a marvellous job, and he had.

"They're really nice."

"Thank you." He seemed to want something more than "nice."

"What kind of paint did you use?"

"Any scraps I could get my hands on."

"You mean house paint?"

"Yep. Mostly from neighbours. Scraping the bottoms of cans that people were finished with. Stuff like that."

"Well they're really nice," I said. "And I really mean it. It's nice to see a patriotic man...in this country."

With that he brightened up.

"I had two others but they blew away in a storm," he said. "We get some awful storms around here."

"Which two?"

"The Northwest Territories and the Yukon."

"Hmm! Isn't that strange? The only two that don't represent real provinces and they get blown away."

"We get some awful storms," he repeated. He sat on his bicycle and looked at me. He had chocolate brown eyes. "This American and his wife were coming through one day," he said, "and stopped. He knew Canada pretty well but his wife knew nothing about it. She was from Oklahoma or somewhere and thought the world ended at the American border. Well, he had me get all the crests and lay them down on the ground and go over each one with her, telling her the name of the province and the symbolism of the crest. I tell you, by the time I was finished she knew a lot about Canada."

"I bet she did," I said. "By the way, which crest gave you the most trouble?" There was a lovely breeze coming off the lake.

"I'd say Manitoba there. I had a helluva time with that damned buffalo. You have no idea."

32. Bruce Eats Stones

We had parked on a gravel road and tied Bruce to the side of the car. We left him with a bowl of dog food and a bowl of water. When we got back from looking at the crests we noticed he was doing something strange. He was eating stones.

He had taken the stones from the road and put them in his bowl, just pushed the stones up into the bowl with his snout. Then he ate the food together with the stones.

We grabbed the bowl off him and picked out all the stones. Then we put the bowl down again. And again he started nosing stones up into the bowl. And eating them with his food.

Maybe he was nauseous. To the canine ear, Gravol might be easily confused with gravel.

33. Ferry to Nowhere

When we got to Amherstburg there were no signs showing where the ferry dock was located so we drove down to the waterfront where a 300-pound black woman dressed in a pink pant suit and a pink sun hat was sitting on the dock fishing with a bamboo pole ten feet long. She had just caught a fingerling and was gingerly trying to remove the hook. She looked worried. She had her pink tongue clenched between her white teeth. It looked as if the fish had swallowed the entire hook and the hook had pierced its little heart.

A white woman about fifty was standing there with her son—or was it her lover? Or, perish the thought, both? He was about twenty. She kept touching his bare shoulders lovingly, lightly, teasingly. She couldn't understand what I was asking her.

"The ferry dock? What do you mean, dear?" Her lipstick was severely smudged.

"The dock where the ferry boat pulls in to pick up passengers," I said. I knew there was one because it was clearly marked on my road map. Well, fairly clearly.

"The dock for the ferry boat? What do you mean, dear?"

"Oh, forget it." I started walking away and she called me back. Her young lover looked so serious.

"Oh, I know what you're looking for," she said. "It's half-a-mile back that way, dear," she said. "Yes, it's a half-a-mile back, dear."

"Half-a-mile back?"

"Yes, dear."

So we went back and sure enough we had gone right by it without noticing it. But that was because it wasn't really the sort of thing we were looking for. For one thing, it wasn't a car ferry. It was just a passenger ferry. And it didn't go right across the river to Ohio. It just went over to an island in the river on the Canadian side where there was an amusement park, a private commercial establishment.

We had passed the signs advertising the amusement park and luckily the kids hadn't noticed them. It seemed odd that this would be marked on an official road map as a real ferry.

The signs advertised a duck that played the piano, a pig that tap-danced, and other "feed-and-touch" animals. God, now we were trapped. The kids wanted to feel, they wanted to touch, they wanted to get on that ferry and sail.

"Does this ferry go across to the United States?" I asked the woman at the gate, who reminded me of the woman at the Point Pelee gate house. But this one had an English accent and an ironic disposition.

"No. It just goes to the island and the island is still in Canada," she said. She wanted me to know she was a nationalist, in spite of having an English accent, and that I was a traitor to want to go to the United States when Canada was so beautiful and even had an amusement park with real live feed-and-touch animals. "It's still only in Canada," she said, a little sarcastically.

"Oh dad, let's go," said Alison.

"Yeah, dad, come on," said Jennifer.

"No kids," said Joan, saving my bacon again. "We're going all the way around Lake Erie, remember, and we don't want to waste time in a tacky amusement park. There will be lots of nicer places than this to visit when we get over to the States." I looked at her and cocked my eyebrow. She smiled sweetly. The gate lady frowned.

The kids remained philosophical about disappointments, as always. Never any temper tantrums with these little angels.

34. Windsor: The Gateway to the North

In most Canadian cities the poor live in the north and east ends. But here in Windsor the really rundown areas are in the south and west ends. Mind you, the east and north ends don't look all that prosperous either.

Windsor is the saddest city. Nowhere is Canada's plight more evident. No matter where you are in town you can look up and see the huge Ambassador Bridge to Detroit rainbowing through the air like a cultural and economic siphon. The bridge doesn't seem to link two pieces of land. Rather it seems to link two levels of land. It's the highest thing in Windsor and the lowest thing in Detroit.

Indeed, the United States from this vantage point gives the impression of being some magic land in the clouds, the magic bridge streaming down from these clouds and condescending to land in the hinterlands, this inferior, nondescript underworld where the land has long been permanently scorched.

And from everywhere in Windsor you can see the skyline of Detroit. When you look up, there it is. In Vancouver when you look up you see the mountains, in Windsor you see Detroit.

As if that weren't enough Detroit is upwind of Windsor. Every fart, every belching smokestack comes drifting like a putrid inescapable river of stench into Windsor. And if you turn on the radio you'll be lucky if you find a little Canadian station in between the giant American ones, sandwiched like an earwig between pairs of copulating elephants.

Windsor is a nice place to visit though. And there are several good American and British writers living in Windsor.

35. What to Wear When You Visit the United States

For our last supper in Canada we went to the Top Hat Restaurant on University Avenue. It was quite posh. There were suits of armour standing around in the foyer looking sadly important. In the washroom there was a blackboard with chalk and eraser and a sign saying FOR POETS & ARTISTS. There were lots of different rooms, lounges and so on. The cutlery, china and furniture was old, rich and well-maintained. The walls were made from pieces of coloured glass and old wine bottles with light shining through. The matchbooks were in the shape of a top hat and bore the slogan: LOBSTERS ENTERTAINMENT NIGHTLY.

"What do you think lobsters entertainment is like?" I asked the kids, who were precociously syntax-savvy and had been correcting our English practically from birth.

"Maybe they tap-dance on their pinchers," said Jennifer.

"They probably square-dance underwater," said Alison.

"I bet they do Al Jolson imitations to keep from being boiled alive," said Joan.

"Shall we order four?" I said.

"Would they have to be boiled alive?" said Alison.

"Of course they would," said Joan.

"No, Daddy, no!" screamed Jennifer. Tears of great compassion were squirting out of her eyes. When she regained her composure she said, "Let's just have potato chips."

The kids were fooling around with the cigarette machine and found a quarter in the return slot. They gave it to the bartender. He was appreciative. "You have very nice kids," he said. He had a Clark Gable moustache. He looked like a refugee from Detroit.

On the way out I looked at the suits of armour and shuddered. Maybe we should get four of these for our trip through the States, I thought. I didn't say anything though.

36. A Horrible Way to Die

I felt a little uneasy. Was I doing the right thing in taking my kids to the United States again?

Be a good citizen, Dave, and don't be such a philistine. Learn to disregard your paranoid feelings about this monstrous country. As Canadians we tend to look at the American underbelly with more loathing than it deserves. For the real people of the earth there are no borders. For the poor people of the world the world is an open book.

But I was thinking of that poor young steelworker from Hamilton who took off for a little Florida vacation on his motorcycle and was found shot to death on the side of the road in Ohio. He had probably made a rude gesture to a motorist who had cut him off and the motorist retaliated by blowing his head off with a shotgun. But a killing like this could have taken place anywhere—even in Canada. Don't hand me those statistics about runaway murder rates in the U.S.A. Everybody knows statistics lie. The European races, famed and feared for centuries for their ferocity, have shown signs recently of regaining their sanity, of becoming, once again, like all the other races.

But I'm far off the track. As we left the Top Hat Restaurant I asked the others if they wanted to enter the United States via the Ambassador Bridge or the Detroit Tunnel. And after lengthy discussion as befits such a momentous decision they opted for the tunnel. But there were certain misgivings.

The entrance to the tunnel was just a few blocks from the restaurant. We followed the signs, then paid our seventy-five cents. As we approached the dark and ominous entrance I suddenly remembered something horrible from my childhood. It must have been connected with the birth trauma. My mother told me I had an easy birth, but what did she know?

At any rate I could remember as a child fantasising about the various ways of dying. And I decided the worst possible way, worse even than a plane crash or falling from a trapeze at a crowded circus, or from a tightrope high above the city streets, would be to have a tunnel cave in on you as you were driving through. Particularly a tunnel under a river. I'd never been to Detroit but I'd heard of this horrible tunnel.

Ridiculous! Do you realise what the odds would be against this tunnel collapsing during the few minutes it would take you to drive through? Don't even think of such a preposterous idea.

But somehow Joan picked up my thoughts. We were both anxiety neurotics, but she'd been taking a course in ESP. On the road were some puddles of water illuminated by ghostly yellow light and Joan said, nervously, "Where is the water coming from?"

A chill ran up my back. We were obviously having the same fantasy. She thought the entire Detroit River was about to come cascading in and sweep us away like so much flotsam and jetsam. Another memory from my childhood: When I was a kid I had a book called *Flotsam and Jetsam*. It was a pretty ordinary book, about a guy who loved his sailboat. He used to sail out in the harbour first thing in the morning and write down his thoughts. One line I particularly remember went like this: "It was a beautiful sunrise this morning—for those of us awake to enjoy it."

"It's just rainwater," I said. We were sailing through the tunnel like a motorised mole.

"Rainwater?" said Joan. "How could rainwater get in here?" She seemed on the verge of clutching my arm and screaming: "Get me out of here right now!"

"I don't know. It just does. Rain falls on the street and seeps down here because it's lower."

"And it doesn't have to pay seventy-five cents," said Jennifer.

"How much does it have to pay?" said Alison.

"But," said Joan, with a quivering lip, "it hasn't been raining. There's no rain on the street."

"That's because it's all evaporated," said I, with the quick thinking that has saved my bacon on numerous occasions. "But this is a tunnel, you see, and in tunnels the water doesn't evaporate as quickly. Everybody knows that."

"Oh," said Joan.

37. A Reasonable Request for Oranges

I don't think my explanation really satisfied Joan, but there was light at the end of the tunnel, as if one has to die a little death before entering the U.S.A. And soon a customs official bathed in golden American sunlight was leaning in the window and asking me for my birth certificate.

"By golly, I left it at home," I said. "It's in my fireproof filing cabinet."

"That's not much good to you there," she said. She was beautiful, or would be if it weren't for the mean look on her face. She figured she was smarter than any carload of Canadians any day.

"The last time we came over you didn't ask for a birth certificate so I didn't bother bringing it this time."

"Birth certificates have been required to cross into the United States at Detroit for almost two years."

"Well, I'll be darned."

She spoke in rather sarcastic tones and it appeared as if we were going to be turned back. But then she asked for our dog's needle certificates and we had all that in order. She found nothing amiss there. How could she have known that the vet's signature had been forged? Then she asked if we had any oranges.

"That's all you asked the last time we came over. Do you have any oranges? We said no and you waved us on."

"I wasn't working here that long ago."

"Oh, I am sorry. I didn't mean you *personally*, I meant you *collectively*. I guess I should have said youse."

"There's a lot of cars behind you. Do you have any oranges?"

"No."

"Okay, move ahead."

"Oh by the way, do you know where we can get a map of Michigan?"

"Try a service station. Now move it!"

I went to pull away and stalled the van. Then we jerked away through the rain puddles out onto the streets of Detroit.

"What a bitch!" exclaimed Joan. "We should report her. Did you get her badge number? She didn't have to be that nasty."

"How nasty did she have to be?" said Jennifer.

"I wonder why they always ask about oranges?" I said.

"Maybe she wanted one," said Alison.

38. Writers Should Respect Their Readers

There were no service stations within sight and so, remembering vaguely the route from our trip to Florida of a few years earlier, we headed out onto the Interstate 75 running south toward the Ohio border. We wanted to stay off the expressways but this was the only road running around the western end of Lake Erie.

As soon as we got onto the expressway we became entangled in heavy fast-moving traffic, were forced to make a premature exit, and found ourselves in the heart of downtown Detroit.

It was just like a Hollywood movie from the thirties. But there were no young James Cagneys or Clark Gables running around. There were just a lot of boarded-up windows and padlocked doors. And a lot of black people standing around waiting for buses.

Another funny story from my childhood came to mind: I was sitting in the Detroit bus terminal. It was the summer of 1959. The place was crowded but there was an empty seat next to me. On the other side of the empty seat a nice-looking middle-aged man was reading newspapers and piling them up next to him. An enormous black girl came up to him and pointed at his papers. "Do you mind if I sit there, sir?" she said.

The guy said nothing, just stood up, picked up all the newspapers and in a fit of temper threw them way across the floor of the bus terminal. You should have seen them slide, slither and scatter. Then he stalked off, black smoke puffing out of his ears. It might have had something to do with the fact that the girl was of African descent, I don't know. She looked hurt and sad, but she was relieved to be able to sit down at last.

I would have said something to her like, "Don't let that nasty bastard bother you," but a lot of people had been warning me not to talk to black people in too friendly a way. It might cause a fight. This was a long time ago. I'd been on the bus from Chicago to Detroit and had been sitting next to a pretty black teenage girl about my age. My heart was thumping and I kept trying to engage her in conversation but she wouldn't speak. Then she fell asleep. And as she did her lovely little head came to rest on my shoulder. I was thrilled as only an innocent, pure-hearted eighteen-year-old could be.

As we rode along like that, her sleeping head like a little black curragh bobbing up and down on the miniature sea of my shoulder, I happened to look up toward the front of the bus and at the same moment the bus driver suddenly noticed us through his rearview mirror, noticed her head on my shoulder, and his eyes started bulging out of their sockets. The bus almost went off the road. Others noticed as well and looked back and soon I was getting all kinds of menacing looks. It wasn't as if I'd had to sit beside this black girl. There were all kinds of empty seats. When she woke up and found her head had been on my shoulder she moved closer to the window and cried. I tried to comfort her but really there was nothing I could do.

When the bus stopped at South Bend, a bunch of hostile-looking guys crowded around me and wanted to know where I came from. When I told them Canada they seemed to sympathise with me a bit. They warned me I'd likely get killed if I kept on acting that way.

I was shattered. What about all the wonderful things I'd been taught in Sunday School? When I got back on the bus I sat by myself. The black girl wouldn't talk to me anyway. Perhaps I wouldn't have been such a moral coward if she'd expressed some interest.

But that was a long time ago. It makes me feel not only like an old man but also as if I've been wasting my life. Ah, but who cares? I'm certainly not wasting my life, not a moment of it. Except perhaps when I dwell on the past too much.

And back in the beautiful moment...but wait! Even as I write this I realise I'm thinking about the past, writing about the past. Things are happening around me as I type but I have excluded them from consciousness: the sunlight filtering through the small bottle collection on the windowsill, the beautiful blue of the walls, the sound the typewriter makes, the sound of the spring warblers warbling on the trees outside the window, the telephone that rings occasionally, the conversations I have. None of this is going into my writing. I'm writing about something that happened several months ago. The kids have come home from school and are making lunch for themselves and asking if I want a sandwich. But I am caught in the past, trying to fix a moment that has already become dead. The one saving grace is that I have a book full of notes taken as the incidents unfolded. I'm engaged in a typing and editing pattern more than a writing pattern. And the typing and editing are taking place in the present.

The end result will be to take something from the past, in this case a trip around Lake Erie in the summer of 1977, and make it permanently a feature of the endlessly unrolling present by writing about it and having it in a book that will never recede into the past. So that 1977, for me, will never be totally dead. And so somehow that justifies what doesn't really need to be justified anyway.

Before we managed to get back on to the southbound expressway we made quite a thorough tour of downtown Detroit. I'd heard some awful things about it but it seemed pretty ordinary to me. I got the impression all the really run-down slums were inhabited by people of European descent. The more expensive-looking areas with stately, well-maintained, brown-brick buildings from the turn of the century and with well-maintained lawns and gardens were inhabited by people of African descent. The whites we saw looked like winos, the blacks like successful businessmen. There seemed to be a lot of poverty in all the sections we passed through but it was the whites who were the victims rather than the blacks. Ridiculous making comments like this based on such small samples. But there comes a time in a writer's life when he has to give up any lingering reluctance to appear ridiculous.

We passed Tiger Stadium, home of the Detroit Tigers, and the Olympiad, home of the Detroit Red Wings, and finally found our way back onto the Interstate 75. The Ambassador Bridge brooded in the background. At one point we found ourselves heading westward on the expressway to Chicago and we considered going there just for the hell of it but decided it wouldn't look good in a story about a trip around Lake Erie. I figure a writer should have some respect for his readers if he wants to have any and I do.

39. The Monroe K-Mart and Garage

We were travelling south-southwest along the flat ledge-back of Lake Erie, receiving occasional glimpses of that tranquil freshwater inland sea. The last time we drove this way it was February and we ran into a massive snowstorm. Giant transport trucks were jackknifing all over the place and our little snow-white Toyota gave up the ghost on Interstate 75 near Lima, Ohio. This trip is commemorated in my famous poem, "A Typical Canadian Family Visits Disneyworld." But this was summer and Lake Erie was winking at us conspiratorially, as if to say you are the only ones who really know me. To these Americans I'm just a body (of water) but you Canadians know my true soul. There's something unreal, unthinking, uncaring about the United States.

We stopped at a K-Mart in Monroe, Michigan. Joan wanted to get some camping supplies. The place was crowded with Americans. I kept wondering if people could tell we were foreigners. I wanted to have a leak and found I had to apply at a special window for permission to enter the public washroom. The girl in the window looked at me blankly, decided I was no security risk (in spite of my extreme self-consciousness), and pressed a buzzer which unlocked the washroom door.

The cubicles were painted dark brown. The graffiti was decidedly strange. "I'm going to see the Teasers tonight and don't try to stop me," someone had written.

When I came out there was a short crippled girl staring at me. She was radiantly beautiful and wore crutches with special arm braces. Both legs seemed to be fused. Her eyes shone and she licked her lips as she looked at me. She was about seventeen. I walked over to the stereo department. The girl followed me. They had some really hot equipment in stock. As I watched, a young fellow about nineteen came in, looked at a stereo set and bought it just like that. He wrote a cheque for $650 and walked out with the set in a huge carton. Monroe is basically a Detroit suburb and I guess a lot of the people work in the motor plants. And who knows, that guy might have been looking at that particular set for a week. Maybe he'd read all the consumer reports and knew exactly what he wanted and what it should cost. It's the only way to buy stuff.

The rear-view mirror on the passenger's side of the van had become loose and on the way out I stopped at the K-Mart garage and asked to borrow a wrench. The mechanic was quite generous about it.

"You certainly may, sir," he said.

He handed me the wrench with no questions asked and I walked out with it and tightened the mirror.

"Thanks," I said when I returned the wrench.

"Don't mention it," he said.

Americans are friendly people.

As we drove off, through the rear-view mirror I could see the crippled girl standing there, still staring at us.

40. The Androids of Luna Pier

We didn't bother stopping at the General Custer Historic Site, nor at the "Frozen Custer" stand nearby. We drove straight back to the Interstate 75 but after a few miles of fast driving I noticed we were low on gas so we had to get off again.

We took the next exit and found ourselves in a place called Luna Pier, a small resort community right on the lake. It was a strange-looking place with a series of scum-covered canals heading nowhere and people repairing the roofs of their cottages. Women in sausage pincurls were standing in the middle of the road talking. I don't know what they were talking about. Maybe they were talking about us.

"Yes, there's a family of Canadians coming through in a yellow van. Here they come now. They're very superior, they think they own the entire rights to Lake Erie. They think we're unreal, somnambulistic, ignorant and jingoistic, living out our dull lives like meaningless androids incapable of self-reflection or compassion."

"How do you know all this?"

"I'm picking it up on my sausage pincurls."

The women smiled mechanically and moved to the side of the road to let us through. They had the blank eyes of extra-terrestrials.

The Luna Pier gas station was hopelessly crowded. It was the only one around for miles. Everyone was smoking around the pumps and I started to get nervous. We waited in line for about fifteen minutes. Geez, why didn't I think to fill up in Monroe?

There was a midget pumping gas. He had a high forehead and was puffing furiously on a midget cigar. I handed him my Chargex card and asked if he honoured it. He couldn't decide and kept turning the card over and over. He was puffing so hard on his little cigar flames and sparks were coming out the hot end. I thought the place was going to blow up. Things like that were always happening in the United States. Two paragraphs in the *Toronto Star* on a slow news day.

So I finally lost patience and said, "If you have to think about it, it's no good," grabbed the card out of his pudgy little hand, and drove off.

We drove inland about ten miles to the town of Samaria before we found another gas station. We filled up and got a map.

41. Dead Wrong about Joan

"I'm glad I don't have to live in that crummy place," said Joan, referring to Luna Pier.

An English friend of mine, when he came to Canada, asked if I would be able to tell he was English just by seeing him on the street. You would be able to tell, but I didn't tell him. He had a certain different way of holding his facial muscles, a slightly different way of walking. His cheeks were English red, and his clothes looked English.

"That's the way I felt in that K-Mart," I told Joan. "I kept wondering if people knew we were Canadians." She said she didn't feel that way at all. In fact most of the time she wasn't conscious of being outside her own country.

As for Luna Pier, I told her she would probably have loved the place if it had been in Canada. It was just the knowledge that it was in the United States that made her dislike it so much.

"Oh no," she said. "You're dead wrong there."

I turned on the radio. "One out of every six adults has high blood pressure," said the announcer.

42. Charging Admission to See an Earthquake Crack

We cut down to Toledo on the Interstate 75 then drove right through the city and across the Maumee River. If you think of Lake Erie as a mouse, then the Maumee River is the mouse's tail. There's the way it looks on the map anyway, or from high in the air. The river starts up somewhere in Indiana.

Soon we were out of Toledo and heading east along the U.S. 280 through the town of Oregon then down to the U.S. 2. The U.S. 2 parallels the south shore of Lake Erie but for the most part not close enough actually to see the lake. Marshy land surrounded the highway and as you drove along you could pick out dozens of varieties of ducks, herons, and other water birds. The kids checked the map and confirmed that yes Lake Erie did resemble a mouse. Then they dozed off in the back seat and Joan put her head down on my lap and fell asleep.

At one point we passed a nuclear power plant featuring a huge hourglass of a building, an eggcup five hundred feet high. It looked as if it had been built by the same guy who builds the McDonald's hamburg places. It had been up quite a while and there had been no maintenance at all. The signs had fallen off. Even the paint was falling off in huge flakes like falling leaves. But the paint was green, which is the colour of leaves but not of falling leaves. I wanted to stop and take a picture of the plant but I didn't want to disturb Joan and the kids. It looked like the sort of place where you could drive in and get fast service on a small nuclear bomb. It looked as if you could pick up a case of leukemia just by leaning against the fence.

We passed Crane Creek State Beach and the towns of Long Beach and Locust Point. At this point there's an interesting peninsula that juts out into Lake Erie, surrounded by four islands. I'd noticed it on the map many times in the past but never visualised myself being there. It's due south of Point Pelee and Pelee Island and forms part of the partial land bridge across western Lake Erie, the flyway which migrating birds find so attractive.

As we drove through Port Clinton and further out along the Marblehead Peninsula it became apparent we were heading into tourist country. It was highly commercialised in a way that Point Pelee definitely was not, though Point Pelee definitely attracts tourists.

Most of the tourism around Marblehead though was of the short-run, day-trip variety. Mostly holidaying Ohio residents. I can't imagine people from other states saying hey, let's head up to Lake Erie for our holidays this year.

Cottages, trailer camps, and tourist traps of all kinds became more and more frequent. Highway signs advertised the attractions. Everything was amazing and unbelievable and fantastic. THE AMAZING PREHISTORIC VALLEY was straight ahead. You could turn left for the FANTASTIC EARTHQUAKE CRACK BRING YOUR CAMERA.

The largest granite cut in Canada is on Ontario Highway 118 just west of Bracebridge but there are no signs pointing it out. The enormous skull-like Bruce's Cave, on the Bruce Peninsula, stares out across the Canadian Shield toward Labrador as if waiting longingly for the return of the Ice Age. It's marked by a feeble little cardboard hand-written sign nailed to a stunted sumac. One time I climbed a medium-sized mountain near Banff and found, when I got to the top, there was a chair-lift I could have taken, had I noticed it. But at the summit were dozens of U.S. tourists milling around. They had come up on the chair-lift. You could see a hundred miles in every direction. It was glorious. A lady American sneered, kicked a small rock and said, "I suppose they'll eventually get this place cleaned up."

Years later I encountered the same lady—at least I have the strangest feeling it was the same one—in the foyer of the Avon Theatre in Stratford, Ontario, following a performance of *Hamlet*. When her friend asked how she liked the play, she replied: "I didn't like it at all, it was too full of clichés."

That crippled girl, who had been staring at us a few chapters back, I wish I could say that we were about to encounter her again. But she had apparently disappeared from our lives forever, as do most of the people one briefly encounters on one's travels.

43. Americans Are Even Friendlier When Drunk

On our Boron map of the eastern states there was a red dot marked East Harbour State Park. It was halfway between Port Clinton and the town of Marblehead. The map didn't really seem all that accurate though.

We drove past an unmarked state park. It was about seven o'clock, time to turn in. So we turned into a side road in order to turn around and go back. Another car pulled in alongside ours. Two guys were in it.

"What're ya lookin' fer?" the guy on the passenger side said. He had blue eyes, sort of unfocussed, and he talked with a slur as wide as a canoe is long. But he obviously wanted to help.

"We were just turning around to go back to the state park."

"Ko shtraight ahead," he slurred. He conferred for a moment with the driver, a darker, smaller fellow with a wacky grin. "Ko down to the shtoplight then turn left. It'll take you to Easht Harbour Shtate Park. Thash where ya wanna ko—erp!"

"Thanks a lot. That's where we were heading but we passed another state park a mile or so back. It wasn't marked on the map. We were just turning back to check it out."

"Ya can't camp there," he said. "But ya can camp all night at Easht Harbour Shtate Park."

"Thanks a lot, eh?" I said. Americans love to hear Canadians say "eh?" They smiled. They had huge beer bellies, like Georgia sheriffs. Then they drove down the side road, weaving a bit from side to side.

I pulled back onto the highway and headed east toward the stoplight.

"Were they drunk or what?" said Joan.

"Hard to say. Just a little drunk maybe," I conceded.

The kids giggled.

44. Canadians Are Really Cute

But we were out of luck. East Harbour State Park was filled to capacity for the night. We'd heard on our car radio all along that hotels, motels, tourist homes and campgrounds were all filled up and people had been sleeping in their cars at the side of the road. It was the July 4 weekend. People were restless, on the move. It was the 201st birthday of the United States of America.

Joan was getting a little edgy. She said we should have started looking for a campsite at five o'clock. "I don't want to leave it this late any more," We kept passing motels and campgrounds with NO VACANCY signs. Every time we saw another NO VACANCY sign Joan would sigh a sigh of great depth, resonance and complexity.

We stopped at the inappropriately named Camp Runnamuck. The guy said he had nothing but he could let us park at the side of the road with no shade and no picnic table. Joan wouldn't go for it. There was a sign saying NO ROWDYISM. Everything was quite quiet and peaceful. "Maybe there will be some rowdyism, and you can kick the rowdies out and let us in," I said.

"You Canadians are really cute," he said. I wondered if he could tell I was a Canadian because of my accent. Or maybe he'd noticed my licence plate: KEEP ONTARIO BEAUTIFUL.

45. October 8, 1686

It was a beautiful area, really. It was the hour before sundown and all the little towns and villages radiated a pristine beauty. People walked along the streets in a trance. Everyone looked as if he or she had just stepped out of a shower and put on fresh clothing.

We finally found a place. It was called Ned's Ledge, just past Marblehead at the tip of this lovely peninsula separating Lake Erie from Sandusky Bay. We were almost due south of Pelee Island. In fact looking out over the lake I thought I saw Pelee Island in the late afternoon sun, It looked the same as it had from the other side, from the west beach of Point Pelee, earlier that day in the early morning sun with Bruce rolling over and over on the dead fish. Could that have been only this morning? We could also see Johnson's Island which contained the ruins of a Civil War prison and cemetery.

The woman's name was Shirley. She charged us $3.00 and solemnly wrote us a receipt. What looked like a seventeenth-century grave marker was propped against a tree outside the house. But it was only a copy. Shirley's husband had cut it from a slab of wood in such a way it looked like real marble. "Ned's good at that sort of thing," she said. "He really is. But he doesn't do it much anymore. He's too busy all the time." She sounded as if she wished he'd slow down and do it more.

Here is what the grave marker said:

JANE SECORD
WIFE TO CAPT.
RICHARD MORE
SENR, AGED, 55
YEARS. DEPARTED
THIS LIFE YE
8 OF OCTOBER
- 1686 -

46. The World's Largest Movie Screen

We set up camp in the middle of a grassy field spread out behind Ned and Shirley's large white frame house. I always feel a little stupid at moments like this. It somehow seems a little less natural than just turning in at a hotel or even a motel. A little less natural even though presumably you're closer to nature.

Anyway it was the July 4 weekend and the other campers were flying U.S. flags and tossing firecrackers all over the place. The kids ran across the field to play on the swings. I tied Bruce's leash to a stake. Joan made sandwiches. I got the sleeping gear ready.

Then came one of the bonuses of this kind of trip: the friendliness of the people. You get to make friends wherever you go. A woman, one of the campers, came over to talk to us. Things like this never happen in motels or hotels.

The woman's name was Evelyn, and it didn't seem to bother her at all that we were not flying a flag. She brought over her shy little girl, Kelly, and her not-so-shy brown dog, Rusty. She told us they'd had a tornado just last week.

"Too bad my friend Russell wasn't here," I said. "He's crazy about tornadoes but he's never seen one."

"He wouldn't have been able to see it if he was here," she said without smiling, as if a dark thought had crossed her mind, as if she were thinking (to herself) that Russell must be a Communist or something. "It was in the middle of the night."

She and her husband were planning to take their kids to Cedar Point the next day. Cedar Point was apparently a semi-Disneyland. They wanted to leave first thing in the morning because it was expensive. Admission was $8.50 per person. They wanted to spend a full day there to make sure they got their money's worth. The parents were more excited than the kids.

She was surprised we hadn't heard about Cedar Point. You could tell she was thinking unpleasant thoughts about the intelligence of Canadians.

"They just have the world's largest movie screen there, that's all," she said.

"How large would that be?"

"Six storeys high, that's all."

She went on to tell us about all the amusements and rides they have there. She told us that every morning in the summer there's a line-up of cars five miles long waiting to get in. We had no reason to disbelieve her. She said she'd been to Point Pelee when she was a kid.

"Want to go?" I asked Joan after the woman left. Meaning to Cedar Point the next day.

"No thanks," said Joan.

I was glad. I always get sick on rides. Even ferris wheels. Or, as the kids used to call them, fairest wheels.

47. Why Bruce Likes to Roll Over on Dead Fish and Eat Stones

An older man and woman came by. They were in their sixties. They had a brown dog with them, part Labrador retriever and part collie. Its name was Rusty.

"That woman who was just over here had a dog named Rusty," I said.

"Popular name for dogs," he said.

"A pop pup name," said Alison.

They were nice, intelligent people and the woman reminded me a lot of Joan's mother, Velma. But they frightened me a little because they thought Canada should be taken over by the United States as soon as possible because of all the communists up there. I just smiled and agreed pleasantly because Joan was giving me significant glances and meaningful looks.

The old fellow said the "socialist" policies of Trudeau's government were going to destroy Canada economically. He seemed to be genuinely concerned about the fate of Canada. He said he and his wife had long been thinking of taking a motor trip into Canada but hadn't got around to it yet. Maybe next summer.

It turned out this man, whose name was Clive, knew a lot about dogs. One might say Americans know a lot about everything. But he seemed to know his dogs all right.

He told us Bruce likes to roll over on dead fish because he wants to get their smell on his fur. It's a way of disguising his own smell so that other animals will be confused and at a strategic disadvantage. The average dog's mind is quite devious when it comes to other dogs. The average dog's mind is located in his nose.

As for pushing stones up into his food bowl, that's just the dog's instinct which tells it to bury its food. He probably is not really eating the stones, he just appears to be. He is probably nosing the stones out of the way and eating the food—that is, unburying the food and eating it.

"Maybe a few go down but it won't hurt him any," said Clive.

We were still a little worried but he said we shouldn't be. "A dog's instinct will keep it out of trouble a lot better than a human's instinct will," he said, ambiguously.

He seemed to be tremendously well-informed on politics and animals.

"You should have your own talk show," I said.

Meanwhile, Bruce was tugging at his stake trying to get a shot at Rusty. Rusty was about three times Bruce's size. But Bruce was baring his fangs and growling at him.

So much for Bruce's instincts keeping him out of trouble. He plays with cats, ignores small dogs, and fearlessly attacks large dogs.

48. Gratuitous Violence

After the kids were in bed Joan and I sat under the full moon. Among other things that must remain unrecorded, unless as some people say everything we say, do or think is recorded forever by a giant recorder in heaven or in another dimension closer to us than our skin, we talked about the United States.

Joan spoke of how awful it must be to be an American, hated by the rest of the world.

"In their own country they go out of their way to be generous, sweet and gentle," she purred. She said they seem to be unusually self-conscious about their nationality.

I didn't know about that. Whenever you make any generality about a race the opposite becomes equally true. All I know is that there is an overpowering sense of boredom in the American air. You feel it, at least I do, as soon as you cross the border. I remember feeling it on my first trip to the United States when I was twelve. For a Canadian the United States is an exotic country and any Canadian travelling through the United States is bound to have a sense of déjà vu about many of the things he sees, as if they were seen before in old Hollywood movies. But that doesn't negate the boredom that hangs so heavily in the air. It's as if all the beauty and excitement one would expect has been harvested by the American film industry, leaving nothing but emptiness and despair.

Canada is a much more exciting country in every way. At least that's the way I felt in the summer of 1977. There is something unformed about Canada. The only people who are doing anything about it are real-estate developers and entrepreneurs of various kinds who don't give a damn about anything except profits.

For an American, despair sets in early, perhaps even before puberty. There's simply nothing left to do. How boring it must be. It's just the same old thing over and over.

Americans always seem to be hurrying home to watch television. In fact, everyone in the campsite had their TV sets on full blast.

49. The Ghost of Jane Secord

It was the evening of July 2, 1977. Near Marblehead, Ohio, Ned's Ledge was situated on a height of land from which could be seen large stretches of Lake Erie and Sandusky Bay. It was a fairly prosperous area. American flags were flying everywhere.

The first explosion came around eight o'clock. By sundown huge skyrockets were soaring through the air and exploding in red, white and blue orgasms. In the campgrounds at Ned's Ledge one camper called several of his neighbours over to help him set up a large heavy

American flag. He wanted it placed on top of his TV-equipped motor home. The flag was so heavy it looked as if the motor home would tip over.

No one would be able to accuse this man of being unamerican. He was proud of his country and cherished the freedoms guaranteed to him by the American constitution. But the enemies of the American way of life were many. Their motivation was not easy to understand but it probably had something to do with satanic envy.

Later I dreamt that the McFaddens were sleeping in their camping van, which wasn't all that strange because we were. And suddenly the door opened.

It sounded so realistic I woke up and checked the doors. They were closed. No one was stirring around the van. So I went back to sleep.

About an hour later Joan woke up and said she just heard the door open. I heard it too. It sounded very realistic. But when I checked the doors they were still tightly closed and again there didn't seem to be anyone stirring around the van. The same story. It didn't occur to me to lock the doors.

We talked about it in the morning. Why should we both have the auditory hallucination that the doors were being opened? Joan said she lay awake for hours expecting someone to open the door and blast us with a shotgun. Only in America could such fears exist in peacetime.

"Why didn't you ask me to lock the doors?"

"I didn't think of it."

A provincial cabinet minister from the Hamilton area once publicly accused the U.S. television networks of conspiring to feature so many shows depicting violence in American life, exaggerating the frequency and intensity of such violence to such a degree that viewers would be conditioned into thinking it was unsafe to go on the streets at night. This was intended to encourage people to stay home and watch television so that the ratings would go up, along with advertising revenue.

But when you look at the statement it can be boiled down to the same old story: the United States isn't such a bad place really. We should establish even closer ties. It would be good for business.

Anyway the guy lost his seat in the next election. Probably more because he was always advocating curfews for teenagers. I mean, who wants teenagers hanging around the house? He was also trying to pass a bill requiring teenagers to carry identification cards, complete with a photograph of the bearer. But that didn't make sense, because, as everyone knows, all teenagers look alike.

I kept thinking about that door opening. Could it have been the ghost of Jane Secord, wandering hopelessly over the face of the earth for 291 years, searching for the guy who made a duplicate of her tombstone?

50. When a Poet Gets a Grant

Off and on for the past year I've been working on the details of a plan that would result, if successful, in great masses of people suddenly paying more attention to the poets of Anglo Canada. The manipulation of the mass mind. Unfortunately I'm not at liberty to divulge details of my plan at this time.

But on the choo-choo train of civilisation, newspapers, television, movies in general, and other forms of pop culture are in the caboose. The poets are up front in the engine compartment. They may not be giving us much direction but at least they are the first to glimpse where we're going.

Ah, to be able to live off royalties! Grants are wonderful, but for every dollar that goes to a poet there's a hundred thousand dollars going to the vast artistic institutions built upon his vision.

The *Hamilton Spectator*, which advocates economic union with the United States, recently ran an editorial saying it was okay for the Canada Council to give money to theatre groups, art galleries and symphony orchestras but grants to individual artists were simply "protecting mediocrity," and simply an excuse for the artist "to do his own thing."

So I fired off a letter to the editor asking what theatre groups and symphony orchestras would perform and what art galleries would show without the work of individual artists. And I told them they were saying that just because theatre groups, art galleries and symphony orchestras advertise in their crummy newspaper while individual artists don't.

I was particularly mad because they ran the editorial shortly after running a news story about me getting a grant. The news story was written in such a way that it would be bound to annoy a lot of people, as if it were begging people to be annoyed. I felt as if I'd been exploited to help sell papers.

When a poet gets a grant he is somehow reduced to the status of an institution and a minor one at that.

SUNDAY, JULY 3

51. The Power and the Glory

Shirley and Ned were up early. They were getting ready for a garage sale. They had a back massager only used once, and some well-thumbed books by Billy Graham and Barry Goldwater. They also had firewood and ice for sale and cottages and boats for rent.

Ned taught English in the local high school, the largest high school in Ohio. He was the head of the English department. "I supervise twenty-four English teachers," he said.

"That's strange," I said. Ned looked at me. "I know a fellow who teaches English in a high school in Picton, Ontario, and he looks remarkably like you." It was true. Ned looked a little like Dirk Bogarde as well, but sadder and with slightly less of an international look about him somehow, more of a heartland U.S.A. look, a little more tired looking—as if he were dying before really having lived. I didn't want to tell him that though. I perversely thought I'd go on and on and give him the impression that Canadians are tremendous bores.

"Actually this fellow, and I'm sorry I forgot his name, he's not from the Picton area—do you know where Picton is? No? It's on the north shore of Lake Ontario, on a peninsula that juts out into Lake Ontario just as Marblehead Peninsula juts out into Lake Erie. But this fellow, and my God he really resembles you, and him being an English teacher and all that, it's really strange, isn't it? He was born and raised on an island in the Bay of Fundy—"

By this time I could see Ned's eyeballs were ready to explode. "When is this guy going to shut up?" he was saying to himself. "Can't he see I've got a lot of things to do? God, Canadians are boring."

But as soon as I said the word Fundy I stopped talking and turned away. I started digging through the books and bought a copy of Graham Greene's *The Power and the Glory* for ten cents. "That's a good book," he said weakly. "It's all about a priest."

"Is it taught in your high school?"

"Yes, it's on one course."

An ideal book for high school, I thought. Pleases the Catholics because it's about a priest and pleases the non-Catholics because he's not a very good priest. And the teacher can go on and on about Greene's humanity until school's out and the kids head home to watch "Starsky and Hutch" and "Kojack" and "Policewoman" on television. Another good novelist bites the dust. Like going before a firing squad.

Anyway it seemed as if Ned had solved some of life's problems. The purpose of life was to make money, at least in modest amounts. And since Ned was a quiet, peaceful man he had chosen quiet, peaceful ways to do so. I would love to know what the twenty-four English teachers thought about him and his ledge and his garage sales and his campgrounds and his cottages and boats for rent and his firewood and ice and old Graham Greene novels for sale for a dime. Probably nothing at all. Oh yes, and I also bought a copy of *King Lear* and *The Winter's Tale* for a dime apiece, and a Horace *Complete Works* for a quarter.

I asked Ned about the grave marker. He said he did it ten years ago on a holiday trip through New England. It took him all day. He enjoyed doing it but he didn't think he'd ever do anything like it again.

52. The Possibility of a Second Edition of This Book

It occurs to me I may have let down my readers by not taking ferry rides to the various islands off Marblehead Peninsula. There certainly appears to be a lot to see on some of the larger islands of this group.

For instance, Perry's Victory and the International Peace Memorial is located on South Bass Island which can be reached by ferry from either Port Clinton or Catawba. None of these islands is as large as Pelee Island on the Canadian side, but South Bass Island boasts a highway, U.S. 357, and a town, Put-In Bay.

The largest of the group of islands is Kelleys Island which boasts a town of the same name and a highway, U.S. 575. Glacial Grooves State Memorial Park is located on this island which can be reached by ferry from Sandusky or Marblehead. Inscription Rock State Memorial is also located on Kelleys Island.

The town of Middle Bass, Ohio, is located on Middle Bass Island which can be reached by ferry from South Bass Island. Isle Saint George is a town on North Bass Island but there is no ferry service. Other islands include Starve Island, Sugar Island, Rattlesnake Island and Mouse Island.

I'm sure if I had visited these islands I would have gathered material that would have considerably enriched this book. And perhaps if sufficient response to this book is forthcoming, I might be encouraged to repeat my trip at greater leisure and with more thoroughness. Perhaps a second trip would yield much material that could be incorporated in a second edition.

To be perfectly truthful with you (as they say in Ireland), I hadn't planned to explore the U.S. side of Lake Erie. I merely wanted to motor around the lake to see, as I said before, what it looked like from the other side. U.S. writers seem to be doing a more than adequate job of exploring their own country. If I wanted to do any detailed exploration of an area I think the area I would choose would be within the borders of my own country, Canada.

And if I may take this opportunity to speak of myself as a writer, I would say that in all my books there has been little exploration of the outer world—in the sense of physical exploration. My way has been to discuss in my writing the things that appear to me in the course of my ordinary existence—the things that find me rather than the things I find. I am a filter. I have to impose certain restrictions on myself if what I am to write is to be in any way intelligible. My choice of what restrictions to impose on myself defines me as a writer. My attitude has always been to treat writing as a peripheral enterprise. My writing has always been concerned with what I can see without turning my head.

After breakfast we broke camp and left Ned's Ledge forever. We drove along the north shore of Sandusky Bay. In the distance we could see the low-level bridge which would soon take us across to the south shore and on to Sandusky. The area seemed a little remote and isolated. Yet it was good tourist-attraction country. We passed colourful, imaginatively designed signs advertising such things as SENECA CAVERNS RAIN OR SHINE, MYSTERY HILL SEE THE AMAZING FORCE OF GRAVITY, and PREHISTORIC CAVERN BRING YOUR CAMERA.

On this day, July 2, 1977, in Montreux, Switzerland, Vladimir Nabokov, the greatest novelist of the twentieth century, breathed his final breath, slipped out of his warm body and entered the chilly waters of eternity.

53. World's Strangest Babies

Sandusky Bay is about three miles wide at this point and there are actually two causeways crossing it, running parallel and about a mile apart. We crossed on the older of the two, a two-laner. There was hardly any traffic on our causeway, which was part of U.S. 269. But the traffic was bumper-to-bumper on the other causeway, part of U.S. 2, a multi-lane controlled-access freeway stretching from Port Clinton to Huron and bypassing Sandusky.

After hitting dry land the road passes through the little towns of Bay View and Baybridge. Then I spotted a much more modest sign at the side of the road. Because of its small size and look of impermanence it immediately engaged my interest. It was merely an arrow pointing off down a dirt road. It bore the words WORLD'S STRANGEST BABIES.

I don't think Joan or the kids noticed the sign. I drove on, wondering. The words kept going over and over in my head: World's Strangest Babies, World's Strangest Babies. I spotted a miniature golf course ahead. "Who'd like to play miniature golf?"

"Oh, could we, Mom? Could we?" said Jennifer.

"That would be *soooo* nice!" said Alison.

"Just you kids and Mommy. I have to go back on the road a bit. I'll be back in half an hour. Play good now."

"It's 'well,' not 'good,'" said Jennifer.

"Yeah, Daddy," said Alison.

Joan looked at me even more strangely.

"It's just something I want to see, something I'm curious about but it's nothing that would interest you or the kids. I'll tell you about it when I get back."

"Dave?"

"Yes?" I knew she was going to say be careful.

"Be careful, okay?"

"Okay. I'll be back in less than half an hour. Don't worry. Enjoy your game. It's not every day you get to play miniature golf. So play…well, really well, okay? And thanks for correcting my English, kids!"

54. A Non-Profit Educational Story

The dirt road leading away from the highway didn't go very far. I passed a house with a swimming pool in the back yard. A huge cement truck had somehow fallen into the pool and some men were trying to pull it out with a tractor. They were up to their ankles in mud. The weight of the truck had collapsed the walls of the pool and the chlorine water had flooded out over the yard. I slowed down then kept on driving.

The road ended at an unpainted barn. There was a sign over the entrance: WORLD'S STRANGEST BABIES.

I parked the van and walked over. There were seven or eight people milling around. There was a little makeshift ticket office inside the door. The sign at the window was neatly drawn:

WORLD'S STRANGEST BABIES

A NON-PROFIT EDUCATION SHOW

ADMISSION

ADULTS 75 CENTS

CHILDREN 50 CENTS

CHRIS MICHAEL CHRIST, PROP.

55. A Brief Conversation with Christ

I guessed the guy behind the window was Chris Michael Christ. He had a hare lip only partially hidden by a wispy moustache. He also had a wispy goatee. He looked sort of Asian. He was wearing a dirty T-shirt bearing the slogan NO THANKS I GAVE AT THE ORIFICE. His fingernails were dirty.

"Jes' whan?" he said with a redneck accent.

"Yes please." I handed him a dollar and he gave me a quarter change, a ticket stub and a small neatly printed advertising flyer. The flyer indicated World's Strangest Babies was a touring show based in Gibsonton, Florida. I walked through into the dimly lit interior.

I don't even remember looking at the swimming pool disaster on the way back out five minutes later.

56. I Decide Not to Say Anything

"It's not very pleasant being left alone like this with two children in a foreign country," said Joan. They hadn't been playing miniature golf after all, for the course was closed. There was a sign over the door saying GONE OUT OF BUSINESS. I hadn't noticed it earlier when I left them there. They'd been standing there all this time, or actually sitting on a bench painted red, white and blue, outside the barred entrance to the miniature golf course. I guess they'd just sat there watching traffic go by.

"I didn't know if you were ever going to return."

"You were worried about me?"

"I was worried about how I was going to get these kids home without a car."

Joan didn't seem anxious to know where I'd been which was sort of a surprise. We got in the van and continued along the U.S. 269. I decided not to tell her until she asked me. But as we approached Sandusky I realised she was never going to ask me. So I decided not to say anything. My resolve lasted less than a mile.

"Don't you want to know where I went?"

"Oh yeah, where did you go?"

I told her about the sign and how I wanted to check it out not for my own curiosity but just for the sake of the book, my writerly conscience. And how I was glad I followed my instinct not to take her and the kids.

"Was it that bad?"

"Oh, it was horrendous. There were about twenty card tables set up in the dimly lit interior of the barn. Each table had a little sign, a jar, and a lamp. The first one was...."

"Don't tell me!"

" ...Called Elephant Nose Baby."

"Don't tell me," she screamed. "I don't want to know."

But I had to tell her anyway. I'm not saying I have to tell Joan absolutely everything but not telling her this would have made me feel uncomfortable. It would have been like keeping something from myself.

Besides, the kids were listening at the back of the van. "Come on, tell," they kept saying.

57. Ordinary Babies

What can I say? They were just ordinary babies. I sometimes collect mushrooms and you quite often come across a specimen that is deformed although still recognisable as a member of a certain species. You don't think anything about it. It's just there. Part of reality.

Elephant Nose Baby was a baby with a nose like an elephant's trunk. The baby was quite large, about six pounds, same size as Jennifer when she was born. It was floating in some kind of preserving fluid. There was no way of knowing how long it had been floating there. Maybe a month, maybe sixty years. It looked strangely alive, more than alive. It looked as if it were perfectly aware of the circumstances of its life and could tell what was going through my mind. Which was nothing really.

The trunk came down to the baby's chest. I wondered if the poor mother had seen it and if so what she thought. I was certain that most doctors' professional groups look askance at the trend toward natural childbirth techniques and midwifery because of awkward situations like this which are probably not all that rare. Imagine the poor doctor. The mother lying there, ecstatic, waiting to be shown her baby.

Its eyes were open. Blue eyes. Curly blonde hair. Oh yes, perfectly formed genitalia. It was a male.

Frog Girl was dark-skinned, of African descent I suppose. A tiny pimple for a nose. A mouth that stretched from ear to ear. No chin at all. Eyes like golf balls staring out through the sugary light shed by the lamp. Perfect silence, stillness, and this unearthly light.

Cyclops had no nose at all. The eye was right where you would expect a cyclops' eye to be: smack dab in the middle of the forehead. No eyelid. It was set in and the flesh just crinkled around it. Under the eye were two nostrils the size of navels.

I was suddenly certain races of these beings had lived at one time and died out. Their genes had obviously not been totally eradicated from the world's gene pool. The genes are still there, here, waiting for an advantageous moment to make their reappearance.

And maybe these races will come back some day. All we need is someone with the good will to let a child like this live, and a world with enough tolerance and kindness to allow it to live without subjecting it to all sorts of cruelties.

Why not? Why are our formal assumptions so rigid? Perhaps they won't always be so.

Cyclops, Frog Girl, Elephant Nose Baby, I wish you'd been allowed to live. Who knows what an incredible future died when you died?

58. In Flanders Fields the Palm Trees Blow

It seemed like any old day out on the road. But as we entered the heart of Sandusky we remembered it was Sunday morning. It was so quiet. And hot.

Sandusky was a beautiful little city. The streets were empty. The few people we saw seemed equally empty. Everywhere you looked there were traces of intelligent life but it seemed to have passed on to another planet.

The lack of intelligent life seemed to have something to do with Lake Erie lapping at a row of brightly coloured docks and pavilions a few blocks from the centre of town. Everything seemed freshly painted in the brightest hues. But one day a decade or two ago, perhaps around 1955, a mysterious underwater tornado had appeared at the lakefront and sucked the soul of Sandusky into the deeps, never to reappear. Since then, no colour has faded, no coat of paint has peeled, nothing has rotted or decayed, and nothing has happened.

The poet Russell Seaworthy has a thing about palm trees growing in Southwestern Ontario. Whenever he visits the Caribbean or Hawaii he brings back palmetto seeds which he plants in various strategic points. He expects the first palm trees to start growing around the tip of Point Pelee. Maybe next year, maybe the year after. But it's inevitable. The tropics will return to Canada.

I don't know if Russell realises this but palm trees can be found growing less than thirty miles south of Point Pelee, on the southern shore of Lake Erie, in the small city of Sandusky, Ohio.

The four of us wandered through the beautiful gardens and parks surrounding the grand old courthouse. We took pictures of each other in front of the palm trees. Joan took cuttings of interesting looking plants in the hope she could smuggle them across the border and be able to nurse them back into life at home.

The children chased each other up the courthouse steps. Everything was so peaceful. We could hear the faint whistle of a popcorn vendor at the curbside.

Then we noticed a bronze plaque standing amid a bed of poppies. The plaque said the poppies had been grown from the seeds of the poppies of France in memory of the Erie County soldiers who had fallen in the Great War. The plaque also bore the words of the famous poem, "In Flanders Fields."

The poem was correctly attributed to Colonel John McCrae. But there was no indication that McCrae was a Canadian, from the city of Guelph, Ontario, and had served in the Canadian

Army. There was no indication the poem was anything but American. That would have been totally out of place on such a plaque.

Let the people assume the writer was an American. McCrae couldn't help it if he wasn't. Surely if he'd had a choice he would have been.

59. An Ordinary Mystical Experience and Two Mystical Experiences Involving Language

Also in the park was a life-size model of the famous Leaking Boot statue. It had been brought to Sandusky from Bavaria by a local pharmacist, Alfred W. Oates, in 1911.

For more than fifty years my grandfather (actually a stepgrandfather, but that's another story) had a china copy of this statue prominently displayed on a shelf in the living room of his humble home on Tragina Avenue in Hamilton, Ontario. It was about eighteen inches tall. The boot was attached to the boy's hand by a thread. When my grandfather died early this year I came into possession of the charming piece. It's sitting on a ledge not ten feet from me now as I type. It appears to have been bought as a souvenir of Cleethorpes. A crest at the base bears the word "Vigilantes."

My grandfather was born in Sheffield, England, in 1900. We were good friends. When he died I felt a sense of absence. I kept looking back at myself and finding myself absent. My energy would go into whatever I was looking at and then it would look back expecting to see me standing there. But I wasn't there. I'd vanished.

Russell Seaworthy was also born in Sheffield, England, but in 1947. One evening a few months after my grandfather's death Russell and I were discussing linguistics. I was telling him that at the beach one day I pointed at the water and asked the kids to tell me what I was pointing at.

"Water," they said.

"No, that's not water. Water is a word. That's not a word."

And suddenly the lake became something else. Our perception of it changed in a flash. It became all the things it has always been but it stopped being water. It became an element, one of the four Zoas. It became light. Its wateriness had been transcended. We looked at it with the innocence of a sandpiper or a painter.

Russell spoke of how writing provides for the absence of the writer. He spoke of how "I" or "you" are essentially matters of direction which map a landscape, the "here" and the "there." And he spoke of what he called the "it that is in everything."

The conversation was quite exciting but it was past my bedtime and I found myself nodding off. I went to my room, crawled under the covers, and expected to fall off to sleep immediately. Surprisingly I didn't. Instead I became absent again. The mind's bubble burst and became a vacuum sucking in all the nameless, wordless aspects of the environment. I was merely a continuation of the ineffably rich "it that is in everything." I lay like that for hours, something warm and soft enclosed in sweet blankets on a bed in a small room on the shore of a great lake. I was simply the "here" gazing at the huge canvas of "everywhere" and zooming in on anything that caught my interest and finding it transpose itself into everything else.

60. The Green Bikini

We left the park and walked along peaceful side streets leading to the waterfront. Everything seemed closed. The only signs of commercial life were the popcorn vendor and an old church beside the courthouse. Small groups of people walked gracefully and silently in and out of the church, up and down the broad stone steps, as if this were heaven itself. The church was made from the same stone as the courthouse.

We passed a drugstore that was open for business. Maybe it was Alfred W. Oates' drugstore. We went in.

There were two black children at the counter buying candy. They were dressed in their Sunday best. The clothes looked homemade but stylish. The kids had about four dollars and were stocking up on the most dreadful-looking candy concoctions.

The girl behind the counter was so beautiful she made my head feel light. She reminded me of a line from the aforementioned Kawabata's *The Master of Go*: "A young poet coming down from Shiga Heights had taken note of the beautiful sisters at Jigokudani and passed on his impressions to me."

Like all truly beautiful creatures she gave the impression of being unconcerned with her beauty, though not necessarily with herself. She was destined to spend the rest of her life in Sandusky, I felt, dressed in a white smock, her cream flesh slowly drying up and dying over the years. And then she would die like a mushroom in the heart of the forest, a once perfect mushroom, now bruised and misshapen, mourned only by those in her own little fairy ring.

A tall, elderly man was leaning over the counter, looking down at the girl and talking to her. I had the feeling he was sexually aroused. His voice had that familiar nervous, hoarse quality. He was about seventy-five years old, maybe older. Maybe he was the Alfred W. Oates who brought that boot back from Bavaria.

"What are you going to do when you get out of here today?" he said.

It was a delicious moment for me. I knew I was about to hear the voice that went with that beautiful form. I couldn't help overhearing, especially when I turned my head sideways (to steal a line from Stephen Leacock). The pause was infinitesimal yet in that pause I became keen with anticipation. What would she say? What would her voice be like? Would it remind me of other beautiful women of my youth, women I'd succeeded in forgetting but whose memory would come back in a flash given the proper set of cues? I prepared myself so that I might detect a hint of the attitude she was adopting toward this old man who seemed to be hopelessly on the make.

Whatever attitude she had assumed was subtly hidden. For all I knew in my innocence she'd been having a sneak affair with this old guy for years. She seemed to be amused, annoyed, bored, and slightly open to his advances all at the same time. All this was buried in a completely ordinary voice, not heavily accented, not particularly beautiful, not overly intelligent and not highly educated.

"Oh, I don't know," she said. "Go down to the beach, maybe go over to Pelee."

"What kind of bathing suit do you have?" The man was smiling one of those "Saxon smiles" the Irish are wary of. He was tall and thin, both elbows and knees bent in a strange combination of angles like in a Wyndham Lewis painting. He looked a bit like the poet Earle Birney, but more to the point he also looked a bit like the old lecher in Ingmar Bergman's outrageously beautiful 1955 film, *Dreams*.

"A bikini," she said.

"Hmm! A really small one?"

"Yeah."

"What colour?"

"Green."

"I'd love to see you in it."

I was standing about ten feet away. I was pretending I was looking at a coin-operated machine which dispensed maps of Ohio, the Buckeye State. I decided it was rude to be listening and watching—even in such a super-subtle manner—so I approached the counter and asked the girl for change so I could buy a map.

I'll never know what I broke up. It might have been the cruelest thing I'd ever done in my life. Joan was calling me over to the magazine display.

"Look at all this pornography," she said.

The kids were looking at the selection of hair dryers. Bruce was outside, his leash tangled around a parking meter. You could hear him barking. "Woof woof," he barked, experimentally. "Woof."

61. Laughed at by a Family of Blacks

Sandusky is the terminus for the ferry which runs across Lake Erie between Leamington, Kingsville and Pelee Island. The Sandusky waterfront was brightly painted and well-maintained. This was a thing you noticed in a lot of U.S. cities. Old stuff is treated with a lot of respect just as a matter of course. You don't have to fight with obviously compromised city councillors to prevent old buildings from being torn down to make room for parking lots.

The Sandusky waterfront was like being back in the 1920s. The ferry departure area was under an old-fashioned pavilion with wooden supports and long painted benches. Someone was silently selling ice cream, and silently licking an ice-cream cone as he did. A few people sat around with ferry tickets in their hands. Joan and the kids sat on a set of concrete steps leading down from the dock and down below the surface of the water. The steps had been built when the water level was lower. And the water level of Lake Erie had risen considerably since I was a kid. North-shore beaches a hundred feet wide had been totally submerged in that time.

Everything looked old-fashioned but new in a curious way. There were hardly any people. It was sort of dream-like. It was like being in another era before the rot set in.

A large family of blacks drove slowly by in a black car. They pointed at me and laughed. I'm not just being paranoid. They really did. They were all looking at me and laughing their damned fool heads off. I couldn't figure out why. Then I thought it might have something to do with the brightly coloured African-styled shirt I was wearing. I forget what you call them—a dashiki? The kind that the poet Dennis Lee wears all the time. Very comfortable. Joan's mother bought it for me. I think these shirts used to be quite popular with American blacks a decade or so back. That, combined with my lily-white face (I can't help it) and the camera I was carrying, must have made me look ridiculous. But that was their problem, not mine. I didn't feel ridiculous. I didn't ask to be born white and with a taste for cheap cameras and colourful and comfortable shirts.

62. And the Streets Were Paved with Words

So much for Sandusky. We were driving southeast on the U.S. 6, a highway that would take us all the way into the mysterious heart of Cleveland. A few miles out of Sandusky we found ourselves trapped in a traffic jam. Thousands of cars were lined up waiting to get onto a side road leading north a few miles to Cedar Point where they have the world's largest movie screen. Remember Evelyn, the woman at Ned's Ledge?

"Sure you wouldn't like to see the world's largest movie screen, Joan?"

"No thank you."

"They might be showing interesting Ohio travelogues."

"No thank you."

"They might be running a special documentary on Pierre Trudeau and the communist menace. Or a special preview of *The Jack Spicer Story* starring Archie Bunker and the Shorty Rogers All-Stars."

"No thank you."

"Imagine! A movie screen six storeys high! What a great country this is! The world's largest movie screen and the world's strangest babies!"

Joan's eyes sparkled. "I'd rather see the world's strangest movie screen and the world's largest babies."

We stopped at a roadside fresh-fruit stand and bought baskets of peaches and plums. They were terrible. They tasted as if chemical flavouring had been added. "We should take these back and tell them to shove it," said Joan. But we didn't. In fact we eventually ate them all ourselves. Grumbling with every bite.

We stopped at a gas station.

"Where ya headin'?" said the guy.

"East," I said. "For years we've been visiting the Canadian side of Lake Erie and we just got a little curious about what this side looked like."

The guy smiled weakly. He looked bored, as if I'd told him a little more than he really wanted to know. If I wanted to be an entertainer I should be on television, he seemed to be saying.

As we passed through the town of Huron, Joan spotted an interesting looking place to spend some money. It was the Wileswood Country Store, a little bit of Americana, a white clapboard house in the nineteenth-century style with Old Glory blowin' in the wind on top of a fifty-foot-high flag staff. A black eagle plaque was nailed above the door. "Nothing unpatriotic about us," the tableau seemed to be saying.

I didn't feel like going in. It seemed a little depressing. So I took Bruce for a little walk. We went over to the Texaco station on the corner. It was on a V-shaped lot wedged into a fork in the road. The sign on the washroom said CUSTOMERS ONLY. Well, I'm a customer. I buy gas quite often as well as a lot of other things although not here.

The door was locked. I walked around the front with the dog. There was a greasy-looking, mean-looking, tattooed fellow about fifty-four years old sitting there looking as if he needed a drink in the worst way. I asked him politely for the key to the men's room.

He pointed at poor little Bruce. In case I haven't mentioned it already Bruce was a West Highland white terrier. There's a lot more about him written up in *A Trip Around Lake Huron*, where he really comes into his own.

"He's not a man," the guy said.

Very perceptive of you, I thought. "No, I guess he's not, but I am," I said.

"You can just leave him somewhere. I'm not having him going in there pissing all over the floor I just mopped up."

I couldn't believe this guy. "I got a huge camping van around the corner with an empty gas tank," I said. "It needs oil. And it needs a new set of spark plugs. You just missed out on a nice big sale. This dog is less likely to piss on the floor than you are by the looks of you. Now, where's the next gas station?"

The guy was about as perturbed as if I'd shot him with an empty water pistol. He coughed up a bit of phlegm and scored a direct hit on the waste-paper basket. The floor of the station was pretty clean. The phlegm dripped slowly down the inside of the basket.

"You can go to any gas station you want," he said. "I've always heard tell this here's a free country. And the best part of it is he"—he pointed at poor little Bruce who was wagging his tail at the guy—"ain't goin' in there."

"Come on, Bruce," I said. We walked away. I fantasised about pulling in with the van, asking for him to fill it up, then driving away just as he went to remove the gas cap. But then I thought he might take off after us in his car and shoot us. Maybe that's what happened to that motorcyclist from Hamilton who was found shot to death on the side of an Ohio road on his way to Florida, though I don't think he had a dog with him.

I wasn't even planning to take the dog in the washroom anyway. I didn't like dogs watching me pee.

63. Fat

We passed through Ruggles Beach and Beulah Beach. Ah, if only William Blake were here! Then we stopped at Vermilion, which, according to a highly educational roadside sign, was "named after the red clay Indians used for paint." We looked at a marine museum overlooking the lake. The Frank Lloyd Wright architecture was nice but we didn't feel like going in. I took a picture of the beach with Lake Erie sparkling in the background. The picture showed people sunbathing on the sand, swimming in the lake, a few sails out there on the horizon, and in the foreground an enormously fat man fully dressed and framed between two thin trees.

"There sure are a lot of fat people in this country," said Joan. "Everywhere you turn—fatties. The United Fatties of America."

It was true that fat seems to have a different meaning in this country. You're simply not a real man unless you have a fat gut bulging out from over your belt. The attitude toward fat is only noticeable in the more rural areas, and is particularly noticeable in the southern states. It seems to be a redneck phenomenon—the huge gut as a sign of power and success.

This attitude toward fat is betrayed by the fact that young men who haven't yet developed a lot of fat on their bellies adopt the manner of walking generally associated with really fat men. Even though they're thin, they imitate the waddle of the truly fat and hold their arms out semi-horizontally like a grossly obese person. It's a dead giveaway. Just as it's obvious that a guy with sideburns, sunglasses and a sneer is an Elvis Presley fan, it's obvious that a thin guy who waddles with his arms held out semi-horizontally at his side is an admirer of fat Georgia sheriffs.

64. Childhood and Home

We'd been warned to avoid Lorain, Ohio, because of the ugly steel mills. It was Ned of Ned's Ledge who had warned us. But I thought that was kind of hypocritical of him. His car was made of steel, the high school where he worked was built on steel beams. How could he talk disparagingly of the city where this steel is produced, a city where thousands of men have dedicated their lives to its production?

Besides, I liked what I saw of Lorain. There were millions of acres of railway yards straddling the Black River which emptied into Lake Erie at this point. And the air around Lorain seemed relatively clean, much cleaner than in the lower east side of Hamilton, Ontario, where the entire McFadden family used to live until they scraped up enough money to move up the Mountain.

But Lorain was a nice little place. It made me feel warm inside. I'll always have a soft spot for densely industrial architecture. The incredible beauty of steel mills, all the more beautiful because they were not intended to be beautiful and were not widely considered to be beautiful. There's something about a dusty, barbed-wire, weed-filled lot surrounding a steel warehouse that makes me think of childhood and home.

65. Mickey Rooney and Judy Garland

We kept going along U.S. 6 and soon found ourselves heading through sedate lakeside Cleveland suburbs with names like Sheffield Lake, Avon Lake, Bay Village, Rocky River and Lakewood. Each had originally been a town in its own right and each had its own brown-brick 1910ish filtration plant. The homes along the route were large and well-built but dull in style, not very imaginatively designed. Yet each had a black eagle nailed over the entrance to the garage, just above the basketball hoop. And there were a lot of U.S. flags flying.

One could imagine Mickey Rooney and Judy Garland, or some of the characters they played in their early films, growing up here. But the original families seemed to have moved out. The lakefront area west of Cleveland seems to have been taken over by ordinary middle-aged lawyers.

66. Edgewater Park

After spending three hours driving through the western suburbs we passed a small sign saying CLEVELAND CITY LIMIT. Then we passed a large park on the edge of the water on the left.

This was Edgewater Park. We decided to stop and let the kids have a swim if the water seemed okay and maybe a picnic.

We parked in the parking lot overlooked by a lovely old Persian-style pavilion suitably rundown. The park was built on a forty-foot bluff at the bottom of which was a wide sandy beach. You could climb down and swim. There were people frolicking in the surf and sunning on the sand.

I went through the pavilion. They sold soft drinks, ice cream, potato chips. There were two large change rooms and toilets. There was a hole the size of a fist in the wall of the men's washroom. Through the hole you had a perfect view of the women's washroom. I looked through and saw Joan looking back.

I sat on a bench overlooking the lake. Some fleas, tiny blackflies, midges, and/or no-see-ums nipped at my ankles as if I weren't there. Or at least as if the rest of me weren't there. I didn't think such animals wandered this far south. It got so bad that when a large beautiful moth landed on my left elbow I expected it to bite me and so I jerked my arm to frighten it off.

When I wandered back to the car a couple of black guys in their early twenties or maybe even in their teens were talking to Joan. "Can you help them fix their car, Dave?" she said. Their battery was dead. Their rusty old heap was even worse than mine.

"We got cables," said one of them. He was wearing a nice black satin shirt with a picture of a beautiful bare-naked black woman on the back.

They pulled the cables out of the trunk and we hooked them up. I started my car and theirs started right away.

As they were putting the cables away the guy with the shirt, Chico, handed me a joint. "You get high?" he said. His friend's name was Bobby.

"No thanks. You keep it."

"I just wanna give you a little gift for helpin' us, man."

"Do you want a joint, Joan?" I said. She was sitting on the blanket.

"No thanks, dear!"

"Sorry," I said to Chico.

"Hey, well thanks a lot anyway," he said. The two of them drove off—but they'd be back.

67. On the Beach at Cleveland

I took some pictures of the Cleveland skyline from the park. There were ships entering the wide mouth of the Cuyahoga River which was lined with steel mills, and the highlight of the skyline was the Terminal Tower building, a 1920ish skyscraper billed as the tallest building in all of Ohio. It was quite a lovely, human skyline fronted by a long, curved beach and a small baseball diamond with bleachers, the steel-mills not belching out black smoke the way they do in Canada, just modest little puffs of purified white smoke, and the buildings of the city itself faint in the distance.

We spread a blanket on the grass under some trees in front of the pavilion and Joan made sandwiches. I took the kids into the pavilion so they could change into their swimsuits. When we returned Chico and Bob were back talking some more to Joan. They asked her if all that food was just for us. Then when I approached they told me they'd borrowed a new battery and the car was working fine now.

"It's nice you've got such close friends you can borrow a battery just like that," I said. I love to pretend I'm even more naive than I really am.

They looked at each other, trying not to laugh. I smiled. They left. Again, they'd be back.

After we ate our sandwiches and drank some tea we walked down to the beach. The water was fairly disagreeable-looking close in to the shore but it became clean after you waded out for about ten feet through the muck. It wasn't as bad really as the Canadian side around Turkey Point and places like that. And there weren't any dead fish along the shore. The city kept the beach clean daily during the summer. And there were quite a few lifeguards, something you rarely see on Canadian beaches.

So the kids went splashing through the scum. Bruce started tugging at his leash. He'd seen a small brown dog nearby, being held on a leash by a small black man sitting on the sand.

"Is that small brown dog's name Rusty by any chance?"

"No. She's Mizz," said the small black man. "Aren't you, girl?"

The lifeguards started yelling back and forth to each other. They were on wooden towers about fifty feet apart. They seemed to be yelling in some kind of code.

The kids finally came out and we started walking slowly up the bluff to the car. The same black guys caught up with us again. Chico said we shouldn't have let our kids swim in that awful water.

"They used to post it but they just can't keep the people out," said Bob.

They walked with us back to the car, then got in their own and took off.

At one point I asked them how come the lifeguards were white and the guys picking up the garbage were black, and how come when you go into a restaurant it's always the waitress is white and the cook out back is black.

"That's just the way it is," said Chico.

"And it ain't never gonna change," said Bob.

68. We Vow to Return to Cleveland

If we'd gone south on the U.S. 42 from Edgewater Park for a couple of miles we could have visited the famous Cleveland Zoo but at the time we couldn't find the zoo marked on our map of the city and if there were any signs on the road we missed them. Besides, it was getting rather late in the afternoon and Joan wanted to get through Cleveland and settled in a campsite before dark. If we'd chosen to drive along the Alternate 6 instead of the U.S. 6 we might have seen signs pointing to the zoo and as it turned out we might have camped in any one of a number of cages, er I mean campgrounds, in the vast Metropolitan Cleveland park system that circles the city. But then we probably never would have met the McFaddens, the other McFaddens that is, the unforgettable McFaddens, the McFaddens of Sheraton Heights.

So we followed the U.S. 6 over the Cuyahoga River which had achieved global fame a few years back when it caught fire. We drove past Municipal Stadium, the home of the Cleveland Indians and the Cleveland Browns, then switched on to the U.S. 20 which becomes Euclid Avenue.

It was Sunday afternoon in Cleveland and there was little traffic. We passed right by the Terminal Tower building I'd photographed in the distance from Edgewater Park, then drove around the Soldiers and Sailors Monument, a spectacular nineteenth-century sculpture located in the middle of a traffic circle which appeared to mark the central point of the city. It made me think of Hart Crane. In fact the whole central section of the city seems to have changed little since his day, and it had been well maintained.

Euclid Avenue ran northeast from the traffic circle and paralleled the lakeshore at a distance of about two miles right out of the city, into the suburbs and eventually into the rural flatlands of the northeastern part of the state.

A lot of stores boasted iron gates tightly locked to prevent burglaries, with black people standing around outside looking slightly humiliated. Further out we passed a beautiful series of buildings including the Cleveland Art Museum, the Institute of Art, the Institute of Music, the Fine Arts Garden, the Garden Centre, the Natural History Museum, the Planetarium, the Western Reserve Historical Society and so on, all surrounded by a series of parks and winding roads. We drove around and around gawking at the beautiful architecture and vowed to come back some day when we had some time to spend. We could write a book called *Two Weeks in Cleveland*,

and people who had spent their entire lives in Cleveland, bonafide Clevelandites, would be lined up around the block to buy their copy.

69. I Love That Kind of Moon

Joan and Jennifer were napping in the back seat. Alison was up front with Daddy. As we drove along we saw what looked like sheets of water lying ahead of us on the road, the images of approaching cars reflected in the shimmering mirrors.

"I love those optical illusions," said Alison.

"Why?"

"Because they remind me of summer."

"I know."

An earlier scene flashed into my mind. I was driving home late at night and Alison was asleep in the back seat. She was about two. In the southwestern sky, just skimming the treetops, was a crescent moon, a thin fingernail of a moon so slight it was easy to miss.

As I carried Alison in from the car, thinking she was in deep sleep, I was amazed to hear her voice.

"Oh, look at that moon," she said. "I love that kind of moon."

Meanwhile, back in the present, another watery mirage appeared on the road in front of us. Alison and I looked at each other and giggled. It was strange. We'd both seen something that wasn't there and it gave us a special bond all over again.

"What causes those optical illusions?" she said.

"You can look it up in the encyclopaedia when we get home. I used to know but I forgot."

"How did I manage to get stuck with such a stupid Daddy?" I imagined her thinking, though she continued smiling sweetly.

"Lots of daddies pretend they know everything," I averred.

"I know they do, dad. They feed vile misinformation to their kids, and then their kids fight with the teachers when the teachers tell them something different."

"So if I don't know for dead certain, I tell you so."

"You don't fake it."

"That's right. The minds of my little ones are too precious to be anything less than perfectly truthful with."

"That's very wise of you, dad."

"You're glad I'm that kind of dad, are you?"

"I sure am. And so is Jenny."

"Oh, good. It's nice to be appreciated."

70. A Festive Atmosphere

It was the 201st birthday of the universe, at least that's what you'd almost think as we drove into Fairport Harbour on the Lake Erie shore. There were flags everywhere. People were sitting on their verandahs waving flags and staring hypnotically into space. Others were milling along the streets in the general direction of the lakefront.

It was a warm evening. The road began dipping down toward the beach. Way off in the distance we could see the amusement park. There was a ferris wheel, rides, carousels, a midway and thousands of people swarming in and out, each with an American flag in his or her hand, or, in some cases, on their heads. You could tell they weren't ants because they were colourfully dressed.

"The kids haven't noticed the rides," said Joan, quietly. "Let's get the heck out of here."

I turned right. The kids were looking out the other window. They were staring at the people sitting on their verandahs with patriotic embalming fluid pumping through their veins. It was Sunday evening.

71. Sex in Ohio

We drove north on the U.S. 44 toward the lake. There was something called Headlands State Beach Park marked on the map. But when we arrived there was a sign saying NO OVERNIGHT CAMPING. People were packing up their cars and heading home after a hard day of swimming and picnicking. Some people were lying on their bellies on blankets under the trees. They were not tourists. They were just local people with the day off. We examined each person carefully from a discreet distance as we drove slowly by. We knew we'd never see any of them ever again.

We drove through an industrial dock area where an old Great Lakes steamer was being loaded with slag. A byproduct of the steel-making process, slag for years was considered useless except as landfill in harbours, to destroy water-basins and provide more usable industrial land. But now it's used in building highways, ground up fine and mixed with asphalt.

We stopped at a traffic signal in a town called Grand River. Joan said something funny, I forget what it was, maybe something about the Grand River on the other side of the lake, a beautiful winding tree-lined river on the lonely and peaceful banks of which Joan and I had frittered away many a rapturous afternoon before the advent of the children, and I smiled. As I smiled I looked out the window at a car parked across the street. There was a beautiful woman behind the wheel. She was looking at me. I guess she thought I was smiling at her because she smiled right back. She looked like someone I'd seen on the cover of *Oui Magazine*, and maybe she was. After all, this was the United States. She had a pretty smile. She turned toward me, sat up straight, and stuck her chest out. She was wearing a white T-shirt with the word OUI on it in huge letters.

"Let's see now," I thought to myself. "Where can I leave Joan and the kids? Maybe I could just abandon them here permanently." Then I erased such an unworthy thought, obviously inspired by satanic forces, and made a spiritual sacrifice toward unknown but certainly glorious ends. We were still looking at each other and smiling merrily when the light turned green.

"The light's green," said Joan.

"All right, all right," I grumbled, driving off. Cursing my miserable fate. Looking back through all three rear-view mirrors at the same time. Hoping she would follow us and tap on my window at 3 a.m. in the next camping site.

A little further on we passed a young man walking along the side of the road. He had his shirt off. He was well-built and well-tanned. He had a perfect body like Russell Seaworthy. We were driving fairly slowly at the time and I noticed Joan giving him as thorough an examination as she could under the circumstances.

"Do you want me to let you out?" I said.

"What do you mean?" exclaimed Joan, angry at my sarcasm and at the same time pleased with my jealousy. She hadn't noticed the little romantic interlude at the stoplight.

"If I let you out you could go back and examine him even more closely. He might even let you have a touch or two."

"Wait a minute. If there was a woman walking along the street with no shirt on you'd look at her too!"

"It's not the same thing!"

"Yes it is!"

"Haven't you ever heard of the double standard?"

"Of course I have, and it just isn't right."

"I know I shouldn't have bought you that subscription to *Ms. Magazine*."

72. Aspirin Consumption in Painesville, Ohio

We bypassed Painesville and got onto the U.S. 20 heading east. "What a name for a town," said Joan. Little did we know we'd be back the next day.

"What's in a name?"

"I don't know. What is in a name?" said Joan.

"I wonder if the people of Painesville consume more aspirins per capita than people in other American towns of similar size."

Joan didn't answer.

"Well?"

"Are you asking me?"

"Yes."

"How would I know?"

"Well, what do you think?"

She didn't answer.

"Well?"

"I'm thinking, I'm thinking!"

"I think they probably would, Daddy," said Alison.

"Why would they?"

"I know," said Joan, anxious not to be outsmarted by her kid.

"Why?"

"Because it would be a pain living in Painesville."

"What about you, Jenny, what do you think?"

"Sh! She's sleeping, Dad."

We kept driving. I could tell they were still thinking about Painesville.

"I was once talking to a woman named Mrs. Payne, who was a yoga teacher," I said. "I told her I thought that was an unusual name for a yoga teacher. She seemed a little put out and said, 'It's a perfectly normal name.'"

"I don't remember you telling me about any yoga teacher named Mrs. Payne," said Joan. "When did you meet her?"

"Oh, that was before I met you."

"And you still remember her after all these years?"

"No, I don't remember her at all. For a moment there I thought I remembered her, but I was mistaken."

"But you do remember her, you just told us a conversation you had with her."

"Forgive me, it was a false memory. Don't you ever have false memories?"

"I guess I do sometimes."

"Well, I just had one."

"You mean you were lying?"

"No, I was telling the truth as I saw it at the time. But a few moments later I realised that I saw it wrong."

73. The Story of O

"What two things do Ontario and Ohio have in common?"

"Lake Erie?" said Alison.

"Good but that's not it. Two things."

"The ferry and the lake?" said Jennifer. Oh, Jennifer, we should have taken you on that ferry! She was still remembering, ecstatically, the numerous ferries we took on our trip through the Maritimes four years earlier.

"Good but that's still not what I'm thinking of."

"They both begin with an O and they both end with an O?" said Joan.

"Joan, you're brilliant!"

"Was that it, Daddy?" said Alison.

"Yeah, that was it."

"Gee, Mommy. You're smart."

Joan smiled quietly.

"She read my mind, that's all," I said.

"What mind?" said Joan.

Traffic on the U.S. 20 was getting heavy. I wondered what was being said in other cars.

74. Miracle on U.S. 20

We were driving east along the U.S. 20. I had my left foot propped up on the dashboard in my favourite driving position and was flicking my eyes back and forth between the road and the Rand McNally map of Ohio I bought for four quarters in that drugstore coin machine in Sandusky.

"Use this map to plan the shortest route," it said. "Please SLOW down. It will save lives as well as gasoline. Don't make unnecessary trips." I figured few trips were as necessary as this one. If more people made trips around the Great Lakes the world would be a better place.

We were looking for a place to camp for the night, and the idea of saving lives was rather appealing as well. Maybe there should have been a warning on the map not to try to read it while driving. I could write to Rand McNally and suggest it.

There was a nice clean dark-blue shiny Chevy van with huge mud flaps passing us on the left. A little girl was looking out the back seat window at our van. I smiled at her and wiggled my nose provocatively.

There didn't seem to be much in the way of campgrounds in this area. It certainly wasn't prime tourist territory like the Port Clinton-Marblehead area where we'd camped the night before.

At a town called Perry the U.S. 20 decreased from four lanes with a median to an old-style two-lane highway without. We slowed down appropriately.

The map showed a little dot called North Skylark a few miles further along the U.S. 20. From there a faint black line marked U.S. 520 went a mile or two north to a place called Skylark-on-the-Lake. Then it made a sharp right, became the U.S. 530 and ran along the lake, hugging the shore past Ashtabula, like an asp hugging Cleopatra's breast, and all the way to the Pennsylvania border at which point, having taken a bite and ejected its venom, it turned south and reconnected with the U.S. 20.

"What do you think, Joan?" I said. "Will there be a greater chance of finding the campsite of our dreams along the highway or along the lakeshore road?"

"Let's try the lakeshore road," said Joan, with the decisiveness for which she was famous throughout the entire Niagara Peninsula and large sections of Southwestern Ontario.

So we went through the green light at North Skylark and pulled into a vacant supermarket parking lot to turn around to go up the U.S. 520. The bloody parking lot wasn't paved. We hit a rut and bounced so hard we almost hit our noggins on the ceiling. As we slowed down and began driving out the exit a nice clean dark-blue shiny Chevy van with huge mud flaps pulled up. The driver, a narrow-faced man with a long broken nose and a full beard, looked at me sternly.

I braked to a halt.

"Where you from?" he said.

"Canada? Ever heard of it?"

He didn't appreciate the joke.

"What street is it on?"

"It's on the wrong side of the tracks."

"Tsk, I know you're from Canada. I see you got Ontario plates. I mean what part of Ontario?"

"Hamilton."

"Oh, we have some relatives used to live in Mount Hope but they moved to Niagara-on-the-Lake."

"That's quite near us," I exclaimed.

He looked at me again.

"I know," he said.

He smiled at his wife.

"Where ya headin'?"

I checked the map. "We're heading up the U.S. 520 to the lake. We're looking for a beautiful campsite (with fantastic views and no rowdyism) at which to spend the night."

"We live up the 520," he said. "Why don't you follow me home and we'll have a cup of tea and we'll phone around looking for a campsite?"

"Jolly good," I said, a little nervously. "We love tea, being Canadians."

"I know, I know."

I just knew it was going to be more than a cup of tea.

"Follow me," he said. "It's not far."

75. This Would Never Happen in Canada

"Did you know there was a town in Ohio called Delightful?" I asked Joan as we followed the Chevy van nervously northward.

"Where?" said Joan.

"In Ohio," I said.

"Yeah, but where in Ohio?"

"About fifty miles south of here on the outskirts of Warren which is on the outskirts of Youngstown."

Joan looked disappointed. I think she wanted Delightful to be close by so we could make a sudden break for it and see if we could find a room in the Delightful Arms Hotel or, failing that, the Delightful Campgrounds of Your Dreams.

"Dave, this is crazy!"

"I know!"

"What if he's a crazy man and wants to shoot us?"

"I don't know. You shouldn't be prejudiced against him just because he's an American. He can't help being an American. Murders happen in Canada too you know."

"I know. But *this* would never happen in Canada."

"And he drinks tea! Now honestly, would a bad guy drink tea?"

"You never know, you just don't know."

"Listen. He's got his wife there and the little kids in the back. He's got relatives in Canada. Very few notorious American criminals have relatives in Canada. They're an average family just like us."

The kids were waving at us out their back window. "Look at that. They're probably just lonely. They want someone to talk to. Maybe they live in a boring neighbourhood, and there are no children for their kids to play with."

Through the rear-view mirror Alison and Jennifer were looking at each other. They both had their lips tightly pursed. It was hard to figure what they were thinking, but it was definitely something.

76. Besides, It'll Look Good in the Book

"Besides," I said.

"Besides what?" said Joan.

"It'll look good in the book."

"Ah, they'll never believe you. They'll think you made it up."

"Oh, come on, Joan. It's not that unusual."

"No, I guess it's not. Not yet anyway."

The Chevy van turned left onto a tree-lined suburban street. We followed.

"You can help me, you know," I whispered conspiratorially.

"How?"

"By observing everything that happens and listening to everything they say so we can write it all down as soon as we leave. They say Malcolm Lowry's wife wrote most of *Under the Volcano*, you know."

"Maybe they'll want us to stay the night."

"Maybe. They'll probably want to check us out first over tea. They might be scared too."

"Yeah," whispered Joan. "But we didn't ask them. And they probably have guns in their house. Loaded guns. Maybe even in their car. You know Americans. You don't fool around with them."

"I know, I know."

"And Dave?"

"Yeah?"

"Don't get into any fights, okay?"

"Okay, okay."

"Agree with everything he says, okay?"

"Okay."

"No matter what he says, okay?"

"Okay."

"Promise?"

"I promise."

"Scout's honour?"

"Scout's honour!"

I put my hand over my heart and made the Scout's sign. The van almost went off the road.

"Take it easy, dad," squeaked Jennifer.

I managed to get the car back on the road. The kids in the Chevy van were laughing at us out the back window.

"What were you guys whispering about?" said Alison.

"Grown-up stuff," said I.

"Christmas presents," said Joan.

"Make up your minds," said Jennifer, that clever little beauty of yesteryear.

77. Joan Gets Drunk

On the Rand McNally map of Ohio, Cleveland is an orange blob in the shape of an American eagle, its wings outspread, its head facing down and its beak open. The town of Skylark looks as if it's about to be swallowed right up.

We were led into the driveway of a small house with a large garage. There would be no room to put us up for the night, unless it be in the garage, I noted, without prejudice. No basement for instance. Ours was a slightly smaller house if I remembered correctly, but it had a basement with a well-appointed guest room, and no garage.

And suddenly there we were: a typical Canadian family from the north side of Lake Erie facing a typical American family from the south side of Lake Erie.

And then I noticed their name on a sign stuck in the lawn. There were two little brightly painted Dickensian figures, a boy and a girl, holding up a sign bearing the family name. I couldn't believe it. The name was the same as ours: MCFADDEN.

"Holy smoke, that's not your name is it?"

"Yes it is," said the guy, again giving me that look.

"Geez, that's my name too." I was opening my wallet to show him my driver's licence.

"I believe you, I believe you," he said.

"Same spelling too," I said.

"What a coincidence," he said, calmly, with a thin smile. "Holy smoke."

"I'd just die if your first name was the same as mine," I said.

"What's yours?" he said.

"It starts with a D."

"So does mine," he said.

"Oh, no. My God, it couldn't be David?"

"It most certainly is."

We looked at each other and smiled. The women were smiling too.

It had been a hot day and the kids were getting into their bathing suits and hopping into the backyard pool. Lamont was seven and his hobby was pulling down girls' pants. Tania was ten and had the same favourite rock and roll bands as my kids: Kiss and Meatloaf. Like Jennifer, Tania could sing all the verses to "Paradise by the Dashboard Light" straight through.

The adults sat around the kitchen table sipping tea and swapping life stories. We could hear the kids singing "Paradise by the Dashboard Light" by the pool.

After her third cup of tea Joan started in on the beer and started to unwind alarmingly.

"My Dave's a writer and he's writing a story about this trip," she blurted out. I cringed, the veins in my neck bulging. "No one who reads the book is going to believe this part."

David's expression didn't change. "When it comes out I'll be the first to buy it," he said. He was a serious person.

"I'd dedicate it to you, but everyone would think I was being extremely narcissistic," I noted.

"You're right," said David, in a tone that indicated he meant well. "You should just dedicate it to yourself."

78. A Lot of Good Men Died in Vietnam

"Why don't you camp in our driveway tonight?" said Chloris, David's wife, a rather plump and plain-looking (but quite complex) woman of about thirty. She spoke with a Scottish accent. She'd met David when he was in the U.S. Navy stationed in Scotland. David had been born in Scotland too, coincidentally, but came to the U.S. with his family when he was five. He quit high school to join the navy.

"I thought I was being really smart," he said. "Now I know better."

He had a polar-bear skin on the living room floor. It was from a small bear. It must have been a mere cub when it was killed. It came from Iceland.

David had served in Vietnam during the sixties.

"I saw a lot of good men killed in that war," he said. His eyes filled with tears. "I'd prefer not to talk about it." My heart went out to him. I understood completely. They'd trusted their leaders. They went to war in droves, not realising that the Americans with money, the more privileged classes, were finding plenty of ways to stay home in droves. David and his friends were sacrificing their lives for something they thought was beautiful. And now the awful truth was out. If they had only won the war.

79. Americans Like to Brag about Their Dogs

Behind the swimming pool was a pen with two dogs in it, huge, vicious-looking slobbering mutts, but really quite gentle. They were chained.

"Why do you keep them chained when they're already inside the pen?" said the ever-inquisitive and highly observant Joan.

"Because that one is the world's best climber and this one is the world's best tunnel digger," said David.

Then Tania came over and stood on my right side.

"See this dog?" she said. "If there was a contest for climbing he'd win it."

Then Lamont appeared on my left.

"And the other one," he said, with a childish lisp, "would win any contest for digging holes."

Then Chloris came over and put her arm around Joan and gave her a reassuring squeeze.

"These are really remarkable dogs," she said. "Bobby here could climb Mount Everest and Ralph could dig a tunnel out of San Quentin Penitentiary."

80. How Do You Like Your Steaks?

It was getting late. Chloris put her kids to bed and Joan and I got our kids settled down in the van.

"You're right, Joan," I said. "Nobody's gonna believe this. Not even your mother."

"What made you change your mind?" said Joan.

"Their name. It's the same as ours. Now that is a thousand times more incredible than simply getting picked up by them."

The kids fell asleep quickly. It was all the swimming.

The four adults were sitting at the kitchen table when Chloris got up and started doing something at the microwave oven. David started telling us about how their old oven had exploded one day and the whole kitchen was engulfed in flames. With the insurance settlement and a little artifice they managed to get a $2,000 microwave unit out of the deal.

Chloris' voice suddenly rang out.

"How do you like your steaks?"

"Well done," said Joan, delightedly, without hesitation.

"None for me, thanks, I'm a vegetarian," said I.

"No he's not, he's just fooling," said Joan.

"Yeah, I was just fooling. I'll have mine well done too."

"That's another coincidence for your book," said David. "We like ours well done too." He was opening a bottle of California burgundy.

I could have killed Joan for telling them I was writing a book. I gave her a menacing look, the sort of look Mr. Quilp is forever giving Mrs. Quilp in *The Old Curiosity Shop*—but I had a reason for it.

"I think Dave's mad at me," she blurted out, "because I told you about the book he was writing."

They all looked at me.

"Heh, heh?" I said, with a fake smile, little beads of sweat popping out on my brow. "Bad luck to talk about a book before it's written, you know?"

81. On the Brink of Extinction

By the time we were finished the meal Joan (who normally drinks next to nothing) was getting pretty unwound on all that beer and wine. But David was even more unwound.

"Ready for a swim?" he said.

"I don't have a shoot with me," tittered little Joan.

"Neither do I," said I. I was expecting them to suggest skinny-dipping but then I noticed the neighbours' windows overlooked the pool.

"I can lend you one," Chloris said to Joan.

"Okay!" said Joan, brightly.

That was a little strange. Joan is usually shy about appearing in a swimsuit. Further, she's pretty small and would swim in any suit of Chloris'.

"And I've got a pair of denim cutoffs that would fit you," said David.

"Okay."

But before we changed David took me into the garage to show me his Honda 350. "It's my pride and joy," he said. He said it was no good on the highway because of the low gear ratios so he couldn't take it back and forth to work. He worked as a welder in a Towmotor plant in Painesville.

"It'll only do about fifty on the highway. But it's really good around town. Nothing will beat it at a stoplight. And it's a good trail bike. Riding along country roads, lanes, nature trails, through the woods."

He started it up. The roar was deafening. Anyone who would ride one of those through the silent woods has got to be pretty insensitive to nature, I thought. But then again we all must be pretty insensitive to nature or we wouldn't be where we are today—on the brink of extinction, and, collectively, doing nothing about it.

I think he was half-expecting me to ask him if I could take it for a spin.

82. Most Americans Look like Someone Famous

We went out into the driveway. I wanted to make sure the kids were okay and to lock the doors just in case. With Joan half-pissed I had to be particularly responsible.

Across the street a woman was taking her dogs out for a leak.

"Hey Tinker Bell!" called out David. "Tinker Bell!"

She walked over, cautiously. The dogs started running in huge circles around her. One was a semi-collie, the other a small white poodle-like creature.

"Is the Ogre asleep?" said David.

"Yeah at last!" said Tinker Bell. She was short, about four-nine with breasts a little too large for her size. She had an unusual face, soft, large for her size, and not unattractive. She was aptly named.

"Wanna come in for a swim?" said David. I just stood there watching as if invisible.

"Is it safe?" she said.

"It's safe."

"It wasn't last time."

"Go get your suit."

It didn't occur to me to ask about the Ogre or the reference to safety. I just wanted to relax and see what happened. I just hoped the Ogre didn't come over with a .38-calibre revolver when he found out his wife had slipped out on him again in the middle of the night.

Most Americans look like somebody famous, I thought. But I never saw any movie star or rock star or television star who looked like Tinker Bell. She was a true original as far as the unusualness of her face was concerned. I thought maybe she should go to Hollywood.

In fact it began to occur to me that most Americans are resentful of not being rich and famous. They watch television and go to the movies to feed their jealousy. That's it. I'm sure. It explains everything. Think about it. Quick before it goes away.

83. The Arrows of Your Heart

Joan was the first one in the pool. I think she jumped in first because she was so shy in the bathing suit Chloris had lent her. It was too big for her and every time she moved her breasts were revealed in all their occult grandeur. She called out to me once she got in.

"How's the water?" I said.

"Beautiful. But Dave?"

"Yes?"

"Will you get me a string for this bathing suit? It's too big for me. I'm swimming in it."

Chloris gave me a shoe lace and I tossed it in the pool for Joan. I immediately felt stupid. It was the sort of thing a man who'd been married too long would do.

"Let me," said David, diving in and picking up the string from the surface of the water.

He laced it through the suit and took up the slack and then tied it gently around Joan's neck. I could see Joan blushing in the moonlight.

Then Chloris and Tinker Bell and I jumped in the pool under the soft summer sky of Ohio in a huge land of endless cities and towns and villages and railway stations and post offices fading away in any direction you choose to send the arrows of your heart. Maybe that's why most Americans look so bored.

84. Chloris Gets Out Her Stamp Collection

I built a little fire in the back yard with bricks to shelter it from the warm night breezes, cool against our bodies fresh from the pool.

"Look at that," said David. "He's really got a good fire going." I was proud. Only one match too.

We dried off and warmed up around the fire, our toes almost touching. In the pool David had been grabbing the three women by the ankles, around the waist and so on, and throwing them into the air and catching them and chasing after them and swimming up to them underwater and scaring them and all that stuff. But I just dogpaddled around keeping out of their way.

Things quietened down after that. We went in the house and sat at the kitchen table. David got out more beer. Chloris got out her stamp albums. She had a nice collection. When David saw how interested I was he knew for sure he had a wimp on his hands.

Chloris had stamps from all over the world. Tinker Bell on the other hand was into macramé. She couldn't get over our names being the same.

"Hey!" she said. "McFadden, McFadden, and McRamé."

"Ohh!" said everyone.

It was very nostalgic looking through Chloris' stamp albums from her childhood. I'd had many of the same stamps when I was a kid.

"See that one?" she said. "That's worth $300."

"Oh no!" I cried. "I had dozens of them when I was a kid but they all got tossed out."

"Are you sure this isn't *Fernwood*, Ohio?" Joan kept saying. She was referring to a television series about some very amusing working-class suburban goofballs. It was popular that year. It was called *Mary Hartman, Mary Hartman*.

"If you say that once more I'll kill you," said Chloris, in a chilling tone. She sounded as if she meant it.

85. A Serious Discussion about the Environment

David and I were two responsible adult male humans having a serious discussion about water quality.

"How does this side of the lake compare with the other side?" said David.

"There aren't as many dead fish on the beaches over here," I said.

"Yeah. After the Cuyahoga River caught fire a couple of years ago everyone panicked and they got started on a clean-up campaign."

"It might have something to do with the prevailing winds as well," I added.

"What, the fire?"

"No, the dead fish piling up on the Canadian side."

"Yeah." said David. "I guess so."

86. We Get Out of the Pool Just in Time

We were continuing our serious talk when there was an immense flash of lightning, a bolt of thunder, and it started to rain with immense abandon.

"We got out of the pool just in time," I declared.

"Yeah," said David. "Otherwise we would have got all wet."

"And just think," said Joan. "The moon was shining not five minutes ago."

"Yeah. Just think."

"Gee," said Tinker Bell. "It's raining cats and dogs."

"They look like drops of water to me," said David.

Tinker Bell cringed with embarrassment. Joan put her arm around her and said, "They look like cats and dogs to me."

87. The Americans Land on the Moon

We took off our wet bathing suits and put on dry clothing. The women were sitting at the kitchen table. David was lying down on one of the two sofas in the living room. He told me to lie down on the other one. "Go ahead, it's comfortable," he said. It was about two-thirty in the morning.

David started telling me about his job, how he works steady nights. This was his night off, fortunately. He said he liked steady nights because there was less stress, you could goof off more, there were no bosses snooping around, there was less traffic to fight going to and from work, and you could sleep any time you wanted during the day or early evening. It was nice to walk around during the day when everyone else was at work. And on top of that you got paid more for working nights.

"I know all that," I said. "I worked steady nights for seven years." I told him about the painter John B. Boyle who, for three months after he left his teaching job to become a full-time artist, couldn't get any work done. All he wanted to do was experience the joy of walking around town during the day when everyone else was working. "That was in St. Catharines," I said. "It's not the same in Hamilton. Almost everyone's a shift worker there."

He started telling me about how sick little Lamont was when he was first born. "After a while I stopped hoping he would live," he said. "I just gave up on him." Tears came into his eyes. "He's pretty good now but he still gets terrible bouts of bronchitis. Did you see him shivering when he came out of the water?"

I did notice that, and that he was the only one of the four kids shivering. He wrapped himself up in the largest blanket, the one commemorating the manned landing on the moon. The one with the American flag sticking out of a yellow crater and the words about man and mankind. I was never good at remembering unforgettable quotes.

88. Moving to Utah

Then David started telling me how sick he himself was. The story about little Lamont was a mere warm-up. I didn't know what to think. It sounded serious. He showed me the scar from his kidney operation. One kidney had been removed. The other was in bad shape. He had to go back into the hospital in a month.

"It's an incurable disease with a name this long," he said. He took another slug of beer.

"Wouldn't it be better if you cut down on the beer?"

"If the doctors told me cutting down on beer would help I'd quit drinking immediately. But if I'm going to have a short life I'm going to enjoy it."

I didn't want to pump him on it although I had a feeling he wanted me to. He looked kind of grey. I asked him about dialysis. He said he couldn't go on it. I didn't ask him why.

Joan later theorised that he was dying and that's why Chloris had indulged his little whim to invite us home. Chloris had made it clear in small ways that it had been his idea totally.

And yet David talked about quitting his job and moving with his family to Utah. Or maybe to New Zealand. He really wanted to move to San Francisco but Chloris wouldn't hear of it. "I don't relish living in the earthquake zone," she said. New Zealand was more to her liking.

David was a Republican and hated the current U.S. President, Jimmy Carter. He was annoyed about the cancellation of the plans to build some new American bomber. It was in the news all that summer. "I have a feeling he's going to start another war, the biggest of all time. And if he does you're going to have another neighbour," he said. Meaning himself.

89. Greasy Little Wop

I told David how the black family in the car pointed at me and laughed as I was standing on a street corner in Sandusky on a warm Sunday afternoon in my African-style shirt. It wasn't as if I'd been wearing a pair of bell-bottomed checked trousers or four-inch Cuban heels, nor did I have some kind of wild quasi-Afro haircut two feet high.

"You're lucky they just pointed at you. You're lucky they didn't point a gun at you. You're lucky they didn't shoot you."

"Aw, come on. Is it really that bad?"

"You better believe it, baby."

"But was it my shirt they were laughing at or was it something else?"

"What were you wearing?"

"Just the dashiki and a pair of Levis, a pair of Italian sandals."

"What were you doing?"

"Just standing there with a camera in my hand."

"Could have been the shirt."

"It wasn't really African anyway," said Joan. "It was made in Pakistan."

"There's good and bad in every race," David was saying. "I work with a lot of black guys. Some really great guys as far as I'm concerned. They ask me how I liked *Roots*, the television series? I tell them I liked it but it was kind of one-sided. We were all slaves at one time. The blacks had it a heck of a lot better than my ancestors at the hands of the Romans. They killed us whenever they felt like it. We were dirt cheap. When they killed one of us another was right there. They didn't have to import us all the way across the sea from Africa."

"You got a point there," I said. I told him about our trip through Cleveland.

"You could have been in a lot of trouble if you'd got out of your car," he said. He looked at me with his serious blue eyes, a light shade of blue almost white, like the movie actor Paul Newman's. "A Canadian is easy picking for them. They'd take you for all you're worth and if that wasn't enough they'd take your life."

I asked what he thought of that incident yesterday in a small town in Georgia where a white guy drove his Jaguar sports car at top speed into a crowd at a Ku Klux Klan picnic. Nobody was killed but nineteen were taken to the hospital. The fellow told the cops he had a lot of black friends and didn't like what the KKK was saying about blacks so he decided to kill a few. David hadn't heard about this, and wanted to reserve comment until he read about it in the paper.

Chloris started talking about one of their neighbours. She said he was a "greasy little wop" who drives around in a pickup truck trying to pick up women.

"Does he have GREASY LITTLE WOP painted on the side of the truck?" I inquired. Joan nudged my knee with her foot.

"No," said Chloris. "He doesn't have to. Anyone can see it's a greasy little wop behind the wheel."

A thought unworthy of me, and undoubtedly wrong, flashed through my mind: She was just annoyed because he'd never tried to pick her up.

90. A Bridge over Troubled Waters

Chloris and Tinker Bell were telling Joan about the Ogre, Tinker Bell's husband, and how he used to be such a great guy but lately he's turned mean.

"He phones her up from work all the time and wants to know what she's doing, the bastard," said Chloris. "He wants to make sure she's doing all the housework."

Tinker Bell nodded. "Yeah," she said, "and if I'm not in he sometimes phones over here."

"That's right," said Chloris. "He often phones here during the day looking for her. I just tell him I don't know where she is even if she's standing right next to me."

David and I were listening from the living room. "He used to be a wonderful guy, really," said David, "He's six-foot-four and she's only four-foot-nine. He throws her around quite a bit. She doesn't like to admit it but he does. Sometimes she comes over here black and blue and sobbing her eyes out."

"God," I said.

"Yeah, we used to be the greatest of friends. He got along really well with little Tania. They used to play together. He was just like a big overgrown kid with her. Then one day they were fooling around and little Tania accidentally kneed him in the balls. He grabbed her like this and began shaking her. When she came home and told me that I was so mad. If he ever does it again I tell you I'll kill him. I know I will. I'll kill him."

"Do they have any children?" I felt as if I should be puffing meditatively on a pipe.

"No. And that's another thing. He wants kids and she refuses to get pregnant. She won't have any kids by him. Can't say I blame her."

"What does he do for a living?"

"He used to operate the merry-go-round at the amusement park but last year he got a job managing a McDonald's."

Tinker Bell came into the living room. She looked uncertain and very timid.

"Come here," said David. "Sit down."

"Your feet are in the way."

He sat up and pulled her down at one end of the sofa. He grabbed her arm and looked at it. Then he frowned. "What are these marks?"

She became even more embarrassed. "I don't know. I can't remember where I got those."

"Okay then. Rub my feet." Now I was getting embarrassed.

She took his bare feet in her hands and began massaging them expertly. I could hear all those tiny bones cracking. My own feet began twitching with jealousy. She kept it up. "Ah, that feels good," he said. "Why didn't you ever do that before?"

"I did," she said. "Don't you remember New Year's Eve?"

"Oh yeah."

She got embarrassed again. "What's your wife going to say when she comes in and sees me massaging your feet?" I think Chloris was in the bathroom.

"She can't complain," said Don. "She never massages them herself. They have to be massaged by someone."

Suddenly in stormed Chloris. "I heard that," she said. She looked really angry and she looked as if she would have expressed her anger a lot more strongly if Joan and I hadn't been in the house.

Tinker Bell got up and came over to sit beside me. She looked as if she wanted to massage my feet. I would have let her but I was a little too nervous. Joan might bean me, perhaps with Chloris' help. There seemed to be a lot of tension in the air. I know it sounds stupid, but I couldn't help feeling as if something awful were about to happen.

91. A Visit to Tinker Bell's Place

Joan and I finally got into the van at four-thirty in the morning and immediately dropped into sound sleep. Two hours later I was awakened by the alarm clock in my bladder. I slipped out of the van and tried to get into the house but all the doors were locked. That didn't seem right.

When you have guests sleeping in a van in your driveway it's only common courtesy to leave a door open. But then I remembered this was the United States. All that suburban paranoia really prevailed. They were afraid of gangs of murderous Mau Maus bursting into their house in the middle of the night. I wandered across the street and peed in some rose bushes. I hoped the Ogre wasn't looking out his window.

When we finally got up Chloris made a glorious July 4 breakfast for all of us. Fried eggs, bacon, mushrooms, orange juice, toast, twelve kinds of marmalade. Yum. As I ate, David handed me his stereo headphones. His beloved Pink Floyd record was playing, *The Dark Side of the Moon*. I thought of the dark side of Lake Erie. But the music was nice to eat breakfast by. I really liked it a lot. He was pleased.

Tinker Bell came over and had tea with us. Then she took us over to her house to show it off. The Ogre was at work. At McDonald's, July 4 is a particularly busy day.

The house was filled with heavy imitation antique furniture. The walls were covered with pieces of silver from the Ogre's collection. There were silver spoons from all of the states, silver plaques representing various episodes from American history, and so on. The atmosphere was airlessly stagnant with dull patriotism.

I picked up the *Cleveland Plain Dealer* and read a front-page exposé on some conniving congressman. The reporter had done an absolutely wonderful job. "God, they've really nailed this guy," I said. "He's finished."

David was less than enthusiastic. He disliked newspapers. "Yeah, they nailed Sam Shepherd too," he said. "They nailed him on circumstantial evidence. That paper gets away with murder." He was referring to a famous Cleveland murder case, nothing to do with the playwright and actor of the same name.

I spent the rest of the visit playing with the dogs. The collie was particularly susceptible to my caresses. I really know what dogs like.

On the wall was a wedding photo. It was a large head shot of the Ogre superimposed on a full-length photo of Tinker Bell in her wedding dress. Very artistic. Tinker Bell looked apprehensive, her head bowed toward her bridal bouquet. The Ogre looked like Robert Redford. It was as if Tinker Bell was a little doll of an idea in his head. Tinker Bell had aged a lot in two years.

MONDAY, JULY 4

92. A Stupid Computer in Buffalo

The heat was horrendous. I felt like an Eskimo lost in the Sahara. I don't know why we did this but we put Bruce in the van along with a fresh bowl of water and rolled the windows up with only about a three-inch clearance. "There's a lot of dognappers around here," said David. "And that's no mutt you got there. They just love to get their hands on dogs like that."

We thought we were only going to he gone for fifteen minutes but it was almost three hours before we returned. They took us to Uncle Bill's, the only department store open July 4. It was the 201st birthday of the United States of America and to celebrate I bought a skateboard for my daughters. Theirs had been stolen in Canada.

Then I saw this vinyl snap-on steering wheel cover for three dollars and I bought it like a fool. It was all sealed in a transparent plastic package. Later when I ripped it out of its casing and tried to put it on the steering wheel it turned out to be the tackiest thing anyone in the history of the world had ever wasted his money on. I threw it in the garbage.

Joan found a bathing suit she liked and I told her she'd probably find a nicer one in Canada. She quietly put it back. What a rat! I'm worse than the Ogre in my own way. Months later she was still telling me she wished she'd ignored me and bought it. She says she's never seen one that suited her so well.

The record shop next door was open as well. They had Bob Marley's new record, *Exodus*, which I bought much to my later regret. After listening to it for five minutes I realised he'd finally cleaned up his Jamaican nationalist act and sold his soul to get on the U.S. charts. Exodus indeed. The next one will be called *You Can't Go Home Again*.

I also bought a blank tape at David's urging. "You can tape my Pink Floyd record and listen to it whenever you want," he said. The strangest thing is this: I didn't feel guilty at the time about stopping Joan from buying that bathing suit.

But to get a tape at that store you reach your hand through a hole in the padlocked transparent plastic door just like in Canadian stores. But then you pull the tape you want toward you and let it fall onto a conveyor belt. I'd never seen that before. The conveyor belt takes it up to the cash register. "What won't they think of next?" I said.

The clerk was standing there. She had a remarkable resemblance to the young lady in the *Oui* T-shirt a day or so back, but she didn't seem to recognise me. "You never know," she said.

She was calling out questions to the head clerk, a black guy. "Are the Heptones soul or jazz?" she said.

"Reggae," I called out.

"No, it's soul," said the black guy, apologetically. "What?" I said. "Who decides that?"

"Oh, some stupid computer in Buffalo," he said, with passion.

"Kee-rist," I said. "Do you play the tape for the computer and it decides what category the music falls into?"

"No, it's not that sophisticated," he said. "The guy who programs the computer knows absolutely nothing about music."

93. Race Relations in Painesville

We were back in David's air-conditioned van. David and I were up front, the women and kids in the back. "That's where we first saw you," little Tania screamed out as we passed that critical point on U.S. 20. I didn't know where we were going and I was beginning to worry about Bruce. "You waved at me, remember?"

"Oh yeah, I remember," I said. I always like to wave at kids we pass on the highway.

We were being taken on a tour of David McFadden's general environment. We went through Painesville. David told us it had been the locale for a famous movie about thirty years before but he couldn't remember the name of the movie. It was something about a white woman who falls in love with a black man. "Back then this was the only town in the United States where a movie like that could be made," he said, without emotion.

"Why was that?"

"The race relations here were excellent."

"That's strange with a name like Painesville."

"Yeah, that is kinda funny."

"And how are the race relations now?"

"Probably about the same."

94. Race Relations in North Carolina

I told him about an incident that happened in North Carolina a while back. I went into a country store and there were four guys sitting around watching television. Two were white and two were black. The white guys were sitting on chairs. One of the black guys was sitting on the floor, the other kneeling on the floor. I was buying a six-pack. There was a little blob of blood on the counter where somebody had placed some fresh meat.

"I don't like the sight of that blood," said one of the white guys. He motioned to one of the black guys. "Clean it up."

"Yessir," the black guy said, scrambling. He ran back with a J-cloth. "Where's the Windex gone?" he said. In a moment he was back with a bottle of Windex. He cleaned off the entire counter, with great expertise.

I was a little embarrassed. I was counting out my change to pay for the six-pack and I dropped a dime on the floor. Before I could bend down to pick it up, the same white guy turned to the other black guy and said, "Pick that up for the man."

The man yet. Imagine! The black guy went so fast he was just a blur. In a split second the dime was back in my hand and the black guy was back at his spot on the floor watching the boob tube. I had the feeling the white guy was showing off. He probably figured I was from the northern United States and he was demonstrating that the Civil War had been all in vain. He still had his slaves. An extremely efficient form of technology. Wasn't I envious? It was quite macho, like gunning a hot rod at a stoplight.

We were staying at a motel right next to the country store. In the morning the good old boy who ran the motel wanted to talk so I decided to try to explore the situation a little in my own sneaky way.

"You know," I said, "I was expecting to see a lot of bad feeling between the blacks and the whites down here. But I haven't seen anything like that anywhere. Why, last night I went into that country store to get me some beer and I saw two white guys and two black guys sitting there watching television together just as if they were old friends. I'm really impressed."

The good old boy started purring like a kitten. "We got some really sweet niggers down here," he said. "I think all the sour niggers went up north. Yes sir, I figure I've got as many nigger friends as white friends. Maybe even more. Of course that was a public place where you saw them watching television. We would never let them in our living rooms. We good friends but not on a social basis. If some niggers wanted to stay at this motel I'd put them right at the back. Of course there are certain white people I'd put right at the back too."

The guy said he felt there was no north and south anymore. "It's just one country as far as I'm concerned," he said. He started talking about some awful disease that had been hitting his hunting dogs. Tears filled his eyes as he told of how they died in agony. Some of them he had to shoot.

95. A Feeling of Utter Death in the Air

"A lot of blacks would have been better off down there than moving up here and spending their lives working in sweatshops," said David. "The guy's basically right. The blacks up here are really sour. That's why they're always killing each other. It's a big problem."

He also said blacks and whites don't even get together in public places in Ohio, never mind privately. "That's good," he said. "The South is really progressing. We're not."

We drove through a couple of shopping centres even though they were closed for the holiday. Chloris showed us the store where she used to work.

"What department did you work in?" said Joan.

"*Exclusive* sports wear," said Chloris. "Quite expensive."

There were stores everywhere. It was like a fix. It was getting sickening. I wanted out of it all. I waxed philosophical. "What a consumer society!" I said. "All we do is work to buy and buy to work."

No answer.

We passed a small factory. "That's Towmotor, where I work," said David in a small voice. It looked like a shoe box with some chimneys.

"Nice place," I said.

We passed the Holden Arboretum and the first Mormon Temple to be built in the United States (still in use). We cut up some back roads and passed a Girl Scout troop on a hike. There were hundreds of them.

We passed through a series of little towns dominated by service stations, shopping centres and McDonald's restaurants. Every time we passed a McDonald's I'd say, "Is that where the Ogre works?" It never was.

It was all getting rather dismal. There was a feeling of utter death in the air. No excitement. Just gloom gloom gloom. This is what Canada will be like some day, when there is nothing left to fight for, I thought. *Les Québécois* had the right idea. Independence wasn't the question, but the fight for independence was. Thank God there is still something left fighting for in my country, still something left to be created. Maybe I was fooling myself. Maybe things were worse than I thought.

96. Naked in a Foreign Country

We were back in North Skylark. We passed a shopping centre. It was about the ninety-seventh we'd passed that day. I noticed a large OPEN sign in front of a pizza store. "Let's order a couple of pizzas," I said.

So we stopped and I ran in and ordered two large pizzas: one with pepperoni and sausage the way the American McFaddens like it and one with anchovies and pineapple and mushrooms the way the Canadian McFaddens like it. We didn't tell them about the horsemeat/pepperoni scandal that hit the Niagara Peninsula and Montreal a few years back.

"What's the name?" said the guy in the red apron and funny hat. He had a thin moustache like Clark Gable but was much fatter. Most Americans look like somebody famous.

"McFadden," I said, feeling naked in a foreign country. Did he know I was a Canadian? I felt as if I weren't a real McFadden, but a counterfeit. The real McFadden was in the driver's seat in the van.

"It'll be ready in twenty minutes," said Clark Gable.

97. Dogs Are Tough

Then I remembered Bruce. We decided to head back, check Bruce, drop off the women and kids, then drive back to the pizza store.

When we reached the McFaddens' place I hopped out of the van while it was still rolling and into mine to rescue Bruce. He was gasping a little, all his water was gone, but he seemed all right.

We let Bruce lie down in the cool shade and rinsed him off with a cold rag. He seemed to enjoy all the attention. Dogs don't hold grudges. They're instantly forgiving. Then David and I went back to pick up the pizza.

While we were gone, Joan later told me, they went around the back and found one of the McFaddens' dogs hanging from the fence. He had tried to climb over the fence and had been hanging there gasping all the time we were gone in all that heat. They released him and he appeared to be all right. That was Bobby, the one who could climb Mount Everest. Unfortunately he was never going to get the chance. Just like the untold geniuses who died in concentration camps.

98. Smoking Hashish in Ohio

As we drove around the corner David pulled out his hash pipe and handed it to me. "You feel like a little toke?" he said.

"Sure." I lit up.

"Don't tell Chloris though. She can't stand the idea of me smoking. She'd go apeshit."

"Yeah, women are really stupid." Imagine a veteran of a major foreign war coming home and being told by his wife what he can and can't smoke. It just wasn't right. We McFaddens had to stick together.

I took one puff and my head melted away until I was cut off at the neck. I handed the pipe to David. He took two puffs. "Want more?" he said.

"Next year maybe," I said.

99. A Brave American

The guy said the pizzas would be ready in another minute or two. David and I waited outside. It was slightly cooler there than inside with all the ovens.

A red Chevy van pulled up. The girl behind the wheel was an incredible sight for someone a little high on cannabis. She was wearing a neck collar, a head bandage, a chin bandage, and she had two black eyes. Her eyes were little swollen slits. Her jaw was wired shut.

She looked at us. "Is this store open?" she said.

"Yes, it is," I managed to get out.

She got out of the van. We couldn't help gawking at her. She was covered in bruises and cuts. Bandages were falling off her. She had one arm in a cast, the other in a sling. She pulled her crutches out of the van.

"Holy Christ!" I muttered. In my state I felt as if she had endured the most incredible atrocities ever devised.

"I bet she was in a motorcycle spill," said David.

She started swinging her body in the direction of the stereo store. It was closed. I thought she'd meant the pizza store. How could I have been so stupid?

"Oh, I'm so sorry," I said. "I thought you meant the pizza store."

The girl shrugged and swung her body back to the van.

"What happened to you?" said David.

"Motorcycle spill," she said.

"I thought so," said David. "Gonna keep ridin'?"

"You bet. Soon's I get these casts off."

"Good for you."

100. A Circle of Light around Lake Erie

Our feet weren't quite touching the ground as we floated into the McFadden back yard with the pizzas. We placed them on a little card table that had miraculously appeared.

"Isn't that wonderful?" I said. "A card table to put the pizza on!"

"Yeah," said David. "What won't they think of next?"

Strangely enough, Chloris and Joan didn't seem to think anything amiss. Everyone grabbed a piece of pizza, except Chloris. "I'm on a diet," she said, sternly.

"A diet? A skinny little thing like you?" I said.

"Yes, a diet," she said, without a trace of amusement. She knew she wasn't skinny, although she wasn't as fat as the average Georgia sheriff.

"Well, you've got pretty good willpower," I said. "This pizza is almost as good as they make in Hamilton, Ontario."

"I don't like Italian food," she said.

"She doesn't like Italians period," said David.

"Oh yeah, I forgot. Well," I said, "you could have said something before we got it." I went on and on. "We could have got something else. We could have gone to a restaurant and all had something different. You could have had a little chef's salad with no-cal dressing...."

"No," she said, wearily. "It's all right." She seemed ready for us to go. Well, we weren't quite ready yet. We'd go when we bloody well felt like it. After all, we hadn't invited ourselves.

Even David was getting a little tired. He had to go to work that night and his body was telling him to prepare for it by having a sleep.

The kids all wanted to go in for one last swim.

"You sure you don't mind, Chloris?" said Joan.

"No," she said. "Let them go in if they must."

So they went in. Chloris' impatience was colouring the whole atmosphere.

"Where's that blank tape?" said David. "I might as well tape *The Dark Side of the Moon* for you."

"Oh yeah." We went in the house. I put on the headphones and listened as he taped. The music sounded absolutely sensational. I floated away on a pillowish cloud of nothingness to the very place we would have been if I hadn't bothered waving at little Tania McFadden on the road. Somewhere beyond the horizon where the planets exert different influences on earthly life and time goes sideways, back and forth. To paraphrase the poet Roy Kiyooka: Thank you, everyone, for helping me dream this dream.

Mentioning other writers in your writing is "a fault of youth and inexperience," wrote the poet Phyllis Gotlieb. Please, God, let me never become old and experienced.

Thank you, Roy Kiyooka, for helping me dream this dream in which we are drawing a circle of light around Lake Erie, a dream in which everything within that circle is ours.

101. Consciousness

Chloris was telling us all about the various races she didn't like and why she didn't like them. Italians were the most disliked. Joan told her don't come to visit us because we were the only non-Italians on the street.

Chloris also hated the Spanish, the Greeks, the Germans and the Irish. She didn't mention Jews, Arabs, Africans or Asians. I think it went without saying that all four would be on her hate list.

Everyone was sitting around in the living room. They were ignoring me. I had the headphones on and was pretending to be absorbed in the music. They didn't realise the right headphone wasn't covering my ear and I could hear every word that was being spoken.

But I didn't realise the kids were paying attention too. Then innocent little Alison piped up. "We have some Irish blood in us," she said. She was wondering if that meant we were no good.

Chloris' brain snapped like a steel trap. "I didn't know Irish had blood," she said. Alison frowned.

I felt sick. I thought of that horrendous line from the Portuguese national poet Camoens. Vasco da Gama has just greeted a flotilla of Moslems from Mozambique and says: "We come from Europe, the home of strong and warlike peoples."

Chloris spoke again about the possibility of moving to New Zealand. She thought she'd really like the country because the people there were all English or Scotch and had little tolerance for people of other racial origins. I thought that was eminently sensible and realistic of her.

"Maybe New Zealand will turn out to be your spiritual home," said Joan, sympathetic as always.

· "I think you might be right," said Chloris.

"I could live anywhere, I could," said David, sweetly.

"Dave's four grandparents were Irish, Scotch, Welsh and English," said Joan. "So he's a real mongrel."

Everyone looked over at me. My eyes were unfocussed and I seemed to be drifting along with the music. I gave no indication I was following the discussion.

"He's British," said Chloris. I don't know whether she decided that on my looks, my name, or what Joan had just told her.

"Don't you hold it against him that he's part Irish?" said Joan.

"Not really. He can't help being part Irish. He doesn't act Irish. That's the main thing."

That got me thinking. I sort of felt Irish. Sometimes in fact I feel like a pure Irishman in exile from the one true church and one true homeland. And I think I look Irish. I think James Joyce had a friend who looked just like me. I like to dress up in clothes I imagine would be in style in Dublin in 1920. In *Ulysses* there's a minor character named Babyface McFadden the Cop. When I finished reading Joyce's letters I strangely burst into tears.

Although there are a lot of McFaddens in Scotland, McFadden is definitely an Irish name. I guess David never told Chloris that. He was probably afraid to, in the same way he was afraid to smoke grass at home. Little did she know she was married to a member of the very race she most despised. Lovely. Her own children were half-Irish. Yuk yuk. All the Scots are ethnically Irish, for the ancient name for the Irish, before they invaded and settled in what is now called Scotland, was "Scots."

But none of us can help what he or she is. A little philosophy here. The personality is the mask. The only thing in control is the unadulterated indivisible consciousness we all share. The stuff that fills the universe like radio waves, the stuff we as biological creatures, as genetic robots, merely receive like radios, like fine tuning mechanisms.

102. The Dark Side of the Moon

There seemed to be some amazing energy transfers going on between Chloris and David. Both were strong, independent personalities. Yet sometimes when David was talking you could see his personality dissolve and Chloris' take over. Other times when Chloris was talking, David's personality would take over. Almost in a hypnotic way.

For instance, David likes Pink Floyd and motorcycles and is decidedly anti-American—at least until someone else starts attacking his country. Yet he found my Bob Marley tapes from Jamaica too nationalistic for his liking. I wish I'd had my Stompin' Tom Connors tapes along. And when he began talking about the Punk Rock fad that was at its height that summer he expressed deep concern that it would have a harmful influence on his children. When he said that his own personality seemed to conk out and Chloris' took over.

Further, Chloris hates Pink Floyd and any kind of rock and roll. She would complain whenever David played his records. She particularly hated David's favourite record, *The Dark Side of the Moon*.

But at one point I was sitting in the living room with Chloris and decided to compliment her on the furnishings.

"It's quite elegant in a regal sort of way," I said. "One glance at it and I could tell you are a monarchist, if you'll forgive me for psychoanalysing you through your interior decor."

"Royal blue would be more appropriate for the British monarchy," she said. "This red would suit the Spanish monarchy perhaps."

Then she began talking about Pink Floyd. She said *The Dark Side of the Moon* represents death and rebirth. She became quite excited about it and used almost the same words David had used earlier in explaining the hidden symbolism of the music. Again, she in turn seemed to have conked out and David's personality seemed to be shining through.

"I thought you didn't like that record," I said. I was astounded when her own personality came back like the crack of a whip.

"I *don't* like it," she snarled "I hate it. But I listened to it carefully and that's just the impression I got."

103. Americans Wouldn't Have Done This

We were finally leaving. The kids looked sad. Chloris looked relieved. David looked tired. Tinker Bell came over to say goodbye and she looked apprehensive.

I took several photos. I got a shot of David holding a hangman's noose over Joan's head. I tried to get everyone in a lineup from shortest to tallest but there was no co-operation. For one thing Chloris wouldn't allow me to take her picture. I kept trying to deke her out, trying to snap a picture so fast she wouldn't notice. But she was too wary for me. I got a couple of good shots of the back of her head. I got a picture of her behind a tree. But no picture of her face. That's all right. I've got a lot of pictures of Margaret Laurence who looks just like her.

When we were pulling out I told them out the window I was going to write to the Ohio department of tourism and suggest they give a gold medal to the McFadden Family of North Skylark—"for by your generosity and fine spirit of brotherhood, your warmth and hospitality and your high regard for the principles of freedom and democracy, you have made a significant gesture that in the long run can serve only to increase the ties between Ontario and Ohio...." I went on and on.

"That's because we're not Americans," said Chloris with a snarl. Americans wouldn't have done this."

104. Infanticide in Ashtabula

We drove down to Skylark-on-the-Lake then east along the Lake Erie shore. We were quiet, looking peacefully out at the vast lake, wondering about the tiny grey rectangles steaming along out at the horizon.

"You know the way Chloris didn't want her picture taken?" I said.

"Yes?" said Joan.

"Do you think I was stupid for trying to sneak a picture of her like that? I was just doing it to try to make her feel better. Do you think I should have let it drop?"

"Yeah, I think you should have."

As we approached Ashtabula the lakefront became more industrialised, with smokestacks and docks all over the place. You know, even now, months later, I still haven't got those damned pictures developed. I should apply to the Canada Council for money to get all my pictures from the past five years developed. Russell Seaworthy once applied for a grant to get organised.

All of a sudden we noticed a young man walking along with a baby in his arms. "Look at that poor young fellow," I said. "He seems way too young to be burdened with a baby." It was as if I had a premonition he soon wouldn't be.

We were just crawling along. Joan looked. "Where?" she said. I pulled over quietly.

"Over there."

"I see the guy but where's the baby?"

I looked again. Sure enough there was no baby in his arms. Had I been seeing things? The fellow was walking nervously and a bit quickly—almost at a run—away from the dock and toward an old bashed-in Chrysler. As he opened the door to get in someone ran up to him and grabbed him from behind.

The guy shot his elbow back and caught his attacker in the teeth. Then several other guys ran up. They looked as if they might be dock workers. The guy got into his car in a hurry and was trying to drive away and lock the doors from the inside at the same time but the dock workers managed to get the door open and pull him out. There were about four of them. They pulled him to the ground and sat on him.

We had an excellent view of the action. When we first looked it was quite a lonely scene. Just a fellow walking at dockside with a baby in his arms. Now there was no baby but the scene was filled with hysterical people running all over the place. A Coast Guard patrol boat pulled up at the dock and someone dove into the water. A moment later someone was climbing to the deck of the patrol boat with a baby in his arms.

So now it was clear. The guy must have thrown his baby into the water and was trying to get away. A lot of people like us must have been watching him from a distance. Some must have been watching more carefully than we were.

We could see the baby in the boat. They were tenderly covering it with blankets. It was obviously alive.

A police cruiser pulled up and then three more. They released the guy from the dock workers' hold. He seemed to be offering no resistance. All the cops had their guns drawn. There were about twenty guns pointing at this poor unarmed hopeless young fellow. One cop stepped up and pulled the fellow's head back while another cop handcuffed him.

We decided to move on. By this time there were dozens of cars stopped at the side of the road, gawking, like us. We couldn't have been any assistance. We hadn't seen the kid throw the baby or drop it or whatever. Others obviously had. So any evidence we could have given at his trial would have been worthless.

Strange thinking about the incident now. Where is the guy at this moment? Where is the baby?

105. The Indian Chief

We pulled into a campground just over the Pennsylvania state line. It was called Shangri-La Holiday Park. Smiling happy faces. Who could resist it?

We bought some milk and bread in the camp store and asked the price of a campsite.

"Four twenty-five," said the woman behind the counter. She looked like Dolly Parton.

"What? That's outrageous," I said jokingly.

"Well, if you don't like it," she said, pausing slightly, "you can go down the road apiece. They're a lot cheaper. But if you want hot-and-cold showers, a pool table, and lots of recreational facilities including canoes, and nice clean campsites, and a lot of other features too numerous to mention, you'll just have to pay four twenty-five at least."

She didn't mention the showers and pool table were coin-operated, and you had to pay extra for the canoes.

"Where y'all from?" she said.

"Hamilton," I said, assuming she'd think I meant Hamilton, Ohio.

"Oh, we've been there," she said. "On the way up to Tobermory, right?"

I smiled. "Right."

"We went over this big bridge and you could just barely see Hamilton through the smog. Smoky city. Whatch y'all doin' down here?"

"We just came down to get a breath of fresh air, eh?"

"Oh!" She thought for a moment. "Hey, you got lots of fresh air up there. Don't try'n fool me. I been up there lotsa times. I jes' love Canadians. They're so much fun. I love to hear them say 'eh?' I start doin' it myself after awhile. Eh?"

I gave her the four twenty-five. She handed me a green garbage bag and said, "That's for your garbage."

"You mean you want us to put our garbage in *there*?"

"That's right," she said, smiling. She was beginning to think maybe I'd be a lot of fun too if she only gave me half a chance.

"But we just like to throw our garbage around on the ground. And in the woods and all that. We don't like being neat on our holidays."

"Oh, you're jes' foolin'. You Canadians are pretty neat people. You never see any garbage on the ground in Canada. You see green garbage bags jes' full to burstin' and neatly tied. You see them everywhere you go in Canada."

She handed me a wooden coin and said, "Now that's a wooden nickel. You just hang on to that and the next time you're down this way you come here and you get a fifty-cent reduction."

I looked at the coin. It had a picture of an Indian chief on it. He had a goofy smile on his face. But all his feathers were in place. It looked as if it had been drawn by one of those guys who draw for *Mad Magazine*.

106. The Black Lung

We found a nice campsite under a little grove of maple trees. The campgrounds had been carved out of what looked like a virgin forest featuring huge elms and oaks among the pine, cedar and spruce.

"Night's falling," I announced. The others, who could see perfectly well for themselves, rolled their eyes.

"Hope it doesn't hurt itself," said Alison, shrewdly.

There was some firewood on our campsite so I started a roaring campfire—again with one match, if that doesn't sound too terribly boastful.

The four of us were sitting there watching the flames.

"I know a girl who has hair the colour of those flames," said Alison, poetically.

"What's her name?" I said.

"Rachel," she replied.

"I know a girl who has hair the colour of that sky," said Jennifer, after a fairly lengthy pause. The sky was dark, no moon.

"What's her name?" I said.

"Hughdelle," said Jennifer.

"I know two little girls who are really tired," said Joan, "and should be put to bed right away."

"What's their names?" said Jennifer.

"Alison and Jennifer," said Joan.

Then along came Morley, the guy who ran the place. He was riding a white bicycle. He had a black heard and a high-pitched voice. He and his bicycle were illuminated by the flames.

"I just came to see if y'all got settled in all right. And you sure are. You've even found some firewood left behind by another camper and got a fire going." He'd been cheated out of a dollar for firewood. That's what they charged. He was a little overweight.

"You're going to lose weight if you ride on your bicycle to every campsite every night," said Joan.

"I hope so," said Morley, proudly patting his paunch.

He told us he came from a town called Grand Rapids, Minnesota, which was a few miles northwest of Duluth. He said he was just passing through Erie, Pennsylvania, one day, met a girl and never left. That was the girl we met on the way in, the one who looked like Dolly Parton.

"You never know when it's going to happen," he told us. We nodded sagely. He said the two of them liked to go skin-diving in Tobermory every summer. "I just love Canadians," he said.

He pointed to a trailer a little down the lane. He said it belonged to a retired coal miner with the Black Lung. He said the miner lives in the trailer all year long.

"In the winter he takes his trailer to Florida and in the summer he brings it back up here to Pennsylvania."

Morley told us he didn't run the campground full time. "I have to do other work," he said. "But I hope maybe in about ten years I'll be able to do this full time."

We asked him about his other job.

"I'm an electrician in construction," he said.

107. Black Motorcycle Gangs

There were a lot of women with beehive hairdos, little dogs that barked too much, and a lot of fat, hairy-shouldered men in baggy undershirts and knee-length baggy shorts. You could see them walking up and down the lane, with flashlights. Flames from campfires and electric lights from campers and great Winnebagos illuminated their features.

Morley was still leaning against his white bicycle. We told him a little about our trip, including our trip through Cleveland. We told him how surprised we were by the city, and impressed.

"The coloured pretty well own that town," he said.

Then he began telling us a long, involved, and seemingly pointless story about two black kids from Buffalo whose motorcycle had a flat on the U.S. 5 in front of the Shangri-La Holiday Park one day.

"They came in and asked us if they could use the phone. I said sure. So they phoned a friend in Buffalo and asked him to bring his van down here and fix their tire. I told them they could just take it a mile up the road to old Smitty's and he'd fix it for them. But they thought I was just tryin' to get rid of them."

"So what happened?"

"I don't know. But the van never did make it. It broke down half way."

I neglected to ask him how they finally got their flat fixed.

"Yeah," I said. "I notice quite a few black people on motorcycles. In fact we saw some black motorcycle gangs. You ever get them coming in here?" The idea tickled me.

Morley looked a little worried, as if such talk could make something that horrible come true. "No," he said. "We don't let any motorcyclists in here, white or black. If they complain we just call the State Troopers. They can complain to them."

"But you never see any black people in campgrounds in the States," I said. "Why would that be, Morley?"

He looked a little nervous again. "I had a black family in here just the other day," he said. "No problem at all."

I could hardly hear Morley any more because someone had jacked up the volume on a radio across the lane. About twenty people from different campsites were crowded around drinking beer and listening to a ball game. They must have been deaf. Or they soon would be.

108. The Prince of Peace

Just after Joan and I jumped into bed and shut the door of the van rain started to hit the roof. Then it really started coming down. I peeked out my window and watched the campfire go down to defeat in the oft-repeated battle of the elements.

It rained all night. About six-thirty I was awakened by a guy gunning his motor about twenty feet away. I couldn't believe it. I was amazed that Joan and the kids could sleep through it. He kept on and on. I was waiting for him to stop so I could go back to sleep but it looked as if he were going to keep gunning that engine for all eternity.

He wasn't stuck in the mud or anything like that. He was just gunning his motor. I pushed aside the curtain and glared at him. He couldn't see me. He was just sitting there in the driver's seat gunning his motor. He must have been in some kind of trance.

So I put on my jeans and went outside in the rain. I told him to keep it down, I was trying to sleep.

He was a thin fellow, wiry, about sixty years old. He didn't say anything. He just got out of his car, slammed the door as hard as he could and went into his trailer.

I noticed he had Georgia licence plates. On the back of his trailer was a sign saying THE PRINCE OF PEACE.

TUESDAY, JULY 5

109. Porky the Coal Miner

I stayed outside waiting for Joan and the kids to begin to stir. If I'd gone back into the van to try to catch another hour's sleep I would have wakened them. So I just sat there selflessly. The rain stopped. But the maples were full of rainwater and every time there was a gust of wind the water came down as if it were still raining.

I kept hoping to catch a glimpse of the coal miner with the Black Lung. He sounded like a really romantic figure. Someone to write about.

Finally I saw him. He came out of his trailer and started swatting flies. Nothing like a little massacre to start the day. He was entirely unlike my expectations. He was short and fat, wore shorts, a baggy undershirt and a funny hat, and had a high-pitched drawl. His wife called him Porky. She was still in the trailer as he continued swatting flies outside and calling out the score.

"Thirty-seven, dear," he called out. Then, after a few seconds, "Thirty-nine, got two that time!"

Finally the sun came over the trees and started to dry things out and shed some warmth. Porky's high-pitched squeal continued.

"The haymaker's comin' out," he squeaked.

I couldn't figure out what he meant at first. Then he said, "The sun's startin' to shine." I guess the haymaker is an affectionate term for the sun. The term had probably been in his family for generations.

Some coal miner! His trailer was called "The Aristocrat."

"Hope you get over the Black Lung," I whispered, insincerely.

110. The Great State of Erie, Pa.

As I sat under the wet trees waiting for Joan and the kids to wake up I felt as if we were camped among the enemy. I couldn't help feeling we were camped among a powerful, complacent race of people who could eliminate other races or cultures at a whim, just for being different. "We can destroy the entire world if we want," they seemed to be whispering.

The people who had been listening to the baseball game the night before weren't stirring. I went for a walk.

A huge fat "male Caucasian" (police lingo) in jeans got out of a small tent trailer with "Little Injun" painted on the side. At another campsite just down the lane a plastic sign was nailed to a tree. On the sign was a picture of a trailer and a coffee pot with a steaming happy face. You can buy these signs in camping stores and they come complete with blank spaces in which you are required to have printed your name and home state. This sign read: HI THERE WELCOME NEIGHBOR'S. DARN GOOD COFFEE. WE ARE THE MARTIN'S FROM THE GREAT STATE OF ERIE, PA.

111. Canoes for Rent

I walked past a filthy, stinking, scum-covered pond about the size of a septic tank. Three freshly painted canoes were pulled up on the grassy shore. They were numbered: 1, 2, 3. Sitting there, they looked just like the number 111 which happens to be the number of this chapter. A little stream trickled out of the woods and into the pond. Just beyond the pond (an overfond blond vagabond yawned) was a building housing the camp store, headquarters and recreation centre.

Morley's wife was behind the counter again. She looked even more like Dolly Parton this morning with her oversized breasts sticking straight out like nose cones and her long hair piled up into a hay stack on top of her head.

"Hello again," I said.

"I usually don't see any campers stirring this early," she opined. "Have a good night's sleep?"

I thought about the Prince of Peace. "Don't ask," I said.

"All right, I won't."

She was a little wary of me, and was waiting to find out what I wanted so early in the morning.

"How much are your canoes?"

"Seventy-five cents an hour."

"And where do you paddle them?"

I guess that was a stupid question. "Why, in the pond," she responded.

"But that pond isn't much bigger than a canoe," I said.

A cloud passed over her face. "Why, we have a lot of fun with them there canoes," she said.

112. Shooting Pool with a Mass Murderer

So I strolled into the recreation hall and Dolly followed me. There was a thin, elderly black woman sweeping the floor. There was a coin-operated pool table, some pinball machines, and a lending library. The lending library was pretty sad: old movie magazines, cowboy novels from the fifties, a battered old copy of David W. McFadden's *A Trip Around Lake Erie*.

I put a quarter in the pool table and the balls fell out of their little cage and spilled onto the felt. Dolly came scurrying over, noticing that Number 10 had failed to drop. She wanted to give me another quarter.

"No, it's all right. Honest. I'm just going to sink a few." Then all of a sudden this little girl appeared. I hadn't noticed her. She had freckles, a cute little dress, pigtails, cute little patent-leather shoes, the whole bit. And she also had the most evil-looking face I'd ever seen. It was chilling. I couldn't figure out what it was about her face that signalled such evil so strongly.

"I'll play with you," she said, grabbing a cue from the rack on the wall. "Let me break them." She pushed me. "No, you break them. I want to see how good you are."

"I'm no good," I said. "No good at all. Last time I played coonskin caps were all the rage."

"I'll break them then. I always like to break them."

The old black cleaning lady stopped sweeping and looked over with a long, crooked, pink-lipped smile.

"You watch out for him, Michelle," she said. "All de sharks say dey no good and dey haven't played since dose coonskin caps was all de rage."

So Michelle broke the balls and I went to take my shot.

"No," she screamed so loud my ears almost started bleeding. "It's still my shot. I sunk one."

"See what ah tells ya?" said the old woman.

This went on and on. I couldn't believe it. The little girl was so bossy and evil-looking I was absolutely certain, as if I'd seen it in a crystal ball, she was a-goin' to grow up to be a mass murderer. Maybe she already was. Maybe I was about to be her next victim.

113. Joan Gets Suspicious

I managed to make a graceful exit and scurried helter skelter back to our campsite, feeling as if I were being stared at from behind the curtains of every Winnebago I passed.

No one was stirring in our van, and so I sat down again under the trees. I was cold and miserable. The sun seemed to be going out.

Finally I couldn't stand it any longer so I whopped open the door to the van and woke up Joan and the kids.

"Let's just pull the top down and pull out," I said. "You can sleep, and then we'll have breakfast in a restaurant. You deserve a break today. I can't stand this place."

Joan was immediately suspicious.

"Have you been in a fight or something?"

"No, no, it's just all muddy and every time there's a gust of wind the leaves drop cold water down your neck."

Joan looked at me strangely. It wasn't like me to complain. I realised I didn't sound very convincing. So I told her about the Prince of Peace and she was sure I'd had a fight with him.

"No I didn't. Honest. He was too old to fight with. He had to be pushing sixty for God's sake."

So we simply pulled the top down and drove away. Never to return. At least we thought we would never return. But from under the back seat, about ten miles along the road, emerged Michelle the future mass murderer, who wanted to know where and when we were going to stop for breakfast and she wanted her eggs sunny side up. We immediately made a U-turn and drove her all the way back to the pool room.

114. The Difference between Ohio and Pennsylvania

We were driving east along Highway 5 looking for a likely spot to eat breakfast. Highway 5 wasn't marked on our Boron road map, but we figured out from conversations back at Shangri-La that it ran along the Lake Erie shore all the way to Buffalo.

"Do you see any difference between Pennsylvania and Ohio so far?" I inquired of Joan.

"Yeah," she said, without hesitation.

I could see it too. The road was a little snakier and not so flat. There were more vineyards and fewer commercial establishments. You could see the hills in the distance, dotted with prosperous old farms.

But I decided to play a trick on Joan. "What?" I said. "You can see a difference between Ohio and Pennsylvania already?" It was a cruel trick. Joan hates to appear stupid.

"No, I was just fooling," she said.

"Oh, really. I can see an immense difference," I said.

"So can I," said Joan.

"Let's stop at a Howard Johnson's for breakfast," I said. "We've never been in one of those yet."

The first Howard Johnson's we came to was at the intersection of the U.S. 5 and the road that runs into Presque Isle State Park on the outskirts of Erie, Pa. We pulled into the parking lot. Down the street was a McDonald's.

"Let's go to the McDonald's," said Joan. "They have nice breakfasts there. We've never been to a McDonald's yet, not for breakfast."

I could read her mind. She thought the Howard Johnson's looked a little too spiffy for us, dressed as we were in dirty old camping clothes. And we hadn't even showered!

"We can go to McDonald's any old time," I said. There was one right around the corner from us at home. (But our first visit to McDonald's for breakfast was to be documented in *A Trip Around Lake Huron*.) "Come on to the Howard Johnson's."

"No!"

"Yes!"

"Oh, all right. Geez!"

115. Sometimes We Say Things We Don't Mean

The Howard Johnson's was painted in red, white and blue. There were American eagle designs plastered all over it. You could tell the management believed wholeheartedly in the American way of life. Oh well, seeing is believing.

Joan was sitting in the car furiously brushing her hair and pensively scrutinising her face in the rearview mirror. Then she brushed the kids' hair. As soon as we went into the restaurant we headed straight for the washrooms to wash up a bit.

But you guessed it. When we finally got seated at our table we looked around only to discover we were by far the best-dressed people in the place.

Sitting at the table across from us was a beautiful woman with beautiful long blond hair. But she was enormously fat, from the neck down, and was dressed, also from the neck down, in a food-stained blouse and threadbare shorts, bursting at the seams. She was drinking chocolate milk. She looked like an overweight Mae West.

I whispered to Joan: "Check out this tub of lard drinking chocolate milk for breakfast."

Well that was it. The woman heard me. She glared at me then tossed her head just like in a 1940s Hollywood movie. I felt overwhelmed with self-disgust.

The woman's daughter who was about five was also fat. She was drinking Coca-Cola.

"She heard you, you know," said Joan, after a suitable pause.

"I know, I know," I said, with desperation in my eyes. "I can't do anything about it now." I cracked my knuckles. "Unless you want me to go over and apologise to her."

"I think you should," said Joan.

"Okay, I will." Joan was so sympathetic. I went to get up.

"Wait a minute," said Joan. "What are you going to say?"

"I don't know. I'll make it up as I go along."

But when I got over to her table I couldn't think of anything to say.

"Er, excuse me, madam," I said, standing there. "I'd just like to apologise for my bad manners." She and her daughter just stared ahead at their plates. They wouldn't even look at me. I felt truly wretched. The atmosphere was very tense.

"Sometimes we say things we don't mean," I said, "and our voices carry further than we thought they would. I certainly didn't intend you to hear that. I'm not a cruel person."

They still refused to acknowledge my presence so I shrugged, said, "And besides, you're not all that fat," and returned to my seat.

116. The S.S. North American

When the waitress, who looked like Audrey Hepburn (my favourite actress), and just happened to be humming "Moon River" (my favourite song) under her breath, came to take our order she brought a huge steaming pot of coffee and placed it on the table. There must have been enough for twelve cups.

But when she took our orders and found out I wanted decaffeinated coffee, Joan wanted tea and the kids wanted milk, she took it away, still humming "Moon River."

She brought Joan one small pot of tea and me one small pot of Sanka.

After we'd finished eating our eggs and pancakes and all that stuff, Joan went to the washroom again. The kids and I started playing catch with my ring of keys. We started giggling and having a great time. The keys went flying across the dining room several times and we had to take our turns bringing them back.

But when Joan came back we quietened down. Joan likes to be sedate in restaurants. She likes to be serious like everyone else.

The dining room was panelled in mahogany, very well put together. I was admiring the carpentry.

"I like it but I think it's too dark for our place," said Joan. We had been remodelling lately with money Joan earned as a supply teacher. The teacher she was filling in for had had a nervous breakdown so Joan got a solid two months in. Russell Seaworthy was doing a lot of the carpentry work.

Set in the wall next to our table was an illuminated glass case containing some old marine bells and a model of the *S.S. North American*. A beautiful model, really well done.

The card said the original was 310 feet long and was launched in 1913. It served as an excursion ship on the Great Lakes until the early sixties. It was lost in "the mouth of the St. Lawrence" (they must have meant "Gulf") while being towed to the Caribbean in 1972.

"I wonder if anyone was drowned," said Joan.

"I don't know," I said. "The first rule in writing is not to leave any unanswered questions—unless you're a poet!"

"Maybe the person who wrote this is a poet."

"Maybe!"

117. A Monument to a Brave Commander

When we left Howard Johnson's we saw two teenage girls with towels under their arms. They were heading for the beach, trying to flag down rides.

"Shall we pick them up?"

"No!" said Joan. "The van's too messy. Just pull up beside them and I'll ask them the best way to get to the beach."

So I pulled over and the girls told Joan the proper directions and all. And then Joan said, "Could we give you a lift?"

The girls jumped in and I drove away, wonderingly. They said there were quite a few beaches to choose from, about nine in all. We dropped them off at Number 1. It was only about a mile from the restaurant.

Presque Isle State Park is a really beautiful series of lagoons, roads and beaches threading through a forest of poplars a hundred feet tall. You can see the city of Erie across the bay on the south side and Lake Erie on the north. We drove right to the end where there was a 150-foot monument "erected by the State of Pennsylvania to commemorate the victory of Commodore Oliver Hazard Perry in the Battle of Lake Erie, Sept. 10, 1813."

I thought of a nice little plaque to put under that one: "We remember our victories, forget our defeats and begin to think we're invincible."

It seemed strange to put such an impressive statue on the end of a sandbar just inches above the waters of a huge lake. The way the level of the Great Lakes is rising annually you'll soon have to paddle out to read the inscription.

By the way, Perry was the guy who, after destroying the British squadron on Lake Erie, said: "We have met the enemy and they are ours," which was altered by the late American cartoonist Walt Kelly, during the famous McCarthy hearings, to read: "We have met the enemy and they are us"—which could mean different things to different people.

118. Junk Food

The fat people were out in force. Hundreds of them. In Canada everyone tries to keep as slim as possible. In the U.S.A. everyone tries to get as fat as possible. That's one of the many (subtle?) differences between the two countries. *Vive le difference!*

All over Presque Isle State Park we saw these enormous men strutting around with their shoulders thrown back and their mammoth bellies sticking out like great hairy flesh-toned beach balls. They all wore undershirts, shorts, hard black shoes and black executive length socks. They carried Polaroid cameras that fold up like notebooks, and they have police-like auras about them. They appear to be on the lookout for unamerican activities. They obviously know nothing about nutrition or if they do they choose to ignore what they know because life is so boring the only enjoyment they get is eating reams and reams of junk food. They don't want to go out at night for fear of getting mugged so they sit home watching TV and mugging the refrigerator.

"Goddammit, Maw, there's no more junk food in the fridge."

"Well listen, dear, why don't we just send out for some? What kinda junk food you wantin'?"

"I don't care as long as it's junk food. I'm just gonna die if I don't get some junk food inside me right quick."

119. The Day Jennifer Almost Drowned

Presque Isle State Park is a thin brush stroke over the bare canvas of Lake Erie. We walked slowly in the heat through the tall poplars and down to the beach. We spread a blanket. There were signs all over saying keep your dog leashed. I hooked the loop on the end of Bruce's leash over my big toe. The kids went running into the grey water. A huge passenger jet on its way to New York City briefly blotted out the sun.

There was a lifeguard every 200 feet sitting high on a wooden platform like in an American movie starring Frankie Avalon and Annette Funicello. We sat halfway between two of them. There were no dead fish on the beach. You could lie on the beach without coming up covered with grease.

"This beach is even better than the ones in Prince Edward Island," exclaimed the ever-enthusiastic Joan. "And no jellyfish!"

It was the prevailing winds, I was convinced. They push all the crap over to the Canadian side. The prevailing winds come from the southwest and that's why during the summer it's always hot on the U.S. side and cold on the Canadian side. The winds pick up moisture and coolness crossing the lakes. And the oil streaks, dead fish, dead gulls, rotting guts and raw sewage gets heaped up on the Canadian side.

But the important thing was to keep my eyes on the kids as they played in the water. Their heads were bobbing in the small waves. Some other kids had joined them. I counted six. So I just had to make sure there were always six out there. The lifeguards seemed more interested in their tans.

I had a copy of Robert Graves' short stories with me so I started reading "A Toast to Ava Gardner" aloud to Joan. Every few lines I'd pause to make sure I could see six little heads bobbing out there.

But we soon became engrossed in the story.

And then I was up to the point where Ava and Robert begin discussing poetry, and Robert says: "Poems are like people. There are not many authentic ones around," when Joan interrupted me. I still can't get over how calmly she spoke.

"Dave!" she said. "Something's wrong. I can't see Jennifer!"

I stood up, still holding the book. I could see Alison, her head bobbing up and down in the little waves. She was out way too far. But I couldn't see Jennifer. My heart started sinking. Then I saw a little head come to the surface about fifteen feet further out than Alison's. It was Jennifer. Then I dropped the book, ripped off my watch and kicked off my sandals as I ran to the shoreline and kept running into the water. I was wearing cords and as soon as they hit the water they became lead casts. I didn't know whether running or swimming would be faster, nor did I know whether to pause long enough to take off my trousers. So I just kept running out until the water came up to my chest then started swimming furiously. I kept my eyes on where Jennifer's head had come to the surface then disappeared again.

When I got close to the spot her head came up again. Thank Christ! What luck! She was crying! "Daddy!" she said. I put my arms around her. I knew she was safe. If she had drowned I would have killed myself. "I got out too far, Daddy!" she said.

When we got back to shallow water a lot of people were standing at the shore tensely watching this little drama. I looked at one of the lifeguard platforms, and then the other. Incredibly, both lifeguards were just sitting there, not even looking in our direction, just peering straight out at the lake. That's all I saw before I collapsed right there on the sand, my toes still dangling in the water. Jennifer just slipped out of my arms, walked over to the blanket, picked up her copy of *Mad Magazine* (the current issue) and started reading.

A girl about eighteen came over after I resumed normal consciousness. She said that if I had been a few seconds later getting to Jennifer, she herself would have saved her. She had seen Jennifer going down and was racing in from another direction. That made me feel a lot better, really. "God bless you!" I croaked, sort of emotionally. "Are you a good swimmer?" She looked like she'd be a good swimmer and there were quite a few badges on her suit.

"I'm on the United States Olympic swimming team!" she said.

"Yeah?" I said, and then burst into tears.

120. The Lifeguard Springs into Action

The girl put her arm around me and suggested I go over to the blanket and sit down. I did. Then Joan put her arm around me too.

It turned out the girl was from Madison, Wisconsin, and was visiting some relatives in Erie. She really was on the Olympic team but I forget which team and I forget her name.

Joan had Bruce's leash looped around her wrist. I started talking non-stop. I started telling the girl about the summer before when Jennifer fell off her cousin's bicycle while riding down a hill. She had been pedalling backward trying to apply the brakes but the bicycle was equipped with hand brakes which she had never seen before. She landed on the concrete sidewalk, on her chin, tearing open a cut larger than her sweet little mouth, breaking her jaw in three places and tearing out a couple of toenails. All she had been wearing was a pair of shorts. She had cuts and abrasions all over her body.

I held her hand in the hospital while an intern stitched up her chin and repaired her tiny toenails. I hate bragging about my kids but she was incredible. Not a whimper, not even when the intern was sewing up her chin or digging out the root of a toenail.

I kept telling the intern Jennifer's jaw was broken but he said that was impossible because she would be in so much pain she'd be screaming. But the lower part of her face looked a lot different so I knew it was broken.

I was so insistent the intern decided to x-ray the jaw, but he made it clear he was just doing it to humour me. And sure enough there was a solid break under each ear and one in the chin area. But by the time the x-rays were developed the intern had conveniently gone home and another presented me with the pictures. I suppose it would have been a little uncomfortable for the first one to have to face me. Many people can't say sorry, I goofed.

I still have some notes Jennifer wrote after her jaw was wired shut.

"Daddy. I didn't fall off the bike. I jumped."

"Why did you jump?"

"Because it kept going faster and faster and I couldn't find the brakes."

During the story, Bruce kept tugging at his leash. He wanted to go down to the edge of the water. I guess he was getting too hot. He finally took his chain in his mouth and tried to chew through it.

Joan couldn't be bothered getting up to take him so she just let go of the chain. Bruce trotted off toward the lake.

Moments later the lifeguard showed up. "Sir, would you mind hanging on to your dog?"

I couldn't believe it. Where was he when my daughter was drowning? I was so mad I couldn't speak. Same with Joan.

"That's not a dog," I blurted out, without knowing why.

"What is it then?" he said.

"It's my son. He's deformed."

Then Joan went back to the van to make a pot of tea. I just sat there on the blanket with the kids. The Olympic swimmer rejoined her friends. I was questioning Alison about how she could have let Jennifer get out so far. Apparently Alison, who is three years older and that much taller, wanted to be up to her neck and Jennifer was trying to stay with her even though it was over her head.

But that all got settled. And all that time I found myself keeping my ears cocked for cries of help coming from the direction of the van. What if Joan were to get raped or mugged or something back there? I was on edge. I could imagine her crying out, "Help! Rape!"

"Daddy?" said Jennifer. She was looking up from her *Mad Magazine*.

"Yes?"

"If I'd drowned would I have had my picture in the paper?"

121. The Natives of North America

The four of us went for a walk along the road. A workman in green denim was standing there holding a portable citizen's-band radio to his face. He kept saying, "21—Roger!" He was sweating.

A green truck loaded with workmen went by. Each workman was furnished with a long spike for picking up garbage. Each workman was being taken to his own special area of the beach.

Two of the workmen were Native Indians with long straight black hair and copper-coloured skin. They had sad faces. They were both wearing denim jackets in all that heat.

Other people kept going by in cars with their car radios blasting.

We got in the van and drove out of the park, back onto the U.S. 5—heading east into even further adventures.

122. How to Become Part of Nature

We were now in New York State. We could see Lake Erie State Park on the left of the highway but the signs for the park said turn right so we did. The cut-off road curved off to the right and then switched back under an old stone tunnel under the highway. Through the tunnel you could see trees lining the road on the other side. It was a regular cloverleaf exit except that the exit was off a two-lane highway. I had a sense of déjà vu about it. It must have been built in the early thirties. Maybe I'd seen a picture of it when I was a kid. Or—and this is always a possibility when you experience déjà vus while travelling—maybe it had been in a movie and made strangely familiar that way although the movie itself had been long forgotten. As Gerry Gilbert says: "Hands up those who have just had a déjà vu!"

It's amazing how quickly even the best movies, the ones we enjoy the most, seep from our minds. So that when we see them a few years later it's as if we've never seen them before. That's especially true with such movies of the forties as *Casablanca* and *The Big Sleep*. Also *Young Man with a Horn* which I've seen once every three years since I was about ten years old. Books on the other hand stay with you. They require a greater expenditure of energy in order to experience them in the first place. And so they lock themselves in more firmly. Movies of the forties always remind me of my Uncle Ed who was shot by the Mafia in 1951. He was about twenty-three years old, about twelve years older than me. But we were strangely close. I was constantly modelling myself after him. He would always take me to see the latest Humphrey Bogart movie as it came out. I think it was for my ninth birthday he bought me my very own trench coat and fedora. With my snub-nosed water pistol I could do a perfect imitation of Bogart saying, "All right, sweetheart. Drop it!"

But Lake Erie State Park was empty except for a human figure lying out in front of an old stone and wood house about four hundred feet away from the parking lot over an immense stretch of perfect green lawn.

We got out of the van and went over. There was a sign over the front door of the building. As we got closer we could read it. It said FIRST AID. It was the largest first-aid station I'd ever seen. It looked more like a hospital. Actually it looked like an overgrown small-town railroad station.

The human figure was sleeping or lying quietly with his eyes closed. He was a park employee. He had a college zoology textbook by his side.

There were two giant change rooms inside the building. I went in the men's on the left. There were two showers on the south wall—no partitions, just showers. On the east wall was a row of coin-operated lockers. And on the north wall were two toilets, a washstand and a hot-air dryer. All this was dwarfed in the immensity of the room. There were marks on the floor where benches had been removed. The park had obviously been an enormously popular place at one time.

One of the toilets was badly messed up and stank. The other was clean and sweet-smelling but had no toilet paper. So I went in the smelly cubicle and took some toilet paper, then went into the clean one. When I pushed the hot-air dryer button water began shooting out of the spout and dripping down from the dryer itself. Someone had poured water into it. I was startled. I had been standing in a pool of water too. Lucky I hadn't been electrocuted. I thought with a shudder that Alison or Jennifer could have been killed instantly that way. Or any way. God, what would I do if something happened to either of them? I'd just fall apart like a swatted fly.

When I went back out the employee was sitting up reading his zoology textbook. I mentioned the water in the dryer. He didn't know what to do except let it dry out.

"Do you know anything about the history of this building?" I said, slapping my hand against the brick wall. "Like for instance what it was before it was a change house?"

"This is my first summer working here," he said. "All I know is that it's been here since before I was born."

I figured the second storey might be used for offices, and other rooms on the first floor for equipment. But I didn't bother asking him. I walked over to the top of the fifty-foot bluff overlooking the lake. There were some sailboats out there and a strong northeasterly wind was blowing cool. I sat on a bench and closed my eyes.

It was very relaxing. My personality disappeared and I became part of nature. The wind rocked my body as if I were a tree. It was such a pleasure not to be getting in the way of pure experience.

When I returned to the van Joan and the kids were making grilled cheese sandwiches. A gust of wind caught a plastic bag and sent it flying across the parking lot and into the trees.

I looked at the map. If you drew a line due north from Lake Erie State Park it would run directly along Yonge Street in Toronto.

123. The Jewel Box

I dropped Joan and the kids off at a vast department store in the little town of Wytheville, a fortunate town indeed to be given the honour of becoming the home of such a store, so big the whole town could fit inside it. I wanted to get a haircut. But first I decided to take my watch into The Jewel Box, a little store on the main street. Moisture had been forming on the inside of the watch. You could see dewdrops inside the crystal.

The jeweller was a fat guy a few years my junior. He was dressed as if he were running for mayor. He put down his *Wall Street Journal* and looked at the watch. "I don't even think I know how to take it apart," he said.

I should have walked out right there but instead, like a fool, I said, "Oh, go ahead, it's probably easier than it looks."

He finally got the back off after much expenditure of energy.

"Oh look," he said. "Here's your trouble. The stem's broken off. That's how the moisture was getting in."

He couldn't find another stem that would fit. He even took it down the street to another jeweller's then finally gave me back the watch in pieces.

"It's pretty unfortunate when your watch breaks down while you're travelling, I know," he said. "You don't know what to do. But there'll be no charge for that."

A few days later, Frank, of Frank's Time Shop on Kenilworth Avenue in Hamilton, Ontario, said there was no way that stem was broken before the watch had been taken apart. "Don't worry," he said. "That guy broke it for sure and was afraid to tell you."

124. You Think It's Easy Being a Barber?

It was a really old-fashioned barber shop. Six chairs, no waiting. It was called the Wytheville Barber Shop.

My guy started cutting away. I almost fell asleep. He was talking about spring floods and all that kind of stuff. I started telling him a long-winded story about a barber who had a nervous breakdown as he was cutting my hair. He burst into tears and started howling. Honest, it was nothing I'd said. He had to be taken away. "The stress must have gotten to him," I said. I must have struck a chord for the guy started purring like a cat.

"Oh yes, it's a hard job, it really is," he said. "People just laugh at you when you tell them but oh, it's a hard job all right." He stopped and looked at himself in the mirror. He held his elbows out as if he were cutting my hair. "It's hard holding your arms out like this all day long," he said. "It tightens your muscles right around the back. It's hard to get them untightened at the end of the day."

I believed him totally. I hope I never have to be a barber. I'd rather be a watch repairman.

"Oh no!" screamed Joan when we met fifteen minutes later. "Your hair looks awful!"

I looked in the rear-view mirror. Sure enough, it was cut at all different lengths. It did look kind of stupid.

125. Nicodemus in Niggertown

We had to pay seventy-five cents to the parking-lot attendant. He was a great fat guy in a neat uniform with white shirt and tie. His name tag said Nicodemus. He had a gun in a holster fastened to his belt.

"Hello there, Nicodemus," I said, handing him the money and my ticket. For some reason that did it: my friendly greeting combined with the Ontario licence plates. He wanted to talk. He wanted us to know he wasn't a native of Wytheville and as soon as he saved enough money he was moving back to his home town.

"Where's that?"

"Jacksonville, Florida," he said, proudly.

"You like it down there better than up here?"

"It's the people," he said. "The people are so much nicer down there. Not as many snobs."

I asked him about his gun. Was it for shooting people who tried to crash through the gate without paying their seventy-five cents?

"No," he said. "But a guard on a toll-gate on the highway was shot and killed for a quarter last week. He wouldn't let them go till they put in their money so they just shot him right between the eyes."

But had he ever had to use his gun?

"Just once," he said. "I'm not proud of this. It's not a very pleasant thing to have to tell and it's not a very pleasant thing to have to remember. I still sometimes lose sleep over it. I had to kill a man once."

"What were the actual circumstances?"

"It was over in what we called Niggertown," he said, without apology although you could tell he knew it wasn't nice to call it Niggertown. "I was night watchman at the warehouse and someone broke in. He drew a gun on me and so I shot him."

126. The Monkey Man

Nicodemus stopped us just as we were about to pull away. "Just a minute, sir. You've given me a Canadian quarter!"

"And?"

"I haven't got anything against it. It's just that I got yelled at once for taking it so I don't take it anymore."

I gave him another quarter—and I couldn't resist blasting off a bit. "Holy heck," I said. "For years when U.S. money was worth a lot less than Canadian we always took silver at par anyway. It just wasn't considered worrying about unless it was over a dollar."

"I know," he said, quietly.

As we pulled away the kids started screaming with delight. There was a man out in the road. He was jumping up and down like a monkey. He was dressed only in a pair of white jeans. He was just bounding up and down as if he had springs attached to his feet.

"Look at that man, Daddy. What's the matter with him?"

"That's a monkey man," I said, making it up as I went along. "Most times they're just like you and me—real ordinary-like—and every once in a while they just can't help it, they have to start acting like monkeys!"

The guy leaped up to a stoplight where a car was stopped. The people in the car were trying to get their windows rolled up. But it was too late. With one bounce, the monkey man jumped right through the back window. We just kept driving.

"Wow! Did you see that?" screamed the kids.

127. A Little Side Trip into the Mountains

As we drove further into New York State there was a gradual increase in the height of the bluffs along the shore. At times it looked like an eighty-foot sheer drop into the pounding surf of Lake Erie. There was a strong northeasterly wind.

To the southeast you could see the foothills of the Adirondacks. These are the hills you can see on a clear day from the north shore of Lake Erie around Featherstone Point.

"What are those mountains?" I used to ask my father.

"Those are the Blue Ridge Mountains of Pennsylvania," he'd say. Now it looked as if he'd been wrong. Those mountains over there were in New York State, not Pennsylvania.

But when I looked at the map I saw that yes my father was right after all. We were in New York State but the state line bends around to the south, and yes those mountains would be in Pennsylvania.

The mountains looked almost as far away from us as we drove along U.S. 5 as they did when I was a kid standing on the beach on the Canadian side.

"Would you care to take a little side trip into the mountains?" I inquired of Joan.

"No. Some other time. I'm anxious to get home. I've got a lot to do before tomorrow."

128. The Michelin Man

We stopped at a Sunoco station in Irving, New York. An enormously fat man covered in sweat came out. Every crease was caked with grease.

There was an old Volkswagen van sitting there. It looked like the one Russell Seaworthy used to have, the one that he smashed up on the Skyway Bridge almost killing himself. The one that used to have the Michelin man sitting up on the roof as if it were navigating. The Michelin man was sort of magic but it let him down that day on the Skyway Bridge when Russell was looking over at the skyline of Hamilton and ploughed into a slow-moving transport truck. Demolished the van and four of his teeth.

It seemed like a good idea to tell Russell about this one, especially if it were for sale. He loves the old-style VW vans but it's hard to find them in good condition.

"Is that van for sale?" I said.

"No, not really. It doesn't have a motor in it."

"What year is it?"

"That would be a 1966. Actually it does have a motor in it. It's got a big Chevy motor in it." He looked at me and laughed. "We're going to take it to the drags."

"Have you raced it yet?"

"No. We took it out but it's too heavy for the van. We're going to have to change the wheels. We put the motor in the back. Maybe we should have put it in the front."

The fat man waddled away in the summer heat, his arms sticking out horizontally like a barber. Imagine doing all that work just for the questionable fun of occasionally taking the van out on a quarter-mile track. Endless hours of toil, sweat, cursing. Then finding out you should have put the motor in the front. What a boring life!

Almost as bad as writing books. Writing a book then finding out you should have put the end at the beginning.

129. Smug Complacency

In front of modern motels in the U.S.A. they have theatre-style marquees so they can put out any message they want and change it as often as they want.

Some of the older motels have signs reading FREE PHONE. Others say FREE PHONE AND TV.

More expensive motels say FREE PHONE AND TV IN EVERY ROOM.

Then there's COLOR TV IN EVERY ROOM.

A few years ago water beds were all the rage. The latest thing is dirty movies, also known as skin flicks.

But you can't put up a sign outside a motel saying DIRTY MOVIES or SKIN FLICKS. It just doesn't sound right. So they put up signs saying ADULT MOVIES—which kind of slanders the brighter breed of adult and makes it difficult to explain to children.

"Daddy, what's an adult movie?"

"Ask your mommy."

"She's sleeping."

"Wake her up and ask her."

Some motels have signs saying ADULT MOVIES AND WATER BEDS.

Somewhere in Ohio I thought I saw a sign reading SUNNYSIDE BROTHEL. But it went by so quickly I could be wrong.

AUTUMN REUNION NURSING HOME and SURFSIDE NURSING HOME are two signs worthy of mentioning.

"Oh look at that," said Joan. "How sick! Autumn Reunion Nursing Home!"

"Oh look, Daddy. Surfside Nursing Home," said Alison. "Does that mean the old people can go surfboard riding?" She was being cute.

"If you were an old lady in a nursing home wouldn't it be nice to be able to hear the surf?" I said.

"Yeah, I guess so," said Alison.

As for the autumn reunion, I thought that was really poetic, not sick at all. I began dreaming of living in a nursing home reunited with all the boyfriends and girlfriends of my youth, all the beautiful boys and girls I've lost touch with. That would be absolutely sensational. Sometimes I just don't understand Joan. She's just too sophisticated for her own good.

I hated the motel sign reading IT JUST LOOKS EXPENSIVE. If that were true they could have just posted the rates on the sign.

But the worst sign of all was in front of a motel near Erie, Pennsylvania. It was the Capri Motel and it reminded me of all the smug complacency that political systems feed upon like grease. PRAY—BELIEVE—RECEIVE. That's what it said.

In other words, don't complain if you're not as rich as I am. It just means you haven't prayed as hard as I have or you haven't believed as deeply as I have.

That's probably the unspoken belief of the American establishment that runs the California vineyards, the Pentagon, and so forth, and refuses to put in an adequate medicare system.

It is more blessed to give than receive—but only if you're giving to me.

130. Father Baker Bridge

There are huge steel mills on both sides of the Father Baker Bridge which leads into Buffalo from the south. The bridge is the same height as the smokestacks. Whichever way wind is blowing the motorist and his passengers get lungs full of sulphur dioxide and poisonous particulate matter.

This is the end of Lake Erie, the anus of a vast grey prehistoric animal which still groans in its sleep and dreams indecipherable dreams. This is where Lake Erie narrows into the Niagara River and through the billowing clouds of smoke we could see the faint outline of some Canadian trees far across the water.

"I can see Canada," I said.

"Where?" said the kids.

"Over there through the smoke."

"Oh yeah," said Alison.

"I wish we were there now," said Jenny. "Daddy?"

"Yes?"

"Do we have to go through the tunnel to get to Canada?"

"Do you want to?" I thought maybe the Detroit tunnel had frightened her.

"No," she said. "You don't see anything in a tunnel."

"No, Jenny. We don't have to go through any more tunnels on this trip. The tunnel was in Detroit at the other end of the lake."

"Oh. What city is this?"

A guy in a yellow English sports car passed us. Then along came a guy in a black German sports car and passed the yellow one.

"Buffalo."

"Oh!"

131. The Peace Bridge

And there at the entrance to the Peace Bridge, just after we paid our seventy-five cents, stood two hitchhikers. A man about twenty-eight who looked like the pop star David Bowie. And a girl standing in front of him, a little girl about Jenny's age, just coming up to his waist. A large thumb and a small thumb sticking out into the wind from onrushing cars.

Something about this apparition made my heart stop.

"Should we pick them up?"

"Yes, let's," said Joan.

But we were in the outer lane and an impatient Cadillac with Ohio plates was nosing past us on our right. We were caught in traffic and couldn't stop, just as we had been in Detroit a few days earlier.

There was something magic and mysterious about these two hitchhikers, lonely, unreal, as if they were floating in the mist, about to disappear. My heart was aching for them. I wanted to know who they were and where they were going and I wanted to help them get there. I would have done anything for them.

That was July 5, 1977. About five in the afternoon. If you were about twenty-eight then, and looked like David Bowie, and were hitchhiking on the Peace Bridge into Canada with a nine-year-old girl, and if you happen to read these words somewhere, sometime, I don't care if it's forty years from now, please try to contact me. I'd sincerely love to hear from you.

132. Canadian Soil

In the middle of the Peace Bridge were three flags: the American flag, the United Nations flag, and the Canadian flag.

"We're in Canada," I said as we passed the blue UN flag. Canadian Soil.

"Yay!" said the kids.

"Joan?" I said. "I know this will sound crazy but I wouldn't mind turning around at the customs booth and going back and picking up those two hitchhikers."

"They'd probably be picked up by now," said Joan, sympathetically.

Anyway, the girl in the customs booth was nervous. It was as if she'd just started that day. Our car wasn't searched. She didn't find out about the geranium cuttings we were smuggling across, snitched by Joan from the park in Sandusky. By the way they have now grown quite a profusion of roots and are ready to be planted in the actual Canadian soil of our cute little Canadian back yard.

133. Things Distinctively Canadian

We drove west along Highway 3 toward Port Colborne and Dunnville and as we drove we amused ourselves by looking for things that were distinctively Canadian. That's what I like about the paintings of John Boyle. He just instinctively paints things that could only be found in Canada. It's not easy.

"There's a maple leaf on the McDonald's sign," said Alison. "They don't have maple leaves on McDonald's signs in the States."

"There's a car with Canadian licence plates," said Jenny.

"There's a Dominion Store," said Joan.

134. Mount Zion Cemetery

Since we were running along Highway 3 we decided to stop off at Mount Zion Cemetery where Joan's grandparents are buried. It's about three miles east of Dunnville.

I never knew Joan's grandfather. He died in 1956. His name was Charles Wilkins. He was a letter carrier. He loved fishing in the Grand River on his days off.

Joan says that just as Charlie was being lowered into his grave a huge fish jumped in the pond next to the cemetery. The cemetery was on a hill and you could see the pond easily. It was in a farmer's field. It was just a duck pond. You wouldn't think there'd be any fish in there.

When we pulled into Mount Zion Cemetery the first thing Joan said was, "Oh, look! The pond's gone. All dried up."

Joan's grandmother, Alice Wilkins, died in 1966. She was a tiny woman who even in old age never withdrew from the moment. And now she was lying under the ground with Charlie.

Joan fixed up some of the plants growing around the tombstone and watered them.

I looked around. There was a fresh grave for a seventeen-year-old boy: A. Brett Cuthbertson 1960-1977.

There was a tombstone for a man who had died at the age of twenty-two. His parents' names were also on the stone even though they were apparently still alive. Peter K. Schneider 1920-. His wife, Martha L. 1922-. Their son George L. 1952-1974.

There was one tombstone facing the wrong way. At least it was the only one in which the lettering faced west, toward the duck pond and the road. All the others faced east toward the rolling meadows and rising sun.

This tombstone facing the wrong way was fascinating. Orlan E. Neff. March 13 1920—October 31 1949. Imagine dying on Halloween 1949 in rural southern Ontario at the age of 29!

I wondered if Orlan E. Neff had ever driven all the way around Lake Erie. I just felt he was a really funny character who died in some tremendously stupid accident. Ah, if only he could speak. If only you could put a quarter into a slot in the tombstone and listen to the shades wail and mumble. My mind was flooded with the possibilities of how Orlan E. Neff would sound and what he would say.

135. It's Okay to Pee in the Cemetery

Joan had to pee. She was trying to walk back to the car with her legs crossed. "Let's go," she said.

"Why don't you just pee behind the tree?" I said. There was a 150-year-old maple right in the middle of the cemetery. And we were totally secluded.

"I couldn't pee in a cemetery," said Joan.

"Why not?"

Joan didn't say anything but she looked thoughtful. Maybe she was worried that the dead people would be offended.

Meanwhile, Bruce, whom we haven't discussed for quite some time, was running around peeing against tombstones left and right, marking out his territory, saying BRUCE WAS HERE in the only language he knew: Urinese.

"Dogs pee in here all the time," I said.

That won her over. "Okay," she said. She went behind the great old maple.

As she was peeing I slipped off my sandals and sneaked up behind her. I was just going to stick my head around the left side of the tree and say "Boo!!!" when Joan stuck her head around the right side of the tree and said "Boo!!!"

I just about died.

136. The Night of the Living Dead

Mount Zion Cemetery reminded me a lot of the cemetery in my favourite movie, *The Night of the Living Dead*.

I lay down in the grass and remained perfectly still. I felt as if I were dead, lying there slowly disappearing along with all the other dead people, along with all the dead fish, leaves, flowers, birds, worms, dogs and rabbits, rotting logs, mysterious memories, haunting thoughts, all dead and dying.

In a thousand years there would be nothing left of us. Our forms will have been totally subsumed by other forms: new trees, new grass, new duck ponds, new people, new phantom fish leaping into the air as an old fisherman is lowered into the ground. The very atoms of our bodies might have been dispersed all over the world hundreds of times, like mushroom spores, and might have temporarily constituted the bodies of dozens of other human beings never mind other animals.

"Hey kids, why don't you lie down here with me and feel what it feels like to be dead." It was like the voice of someone who wasn't there. It was like nothing talking.

"Ech, no thanks," said Jennifer.

Alison just looked thoughtful. She knew she'd be dead some day. Might as well get used to it.

"Joan? Come and lie down."

"No thanks."

"Bruce?"

He stopped running around and cocked his ears.

137. Howard and Velma

"Let's drop in and see my mom and dad for a minute," said Joan. We were almost home. It was only a couple of miles out of our way. But still….

"Aw, Joan," I whined, "why don't we just go home first and then call them. You must be awfully tired." Actually I was anxious to see the house. I had a vague feeling something was wrong. It had burned to the ground in our absence or something like that.

"Okay," said Joan.

But then I began to feel guilty. I was the one who had told her not to buy that bathing suit in Painesville, Ohio, or wherever. I didn't want to rule her life with an iron fist. So when we came to the road leading to Joan's parents' place I turned, with a sneaky smile on my face.

Joan grabbed the wheel. "No, it's okay, Dave. We'll just go home and phone them later."

I turned anyway and we drove up their driveway. We could see them looking out from behind the living room drapes. We couldn't go home now.

Howard and Velma were happy to see us. They wanted to know all about our trip. They particularly wanted to know how Alice and Charlie's grave looked.

"Joan peed in the cemetery," I said.

"Joan, you didn't," said Velma.
"Why you dirty squealer!" said Joan.

138. A Moment in the Lives of Some White People

Howard was telling us about how the blacks were taking over the larger American cities.

I told him we noticed in Detroit that the black neighbourhoods seemed classier than the white.

"Ah, the poor whites," he said.

"The blacks are just as good as us," said Velma.

"They sure are," said Howard. "If they can go through all the persecution they have and still rise to the top they must be as good as us. Some of them are real smart. They're starting to get educated."

139. Go Bananas

Howard wanted to know which cities we'd gone through on our fabulous trip around Lake Erie.

"Detroit, Toledo, Madrid, Cleveland, Erie, New Orleans, Montevideo, St. Petersburg, Ithaca, Troy, Rome, Athens, Lisbon, Cairo, Belgrade and Buffalo."

"Don't forget Copenhagen," said Joan.

Howard and Velma were square dancers and had been on trips to square-dancing conventions all over North America. We're always embarrassed by the large number of expensive gifts they bring back for us. I have a FONZIE T-shirt from Kansas City and a GO BANANAS T-shirt from Atlantic City. The GO BANANAS T-shirt has a picture of a monkey sitting on the toilet and eating a banana. I only wear it on special occasions.

But we forgot to bring them gifts from our trip around Lake Erie.

"We flew over Cleveland when we went to Kansas City," said Howard.

That didn't sound right. "Are you sure?" I said.

"Oh no, I'm wrong. What made me think we'd gone over Cleveland was the pilot was a real card and when we were going over Chicago he announced that we should be passing over Chicago but it looked a lot like Cleveland."

140. Nirvana

One down and four to go. Lakes that is.

We were telling Howard and Velma how we wanted to take trips around the four remaining Great Lakes now that we had been all the way around Lake Erie.

"You'll really like going around Lake Superior," said Howard. "I don't know about the American side but the Canadian side is real pretty."

I said it would be scary going around Lake Michigan because it's the only one that is American on all sides.

Joan happens to have a friend who likes to go to Cape Cod and Joan is sort of interested in going there.

"When we go around Lake Michigan will we see Cape Cod?" she said.

"My God, what a lousy sense of geography you have," I said. "And you a school teacher!"

Everyone laughed. Joan actually takes pride in not having a sense of geography. It's an admirable quality. Not to know where you are geographically is the next best thing to Nirvana.

And it makes men feel secure when women don't know left from right, west from east.

141. Dead Fish

When we pulled into our driveway our next-door neighbour, Audrey, a magnificent stutterer, came running out with a serious look on her face. Oh oh, right away we knew something was wrong. She was wearing a David Bowie T-shirt.

"You better chacha-check your house right away," she said. "There's been an awful smell comink out of there all day." Audrey always pronounced a hard g or almost a k sound on the end of her -ing words. When I asked her about it once she said it was her way of being different.

Sure enough there was an awful smell and it got worse as I approached the door.

When I opened the door there was an avalanche. I was buried in a huge heap of dead and rotting fish. The kind of fish that had been all over the beach at Point Pelee. The kind of fish Bruce had been rolling in and peeing on. The kind of fish I imagined decaying along with at the Mount Zion Cemetery.

For the next hour I shovelled dead fish out into the driveway and buried them in the backyard. The dead fish were in all the rooms. It was ghastly.

Worst of all, I couldn't figure out where all the fish had come from. It was almost as if God were angry, as if He didn't like people to take trips all the way around one of His Great Lakes. It was His way of punishing us. I half-expected to uncover a pile of mouldy loaves of bread under the dead fish.

142. Business As Usual

After I finished shovelling out all the dead fish and burying them Joan and I started scrubbing the floors. We sent the kids over to Audrey's for the night. We threw out our rug. We sprayed Lysol everywhere. It was awful. We were really too busy to begin to discuss or to consider how the dead fish had got there.

Then when we finally had the place back in shape we were too exhausted to think about it.

I wearily checked the mail Audrey had been picking up for us. I had sent out a new book list just before we left and already the orders were starting to pour in. I was pleased.

I even had some orders from other poets which was sort of amazing because poets like to exchange books or get free review copies. They hardly ever buy books.

After my shower I was surprised when I checked our mileage book and discovered it all came out to even numbers. We had been gone one hundred hours and had travelled eight hundred miles. We'd spent $133.31.

As I flopped into bed I wondered how long it would take me to write *A Trip Around Lake Erie*. Would it take me more than one hundred hours?

Probably.

Would it earn me more than $133.31?

Probably not.

Better still, would it be good?

And what lake would we go around next?

A Trip Around Lake Huron

GREAT LAKES SUITE

VOLUME TWO

A TRIP AROUND LAKE HURON

A Trip Around Lake Huron is dedicated to Laverne "Zip" LaFrance—commercial fisherman, photographer and member of the Bahai faith—accidentally drowned in Lake Huron, January 3, 1979.

"He remembered those moonlit evenings, when, leaning back in the victoria that was taking him to the Rue La Pérouse, he would wallow voluptuously in the emotions of a man in love, oblivious of the poisoned fruit that such emotions must inevitably bear."

—Proust, *Swann's Way*

Contents

33. A Family Discussion at the Edge of the Woods
34. A Funny Noise Like a Flute
35. Unamerican to Pick Mushrooms
36. The Difference Between a Mushroom and a Toadstool
37. The Trees at the Edge of the Woods
38. A Beautiful Woman Spurned
39. Grapefruit

SUNDAY, AUGUST 7

40. Vaseline
41. Time Warp
42. Thievery in Canada
43. The Black Killer
44. For Those Without Sunday Clothes
45. Charles Sangster, Canadian Poet
46. The Home of Chicago Steaks
47. If You Seek a Pleasant Peninsula
48. Songs of the American Railroad Man
49. Bliss Carman and the Call of the Wild
50. Actually Experiencing the Call of the Wild
51. Hart Crane, Canadian Poet
52. What We Said While Crossing the World's Largest Suspension Bridge
53. A Respite from the Ordinary
54. As Funny as a Cloud
55. Richard Nixon in Drag
56. Bruce Vomits in My Hat
57. Miller's High Life
58. Bruce Is Not Himself
59. Grape Pudding
60. What Writing Is Like
61. Mickey Mouse

MONDAY, AUGUST 8

62. The Narrator Almost Becomes a Hero
63. Pretty Soon the U.S.A. Will Be as Bad as Canada
64. The Weekly Wave
65. Fifty Years of Service to the Motoring Public
66. The Road to the Sault
67. The Department of Natural Resources
68. So Much for the Government
69. Orange Caps
70. The Body of Someone You Love
71. How to Become Strange
72. False Pregnancy

A Trip Around Lake Huron

1. For the Heart Is Continually Breaking

I've always felt that selfishness is the deadliest sin. The legendary forbidden fruit is the self. Yet when a writer tries to keep out of his writing he finds it impossible. He can go on for years saying this is me, this is not me, and eventually it will all collapse. He'll find his own self in everything. It's something impersonal, at the bottom of everything, creating everything, inventing everything including the illusion of the self-invented personality. His daily attempts to invent his own self and to keep his own self out of his writing are seen for what they really are—a tremendous waste of energy.

It's a matter of perspective. Since the eyes through which I see are located in my body, my body seems unrealistically large, larger than the entire Great Lakes. At times it seems somehow larger and more significant than the entire universe. Our lives are small, yet it's impossible to maintain a sense of that smallness for long. People really do become smaller as they travel away from the viewer.

Which is the better attitude for a writer to adopt, providing he has a choice? The one he knows to be true yet which leaves him with the feeling he is betraying his senses? Or the one he senses to be true yet which leaves him with the feeling of being egocentric? Consciousness of the problem is painful. Yet if the pain is ignored and the consciousness is maintained the pain goes away. For acute pain doesn't last long. And we're left with a sense of vagueness.

This vagueness is not something to be scorned, for the greater the vagueness the greater the need to write with ever greater clarity. For the heart is continually breaking and every breath we draw is a sacrifice.

This is what I wrote in my notebook on the morning of August 4, 1977. I live in the east end of the Mountain in Hamilton, Ontario. The kids were on their summer vacation and Joan and I decided to take them with us on a trip around Lake Huron. It was exactly a month after our return from our trip around Lake Erie.

2. Arthur Hailey

In other words I'd rather write like myself than like Leonard Cohen, Shakespeare or Arthur Hailey.

But am I writing like myself?

3. Fishing for Salmon in Lake Ontario

My next-door neighbour Gene has a heart problem and has had several major operations. Yet he spends all his spare time working on his house—knocking out walls, replacing eavestroughs, painting, laying cement. I tend to do as little as possible in that field. My occupation enables me to work at home in a beautiful, book-lined basement office.

Because I occasionally receive grants for my work a lot of people around here feel I'm defrauding the government and living off their own hard-earned tax dollars. I get called nasty names, and I've been asked how I can justify taking this money when there are elderly people in Hamilton so poor they are forced to eat dog food. Further, I must be quite clever to have so perfected the art of grantsmanship. Too bad all that cleverness couldn't be put into honest work. Also, I must have been very astute long ago in my choice of friends. The latter remark implies that it must be my well-positioned friends who pull the strings that enable me to get all this money. My pleas that I have no such friends—and that since the money is being offered I am forced to compete for it out of a sense of professional duty—draw only ironic smiles.

These remarks are often directed at me through my wife who finds them kind of upsetting. She wants me to become more commercial in my writing so that we could live off royalties and forget about grants. I'd love to but I can't. Every time I try something stops me. And then again maybe no one can deliberately go commercial. Or maybe everyone is already totally commercial, including me. Maybe I secretly expect this book to sell a million copies. Brent Carver and Rebecca Jenkins would be perfect in the movie version.

A friend said I'd be able to sell the book to the movies if I had somebody chasing me around Lake Huron. Even *Lolita* (book or film) wouldn't have made it without Quilty. But I couldn't do that. To me, this series of five books is a fabulous project. In my own world I'm creating something for all time. If I were to add someone chasing me that would destroy everything. To be able to make enough money from a book to be able to retire to a glorious hotel in Montreux, à la Nabokov, would be very nice indeed. But I'd prefer not to make a fool of myself by trying to give a name to the disembodied emanations, fates, furies and demons, all pursuing me around these lakes in the summer of 1977. It would spoil what I see as the transparent nature of these narratives. I knew I could make this story work without some clunky Quilty or an obviously metaphorical axe-murderer chasing me; otherwise I wouldn't have wanted to write it.

Hamilton. Most of the people on our street are spending their lives working at Stelco, Dofasco, Westinghouse, Procter and Gamble, International Harvester, National Steel Car, and so on. In a way I'm seen as a different kind of bird who should have flown away long ago. But I'm tolerated. Sometimes my kids say they wish I had a job in the factory like all the other daddies they know. It would be impossible to tell them how often I wish the same thing.

Every time we drive past some steel plant or refinery or assembly plant, Alison and Jennifer say, "Oh, look at that. Isn't that beautiful?"

As for Gene, we're becoming fond of each other. He has a hot rod which he takes to the Cayuga Drag Strip, and he's even let me race it along the quarter-mile track. He has a special salmon-fishing boat rigged up and he sometimes takes me fishing in Lake Ontario. He told me that when he was in high school he made friends with this strange artistic kid in his class even though everyone else shunned him.

One day I saw Gene's feet sticking out from under his verandah. He was just repairing the footings but for a moment I thought he'd been murdered and his body only partially hidden. It was a warm day and there was the possible murderess, Gene's wife Audrey, sitting on the lawn chatting with a couple of her friends.

"What's Gene doing?" I innocently asked as I walked over.

"He's workink," she said rather loudly and excitedly, with her special way of pronouncing the -ing sound. It was as if she had something she'd been hesitant to tell me and the pressure was building up. Here was her big chance. Perhaps the presence of her pals had given her sufficient self-confidence to speak her mind. There was scarcely a pause before she added the *coup de grâce*: "Some *pfl-flp*-people have to work, you know."

When I mentioned this to darling Joan, she was livid. "You just wait till her friends leave," she said. "I'm going over there and giving her holy heck. She has no right talking to you like that. There's no one who works harder than you."

"Oh heart, how could I have forgotten you?" (Rilke.)

4. I'm With You Always, Dave

When we returned from our trip around Lake Erie we were shocked to discover our house full of dead fish. We'd soon cleared out the fish and buried them in the back yard. Tons of them. But we still hadn't discovered how the fish got there. And a trace of the smell still lingered.

In preparation for our trip around Lake Huron Joan and I were scrubbing the kitchen floor with Boreen Concentrate when Gene and Audrey came in. It was early evening, a few hours after the unpleasant incident with Audrey. Joan hadn't got around to going over and giving Audrey a piece of her mind, although the thought was appreciated. Actually I'd asked her not to because I would have been embarrassed.

But this visit was quite friendly. Joan told Audrey we didn't know where we were going, we were just going. This wasn't unusual for us. Last year we set off for the Agawa Canyon and ended up in Prince Edward Island. Come to think of it one year we were heading for Vancouver and wound up in Florida.

Audrey realised she'd been a little too outspoken and had hurt my feelings. Rather than apologising she became unusually friendly in compensation, obviously so, at one point going so far she actually asked how my work was going. Perhaps Gene had told her off, for he is a sympathetic soul who often finds himself on the receiving end of some volley or another of Audrey's sarcastic barbs. They stayed on an hour, drank a few cups of tea, then left. Everything had been resolved. It's not easy being neighbours, especially when there's a mutual driveway. One can't let things build up.

"Are you sure you don't know where all the dead fish came from?" I asked just as they were leaving. It was about the twelfth time I'd asked them.

"I'm positive," said Gene.

"All's I can be *sluh*-sayink is you must have an enemy somewhere," said Audrey.

"Yeah," said Gene, in a serious tone. "Somebody's trying to tell you something. Maybe it's one of those jealous literary types."

"Can you still smell it?" I asked, sniffing. They were standing at the door.

"Oh, it'll be months and months *be-ba*-before you'll be gettink rid of that *sissa*-smell," said Audrey. "Why *dada*-don't you sell your house so Marg and Johnny can move in?" Marg and Johnny were their closest friends. In fact Marg was one of the women with Audrey on the front lawn that afternoon when I had my feelings hurt.

I wasn't expecting Joan to get angry but she did. "Why you bitch," she said. My eyes bulged and I glanced to see if there was room for me under the table when the kitchen utensils started flying. "What do you mean, why don't we move? Lookit, you better get this straight. We're here forever. If you don't like it you should never have moved in. We were here first."

"Okay, okay, I was only *jaja*-jokink," said Audrey.

"Some joke," said Joan.

"They think they can say anything they want to me, walk all over me. But they're going to find out that's not so," Joan said later. She was referring to Audrey, numerous other unidentified women who were forever flirting with me and otherwise trying to pry my heart away from Joan's, and various bus-drivers with whom Joan had a long and inexplicable history of getting in shouting matches, sometimes even being thrown off the bus, after being falsely accused of sneaking by without depositing her fare, or of having an invalid transfer.

When Joan became angry with others it made me nervous, because it seemed that she was really projecting a submerged anger with me.

That night, the eve of our departure on the second of our five great adventures, I was half-way between waking and sleeping when I heard a beautiful female voice whispering in my mind.

"I am with you always, Dave," it said.

I sat up in bed. The only woman in the room was Joan, and she was sound asleep.

It would appear there is a growing danger of this book becoming all bogged down in analysis. Let's get on with the action.

THURSDAY, AUGUST 4

5. In the Beginning

The footings under Gene's verandah had been rotting away and that's what he'd been doing, installing new ones. In the morning Joan was wondering aloud about the state of our verandah footings.

"Have you ever thought of checking our verandah footings?" she was saying. "Has the thought even crossed your mind? People do notice that you don't take much of an interest in this house you know." She was also a little angry because I'd been playing Othello with the kids instead of helping her get ready for the trip. "Have you had the van checked over?" she said. "What about the tires?"

The kids and I got in the van and took the cat to the boarding kennel. When we returned Joan had a pile of stuff at the door ready to be put in the van.

In a few minutes we were off. Our mileage was 59752.8. My watch was broken again and I was fiddling with the car radio, trying to find the exact time for our momentous departure, so that I could enter it in the log book. "Will you turn that goddamned thing off?" said Joan.

We stopped at a store so Joan could get some books and drawing pads for the kids.

"I don't want to go on this trip," said Alison while Joan was in the store.

"Mommy's such a grouch," said Jenny.

"We have to go back. I forgot something," said Joan when she returned to the car. "I can't be expected to think of everything." I thought of asking her what she'd forgotten, but then figured I'd find out in the course of time.

We pulled into the driveway and when Joan got out of the car Bruce jumped after her. The poor little thing didn't know what was going on. He didn't know he was about to be taken all the way around Lake Huron. In fact he had no concept of Lake Huron. To him it was just a-lot-of-water. Joan caught him before he hit the ground and pushed him back in the van. As she did so she caught her sleeve on the door latch.

"Goddamned dog," she said.

When Joan came back Audrey stuck her head out and said, "That was a short *tata*-trip."

"Very funny," said Joan.

"What did you *flp*-forget?"

"My shorts," said Joan.

"Where are you a-goink? Have you decided yet?"

"All the way around Lake Huron."

The poetry of such an adventure was seemingly lost on Audrey. "Have fun," she said.

It was exactly 6:15 p.m. when we finally took off. The mileage was now 59765.2.

"So it was your shorts you forgot," I said. I was smiling. "What made you remember them?"

"I saw a girl in shorts."

I smiled again.

"Do you think you can turn on the charm just like that?" she said, glaring at me sideways.

"God, this is a veritable reign of terror!"

"Oh shut up!" We drove for a block or two in silence. "She knows you don't like her you know."

"Who?"

"Audrey. You hardly speak to her anymore. She can sense something's wrong."

Silence fell again. We drove for miles in it. It was sort of an inauspicious beginning to what would turn out to be a fabulous trip. But before the trip became fabulous the beginning was to become even more inauspicious.

6. One of Many Incidents That Took Place in the Arlington Hotel on the Evening of August 4, 1977

We stayed on old, historic, winding, two-lane Highway 2 all the way through Brantford to Paris. We pretended that the modern superhighways hadn't been built yet. The sides of the two-lane highway were covered with wild yellow snapdragons. I imagined Don Quixote jumping out of his car and tearing them up by the roots because of their fearsome name.

"I just love Paris," said Joan as we crossed the long, low bridge over the Grand River and began passing beautiful old nineteenth-century homes with eighty-foot pine trees standing in the front yard. "Wouldn't this be a lovely place to live?"

"Especially in April," I offered.

We drove slowly through downtown Paris looking for a restaurant. We stopped at a three-storey brick structure with a sign saying ARLINGTON HOTEL—DINING ROOM—COMMERCIAL RATES.

What a nice little family we were, walking across the main street of Paris, Ontario, and into the front door of the Arlington Hotel. We left Bruce in the car. I wondered if we could get commercial rates.

But there didn't seem to be any dining room in the hotel. Just a bunch of guys drinking beer at ordinary tables, staggering to the toilet, vomiting, coming back, watching "Bowling for Dollars" on television and playing electronic shuffleboard. A tall white-haired old guy was standing there with a silver change-maker fastened to his belt. You could tell right away he worked there. He might even have been Mr. Arlington.

"Mr. Arlington?" I said. I was the natural spokesman for the entire family.

"No. Mr. Arlington's been dead since 1864."

"Then maybe you could help me. I was wondering where's the dining room?"

"Dining room? We don't have no dining room."

"There's a sign outside saying dining room. You can see it for blocks."

"Oh, are you from out of town?"

"Yes."

"Well, we used to have a dining room a long time ago but when we closed it up we didn't bother taking down the sign. Everyone in town knows the dining room has been closed down since 1950 anyway."

"Funny. The sign didn't look that old. In fact it looked pretty new."

"Where you headin'?"

"Sarnia." That's where we were planning to cross the border into Michigan. We'd decided to drive clockwise around Lake Huron. We'd driven around Lake Erie counter-clockwise after considerable deliberation and we wanted to do something different this time, so that we would be less likely to lapse into automatism or somnambulism as we continued to circumambulate these giant lakes.

"Sarnia," he said, thinking, squinting his eyes, licking his lips, fiddling with his silver change-maker. "Well why don't you stop in Woodstock? There ain't no restaurants in Paris. But Woodstock has some. It ain't far."

7. Turkey Dinners Through the Years

And so we drove on to

WOODSTOCK
THE FRIENDLY CITY
AND DAIRY CAPITAL OF CANADA
WITH EVERYTHING INDUSTRY NEEDS

in the early evening, with young men driving muscle cars back and forth along the main street at fifteen miles an hour, and the light from the setting sun bouncing off the green tile roof of the greystone city hall.

We parked across from the farmer's market and in front of Queen's Restaurant, "specialising in good food and good service." Not excellent, not even best in town, just good. A nice Canadian sign.

An old guy in a dirty grey suit and a grey tweed cap and running shoes passed us on the street. He looked as if he knew where he was going. I resisted the temptation to follow him. The first of many pregnant women walked by. She looked sort of Italian.

The Queen's Restaurant was a lovely old gathering place with old-fashioned mahogany booths and a staircase leading down to the washrooms and furnace room and the long, low room liberally draped with cobwebs where they store ancient cash registers and Orange Crush (in the chocolate brown bottles) and Kik Cola signs.

There was a bouquet of plastic flowers in a vase on our table. The vase was an old sundae dish with a piece of foam in the bottom to hold the plastic stems. It was a nice restaurant. There were aspidistra and rubber plants—real ones—in the front windows, gold and black velvet embossed wallpaper surrounding the expensive-looking mirrors on the wall, and maroon and gold velvet drapes everywhere. The acoustic tile ceiling was only slightly water-stained.

Sitting behind the cash register, reading a book, was another pregnant woman who also looked Italian or maybe Greek. There was a plaster model of the Venus de Milo standing on a shelf behind her. At the back of the restaurant there were several people sitting in booths. They were sipping Cokes and talking to each other and to the white-smocked waitress who was also sitting there and drinking a Coke.

So the waitress came over and took our order. The kids and I ordered hot turkey sandwiches while Joan's selection was fish and chips. I said I could remember being in a similar restaurant in Dunnville in 1950. It was total recall of my parents buying me a grown-up's turkey dinner which cost two whole dollars. I remembered thinking that the potatoes were mashed a little creamier than my mother's. And the gravy was the same colour as the walls. "It seemed like such a luxurious place," I told the kids. "I thought I was in heaven. Oh, and I can still taste that turkey. It was delicious."

"I'm surprised they'd buy you a turkey dinner," said Joan.

I pulled a face. "There you go again." Joan has this thing about my parents being a little tight with their money. She didn't know them when they were young and free-spirited.

8. Passing Through Woodstock on a Summer Night

Four guys came in out of the warm night. They were wearing wet bathing suits and bathing caps. Their T-shirts were spotted with dampness from their wet bodies. "Oh God, it's air-conditioned," said one, shivering.

"Well, well," said Joan, under her breath. "The local Aquatic Club."

I paid the bill. The pregnant woman got up. She smiled. I smiled back. "What are you going to call it?"

"Ulysses if it's a boy, Penelope if it's a girl." I looked puzzled. "They're old Greek names," she said. "We *are* Greek, you know."

"And what's that book you're reading? *The Odyssey*? *The Iliad*?"

It was the new, all-improved, revised edition of John Fowles' *The Magus*, which had just come out in paperback.

The Woodstock News Depot was next to the restaurant. We walked by. A splendid display of the new version of *The Magus* graced the sparkling window. A terribly hunched-up and twisted man came out carrying a bunch of newspapers.

"Don't look at that poor man, Joan," I said. "There's something horribly the matter with him."

"Shh. He'll hear you," she said.

"Better he hear me than have you staring at him."

Across the street was the beautiful old city hall with its crepuscular green tile roof, the sun no longer bouncing off it. Next to the news depot was a store bearing a sign with a picture of a blindfolded woman. The sign over the door simply said BEAUTY SUPPLY. There were some wigs in the window and there were also some rare coins on display. A sign in the window read

WOODSTOCK COIN EXCHANGE Strange combination for a store: beauty supplies and coin exchange. I couldn't figure out why the woman was blindfolded. Another pregnant woman walked by on the sidewalk. She was not blindfolded.

"Everyone in this town," said Joan, "is either pregnant, blindfolded, hunchbacked or Italian."

"The people who run the restaurant were Greek."

"Greek? You ordered turkey in a Greek restaurant?"

"Yeah. What's the matter with that?" I said, dull-wittedly.

"Oh Dave. Sometimes I wonder about you." I was supposed to be the young genius but Joan's mind was running circles around mine.

On the way out of town we passed Johnston's Jewellers and Art Gallery, which was another strange combination. We also passed the Oxford County Museum. "Oh there's another restaurant," said Joan. "It looks a lot nicer."

"That's the Oxford County Museum," I said.

"No, next to it," said Joan.

"Well it's too late now. I'm full. What's it called?" I couldn't turn to look because I was driving.

"It just says RESTAURANT SINCE 1935," said Joan.

"It's called the Food-Rite," said Jenny.

"Hey kids," I said. "This is where Linda Curnoe's ex-husband was born."

"Oh yeah," said Joan.

"Were Stephanie and Jessica born here too?" said Jenny.

"No. They were born in Southampton."

Part of me seemed to be floating along beside the van, invisible, listening in. Everything that was being said was profoundly poetic, heavy with the weight of the entire universe.

9. The Smorgasbord of Consciousness

Lake Huron was a rumour of a naked woman lying in the moonlight and we were scurrying toward it like a small party of ants, lightheaded, harmless, full of dreams and sorrows.

There's a certain piece of landscape on the south side of Highway 2 just west of Woodstock that I never pass without feeling a sudden déjà vu. It's merely a house with a hill behind it, a rather long grassy drummond that rises perhaps a hundred feet from the road. It's something about the relative heights of the road and the house and the hill, and the angles of the house and the hill in relation to the direction of the road that inevitably springs a door in my mind. The same trap was sprung by a similar landscape through which I passed years ago while travelling in New Brunswick. In later trips through New Brunswick I could never find that same spot. But strangely enough I think it was just outside Woodstock, New Brunswick, on the New Brunswick Highway 2, while now we were just outside Woodstock, Ontario, on the Ontario Highway 2.

And this time, just a few minutes after sundown, with the sky the colour of the sleeping mind, the landscape had altered. The house had burnt down. The black charred ruins, abandoned, stood there like a grave marker. And still the trap door opened and a chill passed through me. I call it déjà vu but I don't know if it is because I have nothing to compare it with. Suddenly the landscape becomes mythic with unheard music and as soon as I think about it I'm back on the highway with all the problems of my life staring me in the face: like trying to make sure I'm driving in the proper lane at the proper speed and wondering if the family is going to hold together and if the cut worm forgives the plough.

What has happened? And why can't I experience it more fully? Why does it disappear as soon as I think about it? Why have I never been able to hold myself up to it, to let myself be impregnated by its beam? Why for me is it always something that has happened in the past, albeit the immediate past, and never in the present? If it is something that can only happen when part of the mind is asleep why is that part of my mind always asleep when I pass this spot? Is the crucial spot something farther east of this particular landscape, another particular landscape I know nothing about but which serves to anaesthetise that part of my brain by the time I reach this particular landscape which I only mistakenly associate with the experience? And had anyone been killed in the fire? Did this tragedy have anything to do with me?

We continued passing through a series of beautiful Southern Ontario towns and small cities which have been left undisturbed for two decades because the heavily travelled route during that time has been the mighty Macdonald-Cartier Freeway, the famous 401. The towns seemed ghostly, bathed in a pewter cloud of consciousness, a fog-like smorgasbord. And every time we slowed down to pass through another town Bruce hopped up to the window, hoping to see other dogs on the street.

10. Marks of Weakness, Marks of Woe

By the time we reached London it was night. The Forest City was humming with traffic. There'd been some rain and the streets were a little slimy. A cyclist wheeled through a stop sign and I had to slam on my brakes. Joan cursed under her breath. She was still a little angry. It hadn't been one of her better days. I decided to make a joke.

"Shall we camp in my Aunt Beulah's back yard?"

Joan's face went cold. "I don't think they'd appreciate us dropping in at ten o'clock."

"I know. I was only fooling."

"Beulah just isn't the type."

A few months earlier, in April, Jennifer and I took the train to London. Irene Dewdney picked us up at the station. "What do you want for dinner, Jennifer?" she said.

"I won't know until I look in your fridge and see what you've got," said Jennifer.

Irene and I exchanged amused glances although I was a little more embarrassed than amused.

"I was planning to stop off at the supermarket on the way home," said Irene. "So you can have anything you want."

"Anything?"

"Yes, my dear. Anything."

"Can we have hamburgers?"

After Jennifer finished off three hamburgers she started into dessert.

"Would you like another chocolate cake and ice cream?" said Irene after Jennifer had finished her third helping.

"Not right now," said Jennifer. "I'll have it at bedtime."

I had to give a talk at the Forest City Gallery that night. There were maybe forty people in attendance, but none I recognised. There was no one there I knew would be familiar with my work. Christopher Dewdney was in Trinidad, Robert Fones was in Toronto, Greg Curnoe was in

Vancouver, Russell Seaworthy was in Germany (or was it Italy?), and Ron Benner was in Iceland. So the atmosphere was a little on the deadly side. But there was Jennifer, in the front row, nine years old, staring at me with such devotion and intensity.

Jenny seemed to know something one wouldn't expect her to know at that age. At least I could see this knowledge in her eyes. She knew that someday she would be all grown up and I would be either dead or close to it. It was as if she knew that the time would come when she would treasure the memory of her father as he was, and she was trying to photograph with her mind every nuance, every detail of the moment. So I mumbled something about this being such an intelligent-looking group I would read my longest and most boring poem, "The Poet's Progress." It was the first time I'd read it in public. Jennifer's eyes were like black holes into the future. I could feel my heart pumping as I went into my reader's trance. She was the most beautiful mushroom in the forest.

"That was good, Daddy," she said later.

"Thank you, Jenny," I said. I had a feeling she had it all stored away in her cortex forever. And if it turns out that this was nothing but vanity on my part, I don't care.

And so there we were driving at a snail's pace through the slimy streets of London four months later.

"This city looks like Hamilton," said Alison.

It's not really as interesting a city as Hamilton but it's in a healthier state. Decay hasn't set in as badly, nor has cancerous growth. The air is cleaner. And London is substantially more middle-class, both in the look of the residential areas and the people you see walking along the sidewalks of the commercial areas. Everyone looks so ordinary. You don't see as many grossly obese people, people smelling of aeroplane glue, people with horribly disfiguring marks on their faces, casts on their arms or legs, crutches, wheelchairs, electric scooters, or so many people bearing marks of weakness, marks of woe. It's a far less interesting city. The poet Christopher Dewdney once commented that "Hamilton is one big recessive gene pool."

11. The Man in the White Hat

We were heading west toward Sarnia along Highway 22. It was getting late and Joan wanted to know how close we were to the Pinery Provincial Park where we'd been camping the summer before. I told her it was about an hour away.

"Oh, that's too far."

I stopped at a roadside country store, bought some soap and a can of dog food and asked the Serbian woman at the cash register directions to the nearest campsite. She rattled off the directions to about three different spots. She apparently got asked that question a lot. We chose the nearest, about five miles away. The entrance to the campsite was closed for the night but I pried the gate open with my teeth (with some help from my Swiss Army Knife) and drove through. I flashed my flashlight over the giant map painted on a billboard. I tried to figure out where to go. There was no moon and no wind. It was mysterious. We finally camped in the middle of a grassy field surrounded by birch trees. There were quite a few small lakes around. There weren't very many campers.

I filled the kettle for tea and plugged in the cord. Joan began making fun of my new white hat. "It makes you look old," she said. I'd worn it when we visited her parents a few days before.

"My mother told me you don't look like a kid anymore. Dave doesn't look like a kid anymore. That's what she said."

FRIDAY, AUGUST 5

12. St. Mushroom of the Cross

We were in the Coldstream Conservation Area which is part of the St. Clair Region Conservation Authority. We were forty-six miles from Sarnia. This information was provided by two teenage girls who were cleaning out the men's washrooms. It was morning and I wanted to take a shower. They just wanted to talk.

"I'd like to take a shower now," I said.

"Go ahead. We're not stopping you." They were high-school students working for the summer. Their green pick-up truck was parked outside.

There was no door on the shower but it faced the far wall and they couldn't see me from where they were standing. So I took off my clothes and turned on the water. But they moved around and started mopping the floor in front of the shower, copping looks at me and smiling, trying not to giggle. There wasn't much I could do so I just smiled back and acted natural. If I'd acted shy and tried to cover myself I would probably have become more provocative and more in danger of getting indecently assaulted. They were fairly large girls and could easily, in tandem, overpower me.

My strategy worked. The girls quickly became bored and left.

It was still early when I got back to the campsite, my hair drying in the sun. Joan was making a huge breakfast of pancakes and fried eggs. The kids went looking for mushrooms and came back with a bronze cross they found on the path. It was beautiful, about three inches long and two inches wide, with a small hole for putting a string through.

13. A Summer Storm

It was a lovely morning but it was marred by one of those emotional flare-ups that occur in the nuclear family from time to time, the sort of thing that seems horrendous at the time but soon becomes a source of tender amusement in recollection.

We'd been driving about ten miles when Joan put her head on my lap and dozed off. The kids started making a lot of noise in the back seat. I wanted to get them to shut up so they wouldn't disturb Joan but I didn't want to disturb Joan either. So I merely picked up Joan's hairbrush from the dashboard and tossed it softly and silently over my head in the general direction of the kids, hoping to get their attention so I could motion to them to pipe down. Unfortunately it hit Jennifer fairly hard between the eyes and up a bit. She burst into tears.

Joan woke up and started yelling. She wanted to turn around and go home. Nothing I could say made any difference, so finally I turned the van around and started heading back toward London. This made Joan all the angrier and she started calling me names. Maybe I was smiling a bit. Maybe it was just something chemical between us. But she ordered me to pull over and let her out. She wasn't going to ride another minute with me.

So I pulled up a side road and stopped in front of a bunch of guys sitting beside their motorcycles. They were drinking beer and wearing black T-shirts and black leather vests. They looked as if they'd consider Evil Knievel a sissy. They were looking straight at us.

"I don't want to get out here." Joan spoke through the side of her mouth with teeth firmly clenched. She tried to look calm. She was even trying to smile. "Move on, will you," she whispered.

So I drove further down the road. I couldn't help smiling again, and my smile exacerbated Joan's anger, naturally. Learning not to smile in the face of anger was taking me much longer than it should have. She said she resented not knowing the bank balance, she resented not being told when money comes in and she resented me not having a job like normal men. There were other things too. She was throwing the book at me. It was a veritable litany of domestic agony.

And everything she said had a solid point to it.

She said she wanted me to drive her home, she wanted me to let her out of the van so she could go home on the bus, and she wanted me to get out and go home on the bus so she could take the kids around Lake Huron herself. All three.

I didn't know what to do, so I did nothing. That is, I just kept doing what I'd been doing before the storm broke. I drove back to the highway and started heading toward Sarnia. By the time we were in the suburbs of that city the storm had passed, and Joan was smiling.

I checked Jennifer's eye. There was a small bruise but it seemed okay. "I'm sorry, Daddy," she said.

14. The Day-Spring by Orlo Miller

A year earlier I took my little family on a motoring trip from Point Pelee to Tobermory. We went the long way, the scenic route, along Lake Erie to Windsor and around Lake St. Clair to Sarnia. Then we followed the shore of Lake Huron to Tobermory at the tip of the Bruce Peninsula after which our dog is named.

On that trip we got lost in Sarnia. At one point we were parked at the side of the road in Point Edward, a Sarnia suburb, and were trying to get directions from passersby, except there were no passersby, at least none on foot. I noticed we were parked in front of a church, a small white clapboard structure. There was a sign out front saying that the Rev. Orlo Miller was the pastor. That was a coincidence of the first order because only a week earlier I'd been reading an excellent book by the same Orlo Miller, *The Day-Spring*, all about pre-Columbian European influences on the Americas. I'd forgotten that Miller was a Point Edward clergyman. He had also written a book on the subject of the Black Donnellys, though my informants tell me the only person worth reading on this subject is Ray Fazakas, of Hamilton.

On that trip we spent quite a long time driving along the streets of Sarnia, talking about the oil refineries and the high average wage and all that stuff. It was a beautiful day, the sun was shining, the flowers were blooming, and I developed some affection for the place.

So on this trip, as we approached Sarnia once again, I innocently asked Joan and the kids if they remembered being in Sarnia the year before. They said no. I couldn't believe it. Only after I filled them in on the context of our visit to Sarnia did they begin to remember it. Maybe next year they wouldn't be able to remember having taken a trip around Lake Huron. But they'll have this book to remind them!

15. The Road to Hollywood

There we were up in the clouds on the Blue Water Bridge joining Sarnia, Ontario, with Port Huron, Michigan. Actually there were no clouds. We were up where the clouds would be if there were any clouds. The sky was as blue as Alison's left eye. A reversal of sorts.

Looking down you could see the entire southern belly of Lake Huron as it narrows into the St. Clair River just as it looks on the map. However, you couldn't see the names of the cities and you couldn't see the dotted line separating Canada from the U.S.A.

The U.S. customs official was Mr. Casual. He didn't ask for Bruce's vaccination papers and he didn't ask if we had any oranges. I wanted to complain. Where's your respect for tradition?

"So where ya born?" the guy said.

"Canada."

"So where ya headin'?"

"Down to Hollywood to become movie stars."

"Okay. Go ahead."

16. The View from the Back Yard

As soon as we got through customs which didn't take very long we drove into Port Huron, Michigan, and headed for the Lake Huron shore. We were suddenly very anxious to see Lake Huron, a lake we were both familiar with from childhood, from the other side. Even with the bridge hovering above us, it seemed strange, as if we were on the dark side of the moon. The other side of Lake Erie had somehow seemed more plausible than the other side of Lake Huron. It was like looking at yourself from above or behind.

But it was Lake Huron all right. You could sense its symmetry as it grew wider and wider the further north you went. There was something clear and graceful about the atmosphere of this lake. The horrors of the twentieth century really hadn't penetrated its consciousness. It couldn't be anything else but Lake Huron but it was a reverse image, like a memory of the future. It was like when you're a child and you're playing in the back yard. You look up and suddenly realise you're looking at the back of your house for the first time. You know what it looks like from the front but you've never been conscious of seeing it from this angle before.

17. The Answer to All My Problems

The U.S. 25 follows the Lake Huron shore all the way from Port Huron north to Point Aux Barques then, still following the shore, it arcs south to Bay City at the end of Saginaw Bay. This graceful loop is familiar to all who love maps. Without the thumb-shaped arm of Saginaw Bay jutting in from Lake Huron, Lake Huron would be all wrong. Georgian Bay on the other side of the lake would have been untenable.

We drove north on the U.S. 25 through towns like Lakeport, Lexington, Port Sanilac (which sounds like something spelled backwards), Richmondville, Forestville, White Rock, and Harbor Beach—all blessed by being on the shore of this beautiful lake even if they are on the wrong shore. The towns and the countryside were uninspiring, unstimulating. Basically there was a back yard sense to it all. There was all of the drabness and none of the sudden beauty that comes with a similar drive along the Canadian shore of this lake. There was a certain ineffable emptiness.

It was summer resort country even this far south however. The spaces between the towns were studded with cottages owned by people from the Detroit area. There were tennis courts, marinas, little rows of cottages for rent all the same colour. There were signs like HOUSE ON THE KNOLL, COOKIES ACRE, WALLY GIRAREL, TOUZEAU RAMBAUM, LAZE DAZE, and SNAY ROAD.

Joan decided to lie down in the back seat and the kids came up front with me. We passed a dead skunk and a field of fresh sheep manure at the same time. What a formidable coincidence!

"Sacre bleu!" I said. "Did you fart, Jenny?"

"No."

"Did you fart, Alison?"

"No."

Through the rear-view mirror the kids looked worried.

"Then it must have been Mommy." The kids looked back at her. She continued sleeping, a group of little zeds floating above her head.

We passed quite a few rural mail boxes with yellow *Times-Herald* signs.

Then we passed a mail box with the name GRIMES painted on it.

"Grimes rhymes with Times," said Jenny. I laughed. She looked at me. "I'm funny aren't I, Daddy?"

"You bet you're funny. You're funny as um er ah um I can't think just now, but really funny."

"Funny as Alison?"

"I think you must be one of the funniest little girls in all of Southwestern Ontario. And remember what Christopher Dewdney said about you?"

"What was that, Daddy?"

"He said you had all of Southwestern Ontario in your eyes."

"Are my eyes pretty?"

"They're beautiful."

Outside the town of Harbor Beach there was an enormous sign outlining the highlights of the life of Governor Frank Murphy who was born there. We drove down to the City Waterworks Park on the lakeshore. They had just decided to turn the area in front of the waterworks into a public beach and picnic area with canopies, picnic benches, swings, slides, teeter totters (also known as seesaws), and huge horse chestnut trees with enormous spreading branches dense with dark green leaves. We drove right onto the beach and scared away all the gulls except one who was sitting on the back of a giant turtle sunning on a rock about twenty feet offshore. About a hundred feet offshore there was a long cement breakwater. Above that, in a hierarchy of curvature, a long low Great Lakes steamer, going slower than a clock, was barely noticeable on the hazy horizon.

There were a couple of other families picnicking in the small park. Some boys were swimming lazily out to the breakwater. Some children from one of the other families were sitting on the swings. They were calling for me to come and push them. That seemed kind of strange. Why didn't they call on their own father? He was just standing there cooking hotdogs on his portable barbecue, a beer in one hand, a fork in the other, and a cigar in his mouth.

I would have gone over to push them but I had to do something immediately. There was a little wooden outhouse attached to the old stone waterworks building. But there was no toilet paper. There was no one in the waterworks building but in a smaller stone building that led down into an underground generating room a guy was painting a large turbine, as in "the surface of" rather than "a picture of."

"Excuse me," I called down. "There's no toilet paper in the washroom."

The guy stopped painting. He looked up at me incredulously. "You don't say!"

"I was thinking of using the women's washroom and I was wondering if you could sort of watch out for me."

"Are you feeling all right?"

I just looked at him. I had the feeling I was being too polite somehow. It was unsettling. I think if I'd started shouting he'd have been more at ease with the situation and perhaps would have been more eager to help. He on the other hand was saying (to himself), "You never know what's going to happen next in this place."

He held his brush up so it wouldn't drip paint. The paint was red. "Don't go in the women's washroom," he said in a threatening tone. And then, in a milder tone, "There's no toilet paper in there either." He went back to spreading on the paint.

"Perhaps I might use the toilet inside the large building?"

"You stay outta there, you hear?"

I thought of going to the washroom anyway and using soap and water. But there were no paper towels, no soap, and the only water was in the toilet. It was a nice clean washroom though.

Actually the guy seemed fairly calm. He was as angry as he was likely to get.

He might have been nastier if I'd been black. But he knew that an ordinary white man could complain and get him in trouble. They'd listen to me.

"What should I do?" I said.

The guy kept painting for a few strokes, thinking about my question.

"Oh, I'm getting awful cramps," I said.

He rolled his eyes, sighed and put his brush down. He stood up and began climbing up the winding staircase to ground level. "You wait right there," he said. I had a feeling he admired my persistence at the same time that he was critical of me for being such an idiot.

He went into the large building and came out immediately with a nice roll of pink toilet paper. He tore off a piece and handed it to me. "I'll wait for you," he said. His face was blank. No amusement, no anger.

It was a fairly generous piece of toilet paper. Almost two feet long.

"I don't need this much," I said, and gave him back a foot of it.

He looked at me as if I was from outer space. Years from now he'd still be telling people: "Weirdest guy I ever met in my life was a Canadian who wanted to go to the toilet and didn't have any toilet paper."

When I came out he was still standing there with the same non-look on his face.

"Thank you very much," I said.

"You should always carry a box of Kleenex in your car," he said.

"I say, that's a good idea. I'm going to do that from now on."

He smiled a little. The guy's completely zonkers, he seemed to be thinking. This guy makes Woody Allen seem perfectly normal. The guy's gotta be a full-bred Zonko-Rooney from Zonkorooneyland.

"Wait a minute," I said. "I just remembered, I do have a box of Kleenex in the car. I'm terribly sorry to have bothered you."

The guy opened his mouth in a wordless scream then fell to the ground and landed on his back with his arms and legs outstretched. He stared up at the blue sky through the green overhanging leaves.

"Are you all right?" I said. "Shall I call an ambulance?"

"Just go," he said in a slow monotone. "I'll be fine."

18. William Blake

When I got back to the van Joan had the stove on and was cooking hot dogs. I had a handful of *Marismius oreades* I'd found growing in a fairy ring in the grass. I tossed them in the pan. They were delicious. The stems were particularly meaty and they absorbed the flavour of the hot dogs. They tasted like the sweetest, most tender bacon—from free-range pigs, even though Sheila Gostick says she wonders about people who take an interest in the life of the pig they're eating.

The motor age had shrunk Lake Huron so much and yet it still seemed large. How incredibly huge it must have seemed to the indigenous people of the area—without cars, without maps, without even horses. The world must have been magically endless. No wonder they heard voices. Their lives must have been one long déjà vu. Imagine having a déjà vu without having to think about it immediately and see it vanish like a peripheral apparition! What is happening to us and where are we heading? Even with the unprecedented amount of literature and other cultural artifacts we're leaving behind, future civilisations may find themselves unable to understand us. We're leaving them a lot to go on, but perhaps the essentials haven't been understood even by ourselves yet. And so we will be as enigmatic as the builders of Stonehenge, as enigmatic as the Australian aborigine with his dream time, his song lines, his ability to stand on one leg for days. Maybe more so.

And so we passed through the little town of Port Hope and Joan said, "What a coincidence! I was just going to say this town reminded me of Port Hope, Ontario, and it turns out to be Port Hope, Michigan." Neither of us felt the need to rationalise this coincidence by assuming Joan had subliminally detected a Port Hope sign earlier which triggered the thought that the town resembled the other Port Hope, or that she'd seen it on the map, or that I'd mentioned it earlier but the mention was forgotten. We were quite comfortable under our intimate blanket of darkness. In fact we'd be comfortable in a culture that rejected the notion of significant coincidence. I liked the example of William Blake, who was somewhat retrograde in his ordinary daily life. He would personally deliver handbills all over town for his latest sale of pictures. Then he and Elizabeth would sit there all day waiting for people to show up but no one ever came. Someone showed King George III some of Blake's poems and the King said, "Take them away, take them away!" Yet Blake lived a long life and died with a smile on his face.

19. Even Jane Fonda Isn't As Cute As She Used to Be

For those who see significance in the insignificant—omens in entrails, the shapes of clouds, chance occurrences—it should be recorded that the ST—short for saint—had fallen off the post office sign in Port Hope so that it read US PO OFFICE. Was this God's little way of saying there are no saints in this town? Just as we passed the sign the speedometer turned over to 60,000.

"That's a good sign," said Joan. I don't know if she meant the post office sign was a good sign, the speedometer turning over was a good sign, or that it was a good omen for the long life of the car that the speedometer turned over to 60,000 in Port *Hope*. Or maybe that the speedometer turned over as we passed the sign with the ST missing.

We made the northern loop around the heel of Saginaw Bay and when we started heading southwest toward Bay City we ran into a wall of rain. The sky had been churning grey and black for miles. There was a K-Mart in a shopping centre just outside of Bay City and Joan suggested we run in and buy everything we could get our hands on. It was raining hard. I dropped Joan and the kids at the main entrance then went looking for a parking spot. The dog hadn't been let out to pee for quite a while so I let her out and both of us got wet. Then I had to run back to the K-Mart. When I got there no one was waiting for me at the door. How inconsiderate! It took me an hour to find them. And when I did find them I was still wet.

"You could have waited for me or asked one of the kids to wait for me," I said, poutingly and in the most markedly immature manner imaginable. Joan was still a little angry from that unfortunate incident with the hairbrush on the road to Sarnia just a few hours earlier. Her anger flared up again, triggered by mine.

I forget her exact words but it was something like this: "How dare you be mad at me when I have a thousand times more reasons to be mad at you? I've forgiven you for crimes a thousand times as bad as the triviality that has currently aroused your ire." That sort of thing. So we decided we'd meet in an hour in the Captain Andy Seafood Restaurant.

There were about four interesting-looking mushroom guides in the bookstore and I spent most of my hour comparing them before narrowing them down to two. I finally chose the British book over the American one because the watercolours in the British one were so beautiful. I later regretted it because it didn't relate to the Canadian varieties quite as well. No beauty fades more quickly than the unappreciated sort.

The only Canadian book in the store was the RCAF exercise manual. The poetry section was worse than in most comparable Canadian bookstores. There were stacks of Hugh Prather books—*I Touch the Earth and the Earth Touches Me*, *You Just Swallowed My Soul*, and so on—poetry for those who lack the organ for poetry. And then there was a book called *How to Survive in the Suburbs When Your Heart Is in the Himalayas*. I flipped it open. There was a picture of a woman facing a pile of dirty dishes. The caption read: "Even Jane Fonda isn't as cute as she used to be."

Jane Fonda. Hm! For a moment I wondered what Jane Fonda was doing right at that moment. And suddenly I felt as if I'd made contact. My heart turned into a crystal ball and I could see her. She was somewhere in Southern California watching a rerun of *The King and I* on television. Her place was very neat.

It was nice to think that this was the same country that Jane Fonda lived in. There was a guy who looked like the poet Ed Dorn standing next to me. He was reading a book called *Forbidden Cures*.

20. What Joan Would Like Next

Silly me! Why didn't I leave the idea of a trip around yet another Great Lake till next year? Two Great Lakes in one year? Preposterous!

I'd just finished getting the van ready for sleeping. We were in the Bay City State Park. It was raining bobcats and Labrador retrievers. "I don't really like camping, Dave," said Joan. She was in a good mood again despite the rain and all. She wasn't being negative, she was being honest. "I don't like flies in my tea. I don't like being wet and miserable. And when I do camp I like to be able to get up in the middle of the night and pee in the fields. But I won't be able to tonight with all these Jesus big Winnebagos around."

We were in a canyon formed by a circle of these $100,000 monsters with air conditioners humming and televisions glowing away like electronic meatgrinders. They looked as if they might have retractable machine-gun nests on their roofs. And radar to detect people peeing in the fields or making love behind the trees. This was camping?

There was a sign at the entrance to the Bay City State Park reading NO TENTS ALLOWED IN CAMPSITE. This is true! Imagine! No tents allowed in campsite! That's like saying "No ball playing allowed in Tiger Stadium." This would have something to do with the average middle-class American family's dislike, jealousy, envy of adolescents and their adolescence (oh how he loves to generalise on the wing!). The ban was designed to discourage teenagers who usually can't afford $100,000 Winnebagos. They can only afford Toyotas with pup tents on the roof. I know a guy who quit camping because wherever he went he found himself surrounded by rowdy teenagers making love behind trees and stuff like that, or was especially bothered by a guy with shoulder-length (gasp!) hair strumming a guitar romantically by the fire and under a full moon, with his girlfriend's head on his shoulder and peeking up at his eyes with supreme adoration. "They ruin it for ya," said my friend. So there you go.

"I know, Joan," I said. "I was stupid for buying this van. I just thought it would be good for the family, to help us to get to know each other more, to tighten the bonds of our mutual affection. But we'll sell it as soon as we get back."

To be more truthful with the reader than I was being with Joan, I wanted to sell it because I was afraid we wouldn't be able to afford to keep it running. The repairs were incredible. It was out-and-out rape every time I took it in for repairs. It was our only car so it was doubling as a family car and all. It was costing about $200 a month just to keep it in running order. I should have known better than to buy a car invented by the goddamned Nazis (he spits on the floor as he types!).

Joan was conciliatory in the extreme. "But you want to go around all of the Great Lakes, don't you? This is only number two, Dave."

"That's okay. I'm not going to be childish about it. We'll buy a nice sensible little American compact and stay at motels all the way around."

Something I said must have put Joan in a better mood. She knew I was being deeply sincere when I enumerated my reasons for having bought the camper, into which the kids were just now climbing. Joan started joking with them. "Now kids," she said. "Isn't this more fun than being in a motel with clean dry sheets and elbow room and a big bathtub and TV?"

Alison looked surprised. She hadn't been in a motel for a couple of years. She gasped. "They don't have TVs in motels do they?"

"Sure they do. Nice big colour TVs."

"Oh yeah! I forgot!" She began staring out the window into a copse of tall graceful cedars.

"And do you know what I'd like to have next?" Joan had a dreamy look on her face.

"What?" said everybody.

"I'd like to get one of those trucks with the camper cap on top of it. No, you know what I'd like to have?"

"What?" said everybody.

"I'd like to keep the camper but just add a nice big trailer so we'd have lots of room."

21. The Strange Case of Debbie Dobyne

I can't remember why I was standing in the heavy rain in front of the women's washroom with Bruce in the Bay City State Park in Michigan at eleven o'clock on a summer night in 1977. But I was wondering about my sad life. When I was fifteen my most-worshiped hero was William Burroughs and I wanted to grow up to be just like him. I was wondering where I went wrong when a black woman in her early fifties came out with a mop and pail and looked at Bruce.

"Oh, look at the lovely little pussycat," she said.

"That's no pussycat," I said. "That's a full-blooded dog."

"Really. What kinda dog?"

"That's only the best kinda dog in the world, a West Highland White Terrier."

"A what?"

"A Westie."

"Now what makes it the best?"

"It comes from the West Highlands of Scotland. From time immemorial, any dog that doesn't match up they kill it, the Scottish people."

"Oh dear!" She had blonde spots in her black Afro hair. "I had a little dog a little bigger than him about this high. His name was Didhebitecha."

"Didhebitecha?"

"Yeah."

"And did you bite him back?"

Her joke had backfired. She laughed. "Then one day somebody lifted him."

She looked sad. Bruce kept wagging his tail. "So someone we knew had a friend in 'Troit who had a dog they wanted to git rid of. So my son-in-law, he drove me down and we got him. He was a lovely dog."

"What did you call him?"

"Didhebitecha."

"Didhebitecha II?"

"No, he never bit me. Neither did the first one." The conversation was getting interesting. "One day I called him from across the road and he ran out in front of a car and got hit. He was a lovely dog. He never shed. It used to cost me fifteen dollars to get his hair cut. In fact I got his hair cut the day before he got hit."

"What a waste!"

"Yeah, in my line of work fifteen bucks is a lot of money."

"Did you get your fifteen dollars back?" I guess that was a stupid question, making fun of someone whose dog died. But I was getting soaked. So was the woman. She didn't seem to mind though.

"No," she said. "No refunds on that."

She said she had six grandchildren and told me the ages and said she'd lived in Bay City since 1969.

"Where are you from originally?"

"Brummagem," she said. "Brummagem, Al-bam."

"Birmingham?"

"That's right. Brummagem."

"What do you like best, the north or the south?"

"I like the north fine but there's somethin' about home."

"Yeah," I said.

She said she was going to get a Westie like mine the next time she needed a dog.

"What are you going to call him? Didhebitecha III?"

"Maybe," she said.

I told her about my Uncle Bill who calls his dog Askim. "When people say to him what do you call your dog he says Askim. So if they're not too bright they get down on their hands and knees and look the dog in the face and say: 'What's your name, dog?'"

She liked that story. "Oh that's good," she said. "I think I'll call him Askim."

I asked her what her name was. "Debbie Dobyne," she said. She even spelled the last name for me.

"What's it really like for you living up here in Bay City?" I said, conspiratorially.

"It's really a nice place," she said. "It really is. But they's a lot of snobs."

SATURDAY, AUGUST 6

22. Tortured with Razors, Burnt with Cigarettes

Standing next to us was a Winnebago with Florida licence plates. The air conditioner was going full blast even though the night was cold and rainy. I dreamt I was back in Ontario in the nineteenth century. For some reason I knew it was 1830. I was in the woods. It was like my old *Wacousta* dream but this time I had a large trunk that I had to get to Ottawa. There was a narrow macadam road threading through the woods. A bus came along and picked me up. It was the first bus in Ontario. It cost me a dollar-fifty to get to Ottawa. I didn't think it was unusual there would be buses in 1830.

I slipped out of the van at 7:30 and went for a long walk through the woods. There was garbage all over the place. There is a different attitude toward the woods in the U.S.A. Some of this garbage seemed to date back to Civil War days. I could have had a garage sale. There were giant spools of cable, wagon wheels, old cars, bottles, display cases, a stack of old French postcards wrapped in plastic, a porcelain and stainless steel soda fountain set.

It started to rain again. When I got back to the van the kids were awake. The guy in the Winnebago came out and switched off his air conditioner. Then it dawned on me that maybe it wasn't an air conditioner. Maybe it was a furnace. The guy looked miserable like most white people in this land. They always look like they're having a terrible time and can't wait to get home to watch television. They look as if they're just riddled with unnameable and inexpressible fears. As if they just wish someone would shoot them and put them out of their misery. It'd be the nicest thing you could do for lots of them. Debbie Dobyne would understand. They's a lot of snobs.

We drove back through Bay City, past rows and rows of beautiful old homes and churches. We could see the massive First Presbyterian Church across the bay. "If that's the first I'd love to see the second," said Joan. It was still raining. She said she used to watch a soap opera that was set in Bay City. "It seemed to be a very wealthy city and it turns out to be true," she said. The show was called *Another World*. The characters were all impossibly successful architects. doctors, businessmen and other wealthy people who had plenty of time on their hands and could afford servants. Like Debbie Dobyne. "Oh no, not the doctor," said Joan. "He didn't have any servants."

"Why not?"

"I don't know. He just didn't."

We were retracing our steps a bit because somehow Joan decided we wanted to have breakfast at McDonald's, to go to a McDonald's in its country of origin. McDonald's: getting you ready for the synthetic future. We'd never had breakfast at McDonald's and we were sort of curious. When McDonald's first started serving breakfasts they put a great huge billboard up on the Mountain in Hamilton, Ontario. It said GOOD MORNING, AMERICA. There were a couple of complaints and the manager of Canadian operations apologised publicly, saying it had been a human error. So they blocked out America and wrote in Canada.

Inside they were selling helium balloons for a quarter apiece. The kids didn't want one so I bought one for myself. The proceeds were for muscular dystrophy. I decided to pretend I had muscular dystrophy. I limped to the counter with my face twisted out of shape, and in a very poor and tasteless imitation of someone with a severe speech problem told her I had muscular dystrophy and could I get a discount on my breakfast. Joan hit me on the shoulder. "Dave, quit it," she said. "He's just fooling," she said to the girl. The girl looked sick. She didn't think it was in good taste. Neither did Joan. I'm terribly embarrassed to have to report I actually did that, but confession increases self-authenticity.

The breakfast was simply terrible. I'll eat almost anything but I couldn't eat those eggs. I took a bite out of everything and ejected it, as clandestinely (and politely) as possible, on to my spoon. Joan couldn't finish hers either. Even the kids thought the food was pretty grim. It just wasn't to our taste somehow. I'm not saying our taste was right.

There was a copy of the *Detroit Free Press* at our booth. The main story on page one featured the sad story of a Detroit business executive whose body had just been found in a downtown rooming house. He'd been tortured with razors and burnt with cigarettes. The exact cause of death hadn't been determined.

23. An Awful Moment In a Woman's Life

Joan refuses to admit she is hooked on shopping. Whenever she goes shopping it's always out of grim necessity. She refuses to admit that she stays awake nights dreaming up grim necessities that will necessitate further shopping trips. But once in a while the truth comes out.

There was a T-Way behind McDonald's. It was like a Zeller's or a Kresge's or a Miracle Mart or something like that. They're all the same.

But it was closed. It wouldn't open for another hour. It was still early, about nine. Joan was trying to hide her disappointment. It became clear to me that she'd wanted to go to McDonald's for breakfast simply because she knew there was a T-Way behind the restaurant.

"I've never been in a T-Way store before," she said, fighting back the tears.

"That's okay, neither have I," I said. "Tell me though…."

"What?"

"Have you ever heard of T-Way before?"

"No!" She sounded like a little girl. It was an awful moment in a woman's life. She wanted us to sit there in the car until the store opened.

"Joan, we'll probably see another further down the road." I was trying to be gentle. "We'd look pretty stupid, a family of Canadians sitting here for an hour waiting for the T-Way to open. People would think we had no class—while God knows we've got tons of class."

"You're right," she said bravely. "Let's go."

24. Dedicated to the McFadden Family of Ontario

We were heading north again. We were on the U.S. 13 that runs along the west shore of Saginaw Bay. To our right was the famous Interstate 75 that runs from Sault Ste. Marie, Michigan, to Miami, Florida, an expressway wide enough to be seen clearly from 40,000 feet in the air.

We were approaching the village of Pinconning which I guess had something to do with pine cones. You could see we were getting gradually into the north country. Coniferous trees were becoming more and more prominent.

I know this will be hard to believe but just then, magically, Joan flicked on the radio, got a local station, and we heard our names mentioned.

"This next song is dedicated to the McFadden Family of Ontario," said the announcer, "who are at this moment driving north along the U.S. 13. Have fun in Michigan, McFaddens, and get home safely, you hear?"

Joan and I looked at each other.

"How did they know about us?" said the kids.

"Well I'll be damned," said Joan.

"Somebody from home must have phoned them and asked them to say that," I said. I felt a little shell-shocked.

"But no one at home would have known we'd be here at this particular place at this particular time."

"That is kind of funny."

"And how did they know we'd flick on the radio at just that station at just that time?"

"I don't know, Joan."

It was a country song they played for us. The words went something like,

> *I know I won't have to die to know what bliss is,*
> *I know it whenever I feel your warm and tender kisses.*

I started turning the dial to see if we were going to be mentioned on other stations.

"No. Leave on that station," said Joan. "They may mention us again."

But there was no other mention.

"I wonder who it could have been," said Joan. "I just don't believe this. It's simply crazy."

"I guess it's just one of those things," I said philosophically.

25. The Screw Turned Around and Hit the Seahorse

We stopped at a roadside park near Pine River. There was a beautiful woods of pine, birch and maple. The forest floor was soft and spongy with dead leaves and pine needles, cones and dead branches, moss and lichens. A few unbroken Miller's High Life beer bottles lay around on the surface. I shuddered to think of what lay below. Human skeletons, old buses, rifles, abandoned railway tracks, ancient villages, vast middens—and eventually the molten core of the earth.

Pine River is the point where the U.S. 13 becomes U.S. 23 and starts heading east along the north shore of Saginaw Bay, and the Interstate 75 veers off northwest straight to the Canadian border. There was too much high-speed traffic on the road to let the senses open up and enjoy this lovely spot. There were no mushrooms around but I found three beautiful bird's eye fungi—*Crepidotus variabilis*—growing on a dead birch branch.

Joan was making tea when I got back. "This tea's undrinkable," she said.

"It must be the water." I told her about the fungi. She said she'd like to see them so I went back in the woods, managed to relocate the branch and brought it back. In just that time about three more cars had parked and the picnic area was crawling with people. All the men wore Farah Fawcett T-shirts.

A really noisy family set up at the picnic table nearest us. They were hollering things like: "If there's anything I hate it's a bread sandwich. Is that all we've got, bread sandwiches?...Guy pulling that great big boat...all of a sudden the screw turned and hit the seahorse."

"Joan," I said.

"Yes?"

"There was a lilac silk scarf attached to one of the trees in the woods. It was right on the edge of the woods, on the far side. You could see it from the farmhouse over there."

"Do you think it meant something?"

"I don't know. A yellow ribbon means waiting for a soldier to return. What would a lilac scarf mean?"

"I don't know. We'll have to ask the kids in the morning."

"They'll know for sure."

"Or make some very good guesses."

26. The House of Hate

We were heading into Tawas City, which Jennifer was going to have a reason to remember forever. I felt something on my face. I looked in the rearview mirror. It was a pimple.

"Look, kids. Remember that chocolate bar I ate yesterday? Now I've got a pimple. And I'm not even a teenager."

The kids moaned and groaned.

At that moment we passed a house, an ordinary-looking house, with a sign out front saying HOUSE OF HATE.

I saw the sign quite clearly, each letter as distinct as the pimple on your face, and that's what it said: HOUSE OF HATE. I turned to Joan.

"Did you see that sign?"

"What sign?"

"I wonder why that house would be called HOUSE OF HATE?"

"It said HOUSE FOR SALE, you dink. Can't you read?"

27. Bruce Bites Jennifer

Before I had time to respond we heard a fearsome animal growl in the back of the car followed by a scream. Bruce had bitten Jennifer.

Joan rushed back to have a look. "Oh God," she said. I pulled over. But suddenly there were cars everywhere and I was unable to stop. "It's pretty bad," Joan whispered in my ear.

There was some kind of arts festival in Tawas City and the place was crazy with festive merrymakers. Lake Huron sparkled in the bright sun. We pulled into a parking lot adjacent to what looked like the centre of festivities. Joan was covered with blood. "I think he's bitten off her nipple," she said. It was one of those moments. Jenny's eyes looked frightened. But she seemed to be more worried about what we were going to do to the dog.

"It's not the dog's fault," said Joan. "It's our fault for bringing him on this stupid trip. It must be driving him crazy driving driving all day long."

I looked at Jenny's wounds. I put my arm around her and gently pulled her hand away. Joan handed me a damp cloth. "Don't hurt, Daddy," said Jenny. I wiped away the blood. The nipple was still there. There were two ugly cuts, bites. They looked like fair-size stab wounds.

Joan took the kids to a park bench to rest while I went across the street to the police station to get directions to the hospital. When I got back some people were trying to push the van. I'd been blocking about eight cars.

28. Morbid Coincidences in the Waiting Room

Traffic was crawling along as in a nightmare where you can't move. We finally got to the stoplight, turned left, and went past the hospital without seeing it. We'd gone about two miles out of town before we realised we'd missed it. We turned around and finally spotted it, a low white building. We left Bruce tied up outside the car.

Jenny held the damp cloth against her chest as we sat in the waiting room. "I want to go straight home," said Joan. "What's the fastest way?"

"Probably the way we came," I said. "But we could take the Interstate 75 and then the 401 and be back by late tonight."

There was a good cross-section of mildly injured people in the waiting room.

"What's the matter with you?" a nurse said to a four-year-old who was holding his head.

"I fell on my Uncle Joe's chair," he said. "And here comes my Uncle Joe now. Hi, Uncle Joe."

There were three young women all with foot injuries. Sprained ankles, twisted toes, and so on. They were amused at the coincidence. I told them about the Christmas I cut my hand on an oyster knife and went to the hospital only to find three other guys in the waiting room of the emergency ward all with hands cut while trying to use oyster knives.

29. The Six-Dollar Lighter and the Signet Ring

Jennifer sat there waiting patiently with a serious look on her face. Joan became interested peripherally in a fifteen-year-old with a badly swollen hand. "He's really emotionally disturbed," she whispered. "Just look at his eyes. He should be committed."

The doctor came in with x-rays and told the fellow he had several broken bones in his hand. He said he should have come in when it first happened because the bones were beginning to knit and they'd have to break them over again. And because he'd just had a large meal they wouldn't be able to put him under. They took him away to the bone-crushing room.

I asked his father how the kid broke his hand.

"Fightin'. You wouldn't have a cigarette on you would you?" He came over and sat next to me. He was a boyish-looking forty, with long curly blond hair and a strong smell of shaving lotion. I gave him a cigarette and asked him why his son hadn't come to the hospital when it first happened.

"Ah, he's always comin' home with a swollen hand from some fight or another. It's nothin' new for him. He can't stop gittin' into fights. He takes after me."

I backed away a little.

"No, I don't get in fights any more but I sure had my share when I was a kid."

He told me his son had his best friend down on the ground and kept punching him in the head until he punched once too hard and he could hear bones snapping. At first he thought he'd broken his friend's head but then felt pain signalling it was his hand.

I couldn't figure out why his son would be beating up his best friend so viciously.

"He's got a vicious temper, that kid," said the father. "His friend just said somethin' he didn't like. He's always gittin' into fights. He's vicious like his mother. His mother's always flyin' off the handle. She's in the psychiatric hospital right now gittin' shock treatments. She's been in for six weeks."

After a while the kid came back with his arm in a cast. The doctor had told him he'd permanently damaged the knuckle on his left ring finger. Strangely enough his father was missing his left ring finger. He held the hand up. The finger was cut off clean at the hand. "Believe it or not I lost that finger sneakin' into a football game between the Green Bay Packers and the Detroit Lions in September, 1955," he said.

He said he was home on leave from the army and his girl friend gave him some money to go to the game. He went with a friend but half-way there they decided to buy four bottles of cheap wine with their ticket money and then sneak into the game and drink the wine in the stands. It was easy to sneak into football games in those days, he said. He said he used to do it all the time.

"While we were waitin' to be served in the liquor store I showed my buddy the six-dollar lighter my girlfriend had bought me. He started admirin' it and sayin' he wished he had one like it. Six bucks was a lot of money for a lighter in those days. Well, he had this beautiful signet ring and I told him I'd trade the lighter for the ring. So we traded.

"Then we got back to the stadium and he went over the fence and I went after him. When we got inside he said to me, Hey, your hand's bleedin'. I looked and sure enough there was a lot of blood spurtin' out. I figured I must have cut it on the barbed wire on top of the fence.

"Then he yelled out, Hey lookit, you've lost your finger. I got my eyes to focus properly and I saw this long, long tendon comin' out of my hand and danglin' down to the ground and there

145

on the end of it was my finger. I guess the ring must have caught on the barbed wire and just yanked my finger off when I dropped down. Honest to God, I didn't feel a thing.

"Then I'll be damned if my doctor wasn't in the stands. He took me to the hospital, put me to sleep, came back and finished watchin' the game then went back to the hospital and operated on my hand. Then that Christmas my mother bought me a beautiful ring. I said are you crazy? I'll never wear a ring again as long as I live. And I never have."

He was a little guy with a lopsided face. His mouth and eyes were somewhat out of line and his nose looked as if it had been broken several times. His son was really a good-looking kid though. The father bummed another cigarette off me then the two of them left. I told him it was a small price for a great story. "It was real nice talking to you," he said.

30. The National Lampoon

A guy named Dr. Swami sewed Jenny up. He had a heart-shaped birthmark between his eyes. It took just two stitches—one for each cut. He said the scars would go away. But by the look of them now, several months later, he should have used more stitches. The scars are raised and welt-like. They look as if they'll never go away. We rub Vitamin E cream on them every day.

I held Jenny's hand and looked into her nutbrown eyes as the needle went in and out. It wasn't the first time. There was the time she fell off her cousin's bicycle. She brought the bicycle home by herself, with her jaw broken in three places and covered in bloody wounds from head to toe.

"Daddy," she said. "I hurt myself."

I'll never forget sitting in the waiting room with Joan while Jenny's jaw was being wired up. There was a *National Lampoon* sitting on a table. The cover showed a human hand holding a human eye in its palm. I placed my hand over it so Joan wouldn't see it.

31. A Triple Blue Moon

Meanwhile, back in Tawas City. "What happened to her eye?" the nurse said. I looked. It was faintly discoloured.

"That must be where I hit her with the hair brush," I blurted out. "Right honey?" Jenny nodded.

The nurse was tall and white-haired. "Was it an accident?" she said. She was smiling. I guess it was her duty to check out possible child-beating cases.

"Half and half," I said.

Pretty soon we were back on the road heading toward Alpena. Joan decided she didn't want to go straight home after all. She wouldn't let me yell at the dog. "Bruce," I said. He cocked his ears. "You're a lucky dog. A lot of dogs have been shot for less than that." He cowered in the corner.

"Don't, Dave," said Joan.

We were between Oscoda and Greenbush. Lake Huron was still sparkling like a huge pool of 7-Up on our right. We were on the same latitude as Owen Sound, the base of the Bruce Peninsula. The sky was full of planes. Huge B-52 bombers from the nearby Paul B. Wurtsmith Air Force Base were flying around in circles in a pack. There must have been forty of them. It was the sort of thing you seldom see in Canada. Helicopters kept taking off with heart-stopping suddenness from behind little clumps of trees.

"Other than that how did you enjoy the Tawas City Arts Festival?" I asked Joan.

"I wish we could have seen it," she said. "Looked like some nice stuff there for sale."

"Like what?"

"Crafts and stuff."

"Wanna go back?"

"No thanks."

"Next year?"

"I don't think so."

"Never again?"

"Probably not."

We passed an ice cream place.

"Let's stop at the next ice cream place," said Joan. "We need a treat."

The next ice cream place was Jim's Jumbo Cones. Here's what the sign said:

JIM'S JUMBO CONES
CHOCOLATE MILKSHAKES
CHOCOLATE ICE CREAM
BANANA FUDGE DOUBLE MINT
SCOTCH NUT DOUBLE MINT
24 FANTASTIC FLAVORS BY MOODY

We went in. I meant to ask Jim why Double Mint was listed twice but Jim didn't seem to be there. They had unusual flavours like Blue Moon. A young woman standing next to me had a Triple Blue Moon. "What does that taste like?" I said.

"Have a bite." She held the cone under my nose so I didn't have much of a choice. I sunk my teeth in and got almost the whole top scoop.

"Yech, it's awful," I said, pretending I was retching. The kids laughed. I had blue moon all over my moustache. The young woman handed me a serviette. She was laughing too. "Thanks," I said. "I was just kidding. It tastes nice."

It was a funny little ice cream store. There were a couple having an argument about what flavours to get. "What are you getting buttered pecan for, you know you don't like that," the guy was saying to his wife.

"Just mind your own business," she snapped. "I'll get what I want."

When the guy ordered chocolate his wife said, "Why chocolate? You know you'll end up spilling it on your shirt and I'll never get the stain out."

"I'm not going to spill it on my shirt. I'm a grown man."

"You'd never know it sometimes."

A girl about Alison's age got a black ice cream cone. "What is that," I said.

"It's licorice."

She accidentally touched her bare leg with it. The shock of the cold ice cream on her warm flesh made her jump a little and the ice cream fell out of the cone and landed on the floor in a big black blob.

Outside the ice-cream store there was a van exactly like ours, same colour, same model, same year, and with Ontario licence plates. The driver was from Guelph. He too was taking a trip around Lake Huron. He was travelling with his son. The father had an English accent, the son a Canadian. He told me he'd bought the van in June, 1974—the same time we did. He'd gone 62,000 miles compared with our 60,000. His was in a lot better shape though.

32. If You Don't Bellow You Must Be Yellow

In provincial parks in Southern Ontario you have all these helpful students who fill you in on the natural history of the area. Sometimes they even have nature walks at night and show films about whooping cranes and black bears and winter storms.

There's not much of that in the Michigan state parks though. We were getting into the northern part of Michigan, the part that Ernest Hemingway liked to write about when he was young. We told the guy at the entrance to Hoeft State Park, on the shore of Lake Huron just outside Rogers City, that we were interested in mushrooms.

"They're out of season," he said. He handed us a pamphlet with some pictures of various morels. "Morels are the only ones I know of that are edible and you can just get them in the spring." So there you go. I decided against trying to enlighten him. He didn't have the appearance of one who would take kindly to that.

The other campers at Hoeft made us wonder. You could buy a Rolls Royce or two for the money they threw into their huge Winnebagos, and they'd never have to buy another car again as long as they lived. These so-called recreational vehicles are bigger than houses and about as easy to drive.

Sometimes these camping families would go for walks around the campgrounds but they'd only walk on the gravel roads. They wouldn't think of walking in the woods. The women have beautiful hairdos, high heels, pastel pantsuits in fabulous synthetic fabrics, and their faces are caked with makeup, lipstick and eye shadow. They have TVs in their RVs, and they carry immense teddy bears and portable radios when they go for walks. And they always talk loud so you can hear their ordinary conversation three campsites away. Apparently talking quietly is considered unamerican, and one who so indulges could be accidentally taken to be a spy and shot. "Pass the salt, please," they scream at whoever is sitting next to them and you can hear them on the other side of the woods, over the sand dunes by the water, and even out on the loading pier at Rogers City sometimes.

Turncoats, saboteurs, conspirators and Communists talk quietly. If you don't bellow you must be yellow. You must have something to hide. And we don't like that around these parts.

33. A Family Discussion at the Edge of the Woods

The McFadden family was sitting at their picnic bench talking quietly. We were worrying about what to do with Bruce.

"Maybe we should send him to a stud farm for West Highland white terriers," I suggested.

"That's not fair to me," said Alison. After all, she hadn't been bitten.

"I'll never be happy again as long as I live if you do that," said Jennifer.

"If he ever bites Jennifer again or anyone else," said Joan, "pphht!" She drew her hand across her throat.

It seemed funny that several times he'd nipped at Jennifer, although this was the first time he'd ever drawn blood. "Daddy," said Jennifer. "He nips a lot when he's just playing but he's just playing. It doesn't hurt."

We were drinking tea. Bruce was sleeping on the grass under the van. It would have been cooler under the trees, but he had his own reasons for being under the van. We had a nice spot at the edge of the woods. If you walked through the woods you came over a little hill that turns out to be a grassy sand dune and there you are on the beach of Lake Huron.

"I had a little dog named Sniffy when I was a little girl," said Joan. The kids listened intently. "One day a kid on the street kicked him. And Sniffy never forgot it. Until the day he died every time that kid came by Sniffy tried to bite him."

"Did he ever bite him?" said Alison. Good question.

"No. But he was always trying to."

"I never kicked Bruce or anything like that," said Jenny.

34. A Funny Noise Like a Flute

Across from us was one of those Winnebagos. The owner was walking around his campsite swatting flies. Swatting flies out of doors may not make much sense to you, in fact it may seem to you the sign of a weak mind, but in Michigan it's the national sport of campers.

This guy was wearing a flowery hat, flowery shirt, baggy shorts that came below his knee, short white socks, and black oxfords. His Winnebago was part of a Camper Caravan. The spare tire cover said HAPPY BIRTHDAY AMERICA FROM EUCALYPTUS, KENTUCKY. The guy had a curly beard. He started belting out a song as he continued swatting flies.

"When it's cherry blossom time in New Jersey," he sang, "we'll have a peach of a time."

The guy at the next campsite yelled out, "You better not sing any more of that one, Les. There's kids about."

"Oh, I forgot," said Les. "The second verse is even worse." He was so pleased he forgot to swat flies.

The other guy yelled back, "You're a poet and don't know it but your feet show it, they're long fellows." It was nice to see people having fun. There's a movie with Rodney Dangerfield in a hot tub with a bunch of undergrads in bikinis. One says she's majoring in nineteenth-century American literature. "Maybe you can help me straighten out my Longfellow," says Rodney.

Every once in a while Jennifer would slip into the woods by herself. It was only a couple of hours since she'd been bitten. I guess she was still suffering from shock. Why doesn't Bruce like me? She seemed to be mulling the question over.

Suddenly she ran out of the woods. "I saw a big raccoon," she said. Her eyes were as black as space.

"Did he bite you?" said Alison. She usually isn't that cruel.

"No," said Jennifer, still too innocent to notice sarcasm. "It didn't see me, I guess. It just stood there really still."

The next time she came out of the woods she'd seen a brown and white rabbit and a squirrel.

"Did they bite you?" said Alison.

"No. They ran away as soon as they saw me." She showed me a large red berry. "Is this a wild radish?" she said. She stood close to me as I inspected it, and she whispered, "When the raccoon ran away he made a funny noise like a flute."

"I thought you said he just sat there."

"He did at first. I was taking little tiny steps up behind him and when I was this close he looked up at me and ran away and he made a funny noise like a flute."

The two of us went for a walk. We found some fairy clubs. Bright yellow club-shaped fungi that grow about an inch out of the ground. We ate some but Jenny didn't like them. "Let's leave them for the fairies," she said.

We went running down to the lake. Jenny tripped over an exposed root and fell down the sand dune. There was no one at all on the beach. Far out you could see lakers steaming into Rogers City to pick up loads of limestone.

On the way back Jenny made a little collection of mushrooms and berries. "I want to be a botanist when I grow up," she said. She asked if I would buy her a wildflower guide book.

35. Unamerican to Pick Mushrooms

On one side of us were three guys in their early twenties. They had a red Chevy van with a large blue tent. I wondered why they were camping in a place like this rather than in some wilderness area.

On the other side were two girls. They had a grey Pinto and two small blue tents. They were reading movie magazines and listening to schmaltzy music on the radio. They were fat and pimply. They were sunning themselves on blankets and eating potato chips.

Joan and I walked through the woods to the highway where there was a store. We went in and bought some postcards and sent them to friends at home.

One of the cards had a photo of the hospital at Tawas City. We wrote on it: "Thank heavens for hospitals. We're having a hard time identifying mushrooms around here." We didn't mention the dog bite. It occurred to us we were quite a bit further north than Hamilton, so we wrote on another card: "How are things down in Canada?" Hilarious.

We bought stamps and asked the guy where the mailbox was. "It's right here," he said, holding out his hand.

We handed the cards to him. "Don't read them, now," I said.

"I get so many of these I'd never get the chance to read them all," he said.

I had a little basket full of mushrooms I'd picked in the woods. I was going to take them back to the campsite, take spore prints, and try to identify them. Some of them were quite beautiful. Striking colours. I rested them on the counter. The guy ignored them.

Three hitch-hikers came in and bought a six-pack of beer.

I couldn't understand why everyone was ignoring the mushrooms. They looked so lovely sitting there, just crying to be noticed. I guess it's considered unamerican to pick mushrooms. Out of season, as the conservation officers would say.

36. The Difference Between a Mushroom and a Toadstool

I just couldn't understand this park—people sitting around their Winnebagos playing cards, swatting flies, yelling.

"Tomorrow's Sunday and the next day's bloody Monday," one guy yelled out for no apparent reason.

His wife was sitting right next to him. "Now you sound like Bobby," she yelled back at the top of her lungs. Her voice went ringing through the woods. No wonder there were no birds. It's amazing the trees didn't die.

A pack of joggers went by on the gravel road. They were wearing headbands, T-shirts, gym shorts and Adidas running shoes.

Joan wanted to dig up some young pine trees and take them home. "They look so beautiful, and no one ever walks through the woods here," she said. "They don't even jog through."

I walked up to one of the conservation officers. He was wearing an important-looking blue uniform. I wanted to ask him if he could identify a mushroom I found. It was a *Lactarius deliciosus*, considered edible and choice as you can tell from the name, but I didn't let on I knew. "Do you know what this is?" I said.

He examined the specimen closely then handed it back to me. "That's a toadstool," he pronounced, with quiet pride.

"Oh, a toadstool! What's the difference between a mushroom and a toadstool?"

He was completely sure of himself. "You can eat a mushroom but a toadstool is poisonous." He glanced at his fingernails.

37. The Trees at the Edge of the Woods

That night, the bearded guy in shorts, the one who'd been singing the allegedly lewd song about blossom time in New Jersey, sneaked over to our side to introduce himself to the two girls camping on our right. They were bored with him after about thirty seconds and did nothing to encourage him but he went on and on. They sat there listening and he stood there talking. There seemed to be a lot of tension under his words as if he wanted to ask them something but was too shy. Joan and I pretended we weren't listening. But it was hard not to.

"Oh, I've got a wonderful wife," he was saying. He had a florid complexion under his beard. "Love is so important in life." I had the notion he was about to tell them that his wife had a bad back and couldn't make love any more, and would they mind if he....

But no. "You'll find out when you get older," he said. "To love someone without any selfish motives is the best thing life has to offer." Buried in that last line like a hook in a worm was the information that his wife gives him nothing in return for all the unselfish love he gives her.

He went on and on with his hard-won philosophy of life. He thought he was really roughing it in the northern woods in his $100,000 Winnebago.

"I've been camping ever since my oldest son was born and that was 1952," he said. "Every weekend my wife picks me up at work and we drive straight to the campgrounds."

I could read his mind. He desperately wanted the girls to say something, to ask him where he worked, where he lived. But he was out of luck.

"It's what you know about camping that's important," he kept saying over and over. "If you don't know anything about camping you'll go home miserable," he said. "If you know about it you'll always have a wonderful time." Buried in that statement was the information that he knew a lot about camping and would be willing to impart his knowledge to them if only they'd ask—otherwise they might just go home miserable.

One of the girls started turning the dial on her radio. The other yawned audibly. We had our backs to them. I thought the guy was going to start quoting from the Bible.

"One time I remember it rained three days straight and the porch started to sink in the mud...."

I couldn't stand it any more. I gathered up some kindling wood and had a fire blazing away in about ninety seconds. The flames leaped into the sky and cast fantastic shadows on the trees at the edge of the woods. It was dark. The kids had their pyjamas on.

38. A Beautiful Woman Spurned

Earlier I noticed a stunningly beautiful young woman riding along the gravel paths on her bicycle. As the fire died down Joan and I were getting ready for bed when we noticed the girl had dropped in on the three guys camping on our left. She was something off the cover of *Oui Magazine*. Lucky guys.

We got under the covers and listened to their conversation. There was an open screen on the side of the canvas facing them. I thought an electric storm was coming over the horizon but it was just the girl taking flash photos of the guys in the dark.

"I haven't met such funky guys in a long time," she said.

"Yeah," said the guys. They didn't seem funky to me. They seemed sort of slow-witted. But who am I? Merely the invisible one, as always.

"Well," said the girl. "I'm too tired to walk back to my tent. Why don't I just stay with you guys tonight?"

"Ah, I don't know," said one of the guys.

"Okay then," she said, a little hurt. "I'll walk home. See ya."

Joan turned in the darkness. "She's awfully tired, Joan," I said. "Should I run after her and tell her she can sleep with us tonight?"

"No thank you!"

"Ah, that's cruel. Come on, Joan."

"No!"

39. Grapefruit

Sometimes when you've had a Dramatic Insight into the Nature of Things and you try to describe it to others you suddenly realise it was neither dramatic nor insightful at all. You can tell by the look of boredom on your listener's face. But when you're a writer you're free to imagine the look on your reader's face and although I know this won't sound very dramatic at all it struck me as being a Dramatic Insight at the time.

As I was falling asleep the immense futility of all the great emotional crises of our lives hit me right smack in the face. It sort of exploded under my nose like an exploding cream pie. Ah, so that's it! That was my reaction. It's really all so easy. Look how difficult we make it for ourselves.

In a flash I saw that the whole story of the human race was a fairy tale and we were little magic fairies. Three billion of us. Four billion by the time you read this. Five billion by the time the second edition comes out.

We're born and die in a flash, and in that small duration for some inexplicable reason instead of merely enjoying our brief lives we have to take on all the weight of the universe. Each little life thinks it's the centre of the universe and is responsible for everything that happens.

With that realisation a weight slipped off my shoulders. In the corresponding vision I could see the world about the size of a grapefruit. It was covered with tiny lights, three billion of them, each one tremendously worried about its place on the skin of things.

And as I watched the number of lights kept expanding and the grapefruit slowly turned rotten and decayed before my eyes.

SUNDAY, AUGUST 7

40. Vaseline

The washroom was crowded. It was U-shaped with a row of flush toilets, a row of sinks with mirrors, and a row of steaming showers. It was all very luxurious.

All of the showers were in use. I slipped in front of a vacant sink and looked at myself. It was a grey morning and there's something particularly bleak about a men's public washroom on a grey morning in the U.S.A. Everyone was so business-like. No one spoke. Everyone had his own universe in front of him and was hanging on like a lamprey to a pike.

The guy on my right was grey-haired and in his fifties. He had a Velikovsky paperback in his back pocket. I felt guilty for having looked. No one was looking at anyone but himself, in the mirror. This was the U.S.A. on a bleak morning.

I remembered the dream I'd had an hour earlier. I was at home typing out a book of poems and Ezra Pound walked in. He picked up my manuscript and started making changes.

When I got back to the van Joan looked sad. "I'm homesick for Canada," she said.

"We'll be crossing back into Canada tomorrow," I said.

She began telling me about a conversation she'd overheard in the women's washroom. "A woman from one of those Jesus big Winnebagos was in there with a huge case of cosmetics. She was putting Vaseline on her elbows. Why would anyone on a camping trip put Vaseline on her elbows? She was putting it on her eyes too, on her eyelashes, eyelids, ears, throat...."

"I don't know. Maybe in a few years it'll be unthinkable to wake up in the morning without covering yourself with a coat of grease. After all, brushing your teeth in the morning is a relatively new invention."

"And there was another woman there talking to her. She was saying, 'Well, it was just a terrible way to find out. It was really shocking. You know the State Troopers won't tell you.' The woman kept putting on Vaseline. She had a suitcase full of little jars of things. She said, 'Well I know, but I didn't feel it was my place to tell you.' Then the other woman said, 'Well I wish she hadn't told me. It was a terrible way to find out.' I wish I'd heard the whole conversation. Now I'll never know what they were talking about."

Joan was eating a fried egg. She likes to trim all the white first and nibbles away at it until there's nothing left but a fat golden yoke which she scoops up without breaking and pops into her mouth whole. She got that from me. I got it from Saul Bellow.

"It sounds to me," I declared, "as if they were trying to make a big tragedy out of nothing."

Just then I looked up and there was Jennifer standing on the edge of the woods with a plate in her hand. As I watched she tossed her egg into the woods.

"What did you do that for?" I said.

"I thought the raccoon might be hungry."

My heart sputtered a little then started beating again.

41. Time Warp

Joan and I wanted to drive into town to get some gas and just generally be by ourselves for an hour, so we very unwisely and totally uncharacteristically left the kids by themselves. We pulled into Rogers City where the world's largest limestone quarry was located. Neither of us felt like visiting the quarry. It was too touristy a thing to do, even for us.

The price of gas was increasing as rapidly in the U.S.A. as in Canada. It was marked at 80.0 cents a gallon on this pump. While the guy was filling the tank Joan and I decided to go into a public library that was located behind the station. It seemed to be an odd place for a public library.

Actually it was quite a large and spiffy library for a building that looked so small and rundown from the exterior. You walked up the stairs then turned to the right. The walls were made of glass and there were glass tables with plants on them. The library was actually on the second and third floors of the building. I'm not sure what was on the first floor. Maybe some offices.

There seemed to be something familiar about the library, as if I'd been there before, but I knew I hadn't. It was only later I realised that it was similar in structure to a library that has appeared frequently in my dreams through the years.

We didn't have much time to spend in the library. We looked at a display of new books then looked at each other in astonishment. What a hick place Northern Michigan was. All these so-called new books were ten years old. Strange.

When we went back outside I realised, with a sickening feeling in my stomach, that something immensely disturbing had occurred, a cosmic event of unprecedented grandeur. The pumps, the front of the building, the street, everything looked newer somehow than it had a few minutes earlier. The trees looked smaller, and where no trees were a moment ago there were now huge trees. Everything looked cleaner.

The gas was now marked at 38.9 cents a gallon. Less than half what it had been a few minutes earlier.

"We've gone back in time," I said to Joan.

"I know," she said, calmly. She was standing in a very rigid manner, as if afraid to move. So was I.

"We've gone back to 1967. Look at the cars. Look at the licence plates. Even the gas station operator looks ten years younger."

"Never seen a van like this before," the guy was saying. I was hoping he wouldn't notice the 1977 licence plates.

"It's the new Volkswagen camper," I said. I didn't feel alarmed. Joan seemed okay too. My mind just plodded along as normal. "I guess you can't get them in the States yet. They're just trying them out in Canada." I could see he was puzzled. He was thinking to himself, "If it's so new how come it's developing rust spots already?"

I had a feeling we were going to be plugged back into 1977 any moment and it occurred to me we should try to get to a bookstore and buy some first editions. Too bad we weren't in Canada. I didn't know much about American books.

We paid the guy then parked the car and went for a walk. The town had changed incredibly in ten years. Everywhere we looked there were proud buildings from the turn of the century. They hadn't been standing a few minutes earlier. Cheap chain restaurants and muffler shops had lined the main street.

Even the town hall had been torn down. It was a tall Gothic stone structure with a clock. We couldn't find a bookstore. When we got back to the gas station we were back in 1977. The guy looked at us as we got in the van.

"Weren't you people through here before about ten years ago?" he said.

"Yes, we were," I said. "You must remember the van. You made quite a fuss about it at the time."

"Yes, I certainly did," he said. "It was the first time I'd seen anything like it, with the pop-top and all. Now they're all over the place. This couldn't be the same one, could it?"

"No. That rusted out so badly we had to get rid of it. And we bought another just like it."

The funny thing about the whole experience was the change in Joan.

"I like you better now," I said.

"I liked you better then," she replied.

42. Thievery in Canada

On the way back to the campsite Joan began getting nervous and so did I.

"We shouldn't have left the kids there alone," she said.

"I know." My anxiety levels were skyrocketing. "It was insane of us. We should be shot for this."

When we arrived the kids were talking to a couple of campers. A man and his wife.

"Your kids were telling us their life story," said the woman. She was in her late fifties and beautiful. A thin, elegant looking woman. The kids sat there without smiling. They looked kind of subdued as if this couple had been boring them, maybe asking them if they had accepted the Lord Jesus Christ as their Personal Saviour and all that.

But no, the husband was a fat guy with no chin. He wanted to know if we'd visited the world's largest limestone quarry in Rogers City. I felt guilty about admitting we hadn't. W.H. Auden and Christopher Dewdney would have been terribly disappointed in us.

"We went yesterday," said the chinless guy. "We were lucky, real lucky. A quarry employee was up in the lookout with us and explained the whole thing. They have the world's largest shovel there. Eighteen yards. You can drive a car into it and turn it around."

"A full-sized American car?"

"Yes sir. A Cadillac!"

They knew we were Canadians and seemed to think we were in Michigan because we prefer camping in the United States to camping in Canada, as if we thought the facilities were better or something. They just naturally assumed that.

They wanted to know if we'd ever been in Huntsville, Ontario.

"It's a nice place," said the woman. "We used to camp on the French River but we had some unpleasant experiences with thievery in Canada. So we sold our camping trailer and bought a big Winnebago. We just go to the state parks in Michigan now."

"Yeah," I said. "Canada is full of thieves."

Joan started laughing. The couple looked a little confused. "He's just fooling," said Joan. "We've been camping in Canada for years and we've never had anything stolen."

"But you must remember, dear," I said. "We're not Americans."

"Yes, that's true," said Joan.

The couple looked confused again.

43. The Black Killer

Then we got talking to the three funky fellers who'd been visited by, and ultimately (and wisely, no doubt) spurned, the beautiful horny woman the night before. They were from Detroit.

The girl was right. They were funky. You could tell by the way they dressed, the way they talked and the music they listened to that they were hip.

They told me about the Black Killer who lurks in their neighbourhood. They said they were always getting mugged. One had been beaten up at work by black fellow workers. Another said he was playing baseball with some friends when they were attacked by a bunch of blacks swinging baseball bats.

"It's pretty bad where we live," they said. "We try to keep our place in shape but the blacks, when the front of their house falls down, why they just move to the back. It makes you kind of prejudiced."

They wanted to know what we were doing in Michigan. I told them about wanting to go around each of the Great Lakes. They were unusually curious about us, and they thought that was a fabulous idea. So I told them I wanted to write a book about each of the lakes.

"Hey, that's really cool," they said.

I didn't ask them about the girl. Maybe they were afraid she was going to steal their cocaine.

44. For Those without Sunday Clothes

We stopped at the gatehouse on the way out of P.H. Hoeft State Park. A big shining new Cadillac was parked there with a smiling fat fellow in a clerical collar sitting in it. He was a Lutheran minister and he was looking for a family of campers. He had to deliver a message of mercy. Someone had died. I hoped it wasn't someone from Detroit killed by the Black Killer. It was Sunday morning.

"I suppose you're going to church," he said when he saw us getting ready to leave.

"Not bloody likely," I said. He just smiled. He said he was conducting a drive-in church service at one o'clock for "those without Sunday clothes or who have trouble getting in and out of their cars."

45. Charles Sangster, Canadian Poet

We were back on the U.S. 23 heading northwest, skirting the shore of Lake Huron. At one point we could see four Great Lakes steamers steaming into Rogers City to pick up loads of limestone to deliver to steel mills all around the lakes.

I swerved to avoid hitting a porcupine. Then we passed a dead porcupine. You could tell by the tire tracks that some motorist had deliberately crossed the centre line to hit it. I shuddered to think we were sharing the road with idiots like that.

Alison was being nice to Jennifer. "See this ball, Daddy," she said. "Jennifer bought it for Bruce with her last fifty cents."

I got all choked up and asked Jennifer to come up to the front.

"That was very nice of you, Jennifer," I said. "But listen, honey. Don't get close to Bruce until we find out what's the matter with him. Okay?"

"Okay, Daddy."

Joan got the Lutheran minister's drive-in service on the radio. She said she wanted to see if he mentioned us as an example of Canadian heathens. But it got too boring and we turned it off.

We were driving through virgin forest. Thick pine and birch, no development, just a perfect highway cutting through a section of this continent that has been left as it always was. It was so beautiful I put on our eight-track tape of Beethoven's Ninth Symphony as performed by the Berlin Philharmonic conducted by Herbert von Karajan. The last time I'd played it was the summer before as we drove along the glorious Matapedia River in Quebec.

There was a Michigan Registered Historic Site at the side of the road. The plaque said: "Much of the shore is still as wild as when the Huron Indians were the only travellers on this lake."

We walked along the wave-zoned shore. It was quite dreamy. Huge bleached pieces of driftwood had been left high and dry. The beach was about ten feet wide at this point. Behind it was another ten feet of tall grass and then the highway. On the other side of the highway the forest began. There were no cars on the road. Everything was grey and misty.

And silent. There seemed to be a mystical silence that swept through the four of us as if we had never been born. I'd been reading the amazingly derivative Canadian poet Charles Sangster (1822-1893):

> *The feet*
> *Of the Red Man have pressed each wave-zoned shore,*
> *And many an eye of beauty oft did greet*
> *The painted warriors and their birchen fleet,*
> *As they returned with trophies of the slain.*

There were no boats on the lake. Bruce was running free. He took a drink from the lake. We walked for about half a mile and then it started to rain.

Back on the road we passed a sign stating this was the Black Lake State Forest. Occasional large homes had been built on lots cut out of the forest and real-estate signs began to proliferate.

One of the homes had a sign out front saying BEER CAN COLLECTION—BUY, SELL OR TRADE.

46. The Home of Chicago Steaks

Cheboygan is at the top of Michigan's Lower Peninsula, a little southwest of the Straits of Mackinac. If you fly CP Air from Winnipeg to Toronto you fly right over this area, unless you very nicely ask the pilot to fly over Canadian territory all the way.

A large sign on the outskirts of Cheboygan proclaims the town is the Home Port of the Icebreaker *Mackinaw*. Cheboygan's not much bigger than Rogers City and even though it can't boast the world's largest limestone quarry and the world's largest shovel it's a little better known than Rogers City maybe because Cheboygan is a more-interesting name than Rogers City.

It's a nice town with a northern feel about it. It's the Yellowknife of the U.S.A., though there are no signs to that effect, none we saw at any rate. We parked on the main street in front of Wretched's Donut Shop (closed till further notice). We passed Cliff's Live Baits then decided to get something to eat. We went into the Carnation, Home of Chicago Steaks. A sign painted on the window said SINCE 1925—PICK YOUR OWN STEAKS.

"Do we go in the back to pick our own steaks?"

"Oh, they don't do that anymore," said the waitress. She said that was discontinued when the restaurant was remodelled years ago.

"You been here that long?"

"Sometimes it feels that way."

47. If You Seek a Pleasant Peninsula

If you seek a pleasant peninsula...look about you. That is the official motto of the state of Michigan.

The official bird of the state of Michigan is the robin.

The official gem of the state of Michigan is the Isle Royale greenstone.

The official stone of the state of Michigan is the petoskey.

Michigan even has an official fish. It's the trout.

Its official tree is the white pine.

Its official flower is the apple blossom.

48. Songs of the American Railroad Man

Across from the Carnation was a beautifully maintained old building called the Steffins Block, dated 1904. There were four ground-floor stores including the Log Mark, a bookstore and news depot, closed for Sunday. There was a little sign on the door at foot level reading KICK GENTLY HERE.

I looked through the window. Prominently displayed was a book called *Cheboygan—From the Heart* by Jim Cohoe. The title would later be appropriated by no less than an actual Canadian prime minister, Jean Chrétien, for his autobiography, though the word "Cheboygan" was wisely dropped.

There was a photocopy machine and rustic pine display of racks and tables. There were several colour portraits by the local photographer Martha Olechowski.

There was a book of photographs called *Yesterday's Detroit* by Frank Angst, and a biography called *Chief Wawatam—The Story of a Hand-Bomber* by Frances D. Burgtorf. *Isle Royale Shipwrecks* by Frederick Stonehouse, despite its depressing title, had a beautiful cover drawing of an old excursion steamer going down in Lake Superior, with people on deck praying and/or pushing others out of the way to get aboard a lifeboat. *Wood Butchers of the North* by Ellis Olson featured a cover illustration of various brands used by loggers. I guess they'd be called log marks and that's probably where the store got its name.

Regionalism was strong in Cheboygan. Also on display were all three volumes of *Michigan Ghost Towns of the Upper Peninsula*, and *A Treasury of Railroad Folklore: The Stories, Tall Tales, Traditions, Ballads and Songs of the American Railroad Man* edited by B. A. Botkin and Alvin F. Harlow. I said a little prayer that maybe someday *A Trip Around Lake Huron* would be available in the Log Mark.

49. Bliss Carman and the Call of the Wild

Bombing out of Cheboygan we passed a roadside park dedicated "in honour of the great American poet, Bliss Carman (1861-1929)." There was a little plaque telling about Bliss and his work but it didn't mention that he was born and educated in Canada and is known in Canada as a Canadian poet, though it is true that he spent many years in the U.S.A. According to H.P. Gundy, in *The Canadian Encyclopaedia*, Carman worked for the *New York Independent*, "introducing Canadian poets to its readers." Gundy adds that Carman "achieved in his best verse a few finely wrought lyrics of enduring quality."

This reminded me of the plaque in Sandusky, Ohio, which contains Col. John McCrae's "In Flanders Fields" without mentioning that McCrae (1872-1918) was a Canadian and served as a medic with the Canadian Army.

There was a phone booth in the park and the phone was ringing. Since I was standing next to it I decided to answer it even though I was pretty sure it wouldn't be for me.

It was a high-pitched voice. The woman sounded a little drunk. "This is Reenie. How's your weenie?"

"I beg your pardon?" My first obscene phone call and it was in verse. What would Bliss have thought?

"Whatcha doin', you silly ol' pervert? Playin' witcher pecker?"

I hung up.

A few miles further on we stopped at The Call of the Wild, a roadside tourist trap. It was a strange-looking building, plaster sculpted and painted in two tones of brown presumably to resemble a cave or maybe a mountain. There was a stuffed bull moose standing on top of the building and on each side of him was a thirty-foot flagpole, one flying the Stars and Stripes and the other the flag of Michigan.

A woman at the door was taking admission. Two bucks for adults and seventy-five cents for kids. Joan and Alison decided to save their money but Jennifer wanted to see the animals so I gave the woman $2.75.

The woman had a high-pitched voice and was quite merry, as if she had a bottle of gin stashed under the counter. Her name was Irene.

"Do people ever call you Reenie?"

"Sure. Everybody calls me Reenie, but my real name is Madame Irene."

"Excuse me for bringing this up, but I just got an obscene phone call and...."

"An obscene phone call? You?"

"Yeah. What's the matter with that?"

"Nothing at all, believe me."

"It was at a pay phone at the Bliss Carman Memorial Roadside Park."

"Far out!"

"And the girl sounded a little like you. In fact she sounded a lot like you. What's more, she said her name was Reenie!"

"It wasn't me, dear. This Reenie ain't into obscene phone calls. Not yet anyway."

"You want to know what she said?"

"Yeah. Let's hear it, pussycat."

"She said, 'This is Reenie, how's your weenie?'"

"Oh, no. It wasn't me, dear. If I wanted to know how your weenie was I'd just pull it out and look at it."

50. Actually Experiencing the Call of the Wild

The place was full of stuffed animals. It was grotesque and I felt I shouldn't have brought Jenny in. She was silent and wide-eyed as she looked at a pair of snowy owls, one at rest and one with wings spread as if about to take off, mounted on the tops of dead stumps. Since the snowy owl is seldom found south of the forty-ninth parallel it occurred to me the pair must have been shot north of the border.

The black bear was wired to stand up straight on its hind legs. I wondered what our reaction would be if some time in the future the bears take over the world and put stuffed humans on display.

"That would be awful, Daddy." Jennifer had such a serious look on her face.

There were speakers all over the place blasting out tapes of owls hooting, wolves howling, bears growling, and so on. There was even a poetry nook where you could buy cheaply printed pamphlets of nature verse by such American poets as Bliss Carman, Archibald Lampman, and so on.

A beautiful deer specimen was mounted and placed in such a position that it looked as if the front part of its body were running and the hindquarters stationary. Its head was turned straight at the viewer. It was standing in front of a mural depicting a highway cutting through a pine forest. The centre line of the highway continued out on the floor beneath the deer's feet. It looked as if it had been startled by a car and was about to be hit.

"Can we go now, Daddy?"

"Don't you like this place?"

"It gives me the creeps."

"Okay. Let's go."

On the way out was a sign saying CALL OF THE WILD IS AIR-CONDITIONED AND COMFORT-ABLE IN ANY KIND OF WEATHER.

In Kenora, Ontario, there is a stuffed bear dressed up like Santa Claus. It's in the window of a hardware store next to the bus terminal. It's about three feet tall, standing on its hind legs. It's dressed in a red cap, glasses, and a false beard.

51. Hart Crane, Canadian Poet

Mackinaw City looks a little like Banff or Jasper without the mountains. In the summer it's jammed with people who wander aimlessly in and out of restaurants and gift shops and penny arcades. We stopped at Lookout Point under the southern end of the spectacular Mackinac Bridge which spans the Straits of Mackinac where Lake Michigan for the past couple of millennia had been ejaculating its waters into Lake Huron under a solemn New World sky. Once, in Vancouver, a Native Indian stopped and asked if I could direct him to the New World. Turned out he meant the New World Hotel on Powell Street.

Because of the problem with the dog we'd already decided not to bother visiting Fort Michilimackinac. It's actually on the Lake Michigan side and we figured it'd be best to leave it until we took our trip around Lake Michigan.

We got out of the car and put quarters into the coin-operated telescope and took turns peering out at the straits and at the lake steamers, yachts, ferry boats, sailboats, barges, and the occasional canoe all passing through and at the cars and trucks streaming across the bridge high overhead.

Then we looked at Mackinac Island where the Canadian poet Hart Crane spent so many summers as a child. The incredible summer homes of rich Americans, the Governor's Mansion, the Grand Hotel with its mile-long porch shimmering in the haze. I know Hart Crane wasn't really a Canadian just as John McCrae and Bliss Carman weren't really Americans. Mind you, a Canadian, like a Mexican or a Bolivian and so on, is always an American, while an American is very seldom a Canadian.

Mackinac Island from this angle looked more highly developed than the mainland, although cars weren't allowed on the island. Travel was by foot, horseback and bicycle. To the south of Mackinac was the much larger but less highly developed Bois Blanc Island. The high cliffs of Mackinac Island made me think it was connected somehow with the Niagara Escarpment and it almost certainly is. What we know as the Niagara Escarpment is really just the rim of one side of a saucer-shaped geological depression, the other side cutting through Minnesota. But it's not as noticeable on the U.S.A. side because there hasn't been the same kind of glacial erosion working away on it.

With its churches, huge hotels, chalets, castles, old houses, mansions, Mackinac Island looked like Quebec City with touches of Monaco. I kept thinking of Hart Crane.

"That bloody Hart Crane never did a day's work in his life," I said, with mock annoyance.

"Is he still alive?" Joan thought maybe he would be an old man living alone in a suite of rooms on the top floor of one of those hotels.

"No. He drowned himself. Jumped off a cruise ship in the Caribbean."

"What did his father do?"

"He was a candy manufacturer. He made Life Savers. In fact he invented them."

"Life Savers? There you go. He did it to spite his father. His father invented Life Savers but couldn't save his son's life."

"Yeah."

We drove over to the ferry landing and got out of the car. It was busy. Ferries for the island were leaving every few minutes, loaded with tourists. I wanted to go over to the island but Joan was worrying.

"Let's not push our luck with the dog. It's really asking a lot of him. What if he bites somebody on the boat?"

"Yeah. He's tasted blood now."

"Tsk. You're being unfair to the dog. He's sick. Look at him shivering. He's just not feeling right. Remember how sick you were when you had your gallbladder operation?"

We decided to postpone our trip to Mackinac Island indefinitely.

"It'll give my readers something to look forward to."

"Yeah. All twelve of them."

"But twelve good ones."

Joan picked up the dog and put him back in the van.

"Look. He's cringing. He's just not feeling well. He's really tired and lagging and it's not even that hot out. We'll board him out next year when we take our trip around Lake Michigan. And we'll not only visit Mackinac Island, we'll stay the night at the Grand Hotel." Joan was talking big because she was due to start a steady teaching job in September.

"It's a deal," I said. "And we'll probably have more money next year."

"Yes," said Joan, ominously. "If we're still together."

52. What We Said While Crossing the World's Largest Suspension Bridge

To be reminded that something is the world's greatest or the world's largest or the world's sweetest or whatever takes away the pleasure of enjoying it. We'd bypassed the world's largest limestone quarry and the world's largest shovel in Rogers City and Bruce's illness prevented us from visiting Mackinac Island and seeing the world's largest summer hotel with the world's longest porch. But we couldn't avoid going over the world's largest suspension bridge which we were doing right now. The Mackinac Bridge. You can see it when you look down from the CP Air flight from Winnipeg to Toronto. It looks like a tiny pencil stroke joining two peninsulas.

Joan felt a little sick. She doesn't like heights. She was worried that a sudden gust of wind from Lake Michigan would blow us off the bridge. She looked to the left and then to the right, cautiously.

"Is that Lake Michigan right there?"

"Yes."

"And is that Lake Huron right there?"

"Yes."

"Look, kids. That's Lake Huron and that's Lake Michigan, the world's biggest lake."

"No. That's Lake Superior."

Joan misunderstood. "Oh. I'm sorry, kids." She pointed at Lake Michigan. "That's Lake Superior."

"No, no. That is Lake Michigan but Lake Superior is the world's largest lake. Except for the Caspian Sea which is really a lake although it's called a sea."

"Oh."

"And we'll be catching a glimpse of Lake Superior tomorrow."

"Oh."

The bridge seemed to make no impression on the kids. The most incredible feats of twentieth-century technology leave them cold. It's an interesting generation coming up.

53. A Respite from the Ordinary

It seemed as if we should be heading into Canada via this bridge. But no, it just takes you over the Straits of Mackinac to Michigan's Upper Peninsula, a piece of land separating Lake Michigan from Lake Superior. Under the northern end of the bridge was an asphalt parking lot filled with cars, trailers, vans, motorcycles and campmobiles of all sizes. We pulled in and parked but didn't know quite why. Perhaps the others didn't either. Maybe our brain waves were being influenced by some high-frequency broadcasting unit in the U.S. Tourist Bureau.

There were two buildings set in the middle of the vast parking lot. One was a washroom and the other a tourist office. It was hard to tell them apart. The tourist office was merely a storehouse for hundreds of thousands of flyers advertising various tourist traps in Michigan. The kids picked up flyers advertising the Dutch Village and Windmill Island in Holland, Michigan, and immediately wanted to go.

"Oh, children. I'm so sorry. We can't go there. It's 350 miles out of our way."

"Awww!"

"Maybe we'll go next year when we're taking our trip around Lake Michigan."

I looked at the pamphlet. The Dutch Village was advertised as a "world of pleasure" in an "old world setting" and a "respite from the ordinary." You could watch Dutch folk dancers dancing around an old guy in Dutch costume making wooden shoes. You could see windmills, watermills, canals, a Dutch Market, a Dutch Cheese Store, and a Dutch Candy Store.

All this under a tall flagpole flying the Stars and Stripes.

54. As Funny as a Cloud

The place was called the Foot of the Bridge Information Booth. It was strategically located at the intersection of at least two major tourist routes: the route along the eastern shore of Lake Michigan and the route along the western shore of Lake Huron.

When we got back outside there was quite a lot of activity in the parking lot. Dozens of people taking pictures of seagulls. A group of about three people were taking pictures of a deer crossing sign. A lot of people were being pushed in wheelchairs. It appeared to be an outing from some special home for the handicapped.

"It's kind of exciting isn't it Joan?"

"You mean living through an experience you know you're going to write about later?" she said.

"That's exactly what I was thinking. Imagine! What we are saying right now will probably go in the book."

"Not without me giving it the okay."

"Oh, absolutely not. Every word, every comma in this book has to be unanimous."

Alison overheard this last exchange and felt sorry for me. A kneejerk reaction but one I always appreciate.

"Is it going to be a good book, Daddy?"

"Would a guy like me write a bad book?"

"Not every book is liked by everyone."

"That's very true, my little pal."

Jennifer was watching intently and with a serious look.

"I couldn't figure out if it was going to be funny or not," she said.

"Sometimes things that are sad become funny when you write about them, or things that made you laugh make you cry."

"Yes, Daddy, but are you going to set out to make it funny?"

"About as funny as those clouds floating over the Mackinac Bridge."

"Well," said Alison, "Jennifer and I want to be able to have a say in what goes in the book."

"You three get to see every word before anyone else."

Joan jumped back in. "It depends on what happens on the trip. If funny things happen to us the book will be funny. If sad things happen the book will be sad."

Alison: "So far it must be sad then."

Joan: "What do you mean?"

Alison: "The fight and Bruce biting Jennifer and all."

Jennifer: "That was very sad all right."

Daddy: "Yeah. But there have been funny things too."

Alison: "Like what?"

Daddy: "Like this conversation for instance."

55. Richard Nixon in Drag

It was still early in the afternoon but Joan wanted to check out a campground we'd seen from the bridge. It was on the north shore of the Mackinac Straits. A mile east of the bridge. "Let's just look at it and if we don't like it we'll go on further."

It was called Mackinac Straits State Park. "Can you say that, Jennifer?"

"No."

"How about you, Alison?"

"Mackinac States Strait Park?"

"How about you, Joan?"

"Mackinac Strait States Park?"

"Jennifer?"

"No."

The guy behind the counter in the gatehouse took great pride in his uniform and his role in the Michigan state government service. He was smoking a pipe and looked vaguely Canadian, like Bliss Carman. A big line-up was growing behind us.

"The Michigan state parks are the best in the country," he said. "And this is the best of the lot."

"That's what they said all down the line." The ambiguity was unintentional.

"Oh," he said. He took it the wrong way. I had pricked his pride, in his mind (or wherever). His feelings were hurt. This man was very sensitive about his job. It was more than a job.

"No. What I mean is, they said all the way down the line that this was the best park."

"Ohhh, I see!"

"Yes, and so that's why we came here. Whatever you do, don't miss Straits State park. That's what everybody we talked to said."

The guy pulled himself together smartly after that speech. "Which way are you travelling?" He knew we were Canadians. "We came up the Lake Huron shore."

"Really? Most people come up the Lake Michigan shore. It's a lot nicer. Lots more to see."

Joan said she wanted a campsite right on the beach.

"That's not possible," said the guy. "You have to get here at eight o'clock in the morning to get a spot right on the beach." The guy was proud of his park. He told us we could look at campsites 84 and 141 and come back and tell him which we wanted.

But 84 was occupied and when we pulled into 141 someone came in behind us.

"Excuse me but we have this spot." The guy was waving a red token. I looked at it. It had the number 141 on it. He was smoking a pipe too just like the guy in the gatehouse but he wasn't wearing a uniform. Neither was his wife.

When we got back to the gatehouse there was a line-up of campers waiting to get in. The tension was as heavy as the sun was hot. The guy behind the counter had let his pipe go cold. I barged to the front of the line.

"Remember me?"

"Ahem! Yes I do." He was trying to be polite.

"Remember you told me I could look at 84 or 141 and choose one then come back and register?"

"Yes?"

"Well 84 was occupied and you subsequently gave 141 to someone else."

"You looked at 84A."

He took the map out of my hand.

"Eighty-four-A is here. Eighty-four is here. There's no one in it."

"Hooh boy!"

When we got back to the real 84 Joan was getting angry. "I'm not taking this spot. There's no trees and no privacy." I think she was a little put off by the woman sitting at the next campsite. She was wearing a beehive hairdo and was staring at us with a mean expression on her face. She looked like Richard Nixon in drag.

"Let's get out of here. It's all spoiled. I don't want to camp here. Let's not even stop to get our money back. Let's just go."

I was willing to take off but I didn't want to lose my four dollars.

At the gatehouse the line-up was longer and the tension heavier.

Again I barged to the front. Geez, what a guy, eh?

"Eighty-four is not to our liking. Would it be possible to get our money back?"

The guy had loosened his pale yellow government-issue tie. "No you can't. But here. Take number ten. Someone pulled out just a minute ago. It's right on the lake."

"I hope it's to my wife's liking."

"Don't worry. It will be."

56. Bruce Vomits in My Hat

There were little white sailboats bobbing out on the straits, bobbing among the islands in the stream. Cool breezes were bringing in puffy white clouds of pleasure from Lake Michigan. Cars were creeping high up over the Mackinac Bridge like beads of dew along the single strand of a cobweb five miles long. The bridge gradually disappeared into the afternoon mist on the south shore.

I knew exactly where we were geographically. We were located precisely at the centre of gravity of the entire Great Lakes system, the point of balance. We were at the centre of the watery universe. This was the source of all the water in the world. One has felt that feeling at Georgian Bay, Niagara Falls.... Now the water was passing through these straits and into Lake Huron just off to the left.

It was as if we had shrunk in size and what had seemed small on the map was really immense. The Great Lakes really comprised an enormous water system, so enormous the imagination is unable to grasp the immensity of it all and can only reduce it for human consumption. It was the sort of immensity only the gods can truly appreciate. To manage large concepts one becomes very small, if you see the point (groan!).

There were dozens of pretty girls in bikinis lying on the beach. Above them fat gulls were soaring, content with not being human. Suddenly the girls were naked, lying there without even their bikinis, and the gulls were flying up there wearing little swimsuits and with lipstick on their beaks.

Alison came running down from the public washroom.

"I was in the toilet and this lady was talking to herself. She was saying, 'Oh my God, I've got such a headache,' Then I flushed the toilet and she looked startled as if she didn't think anyone was there."

"Was she embarrassed?"

"Yeah, I think so."

"That was very nice of you to flush the toilet."

"Well, I didn't want to get embarrassed."

"I'm not as nice as you. I might have listened to see how the conversation developed. Maybe she would have started telling herself the story of her life. Like, I was born in Elk Rapids, Michigan, in 1927, and things started going wrong right from the start."

Joan wasn't amused. "I don't see what's so funny about that."

"But then Alison could have told me everything she said and it could have made an interesting story for the book."

"To hell with your book. That woman probably did have a helluva headache and I feel bad for her. You don't know what's happened to her to make her have that headache of hers she's got."

"Yes, you're perfectly right. I'm a heel." One of the things about me that has always bugged Joan is my superior attitude. Not that I'm saying I have one, you understand. I can toss darts at anyone, unless it's a woman, then she puts her foot down—unless she has given prior sanction, perhaps by tossing a dart herself. I really don't know how Joan and the kids stand me. I'm not as nice a man as I'm portraying myself in this book. I laugh at other people behind their backs but I never laugh at myself, not even behind my back, and that is about the most despicable stance a human being can take. No one likes a person like that. I like myself though. I think I'm just fine. That's what makes it all the worse. Also I'm very yappy and irritating.

Anyway I went for a shower. Ah such luxury! Canadian parks were never like this. Each shower had its own skylight and there was enough room for me and at least twelve beautiful girls from the beach to shower all at the same time. I left the shower door unlocked hoping that a bunch of them would barge in and join me. After all, it would have made for a socko chapter in the book.

When I got back all clean and cooled off the sun was hot and I began digging around in the van looking for my white hat. When I finally found the hat it was crushed and dirty. There were dogprints all over it. Then I noticed Bruce had puked in it.

While washing the hat out and setting it in the sun to dry I overheard Jennifer having a serious discussion with Bruce.

"Bruce, if you ever bite anybody again we're going to have your teeth taken out. Do you understand? Do you?"

57. Miller's High Life

There was something evil about these two boys, brothers, about six and eight or seven and nine years old. Maybe it was their shaven heads, their narrowed eyes, their identical black bathing suits. They seemed to be grinning at me menacingly. One of them had a toy gun in his hand.

I was sitting on a swing in the camp playgrounds. Alison and Jennifer were playing on the teeter totter. Joan had been with us, holding Bruce on his leash, but had wandered off somewhere without saying anything.

The boys kept looking at me. I was for the moment a key figure in their threatening world, and they were suspicious. I walked over to them and smiled. Their expressions didn't change.

"Can I have a look at your gun?"

The face of the older boy softened somewhat as he handed me his small black cap pistol. It was made in Spain and had the word Pirata marked on it. He told me to look. He pulled a red pellet from a leather pouch I hadn't noticed strapped to his wrist. He took the gun from my hand and placed the pellet behind the cocked hammer. He pulled the trigger.

Bang! It sounded like a starter's pistol. My ears were ringing. The boys looked at me as if I might be fun to kill.

"Want me to shoot you?" said the older.

"No. Not today. Maybe when I'm old and sick you can shoot me."

"You're pretty old now and you look kinda sick."

"No. I'm too young to die."

"I'm gonna shoot you anyway."

He fired at me.

I died dramatically, going down, holding on to the swing then collapsing on the ground. Lying there, face up, I opened one eye a crack. The kids were still looking at me. The older one was recocking his gun.

"I'll shoot him once more just to make sure he's dead." Then I noticed Joan walking across the field with Bruce. "Do me a favour? See that woman? Shoot her for me."

The kid fired at Joan. Oh oh, that was really stupid of me! She was genuinely startled. She grabbed her chest and almost collapsed. Then when she saw it was just a toy gun she became very justifiably annoyed.

I noticed two guys in their early thirties had been sitting a few feet away drinking Miller's High Life beer, listening to country and western music on their car stereo, and watching me intently. They hadn't said a word. They just watched silently. They had Indiana licence plates.

"Did you tell that kid to shoot me?" said Joan.

"I'm sorry, Joan. That was very stupid of me. But it was just a game." We left and walked toward the beach.

"Did you see those guys drinking beer?" said Joan. "They looked really weird."

"I know."

57. Bruce Is Not Himself

The kids threw small pieces of bread into the air and suddenly the beach was solid with gulls. They came from all over Lake Huron and all over Lake Michigan. Some were even swooping down from Lake Superior. Bruce just sat there watching. Joan looked sad.

"I'm worried about Bruce. Why isn't he chasing the gulls?"

"Maybe he's tired."

"I think something's wrong with his mouth. Come here, Bruce." Bruce ambled over slowly, his tail wagging pitiably. When Joan tried to pry open his mouth and look inside he wrenched his head away.

"See? There's definitely something the matter. I think it's from when Jennifer hit him with the broom. He's probably got a sliver from the broom stuck in his mouth."

"When did Jennifer hit him with the broom?"

"Just before we left. She was playing with him, trying to scare him with the broom. She hit him by accident and he yelped. Look at him! He's definitely not himself."

"We'll be in Canada tomorrow. Let's wait till then. We'll take him to a vet in the Sault."

59. Grape Pudding

A man in a track suit had been running along the pathways of the park all afternoon. Running methodically around and around as if he were in training for a marathon run. He wore a T-shirt with ATWOOD ATHLETIC CLUB printed on it. He seemed serious, mechanical, inhuman. I read his mind. It was a total vacuum.

While making sandwiches and tea I quietly observed a family of campers nearby. At first I thought it was a (distant) acquaintance of mine, Tom Ruffo, and his family. The guy was the same shape and size as Tom, a little too neatly dressed and groomed. I was just about to holler over Hey Tom, when I remembered it couldn't be Tom and it certainly wasn't his family because his family was dead and Tom was in jail in Hamilton awaiting trial on a charge of murdering them. The papers were full of this gory murder, with bodies popping up all over Southern Ontario.

As I prepared lunch, the Ruffo look-alike kept yelling at his daughter. His wife just sat there patiently while the guy seemed on the verge of losing his mind.

"Michelle, stop that," he yelled. The little girl started crying. She was only about two and a half.

A few minutes later the little girl started pushing her doll buggy. "Michelle, come here. Come here right now!" The guy slapped her on the behind and said, "How many times do I have to tell you to stop pushing your stroller?" Michelle burst into tears again. His wife just sat there.

I took the tea and sandwiches down to Joan and the kids who were sitting on the beach. There was a lot of stillness in the air. An hour passed without us being aware of time. We watched the gulls floating in the golden air. We watched the sailboats, the occasional swimmer. We watched the changing sky, the bleeding sun, the softening light. Scenes you remember as you lay dying.

A steamer must have been passing through the straits but it was too far out to see. The smoke rose from an invisible point and became a lovely banner of pink in the setting sun. The sun was all red and gold and the clouds were like grape pudding. And somewhere someone must have flicked a switch because suddenly the massive bridge vanishing in the misty distance (and which I'd forgotten was there) became illuminated and the shape of the bridge became delineated by a thousand stationary lights as well as by the moving lights of the tiny cars and trucks passing over it.

60. What Writing Is Like

I was very proud of my fire-building abilities. "Building a fire is like writing a haiku," I thought out loud.

"You can say that again," said Joan, startling me, the flames mysteriously flickering in her eyes.

"There are no two fires alike and never have been. If you think two fires are alike look more closely."

"That's right. Everything's different. Just like writing," said Joan. She was being sarcastic but I didn't care.

"Timing's the thing," I said. "You have to get the right piece of wood ignited at precisely the right moment, the match on the paper, the twigs, the pieces of dried bark, the larger twigs, the softwood logs and finally the hardwood logs. And the better you make it the longer it'll last."

"Just like writing," said Joan, yawning. She once sent one of her poems to the novelist Audrey Thomas. Audrey sent an encouraging note back but it wasn't encouraging enough for Joan. So she stopped writing.

"You can say that again."

"And Daddy," said Jennifer. "There's another way it's like writing. You write on paper, right?"

"Yes?"

"And you use paper to start a fire?"

"Right as usual!" I picked her up and tickled her.

61. Mickey Mouse

Joan and the kids climbed into the van to sleep. It was dark. I sat by the fire reading Rabelais. Everything went still and it appeared as if everyone in the state park, if not in the entire state, was asleep. After a while I noticed a skunk was lying on the ground by my feet. He must have been attracted by the fire. I felt as if I had found the perfect friend. I read for hours. I read much later than I really wanted to because I was afraid of disturbing my friend as he lay there warming himself.

Every once in a while a state trooper drove by in his cruiser.

In the morning I noticed Alison had taken a picture of Barry Manilow, the pop singer, to bed with her. It seemed like only yesterday she wouldn't go to bed without her Mickey Mouse picture. While Joan fried eggs for breakfast I played with the car radio and found a Top 40 station, WIGG from St. Ignace. Barry Manilow was singing his latest hit, inflaming teenage hearts all over the Upper Peninsula. Alison pretended she wasn't interested.

MONDAY, AUGUST 8

62. The Narrator Almost Becomes a Hero

I told Alison what a good singer I thought Barry Manilow was. She thought I was just teasing her at first. But when Joan joined in and said he was right up there with such greats as Tony Bennett and Peggy Lee, Alison seemed pleased.

"Maybe adolescence isn't going to be so bad after all," I said.

"Give it up dad," she retorted.

Joan was making breakfast when a horrendous noise broke out from the next campsite. The guy who looked like Tom Ruffo was having a vicious fight with his wife. I mean they were really fighting and shouting obscenities. Having learned early to stay out of boy-girl fights I tried to ignore it but Joan started screaming, "Oh Dave, look! He's killing her."

I looked. The shy patient woman of yesterday was now lying on the grass and this guy kept dropping on her with his knees, bouncing up and down on her with all his weight, his knees striking her in the breasts, stomach, groin, and thighs.

What could I do? I'm a small person but with an almost perfect body, with a blue-collar ferocity when provoked, tough as a loan shark when I need to be. I ran over and grabbed him around the neck and pulled him off the poor woman.

The guy started swearing at me and pushing me out of the way. Then he turned and jumped on his wife again.

This time I jumped on him with all my weight and tried to pin him to the ground. He picked me up as if I were a kid but I got my right arm free and wound up and hit him in the face. Somehow, though, the punch lost momentum before connecting.

Then the guy took a similar punch at me and the same thing happened. Just before the punch landed it lost its momentum and it hardly stung at all.

Hollywood punches.

"Get this turkey out of here," the guy started screaming at no one in particular, although a small crowd had formed including some guys a lot bigger than I. His wife just lay there, patiently waiting for him to continue beating her.

Then we started squaring off and took turns punching each other in the face. Each punch landed softly somehow. No way could I really hit him. This could go on all day with neither of us getting hurt. I couldn't understand what was happening.

Finally we stopped punching and just stood there staring at each other. The woman was still lying on the grass but she'd propped herself up on one elbow and was looking at us curiously. I looked at her and she gave me a dirty look as if I were the bad guy. I looked back at the guy. His face was full of hate.

"Why don't you mind your own business, you turkey?"

"You're lucky I came over. I stopped you from killing her."

"I wasn't going to kill her. I love this woman. She's my wife. I've got a perfect right to hit her."

"All right, all right." Someone from the crowd put his arm around my shoulders. "Come on, let's go. You can't win in something like this."

I didn't know what to think. I looked down at the woman again. "Do you want me to go?"

"Yeah, get lost you fuckin' asshole."

Back at the van, Joan wanted to know if I was hurt. I said no. She gave me some scrambled eggs with chopped onion and toast. I looked back across the road. The guy and his wife were holding hands and looking smug. I felt stupid.

We cleaned up the breakfast dishes and were starting to get our stuff together. We wanted to clear out in a hurry. And suddenly the wife-beater was standing there, a friendly smile on his face.

63. Pretty Soon the U.S.A. Will Be as Bad as Canada

"You're from Canada?" said the wife-beater.

"Yeah. Ever been there?"

"Hell yes. I go up there all the time on business on account my boss being a Canadian himself and all."

Meanwhile Bruce was at the foot of a cedar tree looking up into the branches and barking at some chipmunks. The guy went over and started tickling him behind the ears.

"Watch it. He might bite you. He's been acting kind of mean lately. I don't think he's crazy about travelling."

"Aw, he wouldn't bite me." The guy kept patting him. "Would you, Bruce?" Bruce wagged his tail.

So we got talking. The guy said he was from Miles, Michigan.

"That's a suburb of Chicago isn't it?"

The guy seemed insulted. "Hell no. Chicago's on the other side of Lake Michigan. Miles is just north of South Bend, Indiana."

So then the guy started telling me all about Canada. He was basing his remarks on a trip he took with his boss to the Maritimes.

"We kept seeing new homes being built everywhere we looked. But there didn't seem to be any people to fill the homes. There were homes for sale all over the place, but new homes kept going up. Real weird, I tell ya. So I asked my boss about it. He said no one can afford to buy homes but the government gives the builders money to build homes anyway just to keep people working. Isn't that terrible? And we're the ones who are paying for all that."

"You said it. It's pretty bad all right."

"And that Toronto. What a dump that is!" He looked at me. "You're not from Toronto are you?"

"Hell no."

"You'd have to be a pig to live there. I couldn't believe it. Garbage all over the streets. I couldn't wait to get back to the States."

I figured it was doing the guy good to get it off his chest. And so I gave him some additional fuel by mentioning President Carter's new welfare proposals which had been announced the day before in a big speech.

"There was a big build-up for this speech on the radio," I said. "And then the speech started. And after about two lines they cut in with a commercial about stereo equipment. A local station cut-in. So we turned it off."

"Yeah, well you didn't miss much. All this welfare stuff is killing us. We're the ones who are paying for it all, you and me, the workers."

I squinted at him. "You're right, pal!"

His eyes focussed a little more clearly as if he wanted to make sure I was the "worker" type. He was thinking hey, maybe this guy's on welfare. He doesn't look that prosperous and his van's a wreck. He doesn't have Bermuda shorts and a golf cap. But I smiled back encouragingly, his eyes went blurry again and he continued his tirade.

"Pretty soon it'll be as bad down here as what you've got up there in Canada. What's that guy's name—Trudeau?—that son-of-a-bitch Commie?"

The trees shimmered in the summer breeze. The guy started patting Bruce again. It was weird standing there talking to the guy without referring to the fight we'd had, or to what I thought was practically the attempted murder of his wife. I wasn't going to say anything—but suddenly I was just blurting it out.

"You're going to kill your wife one of these days you know. Grow up and stop taking all your silly frustrations out on her. She's not responsible for the new welfare proposals or for the garbage in the streets of Toronto."

The guy's expression didn't change. He had a little smile on his face.

"I'd never kill my wife. I love her."

"It looked to me like you were trying to kill her."

"Never. We both push each other around at times. But we love each other."

"A lot of people kill people they love."

"Maybe."

"And who's we? You were doing all the pushing around. She wasn't fighting back at all. And what about little Michelle? She doesn't very often push you back. How old is she? Two? Three?"

"You keep Michelle out of it, you hear?"

Just then Michelle walked up and started looking at the cross around my neck, the one that Jennifer found on the path while searching for mushrooms.

"Daddy, why is he wearing that cross?"

Daddy looked a little embarrassed. I looked down as if I'd just noticed it hanging there.

"It's to ward off mushroom poisoning," I said. "It's a good luck charm. I'm superstitious. Do you know what superstitious means?"

"No."

"It means I believe in magic."

64. The Weekly Wave

We drove into St. Ignace then got on the Interstate 75 heading north to the Sault. What a boring, business-like highway! We got off it and headed east on the U.S. 134 which windingly follows the heavily indented Lake Huron shore out to within a couple of nautical miles of the international border cutting through Potoganissing Bay. In fact from De Tour Village, on the eastern tip of Michigan's Upper Peninsula, you can see St. Joseph Island which is in Canada.

From De Tour Village you can get a ferry to Drummond Island, a fairly large island on the U.S. side. Across from Drummond Island is Cockburn Island which is on the Canadian side. Next to that is Manitoulin Island, the largest freshwater island in the world, and a place of great spirituality to the Native Indians for centuries.

We passed a sign advertising a marathon race that was being held that afternoon on Drummond Island. Joan thought it might be worth crossing on the ferry to see the race. "Maybe that's what that guy was practising for last night," she said sweetly.

We were driving past a lot of coves with beautiful sandy beaches a hundred feet wide. The water looked warm and shallow but there was no one around. No footprints in the sand except for those left by families of Canada geese who seemed to be standing around in a trance. There were occasional fishermen sitting in boats among the reeds with long bamboo poles. And there were lots of islands, rock outcroppings with some stunted cedars twisted by the wind. It looked like driving along the north shore of the St. Lawrence River east of Gananoque and seeing the beginning of the Thousand Islands.

We passed a large grey barn with a sign saying WEEKLY WAVE. "Wonder what that is?"

"That's a hairdressing establishment."

"Oh, I thought it was the local newspaper."

We passed a sign saying CEDAR CAMPUS—IVP WRITERS WELCOME. There was a narrow road leading off into the woods.

We stopped at a roadside park dedicated to Hubert H. Humphrey.

"It's so beautiful around here but so desolate. I wonder why everyone doesn't come here."

"Maybe cuz it's too desolate."

The park was full of huge chunks of granite. There were oak trees, birch, and clumps of spruce and pine. We ran down to the beach. There was a rowboat sitting there complete with oars. We decided against taking it out for a ride.

There were some clumps of long white flower-like fungi. I remembered seeing them when I was a kid but I had no idea what they were called. I had an idea they were edible. They grew something like fiddleheads but were pure white, with sort of a greasy consistency, a mushroom-like flesh. As they grew they pushed aside thick heavy layers of dead wet leaves, just pushed them aside like flaps in a carpet. They had a semi-foetid smell. They weren't in any of our mushroom books. I decided to pick a few specimens and try to get them identified.

65. Fifty Years of Service to the Motoring Public

There was a cute and very bright eighteen-year-old attendant in the gas station in De Tour Village. "You put it in there," I said, pointing to my gas tank.

"I know, I know," she said. "Women can pump gas just as well as men." I pretended I didn't notice her breasts bouncing attractively.

When she finished some gas spilled down the side of the car.

"See this?" I said. I pointed to it.

"Yeah?"

"You think I'm gonna pay for that?"

The gauge was just a fraction over $8.72. "I'll tell you what," she said. "I'll only charge you $8.72."

"Oh. That's okay then." She laughed in an exaggerated fashion and grabbed my arm. "Don't touch me," I said. "My wife'll kill you. She's so jealous."

"Aw, it must be awful for you."

"You have no idea, no idea whatsoever," I said, theatrically.

I went in the little office to pay her. On the wall was a photo of an old guy in traditional service station uniform. Under the picture were the words IN MEMORIAM RUSSELL L. SCHOPP. AWARDED FOR FIFTY YEARS OF SERVICE TO THE MOTORING PUBLIC. The guy bore a certain family resemblance to the girl.

"Is that your grandfather?"

"Yes."

"You look alike."

"Really? Do I?"

"Yup." She looked pleased. "How long's he been dead?"

"About five years."

"Do you think you'll ever get an award for fifty years of service to the motoring public?"

"No way, Jose."

Then I noticed her father. He was in the garage working on a car. He'd stopped work and was glaring at me. I guess he figured I was getting too friendly with his daughter. So before leaving I asked her about Drummond Island.

"I don't know," she said. "It's pretty much the same over there as it is here." She said she'd never heard of any marathon race.

66. The Road to the Sault

Quite a few cars were lined up like weary sheep at the ferry terminal, homeward bound. We decided not to visit Drummond Island. We were getting a little tired of the American side. We drove out of town and headed along a series of country roads cross-country toward Sault Ste. Marie, through Goetzville, Raber, Stalwart, Stirlingville, Pickford. We saw an old log cabin being pulled down the road by a truck. We started singing. The old log cabin, it just keeps rolling along.

Dotted with farms and villages, with occasional narrow strips of thick forest, the countryside was flat but warped slightly like a piece of plywood so that without realising you'd been climbing you found yourself at times able to see great distances from a gentle height. At one point we could see three villages. The shadows of three small clouds crossed the land, again like weary sheep.

The area was fairly prosperous but untouched by the modern era. Sections were heavily wooded. It could have been 1930. It was a little like Manitoulin Island but there were no abandoned farms visible. At one point Joan asked me to stop. There were some interesting weeds at the roadside.

"You don't see these kinds of weeds in Canada."

"Sure you do."

"No you don't."

"I see weeds like that all over the place in Canada."

"No you don't."

"Sure I do. Bigger specimens too."

Joan was getting angry.

"Joan, I'm sorry. I was just teasing. You're right, these are unusual weeds."

She got out of the car and picked an armful. She had about nine different varieties, none of which she could identify. She wanted to dry them out, identify them and use them in her flower-arranging class.

She was just getting back in the car with her armful of weeds when the car inexplicably rolled back a few inches. Honest, I didn't do it on purpose. Joan started screaming.

"Dave! Stop! You're driving over my foot!" I slammed on the brakes.

"Daddy, you rolled over Mommy's foot."

"Oh, oh! Is she all right?" Joan got in the car. "Are you all right, light of my life?"

"Jesus Christ, you're stupid today. You rolled right over my foot. You're lucky I'm wearing these clogs."

"I'm lucky? You're lucky you mean."

"Daddy! Geez, the least you could do is say you're sorry."

"Oh yeah. I'm sorry, Joan. I really truly honestly don't know how that happened. Are there any bones broken?"

"I don't think so but it's awfully sore." She put her foot up on my knee. I looked at it. Sure enough there was a black tire mark, a series of wiggly parallel black lines, over the arch of her foot. I massaged it and she didn't cry out so I figured she was okay. We drove off. I kept massaging her foot.

Just then a turkey vulture, the colour of a tire mark, flew low over the car. It kept crossing and recrossing the road at a height of about thirty feet. We were driving about twenty miles an hour and it was keeping just ahead of us, zigzagging back and forth across the road, its wings held motionless in a broad V.

"Oh Dave, it's beautiful."

It was joined by another. They kept in front of us, flying in tandem, for several miles. Abruptly they flew off into the woods.

We started driving faster and a few miles later another turkey vulture appeared just in front of us and flew along with us for a mile or so before disappearing. Joan was getting quite excited.

We had crossed a height of land and suddenly we could see for miles ahead. There were a pair of turkey vultures on the road ahead of us and so I braked, cut the motor and coasted slowly and silently toward them. They were eating a dead animal. There was no other traffic.

It seemed wrong that they should be called turkey vultures. It's certainly not the name they would give themselves supposing they felt a need to give themselves a name. They were certainly more interesting and much more beautiful than turkeys (though some will disagree), and they flew a lot better than any turkey I'd ever seen. They're closer to a condor although more plentiful. But because of the red wattles around the head they were stuck with this derogatory name. The Latin name, *Cathartes aura*, is much nicer. Then again, they do have a taste for turkey, as many a turkey farmer will attest, and they apparently do originate in what is now Turkey.

As we coasted closer we could see they were more brown than black in colour. We were scarcely breathing, just as in flight their wings scarcely fluttered. The slowness of their wing movements slowed our breathing to almost nil. The kids had climbed up front to get a good view of them in silence. We were just inching ahead. And then without turning their heads to look at us they took to the air.

At that moment there was a loud rustling noise to our right. We looked, and a great blue heron with a six-foot wingspan was rising from a marshy area at the side of the road. It was less than thirty feet away.

"Oh Dave, how incredible! Look at the way it flies."

It lifted off like a basketball player and the sound it made was like the sound of a cheering crowd.

67. The Department of Natural Resources

We rejoined the Interstate 75 just south of Sault Ste. Marie, Michigan. We could feel Canada up there, on the other side, a goal to reach, a symbol of freedom and openness, the end of the Underground Railroad. It was as if we were ants walking along a wall and coming up against the frame of a painting.

Heading into the Sault we passed a nice-looking building on a hill. There were flowers and trees in the lawn out front. A sign indicated it was the field headquarters for the Michigan Department of Natural Resources.

"Here's our chance to get our specimens identified," I said, referring to my mushrooms and Joan's weeds. On the other side of the road and down a bit was a gift shop built to resemble a log cabin.

"Why don't you drop us off at that shop," said Joan, "then go back and get the stuff identified and then pick us up?"

"But what about your weeds? Wouldn't you rather have them identified than go shopping in a dumb little store like that?"

"You can get them identified for me."

"We'll be in Canada in an hour and you can spend your money there."

"I just want to see what's in the store."

"Okay."

"But don't be too long."

"Why not?"

"I'm anxious to get into Canada."

"Why?"

"We have to get Bruce to the vet's. Remember?"

68. So Much for the Government

There were quite a few cars in the parking lot, but there didn't seem to be that many people inside the building itself. Maybe they were all hiding until five o'clock. Maybe they were playing pinochle in the basement. There was a young couple poring over some topographical maps of the region. They were being assisted by a uniformed staff member. It seems the couple had bought a tract of land sight unseen and were now having trouble locating it.

I plunked the weeds and fungus specimens on the counter. The fungus was beginning to turn black. The staff member was a tall brown-haired guy about twenty-four years old.

The couple put down their map. They were suddenly more interested in the plant material. I held up one of the fungi. "I wonder if it would be possible to get this identified."

The guy in the uniform took the plant from my hand. "Hm," he said. His eyes were blank. It was obvious he didn't get requests of this nature often. In the U.S.A. most people don't expect the government to know anything.

"I think it's pretty common," I said. "It just bugs me that I don't know what it is. Any ideas?"

"Well, I've seen it before but I don't know."

"Do you have any books on fungi or mushrooms?"

The guy reached under the counter and pulled out a leaflet. Wouldn't you know it was the same one I'd seen in Michigan state parks all along the Lake Huron shore. It was called

Michigan's Morels and Wildflowers and was put out by the Michigan Tourist Council and Department of Natural Resources. On one side there were pictures of ten different kinds of morels and an article on morels by William J. Mullendore. On the other side were pictures and descriptions of eleven different wildflowers and an article by R. D. Burroughs. There was a little ad in one corner stating that "this folder is a reprint from *Michigan Natural Resources*, the colorful, authentic, non-profit, no-advertising, bimonthly magazine of the state Department of Natural Resources. For a year's subscription send $3 to Michigan Natural Resources, Lansing, Michigan, 48926. It's the last big magazine bargain in North America."

"No," he said. "I'm afraid this is all we've got."

"And I guess there's no way we could get these weeds identified?"

"Afraid not. Sorry."

The couple with the map were just standing there. "We've got some books in the car that might be of some help," said the woman. "You know where they are don't you, Roger?"

"Good idea," said Roger. "Be back in a minute."

When Roger returned he had a pile of books on mushrooms, fungi and wildflowers. My specimen, halfway between a fungus and a wildflower as it seemed to be, was easy to identify. It was the *Monotrepa uniflora*, commonly known as Indian Pipe. A member of the Wintergreen family, it grows everywhere in North America from June to September. The fact that the Indian Pipe was turning black was a positive guide to identification. Like many fungi they turn black when touched. Some psilocybin mushrooms turn blue or purple.

We could only identify one of the weeds. It was the Meadow Parsnip. There was a picture of it in the *Field Guide to Wildflowers*.

69. Orange Caps

Sault Ste. Marie, Michigan, has its own little CN Tower. It's made of wood. It's actually an observation tower about a hundred feet high from which you can presumably see the Sault locks and a wide expanse of Canada across the St. Mary River. But it was closed. Strange it would be closed in the tourist season. There was a fence around it, the door was heavily padlocked and there was barbed wire strung all the way around. It looked like an ammo dump in Vietnam. The wooden stairs leading up to the tower, winding around and around, looked rotten. Maybe somebody had taken a fall and that's why the thing was closed to the public.

All along the riverfront was a U.S. Navy installation. We drove through the town. Joan showed what she bought in the store that looked like a log cabin. It was a plaque with three mushrooms painted on it. The mushrooms had orange caps, yellow gills and yellow stems.

"That'll look really nice in the kitchen."

"But I bought it for your room."

"Darling!"

70. The Body of Someone You Love

From the International Bridge we looked down and saw the rapids far below. "Now we're in Canada," I said.

"It looks just like the United States," said Alison.

"It does?"

"Yeah. It's the same kind of concrete on the bridge."

"Can't you feel a difference in the air?"

"Yeah, I guess you can. A little."

"I can, too, Daddy!" said Jennifer. "Just a little."

There was a long line-up of cars at customs. Already I felt as if we'd come home. It wasn't that we were back in familiar territory. But it was as if we'd arrived back in the kind of strangeness we were accustomed to. No one could ever live long enough to become really familiar with a country the size of Canada. Canada will always be strange. But at least it's my strangeness, the strangeness I'm familiar with (so to speak). The kind of strangeness that is like the body of someone you love, the kind of strangeness you feel free to explore as intimately as you want without feeling awkward or self-conscious about it.

71. How to Become Strange

The rapids of the St. Mary River are a mile wide. We drove around under the International Bridge to have a look at the lock area and at an old power dam that looked as if it had been old when Charles Sangster was a fledgling. I know this is ridiculous but I just felt like getting out of the car and rubbing up against the walls and telephone poles and phone booths. It was so nice to be back in Canada. How embarrassing! But you have to be truthful about these things.

We went further out along a dead-end river road under the International Bridge and stopped so Joan could get out and have a pee behind some bushes. Just as she was having her pee a big excursion boat came around the corner. It was loaded with passengers. They started pointing at Joan and laughing. Passengers came running around from the other side of the boat, which began threatening to capsize.

Joan was infuriated. She wiggled her pink bum back into her jeans and stumbled into the van, her face crimson. "Jesus Christ," she said. "Canada is supposed to be the most sparsely populated country in the world and you can't even find a place to pee in private."

As we sped away we could still see the people on the boat laughing their fool heads off.

72. False Pregnancy

Bruce was sitting on the table looking quite blasé as the vet looked at his ears.

"They're inflamed all right."

This was Dr. S.M. Yogi. His office was on the side of the Trans-Canada Highway a few miles north of Sault Ste. Marie, Ontario.

Dr. Yogi was an Asian Indian as was Dr. Swami. Dr. Swami you will recall was the guy who stitched Jennifer's wounds after Bruce bit her. That was in Tawas City, Michigan, a couple of hundred miles south of the Sault. Yet by one of those strange coincidences that plague my life, Dr. Yogi not only resembled Dr. Swami but he even had a similar heart-shaped birthmark between his eyes.

"You aren't acquainted at all with a Dr. Swami of Tawas City, Michigan, are you?"

"Afraid not. Is he a vet?"

"No, Dr. Swami was on duty in the emergency ward of a human hospital there, and had occasion to stitch Jennifer up."

"Oh well."

"Would the inflammation be severe enough to cause him to bite a child?"

"Who? Dr. Swami?"

"No, Bruce the Dog."

"He'll certainly be in a better temper once the inflammation is cleared up."

He gave us a bottle of eardrop fluid. Then he gave Bruce his annual rabies shot. Then he went into a long discourse on animal psychology.

"To Bruce, Jennifer is the runt of the litter. With many dogs they have to have someone to pick on and it's often the runt of the litter that gets it the worst. To Bruce, the members of the family are his litter and Jennifer, being the smallest member of the family, is the runt."

He went on and on in this vein. He finally came up with a good suggestion. He suggested that Jennifer be the one to feed Bruce. And that she take Bruce for walks more frequently. Since she is the runt it was necessary for her to take greater pains to be friends with Bruce, and her status would thereby be elevated in Bruce's cosmology.

"Do you hear that, Jennifer?"

"Yes." Her eyes were smouldering with seriousness. "Can I take him for a walk right now?"

The vet charged us twenty bucks. In the waiting room was a wide assortment of dogs and cats and people. Joan was talking to a woman with a black Norwegian elkhound named Smoky. It thought it was pregnant.

"It's false pregnancy. She gets like this once a year at least."

The dog looked so mournful. The woman had provided a little stuffed pup for it to play with. The dog was lying on the floor with the pup between its forelegs, gently cradling it.

The woman said she was from Hamilton too. She'd been living for the past two months in a logging-camp cabin with her husband somewhere in the back woods. But their cabin had burnt to the ground earlier that week while they were in town at a bingo game. She was German, six feet tall, strong-looking. She looked as if she'd been working hard all her life, her face tanned and leathery, her large man-like hands gnarled and fingernails black. Yet she was perfectly feminine, exuding a strong female radiance.

"I'm heading back to Hamilton as soon as I get her looked after," she said, nodding at the dog. "I'm sick of the north woods. I want to open a corner convenience store."

73. Raw Material

We were on the Trans-Canada Highway heading south around Lake George. We passed over the Garden River which flows down through the Garden River Indian Reserve into the north channel of the St. Mary River. On the abutment of a train bridge someone had painted THIS IS INDIAN TERRITORY and INDIAN POWER. We had another huge decision to make: whether to travel all the way around Georgian Bay or cut down through Manitoulin Island then take the ferry to Tobermory and then down the Bruce Peninsula.

The kids wanted to take the ferry. In fact it was unanimous. As I drove along I tried to invoke a precognitive vision of this book. If I could see it clearly enough I could flip the pages and find out which route we should take by simply reading in the book which route we'd taken. I'd been writing for a long time out of the raw material of my life. It was beginning to seem as if my life was following my writing rather than the other way around. It was as if the writing came first and the circumstances of my life were merely mechanisms to bring the writing into existence from the place in eternity where it had always existed. I wouldn't say anything about that to Joan. She'd give me hell for being too pretentious. But you understand, gentle reader. Don't you?

74. The New Bridge to St. Joseph Island

We decided to spend some time on St. Joseph Island. The bridge had only been open a year or so. Before that the residents had to rely on a ferry in the summer and skates (and then, in time, snowmobiles) in the winter. When the bridge was built the way of life changed quickly. People who lived and worked on the mainland built permanent homes on St. Joseph Island. It was quite a shock to some of the old-timers who'd been living in isolation all their lives. Some were third-generation islanders.

It was like the shock that befell the fishermen of the upper Great Lakes when the Welland Canal first opened. Niagara Falls had proven a formidable barrier for the sea lamprey. Suddenly they were free to surge into Lakes Erie, Huron, Michigan and Superior, and the prosperous fresh-water fishing industry was destroyed almost overnight.

This was a nice bridge, long and low-slung. The road forms a causeway of sorts connecting several small, rocky, spruce-clad islands in the stream before taking to the air and crossing the main channel on seven concrete supports.

The island is encircled by a road. It's called Highway 548. When we got off the bridge we didn't waste any time figuring out whether to travel clockwise or counterclockwise around the island. Whether we went left or right would have a strong influence on this part of the book. So we simply turned left and decided to go clockwise.

The first town we came to was Hilton Beach. It was like being in Burlington, Ontario, in 1900.

75. Burlington, Ontario

In the dry-goods store at the main intersection of Hilton Beach several elderly women in frilly dresses crowded around us when we said we were looking for a nice place to eat. They seemed to come from the back of the store, the attic, the basement. It was strange. It was as if we were about to be kidnapped, taken back to the nineteenth century, and force-fed all the horrible things people used to eat (and drink) in those days.

But we didn't need to feel threatened. They merely recommended the Hilton Beach Hotel at the waterfront.

There was a clean tablecloth and a bowl of fresh flowers at our ordinary kitchen table in the dining room of the hotel. Through the window we could see a small dock and the low forested hills of Northern Ontario dimly across the wide immensity of the swiftly flowing St. Joseph Channel. It must have been a long way to skate for provisions, but perhaps not that long by nineteenth-century Canadian standards.

We looked at the menu and ordered the baked-ham dinner, all except Jennifer who wanted a hamburger. The waitress was about seventeen. When she retreated into the kitchen I said something to the effect that the girl probably goes to high school and works here part time.

"I'm not going to work part-time when I go to high school," said Jennifer, wisely. "It's no fun."

I got thinking about Burlington, Ontario. If in 1900, seventy-seven years ago, Burlington, Ontario, looked like Hilton Beach does now, which it did, then in seventy-seven years from now, by the year 2054, Hilton Beach will look like Burlington, Ontario, does now. But given the runaway population explosion, it will likely be more like a mere 7.7 years before Hilton Beach resembles Burlington today.

If you've never seen Burlington, Ontario, it's just another of those huge suburban cities that exploded out of a nice small town over the past thirty years. Everyone works in Toronto or Hamilton, commuting by GO Train or car in a twice-a-day ritual of mind-destroying boredom. It makes Delta, B.C., seem like paradise.

In the case of Burlington you can still see what the original town must have been like if you wander down to the waterfront. You can see the nice old houses and commercial blocks at what was then the main corner of town. But now you can drive for an hour in any direction from that point and still be in Burlington, a Mississauga-like maze of monotonous houses, gas stations, junk-food outlets, muffler shops and shopping centres. It's sort of a cultural collision between the Mafia and Simpsons-Sears.

But a lot of people like Burlington. People who live there by and large love it. The poet George Bowering once said that if he had to live in just one place for the rest of his life he would want that place to be Burlington, Ontario. A great tribute to a great little city.

76. Uncle Albert

It's time to break into the present again. Joan's Uncle Albert died last night, of cancer, at fifty-three. He was a man children loved. He was a particular favourite of Jennifer. In the last half-hour of his life his pain stopped, his breathing relaxed, his twitchings stopped and a tremendous peace fell upon him. According to those who were there he remained conscious until the point of death.

He worked at the glass works in Hamilton and was a union official. His big project was establishing a social centre for retired union members. He put an amazing amount of time into it and when people asked him why he said it was for selfish reasons, he wanted to be able to have a social centre to come to when he retired. But he didn't make it.

His fellow workers raised $6,000 to send Albert to the Bahamas for a cancer treatment. When he returned he was convinced he was cured. Even when the cancer started breaking out again he thought it was something else.

77. A Damsel in Distress

Why does this breaking into the writer's present circumstances tend to occur less frequently in prose than in verse? Because in prose one's attention is fascinated by a story line while in verse one's attention is taken up with the music. Even if the verse takes a narrative form the story is secondary. Verse is simply more interesting than prose. Trying to remain submerged in the writing without reference to the present when you're writing verse is like trying to sleep when your room is filled with beautiful, interesting people.

I'm open to misinterpretation here. As a reader you might argue that prose is more interesting than verse. It certainly sells better. Fiction outsells poetry twenty to one according to David

Kerfoot of Duthie Books in Vancouver. However that's because fiction usually attracts the more interesting writers, the livelier minds.

Poetry has become like macramé. A craft that anyone can do, a craft aimed at an audience of two. A lot of smaller Canadian publishers are refusing to publish poetry. As they say at Coach House Press, one prose writer is worth a gross of poets.

But just because the general run of poets are betraying poetry doesn't mean that poetry is something less interesting than prose.

It's just waiting for someone to rescue it again, a damsel in eternal distress.

Imagine a man sitting at a table with a beautiful woman and her two beautiful daughters. And he falls in love with the waitress. Ah, the perversity of the demons that control my life!

The waitress said she was sad the ferry was gone. She said it was now in use in Kingston, Ontario, taking cars and people over to Wolfe Island. She said her big ambition was to travel to Kingston and take one last trip on it.

I shuddered with sympathy. I had to fight the urge to take her to one side and say, "Look. I'm going to drive my wife and kids to the nearest bus terminal and send them home. And I'll be right back to take you to Kingston." But the forces of good once again defeated the forces of evil.

Bridges are beautiful but ferry boats are almost always more beautiful. And the replacement of ferry boats by bridges is all part of the evolutionary plot to strip us of our beauty, and thereby perhaps increase our sense of beauty, our discovery of beauty inside ourselves. This plot has been unfolding for thousands of years. Look at the Acropolis, or some other magnificent structure of antiquity. These were the products of a communal mind so utterly different from ours as to be unimaginable. A mind for whom beauty was an inevitable part of expression. A mind for whom the Homeric line was ordinary speech.

Eventually bridges will be replaced by tunnels. And people will be banding together to protest the tearing down of old McDonald chain restaurants.

"We used to know everyone on the island," the girl said. She just stood there looking at me, her eyes glued to mine. She knew I understood the feelings behind her words. "But not now."

In the front part of the hotel was a bar room where a lot of people were sitting around drinking beer. "Out of all the people in there how many would you know by name?"

"Probably none."

The current of the St. Joseph Channel swept by relentlessly outside the window. Two hundred years ago it was the route of the voyageurs on their way into Indian territory to return with furs to make hats for the beautiful gentlemen of Europe. Far across the channel were the towns of Desbarats and Bruce Mines. Desbarats is where the waitress went to high school. She pronounced it Deborah.

78. An Unsigned Watercolour

We ate our ham, with homemade soup and blueberry pie fresh from the oven. There was a watercolour on the wall showing the same view we had from the window except that the dock in the foreground was shaped a little differently. It was pointing the other way. We asked the waitress about it.

She said the painting was done by a woman from Toronto who used to vacation at St. Joseph Island in the 1940s and often stayed at the Hilton Beach Hotel. The waitress was too young to have known her but she knew of her, being an intelligent waitress with a sense of communal history.

She said the dock shown in the painting had been wrecked in a storm and a new one built recently. The new dock was pointing a different way but the hills on the north shore of the passage were just the same.

"That's a good painting. They should have used it in building the new dock." She laughed. "What was the woman's name?"

"I can't remember," she said. "She was pretty old then. She's probably dead now."

79. Road to Whisky Bay

We left Hilton Beach and drove over to the eastern part of the island, to the Mosquito Bay area, along a narrow, winding, hilly highway which cuts through dense woods. At one point we parked the van and walked into the woods.

The kids pretended they were frightened. I found a World War II army helmet that had been blasted with a hunter's shotgun and was rusting out. I thought someone had been using it to collect berries in 1949 and had left it behind and someone else had been using it for target practice, or perhaps some hunter mistook it for a slumbering armadillo.

The woods were mysterious, maybe because of the isolated nature of the island. I kept thinking we were about to be ambushed by a family of wild mutants or Scottish cannibals or that we were going to come upon a miraculous child wandering around in a daze.

We drove south from Mosquito Bay and across the Kaskawan River and then along Tenby Bay. Without the map we wouldn't have had a clue which direction we were going in or where we were. The road maintained a respectful distance from the shoreline, which was mostly private and taken up by American cottagers, and there were few signposts.

But when we got to the end of the road we knew if we turned left we'd end up at Whisky Bay and so we did.

80. The Cold Waters of Potoganissing Bay

Suddenly the interminable woods opened up and we were driving down a sandy hill to the shore. There was a white frame house, a lot of trailers parked around, some outbuildings, and a dock. Some campers were starting a crepuscular campfire. All the camping trailers and vans boasted U.S. flags and U.S. licence plates. The campfire wasn't going very well so someone doused the flames with lighting fluid then jumped back. Someone else had a huge string of big fat fish.

We immediately felt out of place. For one thing we were Canadians. I think it's natural for a Canadian to feel more out of place in a part of Canada which has been taken over by Americans than he would say in the U.S.A. per se. Also we weren't interested in fishing. So it looked as if we'd come to the wrong place. But it was getting dark and we didn't want to go any further. There is no such thing as a wrong place for a writer, especially one as all-fired serious as I was.

So I went into the office-cum-store and took a campsite for the night. The woman had severe halitosis (sign of stress) and wasn't very friendly. I had the feeling she'd had reports on us all along the road from Hilton Beach and knew we were coming, a family of Canadians. Possibly bad for business. In the back room children were crying and stale-diaper smells wafted out through the open door.

After we got settled Joan read the kids a story and I walked down to the dock. A cabin cruiser was coming in after a day's fishing. A male and female in their early twenties were aboard. They looked quite simple-minded (drunk?) in a violent sort of way. They overshot the dock and it looked as if their boat was going to plough into another boat and cause some damage.

I jumped off the dock into the boat they were rushing toward. I reached out and stopped their boat as it was about to collide. I don't know how I managed to avoid breaking my arm but the tactic worked. There was no collision. No thanks were offered, not even when the couple finally managed to get their boat docked.

"Catch any fish?" I said.

"Nah."

We were standing on the dock. The cold waters of Potoganissing Bay surrounded us and stretched out to the horizon and disappeared between and behind wooded islands of various sizes.

And under the watery flatness we could hear huge schools of fish, giggling.

81. A Small Party of American Ladies

On the way back from the dock I walked through a corner of the woods. I picked a few bright red mushrooms to show the kids. When I got back I built a fire and we sat around it for warmth. This was the most northern part of our trip around Lake Huron and it was chilly.

I began reading aloud from Rabelais, the tame Cohen translation. I was reading Book I, Chapter 13, entitled "How Grandgousier Realised Gargantua's Marvellous Intelligence by His Invention of an Arse-Wipe," when a small party of American ladies walked by. There were about six of them and they were dressed in pastel blue or pink pantsuits and wore their hair in perfect bouffants protected with space-age plastic hairspray. Their make-up was just so. They wore white high-heeled sandals. A very sophisticated and lovely little group, these were the wives of recreational fishermen.

As they walked along in front of us all six suddenly looked horrified and stared at the four-member McFadden family sitting around the roaring campfire. I guess they must have heard me read a nasty word. The kids were laughing their heads off at the story and the women must have been shocked that a father would read such garbage to his children. Let's face it there's something sort of communistic and unamerican about sitting around a campfire reading a book to your children in the first place—unless the book was the Holy Bible (modern American translation).

The proper thing to do is to take your television set with you on camping trips. But actually to read your daughters a story about the invention of toilet paper, well that's almost atheistic in itself.

82. Illuminated by the Flickering Light of a Dying Campfire

As the fire died I sat there wrapped in a blanket, shivering. The others were sleeping in warm sleeping bags inside the warm van.

From where I sat you could see out over the cold waters of Potoganissing Bay the twinkling lights of Drummond Island on which a marathon race was being run that night. I thought it would be nice if I could just lift off from my body and float over the waters to watch the race, to fly up behind the ear of my favourite and urge him on....

People on St. Joseph Island boasted that "half of the states of the Union are represented on the taxpayers' rolls" and that the kids have to go to the mainland to school. I decided there was something about the island I didn't like. It was in the Canadian air that night—a sense of commercial smugness, a sense of commercial enthrallment to the Americans. No one wanted to waste time with Canadians who weren't lugging big boats and who obviously didn't have buckets of money to spend. The natives wanted to be ordered around by the Americans with dune buggies and cabin cruisers and huge Winnebagos with television sets and air conditioners. They wanted to grovel in front of them. What would the original settlers have had to say about the way their grandchildren were conducting their lives?

My mushrooms were drying on the picnic table in the flickering light from the dying fire. I'd been unable to identify them even though I had some excellent guide books.

There were so many gift shops on the island. And so many abandoned farms. It just wasn't right....

TUESDAY, AUGUST 9

83. Elmer Trump and the Navy Bean Market

The heater in the van broke down overnight and in the morning it felt as if our bone marrow was at the point of freezing solid. I asked Joan to go out and light us up a nice roaring fire but she refused so I had to get up.

While I was fetching wood a fellow came by in a green worksuit and matching hat. "You gonna warm it up outside?" he said in a U.S. accent. We got talking.

His name was Elmer Trump and he was from Saginaw, Michigan. He was a farmer. He grew navy beans. He had a dune buggy attached to his Winnebago. He'd towed it all the way up. I guess he was disappointed that there were no dunes on St. Joseph Island. In fact not enough beach to drive on. Just dense woods right down to the shoreline. I asked him about the market in navy beans.

"It was up to $54 a few years back but now it's down to $13.50," he said. He seemed glad I asked. "We've been undercut by all the Canadian farmers getting into it once they saw it was a profitable thing."

"Well," I said. "The last to get in is usually the first to get out." I could see him pause.

Then he got talking about the cold. Turned out he was no stranger to Canada. He told me he was thinking of going in for a swim. "I've been in water a lot colder than this," he said.

"Oh? Where?" Thinking maybe the Arctic Ocean in the middle of winter.

"Lake Erie. That is one cold lake, oh boy!"

Now, Lake Erie is the shallowest and warmest of the five Great Lakes, and during the summer months it's warmer than the Gulf Stream. In fact there are palm trees on the south shore, as mentioned in my excellent book *A Trip Around Lake Erie*. But I couldn't call him a liar, could I?

"I was swimming in Port Colborne one day," he said. "It was so hot under that blazing sun I dove right in. Brr. My body wanted to go back but my momentum carried me forward."

I had the impression this was a story he'd told before, perhaps with a warmer response. The wording was too exact.

"I've done a fair amount of swimming in Lake Erie over the years," I said, "and it's always pretty warm in the summer months. How long ago was this?"

He thought a minute. "Oh about thirty years ago I guess," he said. "I haven't been up to Canada for a heck of a long time. Ever since they started cutting in on the navy bean market. And just about that time I'll be damned if the weather patterns didn't start changing. They started gettin' all the rain in the growin' season and we dried right up. I just don't feel like goin' to Canada any more."

"But you're in Canada right now."

"Well, yes. But this is different. This isn't the part where they grow things. This is just a place for...."

"Americans to fish?"

"Yeah. Right."

84. Elmer's Dune Buggy

I was the centre of attraction, not because of my magnetic personality but because I was the only one with a fire going. Elmer and I stood there talking and keeping warm. Along came Merle, the guy who owned the place, pretending he wanted to talk. But you could see him inching closer and closer to the fire.

Merle was telling us about an elderly man who'd bought a brand new boat. He was a retired school teacher from the States.

"He paid $9,000 and he wants me to launch it for him," said Merle. "I don't think he's quite right upstairs."

"That's the same with my dune buggy," said Elmer. "People think I'm not right upstairs. I'm sixty-one years old you know. People want to know why I bought a dune buggy at my age. I just tell them I always wanted one and when I got the chance I bought one. How old's this teacher?"

"Seventy-two."

85. A Study in Classic Jealousy

So Merle went down to launch the old guy's boat. We couldn't see the old guy anywhere. I made a terrible Freudian slip. "I sure hope it sinks, I mean floats," I said. Nobody laughed.

Then another old timer came up to us at the early-morning fire. At first I thought it was the guy who owned the boat but no. This guy's name was Caribou Jack, and he immediately started sneering at the unseen old guy.

"A boat that big is just to brag about," said Caribou Jack, as Merle let it drop into the water. It bounced back up and then settled in at its proper level. "It's like catching a big fish. You can brag about it lots but you can't eat it."

I couldn't figure out why you couldn't eat a big fish but I didn't say anything. I didn't want to appear stupid. These guys were Americans, even Caribou Jack, and even though they were guests in my own country I didn't want to give them the impression Canadians were stupid. I wanted to be a credit to my country. So I tried to look and sound as intelligent as I possibly could. Maybe big fish aren't as tasty as little ones. Maybe their meat is too tough and stringy. Maybe you can't eat them because then you wouldn't have anything to brag about. So you have to have them stuffed and shellacked and mounted on plaques on the rec room wall over the bar.

The mysterious owner of the new boat walked out on the dock. He spoke briefly to Merle in a businesslike fashion. He went to get into the boat, drew back, and wiped his feet on the wooden dock. Then he got in.

"That's right," said Caribou Jack with a mean look on his face. "That's right. Wipe your feet you silly old bastard. I know people who have *million*-dollar boats. *That's* nothing." This was turning into a study in classic jealousy. The kind of hatred that you seldom hear expressed so eloquently. Usually it just eats away silently at people's hearts.

"Have you got a boat yourself?" I said.

"Yeah." Something had gone out of his voice.

"Where would it be?" I said softly, after ten seconds of silence.

"It's over there."

I looked.

"Where?"

"Behind the dock."

I couldn't see any boats behind the dock so I figured it must have been a pretty small boat. The dock only came about thirty inches out of the water. His boat must have been smaller than that.

"I don't see any boat behind the dock."

"It's right behind the dock. You can't see it from here."

It turned out to be a little rowboat he'd brought up on his car-top carrier all the way from his home in Royal Oak, Michigan. He kept talking out of the side of his mouth, like Henry Miller. He was a short, skinny guy in his sixties. I asked him what his name was.

"Jack," he said. "They call me Caribou Jack way up in Canada."

Like Elmer Trump, Caribou Jack seemed to have forgotten we were in Canada. Then again we were only a few miles from the border. In fact you could see an American island from where we were standing.

"Well," I said, "since this is Canada we're in, I'm going to have to call you Caribou Jack. But when you say way up in Canada where do you mean, Caribou Jack?"

"Oh, way up in northern Canada."

"Where? It's a pretty big country you know."

"Way, way up in northern Canada. Almost to James Bay."

"Oh," I said. "You must mean Northern Ontario."

"Yeah, that's right," he said out of the corner of his mouth. "Yeah, I was up there for quite a while. That's where I got the nickname Caribou Jack. They figured I knew more about the wilderness than a native."

"Really, eh?"

"Yeah. I could smell a caribou or moose or what have you three days after it passed."

"Three days!" I said. "Wow!" I spoke softly and looked right at him. He knew he was making a big impression on me. His chest swelled. "What would a caribou or a moose or what have you smell like, Caribou Jack?"

"Oh, that's easy. Just like my wife. That's what it smells like."

"Don't you like your wife anymore, Caribou Jack?"

"It's like living with a rattlesnake," he said. "She's got that bad bite on her. She's just at me all the time. I can't have any fun when she's along." He thought a moment. He looked as if he were about to cry. "I gotta get rid of her."

I felt a lump in my throat. I wondered how many men felt that way about their wives. "Oh, I bet you say that all the time," I said.

"No, I don't say that all the time," he said. "But I've had enough. Enough's enough. It's true what they say—laugh and the world laughs with you, cry and you cry alone. When I've had enough I've had enough. Yes sir!"

I felt really sad. "She can't be that bad, Caribou Jack. You've lived with her all these years."

"Oh yes she is. I took her to Hawaii last year and all the time we were there she wouldn't speak to me. Wasted $2,500. My daughter's coming up on Wednesday or Thursday. I'm hoping she'll take her home with her."

86. The Knack of Making Friends

I felt ripples of compassion for Caribou Jack, swamped as he was by waves of jealousy toward others for their possessions and self-pity toward himself because of his wife.

"There's always somebody with a bigger boat than yours," I said. "It's true no matter how big your boat is." He looked thoughtful. I could tell he was taking it in. "Even your friends with the million-dollar boats must feel sick when they see a bigger boat go by."

He started grinning. "A friend of mine bought a brand new boat and took it into shallow water and scraped it all up on the rocks," he said. He certainly had a lot of friends. "He made a helluva mess of it. The funny thing is, he did it on purpose though. 'Now I can have some fun,' he said to me." By this time Caribou Jack was smiling gleefully, his eyes sparkling.

"I wish I had some rich friends like that," I said. "It must be the next best thing to being rich yourself."

"Oh I've got friends everywhere," said Caribou Jack. "I have friends among the rich and friends among the poor. Wherever I've gone all through my life I've always had the knack of making friends. Real good friends too. I don't know what it is about me."

87. Caribou Jack Struggles with His Demon

There were several fishing boats scattered among the islands looming out there across the misty morning waters. The retired school teacher was still sitting in his immaculate new boat tied to the dock. He seemed to be reading a book. It was probably the instruction manual. Caribou Jack was watching him from a slight but significant elevation where he was warming himself by my fire.

"Another thing about that damn fool boat," he said. "It's made of plexiglass. I'd never buy a boat made out of plexiglass. The first rough water it'll fall apart."

Merle approached us. He'd heard the last part of the discussion.

"That's right," he said. Merle started telling a story about a guy he knew who drowned in a boat like that while pulling some water skiers. "The boat just fell apart and the driver flew up in the air and landed in the water. It took them all day to find the body."

Merle excused himself and walked back to the dock area.

Caribou Jack hadn't been listening attentively to Merle's story because he was too busy trying to figure out how he would top it. Since I didn't appear to be going anywhere (how could I with such a good fire going?), he decided to start slowly, sneakily.

"Do you know anything about boat regulations up here in Canada?"

"Nope. Afraid not."

"I wonder if you need a vent for your motor and gas tank? My youngest son's wife didn't have one on her boat. The whole thing exploded one day. Awful mess. She was no good for a year after."

"Tsk. That's awful."

I think Caribou Jack was a little disappointed in my response. I didn't find his stories believable. Further, I wasn't giving him a good lead into the next story and he couldn't figure out how to make the transition smoothly. It was as if he were expecting me to say something, as predictable as a chess move, but I wasn't playing properly. We just stood there for a while. Finally he couldn't stand it any more. To hell with transitions—he'd just barge into the next blockbuster of a story.

"You ever fool around on Lake Superior?" he blurted out. "Boy, they have waves as big as those cottages on that lake. I should know. I lost five of my best friends on that lake—in one day."

"No kidding? Wow! How'd that happen, Caribou Jack?"

"There was a storm coming up. You could see it coming. It's easy, don't you know? Whenever I went out fishing my friend and me would take turns watching the weather. First one and then the other. As soon as swells start coming we head in. But this day it was about to storm even before they went out. I told them not to go. But they wouldn't listen. They went out anyway. Then the storm hit. After it was over they still hadn't come in. I knew why not. They were at the bottom of the lake. Two other really good friends of mine went out looking for them—and they never came back either."

"Seven! Holy Mother of God! I thought five was bad enough. But seven of your best friends in one day! Whew!"

Caribou Jack looked pleased. He'd really impressed me, he could tell. He loved the feeling that came with impressing someone. He decided to hit me with another story, even better if that could be possible. I was a good listener. He'd never let me get away if he could possibly help it, as long as I kept that fire going anyway.

The next story involved nothing less than a whole ship sinking in Lake Superior, with the loss of about a hundred crew members, although he modestly disclaimed any great friendship with any of them.

It seems Caribou Jack was on an island in the lake and just happened to see the ship go by. And he just happened to tell his friends—a number of his very best friends were there with him —that the ship was going to sink. It was something about the way it was sitting in the water.

And sure enough they heard the next morning the ship had sunk overnight. Caribou Jack wanted to testify at the inquest but nobody would listen to him.

"It was a big cover-up, don't you know?" he said.

Caribou Jack was probably referring to the U.S. iron-ore carrier *Edmund Fitzgerald*, which suddenly plunged to the bottom of Lake Superior during a great storm two years earlier, on November 10, 1975, with the loss of the captain and all twenty-nine crew members.

88. A Guide Named Beatrice

I could hear stirring inside the van so I told Caribou Jack I wanted to make breakfast for my family. Perhaps I should have invited him to stay. He might have provided some additional stuff for this story. But I was beginning to overdose on him. After a while he made you feel as if you were drowning. Even now as I write this I can feel him out there, making friends among the rich and friends among the poor.

After breakfast we got ready and pulled out. We drove a zigzag route past the bird sanctuary to Fort St. Joseph on the southeastern tip of the island. Or, to be more accurate, the spot where Fort St. Joseph used to be.

Fort St. Joseph was built by the British after the Treaty of Versailles (1783) awarded Fort Michilimackinac to the United States. At the outbreak of the War of 1812 an expedition of traders, British soldiers and Indians set out from Fort St. Joseph, captured Fort Michilimackinac and held it until the end of the war despite intensive American siege and blockade. The Americans were furious. Among other things they burned the vacant Fort St. Joseph to the ground in 1814. It was never rebuilt.

Our guide's name was Beatrice. She met us in the hot, dusty parking lot and we followed her along a footpath leading in a winding manner up over a densely wooded hill, matted with blooming wildflowers and Indian Pipe. When we got to the top of the hill we saw we were on a kind of peninsula. There was water on all sides, and lots of islands out there to soften storms. A pleasant vista, and a good place for a fort in pre-radar days. You could see the army coming from any direction. No wonder the Americans had to wait until the fort vacated before burning it to the ground. They could have attacked during fog conditions and it would have been a different story. But during fog conditions the Americans might not have been able to find the island. They might have wound up in Tobermory.

Stone buildings were rising dream-like from the earth all around us. It reminded me of my favourite Anglo-Saxon poem, "The Ruin," which begins: "Well-wrought this wall; / Wierds broke it." The poem had been written by an anonymous bard—elegantly meditative and tremendously intelligent—passing by the Roman ruins at Bath in the eighth century. The ruins were more than four centuries old at that time—more than twice as old as the ruins here at hand.

University students were digging in the soil under the hot sun. They'd found a gold coin a week or two before but it wasn't available for viewing. It had been sent to Ottawa. Beatrice, under our urging, settled down and began telling us the story of her life. She was tall and thin, freckled and strangely mature despite the braces on her teeth.

She said she'd been born on the island and was studying veterinary science at the University of Guelph. She was going to return to the island and set up practice when she graduated. She was looking forward to being the only vet on the island. So business prospects were excellent. Her father was a teacher at Lakehead College in Thunder Bay.

When we finished the tour Beatrice showed us some sketches of the fort done by artists of the time. She became quite passionate about the poetry of passing time and picked out strange human details in the watercolours and pencil sketches.

We told her about Bruce and his bloody attack on Jennifer. She said she agreed with the vet in the Sault. We told her if we're ever on St. Joseph Island in future years and one of us gets attacked by Bruce we'd be sure to drop in and see her. We told her it would be nice to see her without her braces. She laughed.

Just as we were about to leave she said something strange. "Maybe being in the United States was driving Bruce crazy." She had a totally serious look on her face.

"Do you really think dogs are that sensitive to political situations?" I said, nervously.

"Most certainly. Most dogs are more sensitive to things like that than most people," she said. "But then again for some of the most anti-American Canadians being in the United States is strangely more pleasant than being in Canada."

"Would that hold for anti-American dogs too?"

"I think so." I looked at her. She wasn't fooling.

We walked back down to the parking lot, got in the van and drove off. Except for Beatrice. She stayed behind. She knew what she wanted to do with the rest of her life. I could see her on that island for the next thirty years, practising animal medicine, specialising in gouging Americans whose pets get car-sick during the summer holidays, then taking glorious two-month winter vacations in Hawaii! Ah, what a life! Clever girl.

89. Graveyard Mushrooms

On the way out we stopped at the old cemetery from the days when the fort was occupied. I wondered idly how much would be left of them, what their bones would look like now, but decided against getting the shovel from the van and digging them up.

However, I did pick some beautiful and edible mushrooms in between the ancient graves.

"Oh no, you're not going to eat graveyard mushrooms," said Joan.

"Sure. And so will you. And they'll be delicious."

"I'm not so sure."

"Oh, come on. Remember Marten Hartwell?"

90. A Picture I Took at That Moment

In front of me as I type is a picture I took at that moment. Joan is standing at the back of the van with my collection of mushrooms heaped in her arms. The bumper sticker on the van says GOING TO HELL IS BETTER THAN GOING NOWHERE AT ALL. And in the background you can see the old grave markers mouldering away.

"Say cheese," I said.

"Oh all right. Cheese."

91. What Me Worry?

The dust was awful that day. When we looked behind as we drove along we could see a great automobile-generated cloud of dust flying.a hundred feet into the air then slowly settling over the mixed woods through which the road cuts.

"This couldn't be doing the woods any good," I suggested. "In a couple of years there aren't going to be any trees left."

"Oh don't be such a worry wart," said Joan.

92. Haunted by Caribou Jack's Prophetic Powers

So we finally got back on the one paved road, the one that runs a ring around the island, the one the province called Highway 548. But the island people don't call it that. We were driving along the part the island people call the Fifth Side Road. We were heading due west, feeling the land slope down to the shore on our left and slope up to our right to the wooded height of land in the centre of the island.

The paved portion got closer and closer to the shore. Now we were on what the local people called the Huron Line. We looked out over the channel and saw Michigan across the water in one direction and Nebbish Island in another. And further west, Sugar Island. All part of the U.S.A.

Along the shores of the neighbouring islands and the Michigan mainland you could see boathouses and cottages surrounded by immense green foliage, the blue sky and the deep blue shipping channel. It must be a thrilling sight to see a great ocean liner or a great ore carrier (the *Edmund Fitzgerald* was 222 feet long) threading through these islands but we weren't lucky that day. We could have waited but who knew how long we would have had to wait? There was no one to call to find out when a big one was due through.

Suddenly it hit me. This must have been where Caribou Jack was when the *Edmund Fitzgerald* went through on its way to the bottom of Lake Superior—the ship he predicted was doomed, something about the way it was sitting in the water. He probably actually did see a ship go by here on its way up to Lake Superior a day or so before that ship went down. And his imagination supplied the rest of the story. Takes one to know one.

93. Enough Already About Me

We walked around a village known as Sailor's Encampment. The channel between us and Nebbish Island was only about a hundred feet wide. You could almost pick out the dots and dashes of the international boundary glistening in the waves.

Then we were driving north on C. Line toward Richard's Landing, passing by luxurious summer homes owned by Americans, large boats parked in their watery boathouses. Would a boathouse for a houseboat be called a houseboathouse?

In Richard's Landing I sat on a park bench as Joan and the kids visited a crafts store. Richard's Landing was a town full of dear hearts and gentle people, a town where everyone knew everyone intimately, where even strangers from the great world beyond speak and smile at each other as they pass on the street.

So I sat there on the bench and as people passed I deliberately looked away from them and refused to say anything. I could feel them looking at me, and feeling sorry for me for not wanting to exchange greetings as befitted the friendly atmosphere. In cities I'm over friendly, in villages under friendly. But that's enough about me.

The eastern end of St. Joseph Island was desolate except for American fishing camps and the ruins of an old fort designed to keep the Americans out. The western end was opulent by contrast with a prosperous-looking town or two, yacht clubs, restaurants, expensive summer homes. It was just like most cities and towns all over Canada: the east end rundown and the west end prosperous. But in this case the reason was more obvious than in most cases. The island's western end was closer to the United States.

94. Greasy Bikers from Minnesota

And there we were, back where we started from at the bridge, wondering what it would have been like if we'd decided to go counterclockwise instead of clockwise. But no, such speculation was idle in the extreme. The whole universe came into being so Caribou Jack and I could meet that morning—not to mention Beatrice the Guide.

Soon we were driving east on the Trans-Canada Highway again, following the north shore of St. Joseph Channel. In Bruce Mines we stopped for lunch at a place called the Copper Kettle. It was a small restaurant at the back of a gift shop. There were some greasy bikers from Minnesota in there. They were wearing Nazi insignia. They were laughing and as Joan glanced at them two of them happened to glance at her so it looked as if they were laughing at her.

"Why would those bikers be laughing at me?" she said.

"They weren't laughing at you."

"Oh yes they were."

"Maybe it was your T-shirt." She was wearing a red T-shirt with white lettering. It said on it CENTENNIAL CENTIPEDES and there was a picture of a centipede on it.

"I don't think there's anything funny about my T-shirt," she said. "It must have been something else. Do I look funny? Tell me the truth." She looked at me soberly.

"Darling, you don't look funny at all. They might be wishing I'd leave so they could take a shot at getting you to join their club."

"You mean like run away with them?"

At that I looked terribly upset.

Joan laughed at me.

95. A Kitchen Chair

Joan bought some puddingstone which was a geological feature of the area. It's a grey stone with brightly coloured flaws. There's an apocryphal story about some guy from Bruce Mines who travelled all the way to Texas looking for puddingstone around the turn of the century when the mines were getting started. Little did he know that he could have found all he wanted if he'd stayed in his own back yard.

A girl with long luxuriant yellow hair was in charge of the Bruce Mines museum. There was a skull of an Indian woman with a bullet hole in it. I complained to the girl about the use of the term "squaw" on the card, like a good loyal citizen. She just yawned.

Most of the stuff on display originally belonged to the Cornish miners whose tin mines had become unprofitable and so came to the area around 1850 to work the copper mines. For instance, there was a fabulous homemade kitchen chair. It had been made over a hundred years ago from one peculiarly shaped branch of a tree. The branch was shaped like this:

and the guy who found it merely sliced it down the middle which gave him both sides of the back and seat and four legs. It was a perfect "found poem." If only poets could be that intelligent.

96. Nineteen Wheelchairs

We drove along the back streets of Thessalon and down to the waterfront. It was such a Canadian town, temporary, unpainted, unplanned. It was so different from the sedate old Europeanesque towns of Southern Ontario, Nova Scotia, or the Eastern Townships. In the park was a plaque commemorating the capture of two American warships in 1814.

On a theatre marquee in Blind River was a sign saying A STAR IS BORN RESTRICTED. "Aren't we all?" said Joan. Just outside town was a hand-painted sign reading TRAILER STORAGE AVIABLE, available being a word not often heard in ordinary conversation and therefore easily misspelled.

Then in the town of Algoma we passed a guy wearing a grey jumpsuit, all grease-stained. On the back, in what looked like yellow paint, he'd drawn the words BOBO'S DO IT ALL followed by a question mark daubed on as an afterthought. The guy was walking quickly along the street, his shoulders hunched over, his arms swinging in right angles to his direction of travel. I thought of Robert Fones' Bobo stories and decided to check this guy out. I stopped the car and went into a nearby restaurant ostensibly to get a cup of tea for Joan, whom I left sitting in the car with the kids.

As the proprietor prepared the tea in a white styrofoam cup I asked him about Bobo's Do It All.

"The guy with that sign on his back is Bobo," said the guy. "He's a real interesting fella. He's been around here for years and years. He lives all by himself in a little trailer outside town and he does odd jobs. He washes windows, rakes lawns and all that. Pretty well any little job you want done, he'll do it. But he doesn't need hardly any money at all to live on because he lives all by himself and that. So with the extra money he gets he buys wheelchairs and gives them to crippled people. So far he's given away nineteen wheelchairs."

"Great story! Thanks!"

97. Pleasant Moments In a Small-Town Bus Depot

I couldn't get over the atmosphere in that little restaurant. Everyone was so friendly. The place doubled as a bus depot for the little town and one of the waitresses was filling out a bus ticket for someone who was going to Sudbury. She kept making little mistakes and laughing.

"You should take a coffee break about now," said the guy buying the ticket.

The bus driver was standing there waiting. "She's already had six or seven today," he said.

"It was probably that decaffeinated stuff. What she needs is the real thing," said the guy.

"That's for sure," said the bus driver, leeringly.

The girl blushed. She finished off the ticket and handed it to the guy along with his change.

"Geez, I sure don't feel like working today," said the bus driver as the guy handed him the ticket.

"You don't call driving a bus working, do you?" said the guy.

"Geez, you guys who stay at the Downtowner Inn and get sloshed then figure you can insult the bus driver the next day, eh?"

Just then I went to pick up the tea and managed to hit the edge of the counter with the back of my hand, skinning it in two places. The blood started seeping out.

"Are you insured?" I said to the waitress.

"You just sit down over here and I'll call an ambulance," she said.

195

98. An Old Man on an Important Mission

There was an old man waiting for the bus to get going. He was grasping his ticket as if he were afraid he'd lose it. He reminded me so much of my late grandfather I just had to speak to him for a minute. He seemed so small and feeble.

I'd been thinking of my grandfather anyway because of the great Foreman-Ali fight that had been on television the night before. I'd forgotten all about it until this morning. My grandfather had been a great fan of what he called pugilistics and he used to listen to all the fights on the radio and write them up in his diary. He would write little summaries of the fights just like a real sportswriter. Every time I see a good boxing match on television I think of him and how happy he would have been if he'd lived long enough to see the fights on TV. He was a hardcore fan and knew about all the famous boxers of the first forty years of this century. This old fellow sitting here reminded me so much of him I asked him if he'd seen the fight.

"What fight?" he said.

"The Foreman-Ali fight last night."

"Oh yes, I did see it," he said. "It was good. Better than wrestling. Wrestling's phony you know."

He looked at me as if he'd just given me the secret of the universe. As if he almost expected me to disagree.

We continued talking and he pulled out a piece of paper with an address written in a feeble old man's wobbly hand. It said 27 TERRACE STREET. Then under it was the name of a store: PAUL'S LIGHTING FIXTURES.

He asked me if I knew where Terrace Street was in Sudbury. I told him I didn't know. But I told him someone at the Sudbury bus station would certainly be able to help him.

He said he had to get to that address to buy some wicks for his son's coal-oil lamps. His son lived in some small town in northern Manitoba. He couldn't remember the name of the town. But it had been hit by a terrible windstorm and the power had been knocked out. His son dug out his old coal-oil lamps to use until the electricity was restored. But he found the wicks had burnt out. So he called his father in Algoma and asked him to pick up some wicks in Sudbury and mail them to him as fast as possible.

"It's an emergency you know," said the old timer.

I wondered if the son realised how old and feeble his father had become. I asked the old guy when he'd last seen his son. "Oh, it's been years and years," he said.

I later found out there was indeed a Terrace Street in Sudbury, a short alley in the north end, but Paul's Lighting Fixtures had faded out of business years before. I also found out there hadn't been a serious storm in northern Manitoba since the winter. I felt as if I'd stumbled on a real-life Thomas Hardy novel being enacted just outside the range of my peripheral vision.

99. Alison Falls down a Big Hole

"You were gone a long time," said Joan, sipping her cold tea.

I told her the story about Bobo and the story about the old man.

Bruce and both kids were sleeping. But they woke up as we got back up to highway speed.

We stopped briefly at Serpent River and walked down the smooth granite shoulders of the fast-moving stream. We were parked next to a van like ours except orange. It had Michigan plates and a bumper sticker that read AMERICA NEEDS YOUR PRAYERS. WILL YOU PRAY? We were parked at the edge of a bluff. I looked down. There was garbage strewn all over the place all the way down. People were taking pictures of the famous Serpent River rapids, trying to frame a shot that didn't show the garbage.

Jennifer came running up to us. "Alison fell down a big hole," she said. Our hearts sank like stones and blood drained from our faces.

"I was only kidding," said Jennifer. "She's over there."

"Don't you ever do anything like that again, you hear me?" said Joan.

"Sorry, mommy."

100. Mild Psychic Torture at Serpent River

How nice it was to have Joan and the kids along on this trip. Usually I don't enjoy travelling because of my morbid imagination which pictures all kinds of things happening to the family at home: Jennifer spilling boiling water all over her pretty little face, Alison being hit by a speeding dump truck, Joan collapsing under the strain of it all without me there to comfort her.

And then climbing up from the river was a little kid blind in one eye. You could see the bottom half of the pupil of his right eye bulging up toward heaven, his other eye as bright as a cat's. He kept running up and down the granite slopes. I shuddered. It was unbearable yet I couldn't take my eyes away from the kid. I noticed a pretty girl about eighteen sitting on a picnic bench with her boyfriend. They were mildly caressing each other. Then I noticed she had only one arm. The right arm ended in a steel hook.

I felt I was being tortured. I found myself muttering to God: I know there's a lot of misery in the world, I said. You don't have to rub my nose in it. Why did God or fate or mathematical chance always push misshaped people into my consciousness like fishermen's hooks? I could remember them all: the midgets, the man with no nose who haunted Kenilworth Avenue all through my childhood and once offered to help me across the busy street to the library, the legless girl who wheeled up to my house one sunny June afternoon in her wheelchair with a stack of handwritten poems she wanted me to read, the spastic who stopped me on the street one day and asked me how I would like to be him. And the dreams, where horribly misshapen and tortured little children approach me and call me Daddy. And the deeper dreams where horrendous monsters with black wings and drooling black pus would rise from the depths of Hamilton Harbour where I was stranded at night in a sailboat with no wind. Why me?

101. Sybil's Pantry

Some sweet violin music was playing on the stereo in Sybil's Pantry, a nice little restaurant in the town of Spanish at the mouth of the Spanish River.

"This is where Frank and Percy and his friends wind up their annual September canoe trip," I said. We were looking at the map. "See? They bring one van down here to Spanish and load up all their canoes and gear on the other van and take it up here through Sudbury and up to where the Spanish River crosses Highway 144. Then they canoe all the way back down to Spanish. Then they load up the other van and drive back up through Sudbury and along Highway 144 to pick up the second van."

"Isn't that clever?" said Joan, sarcastically. She doesn't like Frank for several complicated reasons. She doesn't like Percy either come to think of it. It has to do with the way they treat their wives.

There was a nineteenth-century air about this little restaurant—red velvet wallpaper, English brass rubbings on the wall, framed prints of nineteenth-century landscapes. Even the music, although there'd be no stereo in the nineteen century and a place this small wouldn't be able to support a violinist—unless or maybe even if he was playing for his supper.

Sybil was wearing white sandals and a 1940-style dress that came just below the knees. She had a 1940 hair-style and looked as if she should be in uniform. She was constantly laughing at her own jokes and running from the kitchen to the grill to the tables and back to the microwave oven. We were her only customers. It looked as if we might have been the only ones she had all day.

Then she would relax and take long puffs on her cigarette. I was hoping she'd be smoking Players Navy Cut or some other brand from the 1940s like Black Cat Cork Tips, like my mother used to smoke. But they were just Cameos.

She was English. "Sybil means witch you know," she said. "I don't mind if people call me a witch. I think it's true. I am one." She was just babbling on like that in the most unselfconscious fashion. I loved her.

The kids ordered hamburgers, Joan ordered a schnitzel and I ordered steak and kidney pie. "We don't have steak and kidney pie today," said Sybil. She said she was just cooking up a batch of beef and kidneys for the next day.

"Just give it to me without the pastry," I said, feeling like Mr. Leopold Bloom. She said she couldn't do that but offered to mix up some biscuit dough to go with it. It was delicious.

All through the meal Sybil babbled away mostly to Joan. I picked up brief passages of the monologue and then my attention would be distracted by the food. As the meal ended Sybil was telling of the death of her sister in 1943.

Sybil had had a dream three days earlier. She dreamt she was flying over the English countryside and saw an accident. She flew low and followed a speeding ambulance. She saw them pick up her sister's body. Her sister had been riding a motorcycle which was hit by a truck.

"She was only nineteen," said Sybil. "She was to be married in three weeks." You could see tears in her eyes. She took another puff on her Cameo.

102. Watching Television in Massey

An old timer was sitting on a chair with his feet propped up on a table just inside the front door of the museum in Massey, Ontario. He was watching a portable television. A commercial for dog food came on. It showed a tiny stagecoach pulled by a team of tiny horses. The stagecoach came out of a dog-food box and sped across the kitchen floor, a full-sized barking beagle in pursuit.

"How do they do that, Dave?" said Joan.

"I don't know." I looked at the old guy.

"Me neither," he said.

It cost fifty cents to get into the museum but since we'd been in the Bruce Mines museum just down the road we didn't feel like it even though it contained a scale model of the old trading post, Fort Lacloche. We picked up a brochure on Chutes Provincial Park which was just a little north of Massey. It showed kids in bathing suits sitting on smooth slippery-looking granite rocks bordering a fast-moving stream.

"Want to stay at Chutes tonight?" I said.

"No, it looks too dangerous for Jennifer."

Joan went back to sit in the car with the kids while I walked down the street looking for a grocery store. I found a little Red and White. When I came out with a bag full of groceries I saw a terrible accident. I think Joan must have had a vague precognitive sense of this accident when she remarked on the park being too dangerous for Jenny. Danger was in the air.

103. An Ordinary Afternoon in Massey

Here it is exactly the way I saw it happen. I walked out of the Red and White store with a bag of groceries. My attention was drawn to two young women walking diagonally across the street. It should be mentioned here that the main street of Massey is the Trans-Canada Highway. The two women were engrossed in conversation and were paying no heed to traffic. A mail truck came by at about thirty-five miles an hour just as they were about at the centre stripe. The driver honked his horn and a split second later hit the girls. Then he slammed on his brakes and screeched to a stop.

I dropped the bag of groceries and ran out to the girls. They were screaming and moaning. One of the wheels had passed over the leg of the girl closer to me. But there didn't seem to be any serious damage—no bones broken, just shock. I put my arm around her comfortingly and talked to her like a baby. "You're not badly hurt. You'll be fine. Don't worry," I crooned.

"I'm gonna be sick," she said, then vomited all over the front of my shirt. She even splattered my face. I don't know what she'd been eating but it just gushed out of her.

The other girl was in much the same situation—no serious injuries, just shock. But she didn't vomit. I helped my girl to the side of the road and some other guy helped the other girl over. The driver of the mail truck just sat behind the wheel. He looked sick too.

Someone asked if I'd mind directing traffic around the scene of the accident while we waited for the Ontario Provincial Police to arrive. The mail truck had to sit there in the middle of the highway until the official measurements of the skid marks et cetera were taken. So I agreed.

But directing traffic isn't easy. I kept waving traffic on when I should have been signalling it to stop and vice versa. The other guy who was directing traffic further down the street just couldn't get synchronised with me. Then someone else took my place. He was a lot better than me. He talked a lot to the drivers too, or rather shouted.

"What are you waitin' for, Christmas? This ain't a peep show. What's the matter with you? Can't you see a hand signal?... Come on, get her in high gear.... Let's go."

I went back to the sidewalk and picked up my bag of groceries. A big crowd had gathered. They were just standing there watching the girls sitting on the curb crying. Some Indians from the nearby reserve went by but didn't stop. They just kept on walking with hardly a glance at the girls. The girls' parents had arrived on the scene and one of the mothers was near hysterical. "Would somebody please explain how this happened?" she said. It appeared that I was the only one to witness the accident but I didn't say anything. I was just waiting for the police to arrive to give them my statement. The smell of the vomit was still there but I was getting used to it.

104. A Brain Haemorrhage in Massey

Away up the street I could see our saffron-coloured van parked innocently in the shade of a large small-town roadside maple. I expected Joan and the kids to come running down the street, wondering if I'd been hit by a car. But they didn't notice the flashing lights of the ambulance and police cruiser.

The girls were put on stretchers and placed in the ambulance. Nobody complained that it had taken both the ambulance and the police cruiser half-an-hour to reach the scene of the accident.

The police officer was standing amid a good-sized crowd. "Can anyone tell me what time it happened?" he said.

I was standing off to one side. "Exactly thirty-two minutes ago," I said in a slightly sarcastic tone.

The policeman looked at me. "I only got the call seven minutes ago," he said.

The policeman asked me to sit in the back seat of the cruiser next to the driver of the mail truck. His name was Charlie Robillard of Sudbury. He wasn't saying much. I was a little bit mad at him for hitting the girls. He should have seen they weren't going to look. He should have slowed down a lot sooner instead of barrelling through like that.

"It was mostly the girls' fault," I told the cop as he wrote in his notebook. "But the driver had a clear view of them. He should have seen they were engrossed in conversation."

"I know what you mean," said the cop. "You mean he wasn't driving defensively. Right?"

"Right."

"Well there's probably no criminal charges we can lay. There's nothing in the book about failing to drive defensively. But possibly they'll be able to nail him in civil court. Thanks for waiting, Mr. McFadden."

As I got out of the car Joan was standing there. She must have noticed the flashing lights after all. "All right," she said. "What happened?"

I told her.

"Oh God," she said. "You were gone so long I decided to look back and saw the ambulance. I thought you'd had a brain haemorrhage or something. Oh Christ, I thought. How are we ever going to get home now?"

"A brain haemorrhage? Me?"

"You never know."

105. The Girl from Espanola

We threw the groceries in the back of the van and took off out of Massey along the Trans-Canada Highway once again. We were getting close to the point where we'd have to decide whether to head down to Manitoulin Island then take the ferry to Tobermory or continue on to Sudbury and then down the Georgian Bay route.

We finally decided on Manitoulin. After all, it's a fabulous place, the world's largest freshwater island and the dwelling place of the good spirit Gitchi-Manitou and his evil counterpart Matchi-Manitou. People have lived there for at least 12,000 years.

We'd all been on Manitoulin Island before but we'd never driven Highway 68 from Espanola to Little Current. It's really the scenic route with a series of hills so rocky and rugged we couldn't believe we were in Ontario.

Espanola is just south of the Trans-Canada. It seemed like an ordinary town. There was little to indicate it was a ghost town during the Depression and only revived when the Kalamazoo Vegetable Parchment Company opened a kraft paper mill there in 1945. When I was nineteen I fell in love with a girl from Espanola and was always going to come up here and visit the town and find her but I never did. It would have been inappropriate for me to start looking for her now, with my wife and kids along. If I were alone I'd feel the same way, being a married man and all.

The rocky hills south of Espanola had been sitting there like that for two and a half billion years. Huge piles of Canadian Shield limestone, sandstone and crystalline granite. And then, with the highway threatening to turn into a roller coaster, there'd be a sudden outcropping of Niagara Escarpment limestone layers crumbling away before our very weary eyes.

We came out of the hills and onto a plain on the south shore of Birch Island. Across a meadow could see the tops of two sailboats. It looked as if they were sailing on the grass. And then we crossed the swing bridge into Little Current, the largest and northernmost town on Manitoulin Island.

106. The Four Aces

"I still can't figure out what kitsch means," said Joan. We were passing a series of Ojibway gift stores along Highway 68 which runs down from Little Current through Sheguiandah and along the shore of Manitowaning Bay. Most of the Indians who live on Manitoulin Island live on the small section of the island east of Highway 68. They have very good relations with the white inhabitants, many of whom are studying Ojibway.

"I don't think it really means anything," I said. I knew damned well what it meant: it was a German word meaning garbage, and was used to make fun of bourgeois taste in art.

But Joan's feelings would be hurt if I told her that. Joan had been worried about the word ever since a poet from St. Catharines stayed at our place a while back and complimented Joan on her kitsch décor.

"You've got good taste in kitsch," said the poet, who seemed to be an innocent, and who probably didn't know what the word meant either. Joan didn't want to appear ignorant by asking what is kitsch. But she kept thinking about it, and even went to the library and went through a book of kitsch illustrations trying to figure out what it meant. That didn't help at all.

"It must mean something," she said.

"As far as I can figure out it's a word used by the upper middle class to describe the taste of the lower middle class. It's a term of condescension. It's a way of dismissing something you don't want to have to deal with, something you don't want to have to take seriously or to pass judgment on. It's something you don't have to take seriously."

I was merely repeating what my friend the painter Greg Curnoe had told me but I wanted to sound original. After all, Joan thinks I'm brilliant—at times.

We came over a hill and there was the place we were destined to spend the night. The Four Aces Campgrounds overlooked Manitowaning Bay, and you could see Winnebagos and tent trailers parked amid the trees. Smoke was snaking its way from tiny bonfires up through the twilight. This place had an attractive aura about it. I knew we'd get a good night's sleep here. It seemed lucky.

At the front was a low white building that housed the office and a small general store for campers and other tourists. On the lawn in front of the store were four rectangular pieces of plywood, each about five feet tall and four feet wide, painted and set up to represent the four aces of the card pack. And off to one side were two other large pieces of plywood painted and cut out to represent a dog and a fire hydrant.

"This looks perfect," said Joan.

107. The Hamilton Tiger-Cats

As we registered I asked the guy about boats. I thought it would be a good idea to take the kids fishing in the morning. When I was a kid my dad and my uncles used to take me fishing a lot. My kids had never gone fishing. The proprietor said the boat and motor would be twelve bucks. Canoes were three bucks an hour. As for fishing gear, he didn't rent it. "I've never had any call for it," he said.

It turned out the guy was a refugee from Hamilton, Ont. When he saw me writing Hamilton on the registration form he said, "How is that smoky, polluted city?"

"Terrible," I said. "We get away from it every chance we can." It's simpler than trying to explain why you like it.

"I used to live there," said the guy. "I was born and raised there." The guy had a shining bald spot on his head. His wife came up and started smiling. She was about fifty, quite lovely. Even the numerous liver spots on her face were charmingly arranged.

"Are you from Hamilton too?" I said.

"I was born in Toronto actually," she said, "but I lived most of my life in Hamilton."

"You're smart. You got out."

"Oh, I don't know. We quite like it. We still go back quite a bit. Tiger-Cats aren't doing so well this year are they?"

108. The Energy Crisis

We paid our five dollars and they gave us Number 3. It was supposed to be on the front row so we could watch the sun coming up in the morning over Georgian Bay, if we were up early enough that is. But there didn't seem to be a Number 3. There was a camping van with Michigan plates in the Number 2 spot, and another with Ohio plates in the Number 4 spot. The people in Number 2 had sort of spread out along the front of the beach. They had erected two or three tents and a large number of picnic tables and lawn chairs. There was a little pole in front of one of their tents with a rag draped over it. Joan hopped out of the van and lifted the rag. Sure enough. There was a Number 3 under it. So we pulled in, behind the people from Ohio.

Joan was angry. "They just put that rag over the pole so nobody would tell them to move."

"Should we tell them to move over and give us some room?"

"No," said Joan. "We'll be leaving first thing in the morning. Let them be."

We got set up. I plugged in the electrical cord. The outlet was on the same pole. The cord from Number 2 was also plugged in but it didn't fit snugly. It was quite loose. And so was mine. I couldn't get it to fit properly so I changed the two around. That was fine. So I just left it like that.

About an hour later Joan was getting the kids ready for bed and I was sitting at the picnic bench looking at the sky. Some rain clouds were piling up in the west. Then this fat kid about fourteen came over with an unhappy look on his face. He was from Number 2, Michigan. Bruce came running up to him, wagging his tail. The kid said get away and kicked him. I couldn't believe it.

The kid walked right over to the pole. Apparently their ice was melting. The power had gone off. He looked at the pole and started shouting back at the people at his campsite. I was only about five feet away from him.

"Oh, it figures," he shouted. "They took out our plug and switched it around. They've taken the good one and given us the rotten one."

I looked at Joan. She was looking out of the van at the fat kid with the lungs. She looked as if she were about to jump out of the van and start beating the kid up. He stormed back to his campsite and whispered something to his father or big brother. Then they got in their pickup truck and drove off with a roar, scattering gravel from the road. I guess they went to complain to the proprietor. I didn't care. I could always insist they move their stuff out of the Number 3 area. I didn't feel vindictive, even though the kid had kicked the friendly little dog.

While he was gone I took a look at the pole. I switched the plugs back the other way. Even though they fit loosely contact was made. "Have you got power now?" I yelled over to the people from Michigan.

They checked their fridge. "Yup. It's okay now!"

"Fine then," I said.

109. Vaughan Monroe Threatens to Kill Himself

We woke up about two in the morning. The rain was beating on our tin roof. Above the sound of the rain we could hear voices from the next campsite. Actually we couldn't tell where the voices were coming from—the Ohio side (the nice people in Number 4) or the Michigan side (the psychotics in Number 2).

There were two men and a woman. The main character had a rich baritone voice like Vaughan Monroe which merely added to the unreality of what he was saying. Vaughan Monroe would never talk like this guy.

"Fuck this, fuck that," he said. "You fuckin' bitch. Fuck you." We could hear him getting to his feet and knocking something over. This went on for quite a while. Joan had to have a pee. The kids were awake and giggling to themselves. Joan started looking through the curtains. The voices seemed to be neither from the Ohio nor the Michigan camp but from a tent across the path behind us.

The woman's voice: "You just think you're so fuckin' smart because you're drinking." With that Vaughan Monroe let out a yell. It sounded as if he were trying to knock the tent down.

"I didn't ask you," he roared. "Shut your fuckin' mouth."

A few minutes later the spying Joan announced that a couple were behind the tent in a passionate embrace. Meanwhile Vaughan Monroe was inside the tent making himself a tomato sandwich. You could hear him mumbling to himself. He was opening and slamming cupboard doors, slamming down the knife, slamming down the salt shaker. He appeared to be angry because he had to make his own sandwich.

The passionate couple came back into the tent. "Look, Bob. Don't be so fuckin' angry all the time you drink."

"Listen, Arlene. Four months ago I didn't fuckin' well drink at all.... Want another shot, Jim?"

Things quietened down after that and Joan stole out of the van in her flannel pyjamas. She couldn't hold it back any longer. She squatted behind a tree. Just then a big commotion started again and Vaughan Monroe started screaming that he was going to get into the boat and kill himself. He said he was going to take the boat out a mile or two then put it on full throttle and aim it at the concrete dock.

"Go ahead, then," said Arlene. "You'd never have enough guts you silly bugger."

"I wouldn't eh? Well you'll see how much guts I've got. You just wait and see."

110. Racing with the Moon

With that, Bob came charging out of his tent and made a wide sweep around our van on his way to the dock. At the same time, Joan was still squatting there behind the tree. As he swept around the tree, Bob almost tripped over her bare bum. "Oh, excuse me, madam," he intoned, baritone-ishly.

"He even smiled," Joan said when she got back in the van. She giggled.

As we listened a roar from the dock indicated Bob was installed in his death machine and had got the motor going. And vroom off he went in the blackness of Georgian Bay, the motor growing fainter as he went. Soon all we could hear was the rain.

Then the faint sound of the motor floated into our minds again and grew and grew. We lay there wide-eyed in the night as the sound grew dramatically to a roar. We expected at any moment to hear a violent crash as the little boat smashed full speed into the concrete pier. We had a feeling of utter helplessness.

But it didn't happen. At the last minute Bob cut the motor, swerved, and headed back out into the blackness. We realised we weren't the only ones listening. Arlene and Jim were probably sitting there holding hands, wondering if he'd actually do it. A little laughter in the dark is good for what ails you.

Bob repeated his near miss several times until it got boring and we dropped off to sleep. I'm sorry we can't tell you anything of Bob's fate because we just don't know. That's the nature of this sort of book, unfortunately—and of this sort of life.

We pulled out of the Four Aces fairly early in the morning, before the others began stirring. We wanted to get to South Baymouth before 9:10 when the ferry was due to leave for Tobermory.

WEDNESDAY, AUGUST 10

111. A Ferry Tale

It was still raining. That's why we were in a hurry to take the morning ferry. Manitoulin Island is unpleasant in the rain.

"I don't like camping any more," said Joan. "I want to sell the van." I noticed she no longer called it Gus. When we first got the van we always called it Gus the Bus, after Gus McFarlane our big fat Member of Parliament.

We arrived at South Baymouth with plenty of time to spare. Ten minutes in fact. We were the second car in the line-up. But the line-up wasn't moving. Then I realised why. The ferry was already filled to capacity. I walked up to the car ahead of us. It was an MG with Manitoba plates. A guy with a walkie-talkie and a blue uniform was measuring it with a tape measure. "Okay, go ahead," he said.

Then he measured our van. "Thirteen feet," he said over the walkie-talkie.

Back came the answer: "No, he's about two inches too long."

"That's it," said the guy with the tape. "You're going to have to wait for the one-thirty ferry."

"One-thirty! It's only nine o'clock. Oh Christ!"

Just then the ferry started pulling out, a huge boat filled with hundreds of cars, Winnebagos, buses, tractor trailers, motorcycles, bicycles, everything. The gulls were squealing with delight in the morning rain, and all the merry ferry passengers were standing on the wet decks taking wet pictures of the wet loading docks.

I was infuriated. It looked as if they were taking pictures of my van, the only vehicle not able to get aboard. I made a fist at the ferry. One of the passengers shook his fist back at me then snapped my picture.

A rope was dangling from the end of the boat as it moved out into Lake Huron. "Look kids," I said. A ferry tail." They laughed merrily.

112. Scrambled Eggs

We sat in silent gloom in the van for an hour while the rain stopped and more vehicles pulled up to join us in our long wait for the afternoon ferry. Finally we decided it was time for breakfast. The four of us walked across the broad expanse of the parking lot to the restaurant, a large frame building. It looked as if it had been converted from a house. It was called the Ferry Diner.

It was cafeteria style and there were several people sitting at tables stuffing themselves with scrambled eggs. Behind the cafeteria counter was a big chalked sign reading BREAKFAST MENU. We stood there reading it.

SCRAMBLED EGGS

BACON   HAM   OR SAUSAGES

TOAST   COFFEE $2.50

TOAST JAM COFFEE .90

CORN FLAKES .75

Next to it was another large chalkboard sign spelling out a sad fact of civilised life:

WASHROOMS FOR CUSTOMERS ONLY

I walked up to the girl behind the counter. "What about fried eggs or poached eggs?"

"We only have scrambled eggs," she said as if it were extremely rude of me to ask.

"But we like our eggs fried. Is there another restaurant around?"

The girl broke into a smile. "No," she said.

Joan almost hit the roof. "Come on, Dave. Let's go," she said. "I wouldn't eat here if I was starving,"

113. The Secretary of Lakehead University

All around us gulls were squealing with unearthly delight. At the dock two kids were fishing for perch. They caught several little ones. We let Bruce run for a minute and he chased about 144 gulls off the dock.

Joan started preparing breakfast in the van. Fried eggs and bacon, coffee, toast, marmalade, everything. A guy who looked like a real-estate agent and his wife were sitting in a brand new grey Lincoln parked next to us. They gave us occasional snooty looks.

"I'm not the slightest bit embarrassed," said Joan. "Let them pay $2.50 for breakfast and make those slimy crooks rich."

After breakfast, which was delicious, I started writing in my book. Joan became alarmed.

"This is the only restaurant around here. People will know which one you're talking about. You're going to get in trouble."

"Oh Joan, haven't you ever heard of fair comment and malice prepense? Besides, I didn't use the restaurant's real name. It's really called the Summer Kitchen. Besides, they have a perfect right to offer fried eggs only and to charge $2.50, which isn't bad, considering they have a little monopoly here, and they have to make enough money in the tourist season to last all year."

Joan wasn't so sure, and the kids picked up on her unease. "I hope this book never gets published," said Jenny.

"Don't say anything," said Alison. "Daddy'll write it down."

There was a little kid about five running around with a war bonnet on his head complete with eagle feathers. He also had a little Indian drum and a stick. It looked as if he'd been outfitted in one of the Ojibway craft stores on the island.

"This whole thing is making me sick," said Joan.

"I thought you'd feel better after breakfast. More tea?"

"I'll get it myself. And that big fat kid from the States who kicked Bruce. I'd like to punch the shit out of him. Little Brucie wagging his tail for a little attention. Get away! Poor Brucie just walked away with an awfully hurt expression on his face."

I got out and watched the two kids fishing. They caught several more little perch and put them on a string. They'd make a fabulous lunch.

A guy from Timmins came by and began chatting. I asked him what were his favourite fish. He said he liked pickerel best. I told him I liked whitefish and trout.

"That too," he said. The kids seemed worried we were going to steal their fish.

Along came a guy in Bavarian Liederhosen. We got talking and it turned out he was the secretary of Lakehead University. He had come all the way from Thunder Bay along the south shore of Lake Superior. "It's even more scenic than the north shore," he said. He began telling us some funny stories about moose hunting. Then he told an affectionate story about the poet Irving Layton. It involved Irving's famous ego. He seemed to remember Layton with affection.

114. Cheezies on the *Chi-Cheemaun*

We were aboard the *Chi-Cheemaun*. It was only its second year of operation and it was a nice boat. The seagulls were flying at exactly the same speed. A guy with a bag of Cheezies was standing on the outer deck feeding the little orange things to the gulls. He would hold a Cheezie between his forefinger and thumb. The bird would fly up and, still flapping its wings to maintain the same speed as the boat, would put its bill carefully around the Cheezie and swoop away with it as if it were a little goldfish. The guy then looked through the window into the inner decks to see if anyone was watching.

The last time we were on this ferry I saw an Amish farmer doing the same thing, but with more gusto somehow, and less self consciousness. As the gull flew up and took the Cheezie, the farmer laughed with glee and at no time did he look to see if anyone was watching him. It was beautiful to see a totally natural man.

It was also strange that the Amish farmer was using Cheezies as well. Maybe it's a tradition on this boat to feed Cheezies to the gulls. Almost everything we do we have seen someone else do before—all the way back, every word a step in the darkness.

115. A Typical Conversation between Two U.S. Tourists

I was standing on the deck of the *Chi-Cheemaun*, right in the bow. The wind was blowing in my face so hard I had trouble breathing. I was watching the small rocky wooded islands pass us on either side. As we pushed forward the islands revolved like saucers on the ends of sticks. You know that juggler who always used to appear on the *Ed Sullivan* show spinning plates on the ends of sticks?

There was an interesting conversation going on behind me. I chose not to look back at the men talking so I can't describe them visually. But they had Midwest U.S. accents. Here is the conversation as I heard it:

"I've got a big '73 Chrysler New Yorker."

"So have I."

"We left Sault Ste. Marie this morning."

"So did I."

"We had breakfast in a nice little restaurant in a place called, uh, Bruce Mines."

"The Copper Kettle?"

"That's it."

"So did I."

"We're going to take in that theatre at Stratford. *Richard III* and *As You Like It*. I like it myself."

"I like it myself too."

"My son graduated from college and there was nothing in his field so he went to law school."

"So did mine."

And on and on like that.

116. Miss Addleton and the *National Geographic*

I would have listened to this fascinating conversation for a lot longer but it was too cold out there on the outer deck. It was summer and I was wearing a jacket but the jacket was too thin for the cold Lake Huron breeze.

So I went back to the tourist compartment. Joan was sitting on a bench facing two elderly women with blue hair. They'd discovered Joan was a school teacher and since they were retired school teachers themselves they had lots to talk about. They were talking about all the travelling they'd done since they'd retired.

"We've been just everywhere," they said, delightedly.

"Have you been to Mount Hope?" said Jennifer.

"Mount Hope? Where's that?"

"It's near Hamilton."

"Well no, dear. We haven't actually been everywhere."

"She's been like this since the age of two," I said. "She's a bonafide literalist."

They didn't seem to think that was much of a joke. A sense of humour was missing from their lives. Maybe that's why they were living such long healthy lives. Laughter can be harmful to your health. I can't remember where they were from. I can remember them well but not where they were from. Funny because for me that's usually the most important thing about a person.

But we talked for quite a while and I found out about some islands off the coast of Georgia, and Kauai, one of the Hawaiian islands. It was just like reading the *National Geographic*. When I was a kid I didn't care for children's books, and when we had to do book reports I would always do one on the current, or back, issue of the *National Geographic*.

One day the teacher, apparently after some serious deliberation and perhaps some consultation with the principal, wanted to talk to me about my book reports.

"Do you read each issue you review from cover to cover?"

"Yes," I said. I think I was lying.

"Even the ads?"

"Well, no."

"Then I think you'd better review real books rather than magazines from now on if you don't mind. I think that would be a lot better. Don't you?"

"Yes, Miss Addleton."

Funny the way things remind you of things. The two retired school teachers reminded me of Miss Addleton and they also reminded me of the *National Geographic* which also reminded me of Miss Addleton.

As far as writers are concerned, a lot of writers might also have forgotten—as did I—where those two elderly women came from but they probably wouldn't have admitted it and would have made up some place. Like Paris, Ontario, or London, Ontario, or Warsaw, Ontario, or Shakespeare, Saskatchewan. But not me. I'm too honest. Trust me.

115. Ballast Stones

In the cafeteria there was a line-up. It took ten minutes before I reached the cash register. There was a little red heart stuck to it. Then I discovered I had nothing smaller than a twenty-dollar bill and the girl behind the cash register was short of change.

The guy behind me was very nice about it. He pulled out his wallet. "Can I help you?" he said. "You're in the yellow van, aren't you?" He gave me three dollars. "Take this and you can pay me back later, maybe when we dock."

So I paid for the two pots of tea and one Danish. When I got back to the table Joan looked at the Danish and said she wanted a whole one, not half of mine. So I went back to the cashier and asked for another Danish. I still had some change left from the three bucks.

The fellow in front of me this time only had a twenty. But finally he found some change in a pocket he didn't know he had, like in those dreams when you're in your own familiar house and you suddenly discover a room you never before knew was there. And if you're brave enough to enter the room you'll find a priceless treasure.

When the fellow had gone the cashier took my money. There was no one behind me so we chatted for a minute.

"Maybe I could ask the captain to put in at one of those islands," she said, "so you could get some change."

"No. Don't bother doing that for me," I said. "I'm nobody important."

"Really?" she said, teasingly. "I could have sworn you were someone very important. You're not in the movies are you? Or in the arts in some way?"

"Why yes as a matter of fact I am," I said. "In the arts I mean."

"Oh really. I thought so," she said. "Now let me see. Who would you be? I know you from somewhere. Give me a hint. What branch of the arts are you in?"

"The martial arts," I said. "I take kung fu lessons at the Y."

"Hmm. Interesting. I bet you're involved in other arts as well."

This was getting ridiculous. Did I look arty? Should I tell her I'm quite interested in the art of love?

"None that I can think of off-hand. Just kung fu," I said. "But it wouldn't do for the captain to pull in at one of these islands even if he wanted to."

"Why not?"

"They're all uninhabited, aren't they? There'd be no one on them with any change."

"No. But some of them allow overnight camping. And you know if there's overnight camping allowed there has to be a laundromat, with coin-operated machines. And if there's coin-operated machines there has to be a change-making machine. Oh wait a minute. I lie. Cove Island is inhabited. They have a lighthouse there and I'm sure the operator would have some change. Are you interested in old lighthouses?"

"Immensely."

"I thought you might be. There's a really old one on Cove Island. It was built in the early part of the nineteenth century."

"Really, eh? How early?"

"Oh, about 1880."

"That's not early."

"It's earlier than 1890."

I couldn't believe this conversation. She started talking about how the early lighthouses on the Great Lakes were built out of ballast stones which ships carried after they dropped their cargo and had nothing else to pick up. Finally I took the Danish back to Joan.

"You were gone a long time," said Joan.

"Oh. Don't you know what happened?"

"No. What?"

"Somebody fell overboard. That little self-conscious guy who was feeding the gulls? He just reached over too far and fell in. It looked like one of the gulls did it on purpose by holding back a bit at the last minute. Anyway I had to jump in after him and save his life."

"Get off it." You couldn't fool Joan. "Your clothes aren't even wet."

"No. The captain pulled in at one of the islands and I threw my clothes in a coin-operated dryer. Didn't you hear the engines slow down and stop?"

"No. I was too engrossed in my thoughts."

"What were you thinking about?"

"I'm not telling you."

"Well, that's what happened."

"I believe you."

"You do? You believe that? That was just a cover-up. What really happened was I went down to the vehicle level and made love with a beautiful black woman in the back seat of her white Cadillac. She was just like Billie Holliday."

"It's not fair to tell lies."

119. How to Seduce Black Women

I feel sad today. The book-banners are out in force. There's even a town in Ontario where they're trying to ban *Who Has Seen the Wind*. And every time I flick on the television all I see is a panel of dopey-looking U.S. televangelists asking people to send in money.

A guy waving a Bible got up in a meeting in a school gym in Clinton, Ontario, a few days ago and said, "All the English literature anyone needs is right in this book."

It appears these people want to ban literature entirely, perhaps because they're incapable of seeing anything in it. But the time is not yet right for that. So for now all they can do is ban books that contain the word "fuck." As far as this book is concerned, if the title of this chapter has attracted any potential book-banners, I heartily entreat them to ban this book. *A Trip Around Lake Huron* is a perverse, scurrilous book. The author wants to corrupt your kids. At least he doesn't want them to grow up to be mean, crabby and unimaginative people like their parents.

Imagine! This book contains a chapter entitled "How to Seduce Black Women" and to make things even worse it has nothing to do with seducing black women. All it talks about is the attempted seduction of Canadian children by book banners who want to bring back slavery.

120. How to Admire Posh Yachts without Envy

The *Chi-Cheemaun* docked in Tobermory and suddenly the town of Tobermory doubled its population. I looked around for the guy who loaned me the three bucks but couldn't find him. I guess he forgot about it. God bless you, wherever you are. You have true generosity of spirit. I'd be surprised if you were involved in attempting to stifle the imagination of children.

We parked in downtown Tobermory and sat on a public bench in the pleasant sun. And oh, the boats in Tobermory Harbour! This seemed to be some kind of centre for the ostentatious wealthy from all around the Great Lakes. And it's easy to see why. The water is so deep and clear and there are so many thousands of uninhabited islands to explore within a few hours' sailing.

Members of the Boy Scout troop from Mount Olive, Indiana, were wandering all around the town in their olive-coloured uniforms covered with badges. Jennifer and I strolled out on the dock to take a close look at *The Firefly* from New York City. I wondered if it had come up through the Gulf of St. Lawrence or the Erie Canal. I thought of Caribou Jack's friends and their million-dollar boats. Jennifer held my hand. I felt sort of inadequate. For a moment it seemed the ultimate human tragedy that a beautiful child like Jennifer should have a father like me who can't even afford to take her sailing in the Great Lakes. She deserved better than me.

No one seemed to be home in *The Firefly* but there was someone stirring aboard *The Lady* from Troy, Michigan, which was moored right beside it.

"Would you like to have a boat like this some day, Jennifer?" I said.

"Yeah," said Jenny. "But it would cost too much money."

"Maybe you'll be rich some day." I felt like getting down on my knees and begging forgiveness for not having made more of my talents, for not having used my fine mind to amass a fortune for her rather than write these useless books.

Just then someone came out of the cabin. It was a girl about eighteen with a horsy face. She tilted her head back and looked at us along her long nose, a natural look of superiority. She looked as if she expected us to be embarrassed at finding out someone had been in there listening to us. She looked as if we'd said something to offend her. I wondered what she'd heard of our little conversation, and what she'd thought she'd heard.

All she said was "humph." Then she turned her back, ducked and went back into the cabin.

121. I Get to Talk With a Rich Man

We stood there a minute longer looking at the boats. I guess we were making some of the people feel a little nervous. Maybe they thought we were trying to look through their portholes at them. But surely they'd be resigned to being gawked at when they entered any old harbour.

A man about fifty came out of the *Phoenix III* from Beverly Shores, Indiana.

"Are you the harbourmaster?" he said. There might have been a slight sarcastic tone in his voice. I told him no. "Too bad," he said. "You could have collected a lot of money."

"I'm too honest for that," I said. He just looked at me, wondering if I were being sarcastic.

"Which is your vessel?"

Vessel? Why didn't he just say boat? And why did he assume I had a boat?

"The crocus-coloured one over there." He looked. I pointed at the van.

"Oh. Heh."

"Heh."

122. The Purple Moose

We were happy as all get out because it was only a few miles from Tobermory to our favourite place in the whole world: Cypress Lake Provincial Park. After a couple of hours wandering around Tobermory we no longer could postpone our bliss. We got in the van and took off along Highway 6 which, if we kept on it long enough, would pass right by our house in Hamilton.

But after a few minutes we hung a left and began driving down a narrow winding road through the cedar forest toward the edge of the Niagara Escarpment and glorious Georgian Bay. Our hearts were pounding.

Nothing could take away our love for Cypress Lake, not even the misery of our visit last fall. It was early fall and we weren't prepared for such cold, rainy weather. But even worse than the weather were the people we were with. Mind you, they're very nice people and I like them a lot. But they're no fun to go camping with.

You see, Luella and Simon are health-food proponents and teachers of yoga and meditation. Don't ever go camping with health-food proponents and teachers of yoga and meditation unless you're a health-food proponent and teacher of yoga and meditation yourself.

There was Joan frying eggs over the sputtering campfire under an almost-black mid-morning sky. She was wrapped in my hydro parka. Luella reached over and cracked one of her own eggs into a bare spot in the pan. Her upper lip wiggled with glee. "Oh look everybody," she said. "Look at my organic egg beside Joan's ordinary eggs. Mine makes hers look sick. Mine's so much bigger and the yolk is a darker orange."

I was pleasantly surprised that Joan didn't shove the eggs frying pan and all down Luella's throat. In fact it might have been a lot better if she had. After breakfast Joan started doing the dishes.

"Oh, use my soap, Joan," said Luella. "Mine's biodegradable."

We'd been eagerly anticipating a fabulous weekend but it didn't turn out that way. We certainly didn't mind foregoing meat. We're not big meat-eaters anyway. And it was nice to take a holiday from the kids.

But we did take Bruce along much to Luella and Simon's annoyance. Bruce would let out an inoffensive little bark whenever a chipmunk or groundhog would pass by, and it was getting on their nerves despite the fact that they were yoga and meditation teachers. And the blue jays, Joan and I were very happy about the blue jays, they were so beautiful. But Luella and Simon would moan and cover their ears with distaste whenever one would screech. They called them garbage birds. They made us feel we were stupid because we liked blue jays.

All four of us went for a long walk that afternoon, scrambling down the limestone cliffs of the Niagara Escarpment to the cold deep blue waters of Georgian Bay. At one point I fell off a rock and hurt my thumb. Luella applied Rescue Ointment, a homeopathic remedy with brandy and assorted secret organic compounds, and it felt better. I took off my shirt and shoes and dived into the water with just my jeans on. It was incredibly cold. The next thing I knew Luella had taken off her jeans and was swimming beside me in her panties and nothing else. She threw her arms around me and shivered with delight. I looked up at the high rocks and there was Joan standing there fuming, hands on hips.

That was the night of the big Canada-Russia hockey game and I wanted to go into town to watch it but they wouldn't let me go because they didn't want to sit in a smoky pub with beer drinkers. But at 7:30, just before the game was due to start, they had a change of heart. They decided we'd go to Tobermory to get some special vegetarian candy that's made there. The candy store was closed though so we ended up at the only hotel in town—the Tobermory Lodge—and had ice cream sundaes, chocolate milk and cherry cheesecake. You should have seen them wolfing down all this health food! I asked the guy running the place where his TV was. He said he didn't have one. "This is a high-class place," he said.

The next day John and Janet Boyle came up from Owen Sound. They brought their yellow canoe with the purple moose painted on the side—a purple moose being John's trademark as a famous Canadian painter.

"Did you paint that moose yourself John?" I said. It didn't quite look his style.

"No," said Janet. "He had it painted. He can't paint that good."

The Boyles are aficionados of Ontario wine and brought along a few bottles of Tawny Port 1976. The four of us drank it while Luella and Simon looked on coldly and sipped unfermented, unpasteurised apple juice with no additives. The Boyles refused to eat any of Luella's food. Janet had brought bologna and cheese sandwiches.

Simon took me to one side. "He can't be a good artist if he eats like that," he said.

"Well he is," I said. "It takes more than meditation and bean sprouts to be an artist." Simon winced. He paints a bit.

Anyway the Boyles brought too much food and wound up feeding some of the bologna to Bruce. "Here," said Simon. "Feed him this cheese too. It's pasteurised. And the bread. It's store boughten, fulla chemicals." Poor Bruce almost got poisoned.

It was an awful experience. I particularly felt sorry for John and Janet although we had a good canoe trip Sunday afternoon. Janet was several times on the verge of smashing Luella's face in with a rock.

Luella and Simon were totally exhausted at the end of the weekend while Joan and I were more refreshed than when we arrived. Luella was complaining of headaches, stomach aches, running nose, hypoglycemia, tiredness, general allergies and low blood sugar. They even had more mosquito bites than we did. In fact we didn't have any.

And best of all, Luella and Simon came equipped with Kodiak Grebs, which are supposed to be the ultimate in walking shoes. Joan and I had our ordinary loafers. Yet we were the ones who had to show them how to walk gently and avoid blisters. Their feet were destroyed by the time we packed up Sunday night.

"Even if I'd been half-dead I wouldn't have let on," said Joan.

But now it was another year, the warm sun was shining, and we were again driving down the narrow road to the park. The woods were carpeted with a magic display of wild mushrooms. Joan was giving some editorial comment on the news of Luella and Simon's split-up a few weeks earlier.

"You told me I was just jealous last fall when I told you they wouldn't be together a year from now. But I was right wasn't I?"

"Ah, she probably told you she was going to dump him."

"No she didn't. Not her. I could just tell. I'm smarter than you think."

123. The Strange Case of Elwood Washington

After we got settled I went to the toilet and saw this strange bit of pathos scrawled on the wall:

I AM 6'4" 221 lbs
and scored 3 TDs in the 1971
ROSE BOWL
100 yards 9.7 secs
Bench Press 420 lbs
and didn't get drafted by any
pro team! Bastards!

And it was signed Elwood Washington. Under it someone had written "American bullshit."

What increased the strangeness of the message was its location, far from the world of commerce. We were surrounded by dense forests, misty lakes, mystical limestone caverns, the mysterious Niagara Escarpment and deep pure blue Georgian Bay. To quote from a story (par moi!) on the Bruce Peninsula that appeared in *Scenic Wonders of Canada*: "The forest floor is made up of limestone slabs four and five feet across. Between them are cracks a few inches wide, deep and filled with rich soil that has a springy carpet of moss and is topped by a variety of wild flowers in spring and summer. Birds-eye primula, dwarf iris and marsh marigolds spring into bloom in May. The colours of Indian paintbrush, blue-eyed grass and twinflower are added in June. By July the bladderwort and rare ferns such as harts-tongue fern, wall rue fern and walking fern cautiously emerge for their brief season in the sun, along with several varieties of wild orchids…."

I thought I'd check out Elwood Washington. When we got home I phoned the Canadian Football League head office. The secretary-treasurer said no one by that name had ever tried out for any pro team in Canada. Next I checked out the lineups for the 1971 Rose Bowl. He could have been referring to the one played Jan. 1, 1971, or Jan. 1, 1972, so I checked both. No one by the name of Elwood Washington played in either.

124. Canadians Aren't As Smart As Americans

On another wall someone had written something less literate but more poetic perhaps:

SHITE HOUSE POITS
WANE THY DAY
GO TO THE SHITE HOUSE
IN THE SKY

IN TH WAY OVER
THEY WILL RIDE
SHITE MOUNTS
TO THE SKY

When you see writing on the toilet wall, unless there is specific reference to nationality, one can only assume the writer is a native of the country in which the toilet is located. Tourists are more over-bearing and boastful, while locals are less pretentious, and are somewhat absent-minded, repetitive and unselfconscious. Locals are also occasionally political as on the walls of public toilets at rest stops along the Trans-Canada Highway in Quebec where there are many anti-tourist and anti-anglais slogans simply because the writers know a lot of tourists and anglais use these particular toilets. A captive audience.

By this token Elwood Washington, whom we can assume was an American, seemed much more skilled in language, spelling and grammar than the anonymous Shite Mounts Poit. And although I generally speaking dislike generalities one could be forgiven for deducing from these two examples and others like them that Americans are by and large more intelligent than Canadians. At first I thought the Shite Mounts Poit showed more vision and imagination than Elwood Washington, but since it turned out that he didn't actually score any touchdowns at all in the 1971 Rose Bowl, he didn't do too badly in the imagination department either.

You may think I'm hanging my conclusion on very slim threads. But just a few moments after stepping out of that washroom I observed a little tableau that, as far as I'm concerned, proves my point.

I was walking along the dirt road on my way back to the camp. In front of me I couldn't help noticing a very attractive collie on a leash being held by a young woman in the briefest of bikinis. There were signs all over the park reading DOGS MUST BE KEPT ON LEASH. A couple of young fellows in a souped-up hot rod passed me on the road then pulled up alongside the girl and her dog. I couldn't hear what they were saying at first so, without trying to attract attention, I walked a little more quickly and tried to get within earshot.

"Ah come on, baby. Why don't you come to town with us and have a few drinks and maybe dance a little and who knows what else, eh? It's going to be a pretty boring night."

By the way the girl and her dog were walking I could tell the girl didn't know these men and wasn't particularly appreciative of their attention. She kept slowing down, drawing back and then the car would slow its pace and wait for her. Then she would start walking fast and the car would speed up a bit to keep even with her.

Then finally I guess the guys got tired of pleading for suddenly they gunned the motor and sped away, tossing little pebbles and chunks of earth all over the road.

When everything went quiet again the woman stopped, knelt down, and began scratching her dog's ears. "Never mind, Bobby," she said. "They were only Canadians." Bobby had probably been named after U.S. Senator Robert Kennedy, since the assassination took place nine years earlier and the dog looked about nine.

I didn't want to make myself obvious by stopping when the woman stopped so I kept on going right past her as she knelt there scratching the dog's ears. I might have made some kind of friendly remark in passing but since she was from the U.S.A. I felt sort of self-conscious. She might have looked up at me curiously as I walked by but I don't know for sure because I didn't look down.

The poor young woman had suffered enough without me trying to engage her in conversation. What could I have done except reinforce her belief that Canadians aren't as smart as Americans?

125. Typical Canadian Nightmare

That night I had a nightmare. Joan and I were locked in a room. There was one window facing into another room. The rooms resembled cells in a prison. A beautiful young couple in their early twenties were taken into the next room and tortured. We could see them through the window screaming in agony.

We couldn't see their torturers. We couldn't clearly see how they were being tortured. But we could clearly see the intensity of their agony. Their screams were unbearable. They were being kept just below the passing-out level. They were experiencing the ultimate extremes of pain and we were totally helpless. All we could do was watch.

Then I noticed Joan couldn't take it any longer. Her face was losing its normal muscle tone. She began babbling insanely. The horror of what we were witnessing had destroyed her mind. I felt my own mind starting to go. Then I woke up.

THURSDAY, AUGUST 11

126. Sleeping Slugs

The next day the trees were full of blue jays and chipmunks. It was just like being part of nature. There's nothing like being in the woods. I collected some interesting mushrooms and was trying to identify them. It was difficult.

I thought I had some beautiful worm-free specimens of *Boletus edulis* which in Europe are prized to the extent that mushroom lovers charter trains to go into the forests on collecting trips when the mushroom is in season. But when I cooked them up and tasted them they were terrible. So maybe I was mistaken.

A lot of the mushrooms, especially the boletus, came with transparent slugs sleeping in hollowed-out tunnels in the flesh. It was amazing how few mushrooms I could identify. Most of them were in the grey zones between something and something else. It was humiliating. Every time a new mushroom field guide comes out, it seems another thousand varieties of mushrooms have evolved.

127. The Voice of Experience

I took a walk around Cypress Lake marvelling at the variety of mushrooms. It was like skindiving in a tropical sea swarming with brightly coloured aquatic life. The mushroom I loved most was the *Amanita frostiana*.

I brought twelve of them back to the camp. They were each about two-and-a-half inches long, their yellow caps changing to bright orange at the centre and flecked with little white warts. They closely resembled the fabled *Amanita muscaria*, but they were smaller, their stems were thinner and touched with yellow instead of being completely white, and the volva formed a little white boot with a free collar at the margin unlike both the *A. muscaria* and *A. flavoconia*.

It was definitely the *A. frostiana*, which, according to *Edible and Poisonous Mushrooms of Canada*, published by Agriculture Canada, is "said to be nonpoisonous but the danger of confusing it with *A. muscaria* is too great and it should be avoided at all times." But I had a positive identification. There was no doubt.

My twelve specimens sitting there on the picnic table looked delicious. My mouth was watering. And so I fried them in butter and onions. Joan and the kids didn't want any so I ate all twelve. The first few were quite tasty but by the time I got to number 12 I knew something was wrong. In retrospect they caused an almost immediate chemical change in my body which affected my sense of taste. About ten seconds after I finished the twelfth one I realised I'd made a mistake, possibly the mistake of my life. My stomach started turning like a ferris wheel. But I didn't want the family to know I'd been poisoned. They would have been merciless, especially since I'd been trying to get them to share the mushrooms with me, telling them I was almost totally certain it was okay to eat them. I was going to ride this one out. Phew!

It was almost dark and we were going to the amphitheatre to see some nature films with all the other campers. But first I had to go to the washroom. "I'll be right back," I said as cheerfully as possible under the circumstances.

I puked for five minutes straight. It was horrible. I wrote on the wall, under Elwood Washington's jottings, "*Amanita frostiana* deadly poisonous—The Voice of Experience." Then I vomited some more.

But there was something strange going on besides my illness. I knew I was sick, possibly fatally sick, but the curious chemical reaction had rendered me somehow insensitive to my own discomfort. Although I was vomiting fiercely I was at the same time rather delightfully intoxicated. I felt as if I were floating above myself in an opium dream watching some fool down there being sick. The illness and the intoxication tended to cancel each other out. I wondered how intoxicated I'd be if I weren't sick and how sick I'd be if I weren't intoxicated.

"What took you so long?" said Joan.

I decided to go ahead with the big lie. "Bit of constipation," I said.

128. The Buddha Was No Dumb-Dumb

As we walked into the outdoor amphitheatre everything became blue. It was as if I were wearing blue sunglasses. That was the third effect. And then a fourth effect started: a feeling of extreme nervousness. My mind was racing like a Ferrari, thinking of everything except what was going on around me. And I began getting nauseous again. I began having doubts I would survive. But still I wouldn't let on.

We sat in the back row watching National Film Board films. The first was about Martians taking an Earth shot and finding our planet not to their liking. There was too much traffic for their taste. The film was extremely boring, though under normal circumstances I might have enjoyed it.

The sky above the screen was more interesting. It was full of little silver, gold and purple clouds floating in the sunset. But I was having a hard time sitting still. Every atom in my body wanted to be elsewhere but I didn't know where. I envied the clouds.

The main feature was something about the new underwater park off Tobermory. It was called Fathom Five Provincial Park. When it started I knew I wouldn't be able to sit all the way through it. I was beginning to sweat copiously in the cool evening air.

"What's Fathom Five?" said Joan.

"It's a provincial park," I snapped.

"Where is it?"

Was she kidding me? Was she just trying to annoy me? Did she know how uncomfortable I felt? Couldn't she hear my teeth chattering, see the sweat on my forehead? Why didn't I have the nerve simply to come clean and admit I'd made an honest mistake and poisoned myself? After all, even the Buddha died of mushroom poisoning and he was no dumb-dumb. I could tell her that just as I slipped into the Big Sleep.

"It's an underwater park off Tobermory," I said curtly, hoping to convey the message I wasn't in the mood for further chit-chat.

"Oh, come on, Dave. Who would go to an underwater park?"

"Campers."

"But you couldn't build campfires down there. And how would you keep your sleeping bags dry?"

129. Joan Deduces the Cause of My Distress

The film started with shots of a winter storm off Georgian Bay, thirty-foot waves smashing into the naked cliffs of the Niagara Escarpment. It was making me sick.

I decided I had to come clean. "Joan, I have to go and vomit. I might go to the car and lie down for a while or I might come right back. I don't know yet."

Joan tried to look concerned but the big smile on her face betrayed her true feelings.

"Oh! Are you sick, Dave?" she said. "Something you ate maybe? Let's see now." She was pretending to be dumb. "What did you eat that none of us ate? I can't think of anything, can you?" My stomach was on fire. "Oh of course. Those mushrooms! Maybe you've got a little itty-bitty touch of mushroom poisoning from those perfectly safe mushrooms you ate."

I tried to make an elegant exit but I knew I wasn't going to succeed. I was only about thirty feet away from the back row when I resumed vomiting. It came with great heaving chokes and sobs that I'm sure could be heard all over the amphitheatre. It was a quiet part of the movie too. The symphonic soundtrack had gone dead for some dramatic reason. But no one came running to help me. They must have thought I was simply drunk.

When I got back on my feet my legs were like rubber. And again I didn't feel the slightest bit sick. The pressure was off my stomach and I felt totally rejuvenated, marvellous. I felt a total kinship with nature, a mystical identification with the entire universe. And everything was blue. Little blue squares floated in front of my eyes. I walked as if I were drunk but my mind was as clear as the Buddha's. Well, let's say I felt as if I'd finally tamed the ox and was riding it serenely back to the campsite.

Funny thing. As I write this months later my stomach is getting all churned up again.

130. Mushroom Poisoning

All night I slept shallowly, besieged by curious tension dreams about trying to scale the CN Tower, trying to scale a dozen fish for dinner, all that sort of thing. In the morning I felt worn out. My nerves were all swollen. With poison mushrooms the line becomes thick.

At the height of my distress however I realised I wasn't going to die. The symptoms were quite a bit different than the one really severe killer: *Amanita virosa*. Even a small amount of that mushroom can prove fatal, and one dies a horrendous death. Here is what *Edible and Poisonous Mushrooms of Canada* has to say about *A. virosa* poisoning:

> "The danger is increased by the fact that there is apparently no unpleasant taste and no symptoms are manifested until eight to twelve hours, or sometimes even longer, after the mushrooms are eaten. By this time the poison has been absorbed into the blood stream and the usual procedures such as pumping out the stomach are of no avail.... The general symptoms of this type of poisoning are severe abdominal pains, vomiting, cold sweats, diarrhoea and excessive thirst. After persisting for some time the symptoms usually subside for a while and then recur more intensely; the liver is affected as well as the nervous system. There may be delirium, deep coma, and finally death. The patient suffers great pain."

I dragged myself to the toilet just as the sun was beginning to sparkle in the dewdrops. Overnight a poet had been born. Here's what he wrote, right next to Elwood Washington's complaint and above my voice of experience note:

> *Not last night but the night before*
> *Forty Robbers Came Adoor.*
> *Went downstairs to let them*
> *In Hit Me on the Head with*
> *A Rolling Pin. Rolling pin was*
> *made of brass. Turned me over*
> *and hit my ass.*

Question: What does this poem tell us about the poet?

Answer: He lives in a two-storey house and has masochistic fantasies.

Wrong: It could have been a three-storey house. And maybe it wasn't a fantasy. Maybe it really happened. Then again maybe it really was a fantasy and he lives in a one-storey house, or an apartment, or a room at the YMCA.

FRIDAY, AUGUST 12

131. Alison Worries About Me

I ate a hearty breakfast so I guess I was all better. Joan and the kids weren't about to let me off the hook. They remembered that it could have been them just as easily.

I have an occasional problem with choking in the middle of the night, a form of apnea in which I forget how to breathe. I wake up from the deepest level of sleep, sit bolt upright in bed with my eyes bulging. I leap out of bed, and start wandering blindly, bouncing off walls and making rather unusual guttural sounds. Just as I've awakened everyone in the house and am about to turn blue I start breathing again. It's kind of frightening but it's been going on for eight years and I'm getting used to it.

"Did you choke last night, Daddy?" said Alison, slyly.

"No," I said helplessly.

"You should eat poisonous mushrooms more often. Maybe they'll stop you from choking."

132. The Retarded Kid from Sarnia

As we were cleaning up the breakfast dishes a retarded kid from Sarnia came by. He was about sixteen and was camping with his parents. He had a high forehead. He walked right into our campsite and began talking to us as if he'd known us all his life. He told us he didn't like these provincial parks as much as the private ones like the KOA (Kampers of Amerika) campgrounds because there are no swimming pools in the provincial parks.

"Like to swim, do ya?" I said.

"Ya," he slobbered. I was out of matches so he went and got some from his brother.

Then he began complaining about the camp officers. He said they'd been speeding all over the place in their patrol cars earlier in the morning. He said somebody had a motorboat out on Cypress Lake, which is against the rules, and they were rushing around trying to get him out of there. He said he was worried someone would get run over by a patrol car.

"I'm more worried about duh speeding cop cars dan duh boat on duh lake," he said earnestly. You could tell he was quoting his parents. In fact his whole monologue seemed to have been lifted.

"How does your dad feel about that?" I said.

"He feels duh same way," he said.

After he left Joan turned to me. She'd found the kid delightful. "You don't have to have a high IQ do you?" she said.

"Definitely not," I said. "He'd be a joy to have around the house. He'd be worth his weight in laughs."

There was a retarded fellow I used to see on the city bus occasionally. He would always sit at the front of the bus and do his imitations of radio announcers. He would give the morning news and hockey scores just perfectly, almost word for word.

One day he was giving the news as the bus headed down the Jolley Cut. He said a serious accident had just occurred at the foot of the Jolley Cut and motorists were advised to take another route downtown.

You guessed it. When the bus reached the bottom there had indeed been a serious accident. As the bus inched past, an ambulance pulled up. Everyone on the bus just stared at the fellow uneasily.

133. Young Fellows Flirting with Alison

So that was that. We decided our trip around Lake Huron was finished. We decided to drive home. Joan later said she wished we'd stayed a few more days at Cypress Lake but we didn't know at that time that we'd have to get rid of our van pretty soon and that would be our last camping trip. On any future trips around the Great Lakes we'd have to stay at motels.

We drove slowly, keeping just above the speed limit, all the way down the Bruce Peninsula to Owen Sound. The sky was incredibly blue and there were funny little cloud formations here and there that made you laugh out loud. You could see the road climbing up the next long low hill, and we knew we'd soon be climbing it too. We took turns guessing the distances to various points we could see way ahead of us.

How many miles to the top of that hill?

How many miles before those funny clouds block the sun?

To be truthful I was fairly well bemushroomed, to use the term invented by the legendary mycologist Gordon Wasson. There seemed to be a lessening of the separation between me and the rest of the world, between me and the spirit that connects everything. We were all of the same dimension, the same inner pigment. Everything was moving slowly and peacefully as we stopped here and there for soft drinks and just to look at things. I'd eaten the poison mushrooms but my state was picked up by the others. The moment sort of expanded. A single moment seemed to go on forever.

We had lunch in Wiarton. The restaurant was decorated with a series of framed colour photos of a huge iceberg off Newfoundland. It was interesting. We'd heard that Stompin' Tom Connors had a summer home in the Wiarton area but the restaurant owner said he didn't know anything about it.

Some young fellows about fourteen or fifteen at the next table were flirting with Alison. In fact they came in just to get a better look at her. She's getting to look a little like Dolly Parton, but more beautiful. Jenny's more the Jane Fonda type, but more beautiful.

And that's about the way this book ends, folks. When we got home our mileage was 61013.6 which meant we'd gone 1248.4 miles on this trip as compared with 800 miles exactly on the Lake Erie trip.

I see too I'm winding up on manuscript page 252. *A Trip Around Lake Erie* had 252 manuscript pages too. But that one had 142 chapters as compared with Lake Huron's 133.

Don't know where we're going next. Maybe Lake Superior. Maybe Lake Michigan. Maybe Lake Ontario. Maybe nowhere.

A Trip Around Lake Ontario

GREAT LAKES SUITE

VOLUME THREE

A TRIP AROUND LAKE ONTARIO

for Greg Curnoe
1936-1992
"I tell stories."

"Now I myself am about to cut open my own heart, and drench your face with my blood. And I shall be satisfied if, when my heart stops beating, a new life lodges itself in your breast."

Natsume Soseki, *Kokoro*

Contents

35. Upson O'Connell's Farm
36. The Yarn Ear-Scratcher
37. Cabbagetown Elegies
38. Chesley Yarn's Squash
39. Happy and Confused
40. Smudge Butternut and the Arms Race
41. Captain Crack of Terror Lodge
42. Mr. Synchronicity

FRIDAY, OCTOBER 12

43. Gooseberry Jam
44. A Little Brown Dachshund
45. The Bicycling Kinesiologists
46. No One Will Ever Read This
47. Cemeteries at Night
48. Nat King Cole
49. Two Guys in a White Volvo
50. Phone Calls in the Middle of the Night
51. Extreme Emergency
52. A Case of Extra-Strength Benylin
53. Half-Dead Rats
54. The Labatt's Award for the Biggest Fish
55. An Essay on Death
56. The Quiet Little People Who Control the Weather
57. The Fireside Reading Club
58. The Brothers Karamazov
59. Dead Sailors
60. Sensory Crossover

SATURDAY, OCTOBER 13

61. Nigger Shoes
62. Ella Mae Hopkins in the Flesh
63. Herd of Zebras Trample Crippled Boy
64. Mr. Mental Health
65. Several of the Remote Backports
66. Red Wine and Falling Leaves
67. Saturday Night at the Fire Hall
68. Retarded Girl with Bat
69. Louis Armstrong at Port Stanley
70. Septuagenarian Lust
71. Canadian Mist
72. Over the Sea from Ireland
73. Conversation Overheard at Woody Woodpecker's
74. Amazing Soup

75. Hands across the Border
76. Chocolate Chess

SUNDAY, OCTOBER 14

77. Ryokan for President
78. American Mist
79. Marie-Thérèse and Jesus Christ
80. The Causes of War
81. Sexiest Team in Baseball
82. Daphnis and Chloe
83. A Cream Cadillac with Florida Plates
84. Another Cream Cadillac with Florida Plates
85. Curious about Lonesome George
86. Freezers Full of Flesh and Pheasant
87. Whispers from Eternity
88. World's Largest Pencil
89. Bombs over Tokyo
90. White Goat on Green Lawn
91. Do You Really Think I'm Right for You?
92. Rodney Gets Car Sick
93. Discovering Your Own Mind
94. Voices from the Subtle Levels of the Mind

MONDAY, OCTOBER 15

95. The Worm at the Bottom of the Bottle
96. Every Man or Woman His or Her Own Pope
97. Murder in the Monkey Inn
98. You Smell Okay to Me
99. Men with Tiny Well-Clipped Moustaches
100. Rodney Does It Again
101. Boredom and Immortality
102. Weird Swedish Sexual Apparatus
103. Swimming through Molasses
104. Iniquitous
105. A Sad Little Chat with Titania Balmoral
106. Dropping in on Mom and Dad
107. The Disjointed and Confused Supermarket
108. Swimming through Rose Petals

A Trip Around Lake Ontario

1. Death and Resurrection

It was a ridiculous little trip, but it was also strange, terrifying, hilarious and in many ways unforgettable, with those three fine fellows following me in their van, the autumn sun slowly burning through the oozing mists, the Keatsian swallows gathering in the twittering sky.

But nothing really seemed to have any effect on my peculiar sadness.

Marie-Thérèse said she felt as if I would be putting a lot of myself into this trip, that I would be travelling with the stately passion of one who senses he is about to die. (She was referring to my psychological state.)

Ten years ago I wrote a pair of books based on camping trips I took with my little family. Fictionalisation and distortion went into the writing, so much so that I can't remember if, for instance, I really did come down with mushroom poisoning on the Bruce Peninsula in that long-ago summer, or if the house really was full of dead fish when we returned from Lake Erie.

Much of the writing in those books was intimate, inflaming the sensitivities of everyone involved. We formed an editorial committee and met each evening to review what I'd written that day. We negotiated and bargained. Everything had to be unanimous, but I pleaded to be allowed to leave certain things in and was told I could if certain other things were deleted. I didn't want to compromise the privacy and dignity of anyone concerned, but I did want to involve my family in the books in an uncommonly direct way, I wanted to share with them (rather than impose on them) my own sense of the experimental nature of daily life, and I did want to exploit our lives in order to say something vague but somehow important about the life of everyone who would ever read the books.

Like most over-zealous dads, I wanted to share with my family something I found exciting, as if I were forcing a kind of understanding that would remain with us forever. I wanted to create an archaeological document that would freeze our sensibilities and the environments that created them in a way that somehow would be full of meaning (at least for us) far into the future. I wanted to continue the series, wanted to write a book for each of the Great Lakes, as well as some pamphlets on smaller lakes.

But wanting too much is a common failing, and shortly after the first two books were finished something happened, a certain ennui developed. I decided I couldn't write any more books in that vein: the form had exhausted itself, the writing would be too easy and therefore too difficult. There would be insufficient tension, nothing that would push back when pushed.

And now my kids are grown and my wife divorced and remarried. Each of us has been through flames. Love takes many forms, and in some of those forms there is no hope for anything but agony. When the agony becomes overwhelming lovers must separate, solemn vows broken, even if the separation will create agonies even more intense. "Un seul être vous manque, et tout est dépourvu."

Further, the idea of a third trip book, with me travelling alone or with anyone other than those with whom I made the first two trips, was just too difficult emotionally. But that emotional difficulty and the effort it would take to rid myself of such a burden if even for a brief period, somehow brought the form alive again for me—as did the fact that it had died on me in the first place.

One values form for the challenge it presents, and form dies if it no longer presents a challenge, whether artistic or in less fathomable ways. But in death, over time, it can develop the capacity of providing an unexpectedly contrary challenge, thereby demanding resurrection.

Writing a book, even a seemingly simple book like this, is not something to be undertaken lightly. I had all these things to think about. Also the warmth with which a few hundred people responded to the first two books in the series. All of this was going through my mind. How could I compensate for not having my family along this time? I'd been devising techniques for compensating for their (relative) absence in my life for seven years, perhaps this book would provide me with a profile of how successful I'd been.

WEDNESDAY, OCTOBER 10

2. A Record Number of Cop Killings

Maybe I'm making too big a thing about this, but these were serious questions for me. I never wanted to write books, seemingly random events (SRE) pushed me into it, and having been pushed into it I certainly didn't want to write books that attempted to tell certain spiritual truths about my own precious little life, but what choice does any artist do once he's learned the basics and gets to graduate into the cruel world of multiple personalities, each one vying to become the locus of whatever. At a certain point though I was faced with the sickening knowledge that my writing wouldn't be able to provide me with any kind of satisfaction unless I took seriously the proposition that through it I could perhaps tell something interesting about my own dull life, and the attempt would replace the dullness with a bit of snap.

People who are not self-obsessed are not deeply interesting, and writers who are not ultimately preoccupied with their own minds and hearts seem somehow incomplete. I'm not saying these books were divinely inspired, but it's as if SRE made me write them, and ultimately triggered the writing of them like some kind of mechanical device. You're looking at the work of a man whose major commitment is to purposelessness. The man with no ego. But who nevertheless believes with Broadway Danny Rose that no act is so small it doesn't need an audience.

Nigel Walkey, a prime SRE agent, caught my silly act at the Hotel Isabella last spring, April 1 actually, as good a date as any for a story to begin. I rented a cow costume and got up on the stage during a crowded sweaty beer-saturated poetry reading and bellowed out my mock-Chaucerian erotic obsessive mythological epic (but ultimately tender) "The Cow That Swam Lake Ontario," with the audience howling and the legendary poet Buster Crowe just in from Vancouver, his fly gaping open, vomit stains on his shirt, standing on his table and complaining drunkenly as I hollered out my lines that he'd been in Toronto twenty-four hours and hadn't been laid yet. "Get that fuckin' sexist off the stage," he screamed (meaning me, the cow in long eyelashes) when he realised his sexual complaints were meeting with no apparent sympathy.

The next day soft-spoken, sweet-natured Nigel Walkey picked up some of my books, read them, and got the brilliant idea of dropping by and asking if I were planning to take trips around the remaining Great Lakes. He wished to raise some money to hire a film crew to follow me around my next lake—and what lake did I want to travel around next?

"But those books were written a long time ago," I whimpered.

"Not that long ago," he said, his eyes flashing. I fell into silence and he tiptoed away.

Nigel wouldn't be able to raise the money, I figured, but I didn't want to stand in his way of trying. And if he did get the money, which he almost certainly wouldn't, then that would be an undeniable sign from SRE. It'd force me to figure out why I felt incapable of writing the book. It would give me problems to solve.

He got the money, the devil. He bought a Panasonic boom-box (a.k.a. ghetto-blaster) and installed it on a temporary basis in the bird's-eye blue van he rented for himself and his crew. He rented a little old-fashioned blood-red sports car for me. When they had a private meeting and came forward to express their concern that the suspension would prove too rough for me I knew I seemed pretty old to them. This was a fresh new generation coming up and when I told them I wasn't worried about the suspension, I was worried about other things, they smiled sadly, patiently.

I'd lost three watches in the past few months, including a gold watch of immense sentimental value, if anything can have sentimental value any longer, and decided against buying a fourth, I'd just lose it. Now here I was with a car with no clock, no speedometer, no odometer, no radio, and I'd just paid eighty bucks to have my new computer insured because I'd been doing a little job for a peace activist friend and was afraid that when I got back there'd be an axe through it (the computer that is). The film crew had arrived and were telling me under no circumstances, please, do not look at the camera....

The van was parked in the middle of busy Spadina Road, traffic streaming around it, patiently, without honking, which seemed amazing, but people in general respected film crews, these motorists, for instance, were as always merely rushing home to watch television anyway and everything you see on television has been shot with a camera. One guy was handing the camera up to the other on the roof of the van, and Nigel was telling me to act naturally, don't look in the camera. But that doesn't make sense, it's only natural to look in the camera.

"Actors do it all the time," said Nigel. "It's no problem at all for them."

"I'm not an actor," I said. "I can't force myself not to look into the camera. We have ir-reconcilable differences, the trip's off."

"No, no," said Nigel.

I told him I'd decided to write the book in the present tense and he gave me a polite look. He said that was quite a coincidence because they'd already decided to shoot the film in the present tense.

"What can you tell me about this book?" he said.

"You know as much about it as I do. I haven't started working on it yet. We have to take the trip first." This is the sort of situation that arises when you have the state funding artists.

"Where do you think we'll end up tonight?" said Nigel.

"I don't know. Who's the boss here?" said I.

"I am." In Nigel's eye was a self-mocking glint.

"What about me?"

"Yeah, you're the boss. You can do anything you want or go anywhere you want as long as it's within a couple of hundred klicks of Lake Ontario."

"Ontario? I thought we were going around Superior?"

"No, I distinctly remember we've been talking Ontario all along."

"Ah, Superior, Ontario, what's the difference? I guess I'm just nervous. By the way, who's the sound man?"

"I am."

"Who's the cameraman?"

"That guy. Winston. He's really good. We'll have to show you some of his work when we get back."

"That'd be nice. Who's the third guy?"

"Rodney."

"With the red hair?"

"That's Rodney."

"And what can you tell me about him?"

"He's the assistant cameraman."

"I thought the third guy was going to be the sound man. Why do we need an assistant cameraman?"

"It's pure gold. Just like your computer."

"You mean he's indispensable?"

"I mean we couldn't get along without him."

At that point we noticed a girl lying on the grass on the other side of Spadina Road. She was on her stomach, with her face buried in the grass. This was a cold autumn day, the CN Tower enveloped in mist. People were passing by, casting a glance at her, and continuing on. Nigel and I went over and asked if she were all right.

She lifted her head a bit.

"Yeah, I'm all right," she said. "I'm just lying here waiting for a friend." We couldn't figure this out. Was she being sarcastic?

"You don't look very well," said Nigel. "Why are you lying there like that waiting for a friend?"

Her eyes looked sad even though they were closed.

"I got hit by a bus."

"Oh, that explains it. When?"

"Just a little while ago."

We hadn't seen or heard anyone get hit by a bus and we'd been there quite some time. Turned out she was riding her bicycle and the bus sideswiped her and kept on going. She and the bike went flying, she cut her elbow up pretty bad, there was a lot of blood under her shirt sleeve and she was in a bit of shock. Apparently a cabby had witnessed the accident and had gone after the bus driver. People were still walking by without saying anything, so I went in and called the cops on the emergency 911 number, then went back out and stood over the girl with Nigel until help arrived.

Two ambulances came screaming up. The first was the ordinary ambulance and the second was the paramedics team. The paramedics were impressive. They treated the girl so gently. They asked how old she was and she said nineteen. It was really only a cut arm but they took it seriously and took their time going over her gently from head to toe and making sure she was okay. They were afraid of broken bones. They gave her oxygen, for the shock I suppose.

She told them about the friend she was waiting for. They'd been riding together but her friend had stopped at the store for a bottle of Orange Crush. She was wondering when the friend was going to show up.

"What are you going to do with the bike?" I asked the cops, who didn't seem as bright as the ambulance attendants. I lived right there and figured I could arrange to have it stored safely until she got back from the hospital if they wanted me to.

"Who are you?" said one of the cops. Oh oh. He glared at me like an angel of death. Maybe he thought I was scheming to steal the bike, and maybe, if I could get away with it, carry the girl up to my apartment and suck the remaining blood out of her.

"I'm the guy who found the girl and called 911," I said. "I live right here"—in this apartment building where the custodian put a sign up on the fuse box in the first-floor laundromat, saying: DON'T STEAL THE FUSES ANY MORE. IT'S TOO CHEAP TO STEAL.

The cop continued looking at me as if I had personally run the girl over, as if I were the embodiment of all human evil. "The bike will be taken care of," he said with a sneer. Then he continued glaring at me, staring me down. When I realised what was happening, and that I was dealing with someone with a grade 5 mentality if that, I turned my attention back to the girl. A lot of cops had been killed in the past few months in Toronto, and in Montreal too, a record number. Maybe that was a factor in this guy's attitude. But then again maybe this guy's attitude was a factor in the killings.

The cabby came back and said he had caught up with the bus driver at the subway station at Spadina and Bloor. He said the driver had refused to talk to him. "He just said he didn't hit anybody." The cabby was a Jamaican, very sincere. "It was one of those little buses," he said.

The cops weren't interested, didn't even want to talk to the cabby. Maybe because he was black. Maybe they didn't think it was kosher to launch a case against a bus driver. They'd love to be able to charge the cabby and me with first-degree murder and vampirism though.

"A Davenport 127 probably," I said. "Did you get the number?"

"No," said the cabby.

"Oh well, the cops don't seem very interested anyway."

More glares.

Her friend never did show up, but the girl was going to be all right. Would probably live to get run over by another bus some day. Maybe the same bus. Who knows? Life is strange. I don't think any of this got into the film. If I'd mouthed off too much and the cops had started beating me up, that would have made a good opening scene.

Those paramedics were wonderful. So gentle.

3. People Who Weren't Even Born Yet

I was standing in the lobby waiting for Nigel to give me the cue to open the door, walk over to the little car, hop in and take off. It was a strange grey day. My task was clear: I had to write a book about a guy writing a book about someone making a movie about a guy having a movie made about him while he was trying to write a book. Without looking at the camera.

But there was a feeling of depth and calm in the rock-solid air, nothing that could possibly happen could either depress or elate any of us. We were part of the autumnal mist. There was also a sense of deep amusement in the air, auguring some kind of cosmic irony that would unfold as we went along. Life would become weirder, images sharper, conversations snappier. Every scene would be more interesting than the one before, until we couldn't take it any more.

Indians with long ponytails were walking by on their way to the Native Peoples Centre down the street. Punks in dyed red and black hair with shaved sides strolled by as I stood there waiting for my cue. Nigel said he and the crew didn't want to be part of the story at all, but I didn't seriously think there'd be any way I could possibly leave them out and I made sure they knew that. It would be like trying not to look in the camera, you don't turn to books for that kind of artificiality. Everyone who's on the trip gets to be in the book. No exceptions will be made.

A few days earlier I'd gone to a new barber shop down the street and told an enormously fat lady barber I felt like having my hair dyed, because I was going to be in a movie.

She giggled and jiggled approvingly.

"That's a terrific idea," she said. "You could have it done at the barber's college on Bloor. They wouldn't charge much and they'd do a good job."

"What colour should I have it done?"

She thought for a while then suggested snow white.

"Beard too?"

"Uh, let me see now. Yep, beard too."

I was in one of those moods and was asking her intimate questions about her personal life in a slightly loud voice, but not in an embarrassing way. All the other hair stylists and their clients were quietly listening. I asked if she were married, she said no, but she lived with a guy who worked in a factory. I said that must be boring and she assumed (correctly) I meant boring for him (to be working in a factory) and she said no he really liked it. I said what do you do when you go home at night? Do you watch television and if so what are your favourite shows?

Everyone else in the place was quietly waiting for the answer. No, she said she was too tired to watch television or anything else when she got home at night.

Did her arms get sore, having to hold them up like that all day cutting hair?

No, not her arms, she said, just her feet from having to stand up all day.

What did she do on weekends?

She thought and finally said oh I like to go fishing. I asked where.

"Oh God, let me think now. It's been so long…."

But now here I was waiting for Nigel's cue. Acting as if the camera weren't there would be as unnatural as not blinking when a bug lands in your eye or pretending to be sad when you're happy as at certain funerals or vice versa as at certain weddings. Like not hollering when you get your thumb caught in a car door.

The cue came and I walked out as self-conscious as a Seventh-Day Adventist from Orillia going in to watch the strippers at the Zanzibar on Yonge Street, if you'll excuse the foreshadowing. Mild delusions of grandeur filled the air. People who weren't there were watching me. Perhaps people who weren't even born yet.

I tried to forget the camera as I took off my jacket, tossed it in back and jumped over the door (it was stuck) and into the little seat, backed out of the driveway and drove around the corner.

When I got back Nigel came over with a significant frown on his face. I thought he was going to tell me we had to do it over again because I looked too camera-aware.

But no, he was upset because he had told Tilden Rent-a-Van that the van had to have a working lighter because all three members of the film crew were chain-smokers. They assured them no problem there'd be a lighter but there wasn't.

They'd brought about forty tapes for their new ghetto-blaster. They had also brought a modest amount of marijuana (bought with their taxi-driving money rather than with Canada Council funds I hasten to add) and they hoped they could get it all smoked before they hit the border. I thought it would be fun to give away reefers to tourists waiting in line for the Thousand Island Boat Tour in Gananoque.

"So what do you think about the way I walked to the car? Did I seem to be aware of the camera?"

"Yeah, you seemed a little self-conscious. But don't worry. Maybe we won't have to use it. We've got a lot of film with us, and we can get more when we go through Rochester. We'll be going through Rochester, won't we?"

He didn't say anything but I could tell he'd decided not to try to set up any more scenes with me in them. That suited me fine. If I'd wanted to be a trained seal, I'd never have left the newspaper.

4. Dying with a Smile on Your Face

"I've got it. You have to forget the camera and not forget it at the same time, right?"

Nigel was looking forward to getting out of the city and having memorable adventures in search of the Great White Whale of artistic perfection. "That's right, now you're talking," he said. His patient eyes flickered with humour. "It's all a matter of concentration." He gave the impression occasionally of being a touch in awe of me because of my venerable age (more than a decade their senior), but I felt quite at ease with Nigel because he seemed so uncomplicated and energetic, his mind worked so smoothly and rapidly. Nigel was bright, smart, funny, and he made everyone around him feel the same way. Quite a change from most of my friends, more my age, who seemed to be border-line hysterics on the verge of senility. We've realised we're caught in a circular drift, moving in ever-decreasing circles towards the Terminal Whirlpool. The hysteria came from not having resigned ourselves to it yet.

Being with these guys, and having that little blood-red sports car, and being the star of even such a modest little flick, and wearing my sporty old black-leather jacket, made me feel young. My air-cushioned Nikes put a spring in my step even though it was the fall of my life. I was only forty, but the aging process fascinated me. Like the crew, I smoked a lot and probably wouldn't live long. In fact I can feel tingly numb sensations in the tips of my fingers as I type, probably circulation problems caused by arteriosclerosis in its early and undetectable stage, and pre-cancerous nicotine blisters on my tongue. I'd reached the top of the hill and could see my grave down in the valley on the other side. All I had to do was let myself slide down to it, no problem.

People who fear aging, or are embarrassed by signs of age, are people who harbour suspicions that they haven't lived yet. Let's be candid, there are people who simply identify too strongly with their little lives—as if they were responsible for their own creation and it was their own fault that they were falling apart, instead of just revelling in the cosmic law of creation and destruction and identifying with the starry night and the spring breezes.

Just talking to myself here.

5. Bogie and Bacall

When we got to Sheldon's he came out with my reading glasses which I'd left there a couple of days earlier when he had a little dinner party, with mom and dad in attendance, in honour of his birthday. Sheldon was not like me, he was a great cook, full of all kinds of practical knowledge. He would make his own beer and wine (including an excellent sparkling white which he called sham champagne), repair his own cars and bicycles, once even installed a sun roof in his old BMW. He'd buy old wrecked BMWs and cannibalise them to keep his own on the road.

He took after Dad. I was more like Grandfather—a melancholy pipe smoker who was obsessed with the symphony of time and wrote every day in his modest diary. And who, every night after dinner, would insist that the family gather around in the living room and listen while he read the newspaper aloud. With special emphasis on crime news, boxing, wrestling and obituaries.

Sheldon was a nice guy, but he tended to be too touchy, and he'd allow the unavoidable natural sleaziness of urban life get him down. His honesty would get him in trouble with his women (he was a serial monogamist of incredible changeover frequency) and his employers (he was a wonderful musician but found it hard to fake enjoyment when he didn't like the gig) (he once announced he was going to write a book called "How to Fake Enjoyment When You Don't Like the Gig." I took around an old Smith Corona with a broken space bar but at last check it was covered with dust in the basement).

So he came out with my glasses and a big smile. I introduced him to the crew: Sheldon Rodney, Rodney Sheldon, Sheldon Nigel, Nigel Sheldon, Sheldon Winston, Winston Sheldon. I told them I was going to call them all Fred in the book. The three Freds. They said a friend of theirs said they should call themselves Kukla, Fran and Ollie for the duration of the trip, and they could have fun arguing about which one was which.

Sheldon just stood there with a big smile on his face, trying not only not to appear envious but trying not to feel envy, which was understandably difficult for him I'd imagine, because he was just as narcissistic as I and would love to have had a film crew following him around and immortalising his every scratch and snort. Also he was a great lover of sports cars but he'd never owned a real sports car because he played bass violin and you can't fit a bass violin in anything smaller than a BMW. It was all my fault too, and I swear I took absolutely no perverse pleasure, in fact feel downright guilty, that when Sheldon was about twelve and I was seventeen I decided to give up my interest in sports cars and turned my *Road and Track* and *Sports Cars Illustrated* collections over to him, and he was soon hooked on the romance of fine high-performance motorcars, a Grand Prix teenage aficionado. When he got to grade 9 and decided to study music and asked my advice on what instrument to play I suggested bass violin so he took it, only later realising, when he had fallen so much in love with the instrument, in fact had bought a sumptuous old bass violin made in Brighton, England, in 1833 (he recently turned down a hundred grand for it), that it wouldn't fit in a sports car and that the only way he would be able to have a sports car would be to have two cars, one sedan and one sports, but he'd never felt prosperous enough to afford both.

If I could live my life over, the only thing I'd change would be to suggest Sheldon take up the flute.

But he was a wonderful string bassist, and he and his instrument always looked wonderful together, like Bogie and Bacall. He could lug it up three flights of narrow steep stairs with consummate grace in his limbs and a smile on his face. The little blood-red sports car came up to his knee. His shiny eyes looked down at it.

I told him about driving slowly along crowded Bloor Street in an open sports car, following a van with a cameraman strapped to the roof and pointing a big movie camera backwards at you. Everyone would stop and strain to see who was driving the car. Could it be Jack Nicholson? Warren Beatty? Larry Mann? No, it's only Daffy Duck. Sheldon winced and shook his head when I told him two Caribbean hipsters in their twenties sneered at me at a stoplight and snarled out the ugly word "star!" with curled lips, as if they were saying "slut!" If only they knew!

We talked about the project for a while, about the proposed route, clockwise around the lake, Canadian side first, with a little bit of the Canadian side third, and when he asked if I had a map and I said no he went in and brought out a beautiful topographical map of the entire lake. I put it in the trunk so it wouldn't blow away, then forgot all about it till just now.

6. Big Lake

Lake Ontario was a huge animal with magnetic lines stretching out from it in all directions, pulling you towards it, a huge animal that wanted to be looked at and admired by the millions of tiny human fleas (four million Canadian and two million American) who lived around it and dumped their garbage into it. Once you obeyed the pull and arrived with a clear mind at the shoreline the pull would stop and be replaced by a feeling of being blessed, as if by a silent and motionless saint radiant in the darkness.

Lake Ontario was deep, cold, remote, ancient, and always full of strange beauty. You glanced at it from any angle and received your momentary blessing, a moment of clarity, and then you turned back into the murk of your life. A year to walk around it would be better than a week to drive around it, for there would be only so many chances to meet and speak with randomly interesting people who lived close to the lake, people who, although strangers to each other, were being touched in their lives by the presence of the lake and were therefore becoming of one tribe, whether or not they ever thought about it.

In that little blood-red Spitfire I followed Nigel, Winston and Rodney in their fat bird's-eye blue van out to the remote suburban offices of McBerton and Mowat, the old prestigious Canadian publishing company that had fallen on hard times and was on the verge of bankruptcy. Front office was apologetically withholding the tiny $750 advance on royalties for my modest little book of neo-Keatsian verse, *Golden Dewdrops of the Night*, but a call had come from the editor saying advance copies of the book were in and one copy could be set aside for the author. Oh lucky me. It'd be at the front desk.

Before we'd driven off and left him there on the sidewalk (standing) Sheldon had asked why I wanted to do another trip-around-the-lake book, and when I said it was simply an excuse to write, he quite rightly didn't believe me. "Travelling is like reading," he declared, wisely. "There are people who read widely and there are people who read deeply. Some people travel all over the world without seeing anything and others travel around one little lake and see everything. Not that Lake Ontario is such a little lake."

Sheldon didn't read much but when he did read he read with great pleasure. Books about the history of wine, books about cars, the Dialogues of Plato.

I confessed to having recently been hurt a bit by reviews of my work and by poor sales and I really didn't know if I was a writer or not any more.

"Come on, you're a beautiful writer."

"Thanks, Sheldon. It's nice to have a brother to talk to."

"You can talk to me any time. And remember, Dad always said you should pay more attention to the bad reviews than to the good ones."

"Did he say that?"

"Yeah."

"Sounds pretty wise to me, but what does he know? He never read a book all the way through in his life."

"Sure he did. He was a big reader in the early days. They used to call him Benny the Bookworm."

"Benny? Isn't his name Walter?"

"Wally the Bookworm doesn't have the same ring."

"So why Benny?"

"There was a character by that name in Dickens."

"Benny the Bookworm."

"That's right."

"What book?"

"I don't know."

"How do you know then?"

"Somebody told me."

"Okay, what else?"

"When he came by a few weeks ago he started eyeing that old Smith Corona you gave me with the busted space bar. So I'm going to get it fixed up and give it to him for Christmas. He's going to write his memoirs."

"He is?"

"That's what he says. If mom'll let him. And he's been going to the library lately and bringing home books and reading them."

"Such as what?"

"Ever heard of some guy called Marcel Proust?"

"No!"

"Yes!"

"No. I don't believe it."

"Yes. It's true. He just finished *Swann's Way* and he's growing a little moustache."

The McBerton and Mowat receptionist blankly handed me the book in a brown envelope with my name scrawled on it and I thanked her and left. A puzzled-looking seagull rested on the nicely trimmed lawn surrounding the low-slung one-floor warehouse. I stood there looking at the book into which I'd put so much effort. When I looked up Nigel and red-haired Rodney were standing there intently watching me and smiling. Winston was crouching with the camera, filming this great moment in world literary history. I'd been close to tears and felt embarrassed.

"Why are you filming me standing here reading?"

"This is a dramatic moment," said Rodney.

"You're looking at your new book for the first time," said Nigel.

"Tell them about it," I said and nodded toward the door. I handed them the book. They put it in their van and it stayed there all the way.

"Have you got anything to write about yet?" said Nigel.

"No, do you have any ideas?"

"Did you see that sign in front of Mother's Pizza?"

"What'd it say?"

"It said applications now being accepted for drivers. Do you think we should apply for one?"

"Nah, we already got enough drivers. But how about applying for a pizza?"

7. What Was It Like on Earth?

Nigel Walkey was a cabdriver by trade and knew the fastest way to get from anywhere to anywhere, even during evening rush hours when the Gardiner and Don Valley expressways around Toronto would get as clogged as D.H. Lawrence's bronchial tubes.

But even the best get stuck some time.

Nigel's van was stuck about ten cars behind me. I was stuck behind a bus. It was a long two-lane road threading its way through the dreaded suburbs. Nothing was moving except for the occasional car sailing smugly by the other way (toward the city centre), which made me feel like a man with no money looking through a restaurant window, or a lifer watching sparrows fly over the wall or vees of Canada geese way up high heading for the Sunny Southland.

You've probably been caught in traffic jams before and maybe are even caught in a traffic jam right now as you flip through this book waiting for the traffic to clear, but this was an ugly landscape to be caught in, made even more so perhaps because we knew we were heading down to the lake, or the road we were on would lead us to lovely winding tree-lined Highway 2, the highway we had planned to stay on all the way along the north shore of the big inland sea of a lake until it flooded through the Thousand Islands into the St. Lawrence River.

Sheldon, just before we left, had asked if we would be going through Peterborough. He'd always had a fixation on the Trent Canal locks at Peterborough, some kind of mystical otherworldly memory of them. He said that once when he was a kid he was thrown into a state of confusion for an entire year when the telephone directory for that year came out with a picture of the Peterborough locks on the cover. One glance at that cover and he was electrified. Mom told him he'd never been to Peterborough, but he knew he had. Those locks were so familiar to him he must have known them in another life.

Nigel had left his paralytic blue van and was standing beside my little low-slung car.

"Isn't this terrific? Me and the guys were thinking, we're city kids you know and it just feels so great to be getting out of the city for a few days—but then again it might take a few days to get out of the city."

"I thought you cabdrivers knew all the zippy routes. You'll never get big tips this way."

"Ah, even the best get stuck sometimes."

"What? That's exactly what I just finished writing in my notebook. Look."

Nigel looked and shook his head. A stricken look came to his face and a cold shiver passed through his body.

"I love to hear about this sort of thing happening to others," he said, "but I hate when it happens to me."

"Why?"

"I don't know, I just do. It makes me feel that I'm not in control."

"You're not."

"Who is?"

"I am."

"Then get us out of this traffic jam."

"You have to have faith, my boy."

"And patience."

There was a vast open field on the right. No grass, just a sterile stretch containing old oil drums, manhole covers lying around like loose change, uprooted trees with their black roots sticking up in the air like the legs of blackened radioactive cattle, and small irregularly shaped patches of asphalt, as if someone had been trying to build a parking lot or landing strip without really having a good idea how to go about doing so. Someone with visions of big money owned it and was hanging on to it. Becoming rich means you can afford to get out of the mess you made becoming rich. At least you expect you'll be able to.

It was a beautiful Friday afternoon, but there was no one around except for the people huddled in cars, buses, vans and trucks in the traffic jam or hiding inside their apartments in the jungle of brown-brick blocks of flats on the left side of the road, condos full of potted begonias and fig trees, cut flowers on Friday nights, framed prints on the wall, and lots of electronic gadgetry. Everyone was busy watching television, listening to their new compact discs on their stereos, playing with their video cassette recorders, or maybe just feeding the fish. This must be the Afterlife, I thought, but my memories of what it had been like on Earth were vague.

But what wonderful electronic compensations, it almost made up for the ugliness and sameness of the environment. The sign stretching across the back of the bus in front showed a steering wheel, with a nicely manicured hand reaching for the dial of a huge car radio, and a bright golden glow bursting from the dial. The caption said: TURN TO GOLD, 590/CKEY. I didn't bother turning to CKEY but the ad had a strange effect. Suddenly the area didn't look quite so ugly and monotonous. It must have been the golden glow that did it, I have such a suggestible imagination. Suddenly we were all angels dwelling in a brave new world, a golden dawn. There was a little church on the corner, and its roof was covered in gold. There were little groups of trees, their leaves tinged with gold. The sky was blue, with a couple of little puffy clouds trimmed with golden light, and although you couldn't see it the lake was nearby, bringing health and happiness to everyone in the healthy happy community.

For years I've felt that everything that was beautiful and unique was dying and nothing but ugliness and sameness was being born. But, simply by glancing at that silly mud-splattered ad on the back of that bus, that horrible feeling had been put to sleep. As I sat there in an unspeakably adjectiveless traffic jam I felt at the peak of my powers, I could do anything.

But there was nothing I wanted to do.

8. Long Stretches of Time with Nothing to Do

I was in the fast lane, going like sixty, bumper to bumper in the blinding golden light of a late October afternoon, and checking occasionally to see if the bird's-eye blue van was still behind me which it was. But there were several cars separating us. A sign said Highway 2 to the right, Macdonald-Cartier Freeway straight ahead, so I made a mad swing three lanes to the right and cut off then slowed down and looked back. The blue van continued straight on, the guys staring at me and waving sadly. They were blocked from following me at the cutoff and it would be impossible for them to turn around and come back. But earlier on we'd looked at their map and agreed that if we became separated we'd meet at the town hall in Whitby.

There was something absolute about the lake, or it was somehow a symbol of the absolute, and there was little of the absolute in my life, or anybody's life for that matter as far as I knew, and so I headed down to the lake with glee, happy also that I didn't have to worry about the guys, we'd meet in Whitby in an hour or two, and if I were late they'd wait. But first I drove into a small but crowded shopping centre to send a funny postcard with some sweet words of friendship to my friend Marie-Thérèse in her little old convent in Montreal, a somewhat hypocritical note to my editor saying I was pleased with the look of the new book and including a list of people to send review copies to if they could afford it, and a short letter to my former fiancée Hiroko who was living in a Maori Buddhist commune in New Zealand.

The postcard to Marie-Thérèse was sealed in an envelope and marked private. It would be easy for the other nuns to misinterpret the friendship that had developed between us over the last two years, a passionate friendship that had become tremendously important to me. The postcard was definitely X-rated, but cute. Marie-Thérèse would like it.

The post office was a one-person affair (the best kind, perhaps), inside a huge Mister Drug, but it was after 5:30 and the postal counter was closed. Through the window the clerk saw the look of disappointment on my face, and opened up for me.

"All I want is a dollar's worth of stamps," I said.

She was very nice and even though she'd already balanced the cash and had it tied up in a bag she reopened the bag and gave me my change, even weighed the letter to New Zealand and all that. I thanked her profusely and asked if she did this sort of thing all the time. She laughed and said yes. I told her she'd go to heaven for sure when she died. She was pleased and said that was her big goal in life. She'd always been fond of harps and long stretches of time with nothing to do but sit around listening to beautiful music. Sounds boring, I know, she said, but it beats selling stamps.

"Amen," I said, humorously. I handed her the letter to Marie-Thérèse. "Can you see through the envelope?" She squinted. "Can you see the photo on the card inside?"

"I can see it. There's two people...."

"Oh, no!"

"...But I can't really tell what they're doing or what they have on and I can't read the printing."

"Are you sure?"

"I wouldn't lie."

"Okay then. That's all I wanted to know. Thanks."

9. Mexicali Rose

Sentimental music from the thirties and forties was coming over the car radio and when they played Vera Lynn's "Mexicali Rose" I remembered I'd forgotten to phone my mother to tell her I was going away. I phoned from the booth in front of the Mister Drug. "Hi son," she said. She sounded excited. I told her I was going away for a week and she told me to be careful. She said she'd just been watching Billy Graham on television.

"Oh, guess what," she said.

"Uncle Bob sold his house and moved into an apartment?"

"No. What made you say that?"

"You asked me to guess."

Mom always had a lovely giggle. "I don't think he's even been thinking about that. So guess again."

"I give up. It's long distance you know."

The giggling tone turned to frost. "You can hang up any time you want, son...."

"Sorry, go ahead."

"This won't take a minute. Us ladies had our church bazaar last night. You know all that knitting and tatting I been doing?"

"Yes?"

"Well that's what it was for, the church bazaar. Me and your dad went last night. And guess how much money us ladies raised?"

It must have been a lot but I had no idea how much. "I don't know but I bet it was a bizarre amount," I said.

"A bizarre amount? What do you mean, son?"

"Well it was for a bazaar wasn't it?"

"Oh. Very funny." More giggling. "You're a smart one, I almost forgot there for a minute. Come on, guess how much."

"Exactly eight hundred and three dollars and no cents."

"Oh, heck no. A lot more than that. We raised thirty-four hundred dollars."

"Wow! Good going, mom. I'm proudaya. And it all goes to the church?"

"Yep, sure does. To do good works."

"Like sending food to Ethiopia?"

"You mean like the starving people in Africa?"

"Yup."

"Oh, isn't that terrible? We seen it on television. Maybe that's what they'll do with the money."

"That'd be wonderful. And listen, mom. How's grandma?"

"Oh. She's as well as can be expected you know. But I wish you could come and see her before Thursday. Your brother is."

"Why Thursday?"

"Because she's going to be ninety on Thursday."

"Oh really? I'll come and see her after I get back. You wish her happy birthday for me. Bye now, mom. And say bye to dad."

"Walter, your son says bye.... Your dad says bye too, and you take care of yourself all right? And drive safely."

"Okay mom."

"And before I hang up, did you see the Pope on television?"

The Pope was touring Canada.

"Sure did, mom. I watched a lot of it. Did you?"

"I sure did. Your dad did too. Wasn't he wonderful?"

"Who? Dad?"

"Well him too. But I was thinking of the Pope at this particular point in time."

"I thought you didn't like Catholics."

"What ever made you think that?"

"I've got a good memory, I've heard you say a few things against Catholics."

"You've got a terrible memory because I've never said anything against Catholics or Jewish people or anything like that in my entire life. Honestly, I don't know where you get some of your ideas. I like Catholics. They're just as good as we are. Maybe better. We're all God's children...."

"Amen."

"And son, would you like to be a Pope some day?"

She was serious. That was my mom, she'd gone into her cosmic mode again. "Er, I guess it would be all right. But I'm not sure they'd want me. There's a lot of competition. You have to start small, you know. You have to be a priest first. And you have to be Catholic. And you can't have been divorced, at least I don't think you can...."

"You can be anything you want, son." Mom was speaking in her serious cosmic voice. "And don't you ever forget it."

"Okay, I won't. Popes sure get to travel a lot, first class too, and they get a lot of respect everywhere they go. But don't forget, mom, you raised me in the United Church of Canada where everyone has to try to become his or her own Pope."

"Yes, and don't you ever forget you were raised in the United Church, son."

"I won't, mom. I wouldn't think of it, honest."

"And how's Marie?"

She'd been in town at Thanksgiving and at Christmas and we all had dinner together both times at Sheldon's place. Mom and dad fell in love with her. Later when I asked what it was about her she liked so much, mom said it was because I always looked so happy when I was with her.

"She's okay. We talked on the phone a couple of days ago. And I sent her a card today."

"What kind of a card?"

"Oh, just one of those sexy X-rated cards showing a couple of sex-crazed, half-dressed lesbians wrestling around on the floor. And one is saying to the other does your mother know? Just one of those nice funny friendly greeting cards. Just so she knows I'm thinking about her."

"I know you're thinking about her."

"How do you know?"

"I just know. I'm your mother. Are you going to see her on this trip?"

"I don't know, I don't think so."

"Well, I have a feeling you are, even if you don't realise it at this particular point in time. And if you do see her, be careful."

"And if I don't see her?"

"If you don't see her be careful too."

"Okay, mom. That's great advice. I'll try to follow it. I have to go now. Bye."

"I love you."

"I love you too."

"Your dad loves you too."

"I love him too."

"Bye. And be careful."

"Thanks, mom. I will. Bye."

"Oh, wait a minute. Son? Are you still there?"

"Yes mom."

"There was something I wanted to ask you, something you said. What was it now? Oh yeah. Son, what's a lesbian?"

"A lesbian? That's sort of like a lady homosexual?"

"A what?"

"You know, you watch Phil Donahue, don't you? Isn't he always having lesbians on to talk about their lives and tell exactly what it is they do?"

"Well, Marie isn't...one of those, is she?"

"No, I don't think so. I think she would have told me."

"Then why would you send her a card like that?"

"Oh, just as a little joke."

"Hm. All right then, bye now. By the way, you're not going to sleep in your car on this trip now, are you?"

"Definitely not, mom. I'm getting too old for that. Besides, it's just a little sports car with no top to speak of. I like to get into my jammies and stretch out and flop around under the warm smelly sheets."

"Well, listen now. I want you to take care of yourself and get lots of rest and above all, for heaven's sake, son, watch out for vampires."

"Okay mom. You too."

"Don't let anybody bite you on the neck, because they might be a vampire and you wouldn't know till it was too late."

I knew about this one. They had some vampires on the Donahue show recently. You could hardly tell them from ordinary people except their eyebrows met. "Okay mom. Anybody wants to bite me on the neck, I have a whole list of questions they have to answer first. And don't you let anybody bite you. Some of those vampires can be Scout leaders or Jehovah's Witnesses coming to the door or even Girl Guides pretending to sell cookies."

"I know, son. Thanks for being concerned. Bye now. And I hope Marie gets the joke."

"'Cause you sure don't, right?"

"Right."

10. Time's Sharp Little Teeth

The road swept along behind a large sewage-treatment plant through a new subdivision and came to a dead-end surrounded by half-finished houses and abandoned stone-crushing machines a quarter of a mile from the shore of Lake Ontario. There was a book lying all alone on the pristine expanse of gleaming new-pressed asphalt. I hopped out. It was an old German edition of Rilke in excellent condition except that someone had heavily annotated the thirteenth sonnet, with much pencilled marginalia. I couldn't read German, but finding the book gave me a chill. It looked as if it had fallen from one of the bulldozers. Maybe one of the operators was a German poetry-lover and he might be looking for it so I climbed up on the closest bulldozer and placed the book on the seat.

Trying to get back to Highway 2, I got lost in a maze of streets in a subdivision of beautiful brick bungalows from the early sixties, with handsome sailboats and cabin cruisers sitting proudly on car-trailers in the driveways, orange and red leaves beginning to pile up on the nice lawns, and a few pumpkins lying around. An athletic-looking tall blonde woman with a pair of binoculars around her neck gave me some friendly advice when I asked for directions back to the highway. She was getting out of her tout-terrain Jeep and looked as if she'd just returned from a week-long bird-watching and hang-gliding expedition in the Great Smokies and would have loved to tell me, over a bottle of Blue Nun and a garden salad, exactly what it was that fascinated her so much about hawks.

"Straight down this road to the stop sign then three consecutive right turns and you'll be on Highway 2 heading east, four and you'll be heading west." She wanted to know where I wanted to go and when I told her east along the lake, as close to the lake as possible, she offered me her topographical map of the region.

"Come on in, I'll try to find it for you," she said.

But I wouldn't hear of it. It was autumn, and there was something mystical and poetic about being on a long mindless trip in a little open car with no watch and no map. Besides, as I drove off I remembered I did have a topographical map of the area, the one Sheldon had given me. It was in the trunk. Let it stay there. There's a special kind of magic about not knowing where you are. All the myths come alive, the world opens up, and time loses its sharp little teeth.

11. Human Friendship

Finally I felt free, out of the grasp of the mindless octopus of a city, driving east along a two-lane highway with little traffic, green hills with blue sky and fruit stands, one of which I stopped at and bought a bushel of Macs and a bag of roasted peanuts. I wondered if I should have taken that Rilke with me. Had fate intended me to give the book to the blonde birdwatcher? Maybe she spoke German, she looked German and I thought I detected a slight German accent. Maybe I was meant to give the book to someone else further down the line, some German-speaking person who had never read Rilke but was obviously dying for lack of what could be found therein, to paraphrase another poet. You can go crazy this way. Maybe I should go back and pick it up and deliver it to the German birdwatcher. She'd be surprised, but I probably wouldn't be able to find her house again in that subdivisional maze.

It was amazing: there was no traffic on the road and a late-afternoon autumnal quiet was setting in. Where had all the commuters gone? The guy running the fruit stand had a thin moustache and gave the impression I was his first customer in hours. I complimented him on the delicious apple he allowed me to sample and didn't complain when he dumped them all out of the handsome bushel basket and into a thick-gauge plastic bag. He looked pleased and came out to the car with me and watched as I found room behind the seat for the bag. He obviously liked the little sportster and sensed I was on a rather unhurried journey with no goal in mind (except to get back to my starting point), and in such beautiful weather, with all the fall colours exploding. Maybe he wanted to come with me!

"You're going to die of loneliness on this job," I offered.

"It's not always so lonely," he said.

He felt sad because his dog had passed away yesterday, after a very short illness. Her name was Sarah, a close-cropped curly-haired standard poodle, and he went on and on about what a good friend she'd been. Never any trouble, always sensitive, intelligent, affectionate, gentle. I must have looked sympathetic because he pulled a photo out of his shirt pocket and showed it to me. Elegant-looking dog, almost deer-like in appearance, with long slender legs and snout.

She had a friend, he said, a small one-year-old "mix" who had a lot of energy.

"Don't all one-year-old dogs have lots of energy?"

"That's true, but Sarah liked this small dog so much she'd get into escapades she ordinarily wouldn't. About a week ago the two of them ganged up on a neighbour's goose in the middle of the night. Left nothing but a pile of bloody feathers."

"Did you punish her?"

"No, I didn't have to. I just told her that if I weren't feeding her enough she should just let me know, and it wasn't nice to raid the neighbour's livestock. She understood, really. You could see it in her eyes."

"You think she really understood?"

"Yeah, perfectly. But she didn't feel herself for quite a few days after that goose episode, so I took her to the vet and told him what happened. He X-rayed her and said there were no goose bones lodged anywhere. There were some ground-up bones in the stool, but that was nothing to worry about. What did worry him though was that the stool was black. I told him it'd been black for several weeks, and he said it could be serious. Internal bleeding."

"Nothing to do with the goose?"

"Apparently not. They did a lot of tests and found that her bone marrow wasn't functioning, wasn't producing blood. Aplastic anaemia or something like that. Humans get it too and it's pretty well always fatal.... So the vet phoned and said there was no one home in the bone-marrow department, that's just the way he talks, great guy really, and he didn't know what to say. So I asked him what he'd do if it were his dog and he said he thought he'd put her under. So I took Sarah for a long walk and then took her back and the vet gave her the needle."

"Do you figure she knew she was going to die?"

"I think so. I know it sounds ridiculous, and you always hear the so-called experts say that animals have no concept of death, but I think she knew her number was up. We went for that final walk, and she was weak, you could tell she just wanted to go back to the vet's office, and you know that dogs hate to go anywhere near a vet's office normally. So back we went."

"You were crying?"

"Oh...." He paused. "Yeah, I was crying like a baby. I took her in and the vet came out with his needle. She sniffed it as he put it in. She turned her eyes and looked at me for a second or two then closed them. Just like going to sleep."

He went on to say that he lived alone but always had a dog to come home to. Sarah was the third dog he'd had. He wasn't sure though that he was going to get another. He said he'd always had problems maintaining human friendships, people were okay at a distance but when they got too close he felt uncomfortable. And he felt as if he'd been using his dogs as substitutes for human friendship long enough, and maybe if he delayed getting another dog now it would force him to come to terms with this problem. He said he felt sad now when he would go home at the end of the day and the dog wasn't there, he couldn't believe she was dead.

"I don't want to dwell on it, and actually I think I'm taking it pretty well. It was before her time, though. That's what makes it harder to take. And she was such a unique dog. I never knew another dog like her, even in physical appearance she was more like a graceful deer than a dog. Everybody said that."

I shook his hand and said I had to go, wished him luck, and said I hoped he came to terms with his problems with human friendship because I thought he had a whole lot to offer in that department, and I told him I meant it sincerely. He smiled sadly, and when I looked out my rear-view mirror I could see him standing there watching me disappear from view, and he was still smiling sadly.

12. Twenty Dancers from Montreal

I never did get to see the town hall in Whitby. There was the bird's-eye blue van, the same colour blue as on the cover of *Golden Dewdrops of the Night*, parked at a downtown intersection (the van, not the book), and red-haired Rodney and dark-haired Nigel came over with big smiles on their faces and said they'd got tired of waiting at the town hall so they came downtown to check out the action and left blonde-haired Winston sitting on the moss-covered town-hall step to watch for me.

"He's just sitting there?"

"He's reading your new book of poems."

"Oh?" A broad smile snaked its way across my narrow face.

"Yeah, and he really likes it, like I mean really. He wouldn't let us even take a peek at it."

"Good taste."

"Yeah, really. I told you he was a good one."

"But let's get serious," I said. I pulled out the huge green garbage bag full of apples and plopped it on the car hood as if it were a low-slung counter, and the peanuts too. They each grabbed handfuls of both.

"Okay. Why don't you two wait here and try to figure out what we're going to do," said Nigel, "and I'll go and get Winston."

So red-haired assistant cameraman Rodney and I stood there in the brilliant late-afternoon sun by the side of the little Spitfire, with nice well-groomed well-dressed townspeople walking by and smiling at us, and drivers and passengers in passing cars and trucks and even buses looking at us, as if we were something special. Kids were standing on the other side of the road, picking their noses and staring at us. It was just Whitby, just a town on the outskirts of Toronto, but we were attracting as much attention as if we'd stopped in an indigenous settlement in the Brazilian jungle. We seemed to be parked okay. It must have been the huge movie camera Rodney had balanced on the hood of the Spitfire next to the blood-red apples and the peanuts.

"They think Whitby's gonna be on TV," said Rodney.

"You'd think people would be more blasé about that sort of thing by now. After all this is 1984."

"Yeah, they look as if Steven Spielberg has just buzzed into town with a dozen big trailers."

Rodney and I got into a bit of an argument about Spielberg. He thought *Close Encounters of the Third Kind* was his best picture, while I preferred *Jaws*. Just as we were about to start punching each other, Nigel returned with Winston.

"Did you figure out what we're going to do?" said Nigel.

Rodney and I were very embarrassed. We hadn't discussed what we were going to do at all. Winston was peering at me with renewed interest after having read a few of the poems in the new book. Ah, the awesome power of poetry! (At least for the few with an ear for it.) He was looking at me with the same tentative shyness as the townspeople were looking at all of us.

We felt as awkward as if we were on stage. We were actually blushing, the three of us. Sometimes you just think everyone's looking at you. That kind of self-consciousness is a factor of your own interest in people. You like to look at people so you think that everyone is looking at

249

you. But in this case they really were. It was as if the whole town had dropped everything and come out to stare at us. We could see people blocks away shading their eyes with their hands and peering down the street at us and calling their friends to come and look.

I said no, we hadn't figured out what to do. What could we possibly do that might generate something to write about? Absolutely nothing had happened so far. The book would be full of blank pages, like Henry Miller's *What to Do About Sex after Sixty*.

"Do you guys have any ideas?" I inquired. They just shrugged and sighed and kicked the tires and scratched their armpits and sniffed their fingers. They wanted to know if I was hungry and when I said no they said they'd grab something to eat at the restaurant we were standing in front of and meet me at the bar in an hour or so.

They were referring to the bar we'd passed on the way into town. It was a sleazy-looking bar across from a used-car lot. There was a sign above the front entrance saying 20 DANCERS FROM MONTREAL.

13. Vidiadhar Surajprasad Naipaul

From the highway the place reflected the collective condemnation of the whole town and because of that this dark, unpainted, unadorned and unwashed barn of a building with the cinder parking lot became more interesting than the ordinary local bars, pool rooms, video parlours, bingo halls and late-night smoke shops. It exhaled an atmosphere as forbidding as certain places from childhood. "I don't want you playing with the kids who live there," mom would say. It wouldn't occur to you to ask why not. Or if you did ask she would say never mind. You just wouldn't play with those kids—until one time you fell off your bicycle in front of their house and they came out to help you and they were so nice to you and took you in and their mom washed off your scraped knee so gently you knew your mother had been wrong.

"Do not enter if you are offended by complete nudity," said the sign over the front door. The place looked closed and in fact the front entrance was all locked up. This was strange because there were dozens of cars in the parking lot. So I checked the side door, and it was locked too. But the door on the other side of the building opened into the kitchen, and I went in, and through into the large barn-like bar area, with a sudden shower of canned rock n roll and a short bar with no railing or stools, forty or fifty little tables spread around for drinkers, a couple of pool tables, pinball machines, video games. And there was a stage with a long runway sticking out like a tongue along which sat about two dozen men, their elbows resting awkwardly on the runway along which ran a thin ledge marking out the space they could use for their beer and ashtrays and loose change and the Louis L'amour paperbacks they would pick up and read between performances.

There was a sign saying TABLE DANCES $5.00. A girl in a pair of shorts and an open black-leather vest with her naked tits sticking out was shooting pool with a pair of ugly bikers. A girl in a G-string down around her knees was doing a table dance at the next table, with three more ugly bikers sitting at the table and staring at her intently as she pretzeled herself around them, hoping for a fifty-cent tip. A waitress in an innocent little chemise showing her blonde pubic hair and pink nipples brought me a beer. I looked around at the customers, all of whom were men. Half of them were greasy long-haired long-bearded tattooed black-leather-jacketed bikers and the other half looked like high-school teachers stopping off for a beer on the way home. And there was one unclassified guy, his hands clenched in the pockets of his neatly buttoned navy-blue raincoat. He was a short, neatly groomed, unhappy fellow with a white shirt and perfectly knotted silver tie, and he was just standing there staring at the girls with a tense, frozen look on his face, and he would occasionally walk stiffly up to a girl and say something to her with an unpleasant look on his face and she would skip away and call something over her shoulder to him, something like: "Okay, but later, all right?"

There was a great mirror covering the wall at the back of the stage, with another hanging from the ceiling at an angle, so you could see the dancer from multiple angles at any one time. A lone dancer was standing in front of the mirror, her naked back to the viewers who could nevertheless see her naked front in reflection. She squatted down and reached into some kind of container. I couldn't see very well from where I was sitting. It may have been a pail. Out of it she pulled something and rubbed it all over her breasts and thighs as she continued staring at herself in the mirror.

"Who Do You Love?" by Nash the Slash came on over the loudspeakers, and she started to dance, strutting up and down the floodlit runway with naked abandon and a fierce look on her face directed at the men staring up at her from their box seats. After the song stopped she spread a mat on the runway floor. Phil Collins' "Something in the Air" came on, a slower piece, and she got down on the mat and started to roll over and over, slowly spreading her legs wide, her whole body from head to toe pumping in time with the slowly thumping music, her naked crotch about a foot away from the nose of one of the men sitting at the side of the runway. He was watching intently, even pointing and grinning at his neighbours and nudging them awake with his elbows, yet there was a certain innocence about what she was doing. Being so unashamed of nakedness had a childlike quality about it and the fact she was doing it for a living didn't subtract from that quality, in fact it might have added to it. "We've all become like little children," said my friend Zamzam, the celibate Tibetan lama, as we lay naked with friends one afternoon on the nude beach up the east shore of Kootenay Lake. He was perfectly relaxed and open in his nudity, but I could scarcely breathe because I was trying so hard to steel myself so that I wouldn't be so embarrassed. From then on, I only went to the nude beach at night. And then I stopped altogether when, one night, a furry underwater animal—people said it was probably a beaver—tried to bite my testicles off.

After the dance I went up to the girl and as we stood under the sign reading PLEASE DON'T TOUCH THE DANCERS I asked her with a big smile (to hide the embarrassment) what it was she'd been rubbing on her body before the dance. She looked at me a little nervously. She had a French accent.

"Wha' deed I pood on my brezz?" she said.

"Yeah, what was that?"

"Uh, I pood on da ice?"

"Oh, ice!"

She smiled, arched her back and pointed at her nipples.

"Hit make da Naipauls stick owd," she said.

"Hm!" I said. "Very Sexy Naipauls you have there."

14. Big Bob, Gus and Smoky

Kukla, Fran and Ollie still hadn't shown up. There was another room, next to the bar and equally barn-like, and it was empty except for a couple of tables at which some oldtimers sat drinking beer, away from the music and the dance stage, but they could still look at the semi-naked girls as they scampered sexily between the stage and the washrooms and dressing rooms downstairs. At the back of the room, which was the front of the building, the side closest to the highway, sat a grossly obese guy surrounded by racks of brightly coloured costumes. He was friendly, asked me to sit down, and when I told him I was a writer he became even friendlier and bought me a beer. His name was Gus. He travelled around to the strip joints selling costumes while his wife ran their store, the Naked Pearl, in Peterborough.

"Lingerie, swim wear and exotic costumes," said Gus. "Everything for the exotic dancer. Since 1976 I've sold to over fourteen thousand girls. Yep, fourteen thousand."

One of the exotic dancers, a small, brown-skinned Afro-Canadian with a provocative nose and almond eyes, came up and started talking to him. He called her Smoky, and when she glanced at me, he said, proudly: "This fella's a writer. He's from Toronto." She glanced at me again, this time with somewhat focussed eyes. I asked her if she minded him calling her Smoky.

"Everyone calls me that," she said, with a certain displeasure, "even my landlord."

She was playing with a little piece of black elasticised cloth, stretching it with her hands and letting it snap. She turned to Gus.

"How much is this G-string?"

"Five dollars."

"The last one I bought fell apart. I put it in the washing machine."

"Oh, don't do that. Wash 'em out by hand."

I was still thinking about her name. All the black kids I knew when I was a kid were called Smoky.

"Smoky," I said. "You probably don't even smoke."

"Just cigarettes."

"Where do you live?"

"Toronto."

"What part?"

"I never say."

Smoky and I weren't hitting it off. She kept glancing at me but didn't see the purity of my soul. I was just another lecherous hog, someone to keep at arm's length, as if she were thinking: "Oh, not another writer! All these lechers are either policemen wanting information, ministers trying to save your soul, or writers wanting to write the story of your life. But we all know what they really want." She had a business relationship with Gus, and didn't seem to mind when, in the friendliest manner imaginable, he put his hairy fat arm around her naked little brown waist and pulled her down on his lap. She sat there for a minute then bounced up and started going through the costumes on the rack.

"Guys follow me home all the time," she said. I guess she figured she'd been a little sharp with me. "It's a big problem. I can't imagine what it'd be like if everyone knew where I lived."

"Gus follows you home?"

"Not Gus. Guys. Guys follow me home all the time."

Gus looked at me and smiled sweetly.

"Who runs this place?" I said.

"Bob Waldorf," said Gus. "Big Bob Waldorf. He's meaner than catshit. And don't look now but here he comes."

Nigel, Winston and Rodney had come in with him and they were talking to him. He didn't look that big, or that mean.

Gus's voice dropped to a whisper. "He's got one helluva stranglehold," he said. "If you're drunk and acting up he'll snap a sleeper hold on you, and if that doesn't straighten you up he'll put a choke hold on you and you're done for."

"This guy's writing a book, eh?" Nigel was saying to Big Bob. "The guy we're filming. He's just driving around taking notes for his book, so that when he writes the book he might write a whole scene inside this bar."

"No problem," said Big Bob. "We don't mind, eh? We're game for anything. We're not too fussy about people taking pictures of the strippers though, cause you never know what the fuck they're going to do with them...."

"He's meaner than catshit," Gus kept muttering. Big Bob looked at me and smiled.

"So you're the owner?" I said. "It must be nice being around all these pretty naked girls all the time."

"Nah," he barked. "My wife runs the place. I just take care of the car lot across the street." I looked at him. "I've been in this business since 1968. Any hotel owner who drinks or fucks around with the girls will soon be out of business."

"I believe you."

"I don't even look at 'em." He was growling. "If you can't fuck 'em why bother lookin' at 'em, eh?"

"Gus was right. You are meaner than catshit."

Everybody groaned.

Except Gus and Big Bob.

Gus was dead silent.

So was Big Bob.

Big Bob stared at me.

Big Bob turned and glared at Gus.

Gus looked sick.

Big Bob started laughing.

15. Jamaican Cooking

"That guy is really tough, eh? He rules with an iron hand," said Gus after Big Bob had continued on his way out the front door, inexplicably locked from the outside only. "Good guy though. I think he liked you. At least he didn't punch you in the jaw when you told him he was meaner than catshit."

"He's something like you."

"Whattaya mean? I'm not tough. I'm a baby pussycat." Gus looked over as several more dancers had come by and were fluttering around the racks of exotic costumes. "Aren't I, girls?"

The girls ignored him.

"Maybe you're not as tough," I said. "But what I meant was you're like Big Bob because his wife runs the business and so does yours."

"Yeah, that's right. I am just like Big Bob."

"So tell me about your wife."

"She's Jamaican, eh? She used to be an exotic dancer. She came up here from Jamaica. She knows what the girls want, eh? She makes all these clothes, everything, and runs the store."

"You don't look like the kind of guy who'd have an exotic dancer for a wife."

"Why not?"

For one thing, he was enormously fat, but I didn't want to say that. "You just look like an ordinary guy, that's all."

"Exotic dancers are ordinary people too, eh? They got two arms and two legs just like everybody else." He glanced at me sideways. "I only weighed two-oh-five when I met her."

"How much do you weigh now?"

"Oh, about two-fifty."

He looked at me to see if I believed him. I didn't.

"Pardon? Did you say three-fifty or four-fifty?"

"Two-fifty."

Just then somebody in the other room dropped a jug of beer with a splintering ear-splitting crash.

"That wife of yours, I bet she's a good cook."

"One of the best."

"Jamaican cooking by any chance?"

"Yep. And everything else too. French, Italian, Greek."

"Not Chinese?"

"Yeah, sure. Chinese too. Everything, I tell ya. Her name's Hughdelle, that's what it is. And there's another way I'm like Big Bob. I don't drink. You can't drink in this business, eh? I haven't had a drink since 1976."

"Were you a big drinker?"

"One of the biggest."

During the chat I was making signs at Nigel, Winston and Rodney, who had started setting up their lights. The girls' eyes were shining. More and more of them came over. They wouldn't mind being discovered at all. That big camera was magic to them.

16. Pierre Berton's Son

When a girl wanted to buy something, Gus would hand her a slip to sign: "Please deduct from my pay the following amount for costumes."

"How much money do these girls make?"

"Oh lots," said Gus. "They can make a thousand a week, some of 'em. If they work hard, do a lot of table dancing. Yep. It's okay if you treat it like a business. Get in, use your head, and know when to get out."

"Hello, I'm Captain Colourful," I said to the closest girl. I was wearing a yellow Hamilton Tiger-Cat painter's cap, a Hawaiian shirt and a pair of brown-and-green-plaid Bermuda shorts with red polkadot suspenders. It was a phase I was going through. She'd been watching me. She had a cute little all-white costume on, with white stockings, white garter belt and a kind of open transparent white chemise and the normal transparent desire for some attention. She kept snapping her garter belt and whipping her chemise open even further and sticking her pink tits out.

"Well hello, Captain Colourful. Welcome to Big Bob's," she said. She sounded as if she were trying to imitate Bette Midler imitating Craig Russell imitating Mae West. "I'm Ann Valentine."

"Is that your real name or your stage name?"

"It's my real name and my stage name, both."

"Nice double-duty name."

"Thanks."

"So, did you hear what Gus was just saying?"

"Yeah?"

"And what do you think?"

"I don't make no thousand dollars a week but I don't do no table dancing."

"Why not?"

"I hate table dancing. I do it a little but I don't like it. I'm into regular stripping." She looked at me. "If I'm gonna be sticking my beaver into some guy's face it's gonna be because I want it there, not for five dollars."

"Good, your integrity is altogether admirable and I mean that sincerely."

"Oh yeah, I try to avoid table dancing as much as possible."

Another dancer had just slipped into some kind of little blue spangly costume and turned to Gus.

"Is this okay? It makes me look kinda flat. I don't have much to put in it."

"I don't know if it's too big for you or not," said Gus, "but for ten bucks you can't go wrong."

I winced. "Ten bucks. That's two table dances," I said. Gus sighed and looked at me.

"Talk about writers," he said. "About twenty years ago, just outside Bobcaygeon, I picked up Pierre Berton's son." Winston had the camera pointed at Gus from a bit of a distance, outside the floodlit area. Gus made it seem as if twenty years were twenty days.

"What was he doing? Hitchhiking?"

"No, he ran his car into a ditch. A white Volkswagen, it was. He wanted to go to the garage so I took him. He wanted to get a tow truck. I asked him who he was and he sez you know Pierre Berton? I sez yeah. And he sez well I'm his son."

"Hm! Nice guy?"

"Seemed okay."

"His father's terrific."

"You know him?"

"I've met him."

"He's tall, isn't he?"

"Yeah. Real tall."

"So was his kid."

"Life's like that."

"It sure is."

17. Strippers for Jesus

Smoky got into stripping shortly after becoming disillusioned with her boyfriend. They were in the sack making love one night and she looked up and seven of his male friends were standing there quietly watching. He'd left the door open for them, told them that he'd be making love to her at a certain time, the front door would be open and they could let themselves in and watch.

And so about five minutes before the time, he started making love to her, without telling her what was up.

"Most guys really are jerks, you know," she said.

"Not me."

"Maybe you are, maybe you aren't."

"So you were making love and you noticed the guys standing there all of a sudden and then what?"

"So then I jumped up and started screaming. Then I got a few things and walked out and never came back."

She was working in a bank at the time and quit after her fourth holdup. It was something about being black. The robbers always went to her wicket. The first time was funny. The guy said, "This is a hold-up. Gimme all your money."

"Get serious," she said. "Where's your gun?"

"My friend's got it and I'm warning you he'll use it."

"Where's your friend?"

"He's at the back of the line."

"What's he wearing?"

"A brown jacket. Now shut up and gimme all your money."

"There's no one there with a brown jacket."

"Well gimme the money anyways."

"I'd like to but I don't know if I'm allowed to. Wait right there, I'll have to ask my boss."

She went over and told her boss to call the cops, then went back and gave the guy a hundred bucks.

"He said you could only have a hundred bucks," she said. "That'll do, give it to me." She did. He ran for the door and the cops grabbed him. The cops thought it was funny.

But the bank manager wanted to deduct the hundred bucks from her pay.

The second time she was robbed the guy pointed a real gun at her handsome Afro-Greco-Roman nose. She still hadn't recovered from the bank manager wanting to deduct the hundred from her pay so in exasperation she just scooped up all the money in her till and shoved it at him, and the guy got away.

This time the cops were the heavies. They grilled her in the back room, tried to get her to admit the robber was her boyfriend, or a friend of her boyfriend's.

"They asked me a whole bunch of insulting personal questions," she said. "They wouldn't have dared if I was white."

The third time she was so exasperated she just said to the robber, "Oh, go away," even though he had a real gun. And he did go away. But instead of being treated as a hero by the bank officials, she was criticised for not having let off the alarm.

The fourth time she just collapsed and spent a week at home under sedation. She never went back to work.

I thought bank tellers should have a special trap door on the floor at their feet and whenever someone stuck a gun in their face they could just press a button and the trap door would open and they would fall down a chute into a soft place in the basement, a nice soft mattress. The tellers, that is.

"With a stereo and a bar?" said Smoky.

"Right. And a big jar of Librium."

Did she meet a nicer class of men in strip joints than in the bank?

"Don't ask. You meet some nice guys, but most are pretty pathetic. I can't even look at them any more when I'm dancing because you never know what you're going to see. And guys all the time come up to me and ask me to come out with them to their car in the parking lot and give them blow jobs. And they get mad when you say no."

"Do some of the girls do it?"

"You mean go out to the car with them?"

"Uh, yeah."

"Some of 'em do, that's the problem. They do it if the guys offer them dope. They do it for the cocaine."

"The guys offer them cocaine if they'll go out to the car with them?"

"Yeah. Some of 'em do. A lot of 'em do. And so the guys get very furious if you say no. Some of 'em. Some of 'em don't mind if you say no."

I asked her about the strange guy in the navy-blue raincoat and silver tie.

"Oh him, what a creep! He comes in about three times a week and just stands there staring for hours. He's the minister at one of those churches. Pentecostals? Something like that."

"Really? How frightfully curious! What does he say to you?"

"Oh, he always wants to sit down with me and talk to me about Jesus. All the girls. He wants us to come out to his car so he can save our souls from damnation. It's hard to get away from him. Also he's got very clammy hands. Disgusting!"

"Do you think the people at his church know about all the time he spends here?"

"Probably not. He parks his car way around at the back where you can't see it from the road."

"You know what they say, Jesus loves you."

"I know. But he ain't Jesus. He's just another jerk."

18. Imagine

Gus wanted to buy Nigel a beer. "I'm a bad Canadian, eh?" Nigel said.

"Like, whattaya mean, a bad Canadian?" said Gus.

"Like, I don't drink."

"That's okay. I don't drink neither," said Gus. "And I'm a good Canadian, eh? All's I wanted was to buy you a beer, eh?"

"I got a joke," said Nigel.

"Shoot," said Gus.

"You know why Canadians always say 'eh?' all the time?"

"No, why?"

"Because of the first prime minister. Sir John, eh?"

Ann Valentine was stretching her legs out and rubbing her knee.

"Where'd you get that awful scar?" I queried.

Ann looked down at her leg almost as if she didn't know the scar was there.

"It's a burn from a muffler on a bike."

"Are you a biker?"

"Some of my friends are."

I mentioned the sign out front, the one saying 20 DANCERS FROM MONTREAL, and Ann said there used to be twenty but now there were only a couple from Montreal and she was glad of it. Apparently the Quebec strippers weren't making very much in Quebec. So when they started invading the Ontario places they were happy to work for only fifty bucks a night.

"Yeah," said a tall thin dancer with kinky long blonde hair and terrific cheekbones and an innocent air about her. Dressed a little less flagrantly and she could pass for a nun. She'd been listening as she went through the racks. "Up till then we were making more or less like ninety a day, now we're down to fifty."

I liked her with a sudden and disproportionate apprehension in my heart. I tried not to let her know, but she could tell, and I could tell she could tell.

She turned to Gus and said, "I need undersets. I've got all kinds of costumes."

I turned away and looked at Ann.

"Are those real tattoos?"

"Yep. Like 'em?"

"Sure."

"Good. I'm gonna get some more."

"You could bill yourself as Tattoo Annie!"

She liked that. Her face lit up.

Gus was trying to sell some perfume to Smoky. "I don't wear perfume," she said. "The odd time I wear a bit of musk oil. Perfume's too expensive when you're like me and take about six showers a day. Every time you take a shower you have to put on new perfume. I can't afford it."

I wanted them to tell me some stories.

"What kinda stories?" said Tattoo Annie.

"Stories from real life."

"Hey, I could write a book. My life's just fulla stories."

"So why don't you tell me one?"

"Uh, what kinda story you want?"

"Anything. About being an exotic dancer, about your experiences with the clientele or with the owners, about your parents' reaction when they found out you were a stripper, anything."

Another girl sat down and said she was on a TV talk show in Trenton. "My aunt saw it. She didn't know I was a dancer. Boy, was she shocked!"

"What'd she do?"

"Well, she was a Born Again Christian, y'know what I mean? And she was right furious, she truly was. She phoned my dad in Barrie and said do you know what your daughter's doing?"

"And did he?"

"Oh yeah, he knew. He just never bothered telling her about it. But I mean that wasn't very like you say Christian of her, was it?"

"I'm sure she rationalised it to herself."

"Oh sure she did. She'd make it sound like she was doing me this terrific favour by squealing. They're all the same, those hypocrites."

The kinky blonde with the cheekbones came over and sat down on my left, shivered sweetly and put her arm around me. I felt moved, and I'll tell you why. She reminded me a lot, not just a little, of my friend Marie-Thérèse. If her hair were darker and straighter. But it was more than a physical resemblance and it was something deeper than personality that made me feel they were angels of the same high order. I tried not to show that I was attracted, I wanted to be professional about all this, but she picked it up somehow. She liked me too!

"My name's Pinky," she whispered, and she shivered again, even more deliciously this time, and she even sighed a bit. "My real name's Faith but Pinky's my nom de plume."

I smiled, maybe blushed. She gave me a squeeze with her right arm. I involuntarily shivered a bit but was determined not to let on how much I liked her.

"Pinky what?" I said.

"Let's just say Pinky for now."

"How old are you?"

"Twenty-one."

"Is that all? I thought you'd be about twenty-two."

"We age fast in this business."

"I bet."

"How old are you?"

"Er, ah, um...thirty-five?"

"Really? I woulda said about twenty-nine."

Her eyes sparkled a bit and we blushed some more.

"How about some interesting stories for my book?"

"Good stories or bad stories?"

"Hm, bad ones I guess."

"The tragedy and heartbreak of a stripper's life?"

"You got it."

"Actually I really haven't had many bad experiences. I'm a free spirit."

"I could tell at a glance."

She gave me another squeeze and a big smile.

"How long you been dancing?"

"About three years. I used to be called Lil Pink."

"So how do you like the life of an exotic dancer? Or should I say stripper?"

"You can call it anything you want. Not everybody can handle this business. You have to put your mind in the right place." She was trying to look serious but little sparks kept popping out of her eyes and a little smile kept bursting through.

"What do you mean?"

"You have to be open minded. You have to like it or it'll show. I mean, some girls get up there and they don't smile or anything."

She smiled with her whole face, her whole body. I smiled back. She gave me another squeeze.

"Do the owners treat you okay?" I'd kill them if they didn't.

"Sometimes yes, sometimes no. If I go to a place to dance and I don't like the place or the owner I just don't go back. I want to go to Toronto pretty soon. I want to start to feature pretty soon."

"What's feature?"

"That's when they have your name out front."

"More money?"

"Yep, and more respect."

Our eyes met, my eyes said that I respected her a lot and she beamed back at me.

"And respect, that's worth more than money, right?"

"Yes," she said. "Lots more."

Another girl was standing there with her legs spread and her hands on her hips. "I need something that's kinda tight, like a Spandex."

"I've got just the thing," said Gus.

Pinky said she was from Tennessee. Both parents knew she was a stripper, but they had split up and both had remarried and, although she got along well with the new spouses, neither one knew what she did for a living. She thought that was hilarious, and her shoulders shook with glee. Had her mom and dad actually seen her dance?

"My mom has."

"Not the whole thing?"

"To be honest, no. Like, she just saw me go-go, eh? I'd feel really embarrassed if my dad walked in tonight while I was dancing, but my mom, that would be all right. At least I think it would."

She began shivering and giggling again, Pinky on my left, giggling and hugging me, and Ann Valentine on my right, standing up and pulling her garter belt down coyly for the camera, then sitting down and taking her top off and sticking her tits out.

Ann had been listening and wanted some attention for herself.

"I always try to have fun whatever I do, and I have a lot of fun doing this kinda work," she said. "But I never get turned on stripping. I only get turned on with one man." She put on a big tragic pout. "And he's in Millhaven."

I turned to her. "Oh no, for how long?"

"He's a lifer."

"What'd he do?"

"He killed someone. I don't wanna get into it."

"Was he a biker?"

"No."

"What did he do for a living?"

"I don't wanna get into it."

"How often do you see him?"

"Once a month. Whenever I get the time. And we're allowed trailer visits once every five months."

"Tsk. You poor thing."

"Yeah." She sighed. "The only man I ever loved or ever will."

John Lennon's "Imagine" was coming over the loudspeaker and Pinky was pleasantly humming along in my left ear. She paused, then started whispering. I could feel little puffs of baby breath on my ear.

"I get turned on," she whispered. "Sometimes. Depends on the mood I'm in."

I turned to look at her. Her eyes were like little flares going off in mine. My heart burst into flames. She shivered and sighed a bit and squeezed me again.

"And it's good money too."

19. Trying Not to Think about Pinky

It was time to go. I stood off to one side of the room and watched as the girls continued going through Gus's racks and Nigel and the guys unplugged the lights and started putting everything together.

Pinky joined me. We stood together watching all this activity calmly, as if we were standing on the shore watching a glorious sunset over the Pacific. She didn't say anything, just put her arm lightly around me. When I glanced at her she glanced back silently. I glided away without saying goodbye. She watched me go.

It was night. The parking lot was dark. Some of the cars were rocking.

"I think we got some good stuff, eh?" said Nigel.

I asked him if he thought the girls were really hookers who just stripped on the side or strippers who hooked on the side or just plain strippers.

"I don't know," he said. "What do you guys think?"

"I think it's a mighty fine line," said Rodney.

Winston the cameraman smiled slyly at me. He spoke softly.

"You really seemed to get along good with Lil Pink," he said.

I was startled. I had no idea anyone else would have noticed.

"Pinky," I blurted out. "She used to be Lil Pink but now she's Pinky." Everyone started laughing.

"Me and the guys couldn't help noticing how relaxed you were with her," said Nigel.

"And how uptight you were with the other girls," said Rodney.

"I don't know what you're talking about," I said. "I was totally disinterested." They laughed some more. "Well, okay. I liked her because she reminded me of an old friend." The laughter became hysterical. "But I really tried hard not to show any preference. Do you think the other girls noticed?"

"Nah, it wasn't that noticeable," said Nigel. "We just noticed it because we were filming the whole thing. It was more noticeable to us. It'll probably be real noticeable on the film, right guys?"

I groaned. Everybody else laughed.

"Don't worry, you were okay. What are we going to do now? You want us to leave you and we'll meet tomorrow somewhere?" He had his map out.

"Okay, let's meet at noon at the town hall in Cobourg." I was there once looking at some paintings. There was a little gallery on the third floor of this splendid 1860 town hall right on the main drag.

Winston smiled at me sweetly. I smiled back at him. "Are you guys gonna go back in for the rest of the show?" I said.

"No, we're hungry and tired," said Nigel. "We just wanna get something to eat and then get to a motel."

Winston kept smiling. "How about you?" he said, softly. "You going back in to talk some more with Lil Pinky?"

"It's just Pinky. And no I'm not. No way."

"Ah, you'll probably meet her again some time," said Nigel.

"I doubt it very much. You guys have this all wrong. She's twenty years younger than me for Christ's sake."

Nigel started singing and the others joined in. "We'll meet again, don't know where, don't know when...."

"And besides you got so much film of her I'll be able to see her any time I want," I said as I drove off.

"But not in the flesh," yelled out Rodney.

20. Throwaway Lighters

It was pleasant, even poetic, driving along that highway at night in a little blood-red sports car with the top down, even if it was October and had turned cold. I had to dig out a thick sweater and then on top of that I had to dig out my black leather jacket.

Oshawa was the city that "moto-vates" Canada. That's what the sign said. They made cars there. Not this one though. I drove right through the downtown area without being motivated to stop.

On the other side of town I figured I needed some chicken. There was a Colonel Sanders on one side of the street and a Mary Brown's on the other. Mary Brown's was a new chain and so the chicken would probably be tastier. I was still a naive believer in eternal progress. I went in.

"How come Colonel Sanders across the street is so busy and I'm the only customer in here?"

"We just opened. They don't know about us yet," said the girl behind the counter.

"Is your chicken better than the Colonel's?"

"I don't know, I've never had it."

"You've never had Mary Brown's chicken?"

"That's right."

"Hm. Where do you go for lunch?"

"I pack my own lunch. Or sometimes I go over to the Colonel's." She yawned.

I ordered a chicken sandwich. This was one chicken that never felt the sun on its stubby fat little wings. It was nothing like what you get at the Blue Cellar on Bloor Street or Timothy's on Parliament. It had spent its life in a black hood on death's row.

Three folks in their late teens came in and sat down. A beautiful young blonde man about nineteen came in drunk. He looked like a drunken angel, the village Rimbaud, destined to make everyone feel uneasy and also destined for an early grave, and he made a phone call. Whoever he was calling wasn't home.

I was feeling a little embarrassed that we went to a strip joint the first night out. I never went to any strip joints in *A Trip Around Lake Erie* or *A Trip Around Lake Huron*. But strip joints are important cultural institutions: they, along with churches, represent the twin horns of hypocrisy.

At the Mac's Convenience Store next to Mary Brown's, a young woman in a green Mickey Mouse sweatshirt was behind the counter, leaning on it, talking to an older guy in pink-framed sunglasses who was leaning on the counter from the front side. They looked innocent, their noses were almost touching. There were two guys in the corner playing Moon Patrol. There was a hand-lettered sign over the magazine rack saying NO READING ALOUD and the ALOUD was crossed out and ALLOWED was lettered in above it.

Mickey Mouse was looking at me.

"Do you have any of those throwaway lighters?" I said.

"Yep."

"Then why don't you throw them away? Yuk yuk."

"We got twelve colours and two prices," she said.

"Give me a cheap blue one. I always lose them anyway. I've never had one long enough to have to throw it away."

They didn't seem to mind how tiresome I was being. "Yeah, they're like umbrellas that way," she said. "Or ballpoint pens."

"Did you hear about the broken perfume machine?" said the guy in the glasses. "It was out of odour."

"Haw!"

"I made that up myself," he said.

"Just now?"

"No, it was on September 17, the day that rotten stinking son of a bitch Brian Mulroney became the Prime Minister of Canada."

"I see. Well, I just happen to be Canada's top comedian," I said. "Ask me what's the secret of my success."

"What's the se—"

"My timing!"

Groans and moans.

Mickey Mouse held up an empty hand. "What colour is this lighter?" There was no lighter.

"Uh, this is a joke, right?" I said. "I don't know."

"It's blue," she said. "It blue away. Yuk yuk."

The guy in glasses snickered nicely with a sideways look.

"By the way," I said, "you know your NO READING sign over there?"

"Yeah?" She knew this was going to be a joke.

"I read it."

Laughter.

"Well just don't read it again," said Mickey. "Okay?"

21. Freshwater Whales

I drove into Port Hope, looking for epiphany and a place to spend the night. Port Hope was the place from where the seldom-remembered Upper Canadian whalers of the early part of the last century set out in their little wooden ships in search of whales in Lake Ontario, the big blue freshwater whales that were soon to become extinct and after that soon forgotten, an embarrassing part of Canadian history. The whalers didn't wipe them out, though they tried. No, these whales starved to death when the Welland Canal was opened in 1880 and all the little freshwater sardines they had fed on for millennia finally had a chance to flee up into Lakes Erie and Huron, no longer barred by the formidable falls at Niagara. The whales were simply too huge to negotiate the locks of the Welland Canal in pursuit of the sardines, and for the next few years the starving, half-dead behemoths would be found bobbing in the current off Port Dalhousie. The locks-keepers had to shoot them, even though they knew their numbers were dwindling alarmingly, because their bulk would interfere with shipping along the length of the narrow canal. And then they were gone.

The Royal Ontario Museum has the skeleton of one, but it's never put on display.

The night was dark, the town softly illuminated, a vague and quiet glow that kept the demons away, kept them from sweeping in from all the little churchyards dotted throughout the black countryside to wreak havoc on the living. But where were the living? Except for the drinkers in the three or four Port Hope hotels, they were all inside their recently renovated and sandblasted late-Victorian homes, sipping dry autumn sherry in front of the television set and trying to pretend everything was all right in their lives, reminding themselves the emptiness of their lives was the norm, bargaining for contentment. The Ganaraska River flowed quickly but silently into Lake Ontario. The ghosts of the dead were silent.

I too lacked fulfilment, but I had no sherry, no TV, no softly illuminated home, and so I searched for omens. I pulled up in front of the Ganaraska Hotel and found plenty. Everything was deadly quiet, absolutely no one on the street, but the hotel seemed warm and inviting: there would be television, beer, video games, people willing to talk about their lives, great unknown unpublished late-night alcoholic poets. But my little open car had turned from blood-red to black.

I looked at it quite closely in the light pouring from the windows of the hotel. Yes, it was clearly black. Was I going crazy? I knew it had been red all day, and now it was black. I checked the ownership. The car was officially red.

There was a one-ton stake truck parked across the road on a little roadside bluff that dropped six feet down into the cold black river flecked with white. The owner's name was neatly painted on the door: "TITUS I. CANBY, Coboconk."

A fellow came staggering around from the back of the hotel, and he was blindly drunk. He managed to weave across the road in front of me and get into the truck. There were no cops around. I was the only guy standing between him and a drunken driving charge, maybe worse, maybe a head-on collision with innocent people killed. I felt virtuous and hypocritical.

I went over to him. He rolled the window down and tried to focus his eyes on me.

"You're not going to try to drive are you?" I said.

"What?"

"Are you going to try to drive that thing home?"

He'd probably been driving home in a drunken stupor two or three nights a week since 1947. He was a tall wiry dirt farmer. He had the look of a man who had a good crop of potatoes but he couldn't sell them and they were damp and rotting. His eyes were full of bitter memories and resentments. There were patches of grey mould on his denim jacket. He looked like a fifty-year-old Sam Shepherd. Maybe he was a descendant of one of those freshwater whalers.

"Why are you trying to bother me?"

That was a good question. I'd already inadvertently called his truck a "thing," which was an uncalled-for provocation. I didn't want to sound like a cop, but I didn't want to sound like a Sunday-school teacher either. He probably hated both. Nothing abstract or humanitarian would do, nor would insults be in order.

"I don't mean to insult you but you appear to be a bit too drunk to drive, eh?"

He kept staring at me. He remembered other people trying to stop him from driving home in the past. Knuckleheads, all of them.

"Why are you bothering me?"

Perhaps I should have offered, if I felt so strongly about it, to drive him home myself. But then he would have had the problem of getting back in tomorrow to get his truck. He probably couldn't afford a cab, he wouldn't willingly accept a ride home from the cops and he'd probably never had an accident in his life.

"Nobody likes to see a drunk behind the wheel," I said.

That did it. I'd called him a drunk and fire was flashing from his eyes.

"I got a good pair of boots on my feet...."

I froze.

"And if you want me to get out of this truck I'll get out...."

Maybe it was working!

"And if I do I'll kick your fuckin' head in."

I suppose I should have challenged him. It would have gotten him out of the truck. Everyone would have come out of the hotel. The cops would have pulled up. But I might have ended up spending the night in the can. That's the way these things usually work, in my experience.

"Drive then," I said. "Go ahead. Maybe I'll read about it in the paper tomorrow."

The guy wasn't satisfied.

"Why are you bothering me? What business is it of yours?"

"Do you really want to know?"

"Yeah."

"Well it's like this, see? When a drunk gets behind the wheel it's everybody's business."

Being opposed to drinking and driving was ultra-fashionable. Everybody had stickers on their window saying if you drive don't drink. But I never heard a line as schmucky as the one I'd just come out with. Maybe I should go to work for the insurance companies. If there are any cabinet ministers reading and you want me to write a speech for you just give me a call. Schmuck for hire.

"Oh fuck off."

"Look, what if I was drunk and you were sober and you saw me get into the car to drive? I'd hope you'd try to stop me."

I had a sudden vision of my daughters dead on the road.

"Listen," he said. "If you keep bothering me I'll get out of this truck and kick your head to a bloody pulp."

"Okay, drive," I said. "Maybe you'll just kill yourself and then everyone'll be happy."

"Why you!"

"All of Coboconk will have a big street dance to celebrate."

22. Sea of Slaughter

I was about to order a beer in the Ganaraska but it was too bright in there—and what if Titus I. Canby were to come back with a shotgun? Let's face it, I deserved it. A group of mothers whose children had been killed by drunk drivers had recently formed a high-profile organisation seeking stiffer penalties for those who drive while under the influence of alcohol. It was called Mothers Against Drunk Drivers (MADD). Hypocritically, I owned and sometimes even wore, in public, a T-shirt emblazoned with the letters DAMM—Drunks Against Mad Mothers. Yes, it's true; I deserved to be shot.

Around the corner at the Gloucester I ordered a Canadian Club and a Miller from the shyly smiling dark-haired little forty-year-old lady behind the bar.

"We don't have CC. Would Weiser's do?"

"Sure."

In a scene reminiscent of the Seacliffe Hotel on Point Pelee, in my trip around Lake Erie seven years earlier, the sound was deafening from the giant fuzzy TV screen on the wall but no one was watching it. It was the second game of the World Series. Kurt Bevcacque hit a three-run homer in the fifth inning to win the first game for the San Diego Padres. The Detroit Tigers would win tonight and the next three to win the World Series. But nobody was interested in baseball that year, attendance was way down. Two guys were sitting at the bar with their back to the screen, talking intimately about their lives. There was no one else in the place. A quiet night in Port Hope.

"If you put a Weiser's there and a CC there," I said, "I'm not really sure I could tell the difference."

"You mean like if you drank them, eh?"

"Uh, yeah."

"I don't think many people could. It'd be fun to try, but I can't do it."

"Why not?"

"I told you. No CC."

"Oh yeah. Just as well. I'm driving."

"Well space your drinks out and drive carefully, remember you've been drinking."

We were face to face, but had to shout at each other because of the roar from the television. Finally she lowered the volume. I kept turning to look at the photos on the side wall, a series of giant black-and-white blow-ups. One simply showed three guys with their mouths open, as if yelling, or waiting to be fed.

"So what's this?" I said.

"It's the track at Kawartha. People at the track. It was taken years ago. I don't even know who the people are."

There were a couple of shots of buildings on fire. "It was the big fire of 1968. Almost levelled all of downtown."

It was an L-shaped bar so I had a good view of the two guys in intimate conversation. The cut-off list posted behind the bar for easy reference was fascinating, and in large letters right across the top it said: ALL SATAN'S CHOICE. Below that there was a two-column list of names, surnames first, with a date after each name. It appeared that all members of the Satan's Choice Motorcycle Club were barred for life. My friend the dirt farmer was there: Titus I. Canby, Nov. 24.

"What'd Titus I. Canby do?"

"He walked through here in nothing but his boots. Somebody dared him to walk through in his birthday suit. So he did. It was his birthday. We barred him for six months."

"What about Shorty Wachtel? What'd he do?"

"She. She ripped me off for fifty bucks. Barred for life."

"How'd she do that?"

"I keep my money folded under the ashtray here on the beer tray, like this." She pointed to her tray. "I turned around and it was gone."

"How'd you know it was Shorty?"

"The boss saw her."

"Did you charge her?"

"No, we don't bother usually. There's no point to it really. We just bar them."

"What about the Satan's Choice?"

"They got charged. They really got charged all right. You don't belong to the Choice, do you?" She was eyeing my black-leather jacket.

"No, I've had this jacket for fifteen years but I've never owned a motorcycle. They're too dangerous."

"I didn't think you were. You may have a beard, wear a black-leather jacket and drink boiler-makers but you're a gentleman."

"Thanks."

"You're welcome. If you belonged to the Choice I wouldn't serve you. They're barred for life."

"What'd they do?"

"Oh, they just came in here one night and blew a guy away. A good friend of mine. He died in my arms."

She spoke so calmly and matter-of-factly I could scarcely believe her.

"A whole bunch of them got charged," she said. "Two of 'em got convicted. They're still in prison."

"Why'd they shoot him?"

"He was a biker too, eh? But he belonged to the Hell's Angels. The Satan's Choice guys wanted him to join them but he didn't want to. He thought they were a bunch of wimps. So one night he was in here having a beer and they just came in with a shotgun and blasted him away."

Probably one of them was Tattoo Annie's boyfriend.

I took a sip of my whisky and my new friend wiped a few glasses. My ears began adjusting to the quiet conversation of the two guys sitting diagonally from me, at the front of the bar.

"So my mother had five sons, then at the age of forty-eight she got pregnant again and had a little girl," said the little guy with the beard.

"How old's your sister now?" said the big clean-shaven guy.

"She's twelve."

"That's a nice age. Starting to get tits?"

"Yeah, really nice ones too."

"Great."

"And the nice thing is she prances around the house with no shirt on."

"Wow, eh? And how old's your mother?"

"Sixty. And she still has nice breasts too."

"The little girl takes after her?" said the big guy.

"Sure does. In a lot of ways...."

Someone hit a home run. No one looked at the screen, not even for the replay. The bartender stopped work and put an elbow back up on the bar.

"Nice town, Port Hope," I said, when things quieted down. "Very quiet."

"Sure is. Very friendly too. You can say hello to anyone."

"And do they answer?"

She didn't answer.

"And there's that famous Canadian writer, Farley Mowat. He lives here, right?"

"Sure does. The book-writer. He's a real nice guy. Very friendly."

"He must be. I don't see his name on the cut-off list."

"No no, he never drinks here. I don't know where he drinks. He lives just down the street though, or at least he used to."

"Did you ever read his books?" *Sea of Slaughter*, in which he predicts the imminent collapse of Canada's fishing industry, had just come out.

"No, I hear they're really good, but I never read them. I know about his books, they're about animals becoming extinct and stuff like that. It's important that people be aware of that kind of thing, you know, and it's real good that he's writing about things like that. But, you know, a friend of my brother's, he told me something that really made me think. He said it's all very well for Mr. Mowat to be writing these books about conservation and about animals dying out and all that. But what with all this over-population in the third world and all, we're going to have to choose between people and animals. And let's face it, people are more important than animals."

Are people more important than animals? Do fetuses have souls? Should the monarchy be abolished? I always back out of arguments like these. Leave it to the experts. There are enough of them around, they don't need me. All I know for sure is it's not right to drive while you're dead drunk. And you should never never never never never let things get you down.

23. Thousands of Square Miles of Darkness

Titus I. Canby would probably be at home flaked out by now, naked again except for his boots, their heels free of traces of my congealed brain matter, and I was sure he'd arrived safely. My car was still parked in front of the Ganaraska, nobody had let air out of the tires or blasted out the windshield. The car still looked black, however, in the dim light from the frosted windows of the hotel, and it was still a black night, giving the sense of being in a small softly illuminated town surrounded by thousands of square miles of absolute darkness, and rather than drive off into said darkness I thought I'd go back into the Ganaraska for a beer. Maybe something miraculous would happen. It sounds stupid, I know, but if you have a feeling something miraculous is going to happen it always does.

It was a much larger place than the Gloucester, and there were maybe thirty drinkers sitting around in little groups. There was one little room partitioned off with a pool table and a TV set. The ball game was over, the eleven o'clock news came on and I stuck my head through the partition to watch this fellow who had the same name as mine, a Bay Street lawyer from Toronto whose career I'd been following because he was president of the Ontario Progressive-Conservative party, often had his name in the papers, and the coincidence of our names (he was also the same age as me) amused me. I never knew what he looked like, though, and suddenly there he was on the screen being interviewed and he even looked something like me—except that I would never wear such a cheap suit.

It was as if I'd known him for years. It was like seeing myself on the tube. I was always getting calls for him, usually from drunken car salesmen from Thunder Bay or Sault Ste. Marie, and I'd say things like: "Sorry, this is the poet not the politician."

So there I was in a strange town watching someone on TV who had the same name as me and suddenly someone called out my name. The things that run through your mind at such a moment! At first I thought it must be someone who knew the guy on TV and was simply calling out his name because he saw him on TV, but the voice was unmistakably directed my way rather than at the screen. And then I thought it must be someone from the camera crew, but the voice sounded more surprised to see me then and there than anyone from the crew would have been. I turned, a little nervously, and found myself looking into the eyes of someone I hadn't seen for at least ten years. Sly-looking Archie Felix.

He looked old. Archie was the kid brother of Rupert Felix, my friend all through high school, and while Rupert went on to get his Ph.D. in mathematics and become a full professor at Harvard University (and author of some allegedly influential books) Archie at least when I last saw him was threatening to make a career out of writing unreadable and unpublishable poetry that seemed somehow designed to prove that he was more intelligent and had more spiritual and moral integrity than his successful brother. Perhaps I shouldn't say this and I certainly don't want to hurt anybody's feelings but perhaps it needs to be said. Poets as a group, even often-published poets and poets who have received much attention and generous grants, are fairly down-scale in the IQ department, and in the department of ordinary human values as well. You're much more likely, odds-wise, to get into an interesting and lively discussion with an accountant or a bus driver than you are with a poet.

Archie's bitterness took many forms. One look from him could make you feel vaguely uncomfortable for weeks. Behind those sly eyes was a tragedy dying to be unravelled. But that was long ago. Surely he'd changed.

"What are you doing in Port Hope?"

"Picking apples."

"Seriously?"

"Yeah, it's nice work. Fresh air, nature."

"But...."

"I came here three years ago to do carpentry work with a friend who was remodelling old houses. That fell through. Now I pick apples to supplement my welfare cheques."

"I thought you'd never leave Hamilton."

"I'll never go back there now. The very thought of it makes me sick."

He wanted to know where I lived and when I told him Toronto, his face got bright and full of awe. "What's it like to live in Toronto?" he said.

Something told me not to ask him about his poetry. When he asked about mine I told him about the Great Lakes series, and how this was the third and a film crew was following me around. That seemed to bother him for some reason, but I knew better than to ask why.

"I'm not interested in poets like you who go on and on about nothing," he said. "There's only one poet in Canada worth reading. Irving Layton." He shook his head. "Pure platinum." He'd changed all right. Ten years ago he would have said the only poet in Canada worth reading was himself.

Then he started to list all the great poets from the past he could think of—Yeats, Dylan Thomas, a few others—and suggested I might become a better poet if I read them.

I told him I didn't like pretending to have read more than I actually had but I wondered how he knew I hadn't read Yeats or Dylan Thomas. He said he could tell by reading my poetry. I told him I didn't think he'd read any of my poetry, but maybe he had once spoken to someone who once knew someone who had read a poem of mine in *The Fiddlehead* twenty years ago.

He mellowed immediately. "You're right," he said. "the only thing I've read of yours was an article in the Hamilton Spectator somewhere around 1972. With a soft voice I told him I took my writing seriously and had sacrificed plenty for it. A spasm of belief softened his eyes.

On the screen, police chiefs were calling for the return of capital punishment and there were film clips of mourners at the funeral of the latest cop to be killed.

"Why are all these cops suddenly being killed?" I said, rhetorically.

"Maybe people are discovering that cops are human," he said, poetically.

"No use shooting them if they're not human."

"Right."

24. The Man with No Thumbs

John Turner was on the screen telling how he was going to rebuild the "shattered" Liberal Party of Canada. I looked at Archie Felix and could see that I'd grown up since I last saw him ten years ago. I had always thought that Archie was a rather unpleasant fellow to be around, although I never took the trouble to try to figure out why. But now I saw that it was something mutual between us as individuals. There was something wrong about us being in the same room together, a basic chemical flaw, as if we were descended from families that had feuded in the eighteenth century. I always wanted to flee from him, and it now occurred to me that he had always felt the same way. An infinite number of microscopic psychological and physical traits goes into the making of our affinities and antipathies. If we take the trouble to investigate our obsessions we often find they're fuelled by the most trivial banalities. Archie and I had always felt somehow threatened by each other, but the thought of trying to analyse the situation and figure out why, or even bringing it up in discussion, seemed futile.

Right now Archie wanted to know what I felt when I looked at the moon. Maybe I was wrong, but his tone sounded contentious, as if he were seeking to compete with me for some kind of poetic honour, as if he wanted to show his soul had greater nobility than mine.

"I don't know, how about you?" I said.

"I see a battered woman," he said, sadly and with great stateliness. Maybe he wanted to make some horrible confession from the past, about a former wife or lover he'd beaten up. But I didn't think so. He was simply giving me a little peek at his soul, which had the capacity to see the suffering of all the women who had ever lived focussed in the face of the moon.

And yet there was still something unpleasantly competitive about it. He seemed to assume I saw absolutely nothing but a silver guinea in the sky when I looked at the moon. I told him about being on the New Mexico desert during a total eclipse last year, and how it was the most wonderful experience of my life. He didn't seem impressed. And I told him, truthfully and non-competitively, that I too saw a woman when I looked at the moon, but it wasn't a battered woman, it was simply the shocked and horrified face of a sad lunar goddess who at the beginning of time was fated to sail the heavens forever gazing down at the earth, and it's a shocked and horrified face because of all the shocking and horrifying events she had to witness constantly as she followed the night around, and too the simple pain of being human.

We were abruptly joined by a big fat guy named Ed who plopped himself down beside me, pushed over until I was jammed up against the wall, and kept singing over and over, in a silly voice:

I got lucky, oh I got lucky,
I got a pocketful of rainbows.

Archie looked on in silence, a look of pure annoyance on his face. Ed kept wanting to shake my hand. He had huge hands, and both his thumbs were missing.

"What happened to your thumbs?" I said. He wouldn't answer.

"Yeah," said Archie. "I never asked you. What the hell did happen to your thumbs?"

No answer.

There was a lot of antagonism in the air. Apparently Ed and Archie each had a room in the hotel, had been living there for some time, and often drank and ate together. I wanted to be going, but was jammed in, and I couldn't follow the conversation, which was unpleasant and laden with long pauses and incomprehensible private references.

"You're really an asshole, you know," said Archie at one point. Archie hardly ever moved his lips when he talked and his lips were so thin they were almost non-existent. He could be called the Man with No Lips.

"I know I am, but so are you," said Ed.

"No I'm not."

"Yes you are."

"No I'm not," said Felix, "and if you say it once more I'll kill you."

This is the sort of conversation one is forever overhearing in Hamilton.

After a pause, with lots of stern eye contact, Ed said, "Why not?"

"Why I'm not an asshole?"

"Yeah."

Another long pause, and then Archie said, "Because I haven't cashed in my chips like you have."

"Why haven't you?" said Ed. Another long pause, with lots of smouldering eye contact. "Because I've never wanted to," Archie finally said.

It was as if Archie and Ed were usually on good terms. Ed seemed surprised at the antagonism. Possibly Archie was embarrassed by Ed's presence and didn't want me to think that the two of them were buddies. I felt terribly naive and out of it.

Finally Ed, who seemed to have the IQ of a snail but was equally sensitive, left, singing the same silly song but feeling a bit wounded. Archie smiled at me and I smiled back, weakly and with little understanding.

"How old are you?" he said, abruptly. The question caught me off guard. Sudden amnesia. At first I thought I might be twenty-five. No, older than that. I must have looked like an idiot. Thirty? No. Thirty-five? Wait a minute now!

"I'm thirty-nine," I finally said. "Actually, I just remembered. Tomorrow is my fortieth birthday."

Archie looked at the clock. "You mean tomorrow midnight?"

"Yeah."

"You mean like five minutes ago?"

I looked. It was five minutes after midnight. I was forty! Archie reached out and shook my hand.

"Congratulations."

"How old are you?"

"Thirty-nine."

I got up to go and Archie walked me to the door. From the lobby, a flight of stairs went up to the rooms above. He wanted me to come up for a cup of coffee. I felt uncomfortable about saying no, a conflict between professional and personal responsibilities, so I said I had to meet Nigel, Winston and Rodney in Cobourg.

"But it was nice seeing you again," I said. "And what about Ed? Don't you know what happened to his thumbs?"

"No, I never thought to ask him before."

"He must have a terrible time hitching a ride."

"I guess I never really cared before."

He looked right at me. It was one of those moments. My deep heart felt sore inside.

"Cared about what?" I whispered.

"About what happened to Ed's thumbs," he whispered back.

25. Sorry, Mr. Aserfarty

"I couldn't recall what Mrs. Aserfarty was wearing," the lawyer was saying, a lawyer who was acting as a Crown witness in the wonderful old-world courthouse of the Cobourg town hall. The lawyer was testifying on the witness stand that he had witnessed a "vicious fight between a man and his wife."

The fight had taken place in the lobby of the very same courthouse, which was said to be a perfect replica of the Old Bailey in London, a month or two earlier following a divorce hearing. Mrs. Aserfarty was suing Mr. Aserfarty for divorce. The lawyer had just been sitting there in the lobby practising Transcendental Meditation, as was his wont whenever he got a five-minute break or so, when, the divorce hearing being adjourned, Mrs. Aserfarty came out of the courtroom into the lobby, followed, as chance would have it, by Mr. Aserfarty.

"At that point in time," the blissed-out barrister told the court, "Mr. Aserfarty jumped on Mrs. Aserfarty from behind and choked her. Mrs. Aserfarty fell to the ground, with Mr. Aserfarty on top of her."

The man I took to be Mr. Aserfarty squirmed in his seat. Just a glance told me he was guilty. He was wearing a red satin coach's jacket, was balding with a fringe of curly red hair, he was short, fat, about fifty, and had a plastic bag marked IGA in his lap. The bag looked as if it contained empty beer bottles. Mrs. Aserfarty was younger, about forty, blonde, quite attractive in spite of the thick dark circles under her eyes, and was wearing a pink mohair sweater. She took the stand. Her full name was Hilda Hungerford Aserfarty. She corroborated the swami lawyer's testimony.

"He came up to me from behind, grabbing me around the neck," she said. "It was after the divorce hearing. I was waiting for my ride."

The judge yawned, apparently not noticing the little discrepancy. I guess you can be waiting for your ride and walking out of a courtroom at the same time.

But the judge's mind seemed made up. Anybody who'd be stupid enough to attack his wife while a lawyer was watching, even if the lawyer did seem to be in a state of nirvana, or maybe even satori, has to be guilty. As witnesses go, a lawyer is worth two cops, and a cop is worth two ordinary guys (especially guilty ordinary guys with plastic bags full of empty bottles), even if their only crime was to beat their wives viciously every chance they got.

"And he placed his hands around my neck, like this, your honour, and applied pressure and pushed me to the floor. I was very terrified."

"Who pulled him off of you?" said the judge, as if reading from a teleprompter.

"Mr. Flunky pulled him off." Mr. Flunky was the cosmic lawyer. A thin smile appeared on the judge's face. The judge was proud of Mr. Flunky. It'd be Judge Flunky soon—or at least Mr. Flunky, QC. The judge knew Mr. Flunky had pulled him off of her, that's why he asked, he wanted it on the record.

"What happened next?" said Mr. Aserfarty's lawyer. Mr. Aserfarty was waving his arms around as if he didn't want his lawyer to say anything, but his lawyer didn't notice.

"I went to the washroom," said Mrs. Aserfarty. Mr. Aserfarty buried his face in his hands. His bottles clinked some more.

"The ladies' washroom?"

"Yes."

"Why?"

"I was terrified."

"I bet you were," I muttered. "He's a mean-looking little fart."

I was just mumbling to myself as I often do. But there must have been a sudden hush in the proceedings. Or maybe I spoke a little too loudly.

Mr. Aserfarty jerked around and looked right at me. His bottles clinked a whole lot. The judge shot a nervous look my way then a meaningful look at the security guard. Everyone was looking at me.

The security guard came trotting over and asked me to leave. I told him I was getting ready to go anyway. Mr. Aserfarty was eyeing me intently and his lawyer was eyeing him the same way.

"You're lucky the judge didn't call a mistrial," said the security guard once he had ushered me out of there.

"I was just talking to myself. It's a common habit. It wasn't my fault that everything went quiet just at that moment and everybody heard me. It must have been the acoustics."

"It's true the acoustics here are excellent, but what you said was really serious. You could have prejudiced the judge."

"Oh! That would have been awful! How could I have ever lived with myself."

"I'm serious."

"I know you are."

"I mean I really am surprised he didn't find you in contempt of court. Around here that's a five hundred buck fine and ten days in the can."

"I know. It's just that everything's so quiet around here. There's no surrounding traffic noise. You're not wrapped in a cocoon of noise like you are in Toronto. In a Toronto courtroom you can drop a handful of quarters on the floor and nobody notices. People talk to themselves all the time on the street. Nobody hears anything."

"I know. My brother lives in Toronto."

"Does he talk to himself on the street?"

"Probably."

"Get down there very often?"

"Oh, at least once a year. Santa Claus Parade. Sometimes the Grey Cup Parade."

"Like parades, eh?"

"The missus does, and the kiddies."

"So what's the story on this Aserfarty deal?"

"Oh yeah! Hey, you must be the only one in town who doesn't know." Big smile on his face.

"I just got in this morning."

"Well, it wasn't me who told you, okay?"

"It's a deal."

"This Mrs. Aserfarty, she came home early one afternoon and found Mr. Aserfarty in bed with the priest."

"The priest? Oh, no! Not the priest?"

"Yeah, they were going at it like a pair of cocker spaniels."

"No!"

"Yeah."

"Hm. So, what happened next?"

"Well, the priest caught hell. He got transferred."

"Where to?"

"Calgary."

"That'll teach him."

26. Alfonso the Dirty Dog

It was a beautiful summer afternoon in Halifax. I was seventeen years old. I looked up in the sky and saw a sundog, and then I saw a plane flying through it, a DC-9 or something, way way up, just a tiny sliver of silver passing through a sundog, an insignificant event as far as I was concerned. But suddenly, over twenty years later, standing in the lobby of Victoria Hall in Cobourg, Ontario, looking at a bell attached by a bracket to the wall, a bell that had been saved from His Majesty's Canadian Ship *Cobourg* when it was scrapped after the war, and still thinking of Mr. Aserfarty carrying on with that old fat priest, I thought of that old DC-9 again. Funny the way the mind works, eh?

The *Cobourg* had been a revised flower-class corvette, launched July 14, 1943, as part of the Sixth Canadian Mid-Ocean Group. On four occasions it had taken part in underwater sonar contact. It was the pride of the town of Cobourg.

That rarest of beings, a truly happy fellow, was sitting there in the lobby of the courthouse, and he was tilting his chair dangerously back and smiling and talking to himself in a nice friendly way. I watched him out of the corner of his eye, I mean my eye, and heard him smile and say to himself: "I think I'll buy myself a nice hot cuppa coffee." But he didn't get up. He just sat there smiling. As I walked by our eyes met and for a moment I had the impression he was looking into the innermost recesses of my heart. Then a strange thing happened. He smiled at me and said: "Hello Alfonso, you dirty dog."

I was electrified. I returned his look, laughed and kept on walking. But in some funny way I felt as if he had somehow divined my real name, Alfonso, the name that I didn't even know was mine. And when he said "you dirty dog," well that too was real. For a moment I knew that yes I was a dirty dog. Dirty doggish through and through. Dirtier than Mr. Aserfarty and the priest. And it was a lovely feeling. I identified with all the dirty dogs in the world. They were my brothers. You could call me Alfonso the Dirty Dog any old time you wanted and I'd come running.

I'd made it to Cobourg the night before, but it seemed dead and I couldn't find any place to stay in town, so I went back the way I came. I finally stopped at the Lotus Motel, a few miles east on Highway 2. The Chinese man who ran the place was dozing in front of the TV as I pressed the buzzer. He woke up with a start and spilled his tea.

While registering I muttered something about it being a Chinese motel.

"Oh, we've been here a long time," he said.

I checked to see what he'd been reading. It was an old tea-stained *Reader's Digest* edition of *The Good Earth*.

The price seemed steep and I asked when his off-season rates started. "One price all year round," he said.

In my room, I was fiddling with the TV and getting into my jammies when there was a little tap tap on the door. It was a young woman about twenty-five, tall, beautiful, long blonde hair. She was dressed in a CP Air stewardess uniform.

"My sister and I are in the next room," she said, with a bright smile and flashing eyes, "and we saw you coming in and we thought you looked as if you could use a nightcap."

"Oh, that's very nice of you," I said, "but I've had such a long day and I'm just exhausted."

She wasn't discouraged, just continued smiling insistently. "All the more reason you need a nightcap."

"Well all right, let me just get my pyjama top then," I said.

Her sister was just as nice. They were identical twins, from Brighton (England). They worked for British Airways. Both looked and talked a bit like Marie-Thérèse. They were heading down to Lester Pearson Airport for flights into the unknown. When I told them it was my fortieth birthday they got really excited and we turned into little kids, giggling, telling jokes, arm wrestling, tickling each other's bare feet with peacock feathers. All three of us liked good scotch. They were just opening a bottle of Laphroiag. After the second or third drink I still couldn't tell them apart. I couldn't figure out which one seemed more like Marie-Thérèse. I seem to remember them saying something about how their breasts were quite different if I looked closely. I said I was looking closely but I couldn't see any difference. They started unbuttoning and at a certain point of disarray and relaxed intimacy they started playing with my pyjama buttons. I desperately wanted to leave but I just couldn't figure out how to make a graceful exit without hurting their feelings so I just sort of bolted for the door all of a sudden. They had anticipated my move, however, and were too fast for me.

"Rape, rape," I shouted as they dragged me back in. They laughed and said no one pays any attention when a man yells rape, especially in a Chinese motel. One price all year round.

I began to argue vociferously that the Chinese were the same as everyone else but they calmed me down and told me I should prepare for a beautiful experience. Although it would be sleazy if not tacky of me to go into the details, there was nothing sleazy or tacky about what happened, for over the next few hours we became quite good friends and enjoyed ourselves immensely. Those little stewardess sweethearts knew a thing or two about the stratosphere, believe me, and about in-flight safety too in case you were wondering (the AIDS era had begun). In fact, the three of us were still great friends in the morning. Over Wheatabix, canned peaches and instant coffee they insisted on giving me handfuls of airline passes and we made plans to meet in the mysterious and lovely land of Queen Lilioukalani at Christmas. Hope I have this book finished by then. Otherwise, no go.

THURSDAY, OCTOBER 11

27. 10% Discount for Seventh-Day Adventists

Two Budget Rent-a-Buses with big signs on the side saying DANISH BOYS' CHOIR pulled up and sixty boys about ten years old poured out, each with a bulging plastic bag in his hand, and started throwing balled-up pieces of bread and old stale Danishes (with the blob of jam already scooped out and eaten) at the seagulls of Cobourg Harbour. I stopped to let the boys cross in front of me and one of them, a blonde kid with long eyelashes, looked at me sitting in my little Spitfire and gave me such a sweet smile my heart put its little blood-red hands on the bars of my dusty old ribcage and started shouting, "Let me outta here."

The Coast Guard boat in the harbour looked about as big as the HMCS *Cobourg*, judging by the old framed photo under the bell in the town hall, and it seemed silly that the corvette, which at the time was only two years old, had to be scrapped. It should have been sitting there in the harbour with its one big gun, silenced forever in peace, sticking up into the air as a proud reminder that, as a country, although we made a tragic blunder, one we'll never be able to atone for, in not allowing the Jewish refugees to enter Canada before the war, as well as a whole list of other blunders involving Japanese Canadians and indigenous Canadians, we did one heckuva good job in helping get rid of those blood-sucking Nazis.

The sun was shining on the lake and I flicked on the radio and heard about the terrible floods in the interior of British Columbia. I also heard that the final score last night had been 5-3 for the San Diego Padres, the Big Mac team. Little did they know it would be the last game they'd win in this series. It was hard to take the eyes or the mind away from the huge flat mirror of a lake with the sun shining on it under the pale blue Ontario sky, the water calm and sparkling but cold and deep, dreamlike, abstract, lifeless, like a Lawren Harris painting, or a Christopher Pratt.

Nigel, Winston and Rodney had been out on the main street of Cobourg, shooting footage of some workmen laying a sewer. This is what happens when the government gives cabdrivers money to shoot a film. Lots of footage of sewer workers. "We'll fit it in some way, and we can always get more film when we pass through Rochester," said Nigel. "We are passing through Rochester aren't we?"

We agreed to meet at five in front of the town hall in Picton.

I had gone into the liquor store for a bottle of scotch just before leaving town and got into a bit of a conversation with the sole clerk in there, a skinny gentleman in a white shirt who looked ripe for retirement. I told him how much I liked Victoria Hall and how beautifully renovated it was. Just small talk, but he surprised me by saying he hadn't been in the hall since it had been renovated and didn't want to because he thought the elaborate renovations had been a terrible and frivolous waste of taxpayers' money. He was of my father's generation, and might have served on the HMCS *Cobourg* as a young man. He probably would have been more satisfied if the old town hall had been torn down to make way for a Ramada Inn, and he'd probably have been pleased to see the old corvette scrapped rather than be maintained in Cobourg Harbour as an historic museum piece. My father was like that: he was a mild-mannered, mellow man, but he didn't like old things and he once told me (mildly) he thought ivy growing on walls was unsightly.

I gave Marie-Thérèse a little buzz from the phone booth across from the liquor store. She was in a fairly reserved mood, as if she had picked up on her radar all the details of what I'd been doing last night. She offered me none of the squeals of excitement she'd normally dish out when I called her unexpectedly. It was as if I should know why she was being so distant, as if she took it for granted that I knew damn well what was bothering her but I couldn't quite figure it out. For two years now we had had this absolutely seamless mania about sharing every detail of our lives with each other. Suddenly all of this supercharged and over-enthusiastic intimacy seemed to be bogus, counterfeit, illusory and terribly embarrassing all at the same time.

She had to go to Kingston the next day for a meeting with the nuns who work at the women's prison there. This kind of coincidence had been occurring constantly in our lives since our first meeting, so much so that we scarcely commented on it any longer. It was just a day visit, she was coming in by morning bus from Montreal and heading back on the night bus, and I didn't know what time I'd be arriving, but she gave me a couple of numbers I might be able to reach her at and she thought we might be able to have lunch together although she didn't seem enthused about the idea.

But now I was driving slowly through the Pentecostal camp on the shore of Lake Ontario. I passed the NO MOTORBIKES PAST THIS POINT sign. I suppose that meant because of the noise. My little blood-red slipper of a car was in the advanced stages of cancer of the muffler, and so it sounded worse than any motorcycle. But the camp seemed deserted, and it seemed unlikely anyone would complain. There were signs everywhere: CAUTION SPEED BUMPS, and JUNK IS NOT TO BE LEFT HERE TAKE TO CAMP. People need signs more than signs need people, I wrote in my notebook, but I have no idea now what I meant although it seemed profound at the time.

A couple of months earlier, Marie-Thérèse and I spent a weekend on the beach at Lake Huron. There was a notice on the wall of our kitchenette listing a series of eight bizarre commandments: Don't flush the toilet when the television is on channel 6. Don't open champagne bottles indoors, take them out on the porch, and so on. I couldn't resist adding, as number 9, in the same hand: "10% discount for Seventh-Day Adventists."

It might be years before anyone noticed number 9, but we laughed later thinking of a Seventh-Day Adventist family some time in the future trying to bolster their courage to come down to the front desk in the morning to claim their discount, expecting that the hotel was run by a Seventh-Day Adventist family just like themselves, and the poor clerk wouldn't know what they were talking about. Later it occurred to Marie-Thérèse that Mormons, Quakers, Unitarians, Atheists, Presbyterians, Neo-Druids, Sufis, Hinayana Buddhists, Socreds, Hindus (Jimmy Swaggart the TV evangelist says all Hindus are devil worshippers and he should watch it, it's bad karma to say things like that), Devil Worshippers, Neo-Nazis, Midnight Gamblers, Hasidic Jews, Charismatic Catholics, Jehovah's Witnesses and even the occasional Theosophist also would be going down to the clerk and claiming to be Seventh-Day Adventists just to get the discount.

"Gimme a Bible, I'll swear on it I'm a Seventh-Day Adventist. Would I lie about something like that?"

"But but but...."

But this was Lake Ontario, much colder, deeper and less human than Lake Huron could ever be, even though there were four million Canadians and two million Americans living in all the cities, towns and villages along its shore, and humanising the lake with their poisons. The trees at the Pentecostal camp were blazing with colour, elms and oaks and blood-red sumacs, there was a huge white clapboard meeting hall, very handsome, a vast trailer site full of trailers, and scores of handsome Christian God-fearing (why are they always God-fearing, wouldn't it make more sense to be devil-fearing?) summer cottages all around. There were clumps of Canadian marigolds and the kind of random dahlias that always amaze you with their wonderfully variegated patterns and colours, but there were scarcely any cars, all the driveways were empty, and the only person I saw was a gentleman having a pee against a trailer wheel. It must be a different scene in the summer, and I wondered what they did with themselves: no cards, not even cribbage, no dancing, not even a simple joyous Bunny Hop snake dance (remember those?), but every single trailer and cottage sported a tall TV antenna, so there was a good chance that when they weren't busy praying, speaking in tongues or studying the Bible they were watching those soul-stirring evangelists on TV. You know the ones: they stand up there in front of the camera and say things like: "All the other TV evangelists are no good, I'm the only good one, send all your money to me." Or: "People who don't believe that killers gotta get the chair are gonna go to hell just as much as if they had hammered the nails into Christ's hands." Or: "God has revealed to me that if you don't send in a million dollars by next week he's gonna cause my ears to grow to the size of an elephant's." Or: "God has revealed to me that the Russians have a rocket-launching pad in Hamilton, Ontario. So let's send in the troops real fast like before it's too all-fired late and Jesus comes to earth and whisks all us believers off to Tehran where we'll shed tears of joy for 144,000 years and then we'll start to get a tad bored and begin to long for the good old days of secular humanism." To which the crowd roars another "Aaaaaa-men!"

Speaking of speaking in tongues, I had a newspaper assignment one Sunday evening to attend a Presbyterian church service, it was an old church from about 1840 and in recent years had been declining to the point where the good Christian businessmen who ran the church decided it would be more profitable to level it for a parking lot and this was the final service. Everyone who had ever gone to that church was there that night, even the dead. And something dreadful happened.

A large Afro-Canadian lady in the front row began speaking in tongues during a quiet part of the service. Presbyterians didn't speak in tongues, and most of them were decidedly white, but she was decidedly black with big red lips and frizzy hair. And she was shouting up a storm. Unpleasant stuff too. I was at the back taking notes. She was going on and on about how the Lord was going to strike down dead everyone who was there that night, which seemed reasonable enough. But people were getting disturbed, Presbyterians didn't like to be reminded they were going to die, it wasn't nice, and the assistant pastor was ordered to give her the bum's rush. Trouble was, he was just a little guy, and she gave him a bat across the head with her arm (which had a cast on it) and knocked him into the choir. Then she kept on speaking with the tongues of the dead, so to speak, and finally the chief pastor came to his assistant's assistance and with everyone watching in a dazed and vaguely unholy silence, as if watching the news on TV, the two pastors dragged her fairly roughly out of the church, slammed the door and bolted it from the inside.

I was to write a fluffy little sentimental four-paragraph story about the last service of this stately old church but my inner demons found it impossible not to give the story the full treatment. The editors hated it when I did things like that, for they had to take the calls of complaint from outraged Presbyterians the next day. But much to their credit they ran the story. Grudgingly. No free beer at the Press Club for that one.

28. A Poet Lands on a Butterfly's Nose

It was that part of mid-autumn when the grass suddenly in the bat of an eye turns an intensely dark shade of green and gets all wet too (although the corn, curiously, by contrast is pale and so dry it makes your skin itch to look at it) right down to the side of the road, even though there hasn't been any rain to speak of and everywhere you look you see pumpkins oranger than oranges on television commercials (don't you just love books like this?) lying around like poets waiting for inspiration (it was getting close to Halloween), and you also see black cats, curiously elongated in your peripheral vision, suddenly darting out of or into barns or sitting on remote fence posts licking their paws with an air of assumed invisibility, as if they were saying (to themselves) no one will ever notice me here, I'll just sit here all day.

I was wondering how Al Sheepskin's mom was doing. She was eighty-four, bright and in wonderful health, but Al had her going to his psychiatrist because she was having trouble coming to terms with her guilt about her husband's recent death. It wasn't the fact that he had died (which he had) but because he'd been a wolf-crying hypochondriac all his life. She felt guilty because when he started complaining about pains in his back legs arms neck head feet ankles wrists fingers toes knees she just thought he was complaining again, never dreaming he was in the final stages of undiagnosed cancer.

So she'd been telling me that as a kid she'd been extremely religious and felt that her only companion was Christ, He followed her everywhere and she could always rely on Him, until she came to Canada (from County Donegal) at the age of eighteen. All the people she met in Canada were atheists who spent all their time fulminating against the British Empire, the Anglican church, and in fact all churches, and she got sucked into it all and Christ simply departed from her life without so much as a fare thee well.

So I said why don't you just talk to your husband? Tell him you're sorry. She looked shocked, looked at me as if I were crazy and she said, "But he's dead." So I said, "So was Christ dead, and you talked to Him, didn't you? Talk to your husband as if his spirit were with you as Christ's used to be, and I bet he'll answer you. Just tell him you're sorry and all that, and maybe you'll feel better." Her look changed, she looked at me as if I had just saved her a dozen humiliating trips to the psychiatrist. At least I hope that's what that look meant.

The sky was as blue as the grass was green and that little blood-red Spitfire moved along that open road like a veritable blossoming rosebush on wheels. I tried to stop the thought from coming, but finally it came: maybe Al's mom felt guilty because she was guilty. Maybe she suspected her husband had cancer but downplayed his complaints because she wanted him to die! Maybe that's what the look meant.

But I stopped at the historic old Barnum House and read the bronze plaques in order to shake the thought from my perverted mind. There were two plaques, one put up by the provincial government and the other by the federal. What a bizarre system of government we have! Like something out of Jonathan Swift (or maybe P.T. Barnum). The provincial plaque was blue in colour and stated that the house was built "around 1819," while the federal plaque right next to it was copper-coloured and stated the house was built "ca. 1820." Both agreed the house was built for Eliakim Barnum, "an American emigrant," but the federal plaque was more pretentious. It seemed to be aimed at making the reader feel a little stupid, but having the opposite effect:

...Palladian composition of centre block and wings, the house expresses the Neoclassic mode in the temple facade of the principal building, the dominant pediment and the smooth wall surface relieved by blind arcading. The pedimented, pilastered door, the enriched cornices and the tympanum fan are Neoclassic decorative motifs executed here with a delicacy and linearity peculiar to wood....

The provincial plaque was a little more self-congratulatory, with many references to the restoration work done by various provincial agencies down through the years (and, unlike the feds, they correctly used a cedilla in "façade"). For instance, the Architectural Conservancy of Ontario did a lot of work on the house in 1940, and although "the interior has been modified several times since, the façade remains essentially unaltered."

I went up to the front door. Not only was it pedimented and pilastered but it also bore a scrawled sign saying: YES, WE ARE OPEN, COME IN. A thrill went up my spine. But when I tried the door it was locked, there were no cars around, and no signs of life anywhere. So I drove up a narrow lane that led way behind the house, past the fire cart marked GRAFTON FIRE DEPARTMENT 1857, and up the wooded hill kitschily ablaze with autumn colour so extravagant you wish it could be like this always. I drove slowly because I didn't want to aggravate the cancer-ridden muffler any further, and the road stopped at a man-made marmalade bluff overlooking that giant tube of toothpaste known both as the Macdonald-Cartier Freeway and, more popularly, the 401.

I got out of the car and sat on a stump for a few minutes, marvelling at the sudden cosmic stillness (the speeding traffic on the 401 was curiously silent and I felt relieved, as if by blind arcading), until a Monarch butterfly, like a beautiful thought fluttering in the air, landed on my nose and startled me, like the brave soldier in Guy de Maupassant being startled to death by a rabbit.

29. Universal Perfection

Flirtatious butterflies of various sparkling hues, blue skies you could reach up and pinch, dark wet grass sprinkled with autumnal diamonds, trees bursting with pumpkin-coloured leaves, pumpkins each one bigger than the one before, smart cats pouncing on naive birds, clever birds soaring in the downdrafts far above or bouncing from treetop to treetop and whistling "tree-top, tree-top," little wooden houses with freshly chopped wood stacked for the winter, the disinterested sun shining in splendid self-containment, guys in suspenders and longjohns brushing their teeth outside in little washbowls, unlikely hills and valleys, sensual little roads leading here and there with no traffic, huge towering pumpkin trees with giant ripe pumpkins falling from them and landing on the ground with multiple splats, sleeping dogs inexplicably waking up and leaping out of the way just in the nick of time before pumpkins landed on their heads or old tractors ran over them, little villages with elderly shining-eyed ladies waving as if that little blood-red sports car were the final float in the Santa Claus parade....

All my problems had shrunk, I couldn't remember what they were, I wanted to head back to Toronto to get reacquainted with the general agony of my life. But I had a job to do....

Just as I pulled up in front of a tall-spired old Quebec-style church sitting on a hill to the south of the tiny village of Lear, a yellow school bus pulled up as well and scores of delicious little kindergarten kids hopped out and surrounded my little blood-red roadster. There was a modern one-floor schoolhouse called St. Theresa's squatting next to the graceful old church which looked a bit like a miniature Salisbury Cathedral.

Scientists declare that life on earth and in fact the whole existence of the universe is based on a series of inexplicable coincidences and flukes. Just as the temperature of the human body stays at 98.6 degrees Fahrenheit, so most of the Earth's surface stays at between sixty and 100 degrees and has done so for a billion years despite a large increase in the amount of heat received from the sun and despite drastic atmospheric changes.

Just as the salinity of the ocean has stayed at 3.4 per cent for a billion years or so despite the mountains of salt the rivers of the world dump into the ocean every day (if it increased a couple of percentage points life in the oceans would cease), so the oxygen level of the atmosphere has stayed at the optimal 21 per cent (if it increased by a few percentage points spontaneous combustion would start breaking out).

No one knows why slightly more electrons than positrons were created in the Big Bang, but if it had not been so there would have been no galaxies, no stars, no planets, no Lake Ontario, no Marie-Thérèse.

If the Bang had occurred at even a fractionally different velocity, physical matter would never have come into being. At an atomic level, everything happens at just the perfect speed and ratio for complex molecules to form.

And so on. It's as if thousands of millions of years before life appeared the universe was perfectly organised so that some day life could appear, just as my little blood-red roadster was built to run.

But none of these coincidences was somehow as alarming as the coincidence that was about to occur as I pulled up in front of St. Theresa's. I hope you're ready for this. Readers, fasten your literacy belts.

"I like your car, Mr. McFadden," one of the kids called out with a shy little voice.

Volts of electricity ran up my spine. Each hair on my head felt like a mature oak tree. Long sparks shot out of my eyes. I frantically leaped out and looked all around the car to see if maybe Nigel, Winston or Rodney had stuck my name on it. Nothing. My mind was reeling, and I went over to the kids, who were standing shyly in a group watching me.

"Who said that?"

"He did, Mr. McFadden."

It was a little boy, pointing at an even littler boy.

I tried to be calm, smiled sweetly, bent down.

The kid's eyes were shining. "Guess what I'm getting for Christmas," he said.

"Christmas? It's not even Halloween yet and you know already what you're getting for Christmas?"

"He knew a long time ago, Mr. McFadden," said one of the other kids. They were all standing there like tame little deer.

"Well, what are you getting?"

"A Gremlin."

"A Gremlin, eh? What's a Gremlin?"

"A teddy bear."

"Oh, isn't that nice." The kid had a grin on his face as big as all-get-out. "You're just like a little teddy bear yourself." The grin grew even bigger. It was all I could do to restrain myself from picking the kid up and hugging the bejeebers out of him. But how the heck did he know my name? What was going on here?

The school bus driver was watching from a respectful distance.

"How do you know my name?" I said to the little teddy bear.

"He thinks you're the principal," said a smart little girl, a little girl obviously not given to mass hysteria.

"Oh. And what's the principal's name?"

"Mr. McFadden."

Pause. My Adam's apple bobbed.

"Well, isn't that wonderful! That's my name too, and you guessed."

30. The Sweet Little Kids from St. Theresa's

You as a reader are, as always, way ahead of me as a writer. You know what the title of this chapter is. I have no idea what it's going to be. I don't know if I'm going to drop dead before I finish this sentence but you know I lived to finish the book. You know how many pages there are, how many chapters, who published it, what colours are on the cover. I'm way back in the dark dim past, struggling for faith, trying to be serious in the face of overwhelming odds. Is there a picture of me on the back cover? Is there a blurb from Northrop Frye stating my travel books are better than H.V. Morton's? Are the Progressive Conservatives still in power? Is Colin Thatcher still in jail? Is Bill Vander Zalm still out of jail? Are there any trees left in British Columbia? Does the Canada Council still exist? Is Marie-Thérèse still in the convent? Skip that last question, it's a frivolous one, and it's not something you would even care to know, having agonies enough of your own.

It's amazing to think, for instance, that I could simply abandon this book right now and it would never be completed. And I could continue on diligently, and complete it, and it would be published, noticed, read, reviewed, and so on. And if I were to complete the book, I'd be able to feel as if it had existed for all eternity, as has everything and everyone, you, me, this scotch I'm sipping, people not born yet. What fun it is to pretend that time exists! And yet we have no choice but to pretend it exists because there's no way we can get outside time to get a clear look at the pretence we know we're indulging in. You might see the universe in a grain of sand while quantum physicists say that every atom in the universe exists everywhere in the universe. And so we are doomed to spend our long and lonely lives labouring away at what is already completed—or what has already been left incomplete.

As I walked towards that modern one-floor schoolhouse called St. Theresa's squatting next to the graceful old church which looked a bit like a miniature Salisbury Cathedral I remembered a dream from the night before, a dream dreamt while the dreamer was wedged congenially (if not congenitally) between two warm friendly sweetly snoring sisters, who, by day, doubled as airline stewardesses. It was a long dream, I dreamt I was at the convent of Ste. Maria Fidelis in Montreal, and Sister Marie-Thérèse was teaching English there, and I was hanging around, chatting with the other nuns (none better!) in the common room, until I suddenly realised there was no reason for me being there and I began to feel silly and left. It was sad leaving, it was like having to give up something you loved simply because you had no reason for loving it, it was irrational except in a deeply private sense that could not be communicated. There was a feeling of sadness so strong it was like a long note on a dream violin, vibrating in all my dream-time cells, and I got on a bus at the bus terminal without knowing where I was going.

After a sad ride through the long night the bus stopped on the shore of a bay and I got out and stared out over the water. The bay was illuminated in a soft morning dream-light and bordered on the left and right by high steep limestone cliffs. The bay was U-shaped and at the extreme end you could see it open up into a great storm-tossed lake which was full of light and mist, as if there was a break in the clouds. I thought we were on the north shore of Lake Erie, when someone said: "This isn't Lake Erie, it's Lake Superior!" It was a subtle dream that gave an exact description in metaphorical terms of the state of my psyche on this particular trip, I thought. And without bothering to analyse it in any detail here (I'm trying readerly patience enough already) I marvelled at the dream's accuracy.

Lake Erie is the lake of my childhood, Lake Superior the lake of my destiny, the superior lake, and if I do continue this Great Lakes Suite Superior will be the one I leave till the end. After this there's only Michigan, the all-U.S. one, and then Superior. But I had already taken the trip around Lake Michigan, with my little family, by car rather than camper, staying in motels rather than at campsites, and this trip was taken the summer following the summer of the trips around Lakes Erie and Huron, and although I still have the notes from the trip, I still haven't written it up as a book. So the only lake I haven't circumnavigated is Superior, and there it was in my dream. The bay represented the ordinary dullness of life, just another U-shaped bay on the north shore of Lake Erie, but it was made glorious by a sudden accident of light and mist, made beautiful by the presence of grace, passion, love, and Erie is transformed into Superior, as samsara is transformed into nirvana, as our little lives encompass all life.

The principal of the school was Matthew McFadden. He was in the lunchroom with the teachers, sitting around a large table sipping tea and eating apples. He had a small beard like mine, we looked alike, I could understand the kid's mistake. He poured me a cup of tea just as the bell was about to ring, and the teachers left to go to their classes.

Matthew was a gracious man; that is, he didn't entirely share my amazement at what had happened outside (he had even more amazing coincidences of his own to share), but he seemed to be delighted that I dropped in. We talked for an hour sitting at that table, and for the entire hour he held an apple in his hand without taking a bite out of it. He gave the impression of being a Christian first and a Catholic second; that is, he wore his Christianity well. He spoke of taking his kids on summer retreats to a villa in Cobourg, "so they can more fully realise Christ in their lives." The villa had been built by, and for a long time was the summer residence of, U.S. President Ulysses S. Grant (1822-1885). It was one of several crumbling old villas in the Cobourg area, which in the last century (and until the stock market crash) was the most fashionable resort area in North America.

The priest wasn't around so Matthew showed me through the church next door. He spoke of his grandfather, George McFadden, who had been lockmaster on the Trent Canal at Peterborough for years. My grandfather and great-grandfather were both named George McFadden and since Matthew and I bore a certain family resemblance and were both coincidence-sensitive so to speak, we decided we probably had a McFadden ancestor in common and his name was probably George.

I told him about my brother Sheldon always having had a thing about that Trent Canal lift lock at Peterborough. He saw a picture of it when he was a child and he told mother he'd been there. She said he hadn't and he insisted he had. When he finally visited Peterborough and looked at the lock, he said he felt as if he had lived by that lock all through a previous life.

Matthew didn't feel comfortable commenting on that because good Catholics don't believe in reincarnation, and the coincidence he had to tell me certainly eclipsed mine, although the coincidence that happens to you is always more startling than any you hear about happening to others (you know yours is true, the others could be exaggerated). A good coincidence is like a royal flush or a hole in one, but you don't win any pot or praise for it, because it's something you can't share with anyone.

Anyway, Matthew was with his wife in a store in Peterborough one day. "My wife just pointed across the store and said, 'Look at that man, he's a dead ringer for you.' He really did look like me too. We just stared at each other and started walking toward each other. It was funny, we didn't take our eyes off each other. We sort of met half-way. We started talking about how it was almost like looking in the mirror and then he introduced himself. He said his name was McFadden, Steve McFadden, from Ottawa. I just about fell over. Same spelling and everything. Well, it just freaked me right out. Him too."

We got talking about our supposedly common ancestry. He started telling a few stories (some very familiar!) about his Irish forebears. There was a wake being held for a certain Sean O'Malley and everyone was having so much fun dancing that when someone said too bad old Sean can't see us having all this fun, Matthew's grandfather grabbed the corpse and sat it up in its casket. "Now at least he can watch us," he said. And there was the one about someone running outside in a rainstorm and sprinkling holy water around, either to stop the rain or to keep it coming down. He thought that was peculiarly Irish, but then again there are stories about sprinkling holy water during thunderstorms in the work of Quebec writers Victor-Lévy Beaulieu and Jacques Ferron.

Everything was so quiet. We stood in front of the church. I suggested that people from the city might go out of their minds if they had to stay in Lear for a long stretch. "Oh no," he said. "People who move here from the city love it and say they'll never move back." He said there were a lot of people in the area who had moved from the city during the back-to-the-earth movement of the sixties and seventies. An old farmer in the area, one who'd been born on a farm and farmed all his life, said to him: "I hope just because they've bought themselves a pick-up truck they don't think they're farmers."

"And I looked at his hands," said Matthew. "They were covered with thick calluses from working in the fields all his life. No, I said, if they start farming at thirty-five or forty no matter how hard they try they'll never become farmers."

"But they won't want to move back to the city, either?" I felt as if I had thick calluses on my soul from trying to be a poet.

"That's right."

The sweet little kids of St. Theresa's seemed so different from the rotten little monsters around the Spadina-Bloor area where I lived. So sweet and unneurotic, so healthy-looking. The adults too. Matthew's heart, it was obvious, was less troubled than mine, maybe less troubled than almost anyone's you can think of. You can see these things often at a glance, most clearly in the first moment of your first meeting. Maybe Matthew was no saint but he had genuine saintly instincts, and there was none of that odour of sanctity, of merely trying to be saintly; it was as natural as having been hit on the head by a big blob of birdshit, it had something to do with predestined genetic benedictions and childhood environments. I knew he was of my tribe. Not that I was like that, but I knew him immediately, could read him easily, and appreciated him immensely.

"It's true," said Matthew. "The kids here, they're so trusting and open. It's just such a pleasure, such good fortune really, to be in a position to know so many little children and to be able to observe and participate in their growth, to see their minds be born almost, and start to become awake. And you know, they like me, which is just wonderful as far as I'm concerned, and they want to talk to me all the time. They're so excited and enthused about life. And they don't talk about 'Three's Company' or the things they see on TV. They all have TV but it doesn't seem to impress them."

"What do they talk about?"

"Oh, they talk about their horses, their family outings, picnics and so on. You have to restrain them sometimes, they're so loving. They'll tell you all kinds of things about their families."

"Embarrassing things, you mean?"

"Sometimes, mildly embarrassing." He changed the subject. "But it's not just me they like, don't get me wrong. They just like adults. They have no distrust, no fear of big people. Liz, the prekindergarten teacher, they just adore her. They hug her and kiss her and they're always climbing up on to her lap."

He said there were plans to build a large extension on to the school next year. "Maybe they'll make you full-time principal here," I said. He was currently working mornings at this school and afternoons at another, but his heart was with St. Theresa's.

"Oh, that's next year," he said. "Let's deal with this year now."

31. Moonbeam

I'd spent a lovely afternoon a few weeks earlier wandering through the Royal Ontario Museum with Scotty Darling, who was beginning to write wonderfully impassioned and brilliant poetry following a particularly disastrous (for him) marital split-up. Peggy decided she was a lesbian and pulled out allegedly without warning, leaving old Scotty tired and bitter and lonely and suddenly with the eye and heart of a poet. But he was also under the spell of the new Stephen Mitchell version of Rilke. Scotty proclaimed Mitchell the first translator of Rilke into English to give the impression he was capable of *understanding* Rilke, who was notoriously hard to understand, even to Germans. Mitchell's credentials for being a serious translator included the ten years he deliberately spent in a Zen monastery in Japan getting ready for tackling Rainer Maria Rilke.

All this had been particularly exciting for me as a friend of Scotty's because all his life Scotty had professed to hate poetry. He was always saying poets are a dime a dozen, you should use your supposed talent Writing for Dollars. But that's another story, this was just my way of saying the Mitchell edition had been out a few months but I couldn't find it in Toronto stores (though I had it on order), and now here it was sitting proudly in the window of Ye Olde Apothecary Book Store (next to Ye Olde Haberdashery Art Gallery) in Lear.

I picked up a copy and it flipped open to the fourth elegy: "Flowering and fading come to us both at once." Ouch. Somewhat more powerful than MacIntyre's "We understand blooming and withering alike," or the Leishman/Spender "We comprehend flowering and fading simultaneously," and so on. There were only two copies in stock. I bought both.

Eighty years ago, when Rilke was just a gigolo and had never been translated into English even badly, the village of Lear had been larger and had an apothecary and a haberdashery next door to each other and now they were operating as an art gallery and bookstore respectively. The bookstore was more interesting than the gallery, even though the same guy ran both. It was a tiny store but it seemed, almost cruelly, that every book I'd ever wanted to read but hadn't got around to was there in a beautiful old edition and inexpensively priced: Trollope, Fielding, and on and on. I flipped open an old volume of Maupassant and there was a picture of the soldier being frightened by the rabbit. There was a 1930 limited edition of a lovely English translation of Goethe's *Faust*, uncut, and with original wood-block prints.

Lyle Pipkin was the guy who ran the place. He had a soft German accent and didn't offer me a beer though I was casting thirsty glances at the frosty Pilsner Urquell he was sipping. He said he used to live in Moonbeam, way up in Northern Ontario, and ran an art gallery in Kapuskasing. He was a good friend of Neil Armstrong (not the astronaut), who ran Eclipse Press in Moonbeam and who liked to tell fascinating stories about that old Canadian poet Duncan Campbell Scott who all the time he was running the ministry of Indian affairs and stabbing Indians in the back (metaphorically) was writing sentimental neo-Longfellowian poems about the noble savages. Pipkin had a complete selection of Eclipse publications in stock, lovely editions of new poetry for the most part.

The gallery was devoted to Pipkin's landscapes. He thought of himself as the eighth member of the Group of Seven, liked to sketch outdoors in coloured chalk, then make larger paintings in oils in his studio. I was impressed by the strangely fundamental and ultraschizophrenic stylistic differences between his sketches and the paintings based on them. The sketches were spontaneous and sensuous, like Emily Carr's, while the finished paintings were laboured and geometrical like Lawren Harris's. He said he'd never noticed that before. He'd have to think about it.

32. Einstein on the Beach

I drove along Highway 2 through the capriciously cool, cocksure and crazily coloured country-side then turned right at Lakeport and headed down to the beach which was covered with bald flat stones and discarded tractor tires (also bald). A guy was sitting there reading a book, an older fellow with a white beard, corduroy trousers, a thick wool sweater with a dashing silk ascot, and a red beret. He nodded at me and I nodded too then strained to make out the title of the book. There could be no doubt, it was the Stephen Mitchell version of Rilke. I made a U-turn and headed back to the highway. Another bearded fellow in similar garb but thirty years younger was hammering a nail into the door of his little old house, with geraniums in the window. I glanced at him and he looked away as if annoyed. Maybe my muffler was too loud.

Goats were running around and butting each other in the sloping dark green fields. There were orchards full of apple trees badly in need of picking, the trees collapsing under the weight of the apples. There was an enormously great huge fat woman waddling down the front steps of Tubby's Diner (Char-Broiled Burgers) and cradled in her arms like a baby was a large, brown, bulging, grease-stained bag, obviously full of char-broiled burgers with no onion. Azaleas, dahlias, marigolds, pumpkins and fruit stands were blazing away everywhere you looked. Forget the burgers, eat the apples, I shouted but she couldn't hear me over the roar of the muffler. I drove through the town of Brighton and had to stop to let some old veterans of the Korean War stagger across the street from the Royal Canadian Legion to the liquor store, then turned south back out into the country, past a log-cabin camping-supply store surrounded by ten-foot stacks of blood-red pop cases and a stack of four fibreglass canoes, each a different colour (bright orange, red, yellow and shiny black) on the front porch, and through the open gates into Presqu'Isle Provincial Park.

It was flat, marshy, sunny, warm. Great flocks of swallows would burst into the sky and circle for a few minutes then come to rest on another tree. There was no one around. I thought I'd do a little exploring on foot. I hopped out of the car and wandered off the road, following paths through the trees and bulrushes down to the beach, and the lake suddenly opened up in front of me like all of heaven. But when I eventually looked back a van had pulled up by the car, a bird's-eye blue van, with what looked in the distance like a cameraman strapped to the roof. I went back up to the road. The guys were smiling beatifically.

"We've been shooting on the beach," said Nigel, his head sticking out on the driver's side.

"I won't have to do any more exploring then, I'll just look at your film when it's developed."

"Were you planning to stay here long?"

"No, not at all. I just thought I'd pop in for a minute. I wasn't planning to, just decided at the last moment. I was going to drive right down to the end of the peninsula but I don't think I'll bother now."

Nigel just sat there smiling sweetly at me as I tried to explain that these books were intended to be time capsules, and I wanted them to be clear and friendly.

"Yeah, you're pretty clear and friendly yourself," said blonde-haired Winston, from the roof. John and Yoko were playing softly on the boom-box

"Why thank you. Takes one to know one." Good time to ask for a favour. "I just noticed this car has a tape player," I said. "Got any tapes to spare?"

"Oh, we got hundreds," said Nigel. "What do you want?"

"Got any Philip Glass?"

"How about *Einstein on the Beach*?"

"Sure!" That was Philip Glass's most famous piece to date, and even though I'd attended two of his concerts and been sort of following his career I still hadn't heard it. I slipped it into the tape player and jerked the volume up so you could hear Einstein all the way down to the beach. "Wow, that's wonderful! Thanks a lot."

33. Dangerous Vegetarian Propaganda

Winston got down from the roof and the four of us stood there by the side of our vehicles which were parked in the middle of the road, and we were smiling dreamily, Philip Glass blasting away, occasional park vehicles slowing down and pulling partially off the road to get around us without expressing any annoyance.

"Me and the others were talking, eh?" said Nigel. "We figure this is by far the most peaceful shoot we've ever been on."

"Peaceful?"

"That's right," said Winston. "There's no pressure at all."

"Aren't you putting any pressure on yourselves?"

"No."

"Just leaving it all for me, right?"

"Yeah, that's right."

"What about that beating you gave me in Lear?" said Rodney.

"We didn't go to Lear."

"Oh."

When I asked about the colour of the car everyone agreed it was red. For me it had been switching back and forth from black to red all day. When I asked them to stare at it intently for a few moments it turned black and then red for me, but it stayed red for the others.

The blue van, with Winston on the roof shooting film, followed as I drove out of the park and along the lake, but when I stopped to talk to some guys who were sitting around outside Quick Fisheries the van discreetly disappeared.

"How's the fishing?"

"It's no hell."

"What are you catching?"

"Perch mainly, and some whitefish."

"Trout too," said another guy. There were three of them, they looked tired.

"There's lots of pickerel and pike out there but we can't catch them. We're having trouble with the ministry. The angling association won't let us touch pickerel or pike."

"Reserved for the American sports fishermen?"

"That's right. You got it."

"How come you're not out fishing right now?"

"We've been out."

The older guy, the boss, turned to a younger fellow.

"Show him the fish."

"You show him."

We all went inside.

"Those are sunfish, aren't they?" I said. We used to catch these small, brightly coloured, bass-like fish, six inches long maximum, when we were kids, sitting by mythic pools on long summer afternoons with a bluebird warbling away on every fencepost and the smell of dead and dying worms in the air.

"Yeah. We get lots of those."

"You eat 'em?" I wasn't sure you were supposed to eat sunfish. Although they were known as panfish, that could have been for their shape rather than for their supposed destination in the frying pan.

"Nah, we ship 'em down to Detroit. The coloured people eat 'em."

"What about these catfish?"

"They go to Rochester."

We talked about catfish becoming popular, how there were catfish restaurant chains in the U.S.A. now. White folks had discovered catfish, but the fishermen still wouldn't eat them.

"Do you sell anything to restaurants around here?" Sad question, sadder answer.

"No, mostly to the big firms in Toronto and Montreal. They all get turned into fish sticks."

"Yech."

"Yeah."

I drove past the Brighton Speedway—"Exciting Racing at Night"—and the bird's-eye blue van was following me again. There were some pigs in a field at the side of the road so I stopped to feed them some apples. The guys got out and shot some film. The pigs smelled terrible. They were eating the apples and they were also eating each other's shit before it hit the ground. I threw some apple pieces into the pond but as hungry as they were they wouldn't go in after them.

"To think that we humans prefer the taste of pig flesh to the taste of apples," I said.

"Disgusting for sure," said Nigel.

"To think those strippers last night were calling each other pigs," said Rodney.

"They were?" said everyone.

Rodney was suddenly embarrassed. "Yeah, didn't you hear 'em? The ones from Ontario were saying the ones from Montreal were pigs."

We all denied having heard it, which made Rodney, who was a bit younger and less experienced (a recent Ryerson grad in fact), feel a tad insecure. He had that am-I-a-nut-or-what look on his face.

We drove over the Murray Canal and into Prince Edward County, that big rectangular peninsula that sticks down into Lake Ontario like an axe into a pig's back, and we stopped to ask directions from a woman walking along with a child and two griffon terriers.

"Are we pretty close to Carrying Place?"

"No, not really," she said. "It's purdy far. You gotta go straight down to the four corners, eh? Then turn left and you'll see the Carrying Place post office, and then left again and it takes you right into Carrying Place."

"By the way, what kind of dogs are they?"

"They're griffon terriers, very old French breed, going back now to the eleventh century at least. They're mentioned in Flaubert's 'The Legend of St. Julian Hospitator,' eh?"

"Oh yeah, I thought so."

This was a literate county. There were so many of those little informal book clubs you could go to a meeting of a different one every night of the week.

"Did she say her dogs liked to eat hot potatoes?" said red-haired Rodney.

The car was running well. There were two guys walking along the side of the road and carrying double-barrelled shotguns, with a couple of Barbary greyhounds (Flaubert says they're swifter than gazelles but liable to bolt) trotting along with them. Someone suffering from some kind of private anguish had been putting signs up all around Toronto saying: "The Ontario Arts Council is exporting dangerous vegetarian propaganda with your tax dollars." I was no vegetarian, but it seemed strange that people would go out with shotguns and shoot rabbits. I had that old familiar feeling, that there were better places to be than the planet Earth. Preferable would be some planet where you didn't have to kill things to live, some planet where you didn't have to endure. A century or two from now people would look back on us with horror because we ate meat, just as we look back with horror at cannibalism among South Pacific tribes 150 years ago. Even the gentle non-cannibalistic Aborigines of Australia considered kangaroos human yet shot them and ate them (unlike the European settlers who just shot them for the hell of it without eating them, and shot the Aborigines too while they were at it, men-women-and-children in huge numbers, hunted them down like kangaroos). And the Maoris of New Zealand will admit that sure the Europeans stopped them from eating each other but they hint darkly that there are worse things than cannibalism that they do now that they didn't do then.

It was a quiet road so as I drove along I pulled out my little bottle of scotch and had a little snort. Sort of a half-snort, a nip if you will, as befits a serious motorist. I wouldn't get staggering like Titus I. Canby. Just a taste. I looked old in the rear-view mirror, I started feeling sorry for myself again so I practised watching my Buddha breath and my brain quieted down. There was a floating sensation, and when I looked down I could see a little black sports car driving along a little grey sports road among the green sports hills and sports pig farms. And then it went off the road into a ditch.

34. The Songbirds of the Great Forests of Our Youth

We were all hanging around the general store in Carrying Place, eating sticks of licorice and trying not to look too much like tourists. After considerable discussion we decided if there were tourists driving through they would probably think we'd been living in Carrying Place all our lives. There was a phone booth.

Everybody thought a good idea would be to phone Chesley Yarn, the most famous of all Canadian poets. He didn't betray the spirit of poetry by setting out on a vulgar campaign to get famous. He just became famous naturally, because his poems were so danged good. Yarn was a great old guy who drank a lot of hard liquor, and beer too, and when he visited you he wouldn't leave until there wasn't a drop left. He'd wiped me out booze-wise a lot of times.

It's true, there were four of us that day, but altogether we wouldn't drink half as much as Chesley. We wouldn't shout and carry on as much as Chesley either, and we wouldn't argue with him much. I felt sorry for him living way out in the sticks and trying to be a great poet. He had a wonderful wife, but still aside from her there wasn't much input. He didn't seem to need it though. The greats never do. They are the input. Like Mozart. It comes straight down from God, via the songbirds of the great forests of our youth.

When I phoned him he told me to get there right away. I said there were four of us. "Geez-us, are you ever in luck," he said. "Elsie just put on a pot of spaghetti big enough to feed an army. Bring a case of beer, will you?"

"Uh, how do we get there?" I'd been there once before, with my ex-wife before we were married, when we were still high-school sweethearts, more than twenty years ago. I wanted to be a real poet just like him, and wrote and told him. I sent him some of my poems that had been cruelly rejected by the high-school year book. He thought the poems were terrific. He told me to come and visit him (and bring a case of beer) and he'd give me some tips about how to be a real live poet like him. I couldn't believe my luck. I was dying to meet a real live poet. Unfortunately, the high school I'd gone to was one of the very few in Canada that hadn't been visited by another real live poet, Wilson MacDonald of Port Dover.

"You continue along the highway toward Picton," said Chesley, "and you come to two signs. Take the second sign, it's just past the big house on the right, a green sign, make a left turn and go right down the road for seven miles. There are one two three four five turns, go past the village, straight through, go one mile down the road then turn left. You come to a dead end. We are the one two three fourth house down the road, there's a big double garage, a big blue roof —on the house, not the garage. It's an A-frame. Got that?"

I told him I thought so and asked how his arthritis was coming along.

He laughed and snorted, happy I'd remembered. "It's all right. I'm mobile. I just bought a new car. Yeah, a brand new Mercury."

"Nothing like a new car to make you forget your arthritis."

"Right."

He said he wanted to put us all up for the night. The three guys in the spare room and me in the library. "And have you got anything to drink?"

"You already mentioned that, Chesley. You told us to bring a bottle of beer."

"A bottle?!!!?"

"No, I mean a case, sorry."

"Kee-rist!"

I thought it would be a nice idea to zip back to Quick Fisheries and grab a couple of nice big fresh whitefish.

"Fresh whitefish? Where?"

I told him.

"I never see anything like that around here, and I been living here all my life. I guess I'm not looking." He said don't bother with the fish on account of the huge pot of spaghetti Elsie was brewing up, as coincidence would have it. I said where's the closest liquor and/or beer outlet to Carrying Place and he said "Trenton or Brighton, take your pick." I decided to head back to Brighton. The guys waited for me. I was back in short order with a case of the new giant size 500-millilitre Labatt's Blue, and, in honour of the spaghetti, the added bonus of a litre and a half of Chianti.

The liquor store was ironically adjacent to a huge cemetery. I mentioned it to the eager young liquor-store clerk and he said: "Yeah, all summer long tourists—and sometimes short ones too—stop to take pictures of the liquor store and its darkly appropriate neighbour, the graveyard." He said he'd come out and take a picture of me if I wanted, and he would show me where to stand for the best shot and all, showing me standing in the graveyard with the liquor-store sign above the stones. I said that would be nice but I don't have my camera with me. He said he'd take it with his camera and mail it to me for a small handling charge and I said, ironically, nah I don't like having my picture taken.

The guys had a fish-eye lens on their camera and were photographing ants building a hill in the parking lot. I came running up to them and inadvertently stepped right on the hill, thereby thoughtlessly destroying thousands of ant-hours of hard labour and ensuring that I will suffer rebirth as an insect for many incarnations to come for dead certain. Unless I set to work to erase the bad karma immediately by ceaseless praying and fasting and sitting quietly in the lotus posture for twelve hours a day.

"Me and the guys were thinking," said Nigel. "We're not sure we want to be put up for the night—"

"It's okay if you don't want to go—"

"Oh, don't get me wrong. We want to go. But—"

I told them they didn't have to stay the night, they could leave whenever they wanted.

35. Upson O'Connell's Farm

I was following Yarn's instructions carefully, and the robin's-egg blue van was following in the Canadian late-afternoon slanting autumn sun along that dusty one-lane remote rural road, and we pulled into somebody's driveway. It couldn't have been Yarn's place, because it said on the mailbox O'Connell.

A nice-looking fat lady with hives and bald spots was cutting the grass, and she ignored us, although I had the feeling it had been decades since a little blood-red sports car had pulled in there, especially followed by a film crew in a blue van. It was one of those Simpsons-Sears mail-order Black and Decker power mowers she was using. There were kids playing all over the place. Whole teams of amorous frogs were almost drowning out the sound of the mower with their croaking. The smell of blood was in the air. I thought the lady was wearing a flesh-coloured skull cap at first, but it just turned out to be a bald spot. The hair she did have was orangey-white.

A row of cows stood contentedly flicking their tails at plump slow-cruising flies in an old-fashioned decrepit barn. A show of crows was perched on top of the barn. An old guy, the lawn mower lady's husband probably, came out, and his son too, both wiping their hands identically on their identical overalls.

"Invigoratin', ain't it?" said the old guy. "Soon be winter." They'd been milking the cows.

The woman had clicked off the mower and felt safe to acknowledge us from a safe distance. The kids were getting on her nerves. "I'll tan yer hide on the fence," she yelled at one of them.

The farmer's eye told me the time was purdy well nigh for me to state my business.

"I guess this isn't Chesley Yarn's place, right?"

"Nope. Sure ain't," said the dad. "Chesley, who did you say?"

"Chesley Yarn," said the son, and he said it over and over until his father caught on. "Chesley Yarn, Chesley Yarn...."

"Now he's the book-writer, ain't he?" said the dad.

"Yep, that's him. He writes books of poetry."

"Oh yeah. I know who you mean. He lives over there."

"I guess you're Mr. O'Connell?"

"Call me Upson, I ain't Mr. O'Connell. That's my father's name, and he's been dead a long time."

The lady with the lawn mower came over. "Who they be askin' about?"

"Oh, you know that that that book-writer, Chesley Yarn," said the son.

"Oh, *that* fella." She spat on the ground.

"Do you know him very well?" I asked.

"Scarcely knows him at all. He don't socialise much, he don't. Spends all his time in that house of his typin' away at his typewriter and readin' books. I guess he works real hard, he does. In his own way, I mean. Must be very difficult doin' that kind of work. Wouldn't ya say?"

36. The Yarn Ear-Scratcher

Chesley Yarn was dressed in a clean white polyester dress shirt, sleeveless, the top three buttons undone, and a pair of checked bell-bottom trousers with extra-wide cuffs. A postcard was sticking out of his shirt pocket as if begging to be noticed. Yarn had grown a nice grey moustache since I saw him last, and was chewing gum. There's a saying in California: "You can always tell a Canadian, they wear checked pants and chew gum."

When I came to a halt right next to Yarn and flicked off the ignition he held out his hand as if to shake mine. But when I extended my hand he shot his long thin knobby leathery arm past mine, grabbed the case of beer sitting on the passenger's seat, ripped it open, pulled out a beer, twisted off the cap and took a big slug, all with one hand. It was a joke, it was serious, it was getting dark.

The van pulled up behind us and the guys jumped out with their camera shooting away.

A lot of people, even people who admired Yarn's poetry, found him a little hard to take in the flesh with his loud voice, checked pants and country manners. There's no doubt he had a tendency to be obnoxious and belligerent and he certainly had a tendency to clean out your liquor cabinet real good before you could think to lock it up. But to me he was fascinating because he was a natural, that is I was always trying to discover something phony about him but never could. He wasn't playing the role of the hard-drinking loud-mouth poet, he simply was a hard-drinking loud-mouth poet. He was generously and uncomfortably direct and honest, without being self-conscious about it, and he was never thrasonical. Vain but never boastful. Now that he was in his mid-sixties, I wanted to see him deepen, perhaps become more passionate about his writing. But I don't really think he saw any need for it, or virtue in it. He certainly wasn't going to force it if it didn't happen naturally. He was just the way he always was: a big tall skinny loose-limbed sloppy hard-drinking country bumpkin who had read some books and loved to embarrass people, particularly people who were quiet and polite and didn't threaten to embarrass him in return.

Yarn was a poet, and had the air of being outside language looking in, not only at language but also at all the insane ways there are of being human. Animals have no language, and therefore suffer no moral dilemmas, and therefore are natural; their consciousness is absolute and undivided like a poet's.

Yarn's place was on the shore of Waldo Lake, a perfectly round crater about three miles in diameter that drained off into Lake Ontario when the water level was high enough. Yarn said some scientists from the University of Chicago were up having a look at the lake recently and concluded it was meteoric in origin and was formed about the time of Christ. Maybe at the very moment Christ was born Prince Edward County was hit by a giant meteor.

It was getting dark, and we strolled through the trees around to the front of the house, and there was the lake, calm in the dusk, with a little dock for boats, and the unusually tall (for Ontario) spire of a church visible on the other side.

Then out came a dog, an ordinary-looking mutt with a curled tail like a pig, black and white spots and long hair, fairly intelligent-looking thing. It was very happy to be there, very happy to see us, as was its master. There was some kind of contraption attached to its collar. It was an arm with a little plastic hand on the end of it, a plastic index finger sticking out from the hand, and a small battery-powered motor. Yarn reached down and flicked on the motor. The finger started to scratch the dog behind its ears.

"It's my invention," said Yarn.

"What's it all about?"

"What's it all *about?*" he said. "Isn't it obvious what it's all about? I mean the guy at the patent office got it immediately, didn't need any explanation at all."

"Gimme a break, Yarn. We all can't be as smart as patent officers."

"I guess you're right. Well, like all dogs, if you've ever taken the trouble to observe a dog at all, this one likes to be constantly scratched behind the ears, but who wants to devote his entire life to sitting around scratching a dog behind the ears? Would you?"

"No, I guess not."

"No, I didn't think so, not even if you really liked the dog in question as much as I like this one. No! So I invented this ear-scratcher."

"An automatic ear-scratcher!"

"Good for you. You got it. Congratulations. Look, when he comes around wanting to be scratched behind the ear I just turn it on and he leaves me alone. He just lies down under a tree and the finger keeps scratching him until I come around and switch it off or else until the battery goes dead."

37. Cabbagetown Elegies

Chesley's new book of poems had just come out, as had mine, so I got mine out of the van and we compared cover designs. "I sort of wished I'd asked for upper and lower case for the title when I okayed the cover," I muttered and mumbled.

Chesley heard me and exploded incoherently.

"You okayed the cover? Good God, *yaya*-you got the okay on the goddamn cover? I have not had the okay on the goddamn cover. They just send it to me.

"They sent it to you for approval, Chesley. You didn't say anything so they figured you approved."

"Shee-it!"

"But I got the jump on them. I found out who was going to design the book and when he was going to get started. So then like I went into the office, talked to him, and showed him the picture I wanted on the cover, and he proposed this way of handling it, and I said okay, it looks nice." And so on.

Nigel, Winston and Rodney were just sitting there, looking as if all this chitchat was tremendously interesting.

Another guy showed up, someone who was a friend of Chesley's and who wrote book reviews. I think he was a little miffed at first because we were there. He liked the cover of Chesley's book but not mine. His name was Eric Grout.

"It's a completely indifferent cover to me," said Grout.

"What don't you like about it?"

"I don't like anything about it, how about that?"

"Well, what in particular do you dislike about it?"

"I don't like anything about it, did you hear me?"

On the cover of Chesley's book was a picture of a dead bull covered with flies. That was the title of the book, *Flies*. My book had a beautifully designed cover, featuring a detail from Puvis de Chavannes' *The Beheading of John the Baptist*. Eric was probably as familiar with Puvis de Chavannes as he was of Rilke.

In order to change the subject Chesley asked for my opinion on the cover design of his book.

"Is it too late to make any changes?" I joked.

Chesley's wife Elsie was listening from the kitchen area. "It sure is," she said.

"It sure as hell is," said Chesley, who had never been one to appreciate the incredible subtleties of my sense of humour.

This was getting silly. We talked some more about the cover of Chesley's book, then I turned to Grout. "I don't care," I said. "I like the cover of Chesley's book but I like my own too."

"It's important that you do," said Grout, wisely.

We were settling in for a long evening. For some reason, neither Chesley, Grout nor I could stop for one moment trying to one-up each other. I don't know about the others but the tension between wanting to be a polite guest and saying what I felt was getting to me. I mentioned Rilke. Chesley gagged. And so did Grout.

"I'm not interested in Rilke, he seems so dull," said Grout.

So I mentioned that I'd seen Eric's review of Casper Goldhawk's *Cabbagetown Elegies*, which was obviously modelled on Rilke's *Duino Elegies*, although there was no attribution to that effect. It was an interesting and well-written review, and I told him so.

"I figured it was the best book of poetry I'd read in five years," said Eric, beamingly. His high beams dimmed, however, when I mentioned casually (and perhaps, in retrospect, cruelly) that the review unwittingly gave away the information that the reviewer was not familiar with Rilke, since anyone who did know the *Duino Elegies* would see immediately what was going on structurally in the *Cabbagetown Elegies*. What Eric had responded to so well in Goldhawk's book was perhaps mainly the Rilkian echoes, I suggested.

"Had I not read Rilke I too would have been more enthusiastic about the book," I said.

"It was all old hat to you, was it?" said Eric, rightly miffed. Maybe he felt we were in some kind of animalistic competition for the old boy's favour and I guess I was being just a smidge insufferable. But Yarn sensed things were becoming a bit unpleasant so he jumped in.

"I must admit that I have read the *Duino Elegies*, translated by a guy named Leishman," he said, "and I thought it was an awful translation because Rilke couldn't have been so awful. I've read Rilke all through. Don't do it, Eric, it'll leave you unchanged and that's the best thing that you can say about it."

Eric was wondering exactly how the Goldhawk book was modelled on the *Duino Elegies*, and he seemed a bit embarrassed to have so unwittingly exposed a blind spot in his education. I said I had no intention of embarrassing him and I mentioned that whenever Rilke talks about the angels Goldhawk talks about his friends.

Yarn hooted and hollered. "Do you see any resemblance between your friends and angels?" he said. "Look at me, I've tried to stay the same forever, and my sweet innocence has stuck to me like an indelible badge." What a guy!

Meanwhile Elsie Yarn and the film crew had struck up a conversation, probably much more interesting. I heard Nigel say they'd spent $36 times four last night for rooms at the Lotus Motel.

"Tsk," said Elsie. "There are bed-and-breakfast places all over the county less expensive than that and you get a free breakfast."

Eric was complaining how tough it was being a book reviewer. "No one ever says hey I read that review you wrote and it was wonderful, they always say hey I read that review and it was terrible."

"I complimented you on the review," I reminded him. "It's not your fault you hadn't read Rilke."

"I have read Rilke, just not that closely."

It seemed pathetic that book reviewers knew so little about their field. For Eric to be reviewing poetry books in the popular press without having read the *Duino Elegies* would be akin to someone writing an astronomy column without knowing anything about the Asteroids. But I didn't say anything.

Meanwhile, Yarn devilishly grabbed my book and handed it to Eric. "Here, why don't you review this for the *Globe and Mail*?"

Eric had a pretty good answer, although unfair, and I wished I hadn't hurt his feelings so. "No, Chesley. I don't think I could do that. I probably haven't read the requisite historical works."

38. Chesley Yarn's Squash

While Chesley, Eric and I were having this silly macho male one-upping sort of talk men sometimes find themselves involved in, it's more or less encoded in our genes, I glanced at Nigel and Elsie who had been chatting quietly in the corner for the past few minutes. I found myself wishing I knew what they were talking about. It seemed interesting. And I began wondering what Chesley and Elsie talked about when they were alone, for instance on their three-month-long annual winter holidays in the south of France, inseparable.

There was a lull in our conversation and I picked up on Nigel's and Elsie's. It seemed blissfully banal and sweetly honest by contrast. I kept wanting to say hey let's get Elsie in on the conversation (although she was simultaneously listening to every word we said and occasionally breaking off her conversation with Nigel momentarily to make some dead-on and much-needed comment for our benefit), but I thought that was Chesley's duty as a husband and I didn't want him to think I was trying to show him up (when a reporter asked Garth Iorg why he ran so quickly around the bases on the few occasions when he hit a home run he said he didn't want to show up the pitcher), trying to teach Chesley a lesson (he was after all twenty years older than I), or trying to impress Elsie (she was still attractive and I bet lots of men here and there around Prince Edward County and maybe even a few up in Hastings County were secret admirers of hers) (and I bet Chesley hated it, that is if he ever took the time to notice it, and I bet he would, notice it that is).

"We were going to bring some fresh fish, Elsie," Nigel was saying, softly, "but Chesley said you'd cooked enough spaghetti for about ten men."

"That's about right." She got up, took a few steps to the stove and stirred a pot or two.

"We passed some commercial fishermen coming in, Elsie," I said, "and they had a batch of whitefish and perch."

"This is Lake Ontario fish you're speaking of." There was a touch of tension in Elsie's voice. "Yeah."

"We were thinking of getting some whitefish maybe?" said Nigel.

"No thanks," said Elsie, sternly. "Never eat it and don't plan on it, and I wouldn't if I were you either." Ooh, she meant business.

"Don't you eat fish in restaurants?" I said. Women are so much more serious than men—at least in rural Southern Ontario. It's getting hard to get in a serious conversation with a man, and if you succeed in doing so you often regret it.

"Hardly ever." No smile.

"But if you go to McDonald's...."

"Wouldn't be caught dead in McDonald's."

I think Chesley and Eric were seizing the opportunity to discuss something pressing in private, perhaps something urgent that Eric had visited in the hopes of discussing, although earlier when I suggested to Eric that perhaps it would have been better for him if we'd come at another time he said he was quite happy to have the chance to meet, he'd read a book of mine once and wondered what I was like in person. Wasn't that a lovely reply? When Chesley was out of the room, Eric was positively Oriental in his politeness, but it was a different story when Chesley was involved in the conversation. It was, on occasion, almost as if Eric wanted to impress Chesley at my expense, and I was probably guilty of the same nonsense, a beam/mote situation if there ever was one. It was as if he (and maybe me too although I sincerely hope not) were sort of going through a kind of mating ritual with Chesley, as if we wanted to be chosen for his admiration. Everyone wants to be universally admired (especially by those they find admirable) but just then we were concentrating on Chesley. All this was exaggerated by the numerous giant-size bottles of beer we'd been chugalugging. We hadn't been there long but already I'd lost count.

Rodney and Winston came in and joined Nigel at the kitchen table with Elsie.

"These guys," I said to Elsie, "eat at McDonald's all the time, there's a whole generation coming up like them."

"Yeah, we eat there all the time," said Rodney with a downcast look.

"But at least we know it's terrible food," said Winston.

I had the feeling Elsie understood what it was like to be twenty-five, broke, and trying to get established in a weird career like film (she was not an unimaginative woman) but she didn't actually acknowledge whether she understood or not. I think she felt a wave of compassion for people who found it necessary to eat that kind of junk, and who perhaps had so much energy and good health they didn't notice it bothering them.

"All the fish I eat come out of this lake," she said, quietly, meaning the crater out front. "It's a nice clean lake." In the summer they would catch enough fish to have enough left over to freeze for the winter. They could fish through the ice in the winter to have fresh fish on the table but they didn't bother because they considered it too dangerous. The ice is plenty thick but she still didn't like having to saw through it. A lot of people had died that way. So they would catch extra in the summer and freeze it.

For some dark and mysterious reason, Chesley chose that moment to burst into the conversation. "Elsie!" he cried. "Look! Look at the size of this beer bottle! You could shove it up your ass and, and, and...what would happen?"

"What would you do with it there, Chesley?" said Elsie, deadpan.

"You could give birth to, to...." He couldn't think of what to say. What kind of conversations do these two have when they're alone? "It doesn't seem right," he said, a little subdued. "It's like being in Montreal drinking from quart bottles."

"How'd your squash turn out?" said Eric, saving Chesley's bacon with perfect timing.

"My squash? Oh, they came out okay, but the awful part was I gave my neighbours some seeds and theirs turned out huge. We don't have quite enough sun here on our side. But anyway, it was humiliating."

"It's always humiliating when your neighbour grows bigger ones than yours," said Eric.

"This guy" (the neighbour) "said he was humiliated when we got our brand new Mercury." Chesley seemed to have a crush on that car.

"He was just kidding, Chesley," said Elsie, sternly again, although no one would ever describe her as a stern woman at all. In fact just the opposite. She didn't like Chesley's habit of bad-mouthing neighbours. Apparently years ago there'd been an elderly, lonely and extremely talkative lady living next door. Chesley complained to someone that he tried to avoid her because she talked so much you began to think you'd never get away, you were doomed to be nodding and smiling at this non-stop yacker for all eternity. This got back to the elderly woman and she wouldn't speak to Chesley (or what's worse, to Elsie either) for an unspecified length of time, let's say until she was on her deathbed. At which time she called them over and told them that she'd never bother them again with her talking, she was going into the big never-ending Silence, and they would never have her to complain about ever again.

And guess what Chesley said, the rat.

"Promise?"

That's right, that's what he said to her, and moments later she was dead. Elsie never let him forget it.

"Yeah, maybe he was just kidding," said Yarn, still on about the motor-envious neighbour, "but there was something behind his so-called kidding.... He gets a new car practically every year. He's one of these guys whose ego resides entirely in his car."

"We all know people like that," I said. Elsie smiled.

Yarn was on privileged territory. He could get away with anything.

39. Happy and Confused

All we had to do was guzzle beer, eat huge platefuls of spaghetti (as soon as you'd finish one plate Elsie would grab it and place a full one back down in front of you) and argue about writing and writers. I hadn't been involved in a conversation like this in years, it was embarrassing, indecent, I felt a touch of culture shock, but I plunged in and maybe even was the worst offender, arguing, gossiping, cajoling, pretending I'd read books I hadn't.

Now and then Elsie would gently lose patience and ask if we might change the subject and we tried to but it never lasted long.

Eric was talking about his trip to the University of Western Ontario library archives where he was looking through the Yarn holdings and found a letter Yarn wrote in 1967 when he was mad as hell at somebody or another. "Oh, yeah, I remember that," Chesley would say, and he'd be off on some bizarre string of gossipy anecdote designed to make himself look good, and it seemed funny and entertaining, especially when we all weren't talking at the same time as was often the case.

I incautiously suggested that Yarn check out the later poetry of William Carlos Williams because it just might speak to him because Yarn was almost the age Williams was when he suddenly blossomed and began writing the greatest poetry of his life. But I shut up when Yarn said he'd never taken an interest in Williams because his old friend Louis Dudek had always been trying too hard to push Williams on to him. "I don't think Williams was interesting before he was sixty-five," said Yarn. "I think you have to be interesting both before and after you get old."

"Listen carefully, Yarn," I said. "I have been privately predicting for years that you were going to write the best poetry of your life in your old age, and now here you are almost elderly. What do you think?"

He heard me and blinked, flattered. "What can I say? You're scaring the shit out of me. But I do think my best book was my last book, the best I ever wrote, but that's just my own opinion."

I guess a lot of the time I was trying to get the conversation settled down and serious, but come to think of it we all seemed to want to do that at different times, and each time one would try the other two would panic and change the subject or make some goofy remark.

"It's important to talk about these things. There's nothing more important than poetry," I said. Everyone agreed.

"What were we talking about?"

"Poets suddenly changing, making big breakthroughs, as I have been predicting will happen to Yarn in his old age and I hope it does because then when I get to be old I'll have his great poetry of maturity to read and to inspire me."

"People like me who live a long time as apparently I have seldom grow and change." Yarn looked sad.

"Maybe none of us ever really change, but Williams' poetry certainly changed, after he had that stroke."

"Look, I went through a period of ten years when I didn't grow and change at all and I hardly even knew it. I was just content with myself."

Yarn then began professing, as he often did, that he knew nothing about poetry. "If I knew how to write poetry I would do it all the time. I have no idea. I don't know fuck all about fuck all."

"You're just like Socrates," I ventured.

Yarn gave me a suspicious look. "I try to avoid those people," he said. "I do actually." Meaning Socrates. Eric was eyeing me too. It was obvious they didn't catch the Socratic drift so I thought I'd tell them the interesting story about the Delphic oracle saying that nobody in the world was wiser than Socrates, and when Socrates heard that he said that can't be right, there must be a lot of people in the world wiser than I, so he went around to try to prove the oracle was wrong. He went around asking all the wise people he could find very pointed questions and found their answers were no better than his. So he figured the oracle was right. He didn't know anything but neither did anybody else. So it was true. Nobody was wiser than Socrates.

They seemed to like that one in spite of their initial suspicion.

Eric was talking about his book of collected or selected reviews that had just appeared, with a blurb by none other than Chesley Yarn on the back cover, and it was something Chesley was claiming he had never said, it was a misunderstanding on the part of the editor. Something about Eric's criticism reminding him of D.H. Lawrence's. I mentioned I'd just been reading Lawrence. Eric said I looked like Lawrence. I said I hoped I was healthier.

Eric made a comment on *Sons and Lovers* I won't repeat.

Chesley started quoting lines from Lawrence's poetry. Something about delighting in the companionship of fire, a companionship more naked and interpenetrating than love. "Sheer genius," he said. "Anyone who could say that in a poem is a pure genius."

Eric agreed, as he agreed with all Yarn's opinions.

We argued about what critics were worth reading (I was pounced on viciously for calling George Woodcock a hack), and we argued about Ezra Pound and Herman Melville and Rilke some more and William Carlos Williams. We even got into some weird kind of spat about Paul Theroux, and at that point Elsie broke in again, this time in an even sterner tone.

"Isn't there something else to talk about besides writers and writing?" she said.

"Yes, what about this movie you're making?" said Chesley.

"Well," said Nigel, "we're going to come back in a couple of weeks and do some more shooting after Captain Colourful here finishes the book."

"It's gonna take him longer than two weeks to finish the book, isn't it?" said Yarn.

"Heh, it'll take me that long to write this evening up," I predicted.

Yarn just really wanted to tell Nigel how to make a film. Not that Yarn knew anything about film, but it couldn't be that much different than writing a poem could it? If you can write a poem you can certainly make a film.

"Just let yourself go," he said. "Don't worry too much about the subject, indulge your sudden rushes of genius, otherwise you're doomed because your basic material is so, well...." He eyed me meaningfully. I was listening, waiting for the word. He wasn't going to say it.

"Scintillating?" I said.

Laughter.

"One of the nicest things about this trip so far," said Nigel, "was...."

Yarn wouldn't let him finish. "I would have thought your arriving here was the nicest thing so far," he said. "I really think it's nice you came." I suddenly noticed his moustache. Had he had one before?

"Did you just grow that moustache recently?" I said.

"No, I've had it for quite a while."

"Why did you grow it?" I was serious and curious.

"Ah, we're all trying to escape anonymity," he said.

And so Eric wanted to know why I had a beard and so on. Chesley wanted to know about my kids. I brought him up to date, and mentioned that my older daughter had just graduated from nursing college and the younger was studying photography. I happened to mention the older was short, only five feet even.

"Do you want her to be tall?"

"She says when you're tall people expect more of you."

"Is that true, Eric?" said Chesley.

"I'm not tall, ask yourself."

"Nobody ever ever ever expected much of Chesley," said Elsie, who was washing the dishes.

"I bumped into the ceiling yesterday, changing a light," said Eric.

I said I'd never bumped into a ceiling in my life but I'd bumped into a few floors.

"It's not how high you are it's hi how are you," said Rodney. Everyone laughed.

"Now," said Elsie, "do the non-beer drinkers want coffee?"

I told them the story about the kids saying we like your car, Mr. McFadden. Eric accused me of having made the story up, but Elsie appreciated it. "That would be a bit unnerving, I would think," she said.

Chesley brightened up considerably. "No, it's not un-Irving," he said. He'd had this postcard in his shirt pocket ever since we arrived and was continually pulling it out, fiddling with it, then putting it back in. It was obviously something he wanted to share with us and now he had the chance. "Speaking of Irving, I have a postcard I want to read you. I don't think there's enough light to get it on the camera." Hint hint.

Nigel sprang into action. "We can light it up purdy good," he said.

The postcard was from the famous Canadian poet Irving Layton and was in his famous patented insulting style: "Dear Chesley: You miserable cretinous parochial Canucky schmuck."

Apparently Layton was annoyed because some of Yarn's letters had just been published, and Yarn in a letter about twenty years ago had said something unkind about Layton, that he'd never write another masterpiece. "I want you to know I went on writing masterpiece after masterpiece, only to put ulcers in your fat gut and haemorrhoids on your fat stinking ass. So, in spite of your awful limitations, you're an authentic poet and I take my hat off to you. Your last book moved me as few books had. Your friend Irving."

"Hah haw," said Yarn, who seemed to be the only one impressed. "Your friend Irving. Isn't that something? It's typical of Layton that he tears you down then builds you up. Oh well, what can one say about Layton?"

Nobody said anything, not even Eric. We all looked bored silly. Nigel backed off.

"There's coffee here for anyone who wants it," said Elsie, again with perfect timing.

Nigel and the guys wanted to leave. They didn't want to stay over. They had to get to a motel so they could do their inventory for U.S. Customs. We figured we'd be crossing into the States early the next evening. We agreed to look for each other the following afternoon at two in the lobby of the Holiday Inn right on the Rideau Canal waterfront in Kingston.

Yarn became very sweet. "We should give them a sandwich to take along. It would of course be a spaghetti sandwich."

"No, it's okay," said Nigel. He started mumbling to himself. We were standing outside in rural starlight, a little additional light coming from the house and faintly but charmingly from the town across the lake.

"Let's see now, Cobourg eight-thirty. Geez, the days get really long and you forget what you've done."

Yarn and Nigel exchanged a few quiet words and then all of a sudden Yarn started stuttering excitedly, and said, mysteriously, "*Wawa*-what will you do when you fall in love?"

Silence.

"Er, as far as what goes?" Nigel looked puzzled.

"As far as just about anything goes. I mean if you're going to carry...." Obviously Yarn had thought Nigel had said something he really hadn't, but Nigel was trying his best to answer the question politely.

"I'll probably be happy and confused."

"Jesus Christ," said Yarn. "You don't quite know what I mean, do you? As a single-minded pursuit of happiness and so on, being in love with a woman."

Nigel smiled calmly, did a good job of pretending he wasn't confused. "I've been in love with a woman," he said.

"Didn't last long?"

"It lasted five years."

That seemed fairly long, since Nigel was still in his twenties, but Yarn thought that was wild. "Oh, a long time!" he said. "I don't wish to comment further. Do I, dear?"

Elsie looked a bit steamed.

"Chesley," she said, "can't you leave these people's love lives alone, or their sex lives?"

Winston was just standing there looking sleepy and content in the soft Southern Ontario autumn starlight. Yarn turned to him and asked him where he was from. He hadn't said much all night, just listened, occasionally chatting with Rodney.

"From Toronto," said Winston. "English background, actually. Lived in Yorkshire for a few years."

"None of us can help that," said Yarn.

"You mean our backgrounds?"

"Exactly."

"Where are you from?"

"Oh well, from this area. Not here. Trenton, born north of Trenton. But that's irrelevant as you know. What you are is a whole lot more important...."

"Than where you're from?"

"Well, it's wrapped up in it of course." Yarn was suddenly quietening down and becoming peaceful and wise. He must have been tired.

"But you can turn out all sorts of different ways," said Winston.

"Oh yeah, all sorts of different ways. Oh well, I'm gonna drink the rest of the beer. Nice meeting you."

40. Smudge Butternut and the Arms Race

Nigel, Winston and Rodney had taken off, leaving Elsie, Chesley and me to drink the rest of the beer and chat peacefully into the night. Eric had dozed off sitting up and was snoring lightly.

"I have certain thoughts about politics too," said Yarn. "The U.S. and Russia...."

"But not enough to do anything about it," interrupted Elsie. "There's no point."

"I just want to write about things that are important to me personally," said Yarn.

One time my friend Joy, who is a seriously committed Christian, asked me what I figured was the greatest pain in the world. We'd been talking about Buddhist and Christian concepts of pain. I said I'd get back to her on that. I thought about it for three days then called her back and said the greatest pain is the pain you experience personally. Stubbing your toe, at least for a moment, is a greater tragedy than the entire Nazi Holocaust. When poets write about their own little tragedies they're writing about the tragedy of the world.

"I agree, in a way," said Yarn. "Writing about what interests you personally strikes me as being a political act. In a way."

I got carried away with youthful hyperbole. "Writing poetry is the ultimate political act. It's a serious occupation."

"Ah, I don't think that living is a very serious occupation," he said. "It doesn't last long enough to be serious."

Elsie leaped in. "It's only when you've achieved old age...."

"That's me," said Yarn.

"...That you can say that. When you're young life seems endless."

"Yes, I suppose life even to the Captain here seems endless."

"Maybe not endless, but it doesn't seem particularly short at this point."

Suddenly Eric was awake. "I think I could die tomorrow," he said. "I really do. Death doesn't seem far away from me."

"Why? What have you got you never told me about?" said Yarn. Eric just smiled. "But you're young, you're even younger than Captain Colourful. Why, when I was your age...."

Eric was sitting next to me on the sofa, smiling in an intriguingly friendly fashion. He said he had a book to give me for my birthday. I became all flustered. "That's all right," said Eric, "I like giving gifts."

"It's all right, Captain," said Yarn, his voice booming. "We're all friends here, and we forgive you for reaching this age."

"It wasn't my fault. I tried not to."

"I suppose we all try to stop somewhere along the line, desperately try to stop."

Later, Yarn was showing off his book collection. "Look at all my first editions. Whole lot of stuff here. Good stuff. I don't know what you're interested in: Hardy, Jeffers, Auden, Yeats, Dickinson, everything. I have an early Williams here somewhere. I have his autobiography. These are hard books to pick up…."

"Remember when I was here twenty years ago? The only books you had here then were the complete works of Freud in thirty-seven volumes. Did you ever read them?"

"No, Smudge Butternut read them and spoiled their virginity."

Smudge Butternut, who had recently died, was a well-known though penniless poet of the sixties who never bathed (at least he smelled as if he never) (friends of his come to think of it said he used to bathe the normal amount but just couldn't get the smell out, it was genetic), was unbearably argumentative and seemed always on the verge of bursting into mindless violence. He had steel plates in his skull from old war wounds. He used to descend on people and stay as long as he could before being kicked out. He lived for about two decades that way, before inheriting some money and a little house in Yellowknife, giving up booze, and peacefully retiring. This is only a sliver of the true picture, though. Butternut was also a warm sentimentalist who would burst into tears (like the famous photo of Picasso looking at the picture of the dying soldier) and a rampant and rabid anti-abortionist. A friend of mine whose wife had a baby was shocked to find a fifty-dollar cheque in the mail from Smudge. It was a reward for not having had the baby aborted. It was a strange gesture, they scarcely knew Butternut, they weren't grateful for the money, didn't need it, and didn't know what to do with it, since my friend's wife was delighted to have had the baby, and hadn't considered abortion for a moment.

Chesley Yarn had been particularly nice to Smudge Butternut through the years.

Earlier, we'd been having a little argument about Smudge Butternut's poetry, Yarn and Eric defending it and me saying it wasn't all that wonderful. Elsie's eyes told me she was on my side but she didn't say anything. Now I was beginning to feel terribly depressed about having taken such a stand. Why couldn't I be the nice quiet agreeable fellow I always wanted to be? Why couldn't I be more like my Dad?

"I have a feeling I'll change my opinion about Smudge Butternut," I said, trying to rehabilitate myself.

Yarn just stared at me. Eric looked surprised. "It's not good to change your opinions," he said.

"But I'm a guy who's eager to leave his opinions behind," I said, truthfully.

"It's hard to arrive at a final opinion," said Yarn. "If I change my opinion I want it to be reluctantly."

"I hate boring myself with my opinions. I have to change all the time."

"I didn't notice that when we were talking about Smudge Butternut."

"I wanted you to change my opinion," I said. "I was begging you to, didn't you hear me? But you didn't. As far as I'm concerned, all the trouble in the world is caused by people who are too opinionated."

Silence filled the room. Maybe I'd gone too far. I'd just accused these highly opinionated people of being the cause of all the world's problems.

Finally Yarn got up and went over to his desk. "I can show you a poem that means a lot to me," he said.

41. Captain Crack of Terror Lodge

I never thought of Yarn as having anything more than a functional interest in the part of the world in which he lived. It's true his poetry reflected his environment, but only directly as it related to him. He was no regionalist. He was too much of a big talker, he wasn't a good listener, and a regionalist has to be able to listen to the people of a region, listen to their stories and so on. Only when it came to his world travels (he'd been in Greece and Japan and so on and had written wonderful poetry about those lands) did he seem to take any impersonal interest in the world around him.

For instance, when I told him about chatting with the fishermen at the fish house he said he'd never noticed any commercial fishing going on in recent decades. But suddenly that night much to my surprise and delight he began telling stories, stories about Prince Edward County, and it was as if he'd never stop. I don't know where it came from.

He read a long rhyming ballad published locally years ago by someone long dead and it was about a fisherman whose boat sank. This fisherman swam to Timber Island, which was a mile off Long Point on the southeast tip of the peninsula. This was a very small island, and this fisherman was the first human to land there since a pig farm had been abandoned, by death, ill health, divorce, insanity or whatever, twenty years or so earlier. The farm had fallen apart but the island was by then hog-infested, just crawling with pigs, and they were wild, ferocious, half-starved. They were killing the weaker ones to survive, and when they saw the exhausted fisherman drag himself up on the beach, they figured they'd eat him too. But the fisherman somehow managed to climb a tree. There were hardly any trees on the island but there was one old dead apple tree and he climbed it and managed to hang on even though it creaked and seemed about to collapse under his weight. And he had to spend an exhausted and frightened two weeks up there until he was rescued.

The excellence of the poem was only surpassed by the imaginative passion with which Chesley Yarn read it.

I told him about the time in the seventies, when Smudge Butternut was drinking a lot, my wife at the time and I drove him from Collingwood to Guelph and when we went through a hailstorm and the hail was hitting the roof of the old van like shrapnel he hit the floor and buried his head under his arms and started moaning and crying that he didn't want to die.

"Speaking of death," said Yarn, and he went on about how there'd been a rash of teenage suicides last year in peaceful, rural, remote Prince Edward County (population 20,000). Four kids had hanged themselves with their own guitar strings. There were about six definite suicides a year, about three times the national average on a per-capita basis. A farmer committed suicide a couple of years back by burning his barn down from the inside. Earlier, he'd built cement monuments around the farm, and he'd left a note saying he'd built them to help him remember and recognise the place should he come across it in a future incarnation. And there were an unusual number of strange accidents, bizarre car crashes, freak strangulations, electrocutions and so on, drownings, plane crashes, snowmobiles and cars going through the ice, fishing huts being swept away with fishermen inside hollering. Yet cemetery plots hadn't been selling too well lately, said Yarn. He'd noticed recently they'd been using the same receipt pad since 1890.

After we came out of the hailstorm Smudge Butternut settled down and we listened to him whispering to himself. He was rehearsing various ways of inviting us to dinner. "Would you care to dine with me this evening?" he said quietly to himself and then, "Thanks for driving me all this way and as a token of my appreciation could I buy you something to eat?" And on and on. We were desperately trying to keep from laughing. Finally we dropped him off in Guelph without him having worked up the nerve to ask us. He just wanted to be dropped off at the main intersection, had no idea where he wanted to stay or anything, but he had to give a poetry reading at the arts centre on Wednesday and this was Sunday. We felt sad as we drove away.

But Yarn was just waiting for me to quit before he resumed going on and on, this time about how down around South Bay there are two villages, called Milford and Demorestville, which are so tiny now you don't even notice them as you drive through—two houses and a store each. But in the mid-nineteenth century the God-fearing folks in the county referred to these little places as Sodom and Gomorrah. Milford had a population of two hundred people and seven hotels, Demorestville one hundred people and five hotels. Milford had been a carousing place for sailors and boat builders, while Demorestville was for loggers....

One time I ran into Butternut at some kind of literary get-together and he'd been on the wagon for I forget how long but everybody was impressed. Nobody noticed though how much Butternut was suffering from allergies. His nose was running and his eyes were red and burning and finally I took him to one side and asked if he had ever heard of antihistamines. No, he said, what are they? I told him they were little pills, you take one and your allergies stop. I took him down to the pharmacy in Chinatown and sat behind the wheel while he went in and when he came out with the pills he leaned back and said in his high-pitched squeaky voice, comical because it was so unlike what you would expect him to sound like based on his bizarre and rough-hewn appearance: "You know, I'm really tremendously famous. Everywhere I go in this country from coast to coast people recognise me, everywhere! Even that Chinese pharmacist, I asked him if he had any antihistamines and he said yes sir Mr. Butternut."

"Oh, that's Smudge Butternut all right," said Yarn. "He really loved being famous, but with a face like his how could he have been anything else but famous? Everybody who ever saw his face remembered it forever. And you know, back in the twenties there were passenger trains running all over the peninsula."

"What peninsula?"

"This peninsula. This *is* a peninsula, you know. Prince Edward County *is* a peninsula."

"Oh yeah, I know, that's right."

"Now there were for instance three trains a day between Bloomfield and Picton. Imagine! There used to be dozens of little cheese factories all over the county.... At West Lake there was a house called Wishing Tree Lodge, but the tree it was named after was shattered by a bolt of lightning in 1925 then toppled by a storm in 1941. It was supposed to have been the largest and oldest maple tree in the world."

"How old was it?"

"I'm glad you asked. It was seven hundred years old."

"How big was it?"

"I don't know how tall it was but it was eighteen feet in diameter. Like all of us, Elsie, you, me, Eric, and the three boys, might just be able to put our arms around it if we joined hands and stretched. People used to stand in front of it and make wishes. Around 1920 a motorist smacked into it head-on and was killed. The crash forced the crankshaft of the car so far into the tree they couldn't get it out and just had to saw it off inside. The new highway runs right over where it used to stand...."

Yarn was born just about the time the great steamboat lines were being discontinued. Up to the twenties you could catch a steamboat from Picton to Montreal or Toronto, and could take long leisurely tours of the Thousand Islands from Picton....

"What about canned goods, Chesley? Didn't there used to be little canneries all over the county?"

"That's right, there were. Between the wars—that's World War I and II—this county produced a quarter of all Canada's canned goods. One quarter! A little county like this! Amazing! And around 1847 or something like that a schooner filled with dried peas and other vegetables went down in Lake Ontario just off the southwest corner of the county. And for days after, the settlers in the area would go down to the beach and scoop up pails of water, take them home and boil them down for soup. They call it Soup Harbour. That's how it got its name...."

So I told Chesley Yarn that I told Smudge Butternut it wasn't fair that he was so famous when an indisputably superior poet like me was unknown even in his own neck of the woods never mind his own country. What's your name? said Smudge. I told him. Oh yeah, said he, you are a good poet, that poem you wrote about Yellowknife was terrific. I told him I felt a little guilty because Yellowknife was his territory and he had written so many poems about that area that I felt as if I were poaching on his preserves and he wrote an official-looking signed document saying I had the right to poach on his preserves in perpetuity.

"And when you looked at it a week later the ink had all faded out, right?" said Yarn.

"How the heck did you know that?"

"He used to pull stunts like that all the time. He always kept his pen full of invisible ink. Autographing books with invisible ink was just one of his many bizarre habits."

Yarn went on about when he (Yarn) was a baby his mother and father would be up hand-milking a long line of cows by coal-oil lamp by four in the middle of the winter while little Chesley slept all wrapped up in blankets in the straw. And then they would deliver the milk by horse and cart all over the county with little Chesley safely sleeping between the rows of milk cans.

West Lake and East Lake on the southwest side of the peninsula were more like landlocked bays than lakes, and they were separated from Lake Ontario only by long narrow sandbars rising just a few inches above the surface of the water. But they were situated so that they caught the full force of the weather heading up across the lake. The sand was continually shifting from year to year, depending on the severity of the storms, and somewhere under the dunes, which were lightly covered with a layer of poison ivy, was the West Lake Brick Works which was a big booming business in the latter half of the nineteenth century. They made bricks from the sand and shipped the bricks all over the Great Lakes. A thousand bricks cost two dollars in those days. There was no sand like it, no sand that fine and that conducive to making bricks. There are old houses made of those bricks still standing in towns and villages and cities all around the Great Lakes. Yarn said he could be walking down a street in Chicago and spot a house made of bricks he knew came from West Bay. He would recognise the special unmatchable colour and texture....

But the constant storms would be forever shifting the sand dunes around and posing a serious threat to the factory. They tried surrounding the factory with fences made of chicken wire and rotten hay, trying desperately to hold the sand back. But they finally had to admit defeat and they closed down. Sometimes parts of the factory can still be seen sticking up out of the sand....

The outside wall of Holmes Mathie's old house in Bloomfield still bore a bullet mark from the murder of Peter Lazier in 1884. Two men—David Lowder and Joseph Thompsett—were hanged for the murder but there was never any motive found and lots of people still think they were innocent. Yarn got out a book by some county historian and in the book was a copy of a letter Thompsett sent his mother from jail in which he says, among other things, "I never knew that fatal shot was fired nor of that man was killed nor nothing of that murder nor my boots never made them tracks. But the jury says I must die to pay some man's penalty. I am ready to die but I die for something I never done." And die he did. The double scaffold still stands in Picton's historic county jail. The paper called it the "picturesque seat of justice...."

And then they have these black agricultural workers come up from Jamaica every summer, said Yarn. They're known by the locals as skid marks, as in see those skid marks over there? And they're also known as jungle bunnies or jigaboos. One agricultural worker started a romance with a local white woman, who happened to be tremendously fat, weighed 275 pounds or more, and the romance was "enthusiastically discouraged" (as Yarn put it) by the local Orangemen....

About thirty years back during a summer storm a giant "tidal wave" (some people claim there are tides on the Great Lakes) came in at Salmon Point, with boats crashing through the roofs of barns half a mile from the shore....

And there was a retired sailor named Captain Crack of Terror Lodge. His family was putting him in a nursing home and the social worker asked him how he felt about it. "Frankly, I'm so happy I don't give a damn," he said. Yarn laughed crazily. "That's an attitude I'm constantly trying to develop, isn't that right dear?" he said. "Oops, she's gone to bed."

Hamish F. McPartlin was mayor of Picton from 1951 to 1967. He used to buy a lot of votes with cheese and booze. Had his own construction company which always got lots of county contracts. McPartlin's wife had an argument with a cabdriver once, the cabby's licence was suspended. Jack Brett, the editor of the *Gazette*, tried to print the story, with the emphasis on the cabby's side of it, and ended up being fired. The story was never published.

Yarn said he got so drunk once years ago he ended up getting lost in the caves up by Lake of the Mountain. Elsie had to get the fire department to haul him out. There was a legend that this lake, which is perched eerily in a crater at the top of a fairly large volcanic hill overlooking Adolphus Reach, is connected to Lake Erie via an underground stream that goes right under the floor of Lake Ontario. The legend arose when a drowned corpse was washed up on the shore of Lake of the Mountain round the turn of the century. It was the corpse of a black man, apparently, so the locals thought he must have been from Buffalo, which was the closest place where there were any black people, and that he had drowned in Lake Erie and his body was swept through the underground stream right up to Prince Edward County....

Other local legends? "Well, there's the legend of the Northern Lights. The folks around here always used to say if the lights were white, frost would soon follow. Yellow, sickness and much trouble. Red, war and harm to many innocent people. Flashing all colours, especially in the spring, was the best possible sign, because it meant there'd be a good harvest. But there's no truth in that of course, or maybe there is a little."

Yarn said he had a great aunt named Norah Nightingale who died a few years back at the age of a hundred. She was a second cousin of Florence Nightingale and she used to tell a weird story regarding the demise of her dear uncle Ignatius "Nash" Nightingale who lived on Huffs Island. In December of 1866 he was called to jury duty in Picton, and so he skated across the Bay of Quinte to get there. He never showed up. It took a search party two weeks to find his body. They finally tracked him down to a hole in the ice and they lowered grappling hooks and pulled out the body. His small, leather-bound diary was in his pocket (everyone who could read and write kept diaries in those days), and in the last entry he said he had finished his duty on the jury and was heading back home. He described certain aspects of the trial, described the judge and fellow members of the jury, but everyone involved was certain, and in fact the records show, that he had never shown up....

And then there was Yarn's Uncle Randall Clarke who was driving his horse and sleigh through Partridge Hollow one night around 1902 when he had his head blown off by a shotgun. There was no possible motive, no suspects, nothing....

And then there was the time two cars collided in downtown Bloomfield. The driver of one had the unusual name of Henry Sloorz, aged 47, of Toronto, and the driver of the other was named Henry Sloorz, aged 47, of Akron, Ohio.

And then there was the barber in Cherry Valley years ago who was known as the world's slowest barber. It took him an hour and a half to complete an ordinary twenty-five-cent haircut....

But Yarn was most pleased to talk about all the big American celebrities who owned land in the Prince Edward County area, who would build cottages and come up to hunt. Mickey Rooney for instance owned property in Ameliasburgh, Bing Crosby and Dean Martin used to go pheasant hunting on Nicholson Island, and John Foster Dulles used to spend his summers in his cottage on Main Duck Island.

42. Mr. Synchronicity

I tried one of my weirdest true-life stories on Chesley but it was a little wasted on him. I went into Bemelman's on Bloor Street in Toronto for a drink one afternoon and the bartender came over with a little book and handed it to me.

"You must have dropped it when you were over there," she said. She pointed to the far end of the bar.

The book was a little collection of poems I'd published twenty years ago. About two hundred copies had been printed. *The Ova Yogas*. Strange little book. Wrote it just before my younger daughter was born. In fact she was reading a copy of it just recently and wanted to know why it was so weird. "We were experimentalists in those days," I said.

"I *didn't* drop it," I told the bartender. "I just came in, I haven't been over at the far end of the bar." I looked at the book. It was in mint condition, in a transparent plastic envelope.

Someone had bought it from a rare-book dealer. "In fact I don't even have a copy of this book myself."

The bartender at first didn't believe me, but she went and conferred with the other bartender. Turned out someone, not a regular, someone they'd never seen before, and carrying a large bag full of books, had been sitting at the far end of the bar and left just before I arrived. They decided this book had fallen from his bag, out of all the books he had in there it had to be a book authored by a guy who, twenty years later, was about to come in for a drink. They decided I should keep the book and if the guy ever came back they could tell him to call me for it.

I picked up the bar phone and phoned Nelson Ball straightaway. Hadn't talked to him in over a year. Nelson had published the book in his youth, when he ran Weed/Flower Press. When I told him the story he laughed and said, "That story is almost as weird as the book itself."

"Do you still have the book?" said Chesley.

"Yep. No one claimed it."

Now Chesley was a poet, but he was a hard-boiled cynic too, and he probably thought my tale was highly embroidered. When I would tell stories like that it'd usually be to encourage my listener to hit me with a strange one out of his own life and times so to speak, but Chesley didn't take the bait. Moreover he was incapable of appreciating magic and mystery in other people's lives in general, although there was a solid core of it in his own life and in his own work. His magic involved the passing of the seasons, the passing of time, the passing of passion. That's enough for anyone.

But I was the guy who was continually having bizarre coincidences blow up in his life. Chesley wasn't at all interested in that. I was serious about it though. I thought there was some principle involved that it was my duty to express. It was similar to the principle involving the negation of thought. When, as in the ancient tradition of Buddhist meditation, one simply follows the breath and lets the natural flow of thought pass away, the thoughts themselves become more interesting, more seductive, more captivating, as if they do not wish to be negated and they do not wish to pass away, as if each thought is a little being with a consciousness and sense of dignity all its own.

It's a principle similar to the one by which people manipulate each other emotionally. As A. feigns indifference, B. becomes more seductive.

But what was it that had been causing all these interesting, seductive, captivating coincidences to spring up all my life? I was famous for this among my friends who called me Mr. Synchronicity. It was all very serious as far as I was concerned, but I wasn't about to try to convince Chesley of that, or anyone.

In fact Chesley started going on about the lack of ethics in the literary community. He had a good story about a fishy deal between two prominent Canadian men of letters, career poets of modest reputation. One was editing a magazine, the other was editing an anthology. Chesley said he saw the incriminating evidence in a collection of letters at Queen's University. Poet A. sent some unsolicited poems for poet B.'s anthology. Poet B. wrote back and said he did not care for the poems but he would put them in the anthology if Poet A. would put some of Poet B.'s poems in his magazine. Poet A. agreed, in writing.

We felt smug and comfortable about it all. We may be bad but thank God we ain't like that. That was the subtext. Like the time I told an acquaintance who was an ardent hard-core anti-abortionist that the Japanese term for abortion was "thinning the bamboo shoots," his face suddenly took on a pleased look. At first I couldn't figure out why he should feel pleased but I thought about it for a while then decided that the piece of information I had given him allowed him to feel superior to the whole Japanese race, and that was what the look was about.

And then we have the case of Poet X. trying desperately to get into a certain anthology being edited by Poet Y. He sends his poems to Poet Y., phones him up, invites him out to lunch, tells him how terrific it is that he's editing the anthology and so on, but when Poet Y., who uncharacteristically for a poet has a certain sense of ethical integrity, eventually decides not to include Poet X., Poet X. makes sure he gets the anthology to review when it comes out and Poet X. tears it to pieces in a lengthy review in the *Globe and Mail*, calls Poet Y. a complete dud as an editor and as a poet too incidentally (although just last year Poet X. wrote an admiring review of Poet Y.'s new book), calls for a Royal Commission to investigate the procedures for choosing poets for anthologies and so on.

Then Poet X. gets appointed to edit an anthology of poetry and pointedly leaves out not only Poet Y. but everybody who was in Poet Y.'s anthology. These things really happen—all the time.

Forgetting that choosing poems for an anthology is something done in the same spirit as picking flowers for a little bouquet. At least it is for people who live in the spirit. Or who know something about it.

FRIDAY, OCTOBER 12

43. Gooseberry Jam

Everything was transformed, everything was slathered with grey mist so thick you could hose down a burning nuclear power plant with it, mist dripping like sparkling champagne from the spruce boughs, like beer foam from the roof of the house, everything was only dimly visible through a pure heavenly mist you wanted to roll up and put in the trunk to take back to the city. The trees seemed stately and intelligent, like wise old elephants in leg chains at the zoo.

And there was old Chesley Yarn, standing in the door of the outhouse in this brand new universe with a big smile on his face, lazily pissing out onto the grass. At first I thought he had a stranglehold on a loaf of freshly baked French bread then I noticed a stream of water coming out the end.

"Is it always like this in the morning?" I said, meaning the mist, not his you-know-what.

"Of course it isn't. Sometimes it's sunny, sometimes it's snowing, we get all kinds of weather here. Come on, come on in for breakfast. I think Elsie's making coffee."

We sat at the kitchen table again while Elsie served eggs, coffee, toast, homemade jam. Yarn talked about *A Hundred Years of Solitude*, how many times he'd read it and everything. I confessed I'd never read past the half-way mark, it always seemed to me to be so gratuitously made up (Elsie's eyes flashed in secret agreement), and I much preferred a book often compared with it and which was much more real by my lights, *Midnight's Children*. Elsie confessed she didn't like to read books about India for some reason she couldn't figure out, but she wrote down the title.

"What kind of jam is this?" I said.

"It's gooseberry jam," said Chesley.

"It's not too sweet," said Elsie. "I don't like adding much sugar."

"It's good, I don't like it sweet much. Wonder why they're called gooseberries?"

"Because geese eat them," said Chesley.

"Gee, Chesley," I said, "you must know just about everything there is to know in the whole world."

"Oh no, there are certain things I don't know."

"He has an answer for everything is more like it," said Elsie.

Everything was kind of sleepy and slow. My body was adjusting pleasantly to being out of the city for a change. A woman from a couple of houses away brought in three roses, just as a little neighbourly gift. Nobody ever does that on Spadina Road. One of the roses was huge, looked more like a dahlia. I got up to have a closer look. "Is that a rose?" I sniffed at it. "Hm, sure is."

"Hah, look at it wither," said Chesley.

Elsie got out the camera and got some shots of Chesley and me. They gave me their address in Avignon where they were going to spend the winter and suggested I come over and visit them, stay as long as I wanted.

As we walked to my car I put my arm around Elsie and told her I thought she was wonderful, asked her if Chesley really appreciated her sufficiently.

"He has his moments," she said. I admitted I enjoyed having her wait on me.

"I guess you did," she said. "If you've been by yourself for ten years or whatever you've done a lot of waiting on yourself."

The little red Spitfire had lost a certain *je ne sais quoi* overnight, that is it refused to spit fire. All three of us had to push the dead carcass (lucky it was on wheels) up to the top of the hill and I had to jump in, let it roll back down and start it that way. Lucky I didn't have to leave in a hurry.

44. A Little Brown Dachshund

There was no one in the Picton Hotel but a little brown dachshund. I knelt down and tickled its ears. Its eyes melted in ecstasy. A middle-aged woman came in from the kitchen and said, "Sorry, we're not open yet." She wiped her hands on her apron. I liked to see a woman do that.

"What's the dog's name?"

"Schenley."

"Hi Schenley," I said. "What a funny name you got."

"We called her that because we like the whisky."

I kept tickling. "Never met a dog yet that didn't like to be tickled behind the ears."

"No, and you're not likely to, either." She smiled. She sounded a little like Elsie. A county flavour in her voice.

A little brightly lit and brightly painted restaurant across the street looked as if it would serve good coffee. I sat at a table next to a guy wearing a yellow hat which said on it: "International Plowing Match 1977—Hastings County."

I caught the guy's eye and we got talking about the heavy mist of that morning, and how it was still in the air despite the bright morning sun. Just then "Raindrops Keep Falling on My Head" started playing on the radio. Not a terrific coincidence, because the local radio station probably was just playing that song because of all the mist in the first place.

There were brightly coloured hand-painted signs all around the restaurant, with original cartoon characters. Murals depicted the dramatic events leading to the discovery of ice cream and candy and every other sickeningly sweet thing you could think of. No wonder the waitress looked at me funny when I said no sugar in my coffee. Somebody had obviously never read *Sugar Blues*.

BEFORE YOU GO HOME…
—try an Enjoyable Tasty CONE!

SUGAR CONES 10¢ extra

Chocolate Bar Flavours
one third of a bar in each cone: add 10¢
Crispy Crunch
Aero Mint
Aero Milk Chocolate

Cookie & Pie Flavours
Oreo
Lemon Pie
Blueberry Pie

Fruit Flavours
Pineapple
Cherry
Coconut
Rhubarb
Raspberry
Blueberry
Cantaloupe
Pear
Fruit Cocktail
Pumpkin Pie

Candy Flavours
Chocolate Chip
Peppermint
Humbug
Peanuts/Nuts
Blackball/Jaw Breaker
Barley Sugar
Pecans
Fruit Slices
Reese's Pieces
Cinnamon Hearts
Smarties
Malt Balls

They actually didn't have ice cream in any flavour but vanilla. But upon order they'd fish out a packet of special flavouring and mix it with a portion of ice cream in a special ice-cream mixing machine.

"In all my extensive travels over the years I've never encountered a place like this before," I confessed, truthfully. The waitress was about twenty-one, short tight black-leather skirt, eyes like highly intelligent little shooting stars.

"You're not likely to, either," she said, smilingly. Second time in an hour! She wiped her hands on her apron.

The guys who set the place up were Jerry Putman and David MacKay. "They're high-school teachers, eh?" she said, smilingly.

"They seem more like *high* school-teachers," I said, jokingly.

"Yeah, you're right," she said, laughingly. "I never thought of that, my good sir."

"They should be reported to the Canadian Diabetic Association," I stated, grimly.

She looked profoundly thoughtful. "Well, I know what you mean," she averred, studiously. "But it's still theoretical. No direct link has ever been established between eating sugar and diabetes."

"Are you sure of that?" I queried, doubtfully.

"Well of course there are many cross-sectional correlations, but we all know these can be spurious unless supported by longitudinal research."

"You're a full-fledged waitress, it's okay for you to talk like that. But I hope you're not trying to tell me that these high-school teachers have analysed the situation that critically."

"Why not? These teachers are fairly intelligent. They hired me, didn't they? Now take Mr. Putman for instance, he teaches art, he did all the signs. The original idea for the store was Mr. MacKay's, I think. Both of them are smart, but I'll admit they always get a blank look on their face when I break into sociological jargon."

"So where did you pick it up anyway?"

"Oh, you know. It's a small town. Nothing to do but read. There's a good library here and I've practically memorised every book in it."

"Good for you, dear," I said. "Now, suppose you show me how this machine works."

"Certainly, sir. You select your favourite flavour or combination thereof and shove it through this handsome-looking slot."

The machine was called the Count Eddie Magic Machine #1.

Why Count Eddie?

"Because this is Prince Edward County."

A brightly painted sign listed some of the many possible flavour combinations, in case you were having trouble choosing what might taste okay and what might just taste weird. Adventurous pioneers, perhaps a sort of ice-cream censor board, had tried these combos and pronounced them fit for public consumption.

Selected Combos
Strawberry & Banana
Raspberry & Rhubarb
Orange & Licorice
Watermelon & Cherry
Cherry & Smarties
Banana & Peanut Butter

I asked the waitress if banana and peanut butter was a popular combo. Just then I felt something touching my lower leg. Something curiously warm and dry and cold and wet all at the same time. Yes, you guessed it. It was Schenley, the little brown dachshund come over to see me. I knelt down and tickled her behind the ears again and again her eyes went all gummy with joy. Turned out she had a little canine urinary-tract infection and her mistress had been bringing her in for a saucer full of cranberry juice.

Anyway, the waitress said she didn't recall ever being asked for peanut butter and banana. I said it was good on sandwiches. "My Uncle Oscar used to make them for me. He said the banana stopped the peanut butter from sticking to the roof."

"The roof?" She looked up. There was another mural on the ceiling.

"The roof of your mouth, I mean."

"Oh. Wonder if it'd be any good for a urinary tract infection."

"You got one too?"

"Not just now," she said, blushingly. "But I do get them quite often. Actually, I lie. I do have a little itsy-bitsy tiny one right now. Cranberry juice never seems to work for me."

"I don't know. I've never had one."

"Infection or juice?"

"Infection."

"You can have mine if you want." Her eyes were shining with glee.

"Uh, no thanks. I won't have time today."

"Maybe you never had one because of all the peanut butter and banana sandwiches you had when you were a kid."

"Never thought of that but you're probably right."

45. The Bicycling Kinesiologists

The cars were lined up a mile back for the Glenora Ferry, and there, only three cars from the front of the line, was a little blood-red Spitfire with no one in it. Whoever the driver was he better get back there soon or he'd find his car pushed into the ditch. All the other cars had drivers in them, and passengers too. That ferry was almost ready to start loading and the driver of the Spitfire was playing a silly game of Pacman in the Wheelhouse View Restaurant, which was decorated with mermaids and sharks on the wallpaper, on the tables, on the cups and saucers, on the doors of the washrooms—mermaids for ladies and sharks for gentlemen. The driver scored 42190 which was a new high score for this particular machine. There were big pike, bass and pickerel mounted on the walls, and a sailor's cap sitting on a shelf. Through the window you could look down at the cars lining up, and could look across the sun-speckled waters of Adolphus Reach over to the mainland, and could watch the ferry coming through the sun-dappled spotty Persian mist, so you figured you better pay your bill and get back to the car before it ended up being pushed into the ditch if not the reach....

I'd passed the Inn on the Bay, a nineteenth-century mock castle that had been turned into a restaurant, and stopped to have a coffee but they weren't open yet so I had to move on. Somehow I felt glad it was closed, the place had an unpleasant aura about it. Yarn had been saying the old building had been deserted for decades, and when it was being renovated during the forties a pile of old baby-clothes were found along with some faded news clippings about the Lindbergh kidnapping. There was a bit of an investigation. It kept some people busy for a while but nothing came of it. [Editor's note: A few days before this book went to press a mysterious explosion levelled the place and two people from Ottawa were killed.]

This morning at 3 a.m. GMT an IRA bomb had killed three people and demolished the top few floors of a hotel in Brighton (England) where Margaret Thatcher and her entire cabinet were staying. But Maggie and the boys were on a lower floor, and weren't hurt. Maggie was quoted as saying a moment after the blast, "We'd better get out of here," and, a few hours later, "It's business as usual." Aboard the ferry I struck up a conversation with two young bicyclists, a man and a woman in their early twenties. They said they were kinesiologists.

"We're involved in movement."

"Peace movement? Macrobiotic movement? Animal rights? Native land claims? Anti-nuclear power?"

Just then the foghorn let out a big blast and both of them jumped. "Ah! Just plain movement," I said. They laughed. They wanted to know why I hadn't jumped. I said I didn't get much sleep last night and didn't have the energy to jump.

They said they were cycling from Toronto to Kingston then they were going to rent a car and drive back to Toronto. Nice time of year for it. They were a nice young couple, bright young tender lovely kids, like something out of a Mickey Rooney movie from the early forties, sweet as candy and twice as tender, and they said they worked with retarded people, teaching them to swim.

It was beautiful cycling along the north shore of Lake Ontario, they said. "The road follows the waterline, eh?" He was working in Winnipeg, came to spend the summer with his girlfriend. "While she was at work, I was out cycling around. You get to meet really interesting people."

"Like who for instance?" I was wondering if they'd met Nigel, Winston and Rodney.

"Well, uh, just today we met this farmer. We talked to him for thirty, maybe forty minutes."

"What was so interesting about him?"

"Well, oh he was telling us all about his theories about farming."

"What sort of theories?"

"Um. I can't remember."

"Organic farming?"

"Yeah, something like that."

Where were Nigel, Winston and Rodney? Were they ahead of me or behind me? Impossible to tell. Later I found out they were an hour or so behind. They caught a later ferry, stopped the cyclists further along the road and chatted with them. Asked if they'd seen a guy in a little red sports car, and they remembered that they had.

There was also a sweet old fellow on the ferry selling Rotary Club raffle tickets for a new car. He had a surprised look on his face, as if he'd had it since birth. He seemed to be surprised at being alive. Every day he got up first thing in the morning, hopped in the brand new Pontiac Acadian he won in the raffle seven years ago (at least it was new when he won it, and he'd been selling tickets ever since then, with the added selling point that it must be a bonafide draw because look he'd won a car himself), drove down to the dock and rode back and forth on the ferry all day selling tickets. I bought one.

He looked so surprised it made me think it was the first one he'd sold in months.

"That's the fifth one I sold today," he said.

"Fifth one? Then why do you look so surprised?"

"Surprised? I'm not surprised. Lots of people buy these tickets."

"I'll be really surprised if I won it," I said.

"Somebody's gotta win it, it might as well be you," he said.

"Yeah, but I'd still be surprised," I said. "I bet you were surprised when you won."

"Heck yes," he said. "Was I ever!"

"I bet you had a real surprised look on your face for days after," I said.

"Yep, I sure did," he said.

He talked about his theories of raffle tickets but I can't remember what they were. Organic raffles? Yeah, something like that. He did tell me he was a grand nephew of the great buffalo hunter and Métis leader Gabriel Dumont.

"That Louis Riel," he said, "he really got a bum deal as far as I was concerned."

"Aw, every grand nephew of Gabriel Dumont I've ever met has said the same thing," I said.

He looked surprised.

Later, when the film crew came through, they spoke to the old fellow and asked him if he'd mind if they shot some film of him sitting selling tickets by his car.

"How much would it cost?" he said. Ever since he won the car he'd apparently had trouble with people trying to get him to buy things.

"It's free," said Nigel.

The old fellow looked surprised.

"Oh, all right then," he said.

46. No One Will Ever Read This

Adolphustown Park was deserted. I parked the car, walked through the woods to the United Empire Loyalist museum which turned out to be closed for the season, then walked down to mist-enshrouded Lake Ontario and washed my face and hands and brushed my teeth in the silver water, the ripples lapping in, the sun shining through the mist, the mist obscuring the horizon deliciously.

Gradually the mist began backing off and thinning out. Grey rocks with their heads sitting up above the surface (like Kyoto rock gardens with a calm lake instead of calm sand) gradually materialised in my lake-like field of vision, each rock with a seagull perched upon it. It was a quiet narrow stony grey beach between two small scantily treed points jutting out twenty feet or so into the lake and thereby creating a tiny peaceful bay. The point to the left was burdened with two ancient willow trees that had managed to weather many a storm, and a couple of ancient overturned rowboats with red and black paint peeling off, the vibrant tones startling in the greyness. (It was lovely.) Halfway between the points, and at the back of the beach, just before the little two-foot grassy bank rose up as it does much of the way around all of the Great Lakes, not just Lake Ontario, there was a curious wooden cross, about six feet high and with a two-foot cross-beam, all painted white, with a long spike driven in to it just where the two pieces of wood joined, right in the centre. It had been very nicely made by a carpenter, though it'd be hard to guess how many years ago. White flakes of paint were peeling off. And the cross bore a spider web dotted with droplets of dew glinting in the sun. Everything was grey but laden with light. A small black spider was devotedly spinning his little life away.

Stiff weeds were sticking up out of the water. For about ten minutes I watched a turtle swimming slowly around under the water, its snout sticking up about an inch into the grey air. He was looking for insects, but didn't seem to be finding any.

Two white and grey seagulls flew a foot above the calm grey mirror surface of the water, away from the shore, becoming smaller in the distance before disappearing in the sun-drenched mist. Did they have any idea how beautiful they were?

Then the turtle's snout drifted closer to shore and it began to pull itself up onto dry land. It shook itself off slightly, like a dog, but not as vigorously as a dog because it didn't have to, it didn't have fur. Imagine a world where the turtles get around (on land) as fast as dogs. Then it wobbled slowly up the beach toward me. At first it seemed as if it were coming up to be petted, maybe tickled behind the ears, if turtles had ears, or on the belly.

Anyway, the turtle came right up to me, must have been half blind, bumped its head against my foot, then continued on around me. I picked it up and placed it down on its back, brushed off the sticky sand, then took out my black felt pen and wrote in thick dark letters on its already dry belly these words: NO ONE WILL EVER READ THIS. And then let it go. It lumbered blindly up off the beach and disappeared in a little puff of dust up the dusty road leading to the highway.

When I ran into the film crew later in the afternoon they said they'd seen a big turtle on the highway and stopped to take some film of it trying to cross the highway to the other side, with cars narrowly missing it.

"Did it make it across?"

"Yes, it did," said Winston.

"Were you disappointed?"

"Not at all," said Nigel.

Were they secretly hoping to get a shot of the turtle being squashed under the wheel of an automobile? No, such a suggestion was beneath me. Luckily I didn't ask it.

They said somebody had written on its belly, with a felt pen, NO ONE WILL EVER READ THIS.

"It made us feel kind of strange, reading that," said Winston.

"As if you were no one?"

"You've got it."

"You're not. None of us is."

"I believe that," said Rodney.

"Me too," said Winston.

"What?" said Rodney. "You mean like you believe that we don't really exist or something?"

I tiptoed away, and when I came back they were still arguing about weather existence is real or a dream.

"By the way, Dave," said Colin. "Did you print that saying on the belly of the turtle?"

"What makes you think that?"

"You were down there where it came from, and you have a felt pen just the right thickness."

"And it's the sort of thing you'd say," said Rodney.

47. Cemeteries at Night

No matter how old you get you still get a bit nervous in cemeteries at night. Burmese Buddhists practice meditating all night in graveyards, visualising their flesh rotting and bones crumbling. Some friends and I recently drove through a cemetery at midnight on the way home from seeing *Night of the Living Dead*. We got out and ran around scaring each other. You should have heard the screaming when I turned off the lights.

But visiting this elaborately fenced United Empire Loyalist burying ground in the daytime was a learning experience. I learned for instance that where I'd been sitting on the beach was where 250 Loyalists had landed in their little boats after sailing from New York in the fall of 1783 under Major Peter Van Alstin (1747-1811). That was why they called it the Loyalist Landing Place. Peter was a Loyalist of Dutch ancestry. But something was bothering me.

The 250 had passed an intense winter in tents at Sorel and arrived here in the spring of 1784. Peter became justice of the peace and represented the area in the Legislative Assembly of Upper Canada. He built the first grist mill in the area, at Glenora.

Most of the 250 stayed in the area for the rest of their lives and were buried here. There was an old brass plaque at the entrance to the burying ground: "Put off thy shoes from off thy feet for the place whereon thou standest is holy ground." Those Bible-punchers love to tell us ordinary folk what to do. Would it be okay if I just took one shoe off and hopped? Not to be disrespectful or anything.

Willet Casey died on February 12, 1856, at the age of ninety-three. Buried next to him is his wife Jane. On Jane's other side is Samuel Casey, who died on December 19, 1857, at the age of seventy-one. Oh to have a little time machine and be able to go back and chat with them. Both Willet and Casey were members of the Legislative Assembly of Upper Canada, following Peter. I couldn't quite put my finger on what was bothering me.

Jane was the youngest daughter of Willet and Jane Casey of Adolphustown, and she died on July 27, 1837, "in the 34th year of her age." Her father was seventy-four at the time. Her stone was erected by her sister, Margaret Ingersoll.

Hannah Van Dusen died on March 8, 1791. Her age was engraved but close to two hundred winters had rendered it illegible. For sure she wasn't as old as the fossils embedded in the granite that formed the tombstone. "She was the wife of Paul Van Dusen and faithfully discharged the duties of...." Couldn't read the rest. Probably an obedient wife and drudge. There'd been a Van Dusen tavern in the area but there was some uncertainty about its exact location. I later asked Kate Van Dusen, the fiery red-haired ultra-romantic Canadian poet, and she didn't know anything about it. Neither the tavern nor the connection with the Loyalists. All she knew was she'd been born in Ottawa and her dad or was it her uncle worked for newspapers and for federal cabinet ministers, though not necessarily both at the same time.

Two people died the year Thomas Hardy was born: Joseph Alison UEL, born March 20, 1754, died July 23, 1840. Mary Richmond, Joseph's wife, born July 15, 1745 (o.s.), died October 8, 1840.

And there was an interesting little tragedy which must have caused a lot of anguish so long ago: Thomas Hillate, drowned while skating December 27, 1885, in his twenty-first year.

48. Nat King Cole

Most of these names are mentioned over and over again in a book called *History of the County of Lennox and Addington* by Walter S. Herrington (Toronto: Macmillan of Canada, 1913). In this and other books, the Loyalists were pictured as fun-loving simple people who would have been Chaucerian had they not been so puritanical. They voted with their feet when the American colonists drove out the British.

Peter Van Alstin, for instance, lived "in a grand style, and was never happier than when entertaining his friends to a sumptuous dinner. He was a rollicking good-natured companion, a typical Dutchman in every respect." He had been a blacksmith who served on the Loyalist side in the American Revolutionary War.

Willet Casey didn't come to Upper Canada with the Van Alstin expedition. After his father was killed in the Revolutionary War, Casey took off overland and settled on the shore of Lake Champlain. He was putting the final shingle on his log cabin when a pair of runaway slaves happened by on their way up to Killaloe Station. They informed him that he wasn't in British territory, he was still in the United States of America (or at least one of them). So he moved up to Adolphustown, where, in 1792, it was decided that fences would be four feet eight inches high no more no less, and pigs would not be allowed to run at large before the age of three months.

Mr. Herrington gets a chance to show off his colourful, dramatic and heavily ironic style of prose when he describes Black Sunday, August 2, 1819. A flat-bottomed boat filled with eighteen young people "jubilant with the spirit of the season" capsized while on the way across the bay to attend a prayer meeting at Losee chapel. It was the "saddest event that ever befell that part of the country," wrote Mr. Herrington, who was also the author of *Heroines of Canadian History, Martyrs of New France* and *The Evolution of the Prairie Provinces*, and who was Napanee town solicitor for sixty years and chairman of the Napanee public library from 1897 to 1947.

He was described as an "enthusiastic gardener, an amateur artist, an ardent camper, an authority on the works of Shakespeare, a Grand Master of the Masonic Grand Lodge of Canada, and a loyal member of St. Mary Magdalene Church."

"All nature seemed to smile on that bright Sabbath morning," he wrote....

> "With innocent jests and snatches of sacred songs they moved merrily over the surface of the bay until, as they neared the landing-place, the boat began to leak and, in the confusion which followed, capsized, plunging all the passengers into the water.... The service was in progress, and the officiating clergyman had just given utterance to the prayer that "it might be a day long to be remembered" when the congregation was startled by screams of terror, and rushing from the church saw the unfortunate victims struggling for their lives. Every effort was made to save them from their perilous position, but of the eighteen, who a few minutes before were overflowing with the happiness of youth, only nine were saved."

It was as if Mr. Herrington had been there. He goes on to emphasise the day-long-to-be-remembered irony and to show the Reverend Mr. Puffer breaking down and crying at the funeral sermon —"unable to finish his discourse." He gives only the last names of the dead: " ...Two Germans, two Detlors, one Bogart, one Roblin, one Clark, one Madden, and one Cole."

But when Mr. Herrington mentions, briefly, very briefly indeed, that there were a "number of negro slaves" who came along with the Van Alstin expedition, I realised that's what had been bothering me. I must have heard that before, but there was no evidence of it in the graveyard, or in the historical plaques erected all over the area. Had the figure of 250 Loyalists included the slaves, or were the slaves extra? Did the slaves have their own part of town, their own homes? What became of them? Where were they buried? Was the Cole who drowned a leaf on the family tree of Nat King?

After all, Cole was the last to be mentioned....

Or would the slaves have been prohibited from attending the white church?

Check that out and get back to me, okay?

49. Two Guys in a White Volvo

Two tall thin elegant smokestacks, grey with white tips, like giant filter-tip cigarettes in the sky, floated above the billowing whipped-cream light-filled mists of autumn. I was heading east from Adolphustown in a small open sports car. A silver steeple appeared above the mist which appeared above a pale orange line of poplars and maples in wildly nostalgic fall foliage: it was St. Paul's Anglican Church overlooking the St. Lawrence River. There were pumpkins every-where. If the river flooded you could sandbag the banks with pumpkins. Sandhurst Public School, with its flag at half mast, sat right on the water. It must have been awful being cooped up in school listening to idiotic paranoid asthmatic guilt-ridden (but well-meaning) teachers droning on wheezily (chalk-dust allergy) while that wonderful river flowed by right outside the window.

Clouds of mist continued billowing in from the river, clouds of mist with the sun shining through, and an historical plaque at the side of the river told of the Escape of the *Royal George*.

Now the *Royal George* was a twenty-two-gun British corvette, the biggest British warship on Lake Ontario, but on November 9, 1813, or thereabouts, it was intercepted off False Duck Island and chased into Kingston Harbour by a whole fleet of sleek little American ships. Fire was exchanged but the *Royal George* had to withdraw. The captain of the *George* was Commodore Isaac Chauncey, according to the plaque. And so I don't think one should take these plaques as gospel, even if they are cast in bronze, for after all, Chauncey was an American naval officer, stationed in Sackett's Harbour on the other side of the lake. In fact he led the famous attack on York the following year. His poor ghost must be howling mad....

The red velvet patches of little sumac trees in autumn, they were everywhere, and there was a freshly painted and very large yellow and black and white HONEY FOR SALE sign with a picture of a bumblebee the size of a hippo. Three men were repairing a helicopter behind a barn, small herds of Holstein cows scattered round about, I passed a survey crew with a sign saying DANGER BLASTING AHEAD TURN OFF TRANSMITTER, then Ontario Hydro's Lennox Generating Station with a sign saying DANGEROUS WATER KEEP AWAY. Everything was so beautiful, even a nuclear generating station.

This reminded me of a long-ago strangely beautiful day spent fishing for bass with my old friends Ernie and Chink in a large rowboat (heavily stocked with beer and raw-onion sandwiches) among the reeds of the warm clear shallow sandy-bottomed Baie d'Or on Lake Huron while the newly built Bruce Heavy Water Plant and Nuclear Generating Station loomed over us. This had always been a good bass-fishing place and there was no reason we could see that it wouldn't still be. At one point as a seagull took a swoop at a low-flying insect or two a hundred feet away from our boat, Chink inexplicably yelled out: "Watch me get this seagull," and cast his line in its direction. Hard to believe, but he got it. The line wrapped around and around the beautiful bewildered bird, and the hook dug into its upper wing.

"Geez," said Ernie, "now look what ya went and did."

"Is there any more beer?" said Chink.

Ernie and I pulled in our lines and we began the slow job of reeling in that furiously spluttering entrapped gull. We finally got it alongside the boat but Chink couldn't touch it, just didn't have the stomach for it. I picked it up and held it while Ernie unwrapped the line and pulled the hook out of its wing. Then I let it slip into the water and it took off like an eagle suddenly free. Chink just sat there smoking Belmonts and feeling stupid.

Then I caught a huge smallmouth bass, and back at camp when I opened it up to clean it there was so much roe inside it that I felt sick and vowed never to go fishing again.

But that was twenty years ago. Today, at the Canada Cement plant approaching Kingston, Ontario, a long conveyor tube, big enough to drive a beer truck through, led from the plant and over the highway down to the loading dock on the sparkling misty river. And there was Bath. Much nicer than that other Bath, in England. For one thing, no ruins to speak of. For another thing, no tourists. Very clean town. Lakeside Park with the Loyalist Cove Yacht Club. Bath Green Gardens with pumpkins and apples and tomatoes for sale. Even Millhaven prison was sparkling in the sun. I was tempted to take the ferry over to Amherst Island, just to see what was there, but the film crew (and maybe Marie-Thérèse!) would be waiting in Kingston.

A couple of meditative fishermen sat fishing in a grey boat close to the shore, with silver spoons sending sweet blasts of brilliant light across the ever-attentive water in all directions. The narrow two-lane winding highway became the Loyalist Parkway as we got closer to Kingston, with Collins Bay Penitentiary over to the side, the thick grey walls supporting gun turrets on the four corners. Red roof. Blue sky. Green grass. River flowing by. Mist. Country of honeybees, Holsteins and penitentiaries. It must be horrible to be locked up on a day like today.

The sign says KINGSTON POP. 60,500. I'm stuck behind a shiny white Volvo, which is stuck behind some other car on and on into the congested downtown area. The Volvo is sparklingly brand new, with two guys in well-laundered white dress shirts with shoulder seat belts and navy-blue suspenders. I jot down the licence number, for no apparent reason, in my big red notebook. WOF '901. A freshly applied bumpersticker on the back of the Volvo says: PACK UP YOUR TROUBLES COME ON GET HAPPY, WE'RE HEADING FOR THE PROMISED LAND. If you read this book and recognise yourself, I was stuck behind you for half an hour. And then saw you later, several days later, several hundred miles away.

50. Phone Calls in the Middle of the Night

Marie-Thérèse had a dream. The two of us were walking down a street in Old Jerusalem and came upon a blue garbage pail with COD marked on the side in big white letters. It was full of fish. We grabbed a few and ate them with bread.

We tried to analyse the dream but nothing sounded right. The whole joyful process of telling each other our dreams, never mind analysing them, had become a source of embarrassment. We decided the dream was just fine by itself. Marie-Thérèse's face seemed grey, frozen, as if she had been crying and didn't want to show it. As if she had hardened herself.

We were sitting in Kenny's Place, around the corner from the main drag in Kingston. Kenny's Place was where we had gone for coffee eleven years ago after the funeral of Ivan Evangeliste who had been shot by a cop right between the eyes, moments after drawing his gun and aiming it at the cop. The waiter said something about how nice it was to see a couple so obviously in love. We'd just met.

To compress a novel into a paragraph, a few shots had been exchanged and a Hamilton cop had his thumb blown off during the ultimately successful arrest of Ivan Evangeliste, who'd been running stolen furs here and there around Southern Ontario. He got ten years in Millhaven. One day he escaped in the back of a service vehicle by burying himself in dirty laundry and he managed to lose himself in a Portuguese-Jamaican neighbourhood west of Bathurst in Toronto. He had a basement apartment. Great guy. Everybody loved him. But they didn't know what he did for a living.

One time while living there, nervously, imagining he was about to be tracked down at any moment, he was stopped for making an illegal left turn. Ivan hopped out and began firing wildly. He obviously did not want to return to prison. The cop drew his gun and fired a perfect shot right through Ivan's head.

I was a police reporter so had to cover the funeral, talk to the people who knew him incognito in Toronto, and even talk to his wife who was still living in Kingston in a little house as close as she could get to the pen so that she could visit him as often as possible. She was sad, she tried to understand why he hadn't headed straight to her when he escaped, and why he never contacted her, and she did understand, but it still hurt. She showed me his oil paintings (ingeniously mournful little Picasso/Dali blends) and book collection (Sartre, Camus, Dostoyevsky, Chandler, Hammett, Hemingway, as well as a lot of books in Hungarian).

One widow, one priest, one nun, and one reporter who had never met Ivan were the entire cast at his pathetic little funeral. The nun was Sister Marie-Thérèse. At our first meeting I could feel this warm friendly spirit come out of her body and embrace me. It was entrancing. We became friends and things escalated. We began to find ourselves interlocked, we quickly developed an insane passion to share everything with each other. And somewhere along the line, after she decided she wanted to leave the sisterhood, and about the time she discovered she had a bit of a foot fetish (harmless really, but she loved it when I tickled the soles of her feet or when I let her tickle mine), we fell in love. I don't believe I ever encouraged her to give up her vows, or to break any rules of the order. I simply tried to support her in whatever she wanted. And when she made it clear she wanted to leave I made it clear I'd support her all the way. When she had her doubts I had doubts too. But when it came time to act she couldn't do it, she not only stayed but she stayed with a vengeance, getting more involved with life within the convent. She gave up her work with the convicts and retreated into the solemn dungeon depths of the order. She said she was trying to become stronger, she had to become stronger before she could do anything. She had too much character to leave because of a man.

Trouble was I did something forbidden. I phoned her at the convent. Not only did I phone her, but it was at two-thirty in the morning. I'd been over at my friend Zippy Xenophontos' place, drinking the devastating and deadly Mexican mescal. Wonderful stuff, but big blackouts if you go a bit over the limit. Zippy got telling me stories about his grandfather, who had developed the notion that his wife had been cheating on him, and then climbed up to the top of the mountain on the little Aegean island where they lived and prayed to God to give him a sign if she had been untrue. Grandfather and God worked out a deal. If anyone in the family died within six months then that would be a sign that his wife had been unfaithful. It was a large family, though, indefinably large, and naturally someone did die. So that settled it. Grandfather decided to leave, to get as far away from Greece as it was possible to get. He settled on (and in) Montreal. Opened up a restaurant, and then over the next few years succeeded in getting almost the entire family, his kids, his brothers and sisters and their spouses and kids, to join him in Canada. In the meantime, his wife took another husband and had a few more kids. Even today, said Zippy, opinion is divided on whether or not she'd been unfaithful.

I can't remember how I got home that night. And I couldn't remember making the phone call to the convent, or, to be more accurate, phone calls. This was just a week or so before.

So we sat there. In Kenny's Place once again. Something had changed. The milk of human kindness and the cream of love was on the verge of turning sour.

"Why did you phone me?"

"What do you mean?"

Little tears sparkled coldly in her eyes. Apparently I'd called at two-thirty on the special night line, let it ring about twelve times until some sleepy voice answered, then I asked drunkenly for Marie-Thérèse. When she got on the phone I didn't say anything. When she hung up I phoned back and had her dragged to the phone again and this time identified myself. Then hung up and went into a twelve-hour mescal coma. While four hundred miles away Marie-Thérèse lay awake, trying to calm her anger, trying to avoid cursing the day she ever met me.

51. Extreme Emergency

There are limits to how shamelessly I want to exploit my life and the lives of my friends. And so I shall be brief. Marie-Thérèse averred that I had given her unsurpassed pleasure and all of that nonsense, I had become terribly important to her, but a certain concomitant bedevilment was playing havoc with the essential and hard-won serenity of our psychologies. Obsessive patterns of thought and action didn't suit the personalities of either. Knowing each other was a definite impediment to our mutual pursuit of perfect serenity. It was now apparent that it was our civic duty to say goodbye and go incommunicado. No more phone calls. No more letters. No more postcards, naughty or not. My drunken midnight phone-calls served to bring the screwiness to the surface. I was tongue-tied.

As soon as she told me about the calls I remembered them. But it was a memory of an action taken under a state of extremely limited awareness. A sort of subhuman awareness, a state for which one can perhaps feel a certain amount of nostalgia no matter how shameful the actions committed while in that state may prove to have been. There are three kinds of people in penitentiaries: those who didn't do it, those who didn't figure it was wrong to do it, and those who say they were in a state of extremely limited awareness when they did it. I was the latter. It was as if a blind earthworm had picked up that phone and dialled that number. It simply wanted to hear a voice, a certain voice.

"Oh no," I said. It's not a pleasant feeling to find out that in the middle of the night you've been making drunken phone calls to a convent.

Truly, we were both happy to be getting out of each other's way in spite of the pain of a thousand little umbilical cords being torn all at once. I became giddy. She didn't. I started making pathetic jokes. She wanted us to part without saying goodbye. Let's not look in the camera. I kept forgetting and saying goodbye. Finally we walked away from each other. And didn't look back.

Now came the tough part. Learning to stop thinking about her. Learning not to say oh wait till I tell Marie-Thérèse every time a little thought popped into my mind or something interesting happened in the street. Learning all over again to rely solely on myself. Be my own audience. Learning to float again. Weaning myself from her intoxicating and highly addictive squeals of delight. It's an old story. As Pietro Metastasio says to his cruel mistress:

> *You're not always in my dreams*
> *And when I get up in the morning*
> *The first thing that pops into my mind*
> *Is often not a thought of you.*

Sainthood beckons Marie-Thérèse Ah, the manifold virtues of silence!

52. A Case of Extra-Strength Benylin

I wasn't going to weep and wail like certain people I could name. I walked into the Holiday Inn and there were the guys. They wanted to show me some graffiti in the washroom. Someone had written: "Hi fellas. I'm a member of the opposite sex and I would like to make love to you. It's true, I'm a *woman* in a *man's* washroom. Please call me at...." [My wimpy editor insists I delete the number.] And under that another hand had written: "Don't be fooled, it's a fag."

They were somewhat disappointed I didn't laugh more.

My friend Waldo Cove was visiting me once when he found out the woman he was in love with had decided to go on a Caribbean cruise with her husband. Waldo went totally out of his money, I mean his mind (what a slip!). He kept bursting into sobs and belly-flopping on the floor and bashing his head against the wall. I thought I was going to have to call in a plasterer after he left. It was such a tragedy for him but it was hard not to laugh at times, particularly when he kept saying sobbingly what beautiful nipples she had.

I'm beginning to think all the world's problems can be solved by people just individually becoming fed up with wandering around all through their lives in a somnambulistic trance and deciding to wake up, to increase their awareness of the ultra-blessed, dazzling, magic, mysterious, glorious and omnipresent moment. Maybe I always thought that but didn't know it.

Anyway, Waldo Cove never has got over that woman, and it looks as if he's never going to. He's become a deterministic down-and-out Benylin addict, a guy who goes into the all-night drugstore and says gimme a case of Benylin, the strong stuff. I tried it once just to see what it was like, to try to empathise with Waldo, and it was almost impossible to drink it's so sweet and foul-tasting. But with much nose-pinching I managed to down an entire large bottle. I turned into a cloud and drifted around the world for about twelve eternities. But when I tried to walk on the ground it was like being in the initial stages of muscular dystrophy. I thought I was in deep trouble, had suffered some irreversible nerve damage. But it passed.

In fact I think Cove's addictions have created irreversible damage to his immune system. He now has to live permanently in a hotel room in a new hotel, so sensitive is he to dog and cat dander, which he finds almost everywhere. And he has to remove his street clothes and place them in a bin outside the hotel room before entering. He is so allergic to cigarette smoke he has to chain-smoke to deaden himself. And he used to be such a brilliant poet.

"That Chesley Yarn is a real character, eh?" Nigel was saying. I was on my hands and knees inspecting the muffler of the little blood-red sports car. Sounded like a Norton 1000 straight-pipe motorcycle from World War II.

"Yeah, he sure is."

"Me and the guys thought he was really neat. I know when we get back we're all gonna rush out and buy a couple of his books. But right now we're really hungry."

"How about the Colonel?" said I.

"That's just what we were thinking," said Rodney.

"ESP," said Winston.

"Yeah," said Nigel. "I don't know how you do it."

"It's easy when you don't have an ego," said the narrator.

"Oh, that's it!" said the film crew in unison.

"You too can be just like me," said the selfless narrator. "Just get rid of your ego."

"I tried it once and didn't like it," said Nigel.

"It's not for everyone," said I.

"So, let's look for a Colonel Sanders with a Midas Muffler right next door to it, right?" said Nigel.

"How about Speedy Muffler?" said Rodney. "At Speedy you're a somebody."

Rodney was so young at the time he still believed in TV commercials. Little did we know he was destined for international fame as a cinematographer.

53. Half-Dead Rats

The Great Lakes were half-dead rats being slowly digested in the body of the great snake of the St. Lawrence River.

The Great Lakes were small oceans on the way to the sea.

The Great Lakes had a soul, and that soul, like the source of the Nile for other writers, was what I was searching for, and to find it would be to find my own soul, not just in flashes but complete.

The soul is hard to find because it lies upstream of every direction. Every soul is at the exact north pole of its universe, from where every step is a step into hell.

Small oceans on the way to the sea reminds me of the silly arguments I used to have with people in Vancouver. They're so sensitive out there. They would get indignant when I'd say there's no sense of the sea in Vancouver. It's not as much of a seaport as Hamilton, Ontario. It's just that you get great huge violent storms on the Great Lakes, they come out of nowhere. But in English Bay you hardly ever see a wave except when a power boat goes by at full speed. It's as calm as a little lake in Muskoka. There's no sense of the sea's potential for mindless indiscriminate destruction.

When you head east out of Kingston you have to turn right at the Royal Military College and head out past the army base there, past Place d'Armes and the Vimy Barracks and so on. We passed a Canadian Army officer in uniform, a black man, and I saluted as we passed. He looked astonished, and then through the rear-view mirror I saw him saluting back—just in case. Colonels sometimes drive noisy little old blood-red sports cars, eh?

Roadside motels offered "efficiency units" (?) by the day or the week on the boring ride from Kingston to Gananoque. On the left, four white donkeys were standing in a field, grazing on the dark green grass.

And there was the St. Lawrence Slaughterhouse, with an immense sign with the words BEEF PORK and a huge painting of a big white sad-looking bull with a nose ring chained to a stump.

And there in the field a cute little cow with a small udder stood licking her own flanks.

And there, over there in the thick woods, a pair of huge snakes the size of transcontinental trains and with eyes as cold as rooftop satellite dishes were about to awaken from thousand-year naps.

And there, scattered among the trees, hidden from the prosaic eye, dozens of carnivorous sabre-toothed slime-coated snails the size of Ferris wheels each sat silently at the end of a long train track of ooze.

Marie-Thérèse was obsessed with the image of Christ on the cross. She sensed that the image was a map of her own psychic condition, her own heart inside of which God is being hammered to the cross with every breath she takes. But if that was all she saw in it then she wouldn't be a nun. There was more to it. And if I felt sad, I would simply wish her happiness, in the Buddhist manner, and immediately felt better.

In Christianity the central image is the most perfect and most innocent of men suffering the most intensely agonising death imaginable. In Christianity one suffers gladly in the hope of heavenly happiness. But maybe suffering gladly is a form of earthly happiness. After all, St. Francis is famous for his joyful agony in the weeks of pitiful illness leading up to his death. Even Blake reputedly died smiling and sweetly singing psalms.

Simone Weil would say that in the midst of her immense (and self-willed) suffering she would think of Christ on the cross, suffering even greater agony and deserving it less, and she'd immediately feel better.

Buddhism always presents suffering as an illusion that can be overcome absolutely. By following the precepts anyone can become so enlightened that suffering becomes impossible.

All happiness, saith the Buddha, comes from wishing happiness for others. All misery comes from wishing happiness for oneself. Something that sounds so trite it's not worth thinking about —until you think about it.

Oh, Marie-Thérèse, I'm gonna think about you every day for the rest of my life or until I can't think any more, whichever comes first....

"Teach us to care and not to care...."

But oh, the ecstasy....

How it could have been, if only, sob, gasp....

54. The Labatt's Award for the Biggest Fish

Gananoque didn't seem to have changed much since Rudyard Kipling read his poetry there in 1903. When he was there people apologised for the name of the town and told him they were about to hold a plebiscite to change its name to something that would more accurately reflect their essentially Anglo-Saxon origins. Kipling told them to cease and desist, there were enough colonial towns with English names and it was getting kind of boring. Gananoque was a perfectly good name.

He probably wouldn't have minded if they had offered to change the name to Kipling.

Oh yes, it's true there was now a new post office, some U.S. fast-food franchises and video parlours. A bingo was being held that night at branch 92 of the Royal Canadian Legion. But the one Chinese restaurant, the Lotus Blossom, had served Kipling so long ago and hadn't changed at all, in fact in honour of this long-ago event they still had Pineapple Chicken Balls à la Kipling on the menu.

A couple of weeks earlier I'd gone into a kitchenware specialty store on Yonge Street below King to buy a teapot and got into a long conversation about food with the somewhat naive saleswoman. It was her first week in the big city and she had just discovered food. She wanted to know all about Japanese food, for instance, which she hadn't yet tasted.

She'd just moved from Gananoque and hadn't had a chance to try all the new kinds of restaurants. I asked her what she did in Gananoque. She said she'd worked in Andy's Sport Shop.

And there it was, on the north side of the main drag—Andy's Sport Shop, with a sign saying FISHING FIREWORKS SPORTSWEAR.

I asked her why she'd moved to Toronto. She said her father had died. "Oh, I'm sorry."

"No, it's all right; he was *really* sick"—said in such a way you wouldn't want to ask what he had.

"Did he live in Toronto?"

"No, in Gananoque."

She didn't offer anything further. I think she thought I thought she was stupid because she'd never tasted sushi. But she didn't seem stupid. There seemed to be a good story there in the death of her father but it wasn't the time or place to pump her about it.

And so I didn't. Now, I parked the car and strolled down the main drag of Gan, as it's known in the area. Past Heritage Corner where there was a large hand-painted sign proclaiming all the winners, through the years, of the Labatt's award, presented annually for the prize musky caught among the islands of the St. Lawrence River. Most of the muskies listed were between twenty and forty-six pounds, any of which would provide a battle with light freshwater lines and all. But in September 1957, a certain A. Lawton, of Delmar, New York, caught a musky weighing 69.15 pounds. A world record. I made a note to check out Delmar and if it weren't too far out of the way maybe try to look up Mr. Lawton. And if he were still alive he'd have perfect recall, naturally, of the day he caught that fish. It'd be up over the mantel and the film crew could film him.

There was something strange about these small Southern Ontario towns. For instance I walked into D.T.'s smoke shop and there were three grown men, all in their thirties, leaning against the counter and watching Casper the Friendly Ghost cartoons with serious intent on a tiny black-and-white television set. That woman in the kitchen-specialty store in Toronto, her name was Trudy. She was very tall, about six feet, thin and pale-looking. She and her brother were going around trying all the different restaurants from different nationalities but they hadn't reached Japanese yet. "In Gananoque there's one Chinese restaurant in town," she said, "and we make a big deal out of that."

I went to the bank to change my money to U.S. U.S. tourists, they don't bother changing their money when they visit other countries. In Toronto you often see them making a fuss because restaurants only give them 20 per cent on their money. And so they run up a huge bill and don't leave a tip, causing staff to tear their hair out in anguish and perhaps even to retire prematurely, or at least to become ill and have to take a break whenever they spot a group of U.S. tourists marching in.

The Toronto-Dominion bank was crowded, huge line-ups at every wicket. I stood at the end of the line but it didn't seem to be moving at all. In front of me a well-groomed young man with very pink cheeks was telling his friend that he had just sent his big fat manuscript of poetry to Talonbooks for publication. "It's in Vancouver," he said. "I heard they publish poetry but I haven't seen any of their books."

The line still hadn't moved. I looked out the window. Across the street the Bank of Montreal was empty. I went over and bought $300 U.S. for $400 Canadian.

"How come," I said to the teller, "there are no customers in here but the bank across the street is full of customers?"

"We had 'em before," she replied. She said it very clearly. That's exactly what she said. I had no idea what she meant.

I smiled. "What do you mean?" I said.

"We had 'em before," she said.

"Oh," I replied politely. "I see. You had 'em before."

"That's right."

55. An Essay on Death

Just before turning the bend and crossing the bridge into the main part of Gananoque we passed Le Temps Perdu. Trudy from Gananoque hadn't mentioned it. The guys in the film crew had been working hard and decided they wanted a good meal (maybe it was Elsie Yarn's influence) so now we had parked the car somewhere and were walking back across the bridge. A guy was walking toward us.

"Could you tell us what would be the best restaurant in town?" said Nigel. He'd stopped the guy in the middle of the bridge, and he was expecting him to say Le Temps Perdu.

The guy looked as if he might be a cook there. He looked as if he knew a thing or two about food and possibly about other things as well. In fact, he was wearing a black beret.

The guy's reply was instantaneous: "Clark's," he said. He told us to head back. We were a little surprised. "Just around the comer on the right."

"Better than Le Temps Perdu?" we said in unison.

"Better than what?"

"The French restaurant down this way?" said Rodney.

"Oh, that," said the guy. "Well, Clark's is more home cooking, soup and all that. At that French one you just pay for something you don't get."

"That makes sense," we all said, again in unison (exclusive of Nigel).

"Sort of," added Nigel.

When we got to where he'd indicated, there was a restaurant all right but it was called the Maple Leaf not Clark's. Home-Cooked Meals. A kid was going by. We called him over. He was a tough-looking little bugger. Long greasy hair. Long greasy fingernails. Smoking a long greasy cigarette.

"I say there, young feller," said Rodney. "Could you tell us where Clark's Restaurant might be?"

"Right fuckin' here, man."

"But it says Maple Leaf."

"I don't care what the fuck it says. It's fuckin' Clark's."

We went in but we still weren't sure. This was not a pretentious restaurant. People were sitting around eating reconstituted french fries with canned gravy and sipping chocolate milk out of little cartons. Canadian cuisine. The waitress was smiling at us as we stood there looking around. She was wondering why we weren't sitting down.

"Can you tell us where Clark's Restaurant might be?"

"This used to be Clark's," she said. "It's changed owners but everybody in town still calls it Clark's." The cook in the back was opening cans of home-made soup and licking his fingers.

So we grabbed a table and sat there looking at menus, and as sometimes happens just before eating, we started talking about unsavoury things. The guys really didn't want to be there but they were too tired and hungry to bother suggesting we head back to Le Temps Perdu. Sometimes four smart people together are dumber than one.

Winston wanted to talk about cats. This guy he knew was bothered by cats at night. He kept phoning the SPCA but they wouldn't do anything. So he got a raccoon trap. Whenever he caught a cat it'd just snarl and almost go crazy. The first one he caught he pulled it out of the trap and drove it to the SPCA to have it put down. But the cat just went crazy in the car, pounced on him and started clawing. He drove off the road and hit a tree. After that whenever he caught one he'd just take it trap and all to the SPCA. Let them take it out.

"Darn right," said Rodney.

"He shoulda done it the first time," said Nigel.

I told them about my childhood friend Brent Bentley. He was a bird-watcher and, with perfect adolescent logic, hated cats because they killed birds. So he used to shoot them with his twenty-two. Shot hundreds of them. Skinned them, saved their pelts. He was only about thirteen. One day he climbed a high-tension tower and pissed on the wires. "Hey it fizzles," he yelled. Those were his last words. He came down in a ball of flame. Big story on page one the next day.

Nigel and the boys liked that one so I told them one my dad had told me. Dad was sixteen and his best friend was a guy named Woodrow Wilson. It was the Depression and when you were sixteen you had to quit school and get a job. My dad worked at Stelco and Woodrow worked at Wallace Barnes. They took their jobs very seriously. Now Woodrow was a highly conscientious lad, and one night after supper he remembered something at work he hadn't done and he was so worried about it he tried to get into the office but it was all locked up. So he climbed up a pole to see if he could get in through the window. He lost his footing and grabbed onto a power line to stop his fall. Took thirty thousand volts and was killed.

And after Woodrow Wilson died, his dad used to call my dad over to play games in the front room, the games the father used to play with Woodrow. I'd ask my dad, suspiciously, what kind of games? And he'd say oh just little board games like snakes and ladders and stuff like that. Chinese Chequers. Crokinole. Parcheesi. Rummoli. Dad used to go, but finally stopped after a while because after playing for a while Mr. Wilson would start crying and my dad felt uncomfortable. Dad said it never occurred to Mr. Wilson to sue Wallace Barnes.

"That's real sad," said Rodney.

"I bet there'd be a big lawsuit if that happened today," said Winston.

Nigel started talking about the little funeral he had for his cat. Buried him in the back yard and next to the grave he planted a rose plant, a clipping from a bonzai tree, and a marijuana plant. How did it die?

"You sure you want to know this?"

"Yeah, tell us, tell us."

"Okay then. You asked for it. It was a cold day and I parked my car in the driveway and he must have crawled up inside the engine to keep warm...."

"Say no more," we all said, except for Rodney. He wanted to know what happened.

"I turned on the engine, like not knowing the cat was inside? And like his tail must have got caught in the fan belt. He got all ripped to hell. I had to gather him up piece by piece in order to bury him."

Rodney said his sister once went through five guinea pigs in two weeks. One ate an azalea plant and died. The other four were found one morning neatly dissected in the back yard with their vital organs removed, like cattle on the western plains. Tiny flying saucers had been sighted in the neighbourhood that night.

Winston said he stepped on a bunny once.

"Kill 'im?" said Rodney.

"Yeah, he died in agony."

But Rodney had one a lot better than that. He had a budgie that every once in a while would fly in a pathetic little flight path around the room. One time he made a navigational error and flew right into a pot of boiling water.

"Was it an old budgie?" I said.

"It was getting on."

"Well, I know a thing or two about budgies," I said. "We used to have them when I was a kid. In fact one time my mother stepped on one. Its eyes went shooting across the room like little bee bees from an air rifle. Poor mom fainted and hit her head on the floor. And I'd say based on my experience with budgies that that budgie of yours didn't make a navigational error at all...."

"You mean?..."

"Afraid so. Sounds like suicide to me."

56. The Quiet Little People Who Control the Weather

There were three guys sitting at a corner table by the window. They were smoking cigarettes and drinking beer and having an animated conversation. A couple of times I heard New Zealand being mentioned, and so I found myself straining to listen, without showing it, because the night before I'd had a vivid dream about New Zealand. I'd been in a train going down the length of the country, and I could see the ocean churning in on both sides, out of either window, one perfect wave after another, in that special kind of high colour and that special kind of beauty you only glimpse in deep dreams. The sky was as blue as the inside of a giant Ukrainian Easter egg sitting in a chimney nest on a sunny day, and out on the horizon were strange living islands, breathing mountains rising out of the sea, sponge-like, expanding and contracting, with a small cloud touching each peak, and long narrow waterfalls cascading a thousand feet into the sea. We passed through beautiful villages, mythical and timeless, and then the members of a rock group called Wham climbed aboard. There was a group called Wham in real life but I knew nothing about them, except that Marie-Thérèse had told me recently that a man had sat next to her on the Metro in Montreal, introduced himself, in English, and said he was a member of Wham.

One of the musicians stood on a chair, popped a bottle of champagne, and poured the contents on my head. "You can get more smashed on the glasses than you can on the wine," I said, and somehow I thought that was incredibly witty, and I said "Write that down," and one of the musicians said "Don't worry, I'll remember it." And then everything exploded and I was floating through a heavenly sky of golden clouds and rainbows of light, with beautiful music everywhere, and stern god-like voices coming at me from all directions saying: "Quit smoking, quit smoking…." I was so alarmed I woke up, reached for my bedside pack and crunched it up and threw it in the garbage. Almost full pack too.

And then a woman came into the restaurant, a tall thin woman in her forties. She was very attractive, and she looked a little confused. Bare feet. I'd seen her earlier in a pharmacy down the street. She had been standing in front of the mirror in the cosmetics department trying on different sample lipsticks and makeup and giggling gleefully. She was nutty as Noah's Ark.

She stood there shyly at the front of the restaurant, as if this were the kind of place where you were led to your table by a maitre d'. I felt suddenly sorry for her and asked her to come and join us for a coffee.

Almost immediately she started talking about New Zealand. I was alarmed.

She thanked us for inviting her over, and said she'd been afraid she wouldn't have been served otherwise, because the people here didn't like her, she used to be married to the man who owned this restaurant. Not married in the legal sense, she said. Spiritually married.

"Those spiritual marriages, they don't last," said Rodney.

We all laughed.

She said there had been a news blackout but last night at midnight New Zealand had been all but destroyed in a massive earthquake.

She was wearing a straw hat festooned with fresh violets and pansies. Faded blue jeans with knee-holes, a pretty blouse, an over-sized man's maroon suit jacket, and she carried a pair of skimpy sandals in one hand. She looked a little like the actress Jackie Burroughs, though a somewhat more etherealised version and with yellow teeth.

Could it be true about New Zealand? Was that what the men in the corner had been talking about? I became disoriented. These coincidences were getting out of hand. They were going to drive me bonkers. For a moment I was convinced some horrible disaster had befallen New Zealand. And what about the reverberations and tidal waves resulting from an earthquake great enough to destroy an entire country? How many people had been killed? How many more people were to be killed? And where was the next giant quake going to strike?

But if there had been a news blackout, how did she find out about it? I didn't get a chance to ask because for the next forty minutes or so she talked non-stop. I soon realised it was just another ordinary coincidence that the guys in the corner had been talking about New Zealand when she came in and announced that New Zealand had been destroyed, and that I had had that dream about New Zealand last night.

"A plate lifted right out of the sea," she said.

"A plate?" said Rodney. He pointed at his plate of chips and gravy.

"Yes, a continental plate."

Forty minutes of formless freeform monologue followed, a one-way rap based on forty years of dwelling in an intellectual wilderness, in a plastic bubble where nothing anyone can say can make any difference. As for New Zealand, people all over the world, people who belonged to a sort of secret society and who were in psychic communion, the forces of light you might say, had known that New Zealand was to have been destroyed. And they had been praying that it wouldn't happen, but it did.

"It had to happen," she said, solemnly, with a blank face and a lifeless sort of eye contact, as if she was unconscious and in a state of possession. "It was for political reasons."

She spoke sweetly, softly, even though her visions were mind-numbingly paranoid. Hitler was a saint. He had had a twin brother who had died.

"Not everybody has to take acid but everybody has to die," she said. She spoke a lot about Jews and Hebrews. It was never Jews, it was always Jews and Hebrews, and they were out to destroy the world. New Zealand was just the beginning. Vancouver was about to be invaded by the Israeli army, composed of Jews and Hebrews, led by Queen Aereorarara or something like that, from New Zealand. The people who lived in British Columbia before the formation of the mountains and in Ontario before the creation of the Great Lakes were quiet, gentle people. They could fly, they were omniscient, they could control the weather. And so on.

One day recently, say about thirty years ago, she had been walking through Yorkville in Toronto with Peter, Paul and Mary. She told Mary she had been noting lately that there were no men her age. She asked Mary where have all the young men gone. It turned out they were all in Flanders Fields. Then Mary wrote a song with that line in it. Ripped her right off, but that was okay. A little acknowledgment would be nice, though.

We asked her what her name was and she rattled off a whole bunch of names.

"All those names, they're all me," she said. There were a lot of laboratory clones of her running around. People had taps on her brain.

After she left the four of us just stared at each other. Nigel decided she had been suffering from severe unhappiness and loneliness all her life. "It was like everything she said was all a way of dealing with her severe unhappiness and loneliness," he said.

No one could add anything to that.

Except I said you had to sympathise with her because she in her fashion was more concerned about the fate of the human race than she was about her own fate.

And maybe that was her problem. Maybe that was the lesson she was unintentionally offering everyone who listened to her. Your own personal pain, the little problems of your own little life, have to take priority over everything—or else you're liable to be swept away in a sea of insanity. A friend of mine took LSD and went through extreme agony for several hours pacing the floor and holding his head and smashing his fist into the wall as he tried desperately not to think about O. J. Simpson. He had become somehow convinced that if he thought about O. J. Simpson, even for a moment, the whole world would be destroyed in a great global fireball. By the next day he was fine again.

57. The Fireside Reading Club

We decided the restaurant should be filmed: our nutty friend with the straw hat and bare feet, the little vacant pool room in the rear, and the people sitting around gorging themselves. In the corner four little kids were slurping down soggy potato chips from a bowl filled with Pepsi-Cola while mom and dad wolfed down grilled cheese sandwiches with ketchup and hot chocolate. Mom and dad looked so terribly young and weary and were surrounded by an aura of poverty and despair. And so the guys asked permission to film the diners, and, permission granted, shot away. While I stood outside and watched a small convoy of white clouds steaming by in the celestial realms above.

Also sailing in the sky was a crescent moon. When the weary family came out I couldn't resist saying to them: "Oh look, it's daytime and the moon is shining." They all looked up and then turned to look at each other and they all started smiling. It was a little miracle.

Gananoque had been a magic spot for me ever since grade 12 or so when I answered an ad in the paper and found myself part of a crooked door-to-door magazine and encyclopaedia sales team. I think it was called the Fireside Reading Club, and we headed for Gananoque. It was embarrassing to remember now although at the time I thought I was doing the right thing somehow and it seemed like a great adventure in the glorious summertime. We stayed in a tourist home on the east side of town, but we couldn't sell anything, quickly ran out of money, and ended up sleeping in a park on a high bluff overlooking the river. At dawn, with the others snoring in the car, I walked through thick mist and watched it gradually rise until the tiny green islands far below began to emerge and become visible like themes in a Beethoven symphony. The other guys had been talking about robbing a gas station (the crew leader, a guy named Rolf Wintergreen, subsequently became involved in a stolen-car scam and spent some time in prison, only later to become a Mafia hit man, a true-to-life professional assassin) and so I summoned up the little nobility I possessed, left the crew sleeping there, and hitchhiked down to the Maritimes where I got a job in a travelling carnival for the rest of the summer.

58. The Brothers Karamazov

The St. Lawrence River was full of dark islands, the red light from the setting sun turning the water silver. We were heading over the Thousand Islands Bridge. I pulled up at customs and the officer wanted to know the usual: where I was going and why and did I have any oranges. I told him I was just making a trip around Lake Ontario to gather impressions for a little book I was doing. As I said "around Lake Ontario" I made a little unconscious circular motion with my finger which Winston, from his perch atop the blue van behind me, caught on his camera. Looks funny on film.

The inspector, an old guy about to retire, asked me to pull over and go into the office. When I got inside the film crew was unloading all their equipment for inspection.

"Why didn't you tell me you were part of a film crew?" said the inspector. He looked as if I'd hurt his feelings.

"I wanted to keep it simple," I said, which was true. Had he read *The Brothers Karamazov*? He said he hadn't got around to it although he'd been meaning to. I said there was a character in that book who committed suicide because he found himself incapable of simplifying his life. The officer nodded. He said that was interesting and he'd read the book for sure now.

59. Dead Sailors

Things were getting a little tense. It looked as if we were in for a long wait at customs. Every little piece of film equipment had to be inspected. Nobody on duty knew quite what to do. They didn't want to let us in if we were going to be taking work away from U.S.-born filmmakers. They were phoning all over the place for rulings.

Red-haired Rodney had a big grin on his face. He knew I liked funny signs. "Did you see that sign just before we got onto the bridge? It said Thousand Village Island. I think it meant Thousand Island Village, a sort of housing development, but the way they had it printed up, so artistically and all, with Village in the middle in big printing, and Thousand above it in smaller printing, and Island below it, like, in smaller printing too, it looked like Thousand Village Island. Hee hee, eh?"

The customs officials seemed impressed with the equipment the guys were bringing in and piling up on the floor and counter, and they also seemed quite pleased with how well the equipment was itemised. Total value of the equipment came to $66,720, at a rental of $2,500 a week. The camera itself was an Aaton 10-millimetre B41 made in France and valued at $20,000. There were ten lenses worth a total of $20,000, and a Cook 950mm zoom lens, made in England, worth $10,000. There was the Nagra II recorder, made in Switzerland, value $4,000, and three Aaton M327 magazines at $2,500 each.

Nigel was behaving professionally, calm and patient. He pulled out his copy of some old book of mine and handed it to them.

"Here, take a look at this, it'll help you to visualise the sort of work we're doing, the sort of trip we're on."

One of the officers grabbed it and flipped it open. "Hey," he said. "I just opened this book to a chapter called 'Bruce Vomits in My Hat.' He must have friends like the people who work here!"

"Bruce was his dog," said Nigel, "now deceased."

"Oh, I'm sorry."

"That's okay."

The customs officer grilling me was Claude Beausoleil, and I asked if he'd heard of the Quebec poet by the same name. He said he never had but he'd check it out, maybe even before reading *The Brothers Karamazov*. He just looked like an ordinary large-size American customs inspector, with his gun and blond hair and big lazy relaxed American face, nothing French about him but the name. He said his nickname was Big Bird.

"Le Grand Oiseau just doesn't have that ring to it," he said.

He showed me his bullets, special "anti-personnel bullets for shooting a guy without it going through him and killing some innocent person behind him."

"They used to be called dumdum bullets," I said. They were spread all over the counter but I didn't want to touch them.

"Yeah, but that was a long time ago during World War II or something. Now we call 'em anti-personnel bullets."

"They sort of explode inside you, right? Not considered very sporting."

"No, they're not sporting at all. But it's better than killing innocent people."

"Heck, anything's better than that."

When Claude Beausoleil said we had to go to Sackett's Harbour I thought he meant as part of the customs procedure, but no he meant as part of the trip. His voice became soft.

"It's really beautiful and historic, you'll love it, you'll want to write lots about it." I imagined a harbour full of sailboats and crowds of tourists, expensive gift shops and macrobiotic restaurants, a lively place. He suggested I contact Pat Wilder, he'd tell me all about the history of the area, give me lots of good stuff for the book. "He's a good guy to have a beer with."

Claude Beausoleil got excited about me being from Hamilton and said he was part of a group of American history buffs who were trying to get the remains of U.S. sailors back to the U.S., to bury them in good old American soil. The remains had been found a couple of years ago in the twin wreckages of two ships, the *Hamilton* and the *Scourge*, in Lake Ontario, off Grimsby, which was near Hamilton, by somebody who had been out fishing for perch, some Grimsby businessman trying to relax for the weekend. He was an Armenian rug merchant actually. The same rug merchant who had come to my school a thousand years ago, when I was in grade 2, and showed us slides of his last trip to Armenia. We were impressed! He was a good guy. I insisted mother and father buy their next carpet from him.

The *Hamilton* had been stolen from the Canadians and was manned by American sailors in the War of 1812. It was just a coincidence the *Hamilton* was sunk near Hamilton, said Claude Beausoleil. Its Canadian name was something else, he forgot what. When the Americans stole it they decided to name it after Paul Hamilton, the American secretary of the navy at the time.

"The Canadians want to keep both ships, and they have a legal right to them at this point as far as we can see. We just want the remains of the dead sailors returned." I told him I'd write a letter on his behalf.

Beausoleil was saying his group went up to Toronto periodically to put on historical re-enactments. They would take their uniforms and old muskets, and they would go up in buses and drink bourbon and Budweiser all the way, yelling and screaming. And when they got there they would soberly reenact the sacking of York for the tourists. Did they get into arguments with the Canadian history buffs about their particular interpretation of history?

"Oh yeah, we argue about all that stuff all the time," he said. "We thought in those days that if we came up to Canada the Canadians would be glad to join us, throw off British rule."

"Something like Nicaragua, right?"

"Hm," he said. He looked worried and puzzled. "Hm. No, not quite."

Nigel later took a shot of Beausoleil, with his camera that is, and when Nigel asked him to sign a release form he did right away, without any fuss.

"This is the second time I've signed a release form," he said. "You ever heard of Vanessa Williams?"

"Vanessa Williams? You bet we have," said Nigel, and Winston and Rodney came strolling over. Turns out Vanessa Williams was the one who lost her title as Miss America.

"She was Miss America then," said Beausoleil, "before the scandal that is, and she came all the way up here from New York or wherever to promote the Thousand Islands Festival. She was getting paid for it. And we're talking big bucks. So there she was sitting on my shoulders with her legs around my neck, for a TV commercial. It was shown all summer. I loved it but boy, did I ever get teased."

"Oooh, yeah. I bet you did."

"Yeah, everybody saw it. Then when the *Penthouse* thing came out, you know, all those pictures of her making love with another woman, the teasing became just absolutely unmerciful. But it didn't bother me. In fact I kind of liked it."

"Did you really think she was making love to that other woman or was it all just fake, posed for the money?"

"I'd go with the latter interpretation. After all, I know I'm a customs agent and all, and loyal to my country, but this is the Land of Take the Money and Run."

"Did you write her and tell her you figured she got a raw deal?"

"Yeah, as a matter of fact, I did."

Another customs official was posing for Nigel's camera. His name was Inspector Larry Carr. He kept trying not to smile, to look stern and official.

"This is not what I do for a living," he said. "I usually pick on bad guys. In the film you can bill me as the idiot who let you smuggle all that cocaine into the States."

"What?" I said. "Do we look like dope smugglers?"

"Yeah," he said. "You do a little."

60. Sensory Crossover

I'm driving through the night in rain and fog, on the Interstate 81. The darkness is unbearable, and then my headlights fade out and my windshield wipers seize up. As if that's not enough it seems I've missed the Watertown cutoff. I can't see anything but danger ahead, and I can't get the car going at any kind of speed, it seems to be faltering. Muscle cars full of teenagers coming home from the big prom pass me and cut in, with kids hanging out the window with almost-empty bottles of bourbon in their hands and jeering at me, screaming at me to get a real car, and frightening me terribly. I look out the rear-view mirror to see if the big blue van is still safely behind me but a much bigger transport truck loaded down with eight brand-new blue vans, each with a brand-new little film crew in it, is right on my tail, lights on extra-high beam and horns honking to get by. Finally I notice the sign for the Watertown cutoff but it's too late and I've passed it. And now the engine is roaring but there's no power getting through. The clutch has definitely gone. I coast to a stop at the side of the road. The clutch has broken down for no reason at all except that its time had come to die, and I wish it were my time to die as well. I calmly coast to a stop at the side of the road in thick wet dark grass and mud. I pull off as far as I can without turning over in the ditch. In the pouring rain and heavy mist, I can't see anything but headlight beams. I tried to put the top up to keep the interior from getting even more soaked than it already was, and also with the ridiculous idea it would make the car more secure from vandals and thieves in my absence. But I became blinded by the headlights of passing cars and the top wouldn't come up properly. Lucky no one was filming this.

We were supposed to meet at the Holiday Inn in Watertown, New York. The film crew would probably be there right now wondering where the heck I was. I better start walking into town. Nobody would stop on a night like this. But I stuck my thumb out anyway....

The first car to go by pulled over, a little old-fashioned Citroen from the forties. The driver was sympathetic to a fault, agreed to drive me way out of his way back into Watertown, even though he'd just left Watertown on his way home to the town of Adams, five miles to the south. He makes an exit, gets back on the Interstate driving north, then off the Interstate and into Watertown. He quietly tells me he's lonely because his wife and kids went to Ireland for a month, leaving him all alone in the big sad lonely house—first time alone in his life. All his friends are inviting him to their places for dinner, a different friend each night because he can't cook for himself. "Oh, I can cook but it's just so depressing," he says. His wife originally came from Ireland and she took the kids home for her first visit in ten years. She hadn't seen her parents in ten years and they'd never met the kids. I had the feeling he wanted me to come home and sleep over.

"Why didn't you go with them?"

"I couldn't afford to take the time off work. I'm working really hard right now, we're really busy, we really are, I mean it, boy are we busy, whew, it's really something."

"Really busy, eh?"

"Oh, yeah! Incredible!"

"I see. What do you do by the way, just out of curiosity?"

"I work in a manufacturing plant."

"What do you manufacture?"

A Fluke transport truck passed by. He read the sign out loud: "Fluke Transport—if it gets there it's a fluke."

"Oh dear. Where were we now? What do we manufacture? You know those plastic swizzle sticks you get when you order a cocktail in a better class of bar? We make 'em. Our swizzle sticks go all over the world, well the free world anyway."

We pulled up at the Holiday Inn and there was the blue van. The guys would be in the lobby, worrying about me. My new friend and benefactor was a very nice man. He wished me well. He shook my hand. His name was Mike Carmichael and he had a small moustache. Thanks, Mike. Hope your family got back from Ireland okay. Every time I see a swizzle stick I'll remember you and your kindness. And I'll remember your father whom I was to meet in a few days by some kind of cosmic fluke.

So the guys were in the lobby, playing pinball and video games, nervously sipping soda pop, nibbling on potato chips, worrying about little old me. There were no vacancies in the hotel, and the guys hadn't booked anywhere yet.

"Oh, I thought we'd missed you for sure, that we'd never catch up with each other," said Nigel.

We had a little conference and decided the best thing to do before anything was to get the car off the Interstate before somebody ploughed into it in the mist and rain, squashing that little Spitfire like a Sandinista first-aid station. So I phoned the state troopers from the hotel lobby. Maybe they'd have their own tow trucks, or maybe they'd recommend a towing firm. A male voice answered.

"Trooper Cooper," he said.

"Trooper Cooper?"

"Yes? Can I help you?"

Nigel and the guys started smiling.

I told him about the breakdown. He said it was very clever of us to want to give top priority to removing the car from the Interstate, but he didn't want to help at all beyond suggesting that we call Cheeseman's Wrecker and giving me the number. He also suggested we stay at the Stars and Stripes Motel and he gave the directions to get there.

"Thanks," I said. "By the way, I know a Judge Mudge."

"Funny."

So we called Cheeseman's Wrecker, and a few minutes later a mammoth scary-looking bear of a guy with a long cigar picked me up at the Holiday Inn. We went out to pick up the car, towed it in to his garage, and he drove me back to the hotel. He said his name was Tommy Cheeseman.

He'd have a look at the car in the morning and we should come down and authorise whatever repairs were needed. I got in the van with the guys and we went on a long drive all around Watertown and suburbs looking for the Stars and Stripes Motel. The guys had already phoned and made reservations for four rooms, so we had to find it. We had to keep stopping to ask directions from passers-by and everybody seemed dazed. They knew how to get there but they couldn't explain. Giving directions is not a highly prized art in these parts.

But we finally made it, unpacked our stuff, washed up a bit, put on our ties and brushed our hair, then walked in the cool October night air to the Oriental Village Restaurant down the road a bit, a dark rural two-lane highway, for something to eat.

"You'd have to have a lot of nerve to go up to that guy and tell him he was smoking in a non-smoking area," said Nigel.

"Give me asthma any day," wheezed Winston, jokingly.

"What was his name?" said Nigel.

"Tommy Cheeseman," I said. "We'll see him in the morning."

"Hope it's not before," said Rodney.

There were two Chinese guys at the bar of the Oriental Village, and one white guy, all drinking beer and staring blankly at the TV. Coincidentally, there was a Chinese movie on, with subtitles. The waitress was white American. We asked how long she'd worked there and if she'd managed to pick up any Chinese, the language that is. She looked like Ethel Mertz from the *I Love Lucy* show.

"Just a few words," she said. "Now, that's Mr. Lin up there watching TV, he's the boss. They have a different slang in different parts of China, that's why they use Cantonese subtitles, they want to unite the people."

"Who can blame 'em for that, eh?"

The guys were giving the movie the professional eye.

"Lots of zoom shots, eh?" said red-haired Rodney, who was a touch younger than the other guys, in fact was fresh out of college, and was always subtly trying to impress them and win points for his comic insight, film knowledge, and maturity. "That's the Sergio Leone school of zoom technique." The laughter encouraged him. "Yeah, I watched a sort of mythological musical from India once and they really went in for the zoom shots. About thirty zoom shots a minute."

Everyone became lost in thought. Silence prevailed.

"Thirty a minute!" repeated Rodney. "That's a lot!"

The Chinese movie was full of utterly stupid violence, and every few minutes somebody would get his head punched in, usually the nice guy. And we had the additional benefit of being able to hear Mr. Lin explaining the action to the white guy at the bar.

"He beat him up, he make him bad," said Mr. Lin, sort of a Chinese Jay Scott.

The white guy would nod politely and sip at his beer.

All through our meal there'd be the periodic sound of vomiting coming from the television.

"Classic kung fu sound editing," said Rodney.

"Except there's no kung fu."

"Oh yeah, I wonder why not."

"Real cheap budget."

That reminded him. "By the way," said Rodney, "are we still planning to rent a plane to get some aerial views of Dave in the car?"

Nigel cleared his throat as if he had bad news to deliver, and would have preferred not to deliver it at that moment.

"Well, it all depends on what's the matter with the car, eh? If it just needs a new spark plug, okay, we'll get the plane."

Instead of a wine list we got a list of bizarre pseudo-Polynesian drinks, but there was no indication of the ingredients in any of them. One was called the Suffering Bastard—"a different drink but one with many ardent disciples." That was my favourite. But I also liked Mount Fuji—"named after the goddess of the volcanoes, this drink captures her awesome powers." There was also the Navy Grog—"eight separate ingredients go into making this popular concoction."

I had the feeling all these drinks were the same. Whichever one you ordered you got the same drink. So I put it to the waitress.

"No, not at all," she said. She looked as if I'd personally insulted her integrity, but it turned out I was at least half right.

"They all have different mixtures of juices," she said, "but they're all rum-based."

An inexplicable but nevertheless overwhelming desire for a martini struck me so I asked for one. When it came it was red. I thought at first it was just a reflection of the red velvet wallpaper but it tasted funny too, it tasted kind of...red.

The waitress conferred with the bartender. They'd never been asked for a martini before, as it happened, and they'd had to look it up in the book. They didn't have any white vermouth so they thought red would pretty well be the same.

It was as if I had been born for that moment, as I stared at the red martini, to be sitting in that Chinese restaurant in Watertown, New York, complaining about my martini, in a world of earthquakes, famines and wars. As if the whole universe had been created just for that moment.

Rodney had been deep in thought for several lengthy minutes. "People who are born blind must have a remote concept of sight," he finally blurted out. And he started talking about a book he'd read years before, about a guy who had a photographic memory. *The Mind of a Mnemonist* by A. R. Luria, a translation of a Russian book, was in the library at Ryerson where he'd been a film student. "This guy, he put on shows. Someone in the audience would call out a six-digit number, see? And then someone else would do the same. Until about a hundred six-digit numbers had been called out. Then he'd go to the blackboard and write them all out."

"From memory?"

"Yeah, from just hearing them once."

"Wow!"

"But that's not all. He could recall them exactly if you asked him about it ten or fifteen years later."

"Gee. Wow! This was actually in a book, eh?"

"And he also had this thing they called sensory crossover, right? He would hear things you're supposed to see, or even taste things you're supposed to hear. Like he might be walking down the street and see a fence, and say 'My, that fence tastes very briny.'"

"Don't they call those people polymodal synaesthetes?" I said, causing the guys to regard me with renewed respect.

"Something like that," said Rodney.

"I think Vladimir Nabokov was a little bit like that. It's very rare. If you were a true polymodal aesthete, you might perceive colours coming out of your stereo rather than music."

"Don't say anything," said Nigel, when Rodney had excused himself to go to the john, "but this is about the fourth time we've heard him talk about that book, wouldn't you say, Winston?"

"Oh, at least four."

"Yeah, he talks about it every chance he gets," said Nigel. "I think it must be about the only book he's ever read."

"Well, all the way through anyway," said Winston.

SATURDAY, OCTOBER 13

61. Nigger Shoes

I was lying in bed with my eyes closed. There were voices outside. I was listening to them and worrying about the book I was supposed to be writing. It occurred to me I should be listening more and talking less. It must have been about nine-thirty.

"Nobody's waited on him for the past fifteen years and now he wants service," said a woman's voice outside the window of my little motel room. "I have to take him this orange juice."

"Let him wait," said the first man.

"But he wants to wear his snakes," said the woman. Or that's what it sounded like.

"I just got home a little while ago," said the second male voice. "I threw her out last night."

"She's mad at you," said the first man. "Go after her."

Second male: "I got nothing on my feet. Where's my snakes?"

First male: "They're nigger shoes."

Second male: "Here's the paper. Let her read the paper."

62. Ella Mae Hopkins in the Flesh

She was almost as big as (though much older than) Ella Mae Hopkins in Leon Rooke's *Fat Woman*. She was a huge woman with a fine thin long nose, sparkling pepper-grey hair, magnetic deep brown eyes. She was the proprietress of the motel. She seemed easy to talk to. We started telling her about the problems at the border, at least Nigel did. I told Nigel he should write an article for the *Canadian Forum* about all the things that had happened at customs.

Woody Allen's *Sleeper* was on the TV, a small black-and-white set sitting up on a ledge behind us in the motel office. Nigel said the border officials at first didn't want to let us in because they were afraid we were taking jobs away from American cameramen. We could hear someone snoring in the other room.

"I think there should be friendly relations between the countries," said the woman. "We go up there and take your jobs, don't we? Look at all the draft dodgers from the States up there. But but but don't tell my son about it though. He's a real flag-waver. Enlisted in the navy seventeen years ago, the fuckin' idiot. He's a chief petty officer now, served in Vietnam. He's a real patriotic flag-waving Reaganite and he doesn't like to hear about draft-dodgers, or about Canadian cameramen coming down here and making movies. He's liable to lose his temper. And when he loses his temper look out baby."

"Why are women so much smarter than men generally?" I said to Nigel, when Ella Mae went to the washroom.

"I don't know but it is true. She is smart, that's for sure. She's probably the smartest American we've met on this trip. She reminds me of Elsie Yarn."

"I knew you were still thinking about her."

"Oh yeah, she was something else. That Chesley is a lucky guy."

Ella Mae came back. She seemed glad to have someone to talk to, really talk to, someone who would understand her late-life angst.

"I'm in my late sixties," she said. "I was sitting in my rocking chair just a-looking out the window watching the cars go by in the winter, and in the back yard a-watching the clouds go by in the summer. Then my son bought this place and insisted I come and run it for him. He's divorced. I have to take care of his kids. His fifteen-year-old son has to catch the school bus at ten minutes after seven every morning, and is he hard to wake up! He's 250 pounds, plays on the high-school football team. The coach makes him run if he does something wrong, misses a pass or something. Run around the park four times in full gear or something like that. And he's so lazy. He comes home and says I hate that sonofabitch of a coach. I'm gonna kill him one of these days."

"Whew!"

"Yeah. He just might too. Don't be so lazy, I tell him."

There was a colour photo of Ronald Reagan on the wall, and it was signed, "Thanks for your help." The woman seemed embarrassed when we mentioned it.

"Hey, it's Ronny Robot," said Nigel. "Shh," I said.

"Oh that's all right," said the woman. "I call him worse than that—but not when my son's around."

63. Herd of Zebras Trample Crippled Boy

The lead paragraph of the main story of *World Weekly News*: "Two weeks after her teenage son killed himself to give his family one less mouth to feed, an impoverished mom learned her child's tragic death was totally in vain—because she had $1,500 in the bank she didn't know about!"

"Take it," said Ella Mae. "It's my son's and I think he's read it. He mostly just looks at the pictures anyway. Not much of a reader."

I snatched it from the counter and squirrelled it off to my room. It was a strange paper, full of paranoid stories about nature running amok and avenging itself on people. It appealed to deep streams (if there are any) in the American psyche (if there is one).

"Bees Sting Golfer to Death" read one headline and below the story was an ad for "Life Insurance to help pay BURIAL EXPENSE."

"Herd of Zebras Trample Crippled Boy to Death—Along with His Mother" read another headline, and below the story was an ad reading: "Will 6 HANDCARVED elephants fit in one LUCKY BEAN and bring you LASTING GOOD LUCK? Yes!"

Carry our lucky beans and if you're a golfer you'll never get stung by bees, and if you're a cripple you'll never get attacked by zebras.

And there was an article about a guy who sells strap-on cushions for meditators who fly. "You may laugh, but he made $80,000 in profit his first year." There was the "Little Girl Killed in Eagle Attack" story, with this provocative (for Sesame Street fans) subtitle: "Big Bird Is Killed with a Baseball Bat." And there was one about a successfully escaped convict who nevertheless became so lonely he sneaked back into prison—and got caught doing so. Some fishermen were crushed by killer octopuses, and a Japanese tourist at Niagara Falls got hit in the face by a fifteen-pound kamikaze salmon. It was the first fish he'd ever caught. Knocked him right out. It would have been a sockeye salmon.

64. Mr. Mental Health

The little city of Watertown looked sweet and pleasant in the daylight. Many could be seen strolling happily along the warm sunny October streets. We stopped at the V Diner, sort of an old-fashioned streetcar eatery, and out front in the sunshine was an artist painting a new sign for the place, very nicely lettered and in shades of orange, mauve, yellow, purple. This was the United States of America, the way it's supposed to be.

The painter was definitely a pro. He knew exactly what he was doing and he never wasted a stroke.

"Ah, it's nice to see an artist at work," I said. He smiled. I was encouraged. "Nice day for being outside painting a sign, eh?"

"Sure is, especially since I usually work in the dead of night."

When we came out after breakfast, the painter had made amazing progress on the sign.

"Did you have somebody helping you while we were in there?"

"No, just myself."

"That's pretty fast, you should work days more often."

"I'm even faster in the dead of night."

All four of us headed out past miles of junk yards at the end of town to Cheeseman's, with Nigel and Winston saying they were hoping this guy Tommy didn't turn out to be some kind of homicidal maniac, because that's exactly what he looked like, bulging eyes and all. Yet most homicidal maniacs of my acquaintance in reality look meek and mild like Tony Perkins or Boris Karloff, or like Tommy's assistant, Everett, a nice young fellow with smudges of black grease all over his clothes and hands and a pattern of big juicy whiteheads all over his face and neck. He was a short guy, very shy.

"Well, let's face it now, pretty well the only place you can get it fixed is Herb's Service Centre," said Everett, "but Herb don't work Saturdays."

"Hey, don't you know that subjects and verbs are supposed to agree?" said red-haired Rodney, but we all cleared our throats and kicked him in the shins. Everett didn't seem to notice anything amiss. In his manner he possessed a nice combination of patience and nervousness, a sort of nervous patience, a willed calmness.

"Do you think you could sort of sweettalk Herb into at least, uh, having a look at it?" said Nigel. "Like today, I mean?"

"No, but *he* could." Everett pointed at big huge Tommy who was standing up straight on the roof of a pick-up truck with a large rope in his hand. He seemed to be making a noose, but as to why up there on the roof of a pick-up truck I have to confess ignorance and beg my reader's forgiveness. "Tommy could, he owns this place," said Everett. "Almost owns Herb's place too. He and Herb go way back."

So we went over to ask Tommy, who politely (and agilely for such a monster) hopped down. Now Tommy was not a pretty sight, and as for size he was two feet at least taller than Everett and four times as heavy and he was the one who was driving the towtruck last night. He listened patiently then exclaimed like crazy.

"This is Watertown, New York!" he said. "This is the boonies! If you have even an ordinary domestic car like say a Buick and it loses a simple thing like say a water pump you can't get it fixed on a weekend! Not around here, baby!"

His thin curling lips were sucking on another enormously long thin unlit cigar planted along the south side of his mouth and bouncing like a baton as he spoke. He had a big sloppy curly beard, and was covered with grease like Everett, though no pimples to speak of. His curiously stringy thin wobbly spaghetti legs, inside his greasy pants, seemed as if they, along with his lips, belonged to another man—or had originally.

It must have been the way I was looking at him. He turned to me and said, confidentially, "My friends call me Tommy the Terminator."

"Play baseball?"

"Yeah, but they never let me pitch."

"We'd rather pay a thousand bucks than stay around here for three days," said Nigel. There was a Holiday Monday coming up.

Tommy put a poker player's look on his face. "I hear what you're saying!" he said.

"Me too," said Everett, over to the side, eyes clear and shining through the grease.

These guys were smarter than they looked.

Tommy went in and telephoned Herb, then came out puffing smoke. "Herb's agreed to take a look at the car! I'll tow it over for us!" It was a nice big new towtruck, and it had painted on it WOBBLY WEENIE (on the hood) and 23-1/2 HOUR TOWING (on the side).

As Tommy hooked up the car, I turned to Everett. "Why's it called Wobbly Weenie?"

"You really wanna know? It's because it's a useless prick. Or it was when we got it. We had to put a thousand dollars into it before we could put it on the road. But now it really goes." He sounded very serious. "It's got a 340 Ford and a 750 double pumper with a racing cam and a double Holly. Not your standard wrecker."

"I should say not," I said. I didn't know what the heck he was talking about, but I trusted him.

"And do you wanna know why only 23-1/2 hour towing?"

"I was just gonna ask you that."

"We just wanted to be different."

"I know what you mean. You gotta be a little different in this world. Not a lot different, but some, right?"

"It sure helps."

"And you and Tommy are sure different."

He looked pleased.

The four of us hopped in the van and followed Tommy over as he towed the car through the centre of town, over the bridge, and out to the north-end suburbs. Nigel had given him one of the walkie-talkies to make sure we didn't get lost but we couldn't get the walkie-talkies working.

Nigel had been shooting film of Everett and Tommy, and was worrying about how he was going to put the footage together.

"It's a strange thing to make a film about a film," he said. "It doesn't seem to work."

"How'd you like to be Dave?" said sweet, intelligent, red-haired Rodney. "He has to write a book about having a movie made about writing a book."

"Thanks for reminding me," Nigel and I said in unison.

"They were pretty good," said Nigel, meaning Tommy and Everett. "They didn't look in the camera or anything when they knew we were shooting."

"Hm. I didn't notice that. I'm impressed," I said.

"Yeah, so like I'll have to ask Tommy if he's ever been in a film before...."

We rolled along in silence, heading out through the grey dismal broken-windowed junk-yard wasteland of sadness and despair, where skinny women with their hair in pin-curls and bruises under their eyes offered wedding dresses for sale, cheap.

The broken amateurish sign at the front of the faded-out dusty garage said: HERB'S SERVICE CENTER—IMPORTS REPAIRED 782-3972 EUROPEAN MOTOR SALES SERVICE.

But there was no one there. Herb hadn't shown up yet. Big scary Tommy puffed on his cigar, which never seemed to get any shorter, and unhooked the car, which had resumed its familiar blood-red colour. The guys pointed the camera at him. I noticed he didn't flinch. He was solid as a side of beef. I was ready to run for it any moment. In wartime I would want guys like Tommy on my side.

"The guys were talking about how professional you seem to be in front of the camera," I said. "Not self-conscious or anything. They were really impressed. Ever been on TV or anything like that?"

"Yeah, lots of times! I'm very outspoken!"

"On what?"

"Oh, on just about everything you would care to name! The environment! Urban renewal! Race relations! Foreign relations! Military spending! But particularly on gun control!"

"Where do you stand on gun control?"

"Well, I own about fifty guns! Whaddaya think!?"

"Uh, let's see now. You're opposed?"

"Right! *Nana*-nice guess! I used to carry a handgun and a rifle in the wrecker all the time! But I do a lot of towing for the police and they didn't like it! So I leave 'em at home now!"

"What did you want to carry them around for anyway? Afraid somebody's husband going to come up and shoot you?"

At that little joke he smiled and his eyes flashed ironically. "No, not me! I'm happily married! Now, that is! But...if a guy can go in a McDonald's and blow away eighteen people like happened last summer! You hear about that up in Canada!?"

"Sure. We hear about all that stuff. Southam stock inches up a notch whenever some maniac pulls out a gun and starts blowing people away."

"Well, he's not gonna blow me away! You have to protect your family!" We just stood there chatting, wondering if Herb was ever going to show up.

"So, what else should we talk about?" I said.

"So, that was funnier than you thought, hilarious in fact!" he said. "I mean, what you said about me being afraid of jealous husbands! Haw haw haw!!! A few years ago I found my wife and one of my towtruck operators engaged in a little oral sex! Haw haw haw!!! Cost me three years and a helluva lot of money! But today I have custody of my kids!"

His eyes beamed with triumph. That towtruck operator was one courageous fellow to fool around with the wife of a guy like Tommy the Terrible Terminator. Had Tommy killed his wife and her lover or simply maimed them for life? I didn't want to ask but he knew I was dying to know.

"I didn't have my guns with me that day! I carried them around all the time in those days! But I just didn't have them that day! And they were lucky I didn't! All I could do was beat them up! I couldn't shoot 'em! But I beat them up real good! Haw haw haw!!! They were four days in intensive care! Haw haw haw!!! Now I'm remarried! Got five kids altogether now! And my anniversary's tomorrow!"

His spaghetti lips formed into a big hearty smile, his eyes beamed and his cigar bounced up and down.

"Tomorrow, eh?"

"Yup! I met my wife in Mental Health! Our anniversary's tomorrow!"

"Mental health?"

"Oh, it's a long story! Don't ask!"

"We got time. I don't see Herb here yet."

"Well, it was like this! The lawyer told me I could either face assault charges or go to Mental Health! He said what do you want out of this marriage!? I said I want my kids! It cost me my house and my business! I had sixteen towtruck operators working for me when all this happened! Now there's just me and Everett! But I finally got my kids!"

"You were determined, eh?"

"You might say that!" The cigar bobbed and the eyes beamed again. "But some of my customers, they call me crazy! Not to my face of course! But I just say fuck 'em!"

"Why do they call you crazy? Because of the way you beat up your wife and her lover?"

"No, it wasn't that! I got a lot of sympathy around town for that! Maybe not a lot but some! A significant amount, let us say! But when you got my beautiful external features and my lovely way of speaking you can never get universal sympathy on any subject, not even sending your mother flowers for Mother's Day! And of course I've been kicked out of every bar in town!"

He wanted to change the subject. He'd been conducting a serious investigation into acid rain. A solid and responsible citizen, even if he did beat people up for practically no good reason at all, just because his inner child felt a little left out on account of his wife enjoying oral sex with the hired help (not as if it was real sex, eh?), and even if he did use a lot of exclamation points.

"I'm convinced this acid rain's killing the fish! For sure! But I'm not so sure about the forests! I think it's some kinda disease killing the spruce trees anyway! Not sure about the others!"

He'd started a campaign to have hiking boots banned from nature trails in the area. He eyed my feet. "I see you're wearing Nikes!" (Oh oh, hope that was okay. It was.) "We went to Nike and got them designing special soft-soled sneakers for hiking trails! Ones with the high ankles for backpack support! Those damned hiking boots were chewing up the trails something fierce! The rain would wash the soil away! And it left all these spruce trees with their roots exposed!"

Suddenly we noticed Herb standing there as if he'd been there all along but we hadn't noticed him. He was a sensible-height guy (like me, and like Kukla, Fran and Ollie too) with a receding chin and a warble in his voice. Very pale face. Looked a bit like a good-sized tuna. Sort of a pockmarked, froggy, chinless, clammy-faced look, like Davey Johnson (the manager of the New York Mets). You couldn't help trusting a guy who looked like that somehow.

"I'll be up front with you," he said when he'd looked at the car. "Monday maybe. Tuesday for sure.... We've got a clutch for a Toyota, a Subaru, a Honda but no Triumph Spitfire."

"But those are Japanese cars, and your sign says European."

"Japanese, European, it's all the same to me."

Nigel was worried about the rental for the film equipment. "This is going to cost me personally three thousand dollars if we're one day late," he said.

"Three thousand dollars?" said Herb. "Anybody who can afford that kind of money should get a real car."

"This isn't a real car?"

"Not in my way of looking at things. You have to take the engine out to fix the clutch. Basically the design of the thing's all fucked up."

"It's not our car, we borrowed it," said Nigel. "We don't have cars or money. We're artists. We can't afford it, that's the thing. It took us a lot of time to raise the money for this project. All the money we raise we put into our work...."

"Artists, huh?"

"Yeah. Say, do you know anyone who could fix it, even tomorrow, if we got the parts?"

"Nope. Nobody that's any good."

65. Several of the Remote Backports

Herb happened to mention that Trevor Snore Pontiac and Foreign Auto Parts in Syracuse would sell us the parts we needed, and he told us what parts we needed. In fact he phoned Snore to make sure they had the parts, and they said we'd have to hurry, they were going to close at five-thirty. We scrambled into the van and zoomed off in the grandest cloud of dust they'd seen in the Watertown area since the election of Richard Nixon.

"So, we have seventy-five minutes to closing time, and the place is seventy-five miles away," said Nigel. "What do we have to average?"

"Uh, let's see now," I said.

"Come on brain, do yer stuff," said Winston.

"Wouldn't that be sixty miles an hour?" said Rodney.

"Oh God, and we need gas too," said Nigel.

"We're out of gas?" said Rodney.

"Yeah, we're right on empty," said Nigel. "But that's not all, you know. The van's been over-heating when we push it too much."

"Maybe we should go back and get the car," said Rodney. "It's got gas and it hasn't been overheating."

"But the car's broken, remember?"

"Oh yeah, I forgot there for a minute."

"How much of that seventy-five miles is through the city?" said Winston.

"A good part of it."

We pulled into a Sunoco station for gas. There was a sign saying: FREE BOWLING 20 GAMES FREE WITH PURCHASE OF TWO NEW TIRES.

I waited until we were on the road again, and moving along fairly smoothly at sixty miles per hour, and settling down, and feeling fatalistic about the whole thing, and no one was talking, everyone was just quietly engrossed in their own little mental patterns.

"Let's get two new tires when we get back," I said.

"Why? We don't need tires do we?" said Rodney.

"He wants to go bowling," said Nigel. Everyone groaned.

Winston, who was sitting in the back with Rodney, came up close to the front and said quietly and smilingly to Nigel, who was driving, and driving very well I might add, really clipping along: "Were you making pig noises last night?"

Nigel blinked and jerked his head and swerved the van a bit. Straightened out. Turned momentarily to give Winston a look.

"Pig noises?"

"Yeah. Pig noises."

"What time?"

"When you were listening to your Laurie Anderson tapes."

"Sure," said Nigel. "I always make pig noises at night."

"I heard it right through the walls," said Winston.

"Well, it wasn't me," said Nigel.

Nigel had been watching the heat gauge and it had gone well past the red line. We stopped just past the toll gate and I took the opportunity to hop out and answer a call of nature between two transport trailers parked at the side of the expressway. As I was answering away, I saw a car, being driven furiously by a nun who had her long white habit stuck in the door. She slammed on her brakes and make a squealing U-turn on the expressway just a few feet from the toll gate. I guess she decided she didn't want to go through that toll. As her car turned she found herself facing me for a split second and her eyes bulged when she saw she was watching a man peeing right in front of her eyes. Who knows, it may have been a first. Either she didn't have the money for the toll gate, or else she was in a hurry to get somewhere and when she saw the toll gate she realised she'd come too far and wanted to head back right away.

Meanwhile, Nigel was in the phone booth phoning Trevor Snore and asking them please to stay open just a bit longer, we'd make it worth their while, it looked like we'd be a bit late but not too much. And when we got there, after getting off the expressway and making several wrong turns and getting a very good (but unguided) tour of Syracuse, New York, the guys had the parts all ready for us, refused to take any extra money for having to stay open for us, and in fact even gave us a can of cold beer each, free. Nigel insisted on giving them a hundred bucks but Trevor Snore (himself) said, "Nosirree-bob, I learned to walk in Canada, I like Canadians."

He turned to his partner, as we sipped our beers. "You know, up there they don't tell Italian or Polish jokes. They tell Newfie jokes. I can understand why. I met some Newfies once and boy are they thick-headed. It takes them all day to figure out if it's wet or dry out."

Any Newfoundlanders who happen to be reading this book should know that not only do these opinions not reflect the author's, the author in fact disagreed with Trevor Snore very strenuously.

"Some of the finest and most intelligent people I know are from Newfoundland," I said. "In fact when I made a visit to several of the remote back ports just last spring, I was amazed to find in every town groups of people using their spare time to great intellectual advantage, studying the great philosophers and so on. One town had formed an Irving Layton Fan Club and Study Group. They seemed much more intellectually inclined than the people we'd just been talking to in Watertown for instance."

"Oh, don't tell us about Watertown," said Trevor. "Those people in Watertown are dumb as channel cats. They're not Americans, they're not Canadians, they don't know what they are."

"What are you guys calling the film?" said the other guy, Fred, Trevor's partner. Rodney had been explaining that we were travelling around Lake Ontario making a film.

"A Trip Around Lake Ontario," said Nigel.

"Hm. I never would have thought of that."

"What's a channel cat?" I said.

"A channel cat? I don't know. Dumb as channel cats, my father always used to say that. I never thought to ask him what a channel cat was. But whatever they are they must be pretty dumb."

Trevor and Fred started talking about an issue of considerable local (and national) concern involving the American Indian Movement. The Indians had opened a cut-rate smoke shop, using treaty rights to avoid paying state taxes. People from off the reserve were swarming in for cheap cigarettes—and fireworks too. In some states the smoke shops were also offering liquor and gambling.

"The Indians on the Onondaga reserve are really sticking it to the government," said Trevor.

"What do you mean?" said Rodney.

"Hey," said Fred. "They got these big huge signs advertising fireworks and cigarettes cheaper than anywhere else."

"Let's face it," said Trevor. "For the past three hundred years this country has been screwing the Indians. Now it's time they did a little screwing themselves."

Trevor and Fred also couldn't get over how Canadians could prefer American beer to Canadian. They knew Canadian beer was much better. We tried to tell them we found Canadian beer too full of chemicals, American beer lighter and purer. They just thought we were stupid.

66. Red Wine and Falling Leaves

On the way back, driving fairly slowly and in a more relaxed frame of mind, someone started passing around a big one-and-a-half-litre bottle of Chianti Ruffino. Nigel as the driver of record wouldn't take a sip. When I said to the others, who were taking healthy glugs, "I thought you guys didn't drink," they said, "Only on special occasions." They had been saving this bottle for just such an occasion. They were celebrating their pleasure at having successfully got ahold of that all-important new little clutch for that little smudge of a car in such an out-of-the-way and unlikely part of the world. The new clutch, along with replacements for several other smaller but no less important parts that seemed to have snapped off or fallen apart or fallen off on the highway when the clutch went, was in a big box in the back of the van. It was a little disappointing, because I considered myself a good and sensitive driver, one who understands cars and the way they perform, the way they like to be driven. I'd been nursing that car along like the sweet little teddy bear of a car it was, and it just ups and dies under me, long before its time. But a clutch can go any time I guess.

As we drove along, our tummies awash with red wine, I got thinking aloud about the famous war criminal Joseph Mengele and how terrific it would be for him if he were to give up, turn himself in, throw himself on the mercy of the Israeli court, and how much better for Germany, for humanity, and how healing for everyone concerned. He could admit his guilt, blame it on the insanity of the times, beg forgiveness. It sounded hokey, but such an event might go some way to silence the Keegstras and Zundels of the world. The disgust we feel for the Holocaust deniers is compounded by their media images, which show them as treating their trials as a joke, as being consummately smug and frighteningly sure of themselves. The disgust we feel for Joseph Mengele is compounded by the fact that he is still free, somewhere in the world, perhaps laughing at his pursuers, perhaps still a believer. Just then we passed a truck with American flags depicted on its mudflaps and the words THESE COLORS DON'T RUN.

Nigel began talking about some of the famous people he'd met. "You know Hannah Blades, the restaurant critic? I have a friend who is a ghost writer for her."

"Oh no, don't tell me she has a ghost writer," said Winston. "I didn't want to know that. I heard her on the radio the other day and she was terrific, but she really tore a certain restaurant to shreds, and after she went off the air the announcer said something kind of unpleasantly unflattering about her, and I phoned up the station and complained. Now I find out she's got a ghost writer. How embarrassing!"

Just then we passed a burned-out car being towed. It looked as if a team of sumo wrestlers with blow torches had worked it over for several days. But you could still read the licence plates: HOT 729.

"It must be a joke," said Rodney. "They probably hang on to those plates at the towtruck shop for when they have to tow a burned car in, then they just slip them on for a joke."

"No," said Winston, giving a fishy look at Rodney. "Nobody would go to that trouble for such a corny joke. It's a true coincidence."

We kept on like that. We found out that all four of us had been Senior Sixers in Wolf Cubs but when it came time to move up to Boy Scouts we declined, decided it was just for sissies. Nigel started telling stories about when he was an usher at the Original 99-cent Roxy. They were showing *Night of the Living Dead* one Thursday night, the night of the week devoted to horror films, and there was a particularly big line-up because *Night of the Living Dead* was a seldom-shown classic at that time, just a terrific movie if you could stomach the premise.

"This guy was trying to get in without waiting in the line-up, you know?" said Nigel. "I asked him very nicely to please go to the end of the line like everyone else. So this guy gets mad. He says, 'Do you know who I am? I'm Irving Layton. And this is my son.'"

"Wow, no kidding eh?" said Winston.

"Who's Irving Layton?" said Rodney.

Everyone laughed. Rodney looked embarrassed. He figured Layton must have been somebody famous. He didn't remember Chesley Yarn reading the postcard, or maybe he was out in the yard at the time.

"You can't help it, being from West Vancouver and everything."

"Oh God. He's not a poet or a writer, is he?"

"Yeah."

"Oh shit." It was going to take Rodney a while to live this down, at least in his own mind. "Well," he said, "do you know who Jean-Pierre Lefebvre is?" Everyone said no. "Oh well, I don't feel so bad then."

"You just made up that name, didn't you?" said Nigel.

"No, he's a Quebec filmmaker. He's totally unknown in Western Canada but they go wild about him in France."

"What are some of his films?" said Winston.

"The Place Where Rimbaud Died…The Wild Flowers."

"Oh that's not Jean-Paul Lefebvre, that's Michel Gagnon."

Rodney looked stricken.

"It is?" he said. "Are you sure?"

A car went by with a bumpersticker saying I LOVE JESUS. GOD MAKES HOUSE CALLS.

"Funny how quickly you get lost when you're away from home," said Winston. We all agreed, without knowing what he was talking about.

"So what did you reply to Mr. Layton?" I said to Nigel. "Did you let him in?"

"No, I said I don't care who you are, you have to get to the back of the line."

"And did he?"

"Yes, he did."

"You should have said I don't care if you're David McFadden. He would have liked that."

"I couldn't. This was before I knew about you. Does he know your work?"

"Sure he does. Steals my ideas constantly."

"You mean like trying to sneak into line-ups?"

"Yeah, in fact he got that from a poem of mine called 'Ballad of a Queue-Jumper.'"

We just kept driving along the two-lane highway, far from the expressway, taking the lazy slow route back to Watertown. We were starting to get hungry but we were distracted by the wine and the spectacular fall colours. As we drove along we looked down into and across broad valleys full of bright red and orange deciduous forests, stunning to the eye. Isn't it amazing how the fall colours become even more spectacular when you're drinking red wine straight from the bottle?

"This is the most fun I've had in a long time," I announced, truthfully. "Too bad it's not an all-girl crew."

After a mile of silence, Rodney said: *"Wha*-why would you like it to be an all-girl crew?"

I must admit, when I'm with men I still like to get a little chauvinistic. It doesn't mean anything, and I'm certainly not as bad as some of Sheldon's friends. How bad are they? Well, one of them, at least when he's been drinking, yells out "slut!" whenever an attractive woman appears on TV. I've never discussed it with him, or with Sheldon.

"Well," I said, "if this were an all-girl crew we wouldn't be looking for a McDonald's and chugalugging out of this wine bottle. There'd be a great big picnic basket full of all kinds of delicious food: lobster, ice-cold Italian bubbly, fine cutlery, fresh Portuguese bread…."

"And we could save on motel bills, right?" said Winston.

"And it'd make for a better book, eh?" said Nigel.

"Sexier anyway," said Rodney.

The guys, particularly Rodney, wanted to know what I was going to say about them in the book, what I was going to call them. I said I was thinking of calling them all Fred. Fred, Fred and Fred.

"I'll say you're tall thin lazy-looking guys with lazy sleepy smiles," and then because I was in such a good-natured mood, I said I'd describe them as "always good natured, ambitious but quietly so, and with no sense of ruthlessness, always co-operative and calm. More interested in having a good time than stabbing each other in the back."

I was in the back seat. Winston and Nigel turned all the way around and smiled. Rodney smiled too, but he seemed a bit nervous.

"And don't worry, Rodney," I said, "I won't tell anyone about the you-know-what you had last night."

"What are you talking about? I didn't have anything last night. Did I?"

I decided to fold up the road map, but was having trouble because of too much wine. There was a guy named John Robinson who wrote a little humour column in the *Hamilton Spectator* five or six days a week for about forty-five years. In fact, he continued writing the column at least once a week for ten years after he retired. He'd just died recently. At any rate, one of his favourite subjects for a funny column was the impossibility of refolding a road map. He could get five-hundred words out of that any old time. All I know about writing I learned from John Robinson, both when I was a kid and reading him, and later when I shared an office with him at the newspaper and we used to sit around the press club together and he'd tell me his secrets of being funny. Gave me long reading lists of famous and little-known comic writers of the past, and asked me questions on them when I'd finish reading them, all of that.

But alas, I've turned out to be anything but funny. My publishers sent dozens of copies of *A Trip Around Lake Erie* and *A Trip Around Lake Huron* to the jury for the Stephen Leacock Award (for humour writing) and even today they won't show me the letter they received in return, along with the books. "We're going to spare you that pain indefinitely," they said. But they did tell me what the last line of the letter was: "So, having said all that, the next time please send us something funny."

Enjoying the act of writing is the important thing, according to John Robinson. "If you enjoy writing people will enjoy reading you," he used to say. He enjoyed writing his column a lot. He used to sit there typing away and laughing his head off simultaneously. It was a heckuva lot better than covering the police beat. Vladimir Nabokov agreed with John Robinson on the subject of enjoying the act of writing, but Mavis Gallant, whose writing is not very funny at all, claims to find writing hell and claims anyone who claims it isn't is a liar (or not a real writer).

"Are you going to mention that I didn't know who Irving Layton was?" said Rodney.

"Ah, don't worry about it," I said. "I'll do it in such a way it'll seem as if I made it up."

He still didn't seem relaxed.

"Besides, it's not going to be the kind of book that everybody's going to read."

"How many?"

"Only about a hundred thousand or so maximum. And of those, only about one thousand will read it attentively."

"Yeah, well it's just that I don't want to be known for the rest of my life as the guy who'd never heard of Irving Layton."

"It won't be like that, I guarantee it."

"All right, okay, I'll forget it."

"And, oh, by the way, of those thousand attentive readers, probably only two or three hundred will have heard of Irving Layton themselves."

"Yeah?"

"Yeah, it's not important to know who Irving Layton is. More important to know who Leonard Cohen is. Or Mozart."

"Who was that?" said Rodney. "Leonard who?"

67. Saturday Night at the Fire Hall

Herb's wife was all dressed up. And she had Herb's good suit in a bag. She was going to get Herb all cleaned up and into his good suit as soon as they got rid of us. Then they were going to a dance at the fire hall. It was Saturday night in Watertown.

"So you two are going to a dance tonight, at the fire hall," said Nigel. He wanted them to invite us along.

"Yeah," said Herb's wife.

"They have that every Saturday?" said Nigel.

"Yeah," said Herb's wife.

"Do they have a band there?"

"Yeah. Well, they usually have, but tonight there's just going to be a guy playing records."

Herb's wife started talking about a boat tour of the Thousand Islands she and Herb had been on last week. They certainly weren't going to invite Nigel and the boys to the dance.

"Yeah, it was really nice. You could look in the windows of the big houses on the islands."

"Those people are so lucky, eh?"

"Yeah. Luckier than us, anyway."

"Do you ever get up to Canada?"

"Yeah. Well, haven't been up there for years. We have a friend from up there who comes down once in a while and camps with us."

Herb came in and started talking loudly, a bit impatient to get to the dance. "Let's go for a ride, one of you guys. You wanna go? Somebody wanna go? Whoever's going to drive it better come with me." I went with him, took the wheel.

"You got a hydraulic problem, okay?" he said as we spun around under the late-evening northern sky. "By that I mean the master cylinder. I tried bleeding it but I couldn't get it any better than it is. If you go to drive the car, and you wanna back up, you have to put the car in reverse before you start it or it's gonna grind. First gear too. You gotta put it in gear before you start."

"Boy, we really appreciate this," said Nigel when we got back.

"Yeah. He usually doesn't stay this late," said Herb's wife.

"Well, I'm really going to give him an amazing tip he won't believe. As long as we can get back to Toronto by Tuesday. It's really bad, because I'm on a really tight budget, and I'm trying to make this film. It's like my big opportunity, right? And this thing could have ruined my whole project. It wouldn't have ruined it, but it would have made it a lot different than I wanted it to be."

"You can drive it back to Toronto as long as you're careful with it."

"Great. We will be."

"Okay.... What do you guys consider a fair price?"

"Whatever you think, and we'll make it more."

"What is it, eight o'clock?"

"Yeah. Ten after," said his wife. She was following him around with a soapy face cloth and giving his face a wipe whenever an opportunity arose.

"Well, there's forty dollars in towing.... What do you think of two hundred and ninety dollars? That includes the towing. I'll pay Tommy Cheeseman out of it."

"That sounds good to me," said Nigel. He started pulling out his travellers cheques.

"Is there any way you can give me the cash rather than the travellers cheques?" said Herb. "I know the travellers cheques are good but it's a hassle for me going to the bank."

Nigel emptied his pockets and counted. "Let's see...there's a hundred and ninety."

"Okay, give me the rest in travellers cheques." Nigel did. "You want a slip on that?" said Herb.

"A receipt you mean?"

"Yeah."

"Yeah, if you could.... When I countersign this, I guess you're supposed to watch."

"Yeah."

"Who should I make it out to?"

"Herb Martin. What's your name?"

"Uh, just put Great Lakes Films."

"Today's the thirteenth. This was not a good thirteenth for you guys. You know, you're lucky it wasn't a Friday."

"It could have been worse. It wouldn't have been disastrous, but it would have been a lot more hassle if we would have had to wait here. Uh, do you think we should just go to Toronto straight, or hit the first place Monday morning?"

"Well, like I told him," said Herb, pointing at me. "If you're careful when you come into a city, okay? Like about going into first gear, I mean, and if you're real careful when you put it in reverse, you can finish wherever you're going, okay? Without any problems I mean. Because, like I say, we put just the clutch disc in, you might have a weak pressure plate too. Who knows? And if I were you I'd let the original owner take care of it when I took it back to him, I really would."

"By the way," I said, "do you have to pull the motor again just to fix the cylinder?" I thought it'd be best to be prepared in case we found ourselves at the mercy of a less-honest mechanic a hundred miles further west.

"No, not to fix the cylinder. The slave cylinder bolts on to the bottom of the transmission and the master cylinder sits up on top right next to the brake master cylinder. So." He turned to his wife and handed her the cash and travellers cheques. "Here you go, bookkeeper, file it." She laughed nervously. "And remember to pay Tommy on Monday."

"Well, I really really really really appreciate this, really," said Nigel, again.

"Well, it's a lot of money, I know. But for a Saturday, and working this late. You know, I'd just as soon have gone home at noon or one o'clock."

As for the dance at the fire hall, it would have been a great American experience. But it wasn't to be, and we didn't push it. Little did we know what fun we'd be having at a fire hall just down the road the very next day! Isn't that just like life?

68. Retarded Girl with Bat

We spent another night at the Stars and Stripes Motel and late the next morning I was driving alone along a long lonely straight two-lane highway over flat terrain. At the precise point where I was thinking how terrible it was that so much of the world has become so cut off from its past, and that our sense of continuity was all askew, as if we were suffering from amnesia, at that precise point I passed the Home of the Inventor of Chloroform. The sky was perfectly blue, the sun warm. I continued straight on toward the lake and the old eighteenth-century naval fort at Sackett's Harbour. The film crew were in the van a mile back.

I drove past the newly built high school with the football team in lilac-and-white uniforms out practising. They were resting, actually, sprawled all over the dark green wet October grass among the bright orange pumpkins and piles of crimson leaves. And there on the Lake Ontario waterfront was Fort Virginia, which according to the plaques had been armed with sixteen guns against the British attack in 1812. The harbour itself was splendid, they could have built a Hamilton here, with steel mills everywhere belching into the sky. There were marks on the ground indicating where Smith Cantonment used to stand—barracks for 2,500 men. Shortly after the war, it had been deliberately burned to the ground to stem an outbreak of cholera. The barracks had been sandwiched between Fort Kentucky and Fort Tompkins. Now it was just a green grassed park with historical plaques here and there—sleepy and clear, but a bit out of focus, very quiet, nobody around. Still being maintained in good shape were a couple of officers' houses from the time. In fact a naval officer still lived in one.

There was a retarded girl playing with an oversized orange plastic bat and yellow plastic ball on the dark green wet lawn of one of a row of summer cottages that stretched along the south shore of the harbour just west of the town. She stopped playing and stared at the car as I drove by. I waved. She didn't wave back. I kept driving. The road made a dead end, and on the way back I saw the famous blue van stopped in front of the house. The retarded girl's mom had come out, and Nigel was talking to her.

"We're closing up, summer's shot," she said. The daughter just stood there holding the orange plastic bat that was almost as big as she.

"How old is she?" said Nigel. He was getting pretty good at going up to strangers and engaging them in intimate conversations. It was something about his general appearance and manner: gently smiling eyes, direct gaze, sympathetically calm voice that oozed friendliness and understanding, a completely unquestionable sincerity as opposed to the fake sincerity that Americans (and others) are used to from their politicians and clergymen. I think he was more touched by the spirit of what we were doing than I was, at least at that point. He should have been writing the book. Maybe he will.

The mother spoke matter-of-factly. "She's thirty-five." We looked at her more closely. She still looked about thirteen. She swung the bat. She had pretty good form too. Apparently retarded children tend to have an affinity for sports. In *The Boys of Summer*, the old Brooklyn Dodgers ace, Carl Erskine, has a retarded boy named Jimmy, and Erskine says to the author: "Heck, we had an Olympics for all the retarded kids of Madison County and Jimmy won a big event."

"What event was that, Carl?" says Roger Kahn.

"Ballbounce. He bounced a basketball twenty-one times." [Editor's note: You actually get to see the kid on the feature-length videotape of the same title.]

"Sure is quiet around here," we said.

"Yeah, everyone's in church I guess."

Winston took some film of the girl, just standing there. The mother wanted to know what channel the film would be on.

"Do you get the CBC around here?"

"I think so. I think I get it at home 'cause we got cable there."

"Where do you live?"

"Oh, down in Rochester."

"Oh, we have to go there in a hurry tomorrow to buy some film."

354

"They'll have it there."

"Yeah, just by coincidence we're going to run out of film in Rochester. It's kind of a pilgrimage to Mecca for us, this is where it all began."

"It's a good place to run out of film," she said.

I was standing back, just listening. Everything was moving so slowly and quietly. It was wonderful being out of the city and mixing with retarded people. A photographer friend of mine once spent a day in the retarded wing of a psychiatric hospital taking pictures. He put a show of his photos together and it was surprising how good it was, not exploitive at all, in fact just the opposite. In each picture we were confronted by a retarded person, more often a couple or a group, with wonderfully unusual signs of intelligence and dignity clearly displayed in their faces. A different kind of intelligence perhaps, but that same old dignity in a very solid and healthy dose. So I was prepared for something like this.

"Looks like interesting work you got here," said the truly generous woman. She had no problems at all with us zeroing in on her retarded daughter and filming her for public consumption.

"Well, I got lucky," said Nigel. "We got a grant of sixty thousand dollars to make this film."

The woman wasn't that impressed. "Well, that's a nice start."

"Yeah it's a good start."

The daughter was staring at us. Winston had finished filming, and hadn't minded her staring in the camera—an exception to the rule.

"Time to eat, eh Pat?" said the mother.

"Yyhh."

"We're going to have to ask you to sign this release form," said Nigel.

"Oh, we've gone through this before." She signed.

"Where?" Had another film crew gone by?

"Oh, where she goes to school."

"Oh, where does she go to school?"

"It's an adult sheltered workshop."

"Oh, what does she do there?"

"Oh, she works. Every day."

"What sort of thing does she do?"

"Oh, little things for Kodak."

"Like what?"

"Oh, different things."

"For Kodak?"

"Yeah, mostly for Kodak."

"Like packing film?"

"Well, to tell the truth I usually never say anything about this. It's kind of weird."

"What is?"

"This thing I don't want to talk about."

"Oh?"

"Yeah, so.... Isn't this a beautiful day?"

"Yeah, it's a really nice area."

"Beautiful!" The woman's voice went up an octave, charmingly, as she became enthused about the fall colours. "I never saw so many leaves out as this year."

The subject had definitely been changed. "Yeah."

"Look at 'em. I couldn't believe it!" She squealed with child-like wonder and delight.

"We hit the right time to come by here," said Winston. We were all looking at each other and smiling.

"Yeah, it's beautiful. You know, all the way up in the car it was *soooo* pretty. But when we got here all the leaves were…." She began giggling. I think she meant that the leaves on the way up were pretty, but when they got to the lake they were all in colour, but she became so excited she couldn't continue.

Some people are particularly sensitive to fall colours. There's a name for the condition. A sort of sensory crossover thing where one look at a tree in fall colour and it's like a blast of laughing gas. I read about it in *National Enquirer*. People with this condition often have very large earlobes, and this lady had monsters.

"Well, we gotta go now," said Nigel. "Thank you." He looked at the retarded girl.

"You're welcome. Say you're welcome, Pat."

"Yooowekm."

"Bye, now. Good luck on your project. Hope you get some more money." She seemed to have recovered from her autumnal petit mal.

"Yeah, so do I, eh? These guys really hope I get some more money too."

"They're working for free, huh?"

"No. I wish."

"I bet you do."

"Bye now. Bye Patty."

"Say bye, Pat."

She says nothing.

"She's ignoring you."

"Yeah."

Later Nigel said he felt strange shooting film of the girl, and he had no idea if he'd be able to use it in the movie without it seeming to be exploitive or voyeuristic. I told him about my friend the photographer's work with retarded people, in which he succeeded in altering the viewer's image of the retarded. It's natural to want to film something that is unusual.

The mother seemed to have no problems at all about our curiosity about her daughter. As far as she was concerned, mental retardation was just another form of intelligence, a subtler form, one you had to learn to appreciate. There was no question of exploitation. Her mother accepted the girl's limited intellectual development as something natural, something requiring more care, but with an ineffable range of rewards. It was my impression that the mother and her daughter were wonderful pals, and would be forever.

Rodney said he'd had a little cosmic fantasy: the mother and her daughter have been together like this for all eternity, constantly being reincarnated on planet after planet, switching roles each time.

I told Rodney that was wonderful and that I thought he'd been a high-ranking Buddhist priest in Tibet in his previous lifetime, but he became angry one day and swatted a fly and so was reincarnated as a Canadian filmmaker.

69. Louis Armstrong at Port Stanley

A middle-aged black businessman was standing at the side of the road in Sackett's Harbour. He must have been a stranger in these parts because he had a road map outstretched on the hood of his sparkling new BMW. He also had a puzzled look on his face. A much younger man, who turned out to be his son, was standing next to him and was also looking at the map. I couldn't see junior's face but his shoulders also looked puzzled. Although not overly familiar with the area, I stopped to offer help.

They were both wearing black pinstriped suits. They said they were trying to get the ferry over to Canada. They knew there was one but they couldn't find it on their map. I took a look on my map, and there it was, a dotted line indicating a ferry over to Wolfe Island, from which there was a brief ferry ride to Kingston.

The father's name was George S. Peabody, and he was anxious to get back to Canada. He looked a lot like Louis Armstrong, but he was no musician, he was a serious businessman. He was the vice-president and general manager of Howell Press in Vancouver. It was a subsidiary of Southam Press, the big Canadian newspaper chain. Peabody and his son, George Jr., who worked for Katimavik and who also looked a little like old Satchmo, had been driving around looking at the countryside. Actually, they were taking a trip around Lake Ontario but the other way, counter-clockwise, and they were running out of time. They had to make some kind of presentation to the cabinet in Ottawa in two days and had a lot of preparing to do. They said they were originally from around London, Ontario, which is where they rented the car. They had been on a nostalgia trip, visiting old haunts on Lake Erie, and decided to go to Ottawa via the long route.

"Do you know Lake Erie well?" I said.

"Sure," said George Sr. "I just sold a house at Port Ryerse."

"I bet you remember the old Stan Kenton band when they used to play at Port Dover?"

"Sure," he said, "and Rompin' Ronnie Hawkins later, and Louis Armstrong at Port Stanley."

The resemblance was so close he'd probably been told thousands of times he looked like Louis Armstrong. His voice, however, was more like a blend of Brian Mulroney and Bill Cosby. When Peabody said he lived in West Vancouver, where 90 per cent of the Mercedes Benzes and Porsches of Canada are located, I made a nasty comment about the bloody Socreds of British Columbia, the way those barbarians closed down the college where I used to work, and the long sad soup lines of Vancouver in the shadows of the new Airbus system, the new domed stadium and Expo 86. The guy smiled broadly but with sad eyes and said nothing.

"He's a real rightwinger," said George Jr. "He even likes Ronald Reagan."

I liked them both right away. I began telling them about Sackett's Harbour. They didn't seem to know much about history. I had to give them a brief rundown of the War of 1812.

Peabody said he was a friend of Mel Hurtig, often golfed with him in fact, on courses all over the world. "I don't know what you think of Mel Hurtig," he said. I told him I hadn't seen his encyclopaedia yet. "Neither have I," he said. "I don't really think he's got the proper focus yet, but it's good to see he's staying alive."

"Right," I said. I figured he was talking about Hurtig's enthusiasm for publishing books that didn't make a huge profit. Maybe he was critical of Hurtig's nationalism. Anybody who isn't a hundred per cent profit-oriented has to be a little bit out of focus.

"He has a new book out on golf courses in North America. That should sell," he said.

I showed him my modest little book of loss-oriented satiric verse, *Golden Dewdrops of the Night*. He was critical of the cover. "It's the wrong kind of laminated paper for that kind of binding," he said. "See this line? Eventually the cover will crack along this line and fall off."

Nigel, Winston and Rodney were standing behind me listening and smiling. Nigel waited until there was a natural break in the conversation, which wasn't long, then said: "I don't know if you want to explore this area any more, but we really have to go eat a big breakfast."

"Okay," I said, "but before we go to the restaurant let's get the walkie-talkies out." We hadn't used the walkie-talkies yet. They looked like wonderful toys. I was dying to play with them. The others weren't enthused.

70. Septuagenarian Lust

We didn't know where to go for breakfast so I told the guys to wait right there, I'd go into the little old fire hall sitting on the corner of this residential part of town right on the shore of Lake Ontario and ask where was a good place to eat. The guys just stood there talking.

The door of the fire hall was open but just as I was about to walk in I found myself surrounded by a pack of armed kids straight out of *Lord of the Flies*. They were wearing army fatigues and headbands and ammo belts and carried rifles, plastic I hoped. They identified themselves as members of the Children's Liberation Organisation. They were just kids playing but I felt a little nervous and looked back to the van but the guys hadn't noticed anything amiss, they were still just standing there quietly talking to each other.

Anyway, the little terrorists (oops, freedom fighters!) said they wanted to take me hostage in order to bargain for the release of some political criminals in Florida. I wanted to know what kind of criminals. A little red-haired kid about twelve with what looked like a splatter of blood on his pant leg sneered and said, "People whose only crime was to fire-bomb abortion clinics to stop the murder of innocent unborn children, that's all."

Whew. I had to do some fast talking, believe me. These kids looked as if they really meant business. They'd shoot you first and find out why later. I told them I was a Canadian and didn't know anything about the situation. They wanted to know if they had abortion clinics up there in Canada. No, never, I said. We wouldn't permit such a thing. In fact the anti-abortion movement started in Come-by-Chance, Newfoundland.

They conferred with each other and decided a Canadian wouldn't make much of a hostage. I suggested the mayor of Sackett's Harbour would make a more viable hostage and they figured that was a good idea. I told them his office was downtown. Where downtown, they wanted to know. When you get downtown just ask anyone, I said.

As they were about to leave I sighed with relief and told my former captors that I really admired them and their cause and said that with a new generation of kids like you guys coming up, the continued security of the U.S.A. and the entire free world was assured. They seemed happy and I darted into the fire hall.

There was a long bar with a big bald friendly-looking guy standing behind it smiling at me as I entered. It was as if he'd been waiting for me all morning.

"What kept you?" he said.

At first I thought maybe he had me mixed up with somebody else but he had a certain look on his face that spoke of a profound, and I mean cosmic, transcendent sense of humour. This guy looked like a big bald retired wrestler, and he looked a little like W. C. Fields too, but without the meanness. He looked like a retired army officer, which in fact he turned out to be. He looked stupid, he looked as if he had been cultivating looking stupid all his life, as if all his life he'd been hearing himself referred to as a big stupid meathead of a guy, but he also looked totally conscious. Invisible radiance was flashing out of his eyes.

"It was just one red light after another," I said.

He hooted and snorted and insisted I have a beer. It was still early but I was thirsty and chugalugged it right down as he watched then got me another. He gave me directions to the closest restaurant, described exactly what was on the menu and what was particularly good, but all the time he was high-pressuring me into staying for the Fiddler's Fling, the Sunday afternoon hoedown. "Listen, it starts in about an hour, maybe less, and there's gonna be one, two, three, four bands. And lots of snatch." His eyes flashed with septuagenarian lust. I told him I had friends waiting. "Bring them too, come on, go get 'em." But they're hungry. "We got a lunch counter. Hamburgers, fishburgers, all kinds of sandwiches. Fifty gallons of coffee. Two hundred cases of beer."

There were some people in the dance hall through a door off to one side. An enormously fat woman in a red polyester short-sleeved shirt and pin-striped polyester slacks came up to the bar and sat down. "Hi Casey," she said.

Casey put a look of mock exasperation on his face as she sat there smiling shyly at him. "Jesus Christ," he said, "I hope you don't ask for change for a twenty."

"I'd just like some water for my aspirin," she said.

"Geez, she brings her own aspirin and wants you to supply the water." He stared at her in silence for a minute then handed her the water. She swallowed her aspirin and took a sip.

"Cold, isn't it?" she said.

"Oh, did ya want it hot? Why didn't ya say so? I could have given it to ya hot, heh heh!" Their eyes were locked together and little sparks were passing back and forth. Casey's voice dropped and I had to strain to hear. "As hot as you want it," he informed her, confidentially. "I'm a heavy woman lover."

"Tee hee," said the woman. "You better be."

"If you'd asked for change for a twenty you know what I would have done?"

"No. What?" she said.

"I woulda grabbed your left breast."

"Promise?"

"Sure."

"Hm. Well then. Got change for a twenty?"

Casey snorted with glee, grabbed the woman on the right breast, gave it a good squeeze. She had frizzy red hair and wore a little pair of reading glasses on her nose.

"Hey," she said, "I thought you said the left breast."

"Oh yeah, I forgot." He moved his hand over to the left and gave that one a squeeze too.

When the woman left he smirked at me knowingly and said, "See? I told you so. There's gonna be all kinds of snatch here this afternoon." Snatch was Casey's term of affection for ladies in general. I asked him if he were married.

"Me? I been married forty-five years—and we still fight. How old do you think I am?"

"Eighty? Ninety?"

"Hey hey hey, whoa down there boy. I know it's hard to believe, but I have just last week celebrated my seventieth birthday."

"And how did you celebrate it?"

"My son came down from Adams and we went bowling all afternoon and didn't get home till midnight. My wife's still not talking to me about that one."

Would his wife be showing up this afternoon?

"No," he said, "she's getting ready for the big bazaar December 11. I know, it's two months away but she's got a lot of doily-making to do. She's at home making doilies. She just makes doilies all the time." He sounded sad, annoyed.

"Hoedowns aren't for everyone, Casey."

"No, I guess not." A moment of sadness.

"Don't you like doilies, Casey?"

"Doilies? Oh yeah, I like doilies, sure I do, doilies are fine. Everybody likes doilies, right?"

"You don't sound very convincing."

"Well, ya know...."

"Excuse my ignorance, but what exactly is a doily?"

His voice picked up. "Doilies, don't you know what a doily is?"

"Not exactly."

"Jesus Christ, they're uh, oh you've seen them, everybody knows what doilies are." He looked at me. My inquisitive look hadn't faded. "You know, doilies are those sonofabitch little things with holes in 'em that you put things on."

"Oh yeah, I know what you mean."

"Yeah, they're sort of like a grill for a stove except they're made out of thread, very fancy, takes women a long time to make them."

"I bet. And then you wouldn't put them on the stove."

"Oh no, you wouldn't do that. You'd get hit on the head with a frying pan if you did that. Christ, couldn't do that."

71. Canadian Mist

He squirted something from a long black tube into his glass. I asked him what it was.

"Oh, this is Canadian Mist. It's what I always drink. No ice or nothin'. Just Canadian Mist. And a little taste of Pepsi."

Casey J. Carmichael, Chief Warrant Officer (Retired) of the U.S. Army, now more familiarly known as Casey the Volunteer Fireman, pretended he was insulted when I asked him if he'd been born and raised in Sackett's Harbour.

"Me? Born here? Hell no. I was born in Buffalo, New York. No, not really. I wasn't born. I was shit on a stump and the sun hatched me out."

"What?"

"You heard me. I was shit on a stump and the sun hatched me out. Haw haw."

I figured that in all his life Casey had never been able to be anything but funny. He had a genius-level IQ but he refused to acknowledge it in any way. His IQ was so high it frightened him. So he'd spent the past seventy years successfully playing the clown.

We went into the dance hall and watched the band setting up. There were sixteen of them. It was the Sackett River Valley Fiddling Association. Casey went over to the fat woman with the frizzy hair and chatted with her while I watched the musicians. They were all in their cutest cowboy costumes. There were three fiddlers, four guitarists, two banjoers, a washtubber, a mouth organist, a mandolinist, an accordionist, an electric-piano player, a steel guitarist, a twelve-year-old Lolita playing castanets. More were arriving.

Casey took me aside and started whispering out the side of his mouth. "Whattaya think, Dave? This woman, she just took up with me. She was touching my leg and everything. Did ya see her?"

"The same woman who was at the bar?"

"Yeah, the one who wanted me to squeeze both her breasts. Didya see her just now? I hadda tell her to leave me alone. Christ, she wanted to eat me up." He rolled his eyes. "Jesus Christ, I'm tellin' ya, didya see her? There's enough ass there for both of us—and that's just on one cheek. Har har har."

As we walked out of the dance hall back to the bar we passed the hefty woman. She had a satin jacket on the back of her chair and there was a large fiddle insignia on the back of the jacket.

"Are you a fiddler?" I said.

"Yep. Sure am."

"Are you playing this afternoon?"

"Nah, I don't play for square dances."

"Why not?"

"I like square dances but I don't like playing for them. The music's too repetitive. I'm a country fiddler, solo-style."

I grabbed a coffee and sat down with her. She said her name was Penny Coomber and her favourite singer was Willie Nelson. I told her I'd seen all his movies, and she liked that. I asked about her husband and she said he was at home working on his stamp collection. "He spends all his time working on that stamp collection. He has no time for square dancing or any other kind of fun." I said it sounded like Casey's wife all the time making doilies.

When I got back out to the bar Casey had a look of mock alarm on his face. "Are those friends of yers outside waitin' fer ya?" he said.

"Hope so," I said. I was finishing my second beer. "I think they're just fiddling with their cameras and walkie-talkies."

"Cameras and walkie-talkies, Jesus!" He put on his gold-braid NASA cap and told some skinny young fellow in the back to watch the bar for him. The young fellow just smiled. We went out and the guys were standing by the bird's-eye blue van in the parking lot. Casey ignored the camera equipment and with eyes flashing walked up to the guys as if he'd known them all his life and started telling some raunchy story about a woman he met in some park he'd visited when he was in Toronto one time.

"High Park?" said Rodney.

"Aye-e-e-e? Howzzzat?" said Casey. He squinted and cupped his hand to his ear and belched at the same time. Everyone started laughing except for Casey and Rodney who both looked serious and maybe even worried, especially Rodney, who seemed to think he'd said something wrong again.

"High Park?" said Rodney, nervously. "It's in the west end of Toronto."

"Shit no," said Casey. "I didn't say *in* Toronto, I meant way way way out in the slashes—and I'm talking about woods. It's uh south of Toronto and to the left as you're going up the Queen's Highway, comin' out of Buffalo...."

"Is there a Lion Country Safari or something like that there?" said Rodney.

"That's it," said Casey. "The Safari."

"Yeah," said Nigel, "it's near Hamilton."

Casey's mind wandered freely. "I don't know where the hell it is. So we went up to that park up there, what the hell's that park north of Toronto? Oh shit...."

With that we all started losing interest and a lot of noise started coming out of the walkie-talkies. Winston was sitting in the truck about half a block away and was testing the system out on Nigel. "Can you hear me?" said Nigel.

"No, no," said Casey. "It wasn't in a park near Toronto, it was way up in Northern Canada. Oh, you guys'll like this story. See? I was up there on a hunting trip and—now get this—I was with my forty-one-year-old son, see? And we run into this twenty-seven-year-old woman. She just showed up out of nowhere. Never saw her before and have no idea where she came from. Right in the middle of the dag-blamed forest. And so, listen you guys, listen. She kept pressing her tits up against me and saying you not have to go tonight, no? That's the way they talk up there. Now, my son's a nice-looking young man, but she was more interested in me for some dang-blasted reason, I couldn't figger it out no-bloody-how. So I says to her I says, where's your girl friend? She says to me, she says, what girlfriend? Another woman for my son, I says. She says she don't have no woman friend, she's all alone. All alone in the Great Canadian Forest. Jay-zuz, I tell ya."

A car drove up and a bunch of people got out. Casey sprang to life. "There's a fiddlin' party this afternoon here," he sang out. "You know what they're having? Fiddlers playing fer four hours straight non-stop, that's all. Starts at two o'clock, two bucks a person, hamburgers and hot dogs, the bar's open now, go take a look."

"Don't forget to tell them about the snatch," I said, perversely.

"Oh hell no, I can't say that. They're with their wives."

"Can you hear me?" said Nigel.

The walkie-talkie crackled and Winston's voice said "No."

"They change bands every hour and there's four bands," Casey shouted out, even though the people had gone inside already.

"Yeah?" said Nigel.

"Yeah," said Casey, more quietly, "and there's plenty of snatch around too, enough for all of us combined."

"Can you hear this, Winston?" said Nigel.

"No."

"He must be able to hear it," said Casey. "Or how could he answer?"

"That's right, I never thought of that," I said.

"Wrong frequency maybe," said Nigel. "Put it on F-one."

Winston got out of the truck and wandered over with the walkie-talkie.

"Does this little switch have to be on?" he said.

"I don't know," said Nigel. "I've got mine on."

"I'll put mine on too then."

"Can you hear this?" said Nigel.

"Sqzzzrpptlllllllnk!" Ear-splitting squelch. Away down the street you could see a policeman the size of an earwig turn and look.

"Yeah," said Winston. Everyone laughed.

"Can you hear this?" said Nigel.

"Can you hear this?" said Winston.

"Can you hear this?" said Nigel.

"Hear this?" said Winston.

"Yeah," said Nigel.

"All right, I'm going for a little walk," said Winston.

"Okay, don't walk more than a quarter mile," said Nigel.

Red-haired Rodney had meanwhile taken the third walkie-talkie for a walk, and now you could hear his voice saying things like: "Breaker breaker this is Bunny Hutch headquarters come in come in," and "This is the Columbia, Mr. and Mrs. Houston Arcade, height is 24.3 degrees we are directly over the Soviet-Afghan Friendship Pumpkin Patch."

"Okay Winston," said Nigel, "come in for a safe landing now, turn around, start heading back, we'll get a little portrait of this guy with his NASA hat."

"Sounds too good to be true," said Winston.

"Rodge," said Rodney.

"Rodge," said Winston.

"Rodge," said Rodney.

"Rodge," said Winston.

"Rrrrroger," said Rodney.

"Okay now," said Winston. "How's about some squelch?" Another ear-splitting "sqzzzrpptlllll-llnk!" and some crows from the field behind the firehouse took to the air.

"Now your rate of descent is 1.5 million metres per second," said Rodney. Confirm that, over?"

"One-point-four billion confirmed," said Winston.

"No, not billion. Million. Confirm...."

"Come on," said Casey, getting bored. He apparently didn't realise all this was in honour of him and his hat. "I'll buy you a beer. Come on in, come on in. I'll buy you a beer, come on in and have a beer on me, come on, come on in, all of yez, come on, let's have a beer."

"These guys are too young to drink," I said. "They're just babies."

"Is there food in there?" said Nigel.

"Huh? Whazzzat?" More squinting.

"They're starved, Casey," I said.

"Yeah, we're starving to death," said Nigel. "We haven't had our breakfast yet."

"Well," said Casey. "You better go down and eat. Woody Woodpecker's is the place. You see where that grey building is, see it? As a matter of fact, go right down here, this street here, okay? You go down to the main street and go to Woody Woodpecker's Restaurant and go in the back and get a sandwich or somethin' fer breakfast, like. But I don't know if the restaurant's open up above...."

"And these guys want to get to Rochester tonight or tomorrow morning," I said.

"Tonight would be good," said Nigel. He turned to me. "Listen. We could go get something to eat, come back and do a bit of filming, then we could meet you in Rochester tomorrow morning if you want to take it slower. We'll drive through the night and get up early tomorrow morning."

I asked Casey for the driving time to Rochester.

"Two and a half hours," he declared. "But the best time to go to Rochester is after the farmers are off the road."

"What time's that?"

"Well, it settles down after five o'clock. The farmers are on the road up till then, see? They're gettin' all their grain in, y'know? And they're always jes' crawlin' along the road carryin' loadsa cement blocks or whatever at five miles an hour and they won't let ya by."

Winston was standing there with the camera. "We should get a little shot of this guy," said Nigel.

"Sure," said Winston.

Nigel looked at Casey. "Do you mind being in our film?"

"No. Of course not."

"We just want to get a dead-on shot of you."

"Good, but come on in and have a beer. Now's a good time to have a beer to start off a good day on the right foot."

"No, I can't get these guys drunk yet," said Nigel. "I've got to wait till at least two o'clock."

"Jes' one beer," said Casey. "Christ almighty!"

"American beer," I said.

"No," said Casey in an Irish accent. "It's Oirish."

"Why don't you go over and have some eggs and bacon and then come back?" I said.

"Yeah, we'll meet you back here. I'll just stick your walkie-talkie behind your seat there." Casey started walking over to the little Spitfire.

"I'll take the walkie-talkie in with me just in case you want to contact me for anything," I said. The big guys down the street had real neat walkie-talkies when I was a kid but they never let me play with them.

"I don't think we will," said Nigel.

"Aww?" I whined.

"It's a really short range, you know, only about a quarter of a mile. So I'll just stash it here behind...."

"Out in the country they work a lot farther," said Winston.

The fire hall was on the outskirts of the village so it was like being out in the country.

"Yeah?" said Nigel. For some reason he wanted me to keep my hands off that walkie-talkie. I couldn't figure it out. All my life people have been refusing to let me play with their walkie-talkies.

"Yeah, it's in the city, it's a quarter mile."

We were alone. Casey had disappeared. I went into the fire hall looking for him and the guys followed. I told them to go and eat but they wanted to look around first. Casey was back talking to big fat Penny Coomber. It looked as if Casey had been whispering naughty things in her ear. She was blushing.

"Were you always like this?" she said.

"Always."

"Even when you were little?"

"Oh yeah, I was *really* like this then. You shoulda seen me."

Casey temporarily had the job of stamping the hands of people as they paid their two bucks. You had to have your hand stamped.

"Gimme yer hand, gimme yer hand," he said to the woman. She feigned reluctance. "It's so they won't bitch at you, know what I mean?"

"Where do you want it?" she said, meaning her hand. There was a twinkle in her eye. That's the trouble with this older generation. They're just totally obsessed with sex.

"In the middle...." He spread his legs and put her hand solidly on his you-know-what. I was astonished, and Nigel looked pretty amazed too. People just didn't carry on this way where we came from, not people in Casey's age bracket anyway.

The woman blushed and stammered. "Why you dirty...."

Casey changed his approach, but not his intent. "Where do you want it, huh?" Meaning where do you want to get stamped.

"Anywhere."

"That's what she said at the picnic. Har har."

Nigel collected himself and broke into the frivolity. "Er, we couldn't get you to come outside with us, could we?"

"Shore can," said Casey, "as soon as my assistant gets here." He was filling in with the hand-stamp for someone. "Well, here he is now!"

Casey got to his feet and out we went. Nigel positioned the old guy in front of the old school bell, Winston pointed the camera at him and people walked by and made funny remarks.

"Watch yer manners," said Casey. "These here gentlemen are Canadians!"

Everyone smiled. "Hey Casey," yelled out one particularly witty yokel, "you'll break their cameras."

"Yeah, Casey," said somebody else who wasn't all that big on originality. "You will, you'll break their cameras."

"He's a pro, he's done this before, he fought in the first world war!" said someone else. I'd never heard that one before but you could tell it wasn't all that new.

Casey seemed to be one of those guys everyone liked but no one wanted to be friends with. I couldn't take my eyes off him.

"Are you a volunteer fire-fighter?" I said.

"Oh yeah, I have been since Christ was a corporal."

"You mean since Pontius was a pilot."

"Har har har," said Casey. "You guys are great. You can go in and take pictures if you want." The band was wailing away inside, so the guys went in to get some shots. Casey and I stood there in front of the big bell. Casey started talking money. "Now this is some gathering the fire department has, you can put it in your book, Dave. Two weeks ago we dreamt up this idea to make money for the fire department, right? And this building we put up on our own, it cost $50,000 you see, so a guy came up and wanted to buy it with the property for $250,000 but it only cost us one dollar for the property but we can't sell it because we bought it off the village, see? So we turned around and gave the village the property we owned back of the fire department for a dollar, so even steven...."

"That's amazing, Casey."

"Yeah. Now this is a historic village, all of it you know. I bought an 1841 house for $5,900. Now the 100% assessment on it is $31,000. So I told the guy you give me $50,000 for it—tweet" (he whistled)— "and you can have it, I'll just leave everything intact—goodbye, I'll see ya."

"How long ago did you buy it?"

"Twenty-five years ago."

Nigel and the boys came back out and stood there smiling at Big Casey.

"You guys gotta come over in July," he said. "It's always in July we have the field day. Jesus Christ, you guys should bring a gang over, you'll have a ball. The guys come over from Cardinal, you know what they do?"

"No, what?" we all said.

"They put a tent in my front yard. One two three four blocks away. It's the only front yard in Sackett that's shaved. I get down on my knees and shave it with a razor.

"Dave was saying that when he asked you where you were born you said something funny, something about a stump?" said Nigel.

Casey beamed with pleasure. "I wasn't born, I was shit on a stump and the sun hatched me out." Everyone laughed. "No, I was born and raised in Buffalo—that is now all niggers." This last was uttered in a deeply ominous tone, like the British complaining about Saxon encroachments in the sixth century. We looked at him. "Coloured. Gennesee and Jefferson, the roughest goddamned place in Buffalo, New York."

"Hm," said Kukla, Fran and Ollie, in unison, with thoughtful looks on their faces.

"Any black people in Sackett's Harbour?" said I.

"Not so far. Oh wait. Yeah, there's one, and he is now a guard up at Briar Hill, which used to be the air-force radar-station. And, uh, he's the guard up there."

"Good guy?"

"So so, you know? They're still a little touchy, you know? You just say hi to him when you see him. Good mornin'. But to associate with them, hey, you keep 'em at arm's length."

"Why?"

Casey looked downright thoughtful. "I don't know, I don't know, I couldn't tell you, I couldn't tell you, but with me there's goodenbad in everyone, huh?"

"I agree. Don't you guys agree?"

"Yep," said Nigel. "Goodenbad in everyone."

"I agree," said Winston.

"Me too," said Rodney. "Though in some people there's more good than bad and vice versa."

"But when I was in the army, well, I called 'em bad asses. They're bad asses when they're in the army, boy."

Another carload unloaded and Casey greeted them. "This is the fling, the Fiddler's Fling, they started at two o'clock and they don't end till six. The bar is open and you go around and park, it costs you two bucks—to get in, that is. Free to park."

"Okay, we'll be right back."

Casey looked at me. "That's what she said at the picnic."

"You said that before. What does that mean?"

"That's what she said at the picnic?"

"Yeah. What do you mean?"

"Come on, do you wanna screw now or later? Yuk yuk. I'll be right back."

72. Over the Sea from Ireland

The cinematographic trio still hadn't eaten. But there they were, mixing it up in the dance hall, filming the band, filming the dancers. I wandered around trying to strike up conversations. I got chatting with a tiny leprechaun of an old geezer with a serious and intelligent face who was with his daughter. She was about forty and looked just like him. He said he was eighty. "I guess I got the advantage on him, eh?" he said when I mentioned that Casey was only seventy.

The band was playing, the twenty or so fiddlers, guitarists, accordionists and so on all standing and solemnly swaying in time with the beat in a row two deep along the back wall of the fire-hall ballroom. Old Frank O'Hara on the extreme left was strumming furiously on the washboard, his skinny intense body jerking back and forth from the waist up and his foot pounding the floor. Frank was a very serious musician and the toughest, thinnest, and hungriest-looking old guy in the place. He was a ratty-looking guy, and he made no bones about wanting to be discovered by the camera.

"Git a shotta me," he kept squealing, "git a shotta me, and make sure you git me in this film. I've played up in Canada. I can play most anyfing. Waltzes, polkas, anyfing. My name's Frank O'Hara."

All he was doing was strumming his fingers along a washboard, it didn't seem that any special talent was required. But maybe there was. He was taking it as seriously as if he'd been studying with Rostropovich all his life.

"In Canada they play different but I can play wif 'em. There ain't too many can compete wif me."

Everyone seemed happy we were there. Was the band playing better because of the camera? Were the folks dancing better? Hard to say. At one point I was standing at the snack counter and Nigel came up with a full cup of coffee and said to the girl behind the counter: "Would you mind pouring some of this coffee out?" The girl was a little distracted by the music.

"Parn me?" she said.

"Could you please pour some of this coffee out? I can't get enough cream in it."

"Oh, you wanna pour some of it out?"

"Yeah, could you?"

The girl poured some down the drain. "Is that enough?"

"No do more, a bit more."

But she was listening to a particularly snappy fiddle solo. "You want me to pour out some more?"

"Yeah do more." She did.

"Thanks."

"I was telling my friends how this woman came up to you in the bar and started to hustle you," I said to Casey. We were all standing around on the grass in front of the big silver bell again.

"Yeah," he said, a mock look of pained astonishment on his face, as if saying what is this world coming to? "She came up to me and sonofabitch she grabbed my hand and christ-almighty she put it on her leg. She's got enough ass on one cheek for all four of us." Everyone laughed. Rodney got something stuck in his throat and started coughing and flushing a bit. "She's got two axe handles across the ass, hasn't she, Dave?"

"Maybe three," I said.

"Three axe handles?" said Winston.

"You ain't kiddin', you know what an axe handle is? Okay, that's about like that"—he held out his hands a yard apart—"and she's three. I woulda said two but if Dave sez three he oughta know."

"Whew! This guy's the horniest seventy year old in the world."

Somebody said something about the big silver bell. When was it made? "I think it was 1845," said Casey. "We had it cleaned. I don't know just how old it is but we had it down in the old fire hall and they used to sit up and clang it whenever there was a fire."

"Let's give it a good clang right now," I suggested. "Oops, there's no clanger."

"Well, you could just hit it with a rock or something," said Rodney, jokingly.

"Looks new," I said, studiously. "Doesn't look 139 years old."

"No," said Casey, "but they cleaned it, they used brushes and everything."

We found the date stamped on the casing—1845.

"There you go," said Casey. "Okay, you can set up your camera anywhere you want and take any pictures you want, see you mugs later." Casey went back in for another Canadian mist.

Someone had been telling Nigel about Hillbilly Heaven, a place out on the highway where they have country music and a lot of heavy drinking and dancing. Nigel was intrigued, and seemed a little disappointed I didn't want to head out there that evening. But just then a car pulled up with a Hillbilly Heaven bumpersticker, and a woman got out along with two little twin girls in old-fashioned long calico dresses.

"Do you go there?" said Nigel to the woman, pointing to the bumpersticker.

"Oh yeah!"

"What's it like?"

"Oh, they got a good band, wonderful band. But there's too much smoke."

"Tobacco?"

"I hope that's what it is." She wanted Winston to take a shot of her car. "It's a seventy-six," she said. "I just got it a month ago. Just made my second payment. Isn't it lovely?" It looked like an old wreck. "As soon as I got it I painted it." It was a smudgy streaky blue colour, very amateurish paint job to be sure.

"How did you paint it?"

"With a sponge. Isn't it lovely? I never thought I'd ever have a car like this."

Casey came back out looking all sweaty and excited, fire in his eyes. He had something important to report. He called us aside.

"You know what some sonofabitch come up and told me? This bastard just come up and told me the urinals were too high. I told him to use the commode. Harty har har, huh?"

The little twin calico sweethearts had discovered the little red Spitfire parked there on the corner and were jumping up and down with glee. They looked about eight years old. They came running over and said is this your car? When I said yes they wanted me to take them for a ride. Their mother seemed to have gone in. I leered at them with mock lechery and said give me a kiss each and I'll take you for a ride.

They didn't mind. They each gave me a sweet little peck and I propped them up on the lip of the trunk with their legs down inside where the back seat would go if there'd been room for one. I drove them at ten miles an hour down a couple of blocks to the lake, along the lake to the fort, and back the way we came. It was a nice drive with the blue sky, the fall colours, the tall sailboats lined up along the dock, the warm clear sun, the historic charm of the small town, and most importantly there was no traffic, not even pedestrian traffic. Almost everyone was mysteriously elsewhere. They all couldn't have been at the fire hall. There were a lot of people at the fire hall, true, but not enough to vacate the whole town.

One guy put in an appearance during our little historical tour. I guess he'd seen us go by the first time and it got him cursing under his breath, people having fun in anti-American Communistic foreign cars or some such emotion, because this time he came flying out his door onto the porch, down the stairs and down the concrete walk to the road and then out in front of our car with his arms outstretched and a furiously red face. I made a panic stop inches from hitting him, if you can make a panic stop at ten miles per hour.

"You better sit down in that thing," he said with a snarl. God was definitely on his side. I tried to drive around him and he ran in front of the car again. So I got the kids to sit, one on the other's lap, in the passenger seat. He looked somewhat pleased with himself as if he'd won a moral victory, or saved their lives potentially, or saved them from Satan. It wasn't as much fun for them.

"Isn't it fun sitting down so low to the ground?" I said, soothingly.

"No," they said, poutingly.

"Ah come on, that's what's so nice about sports cars, low to the ground. Ask anyone. It's fun. You should ask your mom and dad to buy one for you. Don't pout."

When we got back the Hillbilly Mama came flying furiously out of the fire hall and she looked mad too—well, worried maybe, maybe a bit concerned. I prepared myself for the worst.

"Oh mommy," the kids said, "he said he'd take us for a ride if we kissed him so we both did and he took us for a ride. It was fun. He said we should ask you to buy us a little car like this. Will you?"

The lady looked at me with big question marks in her eyes. I smiled and said, "I told them never never never do this with strangers, just with me." I was refusing to show the tinges of guilt I felt for not at least having asked her permission to take them for a ride, which was thoughtless of me. And I'd just read the Clifford Olson book, too. Tsk, I should have been more sensitive to the moral implications. Four-inch spikes driven slowly into the kids' heads while they were wide awake, gagged and bound.

"You girls know better than that," she said, sternly, but not sternly enough to be impolite to me, a perfectly respectable Canadian visitor. Maybe they're freer with each other's kids up there, but I wish the guy had asked me first. I would have said okay, he's obviously not a sex maniac, which is true although I do sometimes get a touch manic under certain circumstances, never involving kids believe me.

The film crew was filming and taping the little scene. The little girls wanted to sing a song in Rodney's big professional-looking microphone. "Should we sing a rock-n-roll song?"

"No," said the mother, "not rock-n-roll. That's terrible stuff; that's garbage." She put her hand on the shoulder of one of the twins and said, "Mary-Anne here is learning to play the fiddle, and Mary-Jane's learning the squeezebox. The Koreans are teaching them."

"Koreans?"

"Yeah, Korean country-and-western musicians. It's really big over there, and they're all coming over here. And you know they were telling us that over there in Korea when you apply for a driver's licence you have to take your test in a football stadium."

"What?" Everybody crowded around to hear more.

"Yeah, in a football stadium. You have to drive right in and drive all around this complicated little course, backing up, parking and everything, and people pay admission to sit in the stands and watch and laugh...."

"Oh they stole that idea from the Canadians," I said. "Canada's been doin' that for years."

"Really? I never heard about that."

"Oh yeah, it's big business. There's a lot you don't know about Canada. It's not all Commies and Mounties you know."

The little calico canaries had opened their sharp little flattened beaks and started warbling. "I get up but nothing gets me down, / You got it tough but I sing a tough song...." They suddenly stopped. "Oh darn, I forgot it," said Mary-Jane.

"Me too," said Mary-Anne.

Or maybe it was the other way around.

"I'll meet yez back inside," said mom.

"You got nice kids, lady," I said with a smile.

"Thanks."

"Stuck, eh?" said Nigel, to the kids. They right away continued the song on the sidewalk next to that parked blood-red sports car under a perfect blue sky and surrounded by rows and rows of stately maples in full riot of fall colours painted on black velvet, continued it exactly where they'd left off: "And I know baby just how you feel / You gotta rollllll with the punches...."

The twins wanted our address. "We live in the mental institution," said Rodney. "We're all crazy."

"You live in the mental institution?"

"Yeah, we all live there. All three of us. Boo!" The kids jumped. "This guy escaped so we thought we'd follow him around and film him."

"Don't tell your mother," I said.

Just then who should reemerge from the fire hall but....

"Hey mom, they said we're going to be in a movie and in a book. But they all live in a mental institution. They're crazy, mom!" She spun her little forefinger around her little ear.

Casey was suddenly there, and our bacon was saved. He quietly asked me to come over to his car. He wanted me to hear something. "Listen to this," he said. It was his favourite song, Bing Crosby singing "Galway Bay," and Casey just sang along, he knew all the words, every one. "I love that," he said. "Oh the breezes blowin' o'er the seas from Ireland / Are perfumed by the heather as they blow...."

He smacked his hand down on the fender of the car after we listened to the song three times. "What do you think of this little shitbox? I used to have a Blazer, I traded it in for this—$7,980 I paid for it."

"Brand new?"

"Oh yeah! Shit, it's only got six thousand miles on it."

He wanted to talk about what we were going to do with all the film we were shooting. "You gonna let me know when it's gonna be on TV? I'll have the whole goddamned village out to watch it. What channel'll it be on, channel 9?"

"We don't know yet. Probably some Toronto channel you can't get here."

"Toronto, that's a shit-assing town." He meant he liked it.

"I always thought so but it's nice to hear you say it."

He laughed and didn't laugh at the same time. "Nice to hear you say it. You guys are really funny. Now, are ya listenin'? Up there in Toronto my son and I got lost, at the airport. You go north, there's some kind of a park or something there. Oh it's beautiful up there. They got somethin' different goin' for them up there."

"Like what for instance?" Was he about to get thoughtful? No way. "The money," he said. "We call it funny money."

I asked him about his forty-one-year-old son. "Does he live in Sackett's Harbour?"

"No, he got married and moved to Adams, got a nice home there, and he's got two kids already."

"Adams, eh? What does he do?"

"He's an accountant."

"Work for himself?"

"No, he works in the office of a manufacturing plant up there in Watertown."

"What do they manufacture?"

"Swizzle sticks. They make those little plastic swizzle sticks you get in your drink. They send 'em all over the world."

"Is his wife Irish, and, if so, are she and the kids in Ireland right now?"

"Uh. Yeah, how did you know?"

I smiled mysteriously. He looked more and more puzzled.

"Come on now, how'd ya know?"

"I'll tell you some time."

73. Conversation Overheard at Woody Woodpecker's

Fred, Fred and Fred were at Woody Woodpecker's. I never did get to see the place but as I sat at the bar in the fire hall I flicked on the walkie-talkie absentmindedly and suddenly could hear them merrily chatting away over their long-delayed breakfast a quarter of a mile or so away. They had no idea their conversation was being beamed out all over the pretty little village. Who knows who else was monitoring it besides me? Maybe the killjoy who ran in front of the car and forced me to make Mary-Jane and Mary-Anne sit down was furiously listening to it on his special radio monitor used to detect unamerican activities. He would be wearing headphones and sitting in front of his huge assemblage of electronic equipment, and his veins would be bulging out of his forehead as he listened in furious sweaty incredulous frenzy. At first the crew were talking about the giant woodpecker out front and the woodpecker cartoons all over the walls, woodpecker salt-and-pepper shakers, and the woodpecker songs on the jukebox.

"Did you see the jukebox?" Rodney was saying. "Every song has some reference to a woodpecker in it." If they realised the walkie-talkie was on, they soon forgot. I shushed up Casey the bartender so I could concentrate on scribbling in my notebook, trying to record everything they were saying on the other side of town. I can't guarantee any degree of accuracy. At times the sound would fade and drift and trying to record the conversation became an inkblot trick. Often it seemed that what I was writing down was coming out of my mind rather than out of the mouths of the lads. And it kept getting less and less accurate as we went on, the batteries fading and all that....

Black-haired Nigel had apparently just ordered a club sandwich. Think of him as speaking in a low, easy-going monotone punctuated with quiet laughter, think of red-haired Rodney as having a high-pitched boy-like enthusiastic voice, a bit wobbly with nervous excitement at times, and of blonde, blue-eyed Winston as having a slow, lazy, very relaxed, well-modulated and sexy voice. Here's the conversation as I recorded it. Probably tells more about me than about them.

Waitress: "You want minis on that?"

Nigel: "Pardon me?"

Waitress: "Meanies? You want some meanies?"

Nigel: "Er?"

"Mayonnaise," I hollered over the walkie-talkie. I'm not sure they knew where the voice came from, or that it was me, but they heard it all right.

Nigel: "Oh. Mayonnaise. Yeah. I thought you said...."

Waitress: "Did I say something wrong?"

Nigel: "I thought you said minis."

Waitress: "Hah hah, you mean like mini-skirts? No."

Another female voice: "She never wears 'em."

Casey heard this last comment, blinked, then yelled over the speaker: "Ask her if she wears knickers." Everybody heard him. Much static-filled laughter.

Waitress: "Are you guys Russian spies or somethin'?"

Nigel: "Oh no, not at all. That's just our walkie-talkies acting up." (A few moments of indecipherable mumbling ensued.)

Winston: "I'll have the tripledecker as well, on brown bread, with mayonnaise? And does that come with french fries?"

Waitress: "Do tripledeckers come with french fries? No they don't. The turkey's still in the oven but I can get you a tripledecker."

Nigel: "Could I have a clam chowder?"

Waitress: "Pardon?"

Nigel: "Clam chowder?"

Waitress: "Gene, do we have any clam chowder? There's no price on that, is there? No, I don't think so."

Nigel: "No?"

Waitress. "No."

Nigel: "So what do you have?"

Waitress: "A lot of these things we just carry in the summer. You see, we're not open. We're only open on weekends now, I mean. See, I mean we're not open all the time. And clams will ferment."

Nigel: "Oh! What's your soup of the day?"

Waitress: "Vegetable."

Nigel: "Okay, I'll have the soup of the day and an egg-salad sandwich on white and a choco-late milkshake."

Rodney: "And I'll have the special."

Waitress: "Okay."

Winston: "I may as well too. Does it come with gravy?"

Waitress: "Pardon?"

Winston: "Gray-V?"

Waitress: "Yeah, I'm sure there is. And that's fresh mashed potatoes, you know, not instant."

Winston: "Right. Fresh'll be okay I guess. And I'll have coffee...."

Rodney: "I'll have a large chocolate shake."

Winston: "Oh yeah, that's what I'll have too."

Waitress: "Two large chocolate shakes?"

Strange voice (from another table?): "You put lettuce on that I assume."

(About thirty seconds of static.)

Rodney: "All thirteens. It was April 13, 1913, at thirteen hundred hours, one o'clock in the afternoon. Or no, that's when it happened. That's when the explosion happened."

Nigel: "I have a scrapbook and I've got one whole page full of anything to do with the number 23."

Winston: "What's the scoop on 23-skidoo?"

Nigel: "Nobody really knows what it means. It's sort of buried in tradition."

Rodney: "I think we started something. There's a flurry of activity in the bathroom."

(Inexplicable laughter.)

Nigel: "Some people think it means, like, death, right?"

Rodney: "I think somebody explained what that was once, what that means.... Speaking of buried in tradition, do you know what rule of thumb means?"

Nigel: "No."

Rodney: "I think it comes from England. There was a law that you could beat your wife, but the whip or the cane couldn't be any thicker than your thumb. And that's where the term rule of thumb comes from."

Nigel: "Yeah?... Speaking of England, William S. Burroughs wrote this really interesting book called *The Job*, with a guy called Brion Gysin. Brion Gysin's this abstract painter from England. I guess they were kind of lovers or whatever, they lived together for a long time in England. And he was the one who told Burroughs about his cut-up techniques. That's how he writes most of his books. He'll write a story, right? And he'll take newspaper clippings and then he'll just fold them all up and he'll cut them in sections and piece them back together. That's how *Naked Lunch* was written. And he was probably on heroin too."

Winston: "You mean one article will be cut up?"

Nigel: "Yeah, I don't have anything with me, but it's really neat. You can just take anything, right? And cut it four ways and switch them around and get these really weird associations."

Winston: "Yeah."

Rodney: "That's like film editing."

Nigel: "Yeah, and that's where he got *Naked Lunch* from and the term heavy metal."

Rodney: "That's like that Art Garfunkel/Nicolas Roeg film, *Bad Timing*. You got the sense you could have just taken the pages of the script and slit them into pieces like this and rearranged them just anyway you wanted to. Did you see that film?"

Nigel: "Yeah, I loved it."

Rodney: "Yeah, I thought it was great."

Nigel: "It turned me off sex for a couple of days, but it was a pretty good movie."

Rodney: "I thought it was pretty interesting, but the thing I found was most interesting of all though was that if that film had been in a completely linear order it...."

Winston: "It would have been awful."

Rodney: "It would have been terrible. It would have been a completely mediocre film."

Nigel: "He's got another one coming out, eh? Called *Eureka*, that was shot in B.C."

Rodney: "Oh really? Is that right?"

Nigel: "Yeah, where you're from. It hasn't got released yet. I was reading about it in *Sight and Sound*."

Rodney: "And speaking of *Naked Lunch*. You know, if they ever made a movie out of that and if they ever made a movie out of Margaret Atwood's first novel it would be neat if they ran both movies on a double bill at the Bloor Cinema or something, you know the way they do."

Winston: "I don't get it."

Rodney: "What was Margaret Atwood's first book?"

Nigel: "*The Edible Woman*?"

Rodney: "*Naked Lunch* and *The Edible Woman*. Tonight only."

Nigel: "Oh, I get it."

Winston: "Have you read *The White Hotel*?"

Nigel: "Oh yeah."

Rodney: "Who wrote that?"

Winston: "Somebody's making a film of that."

Rodney: "Who wrote that? I meant to pick that up."

Winston: "I thought Nicolas Roeg might make a good candidate."

Nigel: "I thought maybe Roman Polanski.... Yeah, that's a great book."

Rodney: "Who's that by again?"

Nigel: "What do you mean?"

Rodney: "Who wrote that book?"

Winston: "What book?"

Rodney: "*The White Hotel*."

Winston: "D.M. Thomas."

Rodney: "Oh, yeah. D.M. Thomas. Right, yeah. That one...."

Nigel: "This girl at school I went around with, who was a poet and sort of into archery and Hare Krishna, went to see him read at Harbourfront and all these people brought their copies of his books and got him to sign them. And he wrote in her book: From one sexual hysteric to another. She said he was really sexy and everything, this old guy. You can sort of tell from the books he writes."

Rodney: "Sex."

Winston: "I've only read that one."

Nigel: "His other ones aren't quite as good."

Winston: "It's just amazing the way it's structured, the different points of view take over the same story. It's really incredible."

Nigel: "Yeah, I guess I've read it one and a half times. Yeah, it's really neat."

Winston: "I'd love to make a film of that."

Rodney: "Well, that's really the basis for your film, isn't it? The next one coming out, so much of it is different perspectives on things, isn't it? Which is very difficult to do."

Nigel: "I saw you reading that book. You were reading that in the hallway of Women's College in Huntsville. I think you were there the first day we were up there shooting *The Machine*."

Winston: "What was I reading then?"

Nigel: "*The White Hotel*."

Winston: "Really? I guess I was rereading it then."

Nigel: "Yeah, you were sitting there in the hall reading it. That's a great book. I lent it to somebody and they never sent it back to me."

Winston: "Yeah? So did I. This guy, I can't get ahold of him now, I lost contact with him, he's got my original copy."

(Sound of munching on food.)

Rodney: "What's Tracy Ronald's new film called?"

Nigel: "*Subway Symphony*.... Terrible title."

Rodney: "Well, it sounds like his other films. *Opera Singers on the Loose*. Wasn't that it? *Opera Singers on the Loose*?"

Nigel: "Yeah, and *Paradox on Tiptoes*."

Rodney: "I saw *Opera Singers on the Loose* on TV and I liked the whole thing."

Nigel: "You really have to be into that kind of music to enjoy it."

Rodney: "Oh yeah."

Nigel: "I saw it at the Festival, and I went with Larry. It turns out that Tracy was sitting in the aisle and we were the only people that walked out. It was so slow."

Winston: "Which one?"

Nigel: "*Opera Singers on the Loose*."

Winston: "You didn't walk out on *Paradox on Tiptoes*?"

Nigel: "No. But I sort of felt bad walking out on that one. We knew Tracy was there, but we just left quietly. It was the sort of thing where you didn't make any noise, right?"

Rodney: "A friend of mine and I were really up on making a jazz film around this guy, this friend of ours who goes to Berklee College of Music, which is.... Do you know that?"

Nigel: "Yeah."

Rodney: "Down in Boston, right? It's just a really amazing place. And we were going to do that. And we tried so hard and then ultimately when I saw *Opera Singers on the Loose* I thought this was very similar to the sort of thing we would have done, and I'm not enjoying watching it at all."

Nigel: "Did you see it?"

Winston: "Yeah.... I worked on it too."

Nigel: "Oh, did you? What were you doing?"

Winston: "I was a second assistant. I didn't have to do too much at all."

Rodney: "You? You were just a lowly second assistant, Winston?"

Winston: "Lonely and lowly."

Nigel: "Remember that old Werner Herzog movie, Rodney? *Even Midgets Have to Start Small*."

Rodney: "Oh, that last scene with the camel was too much."

The talk switched to someone whose name I didn't catch, someone who'd lost a lot of money on a film. "Holy Geez," said Rodney, when Nigel mentioned how much money had actually been lost.

Nigel: "He's like a technical adviser for some film they're like shooting out in Newfoundland right now."

Winston: "It's scary losing money like that."

Rodney: "Oh God, really!"

74. Amazing Soup

As an occasional writer of imaginative fiction I felt it was my ironic duty to continue jotting down everything I heard on the walkie-talkie even though it (and I) continued to lose power and gain static. Not to mention that my handwriting became gradually sloppier and harder to read.

Nigel: "Everyone says how easy it is to go bankrupt and still just pick up where you left off but I really don't believe it.... This is amazing soup. Home-made vegetable."

Winston: "Oh, I didn't get mine, did I? Is there more soup?"

Waitress: "Yes, would you like some more?"

Winston: "Yes."

Waitress: "Cup or bowl?"

Winston: "The cup is smaller?"

Waitress. "Yes. A cup is ...just a cup."

Casey the Volunteer Fireman, who was still busy behind the bar and hadn't been listening, inadvertently overheard this last line and began whistling "As Time Goes By."

Winston: "Okay, a cup would be okay."

At this point, unfortunately, the walkie-talkie seemed to have been moved and I couldn't hear the conversation clearly enough to get all of it. Rodney seemed to be doing most of the talking at first. The conversation descended into the rather boring (to someone not in the field) realm of trying to make a living in films. Points, credits, investors, and so on. At one point Nigel came out with this line: "So if it ever breaks even and I'm sure by hook or by crook he's going to make it break even I'll get six thousand bucks, and anything over that I'll get half."

The conversation started to get more interesting again, but my hand began to tire and I knew I wasn't getting everything down accurately, but that just made everything more interesting....

Nigel: "There's so much consent off and on for about a year, then by seven o'clock you're completely exhausted, dragged out and dog tired, and you have to do all the shitty jobs as well."

Rodney: "Yeah. Well, somebody's brother, I don't know whose, it might even be mine, my brother that is, he gets a thousand a day."

Nigel: "Directors like Herby Shoemaker get two thousand dollars a day."

Rodney: "Oh, really?"

Nigel: "They're guaranteed seventy-five directing days a year, and they don't have to show up half that time. If they only show up for twenty-five days they still get paid for seventy-five. It's worse at the CBC. I have a friend who lucked into this job as a producer at the CBC and he says it's unbelievable. Like what happens a lot of the time is he'll sign a contract with a director and oh, it's unbelievable what happens a lot of the time."

Rodney: "Wasn't there a lighting exercise or something? And somebody's girl friend, it turns out, was being paid two hundred dollars a day to flick a switch on the wall when somebody told her to. She just had to sit at the wall waiting for somebody to tell her to flick the switch. And she did that all day every shooting day for a whole year."

Nigel: "Are you serious? Really? That's wild."

(More static....)

Winston: "His grandmother appears in one of his films and she slaughters a whole bunch of chickens. She has to tear the head off every chicken in the hen house. It's a horrible, horrible film."

Nigel: "It's so embarrassing. Second-to-last act of violence."

Rodney: "There's nothing worse than a horribly executed exploitive film."

Nigel: "Sometimes they're great. I love checking out Imperial Six. They show films like that all the time."

Rodney: "He really wants us to believe that this was a great film and he's really a serious artist too."

Nigel: "It's so embarrassing sometimes going in there in the afternoon. I like to sit in the balcony, which is usually all full of drug addicts and musicians and stuff. It's not so bad though because you can hide, right? But still it's so nervy and tense, right?"

Rodney: "What's the projection like?"

Nigel: "Oh, you know. They totally screw up the projection. They like to wait for every cut."

Rodney (to Winston): "How do you handle an opening night?"

Winston: "Last time, first time. It all remembers how you cost, at least when everybody's excited."

Nigel: "Yeah. Like at the festival."

Rodney: "As a camera assistant, heh. Big deal. Still...."

Nigel: "It's a shame."

Winston: "You get yourself a total investor and it's a shame when you have to test the final scene and of course he wasn't doing shot action."

Nigel: "And it seemed like I just don't like twenty-second shots and...."

Winston: "Audiences react so differently, according to the energy of the day and certain sequences...."

Nigel: "I saw it the first time, I saw...."

Waitress: "Do you want the cheques separate?"

Nigel: "All on one bill."

Waitress: "All on one bill?"

Nigel: "Yeah."

Rodney: "It's really weird when basically missing sort of films these things are about really weird because what I found was the more stylish the person was I was showing it to, a cinematographer or something much better, much more sort of considerate, terrible, it really embarrassed me a number of times, I mean when I like somebody's work, right? Hey, things like what the heck's going on here? They're getting into. Ryerson. Right while we're watching the film. Edgar Edgar. He's standing there."

Nigel: "The first film I worked on was Edgar Edgar giving Edgar was giving Edgar his big chance, right? Really exotic."

Rodney: "It was really weird, somebody too terrified to show it to you, you know life got a good reason basis for more heavyweight these people are the better either they're completely inconsiderate while they're watching it, a really experienced editor, or they're conscious and completely weird."

Nigel: "I think that's really true."

Winston: "And important too."

Rodney: "I don't know if it's important or not."

Winston: "Apparently most of the applications are totally stupid."

Nigel: "I tried to.... Uh, he's in the next booth right there."

Rodney: "Who is?"

Nigel: "Sven Nykvist."

Winston: "They wonder if your budget is."

Rodney: "They might not."

Nigel: "But the Council, the Canadian Arts Council. A thousand bucks. Stationery and all kinds of crap and it's worth it. Every kind of grant possible. You can't support campaigns."

Rodney: "Number of people, four or five people themselves. Lynn Evans."

Nigel: "Ralph."

Rodney: "No, Nick and Lynn. You could show this in a theatre or anything."

Nigel (to waitress): "We're making a little movie, eh?"

Waitress: "Pardon?"

Nigel: "We're making a movie."

Waitress: "Oh, are you? About what?"

Nigel: "There's this guy taking a trip around Lake Ontario and he's writing a book."

Waitress: "Pardon?"

Nigel: "There's this guy, a Canadian author who's written about twenty books, he's taking a trip around Lake Ontario, and writing a book about it, and we're making a movie about his book."

Waitress: "Oh. Well! Sort of an editorial like?"

Nigel (encouragingly): "That's right, sort of a documentary, and dramatic as well. Sort of a combination."

Waitress: "Oh, well. Thank you very much, sir."

75. Hands Across the Border

I was talking to the fellow on my right, who was a blackjack dealer from Las Vegas home for a holiday, about computers and bragging about my own, and the guy on my left started to make unfriendly sputtering sounds. He was a skinny old guy. I'd been vaguely aware of him eavesdropping there at the bar, and now he caught the worm of my eye in the hook of his own.

"You stole that computer," he said.

He crooked his barbed eye at me. He sounded a little drunk, a little crazy.

"Oh, did I?" I said. I sounded bored.

This was in the town of Woolcott on the south shore of Lake Ontario. I had a room upstairs for the night.

"You bet your fuckin' mother's boots you did," he said. He stuck out his hand and said, "I'm Frederick J. Meriwether III." I shook his hand, a stupid mistake. Never shake hands with a mean-looking guy who has just made a hostile remark. He started squeezing so hard I thought he was going to break every bone in my poor little artistic wimpy hand. I was just about to start hollering when he let it go. I rubbed it.

"That wasn't very fuckin' friendly," I said. He looked really mean. There was a young woman, early thirties, sitting on the other side of him and rolling her eyes. She insisted on trading places with him. He traded, and got back to his beer. But he kept watching me with hatred in his eye and nasty muttering under his breath.

The woman was about eight months pregnant. She started complaining softly in my ear about the old guy and apologising for him. She also started talking about her recent divorce. She was married a year ago and her husband was always beating her up, and now they were getting divorced, and she was about to have his baby. The old guy was a friend of her dad's. He'd been taking an interest in her since the split-up.

"He's really nice when he's sober but he's a bastard when he's had even one beer," she said.

"How come you're here in a bar with him then?" We were speaking quietly so he wouldn't hear and I could sense him getting angrier and angrier there on the other side of her, wondering what we were talking about.

"He offered to drive me to town to pick up some groceries. Then he insisted we come in for a beer. I said no, but otherwise how could I get home?"

The old guy glared at me. "You fuckin' well stole that computer," he said. "You and all those fuckin' Commies up in that stupid fuckin' country Canada."

"Shut up, Fred," she said.

"Don't tell me to shut up, you slut."

The guy kept getting worse and worse. I offered to drive the woman home myself. He was really into the beer now and was in no condition to drive. But she was afraid to let me take her home, afraid of what he would do to her later.

Finally we made the high sign to the bartender and he called the cops. They came just as Mr. Meriwether was starting up his car. They took him away in their cruiser. They said they'd charge him with something, then come back and drive the pregnant lady home. I went up to bed.

76. Chocolate Chess

I couldn't sleep and came down for another nightcap. The place was much quieter. The bartender told me the cops had returned, as promised, and taken the pregnant woman home. He claimed ignorance of the people involved. Said as far as he could remember they'd never been in the bar before.

But then came a poetry recitation on the television above the bar. Everyone shushed up. Prize-winning poet Ronald Reagan was reading but pretending to recite a poem akin to the speeches of some of those politicians in futuristic novels of the thirties, forties and fifties. You know the ones I mean. He was unleashing a Whitmanesque litany of Yankee optimism. Things had improved in the U.S.A. since the old days when Washington was calling the plays and all they ever did was fumble.

> Today, people are back in charge and America is scoring touchdowns.
> Inflation is down, and growth and jobs are up.
> Students are doing better in school.
> Crime is down, our people are united and America is at peace. . . .
> Shucks, I wish I could take the credit, but it belongs to all of you.
> And remember, the one great driving idea for our future:

Economic progress.

This was followed by a little news feature on chocolate. "There's even a seventy-dollar chocolate chess set," said the announcer. "It makes losing easier to swallow." Everyone was beginning to sound like Ronald Reagan. Or was it the other way around? At any rate, people were back in charge. You hear that, people?

The weatherman stood in front of his map. "We have some very serious weather conditions in the country," he said. He began giggling uncontrollably and continued for an alarming twenty seconds. Finally he composed himself and went on to talk about Hurricane Joan being just two hundred miles off the coast of North Carolina, with heavy rain in Texas and occasional snowflakes in western Canada. "But," he said, "the three-day lookout seems pretty doggone good." Then he got the giggles again.

Suddenly a bunch of people on the screen were demanding an end to the arms race. A black man with white hair and a sweet face stepped forward and started reading a speech:

> "We demand of our leaders in the congress and we demand of our President a movement in the direction of peace and tranquillity by ordering forthwith a nuclear freeze to bring sanity to this world. The Pershing II means computerised nuclear war and as the number of computer errors increase it's only a matter of time before nuclear errors occur. We're about to turn our planet into Mars because stupid old men can't get along with each other and settle their arguments with their hairy armpits."

"Hairy armpits?" I said. The bartender was wiping glasses. He just shrugged. "Is this a Reagan bar?" I said to him.

He squinted at me. "This is an apolitical bar," he said, "but Reagan's the only guy in Washington worth a spit." His voice was almost identical to Reagan's.

"But don't you find him kind of scary?"

"You mean nukes?"

I nodded, making a show of nibbling on my nails in fear.

"Don't worry about nukes. They'd never do it. It'd be suicide."

SUNDAY, OCTOBER 14

77. Ryokan for President

The morning was thick and bright with mist. You could hear the ear-splitting roar of that little sports car all over town. People were slamming their windows. Letter carriers were giving me dirty looks. Dogs and cats were pissing in my direction as I drove by. The steering wheel and seats were clammy with dew.

There was a nice little restaurant a block away from the hotel and I stopped there for breakfast, drinking coffee for half an hour and reading the morning paper in a small-town restaurant, with a surplus of waitresses, about four of them, sitting around gossiping. I clipped some articles from the paper. One was about a mass expulsion of students from a local high school because they baked a chocolate cake for the teacher and the cake was full of a powerful laxative. A real writer would make a hilarious seventeen-page short story out of that but I'm too lazy and besides you can imagine it yourself with your eyes closed, right?

The washroom featured wallpaper bearing repeated images of naked women in ornate Victorian bathtubs and peeking coyly from behind baroque toilets. And there was a rack of fairly new skin mags right there in the john.

As I was paying my bill I checked out a framed poem on the wall behind the cash register, a handwritten prose poem in the kind of calligrapher's handwriting the nineteenth-century Zen Buddhist anti-poet Ryokan found so annoying. One of his more brilliant but lesser-known poems goes like this:

> If there's anything I can't stand
> it's songs by a singer,
> poems by a poet
> and handwriting by a calligrapher.

A guy about fifty with a pointed Dali moustache and curly white hair, permed, the kind of guy who should be wearing spats or hosting a game show, watched me reading the poem on the wall. He had a proprietary air about him. I wasn't sure if he owned the restaurant or the poem, or maybe both, or more likely he owned the restaurant and the person who had written the poem. You've had the Ryokan poem, now for the poem on the wall, as well as I could translate the flowery calligraphy:

> Here I sit bored you see but pretty soon I'll be busy as a bee.
> One minute it's slow the next is fast
> but all of a sudden everything is past.
> "Flip those hamburgers," "put down the toast," "get a small milk"
> perfect timing and everything goes smooth as silk.
> It's been 7 years of fun watching all the customers come and go.
> Some are strangers, some are farmers
> but most of them are steady charmers.
> The inspector comes everyone is frantic
> to see if we stay open everyone panics.
> It's a self service station that is not really an obligations
> But everyone still helps themselves and friends
> thats what makes our coffee the style never end!

The poem was signed Cathy Lee Armenian, with calligraphy by Samantha Lee Froom. And stuck in a corner of the frame was Samantha's business card, with an address and phone number in Watkins Glen. You could just phone her number and have her take your poem and do it up real pretty and put it in a frame. I figured Cathy had worked for seven years in the restaurant and wrote the poem on the occasion of her quitting, moving on to better things.

"You like that?" said Salvador.

"Terrific poem, just terrific," I said. "You know the poet?"

"That's my daughter," he said. "She's got hundreds of little poems like that."

"She used to work here?"

"Sure did. She wrote that poem to commemorate the seven years she worked here."

"And what's she doing now?"

His face beamed with pointy-moustachioed pride and pleasure.

"She's at college, studying TV production at Albany College."

I told him her poem reminded me of the Canadian poet Diana Hartog and that I thought Cathy would really like Diana's work and maybe find it stimulating and inspiring. I gave him a few titles and the publisher's name and everything. He seemed genuinely delighted, just kept thanking me over and over and saying this is really going to mean a lot to Cathy.

Who knows? Little things like this can make a huge difference in somebody's life. Every one of us is a blind agent of fate.

As I left I had a funny feeling something was wrong. I felt as if Dali and I had quietly exchanged souls. He had become me. I had become him. And there was no returning.

My heart was extraordinarily light and heavy at the same time.

The feeling lasted only a second.

78. American Mist

The thick morning mist seemed to rise like a curtain to let me pass through it then immediately lower behind me. I kept driving along narrow roads that kept sweeping along the shore then veering through the rolling farmland south of the lake. The atmosphere was moody, strange, full of strange shades of grey and gold. Horses and cows were glaring at me as I roared by. Dogs barked furiously. All of nature was full of malevolent intelligence. Nature has exquisite taste and a total absence of sentimentality. Up there somewhere the sun had its (seemingly) generous and (seemingly) ever-bountiful eye on things.

Sodus was an interesting little resort town on the lake, with gift shops and organic grocery stores. It would be a busy place in the summer but now it was quiet, spooky, with people making repairs. The Quacker Box Gift Shop had an ominous sign on the door, at least it looked ominous in mystic October: ENTER WITH A HAPPY HEART. Egad, these superficial simpleton absolutists who always want to tell you what to do! How you could tell if your heart were happy enough to enter? Was the heart either happy or sad, nothing in between? Did it come equipped with an on-and-off switch?

Halloween was coming and pumpkins were being carved all around town. Yards were full of genial American clutter. There was a sailboat in every yard and a concrete donkey with flower-filled cart on every lawn. Through the trees in any direction you could see grey mist-filled inlets from the lake. The Big Sodus Lighthouse was built in 1870. It was surrounded by cottages named Dunrovin and Dunrovin Too. A show of paintings called "Summer Reflections" was running at the art gallery. Nature's Children was having a sale of women's clothing. A nasty little voice started blabbing away in my head. "All you need to take is one sip," it said. "Don't get me wrong; I don't think he's a genius" (a replay of Chester Yarn arguing about George Woodcock). "Keep thinking that way and you'll go crazy," and so on ad nauseam. The Pig Voice, Marie-Thérèse called it. I guess everyone has one, sort of the superego's dark twin, or maybe the superego itself, the ego's evil brother, the parental image in its perverse aspect, Robertson Davies on a bad day.

The roads in that farm country south of Lake Ontario would branch out and head off like capillaries, transporting that blood-red sports car into further dimensions of silent midday darkness. The roaring engine of the open car made the silence even more silent. Everywhere I looked silent apple-pickers were standing on silent ladders propped against silent trees silently bursting with dark green leaves and wine-dark apples. A black guy with a yellow hat was driving an orange forklift truck silently along the narrow road lined with ancient oak trees and prosperous farmhouses with satellite dishes.

In that little open car everything I passed pierced into me and passed through me. Sometimes it was just the car rolling down the road with no one in it. Life is one immense déjà vu. A single solitary little sailboat was bobbing way out on the lake. The person in the boat was thinking exactly the same thoughts.

Historical plaques offered engraved endorsements of the first white men to visit the area. I stopped to look at an old plaque falling off its post, it had been posted by the New York State Education Department in 1935, and it said, subtly worded to portray the white man as vigorous and active, the Native Indians as sedentary and passive: "From 1687 on, French bateaux men stopped here to trade with the Indians." And there was the Putneyville fire hall, Yahna Trader Antiquarian Books, and little crafts shops all over the place. But I couldn't continue stopping, I didn't want to be too late for the guys, I'd have to continue continuing. They'd have taken the most direct route and would be expecting me to show up at noon at the city hall in Rochester.

79. Marie-Thérèse and Jesus Christ

Such beauty and such a sad smell of ripe apples in the fall. Something clicked and last night's dream flooded into my mind like milk. It was Marie-Thérèse's house, the house she wisely decided not to have. It was spacious, full of light, colour and flowers, set on a high hill overlooking the Pacific Ocean. There were three of us in the house: Marie-Thérèse, me and Jesus Christ. We were in a large living room which was under extensive renovation. I was a carpenter and had been working on the renovations for an indefinite period of time: months, it seemed. Christ had just come home after an extended absence. He was delighted with the work I had done. Marie-Thérèse had been there all along, directing me in my renovations, but I felt now as if my work was finished and I felt a little uncomfortable continuing to be there, and so I wanted to leave, but I didn't want to seem to be in a hurry. There was a certain amount of tension in all three of us, but it was a benign tension. You were shy. It seemed you and I had been getting along well in Christ's absence, and you didn't want to hurt His feelings by letting on how well we had been getting along. And so you kept looking at me with such a sweet smile. It was obvious Christ knew how well we had been getting along but he was not going to let it bother him in the least, and he wasn't going to make a fuss. It appeared that he was going to continue on the renovations himself and I cleaned up and prepared to leave.

The dream was rich and strangely harmonious in atmosphere. Just before I left I was down on my hands and knees picking up my hammer and some nails and I looked up and your cat was sitting there, with a little wagon strapped to his back, like a horse's cart. Just a cute little cat-sized wagon. In the wagon was a pile of dark red raspberries, and it seemed that he had been eating some of them. I just thought oh, what a beautiful image to take with me into the light of day.

And I left. I turned around and there you were standing on the deck looking at me sadly through the morning mist and waving. And I looked at you sadly and waved....

80. The Causes of War

Past the R.E. Giuna Nuclear Power Plant the sign said WELCOME TO WEBSTER WHERE LIFE IS WORTH LIVING. This was perhaps a gentle little daily reminder to the people who ran the plant to keep their eye on those controls. Someone had scrawled under it: "Unlike certain other places we could name" and someone else had scrawled under that: "You better not be referring to Sodus."

Halloween pumpkins and life-sized straw-stuffed dummies were scattered everywhere, giant plastic butterflies (very realistic, except mammoth-sized) were suction-cupped onto rooftops and the sides and fronts of suburban bungalows. Old black guys shaking their heads in sorrow drove by slowly in old black trucks. Smiling white guys with white hair and red cheeks were delivering the mail in special cars with right-hand drive. Signs on mailboxes said things like CALVIN C. GARBER, DIFULVIO, or CURTIS AC SB TL BN.

As I came off the ramp from the expressway into Rochester, the sun broke through, the mist dispersed, and there was First Universalist Church with a sign which tried to make a virtue out of the minister's delusions of grandeur: I MUST FIGHT UNTIL I HAVE CONQUERED IN MYSELF ALL THE CAUSES OF WAR. A few weeks back Scotty Darling had been talking about his latest book and said: "At a certain stage I realised I was writing the oldest book in the world."

81. Sexiest Team in Baseball

There was an ice-cream vendor at the side of the road. A sign on the back of his truck said WATCH FOR CHILDREN. I slowed down. There was a line-up of kids buying cones and with each cone the vendor would hand out a watch. Sure, they were just cheap throwaway digital watches, but still....

Standing in the beautifully maintained atrium of the city hall in Rochester, and looking up, one could see row upon row and tier upon tier of symmetrical marble arches and columns with stone-carved capitals and gargoyles. To one side of the atrium, in a small open area, four smartly dressed no-nonsense business ladies were sitting, having just finished a light lunch. Nigel was there. He asked if he could film them.

They said they would prefer if he didn't since they were just having a little after-lunch chat before going back to work. All four were secretaries in the city hall.

But when Nigel told them we were from Toronto, they brightened up.

"We love Toronto," they said.

We said we really loved Rochester, we'd only been there half an hour and already we loved it.

They were dubious. "Toronto is beautiful," they said. "I just love Yorkville," said one. "Rochester has no night life at all," said another. Women were coming from all over the building to join in on this hot conversation.

"That Toronto is some shit-assin' town," said one.

"You must be from Sackett's Harbour," I ventured.

"How did you guess?" she gasped, her eyes bulging with terror of the unknown.

"I'd move to Toronto in a minute if I had an offer," said a red-haired lady in a wheelchair.

"It's so romantic," said a blonde in a beige suit, with no makeup but lots of gold around neck and wrists.

"Sexy, you mean," said a woman with tiny nostrils and large almond eyes.

"Yeah, dammit. Sexy," said the wheelchair lady.

"Sexy as hell," said Beige Suit.

"Trees everywhere," said Tiny Nostrils.

"And they even got a sexy new domed stadium for the Blue Jays," said a woman with her arm in a cast.

"Sexiest team in baseball," said Wheelchair.

The lady from Sackett's Harbour was silent, musing.

The place where they were sitting having their after-lunch chat was going to be turned into a small cafeteria for secretaries, and they were practising up by sitting there on benches for half an hour after lunch each day, getting ready, preparing the atmosphere, performing some kind of unspeakable magic ritual, only dimly realising what they were doing.

82. Daphnis and Chloe

Rochester was an interesting city architecturally. But it was time to get back to Lake Ontario. So we took off in light traffic and headed for the expressway. We drove along a broad quiet parkway, through vacant campgrounds and golden woods and so on with the sparkling shimmering lake glinting through the trees. I had to turn off the key, according to Herb's instructions, when shifts into first or reverse were required. We turned down a little dead-end road and stopped dead at the end.

There we were, on the sparkling grey shore of Lake Ontario, on the western lip of Ironquedoit Bay, with waves coming in, not high waves but fierce, determined and of high frequency under the low-lying blue-grey sky. These freshwater waves were coming in and smashing against the ruins of well-constructed old stone-and-concrete breakwaters that had been pounded by decades of sinister and sudden storms.

The water was high, with massive old oak trees partially submerged and the waves sweeping right by them on their way into the large bay that had over the years hollowed out a large basin for itself behind the shore of the vast sweetwater sea as we used to call it, lost somewhere under the drifting eye of God.

Birds singing, the soft warm wind blowing.

Daphnis and Chloe right around the bend, splashing each other with rose petals.

And the road led right up to the front door of a ghostly old three-storey white-frame hotel, with a screened porch and green trim. Like something out of a Christopher Pratt painting, or an early Bergman movie, or that D.M. Thomas novel, the one that Rodney hadn't read.

The Elmheart Hotel, it was called. It was freshly painted, but looked as if it had been sitting there untenanted for decades. There was a little red painted slot in the door with the words PAY HERE. But it was hard to figure out what you were expected to pay for and how much so we didn't. We stared at the hotel, stared at the waves coming in, stared at a finger of treed land jutting out into the lake, the mist, the greyness, the whole place seemed like a child's dream of some place he'd heard of but never been. L'Eau Grise as Nabokov, that clever old rogue, suggested the Great Lakes might fittingly be called, and Lake Ontario was grey that day, a colourful grey, a grey that made all the other colours seem more than colours, a silent grey.

I walked out along the ruined breakwaters of solid cement with timber supports. I headed toward an enchantingly long low treed point partially submerged by the high water of the lake, with Ironquedoit Bay calm and shining on the other side of the point. A bird started singing real close and I jerked my head around. It sounded like a nightingale, just as rich and Mozartian, although it was the wrong time of day and the wrong continent. As I jerked my head I hurt my neck and missed my step. I took one heck of a fall.

I fell right off the breakwater onto the fine sand, packed as hard as cement. I hit the ground so hard I wished I'd fallen the other way into the drink.

Winston had been filming me. I had fallen right out of sight. He would still be filming, waiting for me to reappear, hoping that I wouldn't be too badly hurt and also hoping that I wouldn't look at the camera.

I finally got up, feeling terribly old and humiliated, and hopped back up on the breakwater.

And—dark victory—didn't look back at the camera.

And knew I'd never find Daphnis or Chloe. If I were ever going to I would have already and perhaps I had and forgotten or maybe had but didn't realise it at the time.

The scene was so powerful it conspired to turn my mind to the personal past, to my marriage which I might as well confess here and now was doomed after my wife discovered it was I who had hanged the family dog from the cherry tree in the back yard one night. She tried to forgive me, but her deepest instincts wouldn't allow her to, even though she knew the dog was suffering from a terrible skin disease which had resisted the most expensive treatments. And the cats too. Tied them up spread-eagled on the branches of the Manitoba maple and allowed the local sparrows and chickadees to peck out their eyes.

And then calmly helped the police in their search for the perpetrator of these crimes, worked with them for several days, until the finger of suspicion began to point at me. And I finally confessed, to everyone's shock and horror.

83. A Cream Cadillac with Florida Plates

A cream Cadillac with Florida plates pulled up right in front of the lonely old Elmheart Hotel. A woman elegantly emerged from behind the wheel. She was a lovely looking woman in her fifties. She looked pleasantly intelligent and perfectly aged.

She started strutting like Mae West when she noticed the camera. Then she froze: "I don't like that thing pointing at me, it makes me nervous, it might have a gun in it, it might be loaded."

"It's loaded all right," said Nigel, "but only with film."

"Oh, that's all right then. And I'm not in your way?"

"No, not at all. No, we're just shooting everything that moves."

"Oh, well, in that case," she said, and she started performing her cute little Mae West routine again, with her hand on hip, and an outrageously sexy look on her face.

"Do I move right?" she said.

She went prancing and strutting up the steps to the hotel and tried the door.

"We already tried it, lady," called out Rodney. "It's locked." But his voice kind of drifted out to sea.

"I don't think that's open," said Nigel. "Oh you have the key, do you?"

"No."

"Looks like it's closed for the season."

"Lonesome George isn't here, huh?"

"We don't know. Who's Lonesome George?"

She shaded her eyes and tried to look through the screen.

"He's an old guy who used to run this place. He lived here all alone. Was always here. He'd be ninety-four now. I guess maybe he's dead, huh?"

"Yeah, probably," I said. "Most people ninety-four are dead."

She walked back to her car, the camera pointing off in other directions.

"Do you come here often?" I said, in my best gigolo tone.

She smiled and blinked.

"Used to. But now I live in Florida."

"Key West?"

"Miami Beach."

She didn't want to talk. She just hopped back in her car and drove off.

"Probably on some kind of sentimental trip," said Rodney.

84. Another Cream Cadillac with Florida Plates

We went back to standing around quietly looking at the lake, the waves, the sky, the ruins of the breakwater, the hotel, sensing and admiring the simple genius of the place. A few minutes later the same Cadillac pulled up again, but this time another woman was driving. She got out, she was younger, about forty, and she had a little girl toddler with her. Very nice woman, friendly, talkative, but she felt uncomfortable about the camera, didn't want any pictures taken of her.

"You didn't sneak a shot, did you?" she said at one point.

"Just of the child," said Winston.

"That's okay, of the child. But not me. Got that?"

We were extremely anxious to know what happened to the Mae West woman but this babe claimed she didn't know what we were talking about.

She claimed she didn't know anything about the other woman or any other car of similar make and Florida plates. A lonely abandoned hotel in the off-season at the end of a two-lane gravel road, and two women, each driving a cream Cadillac with Florida plates, arrive independently within minutes of each other and just miss each other, and know nothing of each other.

It was something to do with her divorced husband, the reason why the second woman was shy of being photographed. He lived in Rochester, she in Florida. In fact she owned a modest collection of high-rent high-rise apartment buildings in West Palm Beach.

She was fascinated by the coincidence of the two cars, and went on and on about it as people did in such cases. I told her about the Coincidence Club, how we would meet in a Chinese restaurant the first Sunday of every month and relate all the wonderful coincidences that had happened to us since the previous meeting, and discuss our various theories about coincidences. Members report that since they joined the club the frequency and intensity of the coincidences they experienced had both increased dramatically, just as when you start recording your dreams your dreams become more dramatic and vivid and more worthy of being recorded.

She wanted to come up to Toronto for the next meeting.

I told her she'd be most welcome but she could start her own branch down in P.B. if she wanted. She said no one she knew down there was interested in coincidences. It was more of a diamond-and-fur crowd. Also interested in their side-arms.

Not that they weren't a charitable bunch. They were always giving money to the contra-revolutionary forces in Nicaragua.

She wanted to know all about what we were doing. For instance, what was the film about.

I talked to her alone. Her name was Virginia Rabinovitch. The guys walked around with the cute little toddler, whose name was Andrea and who was actually Virginia's granddaughter.

I explained what we were doing and Virginia understood exactly, you could see it in her eyes.

"I'm about halfway through *Blue Highways* but left it in Florida," she said. *Blue Highways* was the travel-book sensation of the season, at least in the U.S.A.

We watched the lake in silence for a few moments, watched it trying desperately, as it never stops doing, to swamp the land. And then suddenly she spoke.

"We took a trip around Lake Ontario once," she said. "Many years ago." And then she sighed. It was when she and her husband were still married.

"We found a park that was just like North Carolina but I can't remember the name of it."

"Algonquin Park."

"You know, I think that was it. Really beautiful." She wiped away a tiny tear. "We loved Toronto," she said. "It's like an American city that never was," she said, "sort of a combination of the best features of all our cities. And when we got home we got a divorce."

Then she and her daughter, who was later to become Andrea's mother, went to Europe. They had Eurorail passes, no itinerary, just jumping on and off trains when they felt like it.

"Sounds like fun."

"It would have been but my daughter was all the time pining for her boyfriend back in the States, writing to him every half hour. It sort of spoiled the trip, but it was still a beautiful trip."

"How old was your daughter?"

"Twenty-two. Now she's twenty-four."

Virginia was nice, and she was excited about the idea of the book. I told her I'd send her a copy when it was finished. She said it would be nice for Andrea to have in a few years when she could understand it and all. I agreed with a serene smile. From the fall my right arm and thigh still throbbed and ached.

85. Curious about Lonesome George

To add to the coincidence, Madame Rabinovitch also knew about Lonesome George. She agreed that he was about ninety-four. She remembered him from the old days. But he was still alive, she said. He lived alone in the old hotel.

"I saw him in there when I peeked in the window," she said, "but he obviously doesn't want to see anyone."

She said he had built the hotel as a young man and managed it for decades. She remembered him from her childhood in the fifties. And she said if he'd answer the door he could tell us about what it was like in the twenties and thirties, with special narrow-gauge trolleys coming out from Rochester, and excursion boats from Toronto and Hamilton, with amusement parks, ferris wheels, merry-go-rounds, shooting galleries, baseball diamonds and bandshells.

I went up and knocked but there was no answer.

86. Freezers Full of Fish and Pheasant

We parked in a paved parking lot precisely at the point where a good-sized river came sweeping brilliantly over the dam and into Lake Ontario with an almost inaudible symphony of gurgles.

We were hungry. There was a large restaurant on the lake. It was an ugly concrete building that looked as if it had been built in 1959 and used for wedding receptions, bowling banquets and election headquarters. A girl about fifteen in pink sweater, pink jacket, pink shoes and blue jeans was sitting on the pink and blue steps.

"Is this place open?" I said.

This was Point Breeze, New York.

"I dunno," she said.

She didn't look at me.

I climbed the steps, stepped around her, tried the door, and it was locked.

A more congenial-looking place, cosy-looking and built from logs, boasted an enormous sign: BLACK NORTH INN. It was across the road from the concrete bunker. It seemed very quiet. It soon wouldn't be.

There were three fellows at a table quietly playing pinochle. One guy sat at the bar quietly drinking Black Russians, and two waiters quietly stood there with their elbows on the bar. They were absorbed in watching "Bowling for Dollars" on TV with the sound way down. This was pretty well the scene as we marched in with cameras and all our equipment. We started laughing and making lots of genial Canadian noise, shooting pool (badly), playing the video games and juke boxes at top volume, and so on. Somebody jacked up the volume on the TV, someone else phoned his mother to tell her to plug in the VCR right away, she was on "Bowling for Dollars," Nigel bought a souvenir musky key ring and a long thin black "beatnick" cigarette holder, the waiters and cooks started scurrying around frantically.

Winston wanted to know what a Northburger was. "It's just a big hamburger with chips," said the waiter. The phone rang, as if for the first time since last March. A woman in a red polyester pant suit and heavily sprayed coiffure came in, took one quick look, and went out again. Two guys in red hunting caps came in and sat down at the bar....

"How much are your hats?" Nigel said to one of the waiters through the din. They were baseball caps with Black North logos on them.

"*Fuffa*-four-fifty," said the harried waiter.

"I'll take one," said Nigel.

He rested the camera on the counter and adjusted the cap on his head to fit.

"You guys from TV?" said the fellow drinking Black Russians.

"No, we're from Canada," I said

Winston was busy with the video games. *Twing. Whirrrl. Whacko. Balalalalalala. Hrng, hrng, hrng. Bfflfflt. Neeeyow!! Behhppp. Zang. Booong!*

"Hey, less noise over there, little guy," I yelled out.

"Bowling for Dollars" was over and the TV was talking about "the German sausage you grew up on."

I wanted to play the video games too. "If you have two American quarters for two Canadian quarters I'll throw in a dime," I said.

"I've just got one," said Nigel.

I got some change from the bar and started playing.

"See that sign?" said Nigel. "Oh! No, it's all right. I thought it said unless accompanied by a priest or guardian. I guess it says parent."

"Yeah."

"This place just went crazy all of a sudden," said Nigel. We were all talking at top volume.

"Yeah," I said, "They were having a nice quiet game of cards and all of a sudden boom. An invasion from the north!"

A fellow ran to the phone and began talking excitedly. "It's only an ad, it's coming on at five," he kept saying. For some reason Nigel thought the guy had called the police.

"Did you call the cops for something?" he said.

"Oh no," said the guy. "My mother won the jackpot on 'Dialling for Dollars,' and it's coming on so I just phoned her to videotape it."

It was Nigel's turn to ask what a Northburger was.

"As I was telling your friend, it's just a big burger," said the waiter, patiently. "A six-ounce burger with big fat chips."

The phone rang again.

The same woman in the red pant suit came in again, took another quick look, and went out again.

The two guys in red hunting caps who had just come in and were drinking beer at the bar, it turned out they both worked at Kodak in Rochester. One was a chemist, the other an engineer. I asked them if they were hunting or fishing.

"Both," they said. "We saw some pheasants but didn't shoot them. That was this morning. Then this afternoon we caught two salmon but put them back."

"Can't eat the salmon, eh?" I said, naively.

"What do you mean?"

"Too full of carcinogenic substances, PCBs and all that stuff?"

"Oh no. We put them back because our freezers are full. There's no problem with the chemicals if you know what you're doing. Quite frankly, the problem is with the way the government analyses the salmon pure and simple." The older of the two was doing most of the talking.

"What do you mean?"

"Well, they put the whole fish in the blender and analyse it. That's crazy, you don't eat the whole fish. You just eat the fillets. I take a fillet and take it down to the shop and analyse it and it's clean. My wife and kids eat them. They're okay."

They started asking about the camera, wanted to know what part of Toronto we were from.

"Around Bathurst and King," said Nigel. "Do you know Toronto?"

"My wife was born in Agincourt," he said.

"Oh really."

"Yeah, I went to the University of Toronto."

"What'd you study?"

"Chemistry."

Winston and Rodney came over and wanted to know more about the fish analysis.

"We use a mass spectrometer," said the chemist. His friend listened and nodded in agreement. "Fillets, they grind up the whole fish, but if you neatly cut the fillets off it's okay. All the contaminants go into the fat and it doesn't stay in the pure meat. You gotta trim those fillets off real neatly. I feed it to my wife and kids...."

"Sure you do," said Rodney. "But do you eat it yourself?"

We all laughed. "Sure I do," said the chemist. "I think there's more contaminants in chicken than in fish."

"We gotta tell Elsie Yarn about this," we said.

He said he'd worked for Kodak for a total of thirty-seven years.

"That's hilarious," said Rodney.

"What do you mean by that?" said the guy.

"I mean we ran out of film just outside Rochester."

"Oh."

His young friend said he worked at Kodak too.

"Are you a chemist?"

"No, I'm just an engineer, I'm just a kid, I only worked there twenty-one years."

They wanted to know about our adventures around the lake. We told them about the hoedown at Sackett's Harbour. They knew Sackett's Harbour.

"Was it in the Sackett hotel?"

"No it was in the fire hall there."

They didn't seem to know about the fire hall. It was fairly new. "But I used to go duck hunting in Sackett," said the older guy. "I've seen that hotel just full of duck hunters."

"What do you do, mostly duck hunting or pheasant?"

"I keep my freezer full of fish and pheasant. Every time it starts to get a little down I go out hunting or fishing...."

87. Whispers from Eternity

I wanted to get the talk back to the University of Toronto in the innocent forties and what Canada was like in those days and how it had changed. But we got interrupted by the ancient mariner who was drinking Black Russians. He called himself Ralph McTrombone. At least that's what it sounded like.

"You guys from channel 10?" he said. He was a mean-looking but sweet-looking old fellow at the same time. He was a greens keeper by trade, worked at a golf course, lots of watering and cutting. His voice came out of the side of his mouth in a kind of whisper, but it was a piercing whisper that could paradoxically drown out a shout. The phrase "whispers from eternity" popped into my mind.

"No, we're from Toronto," said Winston.

"What, you guys work for the government or something?"

"What makes ya say that?" said Rodney.

"You just look like it I guess. And where else would you get all that expensive equipment?"

"Well, I guess indirectly we do," said Nigel.

"No, we're not working for the government," I said. "Don't think that."

"Well, they're helping us," said Nigel. "The Canadian Arts Council gave us a grant."

"It's the Canada Council," I said. Nigel blinked. "And we're not working for them."

"How much that camera cost?" old Ralph wanted to know.

"It's not ours," said Nigel. "We're just renting it, it's worth $30,000."

"You gotta write a good book to pay for that $30,000 camera."

Nigel rolled his eyes.

"As Nigel has already pointed out quite clearly, we're just renting it," I said.

"Is it gonna be a comedy?" said a hovering waiter.

"It will be if you hang around here," said Ralph, "cuz this is the funniest place I ever been in more than once."

"Oh, we've been hanging around some pretty funny places," I said.

"Oh, not as funny as this place, you can't beat this place I wanna tell ya."

"Okay, what's so funny about this place?"

He looked stumped. He took a perplexity sip of his Black Russian. People from Canada really ask tough questions. But not quite.

"The character behind the bar, he's pretty funny," said Ralph. The waiter blushed. He was a big gentle-looking guy with sandy hair and freckles.

"And you should be here when the broads are in the bar," whispered Ralph, "like Saturday night for instance."

"Why, what happened?" Thinking he meant last Saturday specifically.

"Oh, I can't tell you, you just have to be here."

Cute guy. No short-term memory tissue left, but probably had photographic recall of his youthful days.

Turned out that was true.

In fact, his memory was too photographic for his own good.

As it turned out.

88. World's Largest Pencil

Sometimes I just like to say to people I meet, "Say, what's the funniest thing that ever happened to you?" So I said that to old Ralph, the crabby but sweet-looking whispering old bewhiskered guy hunched over his Black Russian at the bar.

"Say, what's the funniest thing that ever happened to you?"

"Me? Oh probably when I was in the marine corps hah hah hah." His laughter was all slidey and whispery like a trombone that had been lying at the bottom of a barrel of Laphroaig for twenty years.

"When was that?"

"Oh a long time ago."

"Vietnam?"

"Oh longer ago than that."

"Korea?"

"No. Before then."

"I know. World War I."

"No. Not that far back. How about World War II? Didya forget that one? Didn't they have that up in Canada?"

"Oh yeah, that one. See a lot of action?"

"Eighteen months."

"Where? Europe?"

"No no, up in the Pacific."

"Oh yeah, up in the Pacific. That must have been an exciting time."

"Yeah." We lapsed into silence, then he whispered out of the corner of his mouth, his face all tanned and crunched up like an old rotten crabapple: "I came up here from Pennsylvania."

"So how do you like it? Up here I mean."

"Ah, there's no trout fishing up here. I miss that, you know."

"And what about the people?"

"The people up here, they're no fuckin' good. Down in Pennsylvania the people are honest, you never lock your house or your car. You have to up here or you come home and everything's gone, your car, your TV set. Different people up here. Down there everyone friendly, you don't have to take your keys out of your car even. Here you practically have to lock your shoes at night."

"You get anything stolen up here?"

"No, I lock up all the time."

"Oh." Pregnant pause. Geez, it was only one state away. There couldn't have been that much of a difference. "So what the heck you doing up here since you dislike it so much? Why don't you go back where you came from? World's largest pencil."

"World's largest pencil? What's that supposed to mean, world's largest pencil?"

"Haven't you ever heard that joke? What's the world's largest pencil?"

"I don't know, what is it?"

"Pencil-vania. Haw haw."

He smiled. "I gotta remember that."

"I'm shocked you never heard that joke, you being from Pennsylvania and all. Write it down." I tried to make it sound like an order.

"I will later." He wasn't in the marine corps any more.

"Okay. But why don't you go back home?"

"Why don't I go back? Well, you know, a job's a job.... And in the winter I go down to Florida for six months."

"Where in Florida?"

"Near Sebring."

"Where they used to have the car races?"

"Did they? They had car races there?"

"Yeah, Sebring. It was famous for car races. Still is, in fact."

"I didn't know that."

"Can't know everything."

"Guess not."

Sebring was very big in the fifties. Big names like Juan Manuel de Fangio from Argentine and Stirling Moss from Britain raced there in their Maseratis, Porsches, Ferraris and Jaguars. They always had twelve-hour races and enclosed-wheel cars. It was a tradition, just as they always have twenty-four-hour races at LeMans and Daytona.

"Do you go down there with your wife?"

"Down where?"

"Florida."

"Hell yes, I'm too old for anything else."

"What do you and your wife do in Sebring all winter?"

"Screw."

"Really? At your age? I'm shocked, appalled, and strangely titillated."

"No. I go around and talk to the greens keepers at the golf courses, that's what I do. See, the reason I go down there is because there's no work for greens keepers up here in the winter. So I go down there. But they don't have any work for me of course, because there are hundreds of greens keepers, no work in the north in the winter, they can't give them all jobs down south, so I just go around and talk to them."

"About the greens keeping business?"

"Yeah, we're all buddies, you know. Like you, you're a writer, I imagine if you meet another writer you talk to him, right? So I'm a greens keeper, and I like to talk to other greens keepers. And I like to canoe. I like going in the woods. I'd rather sleep in the woods than in a motel. I like it quiet. Like to get away from all the madness up here. Life is too fast. Make a buck, that's all they want. To hell with nature."

"Well what about these fishermen up here, what do you think of them?"

"Hey, you take these fishermen who have all this electronic equipment and put them in the woods for one night and they're dead." He made a slashing motion at his neck. "And at fishing derbies they have fights (the silly buggers) over who gets to put their boat in the water first."

"But you like fly fishing, you said."

"Yeah, I like fly fishing, but it's better in Pennsylvania. I don't call it fishing what they do around here, guys with those boats, five, six thousand dollars worth of equipment, scanners, radar, everything."

"They're just salmon-killing machines."

"That's right. Salmon-killing machines. That's what they are."

He said he saw a boat like that and it had everything, scanners, radar, and on the side of the boat was the name Lucky Strike. "Hell," he said, "if they caught a fish with that it wouldn't be a lucky strike it'd be, it'd be . . . ."

"Fishicide."

"That's right, fishicide."

"What else, Ralph?"

"What else? I'll tell you what else. They line up down here at the dam over here, you know?" He pointed at the door. "And they strangle the fish." At least that's what I thought he said.

"You don't mean they grab them out of the water and strangle them?"

"No no no. Not strangle. Snaggle. Means they snatch 'em with big hooks."

"What kind of big hooks?"

"Snatch hooks. They line up with a special line with a sinker and three prongs, no bait, they just drag it across the river under the dam and if they snatch a fish they got it."

"That's legal?"

"Sure it's legal."

"It's not legal in Canada, is it?"

"I don't know about Canada."

"I don't think it'd be legal in Canada."

He complained about commercial fishermen having to pay $3,000 for a licence while the sports fishermen hardly have to pay anything. And then there were all kinds of restrictions so they wouldn't interfere with the sports fishermen. I guess he'd visited Dunkirk on the south shore of Lake Erie because he complained bitterly about how commercial fishing down around there was finished. He figured it was the government.

"And what about Lake Michigan?" opined Ralph. "Up there, that's where they let the Indians fish all year around using any kind of hook or net they want. That's gotta hurt the commercial fishermen."

"Oh, yeah, I'm sure it would."

89. Bombs over Tokyo

Winston had tired of the video games and was walking all around the place filming everything he could lay his eyes on. Ralph McTrombone was huddled over his Black Russian and squinting up sideways at me, with his face all scrunched up, waiting for my next question. I asked him what his favourite fish was.

"To eat you mean, or to catch?"

"To eat."

"Well you know, I don't even like the *taste* of salmon, don't like it a bit."

"That's unusual. I thought everybody *liked* the taste of salmon. What do you like?"

"Just brook trout. Fresh brook trout. Best-tasting fish in the world."

Ralph noticed Winston.

"Hey did you take a picture of the bar?" he said.

"Yeah, you don't mind do you?"

"Hell no," said Ralph. "Is everybody with their own wives?"

Yuck yuck! Everybody sort of laughed. That encouraged him.

"Glad there's no FBI up in Canada, don't want them seeing my picture. But then again, they wouldn't care, less there's a number on your picture they'd never recognise you."

I gave him a look. "Say, Ralph," I said, "after the war did you ever go back to the Pacific?"

"No."

"Didn't you ever want to go back to see those islands in peacetime?"

"Nope, and I don't have nothin' in my house made in Japan neither."

Oh dear!

"Where in the Pacific were you?"

"All over—Guadalcanal, Guam and just all over."

"Why don't you have anything made in Japan in your house?"

"Because I don't *like* them slanty-eyed gook bastards, that's why."

"I'm *married* to a Japanese woman, Ralph," I said, mildly. (I really wasn't, but I would have been if she hadn't cruelly rejected me in favour of my high-school friend Wolf Hansen, who was a much better athlete than I, had a much higher IQ, was funnier, more popular, got better marks, was the school president three years running, and so on.)

"Lucky you," said Ralph. He didn't seem at all embarrassed.

"Yeah, lucky me. She's a very fine person in spite of being a slanty-eyed gook bastard."

"Very simple reason."

"And all the members of her family are very fine people."

"Very simple reason."

"And of course our kids are wonderful, but then again they're only semi-gooks."

"Very simple reason."

"What do you mean, very simple reason?"

"Very simple reason."

I couldn't figure out what he meant and I couldn't figure out what to say next so I just said that Japanese people are people too.

"No they're not, not when they shoot people coming out of airplanes."

"What?"

"In parachutes. People coming out of airplanes in parachutes. And they shot them. We didn't do it to theirs."

"But but but my wife has never to my knowledge shot anybody coming out of an airplane or even wanted to. And you gotta remember the U.S. wasn't being threatened like Japan was being threatened."

"They bombed Pearl Harbour."

"Oh sure, they bombed Pearl Harbour. But that was just a military installation, and it was right in their backyard practically, with all the guns pointing at them. It was like Cuba with all its guns pointing at Washington, D.C., in the Cuban Missile Crisis, remember? October, 1963."

"It was lucky they did hit Pearl Harbour. It's a wonder they could see that good, they're so slanty-eyed."

"Ralph, I can see you're a bit of a military historian. By the way, where were you when it happened? Pearl Harbour I mean. Remember?"

"I wasn't there at the time. I'd just signed up. But I was there right after. They bombed the barracks and the airfields and everything...."

"But they didn't bomb any cities, no civilian centres, did they? Sure, they bombed the heck out of some Chinese cities like Nanking. Did you remember the Rape of Nanking in 1938?" He nodded dully. Who cares about the Chinese, they're slanty-eyed gooks too, right? "But no U.S. cities, just the military installations."

"Yeah, but they being slanty-eyed bastards they could miss once in a while."

On the subject of history I was rusty and he was crusty, a lingering case of psychic numbness brought on by war, and with a belly full of Black Russians to boot. But there was a lot of gentleness about him as well, he was cute, you couldn't help like him even though he was a lunatic on the subject of the Japanese.

"The Americans certainly didn't miss when they bombed Hiroshima and Nagasaki."

He brightened up immensely. "Hell no! I was in Tokyo Bay when they dropped those bombs."

"The war was almost over anyway, they didn't have to do that the Americans."

"But this way we didn't have to invade Japan, and besides they never knew what hit them."

This was one corpse I decided against trying to exhume. "So what do you remember most about those years?"

"I remember playing cards. I did a lot of that. It cost me a lot of money to get educated in poker in the services. I didn't know a full house beat a straight till I got out of the service."

"How much did it cost you to learn?"

"A month's pay...every month."

I laughed and his eyes glistened with pleasure.

"So what were you? An artillery man or something like that?"

"I was a gunner on a dive bomber."

"Wow!!!"

Nigel was eavesdropping. He went "Wow!!!" too, then added: "That must have been a pretty nervy thing."

"Oh, I was so dumb I was happy," said Ralph.

Pretending the Japanese weren't really people was probably his way of handling the guilt, I figured. He'd been on all kinds of dive-bombing raids all over Japan, striking not only the cities but industrial towns and even non-strategic villages chosen at random to be destroyed, and his job was the worst of all, he'd actually have to aim and fire at small groups of old men, women and children as the plane flew fifty feet above the ground, and he would see them trying to scurry for cover, see them be hit, fall, and continue crawling, see their enraged faces, see them shaking their fists as the dive bombers flew over.

"He's from Pennsylvania originally," I said to Nigel, "but he lives up here permanently now. Right, Ralph?"

"Yeah, right. I just live down there in Plumbo. Take the highway down to side road 18 and...."

"He doesn't have anything Japanese in his house because the Japanese used to shoot Americans parachuters jumping out of planes."

"Is that a fact?" said Nigel. "What about the Germans? Do you have German stuff in your house?"

"Yeah, what about the Germans, Ralph?"

"Hey, no problem with the Germans. They were caught up in it. Hitler, he dominated them."

Before we left we made sure he knew that his boss during the war, Curtis E. LeMay, the air force general in charge of bombing Japan, admitted that he would have been hanged as a war criminal if the U.S. had been on the losing side. And that not everybody in Hiroshima and Nagasaki died in a flash.

90. White Goat on Green Lawn

An hour later a little red sports car followed by a blue van with Ontario licence plates zoomed along a two-lane highway south of Lake Ontario. At one point we stopped to look at a white goat nibbling on a green lawn.

The lawn was in front of an old prosperous-looking Victorian farmhouse, at a crossroads, and two guys came out of the house to see what we'd stopped for. It looked as if they'd been watching football on TV. One of the guys was on a pair of aluminium crutches and had skinny little inconsequential legs and a huge barrel chest. They didn't say anything but they thought maybe we were about to steal the goat.

"They eat anything, don't they?" I said.

"Oh yeah."

"Tin cans?"

"Yeah."

"Pretty strong too, aren't they?" I remembered my Uncle George putting on a big show for the little kids on Dominion Day at Aunt Clara and Uncle Cecil's farm by wrestling with the goats and pretending they were getting the better of him.

"Yeah. They give good milk too."

"You milk 'em?"

"Yeah. Once in a while."

"And you drink it?"

"Oh yeah, sometimes."

"Is it good?"

"Oh, it ain't too bad. It's a little rich, but.... They make good lawn mowers."

I told them that when I first got out of the car the goat came running over but when she saw I didn't have anything to eat she walked away.

"Take your cigar over to her."

"You're kidding?"

She gulped down my smouldering cigar without even burning her tongue.

They wanted to know about the camera. The light was getting weak. We could only shoot for a few more minutes. I told them we were going around the lake shooting film.

"Been down to Golden Hill?"

"No, is it interesting?"

He said it was and gave us directions.

91. Do You Really Think I'm Right for You?

Winston and his camera were riding with me. As soon as it got too dark to shoot, Winston spoke about how it was too bad the camera wasn't as sensitive as the human eye, and I became super-aware of what I was looking at. This included fluttering trees silhouetted against the opal sky, a long thin track of lonely road winding over yonder hill, and on the other side of the hill, drifting in the evening breeze, clouds of innocent insects some of whom would soon be splattered and bug-eyed on my windshield. If I hadn't been driving I could have written a six-pack of deathless haiku. The camera wouldn't have caught any of this at all, Winston was right. As for Golden Hill, the directions were too complicated, it was getting dark and the place didn't sound very interesting anyway so we didn't go.

It was a strange night. I had the feeling a new solar system was being created overhead. I didn't want to waste time driving at night. Night is the time to be stopped at interesting places, talking to interesting people, doing interesting things....

So just east of Lewiston we stopped at a variety store. We'd gone for miles without seeing a place worth stopping at and we wanted to see if we could locate a motel. But the young fellow who was running the store was on the phone. He was having a very sexy and important conversation with his girlfriend.

"Do you really think I'm right for you?" he said. "Do you ever think you could do better than me?"

On the other end you could imagine the young lady saying: "Oh darling, don't you realise how much I love you? Nothing in this whole world makes any sense for me without you. I'm yours, I belong to you in every way."

The other guys were scooting through the aisles buying things. They bought cartons of cigarettes. Nigel bought a box of "Reagan's the Right One" bubblegum cigars and the other guys stocked up on long thin black "beatnick" cigarette holders (they were big that year), red licorice and various god-awful confections full of chemicals guaranteed to result in deformed children.

Nigel held out something he bought, something wrapped in cellophane and apparently intended to be eaten. Two baked items, with a shiny yellow glaze filling. "Look how yellow this thing is," he said. It really was the yellow of all yellows, a shiny shimmering archetypal Van Gogh yellow as far removed from the mere yellow of nature as normal yellow is from brown.

I'd just been standing there pretending to look at postcards but really just listening to the conversation the kid (about nineteen) was trying to have with his girlfriend. It got too noisy finally and he said, "Just a minute, honey." He put the phone down and turned to us but just then more customers came in so he picked up the phone again and said he'd call her back in a few minutes.

We paid for our stuff and he said (impatiently) there were no motels around here, we had to go to Niagara Falls, which was twenty miles south.

"Nothing in Roosevelt Beach?"

"Nope."

So the film crew and I split up again, agreeing to meet in Niagara-on-the-Lake, Ontario, on the main street, near the clock, at 10:30 the next morning. That way they could relax and it would give me more freedom.

As I was leaving I confessed to the kid that I couldn't help overhearing his side of the phone conversation. He didn't seem to mind so I asked him what his girlfriend was saying in reply.

"Oh, she was saying you know that she like needs me because the world like doesn't make any sense without me in her life. I'm yours, I belong to you in every way. All that stuff. That's the way I feel about her too. Like, it's a funny thing, huh?"

92. Rodney Gets Car Sick

Earlier we were driving along when Nigel in the van started blinking his lights. We stopped. Rodney had become carsick. He rushed out of the van over to the Niagara Gorge.

"Geez, that's steep. Don't fall in," I hollered. It was a long drop. It'd be awful having to climb down there to retrieve him.

When he got back to the van Rodney said he didn't care if it was going to be in the book or not he simply had to vomit. I said I was going to be writing about me falling off the breakwater so I might as well mention other unfortunate occurrences, and besides what's to be embarrassed about? We're all human, eh? Carsickness is a fact of life. A sign of life in fact. And it's a sign of artistic sensitivity too. Look at Malcolm Lowry, look at Dylan Thomas. And then there's my friend Glenda G. Bendix who is vitally interested in images of vomit in world literature. In fact she's planning an anthology of vomit stories.

"Are you going to put this in the book?" he said.

"Don't worry about a thing," I told him. "I'll do it in such a way that everyone will think you're terrific."

He smiled.

"Really? Gee, that'd be great."

93. Discovering Your Own Mind

I didn't want to drive down to Niagara Falls to find a place to sleep. I wanted to cross over to Canada at the Lewiston Bridge and spend the night in the lovely old Monkey Inn, in Niagara-on-the-Lake. But my plans changed when I stopped at the Sunoco station in Lewiston. The guy pumping gas said that the romantic young fellow in the variety store had given me bogus information. In fact, there were two motels nearby. I chose the Niagara Frontier Motel.

"I wish I was forty years younger and my husband would buy me a nice little sexy car like that," said the Polish lady at the registration desk. She said she was seventy-seven.

Hanging on the wall behind the cash register was a portrait of her painted forty years ago— with a photo of Pope John Paul II, the Polish Pope, tucked in a corner of the frame, under her left breast.

She said she'd started slowing down lately and had given her Polish-Mexican restaurant down the street to her daughter and son-in-law. She was pleased with how well they were running it and the changes they'd made. Unfortunately it was Monday and the restaurant was closed for the day.

She gave me room 2.

"How much would that be?"

"That'd be a hundred and fifty dollars."

"What?"

"Oh dear me," she said. "My husband hates my sense of humour."

I told her I liked it a lot. "But what if I had said okay? Would you have taken the hundred and fifty?"

"Oh no, it was just a joke."

We talked about age. I said I was more like thirty years younger than she and was catching up fast. I said my life was getting more interesting as I got older. She wanted to know in what way. I told her I was learning what is essential: Not working so hard, being lazy, discovering your own mind, thinking about the big picture. She smiled knowingly.

I was unloading stuff from my trunk and putting it in my room when the guys went by in the van, with Winston strapped up on top taking shots of the main street of Lewiston, where the McDonald's restaurant is done up to look like the Alamo. This had something do with the Niagara Frontier theme. Remember the Alamo?

I whistled at them but they didn't look, just went sailing by. They were on their way to Niagara Falls no doubt, believing the kid in the variety store that there were no motels in the area. We're all believers. If we are told there are no motels in the area, we won't see any motels in the area. If we are told there are no angels we won't see them floating around, making fun of our foolishness.

94. Voices from the Subtle Levels of the Mind

Too tired to flick on the television, I sat there, in my motel room.listening to the mysterious voices of my mind. Gradually, the voices became more interesting as they adopted the tone and manner of people I actually knew. I felt as if somehow I had plugged into an actual conversation that might have been going on further down the road, or over on the Canadian side of the bridge. I wrote down the conversation just as I heard it.

The next day when I showed my notes to Nigel he said they were remarkably close to what actually had been said last night at the motel where they stopped, remarkably accurate for the most part, so accurate he didn't want to think about it. He shuddered and turned pale and turned away.

And skeptics say there is no ESP! Hah!

I include a transcription of my notes here, edited and abridged for maximum readability, in the hope that readers will find the conversation more interesting and more plausible than anything that could have been merely invented, or merely transcribed.

Nigel: "How much are your rooms?"

Motel Manager: "How many per room?"

Nigel: "One per room."

Motel Manager: "Three rooms?"

Nigel: "Yeah."

Motel Manager: "Just twenty dollars."

Nigel (trying not to sound surprised): "Twenty?"

Motel Manager: "Just one night?"

Nigel: "Yes."

Motel Manager: "Twenty dollars."

Nigel: "What are your TVs like?"

Motel Manager: "Cable."

Winston: "It's not satellite, it's cable?"

Motel Manager: "It's not satellite, it's cable, but it's good, and we got radios on it too."

Winston: "Cable, and radios...."

Motel Manager: "Get about twelve channels."

Winston: "Twelve channels."

Motel Manager: "Are you from the States or from Canada?"

Nigel: "Canada."

Motel Manager: "We get all the stations. We get Buffalo."

Nigel: "Do you get SCTV? Do you get channel 57?"

Motel Manager: "I don't know the numbers...."

Nigel: "Do you get CITY-TV?"

Motel Manager: "CITY-TV? Yes."

Rodney: "I guess that's it then."

Winston: "Down the road they get satellite TV."

Motel Manager: "Yes, but they charge more than twenty dollars."

Nigel: "I guess we can live with that. Do you have water beds?"

Motel Manager: "Yes."

Nigel: "Do all the rooms have water beds?"

Motel Manager: "No, not all."

Nigel: "We don't want water beds.... We need three rooms on the ground floor with no water beds. Unless you guys want water beds."

Winston: "No."

Rodney (uncertainly): "No-oh...."

Motel Manager: "Is this Monday or Tuesday?"

Nigel: "Tuesday."

Rodney: "It's gonna be a short week."

TV in the Background: "I'd like to get out of this thing alive with my son.... We interrupt this program to bring you a special bulletin.... We repeat a special bulletin."

Nigel: "Is this a fake special bulletin?"

Rodney: "Yeah."

Motel Manager: "Are you from television?"

Rodney: "No, film making, not television. We're going around Lake Ontario making a film."

Motel Manager: "What kind of movie you making, uh geography or something?"

Nigel (wearily): "Uh, sort of."

Rodney (enthusiastically): "We were following this strange character around, a writer. Are we still following him?"

Nigel: "This guy's driving around Lake Ontario writing a book about the trip, kind of a comedy."

Motel Manager: "Oh, it's a comedy."

Nigel: "Yeah, a comedy...."

Rodney: "Is that right? It's a comedy?"

Nigel: "Yeah, you know that. You read his other books."

Motel Manager (perceptively): "It's a Canadian movie, eh?"

Nigel: "Yeah. Where are you from by the way?"

Motel Manager: "Me? I live in the States. But I'm from Poland. I'm kind of lucky. Yesterday I was on a plane and I met a stunt driver, today I meet some movie people."

Winston (ironically): "That's lucky all right."

Motel Manager: "You need someone like a stunt driver, you got it here."

Nigel (impressedly): "Yeah? Are you a stunt driver?"

Motel Manager: "I used to be in rallies and races in the States."

Nigel (suspiciously?): "Are you an American citizen?"

Motel Manager: "Yeah, but I'm moving to Canada now, you know?"

Nigel (doubtfully): "Yeah?"

Motel Manager: "Yeah, I should have my papers soon."

Nigel (dutifully): "How long you been over from Poland?"

Motel Manager: "Me? Oh I was really young. Came over in '73. Canada and the States, I think the only two countries in the world, and maybe Germany and Switzerland too, where you can make a good living. No other countries any comparison. In Ireland a gallon of gas costs you six dollars."

TV in the Background: "I'm sorry, there's no other way."

(Sound of gunfire.)

MONDAY, OCTOBER 15

95. The Worm at the Bottom of the Bottle

The next morning I decided to get a bottle of mescal to take back and share with my drinking and baseball buddy Zippy Xenophontos, to celebrate Detroit Tigers winning the World Series, at home, yesterday, beating the San Diego Padres in five. Hundreds of crazed fans ran onto the field and ripped up the sod for souvenirs, then went out and rioted on the streets. Five cop cars and numerous taxis were destroyed, mostly by taking off the gas cap and tossing in a match. Detroit shortstop Alan Trammell, who grew up in San Diego ironically, was voted the series' most valuable player, with two home runs, six runs batted in, nine hits and a batting average of .450.

But mescal, it still wasn't possible to get it in Canada, and it was illegal to import it. In British Columbia I used to smuggle it across the little undefended border in the back of the poet Lionel Kearns' mother's blue Morris Minor.

I know I spoke about this earlier but you really have to respect mescal. It's mystical and dangerous and it possesses the power to unlock the mysteries of time and space. One sip and the local atmosphere undergoes a radical transformation. Two sips and it's as if you're on another planet. Anything more than that and you're courting magnificent blackouts and memorable losses of memory. Whenever I drink it, once I get going, no matter where I am when I start, I end up, bruised and battered, at the bottom of a fire escape in downtown Hamilton, Ont.

I parked the car in the early-morning silence and crossed the four-lane sunny main street of Lewiston to the liquor store which was dark and gloomy. I walked in, looked around, there was no one there. I turned around, the owner had come in behind me, he'd apparently been next door, and was looking at me suspiciously, as if he thought I was about to take advantage of his absence to pillage the place, as if I'd only entered the place because I saw no one was in.

Thick globs of hostility gathered in the silent psychic ether as he stared at me.

"Do you work here?" I said.

"I guess so. It's my place."

"Oh. Do you have any mescal?"

"No."

"Do you ever have mescal, do you stock it usually?"

"No, we never stock it. No call for it." His voice mellowed. "What is mescal anyway?"

"It's a Mexican liquor, something like tequila but with a harder wallop. You know, it has the worm in the bottom of the bottle."

"Oh that stuff. I heard of it but no we never have that."

I was looking along the top shelf and spotted a bottle.

"Wait a minute, isn't that mescal up there?"

I knew it was. We both looked way up to the tequila shelf. There were several different kinds of tequila and then there was the bottle of mescal.

"That's tequila up there," he said.

"But that bottle with the yellow and orange label. Isn't that mescal?"

"No, it's tequila."

"Looks like mescal to me."

"Well, maybe it's mescal-type tequila but there's no worm in it."

"There's no such thing as mescal-type tequila. There's mescal. And there's tequila. And that up there is mescal. And there's a worm in it."

I got the ladder, climbed up, grabbed the bottle, climbed down. I showed him the label. Mescal. Showed him the worm in the bottom. He became very friendly and embarrassed.

"Well, how about that? I should get to know what I have and don't have. My own stock too. Hm."

I paid the guy, walked back across the street, hopped in the little Spitfire, all the while entertaining the possibility that the fellow hadn't been all that unpleasant, it was just my perceptions that were out of whack this morning. But as I drove off another hostile guy was walking across the street in front of me. I slowed down for him to walk across but he slowed his pace and glared at me. I couldn't understand it. I slowed down to a crawl, gave him tons of room, actually came to a stop, made sure he was across, and as I passed him he had a horribly angry look on his face and he yelled out from the curb: "You fuckin' asshole."

I have no idea what that was about. He was a well-dressed nice-looking old guy too. He looked as if he might have been a retired Pentecostal preacher.

96. Every Man or Woman His or Her Own Pope

In Niagara-on-the-Lake I bought some Pope Products. The Pope was visiting Canada. I bought a Pope Baseball Cap and a Pope Key Chain and a Pope Cigarette Holder (just like the "beatnick" cigarette holder but with a little image of the Pope stamped on it). I'd been considering taking a job advertised in the *Globe and Mail* travelling around to small towns in Southern Ontario selling Pope Products in variety stores and so on. My kind of work.

Then I went in a coin shop and purchased some interesting old postcards, old lapel stickers advertising exotic European liquors and so on. Every man or woman his or her own Pope is my motto.

"People are kinda more reserved or something over there." This was Nigel. We were having bagels and coffee in a restaurant on the main street of town. I'd gotten across the border with my illegal bottle of mescal, no problem. "They hold back."

"People in the States are more reserved than Canadians? Is that what you're saying? That's an unusual observation."

"Yeah, I know it sounds crazy, but they seem to be more reserved. Look at how quiet things were in that pub until we walked in. And I noticed a lot of guns. And a lot of cemeteries. And Americans are much more natural with the camera. A lot of them said they'd never been filmed before but it just seems to come naturally to them. They didn't look in the camera or anything."

He gave me a meaningful glance.

"Well it certainly didn't come natural to me."

"Oh you were fine. Don't worry about it. But it is true that Americans are more natural in front of the camera than Canadians. It's like so much more part of their lives. They seem to have a real strong suspicion of anyone who appears uncomfortable in front of the camera."

"You've been thinking about this a lot."

"Yeah, I have. Well, maybe not a lot. But I've been giving it some thought. They think he's got something to hide. He's a crook."

"Right. Maybe they're right. Maybe that's my problem. Maybe that's why I'm always so awkward when I have to be on TV or even on the radio, my mind blanks out and I start sweating and feeling uncomfortable. Maybe I'm a crook at heart."

"Ah, come on, you're no crook. You're too honest, you can't fake it, that's probably more your problem."

"Nice of you to say it, but there are all kinds of different crooks."

"Well, I don't know. But you know you're definitely right in your other books about them being fatter than Canadians. We thought you were just joking, but when you're looking for it you can't help noticing all the fat people. The percentage of fat people, even kids, is much greater."

"It's prestigious to be grossly overweight among certain socioeconomic groups in the U.S.A. It's sort of an ideal."

"And the women, they're much more made up. They wear more makeup, bouffant hairdos, and everything. And it's really weird but Niagara Falls Ontario is the most beautiful city in Canada and Niagara Falls New York is so ugly and tacky...."

Nigel said that as soon as they pulled into town that morning some guy wanted to know what he was filming.

"We're filming a poet taking a trip around Lake Ontario."

"A poet? Is it Irving Layton?"

Irving for a while lived in Niagara-on-the-Lake and made sure everyone in town knew that a poet was in residence. Not only a poet but perhaps the only real poet of the twentieth century, God bless him.

"No, it's not Irving Layton. But that Layton guy has been haunting us all the way around."

"Yeah, he's like that."

"Layton would never get involved in something like this," I said. "It's not exactly the sort of thing you win the Nobel Prize for."

"The guy wanted to show us the house where Irving lived," said Nigel. "I said to him is it an historical site? And he said no, not yet, but when he lived here it was apparently pretty hysterical."

Nigel wanted to know how I felt about the trip. "I don't know yet," I said, "I haven't even started to digest it. All these raw impressions, all these strange and wonderful people."

97. Monkey Inn

I wandered over to the Monkey Inn. The woman who ran the place was talking to *Eyewitness News*, the guy from Channel 7 in Buffalo. I couldn't take my eyes off the waiter, with his long blond carefully coiffed hair, beautifully manicured nails, delicate feminine voice and manners, tiny hair-line moustache impeccably trimmed. He was about sixty years old.

"Was there a murder here?" I said. *Eyewitness News* was all murders and fires.

"Not recently," said the woman. I knew she wouldn't remember me even though we'd had a couple of long conversations on my previous visits to the hotel. She went back to her interview.

"A fire?" I said to the elegant waiter.

"Oh dear, no."

"Couldn't have been a car accident."

"No, but I know exactly what you mean. Good lord, that's all you see on *Eyewitness News*. It's positively outrageous!"

"So why are they here?"

"They wanted to do a feature on this hotel. Because of its historic value."

Something didn't smell right. I knew *Eyewitness News* better than that.

98. You Smell Okay to Me

Actually I'd talked to the cameraman earlier, out on the street. The situation was simply that they were doing a feature on the whole town, with ten seconds devoted to the Monkey Inn.

There was a powerful smell of ripe grapes in the air. The cameraman was talking to a young retarded man on the street. They looked at me expectantly as I walked by.

"Where's that grape smell coming from?" I said.

"Maybe it's people burning leaves," said the retarded guy. "They do it a lot this time of year."

"Not great smell, grape smell."

"Oh, grape. I don't know. I don't smell very well." He couldn't stop smiling. He was a really cute little guy, with protruding teeth, jug ears, an IQ of about fifty. He looked as if he might have Fragile X Syndrome.

I sniffed at him.

"You smell okay to me."

A joke! He got it! He laughed crazily! I wished I had six or seven just like him waiting for me at home.

"But you don't smell like grapes."

"I don't know," said the cameraman, "but I smell it too. Is this grape country?"

"Sure it is," I declared. "Terrific grape country. This is the Niagara Peninsula. You mean you've never tasted Niagara Peninsula wine?"

"No, I drink New York state wine."

99. Men with Tiny Well-Clipped Moustaches

I heard the woman telling the *Eyewitness News* television team about the painting of her late husband on the wall. He looked like Clark Gable in *It Happened One Night*. His eyes followed me all around the room. Whatever part of the room I was in if I turned and looked at that painting the eyes were looking right at me. I remembered this phenomenon from previous visits to the inn.

The woman was telling stories about her late husband in the same words she'd used when telling the same stories to Marie-Thérèse and me when we were there the year before and the year before that. She didn't know the *Eyewitness News* team only wanted ten seconds.

And then she'd say the place was haunted by a ghost who played the piano through her. She'd never been able to play the piano, never took lessons, couldn't play any other piano but this piano, in this public dining room. She'd sit down at the piano and say: "I wonder if the ghost is in the mood to play." Then she'd start pounding away furiously at some old song from the twenties. Maybe she was wise to what she was doing, maybe she wasn't. Didn't make much difference.

Nigel saw the painting and thought it was the waiter in his youth. There was a strong resemblance. It was as if she'd always been attracted to men with tiny well-clipped moustaches.

She also told some wonderful stories about Irving Layton coming in and announcing to all the drinkers at the bar that he was Irving Layton the Famous Poet and he'd just written another of his Famous Poems and they were lucky they were at the right spot at the right time because they were going to be the first people in history to hear the poem in question recited, and by the poet in question himself. She was probably exaggerating like mad. People like to make Irving Layton seem more egotistical than he really is. It's a form of envy. He's always gone his own way, done what he wanted, now he's an old man but still plays handball and beats people half his age and he's got a young and beautiful wife who dotes on him. Maybe he's annoyingly irresponsible in the way he levels his charges of anti-Semitism, and the way he's so sarcastic about WASP (hate that word) mentality, but the people who are most annoyed are those who wish they could let their hair down and be a little more irresponsible themselves. He's got a right to be proud, it hasn't been easy for him. Sure he writes a lot of bad poems, but so did Wordsworth.

Why was the place called the Monkey Hotel? Simple story. There used to be a monkey who lived there a hundred years ago or thereabouts.

100. Rodney Does It Again

We drove south out of Niagara-on-the-Lake, and stopped at the side of the road adjacent to the Niagara Gorge. We looked down into the historic steaming misty Niagara River.

The guys put the camera on the hood of the Spitfire, with an industrial-size suction cup and a rope thick enough to hang an elephant. They used a little pump to draw air out of the suction cup. Thirty grand down the toilet if it fell off.

"I guess I shouldn't wear my hat," I said. "The shadow it casts will spoil my beautiful features."

"Now he's beginning to sound like an actor."

"Yeah, but I couldn't stand the boredom."

"Boredom? This is nothing," said Rodney. "You should see what it's like shooting a real film."

Everybody turned to glare at him.

"Oops, er I mean a conventional film."

101. Boredom and Immortality

"It's so boring being immortalised on film," I said.

"But the end product will be so satisfactory," said Nigel.

"That's what they always say," said Rodney.

"What do you mean, what Nigel said or what I said?" I said.

"What Nigel said. Or both, actually, come to think of it."

"And just think about how boring immortality itself will be," said Winston.

102. Weird Swedish Sexual Apparatus

So the $30,000 camera was glued to the side of the Spitfire, sticking way out. It was glued, but not by glue, whether crazy or just plain tenacious. It was glued by suction. Please skip to chapter 103 if you're offended by rude jokes about suction cups.

"What happens if a passing car hits it?" I said.

"It'll tear it right off," said Rodney.

"How fast were you going last time?" said Nigel, meaning the last time they were filming me driving.

"I don't know. There's no speedometer."

"Well, go only about sixty per cent that speed this time, okay?"

"It'll look faster with the side shot," explained Rodney.

So I drove up and down the road a few times and they got all the footage they figured they'd need. Probably a lot more.

"You soon get blasé about being photographed all the time," I said.

"If this was a conventional film, a big-budget feature say, there'd be makeup artists and hair-stylists all over the place," said the chastised Rodney.

The guys were working up a sweat trying to get the camera off the side of the car. The suction cup was just too powerful and the pump wouldn't work in reverse.

"Looks like some weird Swedish sexual apparatus," said Nigel.

"I used to have a girl friend like that," said Winston.

"Leave this thing in my motel room tonight, will you?" said Rodney.

103. Swimming through Molasses

I was driving along drinking apple juice from Mexico. It was in a half-gallon plastic container which I'd bought a couple of days earlier and was just now finishing it off. It was from "Behling Orchards, RD #2, Mexico, N.Y. 13114. Keep Cold. No Preservatives added. 64 Fl Oz. Happy Apple's Cider."

Good stuff. Better than mescal. No blackouts.

The camera crew was following me down a narrow winding gravel road in a suburban residential area near Niagara-on-the-Lake. Lots of silly-looking trees, shameless flowers, neurotic dogs, selfish cats with absolutely no social conscience, sheep whose idea of a good time is getting shorn, amoral and possibly psychotic goats, and the occasional bossy cow and know-it-all horse.

Just as I took the last mouthful of juice we approached a garbage truck and I gave the empty jug a little toss to the gap-toothed guy who was running shotgun on the back. He in turn tossed it into the gaping steel-toothed maw with a big semi-toothy grin. This is a nice little scene in the film.

The weary wanderers were almost home. No Penelopes to worry about.

The subtle smell of ripe grapes was wafting through the October air as I drove through the morning talking to myself. The lake was on my right, visible through the trees, and I was saying things like: "Sometimes (if not always) being alive is tough going, slow, and sticky, like trying to swim through molasses. Sometimes a wave you made twenty years ago becomes the same wave you're trying to cut through today."

A rabbit, with fully erect ears, as if he were trying to hear my words of wisdom, ran in front of the little car. His hollow brittle little bones crunched under the wheel.

104. Iniquity

I passed through Port Weller on the Welland Canal and turned right and drove up to Port Dalhousie (which must always be pronounced the Southern Ontario way, Poor DeLoozy) where old married couples (as in Paul Theroux's *Kingdom by the Sea*) sat silently in parked cars watching the Great Lakes steamers, Liberian freighters and little sailboats go by. Also single men sat alone in parked cars pretending to read the *St. Catharines Standard*.

There were two taxis parked next to where a large ship the *Canadian Prospector* was docked. The taxis were apparently waiting to take the sailors to town. But there didn't seem to be any sailors aboard. It was a pleasantly timeless place to be on a lazy warm sunny leafy Monday afternoon. It was sort of like eighth-century India.

A couple of guys were repairing the roof of the old pavilion in Port Dalhousie, the pavilion where we used to eat picnic lunches in the rain on long-ago lake excursions. This would be long before the place was taken over by the provincial government and cleaned up, sanitised, Muzacked, McDonaldised, all the amusements taken out, things like the aeroplane ride and the caterpillar ride and the carousel and all the games.

All that was left was the old dusty baseball diamond with broken-down bleachers, the old pavilion where we ran to eat our lunches when it rained, the old restrooms, the sad old beach.

The old restrooms on the beach were locked up. Someone had made a good-sized (and smelly) statement of protest right in the corner at the locked door. It was like keeping a church locked.

People strolled by in the antiseptic but haunted gloom. I still had some wonderful old photos from high-school excursions in the fifties and from picnics in the forties. We would take the excursion boat from Hamilton Harbour.

I went into the old hotel (circa 1862) adjacent to the park. The hotel had been elaborately restored just recently and they'd done a wonderful job. I made a joke. "When are you gonna get this place fixed up?"

The lady bartender laughed. "Actually, they're making some more drastic changes this winter. The dining room is being moved upstairs."

Back outside there was an old couple sitting on a bench feeding the gulls and staring at the sailboats docked in front of the hotel. One of the boats was called *Iniquitous*.

"*Iniquitous*. Now I used to know what that word meant but now I've forgotten," I said to myself out loud.

"We were just wondering that ourselves," said the old couple in unison.

"I don't have my dictionary with me but I think it means wicked," I said. "The guy who owns that boat probably has a wicked vocabulary."

On the way out I was dumbfounded to see the same white Volvo that had been in the traffic jam in Kingston several days back. Chapter 49, "Two Guys in a White Volvo." I checked my notes. Yes, same licence number: WOF 901. That's one for the Coincidence Club.

The Volvo, however, didn't look so new any more. It needed cleaning up badly. The bumper-sticker with its charming promised-land slogan was almost illegible. The same two guys were in it and they were dressed the same in white shirts but it looked as if they hadn't changed their shirts in all that time. And they didn't have their shoulder belts done up.

105. A Sad Little Chat with Titania Balmoral

I drove out of Port Dalhousie in the golden autumn sun, drove through St. Catharines, took Highway 8, then remembered my old high-school pal Bradley Balmoral. I wondered if he was still living in Jordan Harbour. I called him from a phone booth. His wife Titania answered.

"He's still working. He'll be home in an hour." I told her I was an old friend of his. "Oh, he's spoken of you often," she said. She thought I was phoning from Toronto.

Bradley's prime interests, passions, manias, ever since childhood, had always been freeze-action and time-lapse photography, astronomical photography, and the growing of tropical trees, palm trees, and citrus trees in his back yard.

But he'd been working at the steel mill for about twenty-five years

"He's been working shifts all these years," said Titania. "Yardmaster and relief supervisor. It's a living but there's nowhere to go. It's better than being way down on the ladder but it's still nowhere. He's got white hair but it's better than being bald."

He was hoping to retire within ten years, Titania said, so that he could devote himself to his hobbies full time.

I felt sad for Bradley and for myself. We were getting old.

"When he gets home he likes to be quiet. No loud music from the teenagers or anything. He'd never move from here. It'd kill him. He doesn't like changes. He has his hobbies, that's what saves him."

106. Dropping in on Mom and Dad

"Trees. I do love trees. And horses too. Do you, son?"

"Yes I do, mother. Very much."

"Me too. Trees and horses. Anything that's nature. I'll show you a tree before you go. And sunsets. I love sunsets. Haven't seen one for a while. Do you like sunsets, son?"

"Yes I do, mother. Very much."

"Have we ever been around Lake Ontario, Walter?"

"Sure we have. Don't you remember?"

His new moustache was thin and white, very handsome.

"Oh yes. How come our son hasn't? Oh yes, we had a lovely trip around Lake Ontario once."

"Mother," I said, "I have an important and serious question to ask you, and Dad too. I hope you don't consider it too personal."

"What is it, son?"

"Do you and Dad still do it?"

"Do what, son?"

"You know. Make love."

Mom rolled her eyes. "That's none of your business," she said. "And don't you tell him, Walter."

Dad looked blank. He'd been excitedly telling me all about Proust. He said he'd wasted his whole life not doing any serious reading simply because he didn't enjoy reading fiction. And the reason he didn't enjoy it was because he was always trying to read it too quickly. "You have to find your own pace," he kept saying.

"But I have a very good reason for wanting to know, mother."

"I don't care what your reason is," she said. "What is it?"

"Well some day I'm gonna be as old as you are, God willing, and I want to know what to expect."

"You'll just have to wait to find out."

"Did you hear who won the Nobel Peace Prize?" said my dad.

"No. Who won it?"

"That bishop from South Africa, I can never remember his name."

"Bishop Tutu?"

"Yes."

"That's good, dad. But how can you keep the names of the characters in Proust straight, if you can't remember who won the Nobel Peace Prize yesterday?"

410

"I have a guide to Proust. When I forget who so-and-so is, I check the guide, and then I remember."

"That's wonderful, dad. And are you happy about Bishop Tutu winning?"

"I was sort of hoping Pierre Trudeau would win."

"That would have been nice too. Another Canadian."

"A lot of people were hoping Trudeau would win. And a lot of people were hoping he wouldn't."

We talked about when Pearson won it. Pearson was a great hero of dad's, as was Trudeau. Dad was a Pearsonian continentalist in the thirties before he'd ever heard of Pearson and he hadn't changed a whit over the decades. He even looked a bit like Lester B. Pearson. Everyone told him that, particularly when Pearson was Prime Minister, and at the height of his fame.

"Some people say Trudeau shouldn't have been doing that," said mom. She was referring to his famous Peace Initiative. "They say he should have been at home taking care of the country."

"Is that your opinion, mom?"

"Oh, I wouldn't say that. I don't like to say anything detrimental about anybody."

"That's a nice way to be. Neither do I. How about you, dad?"

"No, I don't like to either, really. Though sometimes I do."

"Well, do you think Trudeau should have been at home taking care of the country?"

"No, I'd have to say I think he was right to go. It's the sign of a good leader that he can let his cabinet take care of things while he takes off."

"By the way, do you know how to remember Bishop Tutu's name?"

"How?"

"He's really a cute little guy, right?"

"Yeah, you could say that."

"Just imagine him dressed up like a ballet dancer."

They both laughed but didn't get it.

"What do you mean, son?" said mother.

"Well, what do you call a ballet dancer's little skirt?"

"A tutu?"

"Yeah."

"Oh, I get it."

107. The Disjointed and Confused Supermarket

I thought about the old retired minister in Lewiston getting so angry, so full of hate. Then in Toronto, heading north on Bathurst from the Gardiner Expressway, I stopped to let a woman with a baby carriage cross the street even though she wasn't at an officially designated crosswalk. She crossed, then turned to me, sneered and said: "You suck!"

Whew! Was it something to do with the little open sports car?

People walking down the street looked at me with disgust, then turned away. Was I driving a disgusting car or something? Was this some weird form of envy? Should there only be one kind of car? Help stamp out sports cars? What was all this about?

There's so much hate in the world. The love you make doesn't last forever. You have to keep making it.

I was thinking of Ed, the Man with No Thumbs. It pleased me that Ed would refuse to answer when people asked what happened to his thumbs. I wouldn't answer either, if it were me. And I would refuse to answer when people asked what happened between Marie-Thérèse and me.

It's the most difficult thing in the world to let go of something you love. Our task as humans is to get over that.

One finds it necessary, maybe mandatory, to sacrifice many things, maybe everything, for the sake of one's ever-more intense and less-expressible spiritual devotions. But one's ghost, a ghost principally of one's own making, perhaps a demon of one's own making, was a huge suction cup one was going to have to tear away from one's heart. Nowhere does nature abhor a vacuum more than in the area of the human heart. I was going to have to create a vacuum and maintain it vigilantly because as soon as I let my guard down it would be filled again with your crazy ghost, my passionate little virgin saint.

All the little hairs of my body still bristle when I think of you and maybe they always will, and maybe that's your true gift to me. Something that can never be apart from me for a moment. On my death bed I'll think of you and start levitating, or start complaining about the food, or start running my fingers through the nurse's hair, as if she were you, or as if she were Pinky, or as if she were one of my stewardess sweethearts or maybe both.

For after all, the love you inspired in me came from my own heart. In fact I spent this afternoon, before resuming work on the last little bit of this book, rereading Rilke's *Duino Elegies*, and all of a sudden I realised that I didn't like Rilke, that I had made a mistake with Rilke, that Rilke was not my kind of person, that what I thought I had found in Rilke was something that was not there but was rather something that the reading of Rilke had helped me to discover inside my own mind, during a very short interval during which I needed to make that discovery, and, without Rilke, would have been unable to. All of this was reminiscent of the famous line from Proust: "And with the old, intermittent caddishness which reappeared in him when he was no longer unhappy and his moral standards dropped accordingly, he exclaimed to himself: To think that I've wasted years of my life, that I've longed to die, that I've experienced my greatest love, for a woman who doesn't appeal to me, who wasn't even my type!"

Not that I want to go that far at this stage, or at any stage, but just as an example of how dependent we often are on others to provide us with what we already have in abundance and have had from the beginning and will have till the end.

But each little chapter in this book was a goodbye to you. Each little chapter tried to embody a certain way of thinking about you, a way of thinking tried on and ultimately rejected. But none of these goodbyes was sincere because I know I can never say goodbye to something that never existed and can never exist. It was aching to exist but we never allowed it to come into being. We knew or more accurately I knew it would have been extraordinary, but I never said anything and now it will never be.

It was like your dream of the boy at the top of the stairs, crying because he couldn't come down into the real (oops I mean conventional) world, we wouldn't let him.

These were attempts to speak to you more perfectly than circumstances would allow but they weren't sincere attempts because they involved me in lies, in betraying my desire for silence and solitude, or in a hoax I played on myself to convince myself I wanted anything but silence or solitude.

And none of these was successful because I didn't have the heart for it.

Sometimes I thought you lacked courage but you didn't. You ultimately exhibited a courage greater than what I counted on your having.

And I never really knew what was on your mind anyway.

Women grew their hair long and sold it to companies that manufactured those dolls in the windows of Yonge Street sex stores, those life-size rubber dolls with their mouths rounded into open full-size ohs. Who would buy one of those dolls? Ever met a guy who admitted to having ever had one of those dolls? What kind of guy was he?

"It's obvious that writing a book about anyone other than oneself is a pretext," wrote Victor-Lévy Beaulieu in *Monsieur Melville*.

But we ourselves were pretexts....

I give my narrator my name but he is merely an invention. As you perhaps are one of his inventions, his only real invention, as incomplete and unfulfilled as he will always be. As the doll in the window on Yonge Street is somebody's strange invention.

This book is not about you, not about me.

I stopped off at the newly opened Disjointed and Confused Supermarket (the semi-organic cooperative without a consistent philosophy) to pick up some groceries. I knew all I had in the fridge at home was a pair of socks and some mayonnaise.

In the supermarket, one woman bashed into the other with her cart and said: "You fuckin' ugly bitch. You know, you're the ugliest person I've ever seen in my life. Just look at your face."

Even if you did exist, I'd want you and not want you at the same time.

Victor-Lévy Beaulieu had his father running around pouring out holy water from a gin bottle during a summer storm, telling the kids about a cousin who was killed when lightning struck her room.

This trip was a goodbye to our love which might have been perfect, the answer to every question.

It always bothered me when people who had read the previous volumes asked me if certain things were true or invented, for whatever we write becomes real, whatever we don't get around to writing disappears forever.

We kill ourselves in order to make ourselves true.

We wanted to give each other so much we were unable to give each other anything.

108. Swimming through Rose Petals

When I got home there was a wonderful smell coming from the apartment. When I opened the door the whole place was inexplicably full of rose petals, just jammed full of them. Acres of red roses had been picked to provide enough petals to get into this room. You couldn't get another petal in there.

And no thorns! I threw off my clothes and jumped in, shouting with delight, and swam through the petals as if it were a swimming pool full of red wine. I figured I'd fill a thousand pillows with these petals and give them as gifts for the rest of my life.

I swam over to the sun room where I did my writing and there was my new computer smashed in half. An axe was sticking out of the remains.